A Dash o' Doric

A DASH O' DORIC

THE WIT AND WISDOM OF THE NORTH-EAST

ROBBIE SHEPHERD
AND NORMAN HARPER

ILLUSTRATED BY GRAHAM MACLENNAN

CANONGATE BOOKS

First published in Great Britain in 1995 by
Canongate Books Ltd
14 High Street
Edinburgh EH1 1TE

Reprinted in 1996 (twice)

ISBN 0 86241 5616

British Library Cataloguing in Publication Data

A catalogue record for this volume is available
on request.

Typeset by Palimpsest Book Production Limited,
Polmont, Stirlingshire
Printed and bound in Finland by W.S.O.Y.

Contents

Foreword

WHEN WE began the research for this book, we thought that, time permitting, we might take a wee detour and see how far back in the annals of humour we could trace a distinctive North-east of Scotland voice. What began as a passing notion became more of a challenge than we realised and, very soon, our plan to investigate the humour of the North-east took a temporary second place to our determination to delve as far back as possible. Anyone who has traced their family tree will be familiar with the problems that we encountered very quickly. After two or three generations, the leads tease out into myriad combinations and permutations, most of which turn out to be dead ends and are extremely frustrating. But we had an ace in our hand.

We were helped greatly by the archives of the *Press and Journal*. The *P&J* is blessed with one of the fullest records and one of the most fascinating vaults of Scottish history. Although it was not catalogued or cross-referenced in any formal way until the early 1950s, the sheer richness of the material available – all the way back to December, 1747 – makes it surprisingly easy to pick up little nuggets.

Finally, we came to the conclusion that the earliest recorded example of the humour of the North-east comes not from the turn of this century, nor even the turn of the previous one, but from almost 230 years ago.

It involves no less a figure than Dr Samuel Johnson, of Johnson and Boswell fame, the man who once described the noblest prospect in Scotland as being the road to England. Dr Johnson, ('author of the English Dictionary, rambler and idler' records an Aberdeen's *Journal* of September, 1773), was visiting Aberdeen and had been distinctly less than impressed with the 'rudeness of domicile' and the 'coarseness of fellow' he had encountered.

Today, such a newspaper item would be known as 'a

colour piece' – a feature which reports very little hard news but, rather, paints an impression of an event, or a person in the news for other reasons. Only in the last 50 years have most daily newspapers favoured the colour piece, so Aberdeen's *Journal* was clearly far ahead of its time.

It was here that we reached our goal.

The journalist who had been assigned to accompany Dr Johnson on his visit noted that the good doctor had been walking down one of Aberdeen's streets when he came upon a labourer doing his best to harl the side of one of the town's grander houses in the Broadgate. With an array of buckets, tools, mounds of stones and slabs around the workman, Dr Johnson had no option but to step out into the dirt, dubs and dung of the roadway. As he passed the workman and picked his way through the mire, he vented his spleen with what he imagined was some telling sarcasm.

'Good fellow,' he said. 'I trust that the impact of my person did not incommode your labour.'

We can imagine the wee Aberdonian labourer looking up at the bewigged Englishman, in all his velvet finery, and sizing him up with that practised North-east eye, for he replied:

'Na, na. If ye're nae in yer ain wye, ye're nae in mine.' And he carried on with what he was doing.

The journalist did not record Dr Johnson's reaction, which is a shame, for it was not often that Samuel Johnson was bettered in conversation, especially by the lower orders. We are delighted, of course, that it happened in Aberdeen.

To the best of our efforts, then, this is the first formal record of the North-east humour – and it shows very clearly the tone that has held, more or less, for more than two centuries.

We would be foolish to try to analyse humour – North-east or otherwise. We might as well try to knit treacle or juggle fog. Freud tried it and even he, the father of psychiatry, made a backside of it. So you won't find any learned or knowing analyses in this book, because only fools would try.

We can make shameless generalisations and say that the North-east humour is wry, dry and often subtle. We can say that it is at its best when cutting pomposity down to size, an age-old North-east trait. We can say that very rarely is it cruel. We can say that it is not above making fun of the North-east itself; an ability lost to too many other regions of Britain and virtually unknown in Europe.

Beyond that, we wouldn't dare insult our fellow-Neasters.

When Canongate asked us to prepare this book, both of us knew at once what sort of book we didn't want to write. Specifically, we didn't want this to be a joke book. There are plenty of joke books packing the shelves of every bookshop in Britain and covering the "humour" of almost every region of the UK. Anyone who is familiar with even a fraction of them will be struck very quickly by how similar the tales are and how most of them recycle the same basic stories and punchlines with only a change of locales and names. Shuggie in Glasgow seems to have a suspiciously similar humour to Cockney Alf, Belfast Billy and Geordie Tom. To the best of our ability, all of the tales you'll find in the next pages are verified, genuine and 100 per cent true. They actually happened, somewhere or another, all involving sons and daughters of the North-east, and the vast majority taking place in rural Aberdeenshire, Kincardine or Banffshire between World War I and the present. They have been told to us with straight faces and looks of the utmost sincerity. Those who wrote to us to share their funniest experiences or family wit generally signed off promising that we could rely on their truthfulness. So we have done. We trust them implicitly. (They were brought up in the North-east, after all.) And we're grateful to everyone who took the time and trouble to write because, without them, this book would not have been so rich a collection of North-east humour (and a lot thinner into the bargain).

Along the way, both of us have learned a very important lesson about humour of any sort. It is simply this: the best way to understand humour is not to analyse it, discuss it or pore over it. Just steep yourself in it and enjoy it.

So here are more than 250 chances to do just that.

Norman Harper and Robbie Shepherd
Aberdeen, 1996

'Stop kickin the furniture.'

Babes and Sucklings

One of the most cheering aspects of sifting through the mountains of stories was the number which proved that even primary-school children and infants are capable of the occasional blinding shaft of Doric humour. Here are a few of the best.

A MRS Yule wrote from Ellon to tell us of a neighbour, a young mum, who visited one day with her unruly son. The boy was clearly in no mood for discipline and scraped ornaments across the sideboard and threw cushions on to the floor.

'I didn't like to say anything,' wrote Mrs Yule. 'But when the boy started kicking the furniture, I coughed and glared at him. The young mother finally decided to act. "Lee!" she shouted. "Stop kickin the furniture. Ye'll spile yer new sheen."'

A THREE-YEAR-OLD from Gamrie was being corrected in his speech by his future aunt. All the best people from Gamrie are very broadly spoken, and he was certainly one of the best. At one point, he began a lively discourse on his 'moo'.

His aunt-to-be remonstrated. 'Andrew, that's your mouth, not your moo.'

He considered this for a moment. His aunt pointed to either side of his head. 'And these are your ears.'

Some time after, his grannie noticed him feeling around his head and asked if he had a problem.

'OK, Grunnie,' he said, feeling his ears, 'if this is ma ears, far's ma lugs?'

A YOUNG father on his two weeks onshore from the rigs was picking up his five-year-old son, who had just started school at a primary not a million miles from Turriff.

'And fit did ye learn the day?' inquired Dad.

The boy fixed him with a stare.

'That ither loons get pocket money.'

A PORTSOY mother was concerned that her eight-year-old, David, had picked up some rather fruity language. As mothers do, she blamed his playmates, and the other mothers blamed David. His mother was still concerned and asked the town bobby to have a word with her son to see if that might scare it out of him.

One day, as David was wandering home alone from school, the bobby spotted him, crossed the street slowly and stopped in front of him.

'Well, David,' he said in the sternest tone he could muster. 'I hear ye've been usin bad language.'

'Fa telt ye that?' said David.

'Oh,' said the bobby, 'a wee bird happened ontil ma windae-sill and he telt me a' aboot it.'

'The dirty bugger,' said David. 'And efter me feedin them ivry mornin.'

IN THE days of thatched cottages, one of the foremost thatchers was Adam Clyne. One morning at school, the children of one thackit hoosie were among a class being taught the Bible.

'Now,' said the teacher, Miss McIntosh, 'does anyone know about Adam?'

'Aye,' said one child. 'He's thackin wir hoose aenoo.'

RETIRED BANKER Edwin Reid tells of a six-year-old who was asked what he wanted for his birthday and who replied: 'An Autobank card.'

'An Autobank card? Fit wye?'

'Because ye get siller fanivver ye wint.'

A CHILD was asked by his primary teacher why his sister was absent from school.

'Please, miss,' said the wee lad, 'she's got a blin lump on her doup and she canna sit doon.'

'Her what?' said the teacher.

The pupil couldn't think for a wee while, then suggested: 'Please, miss, her dock.'

'Try again,' said the exasperated teacher.

The lad replied: 'Her aarse.'

In the end, admitting defeat but pointing out the error in his language, she snapped: 'Oh, sit down on your bottom,' which brought snickering around the class.

At playtime, naturally, the discussion centred on the exchange in the classroom. This brought a pensive murmur from the wee lad, who said: 'Weel, she *his* a blin lump on her erse.'

A FIRST-YEAR pupil at Fraserburgh Academy arrived late one morning for a first-period science class. When asked by the teacher for an explanation for his tardiness, he replied quite naturally: 'Sorry, miss, bit ma mither wis darnin a hole in the erse o' ma brikks.'

No sooner were the words uttered than he flushed, clapped his hands to his mouth and stuttered apologetically: 'Oh, I'm sorry, miss. I mean ma troosers.'

DURING THE war, many city people sought the relative safety of the countryside and, with a post as teacher at a nearby village, Mrs Raey rented a cottar hoose from one farming family. Young Jimmy, a boisterous four-year-old and son of the grieve at Cluny Home Farm, soon made himself acquant with daily visits, and often when the lady was in the middle of baking.

One day, he asked for a drink of milk. Mrs Raey filled the cup and handed it to the little boy, saying: 'Take care now, Jimmy; the cup is full.'

Jimmy proceeded to examine the cup, turning it round and round in his wee hands and said finally in a puzzled tone: 'It's nae fool ata, Mrs Raey. It's clean.'

ONE ASSISTANT editor with the *Press and Journal* tells of games he used to play when his two sons were small and they would try to guess what would be for tea on any given night. If their guess was wrong, he would tell them: 'Wrang spy.'

The game became a regular feature in advance of mealtimes until one day when the second boy was old enough to be asked what he would like for his tea. He thought for a few moments, then said firmly: 'I'd like some o' that Rang's Pie.'

ONE OF your co-authors has a younger brother who is still mightily embarrassed to be reminded of the day, when he was four or five, that the tyres on his tricycle went flat while he was visiting his grandfather, and he became very perplexed.

'Fit'll we dee, Ian?' asked his grandfather. 'Ye've nae air in yer tyres.'

Ian thought for a few moments, then his little face brightened. 'I ken, granda,' he said. 'We'll tak the air oot o' Norman's tyres.'

IT WAS the boy's first day at a rural school and, coming home in a foul mood, he was faced by his mother who was asking how he had got on.

'I'm nae gyaun back,' he replied firmly. 'I canna read. I canna write. And the wifie winna let me spik.'

THIS ONE is a famous North-east story and came to us in several different forms, so we have no doubt that it is true. The most common variation on the theme depicted a mother and a restless son of about four on a bus heading from Aberdeen out to Ellon. Across the gangway from them was another, younger mother and her new baby. It was obviously feeding time – judging by the continuous crying of the little one – which attracted the attention of the fidgety four-year-old.

As nature decreed, the young mum started breast-feeding the baby. The four-year-old stared in disbelief.

His mother pulled his shoulder. 'Feeding time,' she whispered. 'Now stop starin.'

'Bit mam!' he said, his eyes growing ever wider, 'he canna aet a' that athoot a tattie.'

AN ALFORD minister's wife in the 1960s used to tell of being invited to judge a children's cookery contest in the village hall and, unusually for those days, spotted a small boy as one of the contestants. He had made iced queen cakes, and when she stood in front of him she made a great show of tasting the queen cakes and saying how delicious they were. He glowed with pride.

'And tell me,' she said. 'You have such a lovely gloss on your icing. How do you manage that?'

'I lick them.'

A CONJUROR was enthralling his young audience at a Supporters' Club Children's Christmas Party at Huntly in the early 1970s. One of his tricks involved pulling eggs from a hat. As he pulled the umpteenth egg from the depths of his topper, he turned to one wee lad at the end of the front row and called: 'I bet your mother can't get eggs without hens.'

'Aye, she can,' replied the boy. 'She keeps dyeucks.'

A GAMEKEEPER at Duff House, Banff, at the turn of the century was telling his wife one night of the arrangements for the Duke of Fife's return from the Continent, and that the Duke would drive round by his lodge.

Next morning, the gamie's daugher, aged three, looked up into her mother's face and asked: 'I say, mam, will we open the gate for the dyeuck, or will he jist flee ower?'

BILL WILSON, of Peterhead, reports being on holiday in Majorca and staying at the same hotel as a young couple with two children, obviously from somewhere in the North-east.

One sunny morning, the boy, aged about six, ran to his mother. 'Mam, can I dive in the sweemin-pool?'

'No, it's ower deep for ye.'

'Bit Dad's in.'

'He's insured.'

DUNCAN FORBES, now of Elgin, tells a story from almost 30 years ago, when his five-year-old, Selina, was very quiet when she was supposed to be out the back of the house playing. Duncan fancied it was just a little too quiet and was about to go out to investigate when Selina came in through the back door.

'Fit hiv ye been deein, Selina?' asked her dad.

'Cleanin the dog's teeth,' said Selina.

'I hope ye hinna hurtit the doggie.'

'No, dad,' said Selina. 'And I'll pit back yer toothbrush, jist like I aye dee.'

A YOUNG Ellon mother was horrified when her five-year-old returned from school with his clothes torn and dirty and his face, arms and legs covered in bruises. The other boys had been throwing stones at him on the way home, he admitted.

'Well,' said his mother, 'we'd better sort this oot. Fit's their names?'

'I dinna ken their names.'

'Well, ye'd better tell yer teacher the morn. We canna pit up wi this. Bullyin needs nippin in the bud.'

'I dinna like tellin the teacher.'

'Well, if it happens again, dinna you start throwing steens back at them. You come and get me.'

'Bit you're nae eese at throwin steens.'

ONE OF your co-authors still gets mightily embarrassed when a hardy annual tale does the rounds of his family. It concerns his first school football match, when he arrived home tired, sore and dirty, but with a glow of immense satisfaction.

'And foo did ye get on?' asked his mother.

'Jist great,' he said, his little chest puffing out with pride. 'I scored a foul.'

Sweet Bird of Doric Wit

The future of any sense of humour lies in its teenagers and young adults. We're happy to report that the Doric sense of humour appears to be hale and hearty – although often unwittingly.

A PETERHEAD joiner had taken on an apprentice who was full of boundless enthusiasm, but who didn't appear to have a great deal of commonsense.

'Foo d'ye ken if ye should use a nail or a screw?' asked the joiner one morning, by way of a test.

The apprentice thought for a minute. 'Use a nail first,' he said. 'And then?' said the joiner.

'And then if the wid splits, use a screw.'

A TURRIFF lad who had had immense difficulty in finding regular work after leaving school had been signed up to the Shore Porters in Aberdeen, one of the world's oldest, most celebrated and most trusted furniture-removal firms.

When, a few weeks later, a neighbour asked his mother how Norman was getting on, she said: 'Oh, fine, fine. He's jist hid the one mischanter. He broke an expinsive Chinese pot at a hoose in Hamilton Place, and they say it wis worth near three hunder poun. So they've telt him they'll be takkin the cost oot o' his wages at three poun a wikk.'

'What rare,' said the neighbour. 'A steady job at last.'

A CLERK at a Banff law practice had struggled to make ends meet on his meagre income and finally, urged by his parents to do something about it, sought an audience with the senior partner to see if a rise wasn't in order.

The senior partner listened to the tale, but declined to offer any more money, saying that times were difficult, and so on.

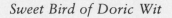

'A steady job at last.'

As the dejected lad turned to go, the partner said: 'I can see you're disappointed, and I suppose you've often wondered what you would do if you had my salary, eh?'

'No,' said the lad, closing the door, 'bit I've often winnered fit ee wid dee if ee hid mine.'

AN ABERDEEN florist was waxing proud about his two children, one of whom had been accepted for Glasgow University to study medicine.

'Aye,' he said, puffing out his chest. 'I suppose ye could say – me bein a florist – that I've produced a buddin genius.'

'Aye,' muttered one nearby man to another. 'A peety the ither een's a bloomin eediot.'

ONE SMART young chap from Banchory was a student on a business-studies course at the old Robert Gordon's Institute of Technology in Aberdeen, and had been asked by the lecturer which magnate he would nominate as the world's most successful businessman.

The Deesider thought for a few moments, then said: 'Noah.'

The lecturer and all of the class were surprised, to say the least, and the lecturer demanded to know how the student had come to that conclusion.

'Well,' grinned the student. 'Noah managed to float a limited company at a time when the rest of the world was going into liquidation.'

A MR ELLIS, from Ballater, wrote to tell us of the summer he was out walking in the Deeside woods when he came upon a group of seven or eight primary-school boys flinging sticks and stones up a tree. As he drew closer, he realised their target was a red squirrel, now beside itself with fright.

'Hie!' he shouted. 'What do you think you're doing?'

The boys spun round, saw him and were decently embarrassed. It took the ringleader to explain: 'It's OK mister, we wis only tryin ti knock it doon so we could stroke it.'

ONE RECRUITING sergeant at the Aberdeen Army Careers Office tells the story of the raw North-east country lad who turned up determined to be a soldier. Despite his scrawniness and a suspicious look of being under-age, the sergeant was impressed with the lad's determination.

'How fit are you?' he boomed.

'Five fit, three inch.'

NOW THAT it is more common to see young dads pushing prams in the park, Ethel Baird, of Kincorth, tells us of seeing a young father pushing a pram round the Duthie Park in Aberdeen and mumbling something gently towards the occupant.

As he came closer to the park bench where she was feeding pigeons, she heard that he was saying: 'That's it, Darren, ye're deein fine. Jist relax. Ye're deein gran. Nae bother, Darren. It'll be OK.'

She smiled and, as they passed, congratulated him on keeping up a dialogue with his son. 'You fairly know how to speak to a baby,' she said. 'Quietly and gently.'

She stood up, leaned over the pram and said: 'And what seems to be the matter with Darren, anyway?'

'No,' said the young dad. 'He's Alan. I'm Darren.'

AN OLD farmer who didn't believe in bad weather set the men to work one absolutely foul day.

'A' them that his ileskins can gyang oot and pu neeps,' he barked.

'And fit aboot us that disna hae ileskins?' said one young lad.

'Aye,' said the farmer, 'you can dee likewise.'

THE SAME farmer was dead against smoking, and when
he caught the orraloon lighting up a Woodbine up the farm
close, he stopped:

'Ye can tak that thing oot o' yer face, min, and keep yer
win for yer wark.'

NANCY FORSYTH wrote to tell us of her brother,
Frankie, starting his apprenticeship in a garage. One day,
an extremely elegant and self-important woman couldn't
get her car into the garage because a lorry was parked
across the entrance. She asked the lorry-driver to move the
lorry, but he replied that he couldn't for a few minutes and
that she would have to wait.

The woman was indignant. She puffed herself out to her
full girth and snapped: 'Do you know who I am?'

The driver leaned round the side of the lorry and called
to the new apprentice: 'Frunkie, awa and phone the doctor.
This wifie disna ken fa she is.'

A YOUTH was lounging at a country crossroads when a
man in a Riley Pathfinder stopped and asked for directions
to Kinnoir. The youth never took his hands out of his
pockets, but jerked his elbow in the direction of Kinnoir.

The Riley man was taken aback at the youth's slovenli-
ness and said: 'You know, if anyone can show me a lazier
trick than that, I'd be bound to give them a fiver.'

The youth, still with his hands in his pockets, stretched
the pockets enough to show a space between his hands and
the material and said: 'Pit it there.'

NORMAN MELDRUM, from Banff, was a champion
schools debater, representing Banff Academy several times
in the *Press and Journal* schools debating competition in
the mid-1980s.

In 1987, he was part of the year's runner-up team, for
whom the prize was a weekend's all-expenses-paid trip to

London. Part of the trip involved visiting the Greenwood Theatre for the Thursday-night taping of *Question Time*, the BBC TV discussion programme chaired then by Sir Robin Day.

Out of an audience of 300 people, it was Norman who was chosen to put the first question of the evening, on national television, to a panel of four of the country's most senior politicians, including David Owen and Joan Lestor. It was quite a task for a 16-year-old, but he carried it off with customary aplomb.

After the taping, the *Press and Journal* guests were invited into the post-recording canapés-and-wine party, attended by the production team, the political guests, a couple of Government ministers and one or two other VIPs. When Sir Robin was told that there were champion schools debaters in the assembly, he made a point of crossing the reception room to talk to them, and remembered at once that it was Norman whose question had opened the show. He congratulated him for the way he had phrased it.

'But tell me,' he said, 'I hope you weren't nervous at posing such a tough question to four of the country's most exalted notables – and on national television, too.'

'Na, na,' said Norman. 'I've been on the stage wi Robbie Shepherd.'

ONE DEESIDE builder was growing more and more frustrated with his teenage son and the lad's seeming reluctance to fix on any career. Eventually, the father decided to start him off on an apprenticeship in the building firm.

When a builder from a nearby village called in one day looking for some spare supplies, he spotted the young lad slouched in a corner of the yard, looking glumly at some two by four.

'How's the loon gettin on?' he asked.

'He's a miracle-worker,' said the father.

The visitor brightened. 'Is that so?' he said. 'Well, I'm

richt pleased ti hear it, for I kent ye werena affa sure aboot the deal ata.'

'No, he's a miracle-worker, richt enough,' said the father again. 'If ivver he dis ony work, it's a bliddy miracle.'

Kissies and Bosies

... otherwise known as Love and Marriage. North-east men are not overtly the most romantic, but deep beneath that gruff, diffident exterior beats a heart of pure mush. What woman could resist the blandishments that have worked their poetic magic and run shivers along spines down the decades, everywhere from Inverbervie to Inverallochy? Quite a few, by the sound of things.

MRS JEAN Macfarlane was a census-taker at Peterhead in 1971 before moving to Edinburgh. She recalls visiting one home in the town where a trachled-looking woman with six children aged between about two months and seven years came to the door. She was invited in and installed herself on the living-room settee.

In the course of the interview, the woman explained that her husband had died four years previously.

Mrs Macfarlane looked at the brood and wondered.

'I'm sorry,' she said. 'Maybe I misunderstood you. Did you say your husband died four years ago?'

'Aye,' said the woman then, catching the drift, added:
'He deed. I didna.'

A FRASERBURGH woman of somewhat slack reputation between the wars became the object of great interest in the community after she claimed she had been raped in the dark by a council roadman while walking home from a dance at Strichen.

'I dinna believe a word o't,' said one bustling matron to another as they queued for their groceries. 'I mean, foo did she ken it wis a roader if it wis in the dark?' 'Weel,' said the other. 'She'd likely hid ti dee a' the work.'

A NEW Pitsligo man had been discovered in flagrante with a rather attractive widow from a nearby parish. Small

The bride's mother.

villages being small villages, his wife got to hear about it and confronted him as he arrived home from work.

'There's nithing atween's,' he protested.

'Aye,' she said. 'Nae even a bliddy nichtgoon.'

A WOMAN wearing a large flowery hat arrived at a wedding at Portgordon Church in 1962 and was met by a very young and nervous usher who stopped her and asked: 'Are you a frien o' the groom?'

'No,' said the woman. 'I'm the bride's mother.'

JOHN AND Jean from Buckie had been courting for a long number of years – 30, to be exact – but there had never been a word of marriage until one day John said shyly:

'Jean, is it nae aboot time we wis thinkin o' gettin mairriet?'

'Behave yersel, John,' said Jean. 'Fa wid hae ony o' us noo?'

JIMMY HAD taken a fancy to a young lass from near Alford, but couldn't quite work out how to ask for her hand in marriage, for these were the days when fathers could still make or break a courtship.

Meg's father had a forbidding bluntness and brusqueness about him, like many farmers of his vintage, and he wasn't about to give his daughter's hand to just anyone, least of all anyone who couldn't stand up to him.

As a result, Jimmy had been slow to pluck up the courage. Little did he know it, but he had an ally in Meg's mother, who had a soft spot for him and thought that her husband had been bordering on the cruel towards the young suitor.

'I widna be surprised supposin Jimmy his a question ti ask ye, Wullie,' said Meg's mother idly one day, beginning the softening-up process.

'Oh, aye, and fit wid that be?'

'I think he's maybe hearin waddin bells.'

'Is he noo? Waddin bells? We'll see aboot that.'

'Now, Wullie. You behave yersel. And fin the time comes and he asks yer blessin, dinna you be coorse til the loon. Be nice til him.'

A few Sundays later, Jimmy turned up at an uncommon early hour before church. Meg and her mother were in the scullery.

'Is he in?' said Jimmy wanly.

'Oot the back shavin afore the Kirk,' said Meg's mother, urging him through.

Jimmy took a deep breath and shambled through to where Wullie was stooping over a basin.

'Aye-aye,' said Jimmy, by way of introduction.

Wullie looked round, then carried on shaving.

'Fine day,' said Jimmy.

'Mmphmm.'

There was an awkward pause. 'I've something ti speir at ye.'

'Oh aye.'

'A question, like.'

'Speir awa.'

'Well, I wis winderin if we could get mairriet.'

Wullie wiped the last of the soap from his face and turned to face Jimmy square on. 'Fa?' he said. 'You and me?'

A DONSIDE farmer's wife had been putting on a little more weight than was healthy and had amassed a formidable array of double chins. Still aware that her looks should be important to her, she sought a little reassurance from her husband that he still found her attractive.

'Div ye think I'm affa fat, Jock?' she inquired tentatively.

'Not a bit, quine,' he assured her.

'Is that richt, Jock?' she asked, secretly delighted.

'Richt enough,' he said, turning back to his paper. 'Mind

you, there's whiles I think ye're keekin at me ower a pile o' bannocks.'

NORTH-EAST man (and woman) are not known for being very demonstrative with their public affections, but one woman was a little more forthcoming with her marital *dis*affections. Overheard at a Garioch flower show in the late 1980s, she told her companion in a stage whisper: 'Aye, the only thing ma man and me's got in common is an anniversary on the same day.'

AN OLD couple decided they would try to recapture the vigour of their courtship and romance by booking into their honeymoon hotel for the night, decades after the event.

At bedtime, Teenie was lying impatiently in the bed, waiting for Wullie, whose arthritis was making his disrobing a little slow.

'Oh, me, Wullie,' said Teenie sadly. 'I mind fan we got mairriet; ye hardly gied me time ti tak aff ma stockins. Noo I could near wyve a pair.'

A FARMER became fed up with the state his wife kept the wee bit of garden they had round the farmhouse and found himself inveigled into tidying it up. Since he felt he should be involved in the farm itself, this irked quite a bit.

One day, when the weed problem had got out of hand yet again, he decided the time had come to put his foot down.

'Na, na, na,' he stormed at his wife, 'ti hell wi this. If ye let the gairden get intil a sotter lik this again, I'll gie't a damnt gweed splash o' weedkiller.'

'A'richt,' said his wife, 'and I wid jist start pittin yer fool draaers til the cleaners.'

The Shoppie

The lifeblood of many a small village and hamlet through-out the North-east was the shoppie – fixed or mobile. Sadly, these institutions are becoming fewer and farther between, and even those that remain are losing their character and the sparkle of wit that crackled back and fore on a good day. Here are a few remembered fondly.

THE TRAVELLING fish van is still a feature of North-east life. Most come from the small fishing ports of the Moray and Banffshire coasts and ply their trade deep into the heart of Upper Banffshire, and Central and West Aberdeenshire.

One morning, at Gartly, the fishman bowled up at one of his regular customers, who appeared with a stranger at her side. This turned out to be a visitor from Aberdeen, and rather a plummy visitor, at that.

When the lady of the house had received her usual order, the fishman turned his attention to the visitor. 'And fit aboot you, ma dear?' he inquired.

'Is your fish really fresh?' she said haughtily.

'Really fresh?' he said. 'Look at them!'

Then he turned to the fillets, lying there on a tin tray, and slapped two or three.

'For God's sake!' he shouted at them. 'I've telt ye afore! Can ye nae lie still!'

SIGNS in a shop near New Deer. The outside of the door bears the legend:
N S Y
The inside of the same door reads:
S Y OOT

TINKER FAMILIES plied North-east doors for trade as late as the early 1970s, and one squad was out near Keith

'Can ye nae lie still!'

trying to get rid of as many carpet offcuts and, frankly, moth-eaten fireside rugs as they could. When they stopped at one abode in Moss Street, the lady of the house was having none of it.

'Certainly not,' she said imperiously. 'Michty, yer carpets is stinkin.'

'That's nae the carpets, wifie,' said the tinker. 'That's me.'

ADAM REID was a tailor in Alford. One day in the early 1950s, he told a prominent farmer and church elder who had been fitted for a suit that the suit would be ready in six weeks.

'Sax wikks?' said the farmer. 'That's nae eese ti me; I need it for a waddin in a fortnicht. Michty, it jist took the Lord sax days ti mak the warld.'

'Aye,' said Adam, unimpressed. 'And look at fit a sotter it's in.'

BILL DONALD ran a shop selling, installing and servicing TVs. One day, in the mid-1960s, he took a call from a woman at Glenkindie who was complaining about the quality of her picture.

'Fit exactly's wrang wi yer picter?' he inquired.

'Weel,' said the woman, 'I've the news on aenoo and the blokie readin the news his got an affa lang face.'

'Aye,' said Bill, 'if I wis readin the news nooadays, I wid hae a lang face, tee.'

A BETTERWEAR salesman who had taken a job in the Inverurie area in the 1970s – and is now a prominent Aberdeen businessman – was out in the Garioch trying to drum up trade when he went up to a cottar hoose and knocked sharply. A small boy came to the door.

'Hullo, ma wee lad. Is your mummy in?'

The boy shook his head.

'Is your daddy in?'

The boy shook his head again.

'Well, is there anyone else in that I could speak to?'

The small boy nodded and said. 'Ma sister.'

'OK, can I speak to her?'

So the small boy trotted back into the house and was gone for fully five minutes. Then the boy returned alone and said: 'I canna lift her oot o' the playpen.'

A SHOPKEEPER at Banff who happened also to be a prominent after-dinner speaker along the Moray Firth coast remembers being overcome at a football-club dinner at Fraserburgh and falling back into his seat. A large crowd gathered round about him and, in his daze, he remembers hearing them clamouring: 'Move back! Move back!'

He also remembers the wife of one of the club officials shouting: 'Gie him some whisky! Gie him some whisky!'

Others began shouting: 'He needs air! He needs air!'

But still the woman insisted: 'Gie him some whisky! Gie him some whisky!'

Up went shouts of: 'Get an ambulance! Get an ambulance!'

And still the woman insisted: 'Gie him some whisky! Gie him some whisky!'

'Eventually,' he said, 'I raised my head and said: "For ony sake, will somebody listen til the wumman?"'

AN ABERDONIAN who had been imprisoned in Singapore during the war returned to the Granite City after being repatriated and decided that the first thing he wanted to do was to buy himself the bottle of whisky he had dreamed about for so many years in captivity.

At that time, whisky was still in short supply and could be sold only in licensed grocers and pubs within stated licensing hours. A man who had been a prisoner of the Japanese for so many years was a little out of touch with the new customs and went into a back-street Aberdeen grocer who had one bottle of whisky on display in his window.

The PoW went in and said that he wanted to buy the bottle.

'Ye canna buy it,' said the young man, mindful of the licensing laws. 'It's nae 'oors.'

'Well,' said the mystified PoW, 'if it's not yours, why have you got it in your window?'

MAGGIE AND Bessie were two sisters, both now deceased, who were among the most colourful characters in the Howe of Alford. Having been invited to a wedding, Bessie made a rare visit to the hairdresser and announced that she wanted 'the works'.

Worried that an old lady might be alarmed at having to lean backwards over the sink to have her hair washed, the hairdresser asked thoughtfully: 'Wid ye like the back wash for yer hair, Bessie?'

Bessie glared at her.

'The back wash? I'm needin the hale lot washed!'

MAD COW Disease has frightened too many North-east butchery customers for the liking of the trade or of beef farmers, most of whom blame the media for blowing a problem into an epidemic.

One well-known Inverurie lady visited one of the town butchers early in 1993 and was greeted by the usual cheery voice from behind the counter.

'Weel, Mrs Mc——, fit'll it be the day? The usual bit silverside for yer broth?'

'Damn the linth wi yer silverside,' snapped the customer. 'I've heard a' aboot this Mad Coo Disease. Keep yer silverside. I'll hae a pun o' mince.'

THE SAME butcher reports his experience with a very difficult customer, known with shopkeepers throughout the town for finding fault with everything. There wasn't a please in her.

The butcher had employed a new apprentice and was interested to see how the young lad would cope with Mrs Difficult. He gave the lad no warning when, as usual, she turned up for her Thursday morning bit of brisket and a hen for the broth.

'Hmm,' she said, peering at the chicken the lad had offered her. 'That disna look affa fresh. It's a bit scrawny. Hiv ye nae nithing better?'

The lad said that that was the last hen they had in stock until later that day. Mrs Difficult asked to see the hen again, and peered at it all the harder, from every angle.

'Ye can see fit I mean, I'm sure,' she said. 'Its skin's a' slack and there's nae muckle meat on it.' She leaned a bit closer and sniffed. 'And I'm nae sure bit fit it's on the turn.'

The butcher says he could hardly control his pleasure when the lad said: 'And could ye stand the same inspection yersel?'

A CULLEN fisher couldn't get rid of a sore throat, so his wife went down to Balfour the Chemist for some pastilles or similar soothers. The chemist recommended a particular brand and gave the wife instructions to dissolve one tablet in the mouth as required.

She was back at the chemist within the hour.

'Excuse me, cheemist,' she said, 'dis he swalla the bree?'

JOHN MUSTARD had the souter's shop (shoemaker) at Cullen a few years back and was working away in his back shop one day when he was surprised to see at the counter a young lad asking if he could come and see his father in a hurry.

John knew of the family, but he was not well-acquainted

with them. Whatever, he decided he had better do as he had been bidden and see what the problem was. He left his brother in charge of the shop and set off with the wee lad.

It was a wasted journey. The boy had been following instructions from his father, who had been about to sit down to his tea and had told his son: 'Awa and get me mustard.'

AN ABERCHIRDER shop assistant was heard discussing how hard it was to get by on a shop assistant's salary and was drawing much sympathy and empathy from one elderly customer, who said: 'I ken fit it's like. In my young day, I'd an affa job makkin ends meet.'

'I'm nae sae much worriet aboot makkin the ends meet,' said the girl, 'though it wid be real fine if they could get close enough ti wave at een anither noo and again.'

LONG BEFORE the days when we all became so sophisticated, and we all believed in the healing powers of the weird and wonderful cures hawked round the doors by quack doctors, one tinker was plying his trade round homes at Stonehaven, trying to sell bottles of so-called hair-restorer.

Ethel Baird, now of Kincorth, wrote to tell us that her mother had gone to the door to be confronted with the salesman and was not slow to point out that if his hair restorer was so marvellous, why did he not use some of it himself, for he was as bald as a ladle. 'It's a funny salesman that doesn't use his own product.'

Without dallying, the tinker replied: 'Aye, but why should I? Hugh Ramsay (the town draper) sells corsets.'

Down on the Farm

Although you would never think so to listen to them, some of the best of North-east humour comes from farming circles, particularly once the farmers get together socially, and any non-farmer who manages to inveigle himself into their company is assured an entertaining few hours.

AT A DINNER held by the National Farmers' Union in Aberdeen, and attended by some of the wealthiest tillers of the soil the North-east of Scotland can boast, the guests were not greatly impressed by the after-dinner speaker – a dull, wordy and not particularly entertaining councillor.

A Huntly farmer leaned to the man on his right and said: 'I've nivver really heard an efter-dinner speech worth listenin til. Hiv you?'

'Michty aye,' said the other. 'Last wikk, I wis oot wi the bunker and he said: "I'll pey the bill."'

A VET near Inverurie had been attending the very difficult birth of a calf. The labour had taken most of the night and everyone in attendance – vet, farmer, wife and son – was exhausted.

Finally, at six in the morning, just as the farmer's youngest son, aged seven, appeared in the doorway, the calf fell on to the straw to a great cacophony of mooing from the proud mother, and sighs of relief and tiredness from the four humans.

The farmer's eldest son, leaning on a byre post, exhausted, said: 'Fit is't?' – meaning was the newborn male or female, for in all the excitement they had been too busy to take note.

The small boy who had just appeared was standing by and said shyly: 'Gies a look at the calfie. I ken foo ye can tell.'

A FARM labourer convicted of lewd behaviour involving a cow had been fined at Banff Sheriff Court and – somewhat unwisely, it must be said – had decided to visit a café in the town for his lunch before returning to the farm.

Without a word, a waitress appeared and laid in front of him a plate of carrot tops, oatmeal, grass and dockens.

He stared at the plate and looked up at her, incredulous. 'Fit's this?' he demanded. 'I canna aet this.'

'No?' she said. 'Well, if you canna, jist gie it til yer girlfriend.'

A FARMER had been refused planning permission for a new house for his son, and so had to resort to finding a cottage somewhere near Rothienorman. He had inquired with all the nearby farmers to see if they had anything spare that they might sell, but none had.

Eventually, he took his son to see an estate agent at Inverurie, but everything on the agent's books was either too far away, too big or, more often, too expensive.

By the time they came to the last property on file, the farmer took off his bunnet, sighed, and ran a hand through his hair. 'Lord,' he said. 'Hiv ye nithing for aboot twa thoosan?'

'I'm sure,' said the estate agent. 'Come oot wi me the morn's mornin and we'll see if it's still stannin.'

A PROMINENT farming family in Aberdeenshire (whom we won't name because they are still in situ) were mildly resented in the nearby community for the way they spent their money in what the townsfolk judged was the flashiest way possible. The family's children, according to local opinion, were indulged right from birth to the time each made its own way in the world.

When the business venture of one collapsed, it became the speak of the place, particularly at the mart, where one farmer observed drily: 'Life hisna been easy for young ——.

The girlfriend's special

He'll ken aboot problems noo that it's a' collapsed roon aboot his heid.'

'Aye,' said the other. 'Problems, richt enough. I doot he'll jist hae ti grit his teeth, roll up his sleeves and ask his faither for anither fifty thoosan.'

THE GREAT drought of 1976 reduced virtually all the North-east farming population to despair, to such a degree that one Ellon minister prayed from the pulpit for rain. On the Monday, one of the most violent thunderstorms in years drenched the area and ruined a large acreage of what crops existed.

'And that's the trouble wi the meenister,' one farmer announced to another at the mart later that week. 'He aye overdis things.'

A FORMER lecturer at the North of Scotland College of Agriculture in Aberdeen swears that this story, from the early 1960s, is true. A chicken farmer near Laurencekirk was losing a lot of his stock, despite the intervention of vets, and decided as a last resort to write to the college to see if they had any advice.

'Every morning, when I go out, I find two or three more lying on the ground, cold and stiff, with their legs in the air. Can you tell me what is the matter?'

A few days later, he received a reply: 'Dear Mr ——. Your hens are dead.'

A FORMER waitress at the Northern Hotel, Kittybrewster, Aberdeen, wrote to us and sought anonymity for her tale from the days when the biggest mart in the North of Scotland was held every Friday just a few hundred yards along the road from the hotel, and farmers from five counties and beyond converged to do business or just have a news.

One particular Strathbogie farmer was a notorious twister, who was never slow to try to get something for nothing.

Our waitress recalled him turning up and asking for a plate of mince and tatties. This was duly served him but, before he started tucking in, he asked if he could change his mind and have a plate of the steak-and-kidney pie, instead. The waitress obliged; removed the mince and tatties, and returned five minutes later with the pie, which he ate hungrily.

He stood up and was walking out when the waitress caught him near the front door and reminded him that he hadn't paid.

'Aye, aye, lassie, bit if I mind richt I gied ye a plate o' mince and tatties for the steak-and-kidney pie, did I nae?'

'Well, yes, but you didn't pay for the mince and tatties.'

'Bit I didna aet the mince and tatties, so fit wye should I pey for it?'

THE DRAM after paying the hairst bill is a custom throughout the North-east, and probably far beyond. One farmer's wife from near Oyne told us of the evening in the late 1970s when the combine-owner had called to seek his due and her man had reached for the bottle of Grouse to seal the deal.

Both men sat down, but the visitor was looking into the dram very glumly.

'Is there something adee?' inquired the farmer.

'There's a flee in ma dram, min,' said the visitor.

'Oh, I'm sorry aboot that,' said the farmer's wife, stepping in to retrieve the glass.

'Na, na,' said the visitor, pulling the glass back closer to himself. 'I'm nae bothered aboot the flee – jist the wye it's widin across the boddim.'

A CROFTER from Craigievar paid an evening visit to a

neighbouring farm. The crofter had spent most of his life as a cattleman on various farms, breeding Aberdeen-Angus and Shorthorn cattle.

On being asked into the farmhouse for a fly cup, the conversation between the two men inevitably was of pedigree cattle.

After a considerable time, the farmer's wife felt the need to change the subject of the conversation and tried to steer it round by asking the crofter how his niece was getting on now that she had gone to Aberdeen to work.

'Deein gran,' said the crofter. 'She's got a job as a shorthorn-typist.'

TWO CROFTER brothers were drying off at the fireside in their wee hoose after a pouring wet day in the fields.

'I winder if the rain's stoppit yet,' said one.

'Dinna ken,' said the other. 'I hinna been oot since I come in.'

IN THE 1990s, it is known as 'an insurance job', but several decades ago no one could be so openly suspicious of a neighbour or friend, least of all in the farming community, but there were ways and ways.

A fire broke out in one Buchan farmer's strae-ricks early one morning, and a troupe of neighbours turned out to do what they could to douse the flames, but to little effect.

The farmer stepped away, looking extremely calm, took out his pipe and lit his tobacco. One of his exhausted neighbours turned to him.

'Weel, weel, Geordie,' he said. 'I doot that's nae the first time yer spunks hiv been oot the day.'

WE HAD better keep the names here secret, but the story involves a farmer near Dunecht, whose farm was being inspected by a representative of the Ministry of Agriculture.

Being invited into the farmhouse, the ministry man said he would be delighted to meet Mrs G——.

'Aweel,' said the farmer, 'come awa in. I hinna a bonnie wife, bit I can show ye some real bonnie coos.'

JUST BEFORE the end of World War I, a group of Garioch farmers were at the mart discussing what punishment would be suitable for the Kaiser for all the havoc, death and destruction he and his like had wrought.

Many punishments were dreamed up, each more vicious than the one before, but they fixed on what they thought was the best of the lot.

They would give him an overdraft on a small, north-facing croft at Rhynie.

WE DEBATED long and hard over whether or not to include this one at all, for it is easily the least tasteful story in the book, but on the grounds that North-east people are not easily shockable, it is included. We won't embarrass the contributor by naming him. If you are easily shockable yourself, close your eyes now.

A Peterhead farmer went into the chemist in 1962 for a packet of condoms, 'Foo muckle's that?' he inquired.

'One pound, plus tax,' said the assistant.

'Nivver mind the tacks,' he said. 'I'll jist tie them on wi binder twine.'

THE DAYS of the travelling threshing-mill round the crofts showed North-east community spirit at its best, with neighbour helping neighbour. At dinnertime or teatime, the small living room of the croft being hairstit would be full to overflowing.

Always, two men would arrive the night before with the steam mill so that they could set it up in fine time for an early yokin the following morning.

At this particular croft, the two steam-mill men were not

known to the crofter's wife, but she was mindful of her duty in making sure that they felt welcome when they arrived for their meal.

'Aet up stem-mull man,' she said. 'Aet up at man aside ye.'

IT HAD been a particularly boring football match at Pittodrie. The Dons certainly had not been at their best, and the final whistle blew with the scoresheet blank.

A group of Kemnay farm workers was making a slow, dejected exit, when one looked at another and said: 'We'd hiv been as weel at hame githerin steens.'

IT HAD been a most enjoyable day at the sheepdog trials at Monymusk. The competitions were over and the post-mortems had to be conducted over a sociable dram. This meant that Dod stayed longer than he had intended, and all thoughts of the raging wife at home had long since evaporated.

It wasn't until he was dropped off at the end of the road that he began to panic. We didn't discover what happened next until the following sheepdog trial when Dod, fortified with the barley bree again, explained.

His wife, apparently, had gone to bed already by the time he had got home. He crept upstairs as slowly and as quietly as his delicate state would allow. He had just reached the top of the stairs and had pushed open the door gently when his wife stirred.

'I jist crawlt in on all fours til the bedside,' said Dod, 'and the wife pit oot her haun, sayin: "Is that you, Flossie?"'

'Did ye get aff wi't, Dod?' inquired a crony.

'I did,' said Dod. 'I hid the presence o' mind ti lick her haun.'

TWO Oldmeldrum farmers had met at the local smiddy in the late 1950s. One was known to be very young, thrusting and ambitious, with an eye to maximum productivity and new methods. The other was of the old school.

Passing the time of day while the smith attended to their needs, the younger was heard to remark that he was planning to erect a massing building on his land. It would be hundreds of yards long and hundreds of yards wide and a good few yards in height. It would be one of the grandest buildings in the Garioch. And what scope it would give him once it was finished.

After he had finished telling of his plans, he waited for the older farmer to be suitably admiring, but the reply was:

'Aye, aye, aye. Bit far I come fae we like ti ploo a bit o' the grun, an a'.'

MANY YEARS ago, there was a particularly impressive bull at Tarland, which gave the farmer immense pride and, in truth, caused a lot of admiration around the Howe of Cromar. One day, the minister called and asked if he might see this bull that everyone was talking about and the farmer agreed readily and began walking towards a nearby field.

'Oh,' said the minister, 'I had assumed it would be safely locked up in a stall, where I could see it at close quarters.'

'Na, na, meenister,' said the farmer. 'It's oot in the park.'

The minister followed, a little more reluctantly, and soon saw the massive animal, standing alone in the centre of a field. He swallowed a little.

The farmer stopped beside the gate and bade the minister jump in over. The minister clambered in over with a little difficulty and waited for the farmer to join him. But the farmer stayed where he was, leaning on the outside of the gate.

'Are you not coming, too?' inquired the minister.

'Na, na,' said the farmer. 'I ken fit he looks like. I've seen him plenty o' times. Awa ye go.'

The minister thought for a moment, summoned his courage and began stepping gingerly towards the centre of the park. Half-way, he stopped, turned and said: 'What if he charges?'

'He winna charge,' said the farmer. 'Ye dinna think I'd pit ye in there yersel if he wis the kinna bull that charged.'

'No, but just supposing he does charge. What do I do?'

'Weel,' said the farmer. 'I wid turn roon, pick up a handfae and fling it at him.'

'A handful of what?'

'Dinna worry,' said the farmer. 'It'll be there.'

Characters

Every city and region has its characters, and Aberdeen and the North-east would appear to have more than their fair share.

BERT DUNCAN, from Woodside, Aberdeen, became celebrated in the shadowy world of London boxing as one of the finest corners a boxer could hope to have supporting him. During one fight, in the mid-1950s, Bert was accompanying a distinctly unimpressive boxer from the dressing-room to the ring.

'It's a long way, isn't it?' said the boxer.

'Dinna worry,' growled Bert. 'Ye winna be walkin back.'

ONE OF the North-east's most celebrated auctioneers is Bill Lippe, whose evenings at Kemnay draw crowds for miles. One evening, the story goes, a handsome stuffed parrot in a large cage appeared. Bidding for Lot 165 began at £10. Bill was surprised that interest took off quite as spectacularly as it did – and certainly far in excess of what he judged the lot was worth.

Finally, just two bidders were in competition with one another: a farmer's wife from Blairdaff and an unknown voice across at the front, right-hand corner of the village hall.

People round about the Blairdaff woman were growing gradually more incredulous that she should be thinking of spending such money on a stuffed parrot, but she had a determined set about her jaw and was clearly intent on winning.

Finally, at £85, the prize was hers and two farmers nearby leaned across to congratulate her. 'Well, Mrs——,' said one. 'At that price, I hope he's a good spikker.'

'Och, he's a rare spikker,' said the other. 'Fa div ye think she wis biddin against?'

PAT BUCHAN, who used to teach dancing around Edinburgh before retiring back to his native Peterhead in the mid-1950s, used to tell of teaching a class of novices at a well-known school for the well-heeled young lady and taking, as a partner, a very nervous and easily embarrassed young deb.

He instructed her to watch his feet carefully and to try to follow everything he did.

She was so desperate to do well that she kept one step ahead of him all the time, without waiting for his lead. After several stops and starts, he admitted to growing a little impatient and eventually stopped, sighed and said: 'I'm sorry, but yer problem is that ye're anticipatin.'

'I am not!' she blushed. 'I'm not even married!'

WILLIE LUMSDEN was a passenger porter at Inverurie Railway Station for almost half a century, a well-kent figure and known to almost everyone who travelled on the line, and certainly to every soul in the Garioch.

He also dabbled as an amateur chiropodist, in days when farmers and farmworkers suffered all manner of problems because their feet were expected to withstand the harshest of winters, the poorest of footwear and the most neglectful of care.

One evening, an unnamed farmworker turned up to have a particularly ugly foot attended to. Willie did the best he could and the client put his sock and boot back on again.

'Oh, what fine, Wullie,' he said, sighing with pleasure. 'I wish noo that I'd washed ma ither fit.'

MAGGIE, A waitress at the former Gloucester Hotel in Union Street, Aberdeen, reports working for one summer season with a country-bred waitress who stood no nonsense from anyone.

When one diner complained that he had detected no hint of oxtail in the oxtail soup, she glared at him, snatched

One step ahead

the plate and announced: 'And ye'll be disappintit ti hear there's nae horse in wir horseradish, eether.'

MAGGIE'S COLLEAGUE had been asked to stand in for an afternoon behind reception to cover for a receptionist who had become ill. When one guest approached to ask if he could buy stamps for a parcel, Maggie's colleague raked about among the drawers and found a sheet of stamps.

She tore off the requisite amount and the man pushed the right number of coins across the counter, as well as the parcel. Maggie's colleague's stare told the man that she was not prepared to do anything more for him.

'W-well,' he said, hesitating. 'Will I stick the stamps on myself?'

'Please yersel,' said Maggie's colleague. 'Though ye'd likely be better stickin them on yer parcel.'

THE SAME lady was back in the dining-room and had been confronted by a QC up from Edinburgh who was having a quick lunch during recess from court and who was clearly not impressed with the cuisine and called her over to say so.

'I have a complaint,' he said.

'This is a hotel,' she said, cruising past. 'Nae a hospital.'

IT WAS the night of the Harvest Home dance at the big hoose, when the laird and his entourage mixed with tenants, estate workers, guests and villagers to celebrate the end of the harvest.

In the middle of an eightsome reel, the second horseman, fortified with the dram, engaged the laird in conversation.

'Man, fit a gran nicht. I'm fair conspirin.'

'Conspiring?' queried his lordship. 'Conspiring means "to plot".'

''At's richt, min,' said the horseman. 'I'm fair plottin.'

JOHN DUNCAN, of Dubbieford Farm, near Torphins, enjoyed long and strong friendships in the community and was highly regarded by all who knew him. Jack Kellas, of Torphins, wrote to tell us of a bit news he had once with Dubbie when the subject worked its way round to fenceposts.

Jack offered Dubbie the chance to buy some surplus that he happened to have after buying more than he found he needed.

'Fit like a price wid ye be needin?' inquired Dubbie.

'Twa shillins apiece,' said Jack. 'They're oak. They'll laist for ivver.'

Dubbie rubbed his chin. 'Ah, bit ye're gey strong in the price, Jake. Dam't, ye're needin ower muckle, I'm thinkin.'

Jack thought for a moment. 'Well, fit aboot a shillin each? A real bargain.'

'Weel, ye are saftenin a bittie bit, ach, ye ken, I'm nae sair-needin posts aenoo. Ma fences is real snod.'

'Right, John,' said Jack, 'I'll tell ye fit: ye can hae the twinty posts for nithing. Will that please ye?'

Dubbie grasped him by the shoulder, grinning. 'Now, haud on Jake, haud on,' he said. 'Is that delivered?'

JACK KELLAS tells also of another good neighbour, farmer George Anderson, who was summoned to attend the Inland Revenue office in Aberdeen for an investigation of his accounts. George was reluctant to go, but was persuaded that it would be better in the long run to get the matter cleared up. Not every farmer in those days had a car, but a neighbouring farmer, Hilly, offered to run him into town.

The two set off on Friday morning and, after attending the mart at Kittybrewster, made their way down town to the Inland Revenue office. On arrival, Hilly suggested that he would sit outside in the car while George set about his business with the tax man.

'Na, na,' insisted George. 'Ye're nae sittin oot here stairvin. Ye'd better come awa in and see fit this bliddy mannie his ti say.'

Once the tax inspector was persuaded that it would be all right for a third party to be present while Mr Anderson's accounts were examined, they set about taking the books through hand.

'Now, Mr Anderson,' said the inspector, poring over sheets of figures. 'I see that at the start of your year you had six hundred head of poultry. Is that correct?'

'Michty aye.'

'And you bought four hundred and fifty during the year?'

'Aye.'

'Well, there is something far wrong here, it seems to me. You have no sales recorded during the year and your closing valuation number is only seven hundred. What happened to the other three hundred and fifty? Do you still have them?'

'No,' said Geordie, becoming a little uncomfortable. 'I hinna.'

'You don't have them?'

'No.'

'So where do you suppose they might be then?'

'I suppose they must hiv dee't.'

'Died? Three hundred and fifty of your poultry have died? What on earth could they have died of?'

Geordie fixed him with a stare.

'The skitter.'

WE'D BETTER not reveal the man's name, but we'll call him Jock the Coalman. A week before Christmas a few years back, the conversation in the village pub got round to finding a bird for the Christmas Day table, and memories of the size of some turkeys they had seen over the years.

Jock listened in silence as one of the worthies continually topped everyone else's stories with a 30-pounder he'd had a few years previously.

'And fit aboot yersel, Jock?' somebody asked. 'Fit's the biggest turkey ee've ivver seen?'

'Weel,' drawled Jock, 'fin I come awa fae the hoose this mornin, the wife wis dressin oor turkey, and it wis that big she wis rowin stuffin up its erse wi a box barra.'

BRYAN SMITH, now of Aberdeen, tells a story from his wartime days in the Far East, much adapted by after-dinner speakers ever since, but this is the original.

It concerns Waddy, third horseman at Drumdelgie, and then in the 9th Battalion Gordon Highlanders. In January, 1945, they were crossing the Irrawaddy when they were divebombed by six Japanese Zero fighters. Mr Smith's batman was shot through the head. Waddy received a leg wound and was removed to a forward casualty-clearing station behind the lines.

Who should appear shortly afterwards but Field Marshal Sir Bill Slim. The great man spotted Waddy, lying there, smoking the ubiquitous stubby pipe so beloved of farm servants between the wars, and wreathed in clouds of XX Bogie Roll. The field marshal bent down and inquired of Waddy: 'Tell me, man, where exactly were you wounded?'

Waddy pondered for a moment, sat up and replied: 'Weel, sir, I jaloose it wid hiv been a twa-three mile the Huntly side o' the Irrawaddy.'

THE LATE Jock Strachan was a well-known and well-respected farmer in the Fyvie area. One evening, he turned up at a concert at Fyvie and the compere of the show noticed that Jock was present. Between two of the acts, the compere told the story of a teacher asking her class for definitions of words, and she had asked for a definition of the word Nothing.

A boy had shot up his hand and had said: 'Please, miss, it's fit ye get for haudin Jock Strachan's horse.'

ONE EVENING, a group of Oldmeldrum worthies were discussing the forthcoming Oldmeldrum Sports, that annual gala which is as much a part of North-east culture as the Turriff Show, the Lonach or the Braemar Gathering.

'Ach, I'm nae gyaun this eer,' said Jock. 'It's aye the same. Quines duncin. Bill Anderson throwin his haimmer farrer than the neist lad. Tugga-war. Pipers dirlin a'b'dy's lugs. Nithing new. Na na, nae for me.'

'Oh, bit ye're wrang,' said Sandy. 'For instance, tak the pageant. This year, the theme's Legends Throweoot The Centuries, and I hear say that the Meldrum Rural wifies are gaun as Lady Godiva – ye ken, the wifie that rode throwe the streets bare-nakit, tirred til the skin o' a fite horse.'

'Ach,' said Jock, 'maybe I will ging. It's a filie sin I've seen a fite horse.'

WILLIE WEBSTER was the joiner at Methlick and, in the 1950s, was visited by the factory inspector who demanded to see the joinery's fire extinguisher.

'Up in the laft,' said Willie.

The inspector was perplexed, for he could see no stair to the loft. 'Mr Webster, how do I get up there?'

'Use a laidder.'

Willie produced a ladder and the inspector proceeded, shakily, into the loft, where he found the extinguisher under a pile of old sacks – hardly the most accessible point in case of emergency.

But, worse, it was empty.

'Of coorse it's impty,' snapped Willie. 'If I kept it full, it wid jist roost.'

'And what would you do if there was a fire?'
'Fill it, of coorse.'

AT INSCH Station, one gate of the level crossing was shut, but the other was left open. Peter Scatterty, on duty as signalman, was asked by Harry Usher what was going on.

'Well,' said Peter. 'I'm half-expectin a train.'

AT A major Fiddlers' Spectacular at HM Theatre, Aberdeen, there was an age gap of 85 years between the youngest and the oldest of the 100 assembled musicians – the youngest was nine and the oldest, Harry Nicol, of Cults, a mere 94.

After a day-long dress rehearsal before the week's show, Harry went into his local at the Ploughman, Culter, for a wee dram to ease away the other elbow exertions on the stage. His trusty fiddle was in its case under his arm as he made his way to the bar. The proprietor greeted him with: 'Michty, Harry, far hiv ye been?'

'I've been awa for a practice,' said Harry.

'Michty,' said mine host, 'at your age, min, if ye canna play the damnt thing afore this time, it's hardly worth yer file yokin.'

IN THE mid-1960s, BBC Scotland staged a grand fiddle concert at Blair Castle, home of the Duke of Atholl. The concert featured fiddlers from throughout Scotland and producer James Hunter had persuaded noted virtuoso Yehudi Menuhin to take part. Menuhin was, and still is, most appreciative of the Scottish style of fiddle-playing, but expressed reservations on being able to handle the technique at short notice.

Some of the fiddlers on stage, to put it mildly, were more enthusiastic than expert, and so it was at rehearsal

that the guest was shown a seat between two elderly
fiddlers of rural stock, who fitted in well in strathspey-
and-reel circles, but never professed to being individual stars.

'Gentlemen,' said Menuhin, 'thanks for the honour, but
I must confess to being a little apprehensive and nervous
in following your music.'

'Nivver ee mind, chiel,' said the lad on his right. 'Ye're
atween twa gweed men.'

NO TRUE man or woman of the North-east has not
heard of Jamie Fleeman. The Laird O' Udny's Feel, as
he was known, was born in 1723 and spent most of his
working life as manservant to the Laird of Udny Castle
in Aberdeenshire. He was of simple mind, but his loyalty
to the laird was staunch, although he often despised the
laird's friends, perhaps because they thought they could get
away with poking sarcastic jibes at 'the fool', but it was
Jamie who always got the better of them, and the stories
are legend.

One of the landed gentry had been a guest of Udny and
had made some remark that had upset Jamie. Revenge came
the next morning as Jamie was having a wee snooze on the
banks of the Ythan when the guest appeared at the other
side of the river with his horse.

He shouted across and asked Jamie where the best
crossing-point would be. Jamie directed him to the deepest bit of the water. The gentleman urged his horse in
and both promptly disappeared. The gentleman nearly
drowned.

Spitting with rage, and utterly drenched, he hauled
himself back out on to the bank and shouted that Jamie
had tried to kill him.

'Gweed be here,' cried Jamie, 'I've seen the geese and
the dyeucks crossin there hunders o' times, and surely yer
horse his langer legs nor them.'

THEN THERE was the time Jamie was staying at another house and the proprietor and his factor were nearby, discussing a poor crop.

'I've tried many things,' said the factor, 'but nothing seems to grow.'

The man of business, with scant knowledge of farming, mused for a time and was about to give his considered opinion when Jamie interjected, counting factors well down his list of useful articles.

'I cwid tell ye fit wid thrive in't. Plunt it wi factors. They thrive onywye.'

JAMIE, OF course, got his by-name of The Laird o' Udny's Fool when he met one of the laird's titled friends in the grounds of the castle.

'Who are you?' asked the gentleman with a superior air.

'I'm the Laird o' Udny's feel,' said Jamie. 'Fa's feel are ee?'

REUBEN RAE was a character well known around Kintore in the 1920s, and there was nothing he liked better than to get a lot of young lads round about him so he could boast of all his achievements. The lads were in awe of him, swearing that he was surely in league with the devil.

One of Reuben's tales was of the time a Kintore farmer sent for him as the farm was over-run with rabbits. The farmer met the newly employed trapper a few days later and asked how he was getting on.

'Weel,' Reuben replied, 'last nicht I set thirty-sax snares, and this mornin I hid thirty-sax rubbits and twa wytin ti get in.'

ANOTHER KINTORE worthy was Jamie Will. One day, the young lads had congregated round the fountain when Jamie came past aboard his rather ancient wreck of a bicycle. It was rumoured that he was courting a lass at Balmoral and was en route.

One of the lads suggested: 'It'll tak ye a gey file on that bike, Jamie.'

'Na na,' replied Jamie, sailing past, 'this is ma Sunday bike. Nineteen gears, and fin I get into tap gear, ilky crunk's a quarter o' a mile.'

WILLIE LOW, of Glassel, was a well-known dealer, and plenty of stories are attributed to him. Willie had sold a heifer to a neighbouring farmer for £440. Unfortunately, the heifer died a week later, so back came the purchaser to complain and seek recompense.

'Man, Wullie, this is nae damnt eese,' stormed the farmer.

'Fit's adee?' said Willie.

'The heifer's dee't.'

'Man,' said Willie. 'It nivver did that fin I hid it.'

THE INTERNATIONALLY known firm of R.B. Farquhar Ltd. was founded by Rab Farquhar, of Rhynie, who started out his business life selling firewood round doors. He never lost the common touch as he became a millionaire, flying the globe to do oil-industry deals. To his immense credit, neither did he lose his strong North-east accent and ways.

Retired banker Edwin Reid had introduced Rab to a British government minister after the minister had made an important speech at the Whitehall Hotel, Houston, Texas.

'Pleased to meet you Mr Farkwar,' said the minister, 'and what do you do for a living?'

Rab didn't like being referred to as Farkwar, but he replied: 'Oh, I jist mak things beginnin wi S.'

'Things beginning with S?' said the minister. 'What sort of things beginning with S?'

'Oh,' said Rab, 'sheds, chalets and shitehooses.'

ON ANOTHER visit to Houston, Edwin took Rab up a

downtown skyscraper to view the big city and Mr F. was duly impressed. On their way out, the commissionaire said to the pair of them: 'Y'all have a good weekend, hear?'

Bob turned to Edwin and remarked: 'It was affa nice o' that chiel ti say that we maun hae a nice wikkenn,' so Edwin suggested that when Rab got home he should stand at the gates of his factory and greet all his workers with: 'Have a pleasant weekend.'

'Na, na, na,' said Rab. 'I couldna dee that. They wid say that Farquhar's aff his heid.'

RAB BUILT and owned a chalet holiday complex at Callander, and would make frequent runs down in his Rolls-Royce to check up on standards and to be sure that everything was in order. One day when he arrived, he found that the handyman was missing, so he went into the shed, put on a pair of dungarees and started up the mower.

The sound of the mower brought out the slumbering holidaymakers, who were delighted to see a member of staff so that they could bring to his attention whatever little problems they had encountered, from blown light bulbs to new supplies of toilet paper.

Rab delighted in finishing this tale with: 'Ye ken this. I workit real hard aa day and finished up wi a fiver in tips. Then I went back intil the shed, took aff ma dungars, went roon the back, climmed in ower the Rolls-Royce, and I wis jist drivin oot fan a twa-three o' them saw me.

'So I wound doon the windae, gied them a wave and I said: "That's me awa hame, than."

'And I could see them starin at me, and then at the car, so I jist said: "Aye, I've an affa good boss."'

The Toon

The humour of Aberdeen is quite distinct from the humour of the countryside. Toonser humour is supposedly quicker and sharper than the rural variety, which is drier and slower, although each can be either, it sometimes seems to us. Here are a few of the best examples of Granite City anecdotes that were sent to us.

SHORTLY AFTER Aberdeen set fire to its trams in that disgraceful ceremony at the beach in the early 1960s, the city's public transport became all-bus. Some of the less-swack Aberdonians complained that some of the bus platforms were too high for them to negotiate and, for several months, conductors and clippies had to bear the brunt of the moaning.

One afternoon, outside Watt and Grant's store in Union Street, a particularly fat woman was struggling to haul herself aboard.

'Come awa, mither,' said the conductor, offering her a helping haul. 'I doot ye need some yeast. It'll mak ye rise better.'

'Tak some yersel,' puffed the woman. 'It'll mak ye better-bred.'

A FIRM of Aberdeen electricians had been rewiring a council scheme on the outskirts of the city in the early 1960s and one of the sparkies, a lad so good-looking that he should have been a model or in films, had taken the fancy of a bored housewife. To the amusement of his mates, he would often repair for an hour in the afternoon to the lady's boudoir and return looking flushed, but relaxed.

One evening, back at the yard, one of the foremen shouted across to him:

'Aye, Jack, ye'll be awa back til yer new girlfriend's the nicht?'

'Na,' he called back. 'Ye dinna think I dee that kinna thing in ma ain time, d'ye?'

ONE CHRISTMAS in the early 1950s, the famed Aberdeen department store of Esslemont and Macintosh offered an embroidery service for silk stockings. Most women who took up the offer chose to have their initials or monogram embroidered around the stocking tops.

An authoritative source reports that one sparky young woman came in and asked if there would be enough room to embroider:

If you can read this, you are too close

She was being attended by two assistants, a senior man and a middle-aged woman. The man, professional to the last, didn't turn a hair and inquired simply: 'Block letters or script, madam?'

His colleague added drily: 'Or Braille, maybe?'

EVERY LORD Provost of Aberdeen dreams of the affection and regard offered to the most celebrated of his predecessors, Tommy Mitchell, who was Lord Provost during World War II. The most celebrated story, perhaps apocryphal, but with a ring of truth, tells of Lord Provost Mitchell at the Joint Station meeting the Royal Train as King George and Queen Elizabeth arrived with Princesses Elizabeth and Margaret for a short and well-earned break at Balmoral.

As the party turned to make their way from the platform, Tommy drew the Queen to one side and inquired: 'Is ony o' the twa quinies needin the lavvie?'

ONE OF Aberdeen's most notorious post-war prostitutes was spending one of her many nights in the Lodge Walk cells when, on the Sunday morning, a great racket got up as she banged a tin cup repeatedly against the cell door. During the night, her period had arrived and she bawled at the top of her voice: 'I want Tampax! I want Tampax!'

The duty officer rushed up and told her to be quiet. 'Ye'll tak porridge like a'body else.'

WHEN PROVOST Mitchell was well into his tenure, it is said that he became very concerned about the drinking of one of the city councillors, who tippled so heavily that he could become a great embarrassment on ceremonial occasions, or when dignitaries were paying official visits to Aberdeen.

At one Town House function, when a party of French politicians was being honoured with an official dinner, the councillor approached Tommy during the cocktails, before the dinner had even begun, and said: 'Well, Lord Provost, I must be saying goodbye and thank you.'

Much relieved, Tommy made a pretence of being disappointed and said: 'Must ye be awa this early?'

Then he paused. 'Or are ye bidin and jist sayin cheerio as lang ye can still recognise me?'

A RETIRED civil servant reports taking his car to one of Aberdeen's newest dealers where he sat beside a huge internal window to watch the goings-on in the service bay.

While he waited, he was struck by the work of one particular mechanic, who seemed to be more painstaking than the others.

The mechanic changed the oil without spilling a drop. He lifted the bonnet and placed the prop with the greatest care, checked the water level, then lowered the bonnet gently and clicked it shut.

Then he cleaned the windscreen and, after washing his hands, drove the car carefully out of the service-bay door and into the car park.

Just then, the service manager came to tell the customer that his car was ready.

'I must be saying goodbye.'

'Well,' said the customer, 'I can't help admiring the quality of that man's work. I just hope he was the man who worked on my car. I couldn't believe how careful he was with that one.'

'Aye,' said the service manager. 'That wid be because it's his.'

A RETIRED farmer had moved into one of the leafier parts of Aberdeen's West End to stay with his son and daughter-in-law and was in the habit of taking an afternoon constitutional. Not many doors up the street, a young couple had moved in and word had got around that the wife was from Stuttgart, which was enough for the old boy to go for an investigative stroll.

One afternoon, he spotted the young wife working in her front garden and he set off down his garden path, walking slowly. Once out along the pavement, he stopped beside her and leaned on her garden fence.

'Aye-aye,' he said.

She looked up into the sun, smiled and said hello.

'Ye're German,' he said.

'Well, yes, I am,' she said, and a silence hung heavily between them for a few moments.

'The Germans drappit a bomb on this street durin the war.'

She wasn't quite sure what she was supposed to say, so she waited. And he waited.

Then he stepped back and, just as he was about to leave, said: 'Dinna fash yersel. It didna ging aff.'

AN ABERDEEN taxi-driver, a Mr Duncan, was sitting in the Back Wynd taxi rank in the wee sma oors when a group of four young men, almost unconscious with drink, were led down the street by two of their slightly more sober friends.

The men collapsed into the taxi and one of the half-sober

chums leaned into the window and gave Mr Duncan a list of addresses and pointed out which drunk was to be deposited at which address.

Mr Duncan drove off but, for a bit of fun, drove round the block and back in time to see the two half-sober men still standing there, chatting to two young women. He wound down the window and called the two lads over.

'Ye hinna forgotten the addresses?' said one.

'No,' said Mr Duncan, 'could ye sort oot yer pals again? I hit a bump.'

A TORY candidate between the wars was fighting the unwinnable seat of Aberdeen North and was addressing a largely hostile meeting. One Fittie woman was particularly disparaging about Conservative policy and the party's promises for the area, and was not shy of heckling him to tell him so.

The candidate took it for so long, but eventually snapped. 'Madam,' he said, fixing her with a glare from the platform, 'you have enough brass in your neck to make a kettle.'

'Aye,' shouted the fisherwife, 'and you've enough watter in yer heid ti fill it.'

DURING THE war, Mrs Chris Clark had a job in a work-men's café with another assistant, Lizzie, who was allowed to take her four-year-old daughter, Betty, in for meals.

One day, Mrs Clark heard Betty being reprimanded for her table manners.

'Noo, Betty,' said Lizzie. 'Foo often div I hae ti tell ye? Ye dinna pit yer moo doon til the sasser fin ye drink yer tea.'

'No?'

'No. Ye lift the sasser up til yer moo.'

IN THE late 1950s, or perhaps early 1960s, the then Lord Aberdeen ventured to the telephone office in Aberdeen to pay his account. The male clerk behind the counter accepted the cheque, which had been signed 'Aberdeen'. Unfortunately, he did not recognise Lord Aberdeen and pushed the cheque back towards him, saying:

'Aye, aye, aye, we ken this is Aiberdeen. Now sign yer name.'

BILL SIVEWRIGHT and Ernie Laing were well into their eighties and were sitting in the funeral cortege in the car behind the hearse as it made its way towards the new Aberdeen Crematorium at Hazlehead.

Bill turned to Ernie and said nostalgically: 'Ernie, div ye mind fan we were young? We used to waak ahin the funeral procession. Then a puckle years efter that, we'd be in een o' the back cars. Now here we are in the car next til the hearse.'

'Aye,' said Ernie. 'We're weerin closer.'

TOMMY TOSH, now deceased, used to tell of watching the world go by at a street corner in Middlefield one day when he saw a blind man approaching, led by his guide dog. At the street corner, just a few feet from Tommy, the dog lifted its leg and urinated all over his master's trousers. The blind man felt in his pocket and took out a biscuit, which he gave to the dog.

'Aye,' said Tommy, 'I've seen some real kind things, bit that's real touchin. Yer dog peed a' ower ye and ye still gied it a biscuit.'

'Kind be damnt,' said the blind man. 'Now that I ken far his moo is, I can kick his erse.'

ADAM DUGUID, of Hazlehead, Aberdeen, reports attending a concert at the Tivoli Theatre, Aberdeen, in the early 1960s. It was a variety show, but he specifically wanted to see one of his great heroes, trombonist George Chisholm.

Adam was enjoying another masterly performance by George, when he heard the young woman sitting in front of him lean closer to the lad next to her and say: 'Is he really swallyin that thing?'

WHEN JACK Robertson, of Middlefield, ran out of ciga-rettes at the Fish Market one day, he asked a fellow-porter for a match, thinking that that would spur the man into offering a cigarette, too.

Jack took the offered match, patted his overalls and said: 'Dash it, I doot I've left ma fags at hame, as weel.'

The colleague reached over. 'In that case,' he said. 'Ye winna be needin the match.'

The Papers

If an area is reflected best by its newspapers, then the North-east can claim a healthy clutch of weeklies, but principally the Press and Journal *and* Evening Express. *It's not generally appreciated that the* Press and Journal *is the highest-circulation regional morning paper, not just in Britain, but throughout the UK; it is one of the three oldest English-language papers in the world, and far outstrips the* Scotsman, Herald, Yorkshire Post *and other dailies that spring to mind. Now that the shameless plugging is over, here are a few tales shared by North-east journalists present and past.*

WHEN A writer from the *Press and Journal* was dispatched to tell first-year pupils at Turriff Academy about life as a journalist, the class sat dutifully through his talk as he explained about training, use of English, knowledge of law, an ability to get on with people, persistence and long hours.

When he finished, he invited questions, but, as in many North-east schools, the class was too shy. Despite repeated requests, no one could be persuaded to ask anything.

The *P&J*'s man decided to go into a little of the history of the paper, for it's not commonly understood that the *Press and Journal* is the third-oldest English-language newspaper in the world. He explained that it had been established in December, 1747, and had published its first copy in January, 1748. It had been founded by a man called James Chalmers.

At that, a ripple of laughter started in one of the back corners and many others in the class turned to see what was happening.

'What is it?' asked the *P&J* man. 'Have I said something funny?'

'No,' said one of the class pointing at a fellow-pupil, 'but his name's Chalmers.'

'Oh, well,' said the *P&J* man. 'It could even be that the P. and J. was founded by one of your ancestors.'

'Nuh,' said the pupil in question.

'Oh, but how can you be so sure?'

'Hinna got ony ancestors.'

AT ANOTHER schools talk, the same writer invited questions and, again, no one could be persuaded out of their shyness. 'Come on, now,' he said. 'Surely someone has a question.'

Eventually, a shy little thing in the front row put up her hand.

'Yes,' he said. 'What would you like to know.'

'Far did ye get yer sheen?' she asked in a very small voice.

'My shoes?' he said, trying not to look surprised. 'Well, I think it was a shop at Inverurie. Why? Do you like them?'

She looked at the shoes and then looked up at him.

'Nae really.'

THE SAME writer was dispatched to a Donside school to talk to pupils there and found them in the middle of a maths lesson. Being a forward-looking school, the maths lesson took a practical form. The teacher had written out a cake recipe and had asked the pupils to work out a proportion sum by converting a recipe for 10 servings to a recipe for 16.

To test their skills, the cake had been baked. As guest for the afternoon, the *Press and Journal*'s man was invited to cut the cake and sample the first slice, so he pointedly made a fuss of how tasty it was.

Then teacher invited all the others in the class to have a piece, and all clamoured forward. All apart from one boy, who stood at the back, not eating.

'What's the matter?' said the *Press and Journal*'s man, 'are you not having a slice of your delicious cake?'

'Na,' he said. 'I ken fit I put in it.'

THE SAME man reports attending a small WRI in the middle of Aberdeenshire, again for the purposes of giving a talk. After speaking for 40 minutes, he was invited to take tea with the committee. Somehow – he is not entirely sure – a strip of raffle tickets appeared at his side and, worried in case someone had mislaid them, he drew the president to one side and pointed them out.

'Na, na,' she said. 'That's your strippie, that. We aye buy a strippie for wir guest spikker.'

He thanked her kindly and sat back, waiting for the numbers to be drawn.

Then she stepped back towards him and said: 'And we hope ye dinna win.'

ONE MORNING in the mid-1980s, all the radio-network wavelengths in North-east Scotland changed to try to tidy up the airwaves. Realising that great confusion was likely as the region tried to retune thousands of radios, the BBC and the IBA had been plugging the changeover for weeks and, on the Monday morning, the *Press and Journal* published a big notice explaining as much.

Shortly after 12.30pm, the features editor of the paper took a call from a very frail, elderly voice. 'I canna find Robbie Shepherd,' she wailed.

'Well, all the radio stations changed today,' said the features editor. 'Have you retuned your radio?'

'Oh, I did hear something aboot that, bit I dinna ken nithing aboot radios,' she said.

'All right. All right,' said the features editor. 'Do you have your paper in front of you?'

'Aye.'

'Is it open at the TV page?'

'Aye.'

'And do you see where it says Radio Aberdeen?'

'Na. I ken fit I put in it.'

'Aye.'

'Do you see a three-figure number next to Radio Aberdeen?'

'Aye.'

'Well, if you turn the dial on your radio to where it says that three-figure number, you'll get Robbie Shepherd.'

'Bit I dinna think it says onything on ma radio.'

'Does it not say anything on the top of your radio?'

'Wait a mintie.' And he heard the sound of footsteps walking slowly over to the other side of the room. A few seconds later, they returned and the phone was lifted.

'No, it disna say nithing on the top o' ma radio.'

'Does it not say anything on the front of your radio, then?'

'Jist a mintie.' And the footsteps went off again.

Back they came. 'No, it disna say nithing on the front o' ma radio, eether.'

'Well, what about the back of your radio?'

'Jist a mintie.' Off she went and back she came, this time with a note of triumph in her voice.

'Yes, it dis say something on the back o' ma radio.'

'What does it say?'

'Made in Taiwan.'

THE FAREWELL gift is a tradition in offices up and down the land but journalism, in which the pool of available professional talent is remarkably small, frequently sees careers move in spirals, with some hacks returning to the scenes of their cub days before moving onward and upward yet again.

The *Press and Journal* was home to one particularly nomadic chap, who stayed for a few months, moved on, and returned every couple of years to stay for several more months, before moving on, and so on.

Each time, a whipround provided him with a handsome farewell gift until, on the fourth occasion, the large buff envelope presented to a particularly gruff sports writer brought a curt wave-away and: 'Season ticket.'

JIMMY GRANT was one of the most celebrated journalists the North-east has ever produced, and was editor of the *Press and Journal* until he retired in 1975. Once invited to a garden party at Holyroodhouse, he accepted, but was determined not to be outdone by the great and the good who, he knew, would be sporting chestfuls of medals.

On the day in question, Jimmy turned up wearing a large silvery medallion which impressed all who saw him. It caused great interest, and when one acquaintance bumped into him and commented on it, he winked and held it out for study.

It had belonged to his mother, as the legend explained:

Turriff Show. Best Butter. 1933.

ONE YOUNG journalist once asked Jimmy Grant why so many people bought the *Press and Journal* in small country villages and towns when, one would expect, everyone knew everyone else's business, anyway.

'Aye,' said Jimmy, 'they do. But they read the paper to see fa's been caught at it.'

A FORMER *Evening Express* reporter remembers going to a tenement in Torry to interview a former fisherman who had reached the ripe old age of 100. As is customary, he asked the birthday boy to what he attributed his old age.

The man thought for quite a while and said: 'Faith in the Lord. Get up early. Dinna sweir. Dinna drink. And dinna smoke.'

The reporter duly noted all this down, saying: 'Well, that's marvellous. Mind you, I had an uncle at Elgin and that was exactly the way he lived and he died at eighty-two. How do you account for that?'

'Aweel,' grinned the fisherman. 'He surely didna keep it up lang enough.'

ONE OF the facts of newspaper life is that everyone will disagree with something. Some say that a newspaper that doesn't annoy a good few of its readers every morning isn't doing its job properly. These days, provided that a complaint is genuine and proven, any newspaper will do its best to correct any error for which it is responsible.

The complaints which are merely differences of opinion are another matter. In these days of customer care, readers whose complaints are merely prejudices will be let down as gently as possible and told why a 'correction' is not possible – because nothing was wrong in the first place.

It was not always so gentle. One editor of a daily paper happened to be passing the newsdesk phone ringing one evening and picked it up. He was treated to a tirade of abuse for the coverage of what had seemed a perfectly innocent report of a minor political meeting. The caller felt that his party had not been given due credit and space. The editor, whose job it is to decide who gets what coverage, listened stoically while an aspiring politician lectured him on how to do his job.

He tried several times to interrupt and explain the paper's policy, but the party man was determined to have his say. Eventually, the editor decided to wait for the flow of invective to falter, then said: 'Excuse me, do you know who you're talking to?'

'I do not.'

'Then bugger off.'

A *PRESS and Journal* man was dispatched to a schools careers evening at Inverurie Academy and was duly manning the stand when an extremely reluctant and gangly youth was propelled towards him by a portly gent with the ruddy face and gnarled hands of a man of the soil.

The *Press and Journal* man took them for farmer father and son.

He went through a five-minute explanation of the demands of the job, the qualifications needed and how competitive it was even to get a place on a training programme, let alone a job. Then he asked if the boy had any questions.

'Go on, Gordon,' said the farmer. 'The blokie's askin if ye've a question. Speir awa.'

Gordon did not look up, but mumbled a good North-east question: 'Fit's the siller like?' The *Press and Journal* man explained the salary scales and merit awards, trainee indentures and senior-journalist rates.

'And foo muckle div you mak?' asked Gordon.

The *Press and Journal* man gave his stock answer: 'Well,' he said. 'More than a pittance, but not quite as much as a fortune.'

This time, the father leaned forward, with a farmer's gleam in his eye:

'And foo muckle's that exactly?'

THEY SAY in the Classified Advertising department of Aberdeen Journals that during a sales promotion offering seven words for £2, a Buchan family phoned up to place a death notice and suggested as wording:

'John Reid. Bogheid. Deid.'

'Well, yes,' said the tele-ad girl, 'but that's only four words and you can have seven for your two pounds.'

'We'll phone ye back,' said the family.

Five minutes later, the phone rang again.

'Right, we've sortit it oot. We'll say:

'John Reid. Bogheid. Deid. Volvo for sale.'

Aches and Pains

The doctor, one of the honoured North-east triumvirate which includes dominie and minister, is held in great respect in villages and towns throughout the North-east to this day. This privileged position gives a doctor a marvellous perspective for seeing North-east wit at its most unwitting.

THE DOCTOR at Tarland, shortly after World War I, was called to the deathbed of a farmer's wife near Coull. The lady was in great pain and it became clear very quickly that there was little that he could do except make her more comfortable. The farmer, a stocky, unexpressive man, stared solidly from the foot of the bed. Three hours later, the lady breathed her last, the doctor performed the duties necessary and the farmer, quite out of character, broke down in tears and fell to his knees.

Three days after the funeral, the doctor met the farmer in the street at Tarland and said: 'In view of your bereavement, I'm prepared to forget about half my bill.'

'That's rale decent o' ye, doctor,' said the farmer. 'And seein as it's yersel, I'll forget aboot the ither half.'

SHORTLY AFTER Aberdeen's spanking new Royal Infirmary was opened in the mid-1930s (largely by public subscription, which gives the lie to the North-east reputation for grip), a workman's bothy caught fire at the eastern end of the site.

Rather than cause a panic in the nearest wards, nursing sisters instructed their staff to draw screens round the beds so that patients need not become overwrought.

One patient who came round after an operation saw the screens and asked: 'Fit wye the screens? Did ye nae expect me ti recover?'

'No,' said the nurse. 'It's nae that. A bothy ootside the

'Fit wye the screens?'

windae catched fire and we didna wint ye ti see the flames and think the worst hid happened.'

ONE RETIRED Donside doctor reports a tale from his days as a medical student at Aberdeen University, when a tutor inquired of his tutor group if any of them intended to specialise.

'Oh, yes, indeed,' said one ambitious young Englishman. 'I feel the area that will offer the most interesting medical advances in future will be the diseases of the nose. Most certainly.'

'I see,' said the weary old doctor. 'Just the nose? Not Ear, Nose and Throat?'

'Just the nose,' confirmed the student grandly. 'I feel that the ears and throat are too complicated to be combined with the nose for the purposes of study and treatment.'

'Hmm,' said the old doctor. 'And will you concentrate on any nostril in particular?'

A SMALL boy who was exceptionally keen on fishing had managed to get a hook fouled in his hand and was taken to the doctor to have the hook removed.

The doctor managed the operation reasonably quickly and, as mother and son made towards the door, he noticed that the boy was hanging back. 'Is there something else?' he asked the boy.

'Aye,' said the lad. 'Gies back ma hook.'

DURING THE war, men of a certain age had to go through a medical before being enlisted. The medical panel came across one chap they thought was skiving and decided to try to catch him out.

'What is the time on that clock, Mr D——?' they inquired.

He looked at the clock and replied: 'Couldna tell ye. The

only time I ken is fan the twa hans is at the top, and that's
dennertime.'

DR DANNY Gordon was a country doctor who practised
at Ellon for many years and was held in the highest regard.
He used to tell a story, from pre-NHS days, of how he was
called out to a confinement and it was to be the arrival of
a fifth child to a Mrs MacGregor.

The midwife was waiting anxiously by the front door.

'Fit ail't ye, doctor, and Mrs MacGregor wytin sair
for ye?'

Dr Danny made little comment, but went about his own
couthy but professional way.

'What kept me?' he used to chuckle many years later. 'I
could have said plenty, bit I wis there in time for the call
o' duty and, to tell ye the truth, I hidna been peyed for the
safe arrival o' the ither fower.'

AUL RIDDELL was a gamekeeper on a Donside estate just
after the war and was persuaded by his wife, after much
pressure and nagging, to visit the doctor to see about his
shortness of breath and stomach pains. After 70 years of
never a day's illness, he knew himself he wasn't any longer
in the best of condition. He wasn't able to tramp the hills
in pursuit of the grouse, and was beginning to fail in his
duties in organising a shoot.

After the usual examination and questions about lifestyle,
the doctor got to the truth of the matter. Putting the
stethoscope aside, he felt around the gamie's rotund frame
and sighed.

'I suggest, Mr Riddell, that you'll have to cut out the
drink and the cigarettes.'

Looking up from the couch, the gamie grunted and
mused. 'I see. I see. And hiv ye a knife, doctor?'

The doctor, somewhat taken aback, asked why.

'Because if ye're makkin me dee athoot ma drink and

ma fags, ye micht as weel cut aff the mannie and get rid
o' a' ma pleesures at the same time.'

IN THE days before the National Health Service, not a
million miles from the Cabrach, Dr Scott was called to
attend a farmhouse where a young maidservant seemed to
be suffering from severe depression.

On arriving, the good doctor tried out the psychology
and experience of a rural practitioner – the techniques these
kindly men had in abundance. After a lengthy chat in his
best bedside manner, he realised that the kitchie deem had
simply taken to bed in the sulks because the farmer had
not paid her wages for five or six weeks. It was an early
and inspired form of industrial action.

'I'll lie him oot,' she confided. 'He'll pey up afore I tak
ma body aff this bed.'

'Noo lassie,' said the soothing tones of the doctor. 'Jist
ee lie ower a bittie and I'll get in aside ye. He hisna peyed
me, eether.'

THIS ONE comes from a relative of one of your co-authors'
families. Aunt Mary was a nurse and on duty in the
out-patient's department of Aberdeen Royal Infirmary. An
elderly lady, a litttle confused, was ushered into the ward,
told to lie down on the bed and the consultant would be
round to visit her shortly.

Along came the man of authority and, with the screens
round about the bed, he started the usual pleasantries with
a remark on how well she was getting on.

'Now,' he said gently, 'if you would just take down
your pants.'

There was no response; not even a flicker of an eyelid
from the old lady on the bed.

'I say, please take down your pants.'

Still nothing.

After repeating the request at least twice more, the

exasperated consultant was almost shouting when he said: 'Mrs B——, I have a long list of patients in front of me and I really must hurry you up. Will you please take down your knickers?'

The woman on the bed finally stirred.

'Oh, I'm affa sorry, doctor. Are ye spikkin ti me? I thocht ye wis spikkin til the nursie here.'

IT WAS the first time in hospital for old Willie. He had never had a day's illness in his life but then, without warning, he was felled by a stroke. The first few days in hospital were a blur, but then he recovered sufficiently to play his part in the daily ritual of hospital life.

Wakened at the crack of dawn, as is the wont of nursing staff, he was surprised to find the curtains drawn round about him, with a cheery nurse beside him with a basin full of steaming hot water and all the required toiletries.

'Now, Willie, ye're gettin a bed-bath.'

'Michty, nursie,' said Willie. 'Ye'll nivver get ma erse in that sma basin.'

THE NEXT three are not so much Dashes of Doric, but they are all genuine transcriptions of reports from Aberdeen Royal Infirmary, as told to us by a receptionist.

1. A doctor had dictated on his machine: 'The old man was admitted with severe lower abdominal pain due to constipation.' The resulting transcription read: 'The old man was admitted with severe lower abdominal pain due to constant passion.'

2. A phone call from a GP to the hospital stated that: 'The patient's got a renal colic', which was transcribed into the daily written report for hospital staff as: 'The patient's a real wee comic.'

3. Again from a rural doctor: 'My patient, I'm sure,

has a chest complaint, perhaps emphysematous.' This was transcribed on the word-processor as: 'My patient, I'm sure, has a chest complaint, perhaps with his semmit on.'

Law and Order

We have included this chapter to prove that even lawyers, judges and policemen have a sense of humour. Unfortunately, the planned chapter on accountants had to go by the board.

ONE ABERDEEN lawyer between the wars used to tell a deliciously self-deprecating story of walking down Union Street, Aberdeen, with his wife one Sunday when a voluptuous young blonde whom he had managed to defend successfully in court, shouted and waved a cheery wave and blew him a kiss across the street.

He waved back before he realised that his wife was glowering.

'She was that case a few months back,' he said hastily. 'And before you ask it was purely a professional relationship.'

'Aye,' said his wife. 'Your profession or hers?'

SHERIFF MUIR Russell was one of the more entertaining dispensers of justice at Aberdeen Sheriff Court. One one occasion, passing a sentence of two years' imprisonment on a notorious old thief and drunk in his 70s, the guilty man wailed: 'I'll nivver live ti finish twa years ma lord.'

'Never mind,' said Sheriff Russell. 'Just you do what you can.'

SHERIFF RUSSELL was also in situ when a young hooligan was being fined £50 for breaking the peace. 'Do you need time to pay?' inquired the sheriff.

The youth, either sullen or unable to understand the question, stood there glowering silently.

'Do you need time to pay your fine in instalments?' inquired Sheriff Russell again.

The youth stood in glum silence.

Eventually, the sheriff addressed the court. 'Is there anyone present who can speak for this young man?' A middle-aged man in anorak and jeans stood and raised his hand. 'I'm his da, yer lordship.' Sheriff Russell beckoned him down and the man stood beside his son.

'I was asking,' said Sheriff Russell, 'if your son needed time to pay his fine in instalments. I shall assume that he does. Now, would five pounds per week be in order?'

The man and his son went into a huddle of intense discussion, which broke a few seconds later and the father announced: 'No, yer lordship, not acceptable. I'm sorry.'

'What?' said Sheriff Russell, 'an apprentice tradesman with a reputable city firm and he can't manage five pounds a week? Why ever not?'

'Be fair, sir,' said the father. 'Fags and drink's an affa price nooadays.'

ONE BRIGHT spark at the Tulliallan Police College was asked what action he would take to help disperse a crowd.

'Well,' he said. 'In Aiberdeen, we'd start a collection.'

IN THE 1940s, James Simpson, a Banff solicitor, had an office at Foggieloan, where he did a few hours' consulting each week. A Foggie couple called one afternoon to arrange a defence on a charge of poultry-stealing. They sat down and gave an account of the incident, which Mr Simpson began to ponder.

He sat pensively with his elbows on the desk and his head cupped in his hands, eyes closed, considering the best course of action. He must have been sitting that way for a good few minutes – certainly longer than he realised – because he was startled to hear the wife say:

'Come on hame, Jim. The bugger's sleepin.'

MARY HAD a shoppie in a small Buchan village. One

How to disperse a crowd in Aberdeen

night, it was raided and the drawers ransacked. The village bobby arrived the following morning to make inquiries and, not noted for his sensitivity, asked: 'Weel, Mary, so somebody wis interferin wi yer drawers last nicht, eh?'

TWO BOBBIES were attending a road accident at a country crossroads which, in those days, was bounded on all sides by drystane dykes. The driver of one car, an old Austin Seven, said he had not seen the other car coming because of the height of the dyke.

The bobby was suspicious, and thought that the driver should certainly have been able to see the other car coming, because the driver's seat in an Austin Seven was not that low. But how could he prove it?

Shortly, he hit on a plan. He squatted down in the middle of the road and said to his colleague: 'Measure the distance fae the grun til my erse, then we'll measure the hicht o' his seat fae the grun. Then we'll fin oot whither he saw the car or no.'

MANY YEARS ago, there worked in Aberdeen a police inspector who stood no nonsense from lower ranks and who never missed an opportunity to put them on the spot. One day, he was out in a patrol car with his driver, as well as a crewman and beatman in the back seat.

A call came over the radio. 'Control calling East Car! Control calling East Car! Go right away to the Boathouse Briggie. There's kids throwing stones at the trains.'

'Roger,' said the inspector.

Eager to impress his three colleagues with his knowledge of the city, he asked the driver: 'Do you know where the Boathouse Briggie is?'

'No,' said the driver, honestly.

He turned to the crewman. 'Do you?'

'No, sir.'

He turned to Peter, the beatman, convinced that total

victory would soon be his. 'And you, Peter? Do you know where the Boathouse Briggie is?'

'Aye,' said Peter.

A fleeting look of disappointment crossed the inspector's face. 'Far is it, than?'

'It's far the kids is throwin steens at the trains.'

CONGRATULATIONS TO John Stewart, formerly of Grampian Police, who had the guts to tell a fine story against himself. When he was a beat bobby in the Mastrick and Northfield districts of Aberdeen, he covered his area on a bike – a great, black monster of a bike, he reports, with a seat like a Fordson Tractor.

One snowy day, he was cycling round the Cornhill prefabs and noticed a group of children enjoying themselves sledging down a short slope. However, John spotted that the slope ended beside a busy road, and he was concerned that an accident would occur.

He rode his big, black cycle towards them, intending to point out the dangers very gently. When he was about 20 yards from them, they became aware of him, stopped their sledging and gathered into a little guilty huddle at the foot of the icy slope.

'Now, kids,' he shouted, still cycling. 'You shouldn't be sledging here. It's dangerous.'

At the precise moment of uttering the word 'dangerous', the bike skidded from under him and he travelled the last few yards flat on his back and into the group of children. He looked up at a sea of frightened and innocent faces. And all he could think of to say was:

'Ye see fit I mean?'

BOB MILNE was butcher at Dunecht for many years and ran three vans delivering all round the area. He was out in one of them every day of the week, and it meant long hours. As is the way of country mobile shoppies, he was more than just a butcher; he carried news and did messages and all sorts of other community good deeds that go unsung too often. As a genial character, he was often invited into homes for a fly cup and news, or perhaps something stronger in the bitter days of winter.

There was a by-law at the time that prevented a vanman blowing his whistle to give notice of his arrival after 8pm. The Echt bobby had warned Bob many times, but Bob needed to speed up his rounds late in the day and the whistle was the only way to do it.

One night at Echt, Bob fussled his fussle once too often and the bobby stormed out of the station and up to the van: 'Dammit, butcher,' he said, 'I've tellt ye again and again tae tak that infernal fussle oot o' yer moo at this time o' nicht, and eneuch's eneuch. I maun chairge ye.'

An hour later, Bob was still delivering, this time at Midmar, just two or three miles up the road from Echt. The last delivery was a parcel of beef to the hostelry at Midmar – at the time licensed only for beer. As usual, Bob made his way into the kitchen for his nightcap to find the self-same bobby plunkit down at the table, diced cap on his knee and a liberal dram of whisky in his hand.

Revenge, when it comes, comes swiftly.

'Aye, aye, bobby,' said Bob. 'I didna ken the law allowed ye ti drink fusky in a porter and ale hoose.'

Bob was never charged.

IT'S A hot day at Aberdeen Beach and one bobby is striding along the Esplanade licking surreptitiously at an ice-cream cappie while enjoying the balmy breezes. Unfortunately for him and for his career prospects, the inspector is out on the prowl and spots his constable in a near-deserted part of the Esplanade carrying an ice-cream cone.

He directs the driver to draw up beside the constable.

'Now, min,' said the inspector. 'Ye ken fine ye shouldna be aetin an ice-cream on duty. I dinna care foo het it is. And fit the hell are ye deein awa up at this end, onywye? There's nithing up here. You should be doon at the ither end, in amon the folk, spikkin til them and makkin yersel seen.'

'Oh, aye, sir,' said the bobby, licking the rapidly melting remains of his ice-cream while being reprimanded. 'I tak yer pint. Fairly that. Aye.'

'Well, than, awa ye go,' said the inspector. 'And dinna let it happen again, or we'll hae ti see aboot it, and I'll mind on this caper the day wi yer ice-cream.'

'Aye, sir,' said the bobby. 'Fairly that. I tak yer pint.'

Then the bobby stopped. 'Eh, there's jist ae thing, sir.'

'And fit's that?' said the inspector.

The bobby popped the last of the cone into his mouth and swallowed it.

'Far's yer evidence?'

THERE IS a hardy annual story among the boys and girls in blue at Grampian Police of the slow-witted North-east cadet sent off for training to the police college. He was struggling with the phonetic alphabet (A Alpha, B Bravo, C Charlie, and so on), and was asked in a rapid-fire, random question session in class what the E stood for.

Quick as a flash, he shouted: 'Aeple.'

THE LAST winter before the Kittybrewster Mart closed in Aberdeen, two farmers from Insch and Kennethmont were heard discussing how sharp the frosts had been, and the Insch man wondered if this wasn't the coldest winter they could remember?

'Nivver,' said the Kennethmont man, 'div ye nae mind the winter o' 1947?'

'Wis it caul?'

'Caul? I'll say it wis caul. Ma wife saw twa solicitors walkin doon Union Street and they'd their hands in their ain pooches.'

Please, Miss

Of all the professions, the one that has the most profound effect on any community is the teacher. Teacher's grip lasts a lifetime, well after the confines of the classroom. But even teachers have a sense of humour. In fact, it's probably a professional necessity.

A TEACHER who spent a large part of his career at Ellon Academy recalls marking an exercise in which one of the questions had been: 'What is rabies and what can you do about it?'

One answer was: 'Rabies is Jewish ministers. You can't do anything about it.'

A PRIMARY teacher in a North-east rural school was having terrible trouble stopping one of her broader-spoken pupils from using the word 'putten' when, as we all know, the word is 'put'.

To correct him once and for all, she wrote on the board:

I have just putten on my shoes

. . . then asked him if he saw anything wrong with the sentence.

'Aye,' he said confidently, 'ye've gaen and putten putten far ye should hiv putten put.'

A TEACHER at a primary school in Upper Donside was having quite a job persuading one young farmer's son to speak English and not lapse into the Doric. The last straw came one afternoon when they were discussing parents' hobbies.

'Ma mither maks her ain wine,' he told the class. 'Bit she's hid ti stop for a file, for she hisna nae bottles.'

'No, no, no, no, no,' said the teacher, standing up. 'Not:

The putten down

"She hisna nae bottles." It should be. "My mother has no bottles." Now, start again.'

He began again, treading a little more warily. 'My mother makes wine but she has had to stop for a while because she has no bottles.'

'Much better,' said the teacher approvingly. 'Anything else?'

'Aye,' said the boy. 'She's gey ticht for corks, tee.'

TWIN brothers were sitting in a circle of fellow-pupils during a primary-school reading lesson. They stuck at the word GRACE. The teacher tried to coax one of them out of the stall, saying: 'Come on, now, Robbie. What does your father say before a meal?'

Robbie looked at Frankie and Frankie looked at Robbie.

Robbie looked at the teacher. 'Please, miss, ma faither says: "Robbie and Frunkie, blaa yer noses."'

MISS MACKIE taught near Monymusk in the early 1950s and was annoyed one day when two small brothers turned up late for school. Miss Mackie asked the older one why.

'Well, Miss,' he said, 'I was half-way to the school but I took an awful sair belly and had to run intil the woods.'

'I see,' said Miss Mackie, turning to the smaller boy, 'and what about you, Sandy, did you have a sore stomach, too?'

'No, miss,' said Sandy, 'bit I hid ti pu the grass.'

MANY YEARS ago, the bakery at Tarland was Grant's the Bakers. The infant class at school were working their way through a lesson about animal noises. The cow moos. The sheep baas, the pig grunts.

'Now,' said the teacher, 'does anyone have a story about moos, or baas or grunts?'

'Please, miss,' said one lad, 'I get ma playpiece fae Grunts.'

JAMES MICHIE, long-time director of education in Aberdeenshire and then for Grampian Region, and an ardent proponent of the Doric, tells a delicious story of paying an official visit to Braemar Primary School and accepting the teacher's offer of keeping his hand in by teaching a class of eight-year-olds for a short time.

Mr Michie enjoyed the 40 minutes back at the blackboard thoroughly, and asked the boys and girls if they had, too.

'Oh, yes, sir,' they chorused.

Mr Michie thanked them all and began walking towards the classroom door when a small voice piped from the back: 'Hey, min, ye're awa wi wir chalk.'

AT THE handwork class, a teacher not from the North-east was having difficulty getting the boys, in particular, to hurry up making placemats by threading laces through holes in pieces of card.

Eventually, she said: 'Come on, Ian; hurry up threading that lace through those holes.'

Ian looked at her thoughtfully. 'That's nae lace. That's pints.'

THE SAME Ian was listening to the same teacher telling the Bible story about the lost sheep. She told the class that the wee lamb had said to itself that it would leave the other lambs and go on to the rocks and explore, and that was why it got lost. 'Now,' she said to the class, 'what do you think of that?'

'I dinna believe it,' said Ian. 'Sheep canna spik.'

AT GALLOWHILL School, a small boy wandered into the headmaster's room. 'Are ee the dominie, sir?'

'I am.'

'Div you ken this: the grieve shot oor cat last nicht.'

'Oh, my, that's a terrible shame. Did you cry?'

'Fit wid I dee that for? It wis the cat he shot, nae me.'

PUPILS ARRIVED at Rhynie School as usual one morning and sat down in their usual places, except for one older boy who stood. The teacher told him to sit down.

He said he couldn't, because 'if ee'd a blin lump on yer erse as I hiv, ee'd be gled ti stan, tee.'

FORMER TEACHER turned writer Lilianne Grant Rich tells of six-year-old Robbie, who came from one of the outlying crofts and had to walk two miles to school and two miles back every day. Lilianne was in no doubt that Robbie was turned out impeccably by his mother every morning but, by the time he had investigated all the dykes and burns and ditches on the two miles, he arrived always in need of a good encounter with soap and water.

Although he said nothing, Robbie's face for the first few mornings in Lilianne's class indicated that he regarded the calling of the class roll a daft-like ploy and that he, for one, would have nothing to do with it if at all possible.

For a week, Lilianne ignored it, thinking that he would soon feel left out and would want to join in like the others.

Then, one day, she called his name three times, fixing him with a stare.

Eventually, and extremely reluctantly, Robbie said: 'Present.'

Lilianne noted it with satisfaction.

'Aye,' said Robbie, 'bit ye saw me a' the time.'

THE SAME Robbie was in class one wintry morning during hymn-singing. As Lilianne played piano, Robbie rose from his seat and strode over to the classroom fire and stretched his hands to the blaze.

She took no notice for a few moments, but eventually stopped in mid-verse and looked towards him inquiringly.

A few moments later, Robbie realised she had stopped playing. He gave her a brief glance over his right shoulder and said, in a completely matter-of-fact and reassuring way: 'Aye, on ye go wi yer playin. Nivver heed me. I'm fair frozen.'

ROBBIE HAD difficulty with arithmetic, and no matter how Lilianne tried to explain to him that a number subtracted from itself left nothing, he couldn't grasp it at all. She tried counters, dots and fingers, but it just wouldn't sink in. Eventually, summoning another waucht of patience, she said: 'Now, Robbie, we'll pretend it's market day. You have six pigs at home and I'm going to take a lorry and take six pigs away. How many would be left?'

At last, a look of radiant understanding illuminated Robbie's face. 'Man,' he said, 'that wid be gran. There wid be neen left, and I could bide in ma bed til eicht ilky mornin, for I wid hae nithing ti feed bit masel and ma rubbits.'

ONE WEEK, Robbie arrived late every morning, and Lilianne began to wonder if he was taking a dislike to school. As the bairns were leaving for home on the Friday afternoon, she said with a laugh: 'Well, Robbie, do you think you'll be on time for school on Monday?'

'No, I dinna think so,' he said. 'Ye see, I *div* like ti come in late and get a "Good Morning, Robbie" a' til masel.'

IN ANOTHER of Lilianne's classes was Jean, a small chatterbox, almost to the point of disruption. In those days, removal of tonsils and adenoids was not as common as it is today and Jean went round bragging about her forthcoming visit to hospital. Some weeks later, she was back in her usual place, blethering non-stop.

Sandy, who shared her desk, looked up imploringly at

Lilianne and said with a sigh that indicated real disappointment: 'Yon doctor mannie maybe took Jean's tonsils awa, bit I'll sweir he nivver took her tongue.'

ONE MONTH, the headmaster delivered the teachers' pay cheques personally, and laid Lilianne's on her desk.

Billy interrupted. 'That's yer pey, isn't it?'

Lilianne just nodded.

Billy thought for a few moments more. 'My dad gies me tippence a wikk. Foo muckle dis he (with a jerk of his head towards the headmaster) gie you?'

LILIANNE ADMITTED to the butterflies all teachers experience when HM Inspectorate pays a visit to the classroom, but was charmed when six-year-old Valerie was standing beside one inspector, reading to him, when the inspector took hold of one of her gorgeous red curls and pretended to cut it off and put it in his pocket.

Valerie laid down her book and contemplated him closely for a moment. Then, taking him by both lapels, she gave him a gentle shake and said: 'Oh, my! Fit'll we dee wi this great big coorse loon?'

DAISY WISEMAN was a teacher at Folla Rule School between the wars and used to tell of a farmer's son, Jimmy Grant, who was among the new intake listening to her explaining about the standards of behaviour she would expect from them.

Suddenly, Jimmy rose from his seat and stamped towards the door. 'And where might you be going?' asked his teacher.

'Nivver you mind,' said Jimmy. 'I'll be back in twa ticks.'

Sure enough, Jimmy was back two minutes later and said to Miss Wiseman.

''At's better. I wis fair burstin.'

AT WOODLANDS School on Lower Deeside in 1944, the class was having a geography lesson from their teacher, Miss Spark, when the dominie, Mr McKelvie, appeared and said to one pupil: 'Geography is it, James? All right, then, can you tell me what a cape is?'

'Yes, sir,' said James. 'It's a cap ye weir on yer heid.'

IT WAS coming up for the annual school concert at a Buchan primary school. We believe it was at Longside, but we can't be absolutely certain. The teacher in Primary One was holding informal auditions for a farmyard scene as a backdrop to the nativity play.

'Now, who can do farmyard noises?'

Up shot a few eager hands. 'Please, miss, I can moo,' said Jean.

'I can clock lik a hen,' said Annie.

'Me, miss! I can grunt lik a pig,' cried Airchie.

'And I can baa,' said Tommy.

Then up shot the hand of wee Johnnie, whose domain was his father's farm.

'All right, Johnnie,' said the teacher. 'Let's hear your farmyard noise.'

'Get aff that bliddy tractor!'

SOMETIMES, TEACHERS don't get the answers they expect. One woman in charge of a primary class, who asked not to be named or credited, asked in the late 1940s for a sentence using the word 'exaggeration'.

A hand went up. 'Please, miss, my faither says ye're guid-lookin, bit ma mither says that's an exaggeration.'

Good for the Soul

As in many other areas of Scotland, the minister is still regarded as one of the three buttresses of community; the others being the dominie and the doctor. Most of the stories in this section came from ministers themselves, all of whom requested that they stay anonymous, which goes to show, we suppose, that a dog-collar and a sense of humour are not mutually exclusive.

A KINCARDINE minister was also a keen golfer and had accepted an invitation for a Saturday round of golf at Inverurie. Unfortunately, the minister was playing very badly and was becoming more and more frustrated until, by the time he missed an easy putt at the 14th, he could contain himself no longer and let go a minor expletive or two.

His golfing chum – also a member of his flock – was mildly shocked that a man of the cloth had such a ripe vocabulary, and said as much.

'You're quite right, of course, Peter,' said the minister. 'In fact, I've been thinking for a while that I'm going to have to give up the whole thing. It's just getting too frustrating for me.'

The chum was just as horrified. 'Michty,' he said, 'surely ye widna gie up yer golf?'

'Certainly not,' said the minister. 'I meant the ministry.'

OLD MAGGIE had forgotten to put her clock forward an hour at the end of March and arrived an hour late at the kirk. She stepped down the aisle in a fine new hat just as the minister raised his arms and pronounced: 'Jesus Christ! Hallelujah!' at the end of the service. Maggie about-turned and marched out.

The minister became worried when Maggie did not turn

The Sunday golfer

up for the next few weeks, so he visited her and asked why she wasn't in church these days.

'Weel, minister,' she said, 'the last time I turned up ye raised yer hauns and cried: "Jesus Christ, I hardly knew ye!" and that wis an affa thing to say aboot ma new hat.'

ONE WEARY minister at Forglen had noted that a spate of break-ins around the parish had happened over the weekend and had caused great concern. After the Sunday service, he was chatting to parishioners when one elder asked: 'What would you do, minister, if someone broke into the manse one night looking for money?'

'Well,' said the minister, 'I'd rise and help him.'

A FORMER prison chaplain at Peterhead noticed that one of the prisoners never received any visitors and, as the weeks wore on, began to feel mightily sorry for him.

'Tell me, Jim,' he said one day. 'I notice that nobody ever comes to visit you. Have you no friends or family?'

'Aye,' said Jim, 'bit they're a' in the jile, as weel.'

A COUNTRY woman who had moved into a granite villa in the West End of Aberdeen after her husband had shown a talent at playing the stock market was about to be visited by the new minister. Unfortunately, a gang of ruffians was playing about in the street outside.

The lads began taunting the minister for his odd style of dress and for having a very old car. The minister (the man who wrote to tell us about the story) was quite amused by it and chose to sail through it towards the front door, but his hostess-to-be was horrified, and lost no time in telling the ruffians so.

Unfortunately, she made the common mistake of trying to pan-loaf it.

'You! You ruffians! Get away with you! Away home to your mithers! I'll call the police!'

Then she turned to the minister and apologised profusely. 'Come away inside for your tea, minister,' she advised, 'and don't bother your erse with them.'

THE MINISTER had been telling his Sunday School about the lost sheep and how Jesus had had ninety-nine of them, but had been distraught to have lost one and had been determined to find it.

'Now,' said the minister. 'It was very important to Jesus that he find the lost sheep, even although he had ninety-nine others. Does anybody know why?'

One wee lad from a nearby croft put up his hand and offered: 'It wid likely hae been the tup.'

A MINISTER in entirely another part of Aberdeenshire had been telling his Sunday School children about the importance of love against hate. 'Now,' he said, smiling, 'let's see if you can tell me the difference between love and hate. Can someone give me a sentence with the words Love and Hate in it?'

'Please, sir! Please, sir!'

'Yes, Willie, what's your sentence?'

'Please, sir! I love het pies!'

A VILLAGE worthy attending a funeral at Essil Church-yard, Garmouth, thanked the minister for the lovely address then, gathering himself up against the cold, sighed and said: 'Aye, I wid like fine to be beeried here in Essil. If I'm spared.'

ON A crowded railway carriage into Aberdeen in the late 1940s, a young minister was holding forth about how well he knew his Buchan parish. Somewhat ambitiously, he declared that he was sure he knew everything that was going on there.

An old chap leaned across and tapped him on the

knee. 'Excuse me, meenister,' he said. 'I ken something ee dinna ken.'

'Really?' said the minister.

'Aye. My wife's yer washerwumman, and I'm weerin een o' yer sarks.'

BEFORE THE war, in one particular North-east village was a garage staffed by a man called Bob who drove the village taxi and specialised in repairing bicycles. He also had an extremely pronounced stutter.

One night, the elderly village minister arrived with his equally elderly bike, wheeled it up beside the inspection pit and tapped Bob on the shoulder.

'Robert,' he said, 'would you have an old seat for my bicycle?'

Without turning round, Bob replied: 'Fit wye? Is the bu- bu- bugger ye've got nae aul enough?'

A RUNDOWN croft in the heart of Buchan was the home of Mrs Eppie McIntosh, her hens, her cows and her numerous cats who had the run of the house. Seeing the minister coming up the road towards the croft, presumably on his annual visit, she had just enough time to stuff the scattered papers and clothes under the cushions and rush to the door to greet him.

'Gweed morning, minister. Come awa in.'

Having settled himself in a chair by the fire, scattering cats in all directions, he was asked by Eppie if he would like a cup of tea. He had been warned by the kirk session of Eppie's standards of hygiene, but he accepted, albeit reluctantly.

Through to the kitchen she went and came back with a cup which was accepted graciously. Thinking that maybe it hadn't been near a sink for a wee while, the minister turned it deftly round to the other side and took a sip, only to hear Eppie remark:

'Aye, meenister, I see ye're left-handit lik masel.'

A VISITOR to the country met up with a farmer from the area round Mormond Hill and, in the course of the conversation, asked to which church he belonged.

'Oh,' said the farmer, 'that aa depens far the waddin or the funeral's bein held.'

A COUNTRY minister was taking a morning walk and came upon one of his Sunday School pupils feeding the farm poultry.

'Are all these hens yours, Willie?' he asked.

'Yes, sir,' said Willie.

Just then, the cock started crowing.

'Now, Willie,' said the minister, 'when the cock crows in the morning, do you know what that is invariably a sign of?'

'Yes, sir,' said Willie. 'It's a sign he's nae sleepin.'

IN THE days when there were no such things as linked charges, and every country church had a minister of its own, three of the most remote ministers turned up at the quarterly presbytery meeting, began chatting and discovered that all their churches had bats. They began swapping tips on how to contain the problem, and perhaps even get rid of them.

'I did suggest to a farmer nearby that he might be able to shoot at the creatures as they came out at night,' said the first minister, 'but I must confess it was not the most efficient solution, and I do feel a little guilty about it.'

'We strung a strawberry net over the hole under the eaves where they were nesting,' said the second. 'It worked up to a point, but there were still one or two who were able to wriggle free.'

The third minister put down his cup of tea. 'Jist baptise them,' he said. 'Ye'll nivver see them again.'

A RETIRED Donside minister who asks not to be named says that he visited a sheltered-housing complex in 1992 to see one of his old parishioners, a spinster who had just reached her 100th birthday.

The conversation wore round to marriage, and the minister observed that she had never been courted or betrothed. Had she never thought that the companionship of wedlock would have been a comfort in her old age?

'Meenister,' she said, 'I'd a dog that snored, a lum that smoked and a cat that wis oot a' nicht. Fit need hid I o' a man?'

AFTER A wedding at Lumsden in the mid-1950s, the minister was doing the social rounds of the guests and came upon two Kildrummy worthies propping up the bar. Both of them were known for long marriages. Sandy, in fact, had celebrated his golden wedding not two weeks before.

'Well, Sandy,' said the minister, 'another happy day, eh? How does it make you feel seeing this young couple setting out on the long path that you've travelled yourself these last fifty years. They're in for a lot of happiness, eh?'

'Meenister,' said Sandy. 'Wullie and me here wis jist sayin we didna ken fit happiness wis until we got mairriet.'

'Aye,' said Wullie. 'And then it wis ower late.'

THE SAME minister reports that later at the same wedding reception he overheard Sandy and Wullie conversing with another Kildrummy farmer, when Sandy turned to Wullie and said: 'No, Sandy, like yersel, I couldna ask for a better wife.'

Then he took another sip of his dram. 'I'd like til,' he added, 'bit I widna dare.'

A MINISTER who preached once in the Church of Scotland in London in 1959 says that he noticed that there were three pennies in the collection plate and joked from the pulpit: 'I see there are three pennies in the collection this morning. We must have an Aberdonian in our midst.'

'No,' said an English voice. 'Three of them.'

BILL DUGUID was travelling by train from Maud to Aberdeen in 1938 and found himself seated to what looked like a very stern-faced gentleman when a farmer in the seat opposite took out a bottle of whisky and began taking a swig.

The clergyman looked at the farmer disapprovingly. 'I'm sixty-five years old,' he said, 'and do you know I've never touched a drop of that awful stuff.'

'Aye, weel,' said the farmer, taking another swig. 'And ye winna be startin the day, eether.'

THE KIRK elders were not at all impressed with the sermon preached by the new minister, and said so to each other as they discussed it afterwards.

Opinions were many, but the general view was put most succinctly by the village grocer, who said: 'In the first place, he read it. In the second place, he didna read it weel. And in the third place, it wisna worth readin.'

Many a Good Tune

If some of the finest shafts of North-east wit come from old folk, that's probably because they have been steeped in it for far longer than the rest of us. We were sent more examples of senior-citizen humour than of any other category. The difficult decision was in choosing what to leave out.

BILL FROM Buckie was in his mid-70s when he suffered a massive heart attack while walking in the town square. He was rushed to the local hospital and from there by ambulance to Aberdeen Royal Infirmary.

The event was the speak of the Banffshire coast for some days until it became clear that Bill would pull through and would soon be back at his regular seat in his favourite bar.

On the day that he was due to be discharged from the ARI, a nursing sister visited him just to be sure that he was happy about the changes to his way of life that he would have to make. Bill nodded solemnly throughout the lecture.

'But I don't want to suggest that it's all gloom and doom,' she concluded. 'I mean, a lot of heart-attack patients go to ridiculous lengths to keep as inactive as possible. They wrap themselves in cotton wool, which is almost as bad as going out disco-dancing. You mustn't be scared of physical exertion just because of one heart attack. Nowadays, we think regular light exercise is possibly the best way to a speedy recovery.

'Heavens, there's no reason why you shouldn't resume sexual relations as soon as you get home.'

Bill looked at her. 'I'm sivventy-six,' he said. 'Wid it be OK if I hid a cup o' tea first?'

AN ELDERLY man from the heart of Aberdeenshire had

'Wid it be OK if I hid a cup o' tea first?'

decided to blow a substantial sum of money achieving his lifetime's ambition. He went on a Caribbean cruise and had a high old time, even although his thick country accent made communication difficult with a boatload of English, American, German, French and Canadian travellers.

At one port of call, many of the passengers were going ashore for a conducted tour when one man collapsed, unconscious, at the foot of the gangway. Heatstroke, was the verdict.

Our Aberdeenshire man, half-way back up the gangway, realised what was happening and was alarmed to see that the man had fallen very awkwardly, with one leg away to one side, his arms buckled under him and the other leg twisted to the left.

He knew enough about first aid to worry for the patient's comfort, and decided that the man had to be rearranged properly to make breathing easier. He had to be straightened out.

'Strachenimoot!' he cried. 'Strachenimoot!'

A ship's officer stopped him before he could reach the invalid. 'It's all right, sir,' he said. 'It's all right. Keep calm. We'll get you a German-speaking doctor.'

A TORPHINS woman was celebrating her 90th birthday but, unfortunately, had been bedridden and confused for several months. When her son and daughter-in-law visited to prepare her for a day of callers and wellwishers, they found her sitting up and looking immaculate. They reminded her that the new minister would be calling on her shortly.

A few moments later came a knock at the door and the doctor arrived for the old lady's weekly examination. The son let him into the house and the doctor showed himself into the bedroom.

After the doctor had examined her, he bade her good-day and left the room to explain to the son that the elderly lady was as well as could be expected. With the doctor gone, the son went in to see his mother and found her mildly upset.

'Fit's wrang, mither?' he inquired.

'He wis affa familiar for a minister,' she sniffed.

TWO WOMEN were in the queue at the Summerhill Post Office and were heard to be discussing their ailments. The larger one had clearly been to the doctor to see about a sore leg, and reported:

'He jist said that if it wis his leg, he widna worry aboot it.

'I jist telt him that if it wis his leg, I widna worry aboot it, eether.'

A RETIRED Garioch vet recalls attending a call to the home of a spinster at Inverurie who was celebrated for her devotion to her two cats. Apparently, one cat had been listless for a long time and was now miaowing and in great pain.

Almost as soon as the vet clapped eyes on the cat, he realised that the animal was heavily pregnant and told the old woman as much.

She was aghast.

'Oh, bit foo could that hiv happened?' she said. 'I dinna let her oot o' the hoose, for I'm feart for exactly that kinna thing.'

The vet looked across at a big tomcat filling an armchair on the other side of the living-room.

'What about him?' he suggested.

'Och, nivver,' said the woman. 'That's her brither.'

AN ELDERLY gentleman turned up at a travel agency at Peterhead and seemed reluctant to seek advice, but stood poring over racks of brochures against the wall. Eventually, an assistant went across to see if she could help.

'Aye, lassie, I wis jist winderin if ye dee holidays in Scotland.'

'Yes, we do,' she said. 'Come and take a seat.'

While the old chap seated himself, the assistant gathered together a pile of brochures and spread them on the counter before him. 'Were you thinking of anywhere in particular?'

'I'd a notion for a wikkend at Dunbar.'

'A very nice place. Would you be going yourself?'

'Na, na, I'd better tak the wife wi me, seein as it's wir ruby anniversary.'

'Oh, a celebration, that's marvellous. Does she know or is it a secret?'

'No, she disna ken yet.'

'Oh, super. She'll get a real surprise.'

'She will that. She's expectin a fortnicht in Tenerife.'

A BLIZZARD was blowing up the Cabrach and the scatter of crofters were becoming increasingly worried about Dod, who stayed by himself and whose but and ben at the heid o' the glen was prone to being covered by drifts.

A concerned group gathered and set off to be sure that Dod was all right. They struggled on foot up the glen to where they thought the house would be, but there was no sign. They began probing the drifts with the long sticks they had brought and, eventually, one of them hit the corrugated-iron roof. After a few moments digging, they cleared the lum.

'Are ye a'richt, Dod?' shouted one man down the lum above the raging storm.

'Deein gran,' came a faint voice from inside. 'I'm cosied up and I've plenty o' a'thing.'

'We wis thinkin we'd dig ye oot,' shouted the neighbour. 'It's a hell o' a nicht oot here. The sna's blaain lik the verra deevil. We'll be as quick's we can. Can ye wyte or we dig ye oot?'

'Dig me oot?!' came the indignant reply. 'Fit the hell wid I dee oot on a nicht lik this?'

BETWEEN THE wars, Maggie and Tam lived on Deeside and, once a month in the summer, Maggie demanded that Tam yoke the pony and trap and drive her for the day to visit her numerous relatives in Buchan. Bored to tears, Tam passed the days sauntering through the unfamiliar villages.

'Fit kinna placie wis it that ye visited yestreen?' inquired one of Tam's friends the following day.

'Nae worth a damn,' said Tam. 'Nae even a decent war memorial ti read.'

WILLIE LIVED a very spartan life near Keith in a ramshackle but and ben at the back of beyond. His dog was his companion, with two hens that used to lay his breakfast eggs every morning, but his diet consisted of tins of this and tins of that.

After one kind lady's Christmas lunch, she packed her family's leftovers and trudged four miles through the snow to Willie's cottage. His face was a picture when he saw the spread being laid before him, but he still gave her a stern telling off for venturing so far in the snow.

And Willie had a substantial repast, with a paper table-cloth over the wooden teachest which served as his table, then Christmas cracker, dram, soup, turkey and trimmings, trifle, Christmas pudding with brandy and a cup of tea. She had brought candles, as she knew Willie's old Tilley lamp was unreliable; bones for the dog and crumbs for the hens.

After everything had been done to perfection, she decided she had better get home, as the snow was falling more heavily. She left, telling Willie that she would return in a few days to pick up her containers and dishes once the roads were cleared and the snow melted.

Two weeks later, she ventured back and Willie was sitting at the fireside, puffing on his pipe. Words were scarce and she suspected that something was amiss.

'Foo are ye, Wullie?'

'A'richt, I suppose.'

She collected all her containers and dishes and, after half an hour, when still no reference had been made to the meal, she inquired gently: 'Did you enjoy the Christmas dinner I gave you?'

'I did,' he said, 'bit ye'd ower muckle saat in yer gravy.'

GERTIE LOST her teeth after the war and never bothered to replace them. She was happy with her lot and never minded that she was gumsie. Her neighbour, however, was embarrassed about it and invited Gertie over for an afternoon fly cup.

Gertie was a little suspicious, especially since the neighbour was not in the habit of inviting the lower orders in for afternoon tea. However, she knew that the woman's father had not long died, and decided she should at least call to pay her respects to the family.

'Now Gertie,' said the neighbour, sitting her down on the settee, 'I've kent ye a lang time, and I've a proposition for ye.'

'Fit wid that be?'

The neighbour produced a fancy box and pressed it into Gertie's hands. 'Here ye are,' she said, 'as ye ken, ma faither is nae lang deed, and his teeth were barely twa month aul. There wis nae pint beeryin him wi a dear set o' teeth, so I jist said til ma man that we'd gie Gertie first refusal.'

ONE DISTRICT nurse wrote to tell us of old Jock, who kept a rusty chuntie (chamberpot) on the sideboard with a beautiful show of lillies growing out of it.

'What a bonnie show o' lillies ye hiv, Jock,' she said, and she ventured closer for a sniff, only to discover to her horror that the compost was somewhat pungent, to say the least. In fact, it overcame the scent of the lillies.

'Weel, quine,' said Jock, noticing her distress. 'The secret's a kniv-fae o' dung stappit weel doon, bit ye're likely smellin the twa mothballs at the boddim.'

A QUEUE had developed at the chemist's and people became most alarmed when an ill-natered old-timer got to the front and demanded 'a tube o' Semtex'.

The pharmacist suggested that he must have got it wrong. Semtex was a highly unstable explosive much favoured by terrorists. What did he want it for?

'I've a sair-blockit nose and I'm needin it unblockit.'

'Ah,' said the chemist, the mists clearing. 'You mean Sinex.'

A RETIRED farmer was walking through woods near Cults on a Sunday constitutional when a wood pigeon spotted him and covered the lapels of the old chap's brand-new Sunday suit liberally with droppings.

The man's wife, who was strolling with him and who wrote to us, said she had a hard time keeping a straight face when her husband looked disapprovingly at the clartit lapel, then looked up at where the bird was still sitting on the branch of a tree and said simply:

'Min, fit wis the eese o' that?'

TWO WOMEN – one as big and bosomy as the other was small and mousy – were standing at an Inverurie bus shelter on a wintry day when slush lay in the gutter and icy winds whipped down West High Street. Our confidant doesn't know how the conversation began, because he joined the queue behind them half-way through, but he jaloused quickly that it concerned a bus running over and killing a small girl's pet dog.

'Of coorse, the bus driver wis affa sorry,' said Bella.

'Affa sorry,' repeated Violet, hanging intently on her companion's tale.

'He couldna stop, ye see. He said there wid hiv been an accident if he'd stoppit. The doggie jist ran oot in front o' him. Even the bobby could see that.'

'Even the bobby,' repeated Violet.

'Of coorse, the quinie wis jist brakkin her hert. Brakkin her hert, the quinie. She couldna hiv been mair nor eicht. And what sorry I felt for her. It wis her doggie, ye see. She wis sobbin. I wis sniffin. Michty, the bus driver wis near greetin, tee. It wis jist tragic.'

'Jist tragic.'

At that, the bus hove in sight. Bella peered at a handful of small change and strode out over the slush and into the roadside. 'Aye, weel,' she said, 'a bonnie little doggie it micht hiv been, bit it's flat as a kipper noo.'

THE WHITE Settler phenomenon – people arriving from outwith the North-east and installing themselves on all sorts of committees within five minutes to run organisations in communities about which they know comparatively nothing – is not new. Many years ago, a Cockney family arrived in Lower Deeside.

One evening, the mother and daughter of the new family decided it would be nice to get to know the neighbours and paid a visit to the neighbouring farm at Newton.

The tenant farmer of the Newton put up with the conversation for some time, but the two visitors were terrible blethers and, anyway, he had great difficulty in understanding the Cockney tongue.

Eventually, impatience got the better of him and he stormed out with: 'Gweed sakes, wummen, will ye haud yer tongues an lat fowk that can spikk, spikk.'

ERNIE, FROM Stonehaven, was proud that he had kept himself in much the same physical condition that he had enjoyed during his Army days, when he had been a physical-training instructor with the Desert Rats. He prided himself on his good health, youthful looks and general trimness.

While on a visit to Aberdeen, he spotted that one of the cinemas had a special deal on for matinee showings, offering cut rates for pensioners. He decided he would take his wife to see a weepie, just as they had in their courting days.

He told the assistant in the ticket booth how old he was and said he would easily show her his bus pass if she needed more proof.

'No, it disna maitter,' said the young girl, 'I can see yer face.'

BILL HENDERSON, an Aberdeen-based financial adviser, told us of visiting a 93-year-old man at Inverurie to go over his investments. The old chap listened carefully as Bill ran through everything in fine detail and eventually pronounced himself happy. Ever the salesman, Bill tried to introduce him to a new five-year bond.

The old boy listened patiently while Bill ran through the sales pitch, then he leaned forward and said quietly: 'I dinna think so, Mr Henderson. At my age, I dinna even buy green bananas.'

Mixter Maxter

On the grounds that every decent filing system has to have a Miscellaneous section, we're not going to disappoint anyone. Here are the tales that did not fit easily in one of the other chapters. Look on it as the Lucky Dip you enjoyed so much at the agricultural shows of your childhood.

IN THE mid-1960s, it was not uncommon for small travelling circuses to set up their marquees in showparks even at small North-east villages. On two summer evenings in 1964, the Showpark at Alford was host to one such circus and most of the village young fry and their parents turned out to attend.

At one point came the obligatory spectacle of sawing a woman in half, and the ringmaster announced that the swarthy young man performing the trick had been perfecting his art for more than 15 years, for it had been his ambition ever since he had been a small boy.

Jimmy Harper, sitting in the audience with two of his four daughters, turned to the man sitting next to him and said: 'That'll be the laddie wi fower half-brithers.'

IT IS said that one elderly member of the aristocracy, whose seat was in Aberdeenshire, had been attending the village show one summer in the 1930s when he had approached the 'Penny A Kiss' stand, behind which stood a pretty young lass of about 16. His lordship, who had an eye for the ladies and a wicked sense of humour, approached the stand, fumbled in his waistcoat pocket for sixpence, and presented to the girl, then puckered his wizened lips.

With great presence of mind, the girl turned to an elderly woman in her sixties next to her and said: 'Grandma, maybe you could attend til Lord ——?'

His Lordship opened his eyes and then, quite unruffled,

turned to his manservant and said: 'Please attend to this purchase.' And walked off.

ANDREW CRUICKSHANK, the Aberdeen-born actor who went on to play Dr Cameron in the BBC TV version of Doctor Finlay, used to tell a story of attending Aikey Fair as a small boy and being mesmerised by a stall set up by a quack doctor.

The quack was peddling a muddy-brown liquid in small bottles, and hoardings to left and right proclaimed the liquid as a cure for what seemed, to the young Cruickshank, like every ailment and affliction known to man.

'Roll up! Roll up!' shouted the quack 'This miracle liquid will cure every ache, pain and disease known to medical science. It will even cure old age.'

When the crowd began to look sceptical, he announced, with barely a hint of a smile: 'If you don't believe me, I can reveal that I am more than a hundred and twenty years old.'

The crowd's scepticism grew even louder, until one woman looked at the teenage girl taking the cash behind a table stacked with the bottles and demanded: 'Is 'at true?'

'Don't ask me,' said the girl. 'I've only been working with him for sixty-two years.'

AN ESTATE agent was showing a young professional English couple round a country cottage not a stone's throw from the knackery near Kintore. Clearly, the knackery had been busy and, to make matters worse, a nearby farmer was muckspreading.

The couple stood it for 20 minutes until they could stand it no longer. 'Frankly,' said the husband, 'I'm a little surprised you bothered to show us here. Is it always like this?'

'Nae aye,' said the estate agent. Then, realising he had probably lost the sale, added: 'But think on the advantages.'

'What advantages?'

'Ye aye ken fitna wye the win's blawin.'

ONE RETIRED Inverurie woman teacher reports taking a long-weekend cruise to Shetland with a female friend. The North Sea can be incredibly rough and, on this occasion, lived up to its reputation; barely anyone aboard escaped sickness.

'Don't worry,' said the teacher to her green-faced companion, 'nobody's ever died of a wee bit of seasickness.'

'Oh,' groaned the woman, 'what a peety. It's only the thocht o' death that's keepin me alive.'

THE CLERK of works at a North-east town council (who is still alive, so no names) had an office worker who would nip out in the middle of every morning for a swig from a bottle of whisky he kept in the basket of his bike. He would also eat a peppermint to try to hide the smell.

One morning, one of the office-worker's colleagues went out early and swopped the bag of peppermints for a jar of pickled onions. At 10.30, the man duly had his swig of whisky and was aghast to find no peppermints. With no option, he bit into a pickled onion.

A few moments after his return, the clerk of works called him across. 'How long have you worked here?'

'Six years.'

'Exactly. Six years I've put up with whisky and peppermint, but if it's going to be whisky and pickled onion you'll need to find another job.'

IN THE days when Keith was a busy railway junction, one of the platforms was notoriously high and open, and one visitor, accompanied by a Keith woman and being seen away after a holiday, commented on the potential dangers to one of the station staff.

'Ye aye ken fitna wye the win's blawin.'

'It's a wonder there isn't a warning sign,' she said.

'There wis a sign,' said the railman. 'Bit naebody at Keith's as stupid as they wid fa aff a platform, so we took it doon.'

A MEMBER of a Central Belt Rotary Club wrote to tell us about attending a national convention in 1988 and meeting a delegate from the North-east. One evening, they fell to talking about life, love and families and the man from the Central Belt took a picture from his wallet and showed him three boys, pink, scrubbed and smiling.

The man from the North-east took the picture and studied it, smiling. 'That's a nice photie,' he said. 'I wish I hid three loons.'

'Have you not got any family, then?' said the Glasgow man, taking the picture back.

'Aye,' said the North-east man. 'Five quines.'

DEESIDE BETWEEN the wars was known for its Royal connections, but it could claim fame also at the other end of the social spectrum; communities everywhere from Banchory to Braemar were favoured spots for Scotland's tinkers and travelling families each summer.

One tinker was supposedly stopped on the road one evening by a solitary figure, who had obviously been out shooting, and was asked for a match.

Someone who witnessed the incident informed the tinker later that he had had the privilege of being in the presence of the Duke of York.

Shortly afterwards, tinker and 'sportsman' met again. Once again, the sportsman was without a match.

On being asked, the tinker once again produced a match but, as he handed it over, remarked: 'It's a terrible thing that a man lik me is supposed ti keep the king's bairn in spunks.'

THE SCENE is a roup (auction sale) at a craftie at Rora. Sandy Bell is auctioneer and George Mackie is showing the goods. 'Right,' says Sandy, as George holds up a double-burner glass lamp, three-quarters full of paraffin, 'fit for this lump, noo?'

There is some mildly animated conversation, but no concrete interest.

'Come on, noo,' says Sandy, 'there's aboot a gallon o' paraffin in't.'

'Aye,' shouts Willie Duncan from the floor, 'and aboot a fortnicht o' wikk.'

SANDY WAS forever fa'in doon throwe his English. One evening, while about to start compering the local-hall concert, he announced:

'We're affa sorry, bit Mrs Soutar canna be wi's the nicht ti play the pianna. She's decomposed. Hooivver, Mrs Mack, the doctor's wife, his agreed ti be the prostitute and, as a'body here kens, she'll dee a gran job o't.'

FORMER PAGE Three girl Linda Lusardi was invited one year to open the Oldmeldrum Sports, a considerably brave departure from the normal roll of celebrities invited to do duty.

'Fa's this openin the show?' one worthy was heard to ask his companion.

'That's that deem that taks aff her claes in the papers,' said the other.

The two of them studied the ample Miss Lusardi for a few moments as she walked round the ring, then the first turned to the second:

'A gey change fae Maitland Mackie, onywye.'

A TAXI firm in the glens of West Aberdeenshire was asked for a good, safe driver for a wedding, and he had to be a teetotaller so that the bride's parents could be sure that their daughter's day wouldn't be spoiled.

'Canna help ye there,' said the boss. 'We hinna onybody lik that, bit I can gie ye a driver that ye'll nivver fill fu.'

THE REASON Aberdonians like golf, Edwin Reid informs us, is that the better they get the less wear there is on the clubs.

THE SCENE is Briggies, the local name for the Allargue Arms at Cockbridge, and mine host Airchie is sweelin the glasses waiting for the men of the Lonach Pipe Band to return from their outing to the Nethybridge Games. The last of the tourists have bedded down and suddenly, on the stroke of midnight, the Lonach Men explode on the place to tell of the success or otherwise of the piping competition across the hills.

As if to prove the exercise, out come the pipes, drums, busbys and all and soon the bar is filled with music and marching – a dirl enough to wake the dead.

It certainly stirs one couple whose bedroom is right above the action. They uptail and slink off into the night without so much as a goodbye.

Three weeks later, one of the pipers asked Airchie: 'A'thing a'richt, Airchie?'

'Michty aye,' said Airchie. 'A couple walkit oot athoot peyin on the nicht o' the Nethybrig Games, bit I got the best o' them; he left his pyjamas ahin, and I've been weerin them ivver since.'

THE LONACH is celebrated as one of the most historic community events in Scotland, drawing an audience from around the world. Its traditions are many and various, but the most notable is the march of the Men of Lonach, when 130 kilted hielanders tramp seven miles of Strathdon, stopping off along the route to partake of drams provided by hosts of castle and ha'.

Dr Innes, a son of the schoolhouse, was actually domiciled in Humberside, but dutifully travelled north on the appropriate August Saturday to be sure that tradition was upheld.

'Tell me, Dr Innes,' one of his Yorkshire colleagues asked him one year, 'what is it that takes you north at the end of August every year?'

'Ah, my freen,' he said. 'It is my most pleasant duty to dispense one hundred and thirty drams to the Men of Lonach on their march.

'And then I spend the rest of the day trying to avoid one hundred and thirty thirsty highlanders determined to stand their hand back to me.'

NOT OFTEN is the Lonach spoiled by bad weather, but when the heavens do open stories abound of previous experiences in the rain. Willie Gray, the bard o' Briggies, regaled those within earshot as to how rain seldom stopped work on farms. He took his fellow-clansmen back to the days when steam-driven threshing engines powered the threshing mills on visits to farms at the tail end of the hairst.

'Aye,' said Willie, 'I mind ae eer fin the hivvens open't and the rain nivver deval't. We stoppit in the efterneen for wir fly-cup and nivver got yokit again.'

'Oh?' said an attentive clansman next to him. 'Wis it ower coorse ti yoke?'

'Na,' said Willie. 'Ma cup widna teem.'

WHEN YOUR co-author (the one that presents radio programmes) visited the Edinburgh studios of BBC Radio Scotland to record a dance-music programme, he went into the reception area to ask if he could use the phone to contact home.

Mission accomplished, the receptionist asked him: 'Tell

me, are there words that cannot be translated from the English into the Gaelic?'

'Oh, aye,' he said. 'Wirds lik television, ile rigs, helicopters and the like, I wid imagine.' Then he thought for a moment. 'By the by, fit wye are ye askin me? I dinna hae the Gaelic.'

'Oh,' said the receptionist, 'so what was that you were speaking on the phone to your wife?'

And they say the Doric is not a language.

THE DAYS of the travelling dramatic societies in the North-east are sadly over. The favourite plays were in the Doric, of course, and included such as Mains Wooin and The Wee Reid Lums.

Abbie Moir had been a leading light with his Culter group over many years and recalled a visit to the Powis School Theatre in Aberdeen, where they were staging The Red Barn Mystery. Abbie, as William, had gently persuaded Maria out to the barn. The sound and lighting effects denoted a terrible night of thunder and lightning, and heightened the suspense, as the audience was aware that William had murder in mind.

The villain was down on his knees with his hands round Maria's neck. Abbie's acting must have been powerful and compelling, indeed, for one lad up in the balcony, for he jumped up, unable to contain his temper any longer, and shouted:

'Let er go, ye bugger! Ye're chokin er!'

UNTIL THE early 1980s, Aberdeen cars had the registration letters RS and RG, while Aberdeenshire had AV and SA. Naturally, the registration autorities had to be careful of any offensive combinations of letters, which was why the registration LAV was never issued. They also decreed that ARS should never be issued, which shows presumably that the diktat came from Down South.

They were certainly quite unaware of the local pronunciation, because they permitted (and still do) ERS.

ALL NORTH-EAST villages are fuelled on gossip. In many cases, what is not known is made up or embellished into a decent scandal out of all proportion to the truth. There are many stories, but the most succinct came from a native of Rhynie, describing her village.

Both of us would like to stress to Rhynie residents that we have nothing against Rhynie, and that this came from one of your own.

'If ye fart at the tap eyn o' Rhynie, it's intil a heap o' dirt by the time it's oot at the fit.'

A MEMBER of the check-in staff at Aberdeen Airport was said to have been treated to disciplinary action after he hung a piece of mistletoe over the check-in desk. When departing passengers asked what the mistletoe was there for, he would tell them: 'So you can kiss your luggage goodbye.'

BILL WAS a fiddler who owed more to enthusiasm than expertise, but still he persisted in entertaining at concert parties. In the early 1960s, he established himself down the bill in a short variety season at the Tivoli Theatre, Aberdeen, largely by diversifying into comedy, at which he was considerably better than the fiddle-playing.

One evening, he arrived later than usual for his call, and a new stage-door hand stopped him, pointed at the violin case and asked what was inside.

Bill was indignant. 'It's a machine-gun,' he said.

'Thank hivven for that,' said the young lad. 'I wis feart it wis yer fiddle.'

JIM LAWRIE was a doyen of Aberdeen hotel porters in the early 1970s, and did duty at several city hotels, but the famous story about Jim concerns the time he showed an important American gent up to his room.

The American was one of the most awkward customers Jim had encountered, putting him to all sorts of needless trouble, changing his mind about the order in which his cases had to be brought up, and so on. To cap it all, he didn't even offer a tip.

Half an hour later, the American called down to reception and asked for the bellboy to be sent up. Jim duly appeared at the door.

'Say, maybe you could come in and show me where the air-conditioning controls are,' drawled the Yank.

'There's nae air-conditionin in this hotel, sir,' said Jim drily.

'No air-conditioning?' gasped the Yank. 'Ya hear that, honey, there ain't no air-conditioning in this hotel. Tell me, boy, what am I supposed to do if it gets too hot or too cold?'

'Weel,' sighed Jim. 'I suggest ye open a windae or fart.'

The Ones That Got Away

We're certainly not suggesting that the people who sent us these tales were passing them off as the genuine article when they owe more to myth and fancy, but let's say both of us had heard variations on these themes over the years and we didn't want to risk the truth of the rest of the book by including them among the others. Still, some of them were too good to waste so, with a warning that you enter this chapter at your own risk, feel free.

KEEPING A nationally-renowned pipe band going is a costly business and needs a good deal of investment and fundraising. The story goes that the Oldmeldrum and District Pipe Band decided on a door-to-door collection, and each band member was dispatched to one particular part of town.

One came to a neatly kept pensioner's house and knocked on the door. An old body came and asked what he wanted.

'I'm collectin for the Oldmeldrum and District Pipe Band,' he said.

She cupped her hand to her ear. 'I'm a bittie deif,' she said. 'Ye maun spik up.'

'I'm collectin for the Oldmeldrum and District Pipe Band,' he said a little more loudly.

She screwed up her face in puzzlement. 'Na,' she said. 'Canna mak ye oot ata. Fit is it ye're sikkin?'

'*I'm collectin for the Oldmeldrum and District Pipe Band!*' he shouted.

She shook her head again and, realising he was working against impossible odds, he shook his head, gave her a weary wave and turned and walked back down the path. He clattered the gate shut behind him.

'Watch ma gate!' she shouted angrily.

'Ach, bugger yer gate,' he said.

'Aye,' she said. 'And bugger yer Oldmeldrum and District Pipe Band.'

THE MOTHER of a kitchie-deem at a big country house in Formartine marched up to the door and demanded to see the laird.

'It's oor Nellie,' she said. 'We think she's pregnant wi a' yer capers and we'd like ti ken fit ye intend deein aboot it.'

The laird looked flummoxed for a moment then said: 'All right. All right. If she really is pregnant, I'll give her ten thousand pounds and put another twenty thousand in trust for the baby. Will that keep it quiet?'

The woman had the wind taken from her sails, but recovered enough composure to say: 'Fairly that. And if she's nae pregnant, will ye gie her anither chunce?'

AN ABOYNE man went in for his morning paper, whistling. The newsagent was struck by how cheery the customer was, and said so. 'Aye,' agreed the man. 'It's ma birthday the day.'

'Well, congratulations,' said the newsagent. 'How old are you?'

'Foo aul d'ye think I am?'

'Fifty?'

'Na, I'm jist forty.'

The man went along to the baker, for his morning butteries, still whistling.

'Ye're real happy the day,' said the baker.

'Ma birthday,' explained the man.

'Congratulations,' said the baker. 'Foo aul are ye?'

'Foo aul d'ye think I am?'

'Fifty?'

'Na, I'm jist forty.'

The man went along to the grocer, for his pint of milk, still whistling.

'We think she's pregnant wi a' yer capers.'

'Ye're real happy the day,' said the grocer.

'Ma birthday,' explained the man.

'Congratulations,' said the grocer. 'Foo aul are ye?'

'Foo aul d'ye think I am?'

'Fifty?'

'Na, I'm jist forty.'

The man went out to the bus stop, still whistling and stood behind a woman in her eighties, waiting for the bus to Ballater.

'Michty,' she said. 'Somebody's affa cheery the day.'

'Ma birthday,' explained the man.

'Congratulations,' said the old woman. 'Foo aul are ye?'

'Foo aul d'ye think I am?'

She studied him up and down. 'Well,' she said warily, 'I widna like ti say, bit I ken a foolproof wye that I can tell.'

'And fit's that?'

'If I gie ye a richt slubbery kiss and then rub yer backside.'

The man was a little taken aback, but looked at the little old lady and thought there was no harm in it, so he bent forward to receive a wet slubbery kiss and then stuck out his behind so she could give it a good stroke.

'Now,' he said. 'Foo aul am I?'

'Ye're forty.'

He was amazed. 'Foo on earth did ye ken that?'

'I wis stannin ahen ye in the queue at the baker's.'

WE WON'T trouble you with the famous-but-hoary old 'Aa ae oo?' story, but we liked the tale of the country loon visiting the Lecht ski slope for the first time, struggling to put on his skis and looking up plaintively to ask:

'Fit fit fits fit fit?'

THEY SAY that a farmer visited the Smithfield Show for the first time late in his career and was amazed by the sights and sounds of the Big Smoke. He decided to stay on for an extra day just to savour London life.

All was going well until his braces snapped, perhaps with the exertions of climbing up and down the steps into the Underground. He nipped into a post office just off Regent Street.

'I'll tak a pair o' yer galluses, ma dear,' he informed the woman behind the glass once he got to the head of the queue.

'I beg your pardon?'

'A pair o' galluses, ma dear. I'll tak a pair o' galluses.'

'Galluses?'

'Galluses. Ye ken. Braces. For haudin up yer brikks.'

'Braces? I'm sorry, sir. This is a post office.'

'I ken that fine.'

'But we don't sell braces in a post office.'

'Well, they div at Auchnagatt.'

A YOUNG mother from Fraserburgh was becoming increasingly fed up with her brood's incessant demands for sweeties. On one shopping trip to Aberdeen, her patience finally snapped. 'Lord,' she shouted. 'If ye dinna stop aetin a' that gulshach, ye'll be that fat that folk'll aye be lookin at ye.'

On their way home on the bus, the boy noticed a very pretty, but heavily pregnant, young woman getting on, and he began smiling to himself. Not many miles along the road, she caught his gaze and he smiled at her. She smiled back and his smile broadened into a grin and a steady stare.

Eventually, she became puzzled and leaned across to him. 'Div I ken you, or div you ken me?'

'I dinna ken ye,' said the boy, 'bit I ken fit ye've been deein.'

A MACDUFF skipper put to sea and after a few hours decided to grab a bit of sleep and instructed the youngest and greenest member of the crew to keep watch and report if he spotted anything that he thought the skipper should know about.

The lad scanned the horizon intently and eventually, just after the skipper had nodded off, burst in on him and said: 'Skipper! Skipper! There's a seagull!'

'For ony sake, laddie!' stormed the skipper. 'Ye wakken me up ti tell me that! I telt ye that ye should only disturb me if it wis something that wid interest me! And ye wakken me for a bliddy seagull!'

'Oh, bit I think ye'll be interestit in this seagull, skipper. It's sittin on a rock.'

TWO FARMERS boarded the train at Torphins and were sitting smoking their pipes in silence when a commercial traveller entered.

'Good morning, gentlemen,' he said brightly. He was met with glares and silence.

The traveller left the carriage at Banchory and bade the farmers farewell with: 'Good day, Gentlemen. A very pleasant day to you both.'

One farmer looked at the other, took the pipe from his mouth and said: 'A gabbin vratch.'

THE MAN from Littlewoods called to tell the Donside farmworker that he had won almost £1 million on the pools. The man was shocked and delighted all at once, and invited the Littlewoods representative inside, apologising for the state of the house, but his wife was away visiting her parents for a few days.

They went through the paperwork, then the Littlewoods man asked him how he thought he'd spend the money.

'Oh,' said the farmworker, 'This his a' happened real sudden. I hinna hid time ti think. I suppose I'll likely hae a holiday. A new car. Maybe I'll buy masel a new hoose. See ma relations in Australia. A cruise, maybe.'

'And what about your wife?' said the Littlewoods man. 'What will she be buying herself?'

'Lord,' said the farmworker, 'dinna tell me she's won the pools, as weel.'

ANOTHER POOLS winner – this time a Buchan farmer – was asked how he would spend his windfall. Would he buy a fancy car? A villa in Portugal? Go on a world cruise? Or just retire?

'Na, na,' he said. 'I'll jist fairm awa til the money gings deen.'

WHAT'S THE difference between stubborn and that good Doric word thrawn? The dictionary will tell you that there is no difference; that thrawn is merely another word for stubborn (a N. Brit. Dial. word, to be precise).

But there's a big difference between stubborn and thrawn, as the following apocryphal story shows. An illness had threatened to disrupt the activities of a Formartine primary school. Two boys had very sore tummies, which the school nurse put down to constipation. Both were sent home with wee notes of the ailment and the suggested remedy.

Mother No. 1 read the note and went for a bottle of syrup of figs from the chemist. 'Noo, Johnnie,' she said. 'The nursie says ye maun tak yer syrup o' figs for yer constipation.'

'I will not.'

'Ye will sut.'

'Winna.'

And so the battle commenced with no suitable outcome. That's stubborn.

Over at Mother No. 2's: 'Noo, Billy, the nursie says ye maun tak yer syrup o' figs for yer constipation.'

'I will not.'

'Ye will sut.'

'Winna.'

And so a ding-dong battle ensued, much as before, except that in this case, Billy was worn down eventually by sheer fatigue and, to get the matter over and done with, relented slightly.

'OK,' he said. 'I'll tak the syrup o' figs.'

His mother duly administered it.

With a furious scowl on his face, half born of rage and half of the dreadful taste of the medicine, Billy stormed off, saying: 'A'richt. I've taen it noo. I've taen the bliddy syrup o' figs.

'Bit I winna poop.'

And that's thrawn.

THERE IS nothing more enjoyable than a country wedding reception in a village hall. North-east folk seem to be more at home there than at a posh hotel, yet the food, the decoration and the formal proceedings are the same.

At a wedding a few years back up Deeside, the main guests were seated at the top table, including the minister beside the bride's mother and the bride's father seated next to the groom's mother, and so on, and so on. The usual set-oot.

Along came a waiter with the drinks and he asked the bride's father if he would care for a whisky.

'Michty aye. Fairly, fairly,' said the father, and a dram was duly set down in front of him.

The waiter moved along the top table and, coming to the minister, asked if he, too, would like a dram.

'Do you not see I'm a man of the cloth?' said the minister. 'And you offer me whisky? How disgusting. How inappropriate. I would rather commit adultery.'

At which the bride's father handed back his glass, saying: 'Michty, I didna ken we'd a choice.'

THE YEAR that Aberdeen's seagull population exploded was certainly 1995, when glorious weather brought a most unwelcome problem to The Toon – fouling, scavenging and din throughout the city. The letters columns in the newspapers were full of debate for weeks.

Two lads of simple mind were having a walk around the Harbour when a seagull spotted one of them well and truly, and scored a direct hit, all over the lad's head and shoulders.

'God dammit,' he said. 'Look at me noo. Hiv ye bit paper, Sandy?'

'That winna dee ony good,' said Sandy. 'The damnt bird's miles awa or noo.'

TWO SONS of New Deer, who had left for work in London and had retired there, had been unable to make it home for the funeral of one of their former cronies who had died, but they turned up together the following summer, by which time the headstone was in place, but it had subsided badly and was leaning at a jaunty angle.

Davie found a piece of wire at the gravedigger's bothy and managed a makeshift repair by tying the wire securely to the headstone and tying the other end to a nearby fencepost. He intended going round to see the widow and explaining that maybe someone had better try a more permanent repair.

The two of them were just about to leave the cemetery, when two of the village's older ladies walked past the stone and stopped to look.

'Wid ye credit that?' said one to the other. 'Geordie dee't nae sax month syne, and he's got the phone in already.'

GIBBY AND Erchie had gone on a package holiday to Rome with their wives. One evening, while the girls went sightseeing, the lads repaired to a bar and asked the barman for a sample of the local brew.

'What about this?' said the barman, showing them a bottle of creme de menthe. 'This is what the Pope drinks.'

'If it's gweed enough for His Popeness, it's gweed enough for us,' said Gibby. 'Gies twa pints o' yer creme de menthe.'

The barman obliged and watched them, amused, as they struggled through the creme de menthe and were soon near unconscious. The next thing they knew, it was six in the morning and they were streaked out on the floor of a bus shelter in a Rome suburb, both with splitting headaches, dry mouths and shaking limbs.

'Michty,' said Gibby, trying in vain to haul himself upright. 'If that's fit the Pope drinks it's nae muckle winner he gets aff planes and fa's on his knees.'

A WIDOW was being comforted on the night before the funeral by her daughter and two of her closest neighbours. One of the neighbours remarked that the widow seemed to be remarkably composed, and hoped that the grief wouldn't hit when all the friends and family had departed and suddenly she realised she was on her own.

'No,' said the widow, looking at her husband in his coffin. 'I'll be fine. Geordie spent a' wir mairriet life oot drinkin and bowlin and gamblin and playin aboot wi ither weemin. This is the first nicht in years I've kent far he is.'

MYSIE AND Dod from Strathbogie had been trying for almost 10 years to start a family when, one day, Mysie decided she had better go for a pregnancy test. Later, the doctor studied the results, then leaned across the consulting desk and patted her hand.

'Well, Mysie,' he said, 'I'm delighted to tell you that after all these years, you're expecting.'

Mysie was overcome, almost on the point of tears with relief and happiness. 'Oh, doctor,' she said, her voice quavering, 'that's the best news we could hiv hopit for.

I winder if I could hae a shottie o' yer phone so I could phone Dod at his work.'

The doctor smiled and pushed the phone towards her. She dialled the number, waited a few moments and asked to be put through to Dod at his desk.

'Oh, Dod, Dod,' she said. 'I've got news for ye. I'm pregnant!'

There was a deep silence at the other end, followed by a cautious: 'Fa's spikkin?'

BERTIE WAS one of those townspeople before the war who were celebrated for their slow wit, but who were never really as slow as townsfolk liked to think. Bertie's stance was on the Plainstones at Banff, where he would lean and watch the world go by, and most of the townspeople would give him a cheery wave as they went about their business.

It was a favourite sport of the more exalted townsfolk from the southern end of town to go for a Sunday stroll, see Bertie in his usual spot on the Plainstones, and go up to try a little test to amuse their wives. A man would hold out a shilling in one hand and a threepenny bit in the other and tell Bertie he could have his pick to keep.

Bertie always chose the 3d.

When a nearby shopkeeper could bear the insult to Bert no longer, she bustled out of her shop the following morning and said: 'Bertie, surely ye ken that the nobs are jist takkin ye for a feel. I saw them yestreen, jist like I've seen them ilky Sunday. They offer ye a shillin and a thripny and they think it's great fun fin ye jist tak the thripny. Fit wye div ye nae tak the shillin? It's worth four times as muckle.'

'I ken that, mistress,' said Bertie. 'I ken that fine. Bit if I took the shillin, they widna come back the next Sunday.'

CHARLIE AND Mary were out for a Sunday runnie in their new Austin one day when a police patrol car pulled out of a hiding place at the end of a farm road and began following them. Sure enough, a few miles later the blue lights went on and Charlie drew into the side.

The bobby strolled up and tapped on the window, and Charlie rolled it down.

'Fit's yer hurry?' said the bobby. 'This is a forty-mile-an-oor area. Ye were deein at least sixty.'

'I wis jist deein forty,' said Charlie firmly.

'Oh, bit I'm sorry sir, ye were deein sixty, onywye.'

'Forty,' repeated Charlie.

'And I'm tellin ye sixty.'

Mary leaned across. 'Oh, for ony sake, officer, dinna argy wi him fin he's been drinkin.'

IN 1974, just before the last local-government reorganisation, households in places where boundary changes were likely were sent explanations from the Scottish Office as to what was being proposed, how it would affect them and also inviting representations.

At one out-of-the-way farm in the Cabrach, the son of the house took the letter to his elderly mother and read it out to her. She listened closely, without saying anything. When he had finished, she thought deeply for a few minutes.

'So fit dis it bile doon til?' she asked.

'Well,' said the son, 'fae fit I understand, we winna be in Banffshire efter next year, we'll be in Moray District.'

'I see,' mused his mother.

'Bit it says here that if we wint ti complain, we should write til this address.'

'I see.'

'So will we complain?'

'No, no, we'll jist leave it. I couldna thole anither Banffshire winter.'

ELSIE WAS happily married to Bert and they had five children. Then Bert died. Shortly, Elsie married Dod, and they had four children. Then Dod died. Before long, Elsie married Chae and they had five children. Then Chae died. Not long after, Elsie died.

At her funeral, friends filed past the casket, and one lady murmured: 'See foo nice Elsie looks in her goon, and isn't it nice they they're together again?'

The woman behind her asked: 'Fa div ye mean? Elsie and Bert?'

'No,' said the woman.

'Well, ye mean Elsie and Dod?'

'No.'

'Elsie and Chae?'

'No,' said the lady. 'I mean her knees.'

WHEN AN Aberdeen woman gave birth to triplets, the story was reported in the Press and Journal, and a medical expert interviewed explained that it was still a rare occurrence and happened probably only once in 20,000 times.

'Michty,' said one reader to another. 'I'm amazed she'd ony time for her hoosework.'

AT ONE Aberdeen Airport open day, a flying club from down south was offering pleasure flights in a World War I biplane and was doing a roaring trade, despite the fact that, as the day wore on, the wind was getting stronger and stronger.

Last in the queue were a farmer from New Pitsligo and his wife. By the time their shottie came round, the wind was really quite strong. 'It's up to you,' said the pilot. 'Air Traffic Control says we're OK for the moment, but I have to warn you that it will be quite bumpy. You won't be frightened?'

'Michty, nivver a fleg,' said the farmer. 'I'm a fairmer fae Pitsliga wi a big overdraft at the bunk. There's nae nithing can scare the likes o' me. Dee yer warst. Bit if it's gaun ti be really bumpy, we'd be due a special price, I'm thinkin.'

The pilot said he would cut his usual price of £30 to £10. Then, to add a little piquancy to the proceedings, said that the special price would apply only if the farmer was able not to scream or shout throughout the whole of the flight. The farmer accepted the challenge readily.

Not wanting to lose the £20 difference, the pilot put the plane through the worst of the windy weather, and then tried a few aerobatics, with spirals, rolls and loop-the-loops.

But the farmer said nary a word throughout it all.

When they taxied back to their part of the airport apron, the pilot helped the farmer out and accepted the £10 note that was offered.

'Well,' said the pilot. 'I must say I admire your cool. I certainly wouldn't have expected you to be able to stay quiet through all of that.'

'Weel,' said the farmer, 'I will admit I near said something fin the wife fell oot.'

IN THE days when the sleeper service south was used far more than it is now, it was a regular occurrence for the sleeping-car attendants to be asked to rouse passengers in time to get off at a particular stop.

One October evening, a sales rep boarded the train at the Joint Station, Aberdeen, and went immediately to find the attendant to impress upon him the importance of being in Berwick the following morning and told him that no matter how fast asleep he was the attendant was to kick him off the train, if necessary.

In the morning, the sales rep awoke to find himself in King's Cross, London. He went to find the attendant and the language he used was bluer than a Rangers shirt.

When his fury finally died and he stamped off, the attendant's supervisor came round and asked what all that had been about. 'I've never heard language from a passenger like that in all my career,' he said.

'That's nithing,' said the attendant. 'Ye should hiv heard the mannie I threw aff at Berwick.'

FINALLY, THERE s no truth in the rumour that when Robbie Shepherd found an old bottle of cough mixture in the bathroom cabinet, he sent his son, Gordon, out in his pyjamas to play in the sna.

Glossary

A gentleman's guide to Doric as she is spak

Acquant	Familiar
Aenoo	Just now
Aetin	Eating
Affrontit, black	Ashamed, embarrassed
Aneth	Beneath, below
Athoot	Without
Aye-aye, min	Hullo there, good fellow
Bannocks	Large, thin pancakes
Ben	Through
Bide	Stay
Birstled	Burned, sizzled
Boddim	Bottom
Bosie	Embrace, hug, cuddle
Bree	Liquid residue
Claik	Gossip
Clappit	Clapped, patted
Clart	Slap on to excess (v.)
Clart	Farmyard manure, slurry (n.)
Climmed	Climbed
Contermacious	Awkward, deliberately difficult
Coorse	Bad, coarse
Coup	Tip, topple, empty out

Craiters	Creatures
Crochlie	Infirm, unsure of step
Damn the linth	(mild expletive)
Dirlin	Rattling, ringing
Dockens	Dock leaves, a tenacious weed
Dominie	Headmaster (usu. male)
Doon aboot the mou	Depressed, out of sorts
Dother	Daughter
Dowp	Backside, posterior (anat.)
Dyeucks	Ducks
Ee	You
Eese	Use
Efterhin	Afterwards
Eyn	End
Fash	Bother, upset
Ficher	Fiddle, interfere (v.)
Fit's Adee	What's wrong?
Flechy	Infested with parasites
Fleg	Fright
Footer	Fiddle, nuisance, waste of time
Forrit	Forward
Fusslin	Whistling
Futret	Weasel or stoat (not a ferret). Now usually derogatory

Gad sakes!	Yeuch! (exclam.)
Gadgie	Chap, fellow
Ganzie	Sweater, cardigan
Gaur	Make
Gey	Quite, really
Grieve	Farmworker's foreman
Gulshach	Sweets
Gype	Idiot, poltroon (usu. male)
Hairst	Harvest
Hale	Whole
Hinder end	End (taut.) pron. 'hinner'
Hirply	Hobbly, unsteady
Ilky	Each
Ill-natered	Not of sunny disposition (usu. married female)
Ingin	Onion
Intimmers	Insides (anat.)
Ivnoo	Now, at this moment
Jaloose	To reckon or fathom
Jinkin	Ducking and diving, chicaning
Jints	Joints (anat.)
Keekin	Looking impishly
Kirn-up	Mess
Kittle up	Enliven, invigorate

Kniv-fae	Fistful
Loon	Boy
Losh be here!	My goodness! (exclam.)
Loup	Jump
Mairriet	Wed, married, betrothed
Mischanter	Mishap
Mochey	Grey, drab, dreary
Neuk	Corner
News	Chat, discussion (n.)
Nickum	Imp, mischief-maker
Oots and ins	Kirby grips, hairpins
Orraloon	Young farm labourer
Ower the heid	A surfeit, in excess
Pints	Laces
Plooky	Pock-marked, enjoying a surfeit of pimples
Plottin	Sweating
Poodin	Best part of any meal
Priggin wi	Pleading with
Puckle	A few
Pucklie	Small amount of
Pyokie	Small bag containing something
Quaet	Quiet, peaceful
Quine	Girl

Riggit	Ready (usu. sartorial)
Rikkin	Smoking, steaming
Rive	Rip, tear or wrench
Roost	Rust
Rooze	To anger, inflame
Rowin	Transporting (also wrapping)
Saat	Salt
Sair	Sore, painful
Sair-made	Troubled, in pain
Scuddlin	Idling, lazing (usu. while sartorially challenged)
Semmit	Vest
Sharn	Slurry (usu. agricultural)
Sheen	Shoes
Shooed	Sewed, sewn
Sikkin	Needing, requiring
Siller	Money, cash
Skirlie	North-east delicacy, best with onions slightly burned
Skite	Slide
Skitter	Diarrhoea
Slubber	To slurp (onom.)
Snod	In good order
Sookit-lookin	Puckered, wrinkled (usu. corpses or accountants)

Soss	Mess
Sotter	Mess
Spad	Spade
Speir	Ask
Spew	Vomit
Spile	Spoil, damage
Spunks	Matches, lucifers
Stairvin	Freezing
Stappit	Rammed, jammed, forced
Stots	Bounces
Strae-ricks	Straw stacks
Styter	Stumble, stagger
Sup	Small amount (usu. liquid)
Swack	Supple, fit
Sweir	Reluctant (adj.)
Sweir	Swear (v.)
Teem	Empty
Tekkie	Outing, trip, visit
Toonsers	Indigenes of Aberdeen (derog.)
Trachled	Troubled, worn out, exhausted
Trock	Rubbish, debris, garbage (usu. concrete n., not abstract)
Trumpin	Tramping
Twa pun	Two pounds (weight)

Tyauve	Struggle (pron. 'chaav')
Vratch	wretch
Waur nor	Worse than
Weerin	Wearing
Wheen	Good few
Wheepit	Whipped
Widin	Wading
Wrang spy	Mistaken identity
Wyte	Fault
Wytin	Waiting
Wyve	Weave
Yestreen	Previous evening
Yokie	Itchy
Yokin	Starting work

Where Credit's Due

AS WE said in the Foreword, we can't claim all the glory for the tales you have read here. This book wouldn't be as full and varied as it is without the help of the many people who took the time and trouble to write down their favourite family stories, professional stories, schoolday stories and chance eavesdropping stories and sent them to us. We are exceptionally grateful, and the least we can do is record their contribution. If we have missed anyone out, we're sorry.

Thanks to Esma Shepherd, Alison Harper, Jack from Kincorth, Les Wheeler, Frances Patterson, Peter Nicol, Andy Duff, Norman Connell, Jack Kellas, Mrs M. Robertson, Peggy Veitch, Sandy Mackie, Margaret Ross, Major Rory Haugh, Leslie Innes, Joyce Everill, James Stewart, A. Gill, Ian Middleton from Arradoul, Alistair Ross, Hamish Mair, Johnnie Duncan, T. Munro Forsyth, Geordie Stott, V.B. Taylor, R.P. Nicol, A.J. Harper, Norman Harper sen., Isabel Ford, Bill McCormick, Nancy Forsyth, Ogilvie Thomson, Bryan Smith, Chris Clark, Gordon Argo, Ron Anderson, Eric Stevenson, Bill Duguid, Ethel Simpson, Mary Kennedy, Margaret Black, Nan Sandison, G.E. Smart, Douglas Mutch, Lilianne Grant Rich, Ray McIntosh, Edwin Reid, Mary Campbell, Carolyn Smith, Rena Gaiter, Mrs L. Christie, Ron Knox, Alec Cameron, Gordon Milne, Eileen McHardy, Miss B.H. Ritchie, P. Dawson, Willie J. Taylor, P.J. Duncan, Helen Walker, Graham MacLennan, Chrissie Sutherland, Chrissabel Reid, John Stewart, Frances Jaffray, Sandy Watt, Lorna Alexander, Sybil Copeland, Aileen Jason, Sandy Mustard, Evelyn Leslie and dozens of others who wrote and requested anonymity, as well as thousands who, over the years, have entertained each of us with their conversation.

Norman Harper and Robbie Shepherd
Aberdeen, 1995

And Finally . . .

A sequel is in the planning stages already. If you know of a classic example of North-east humour – true stories only, please – do write to us. If you seek anonymity, it's guaranteed, but we don't want your stories to go to waste.

Drop us a line at: Dash o' the Doric,
                      Canongate Books Ltd.,
                      14 High Street,
                      Edinburgh
                      EH1 1TE

Frommer's®

Scotland

12th Edition

by Lesley Anne Rose,
Michael Macaroon &
Vivienne Crow

WILEY

John Wiley & Sons, Inc.

Published by:

JOHN WILEY & SONS, INC.

Copyright © 2012 John Wiley & Sons Inc, The Atrium, Southern Gate, Chichester,
West Sussex PO19 8SQ, UK
Telephone (+44) 1243 779777
Email (for orders and customer service enquiries): cs-books@wiley.co.uk. Visit our Home Page on www.wiley.com

Editorial Director: Kelly Regan
Project Manager: Daniel Mersey
Commissioning Editor: Mark Henshall
Development Editor: Myka Carroll
Content Editor: Erica Peters
Cartography: Andrew Murphy
Photo Research: Richard H. Fox, Jill Emeny
Front Cover photo: Rannoch Moor in the Highlands, Scotland / © Adam Burton/PhotoLibrary
Back Cover photo: House for an Art Lover in Glasgow / © Urbanmyth/Alamy Images

Wiley also publishes its books in a variety of electronic formats and by print-on-demand. Some content that appears in standard print versions of this book may not be available in other formats. For more information about Wiley products, visit us at www.wiley.com.

For information on our other products and services or to obtain technical support, please contact our Customer Care Department within the U.S. at 877/762-2974, outside the U.S. at 317/572-3993 or fax 317/572-4002.

British Library Cataloguing in Publication Data
A catalogue record for this book is available from the British Library
ISBN 978-1-119-99276-9 (pbk)
ISBN 978-1-119-97259-4 (ebk)
ISBN 978-1-119-99455-8 (ebk)
ISBN 978-1-119-99472-5 (ebk)

Typeset by Wiley Indianapolis Composition Services
Printed and bound in the United States of America

5 4 3 2 1

CONTENTS

6 THE BORDERS & DUMFRIES & GALLOWAY 124

7 GLASGOW & THE AYRSHIRE COAST 158

8 ARGYLL & THE SOUTHERN HEBRIDES 207

9 FIFE & THE CENTRAL HIGHLANDS 236

10 ABERDEEN & THE TAYSIDE & GRAMPIAN REGIONS 272

11 INVERNESS & THE WEST HIGHLANDS 314

12 THE HEBRIDEAN ISLANDS 353

LIST OF MAPS

ABOUT THE AUTHORS

Lesley Anne Rose is a travel and script writer who has lived in and explored Scotland for a number of years. She has written guidebooks, articles, travel columns, and website copy for various publishers and organizations on areas as diverse as Florida and Malta, Canada, the Caribbean, and the U.K., where she specializes in the Lake District and Scotland. While she enjoys writing about independent travel, food, traveling with children, the arts, and eco tourism, her real passion is cycling and exploring new places by bicycle. Lesley Anne has seen her scripts produced in regional theatre and teaches travel and creative writing. Lesley Anne is responsible for the chapters on The Best of Scotland, the Trip Planner, Edinburgh & the Lothians, the Borders & Dumfries & Galloway, Glasgow & the Ayrshire Coast, Fife & the Central Highlands, and she wrote the planning chapter with Michael.

Michael Macaroon is a writer who specializes in travel and the arts, and has written a variety of books and many articles for newspapers and magazines. His Scottish ancestry is on his maternal side: his great-grandfather was a grazier in the Borders, and his grandfather ran an unsuccessful ice-cream business in Glenrothes. Michael wrote the Scotland in Depth chapter, Suggested Scotland Itineraries, Argyll & the Southern Hebrides, Aberdeen & the Tayside & Grampian regions, Inverness & the West Highlands, and the Hebridean Islands.

Vivienne Crow has been a journalist for more than 20 years. She specializes in travel and the outdoors, and has written for a variety of publications including *The Scotsman* and *The Sydney Morning Herald.* She is the author of nine guidebooks, and currently lives in northern England, about 8 miles from the Scottish border. Vivienne wrote the chapter on the Orkney & Shetland islands.

ACKNOWLEDGMENTS

Lesley Anne would like to thank all the PR agencies, organisations and individuals that helped with travel and research. These include: Kit Reid at Historic Scotland, Beth Kendall at Citrus PR, Gemma Nicholson, Megan Davidson and Lauren Cormack at Crimson Edge, Lee Todd at the Azalea Group, Emma Trimble at Brazen PR, and Helen Fraser. Many thanks, as ever, to Martin Chester for his continuous support and advice.

Vivienne would like to thank Misa Hay of Promote Shetland.

ADVISORY & DISCLAIMER

Travel information can change quickly and unexpectedly, and we strongly advise you to confirm important details locally before traveling, including information on visas, health and safety, traffic and transport, accommodations, shopping, and eating out. We also encourage you to stay alert while traveling and to remain aware of your surroundings. Avoid civil disturbances, and keep a close eye on cameras, purses, wallets, and other valuables.

While we have endeavored to ensure that the information contained within this guide is accurate and up-to-date at the time of publication, we make no representations or warranties with respect to the accuracy or completeness of the contents of this work and specifically disclaim all warranties, including without limitation warranties of fitness for a particular purpose. We accept no responsibility or liability for any inaccuracy or errors or omissions, or for any inconvenience, loss, damage, costs, or expenses of any nature whatsoever incurred or suffered by anyone as a result of any advice or information contained in this guide.

The inclusion of a company, organization, or website in this guide as a service provider and/or potential source of further information does not mean that we endorse them or the information they provide. Be aware that information provided through some websites may be unreliable and can change without notice. Neither the publisher nor author shall be liable for any damages arising herefrom.

HOW TO CONTACT US

In researching this book, we discovered many wonderful places—hotels, restaurants, shops, and more. We're sure you'll find others. Please tell us about them, so we can share the information with your fellow travelers in upcoming editions. If you were disappointed with a recommendation, we'd love to know that, too. Please write to:

Frommer's Scotland, 12th Edition
John Wiley & Sons, Inc. • 111 River St. • Hoboken, NJ 07030-5774
frommersfeedback@wiley.com

FROMMER'S STAR RATINGS, ICONS & ABBREVIATIONS

Every hotel, restaurant, and attraction listing in this guide has been ranked for quality, value, service, amenities, and special features using a **star-rating system.** In country, state, and regional guides, we also rate towns and regions to help you narrow down your choices and budget your time accordingly. Hotels and restaurants are rated on a scale of zero (recommended) to three stars (exceptional). Attractions, shopping, nightlife, towns, and regions are rated according to the following scale: zero stars (recommended), one star (highly recommended), two stars (very highly recommended), and three stars (must-see).

In addition to the star-rating system, we also use **seven feature icons** that point you to the great deals, in-the-know advice, and unique experiences that separate travelers from tourists. Throughout the book, look for:

special finds—those places only insiders know about

fun facts—details that make travelers more informed and their trips more fun

kids—best bets for kids and advice for the whole family

special moments—those experiences that memories are made of

overrated—places or experiences not worth your time or money

insider tips—great ways to save time and money

great values—where to get the best deals

The following abbreviations are used for credit cards:

AE	American Express	DISC	Discover	V	Visa
DC	Diners Club	MC	MasterCard		

TRAVEL RESOURCES AT FROMMERS.COM

Frommer's travel resources don't end with this guide. Frommer's website, **www.frommers. com**, has travel information on more than 4,000 destinations. We update features regularly, giving you access to the most current trip-planning information and the best airfare, lodging, and car-rental bargains. You can also listen to podcasts, connect with other Frommers. com members through our active-reader forums, share your travel photos, read blogs from guidebook editors and fellow travelers, and much more.

THE BEST OF SCOTLAND

Scotland delivers on every expectation of a deeply romantic land filled with misty lochs, fields of heather, and moody mountain ranges, while its thoroughly modern cities are welcoming cultural hubs. Whether you're in the heart of Edinburgh at Hogmanay, alone in Iona Abbey, or teeing off at Carnoustie, you'll experience a nation that champions its history and believes in its future. Our picks of the best include many world-famous attractions as well as a few well-kept secrets.

THE CITIES   Scotland's cities are among the most dynamic in Europe. **Edinburgh** never fails to dazzle with its Old and New Towns, port of Leith, and some of the nation's top cultural attractions. Equally vibrant **Glasgow** claims the top art galleries, best nightlife, and unbeatable shopping. **Stirling** links Scotland's high and low lands and is a magnet for history lovers.

THE COUNTRYSIDE   Strewn with royal palaces (**Falkland** in Fife), ruined castles (**Caerlaverock** in Dumfries and Galloway), Neolithic settlements (**Skara Brae** in the Orkneys), and modern feats of engineering (**Neptune's Staircase** near Fort William), the wilds of Scotland have something for everyone. Outdoor enthusiasts can choose from mountain ranges, river valleys, and rugged moorland where top golf courses, first-class fishing, and limitless hiking blend with tales of clan feuds and a rich variety of wildlife.

THE COAST   Mainland Scotland alone claims 6,158 miles of coastline. Add on the shores of its many islands and it would take a lifetime to discover all the deserted beaches of the Hebrides (**Tiree, Harris,** and **South Uist**), the sea lochs of the west coast (**Linnhe, Sunart,** and **Etive**), and craggy cliffs to the east (**East Neuk**). Unbeatable coastal walks lead from **Eshaness** in Shetland and excellent sea fishing lies off the shores of **Portpatrick.**

EATING & DRINKING   Scotland's culinary scene has excelled in recent years with many establishments championing local and in-season produce. Fresh seafood is hauled ashore at **Loch Fyne,** melt-in-the-mouth lamb is reared in the Borders, and crumbling cheeses mature in dairies across the Highlands. Your local pint could be a dark ale from **Traquair** or a wheat beer from Glasgow's **West.** And no visit is complete without a wee dram of the liquor named after the nation itself: Scotch.

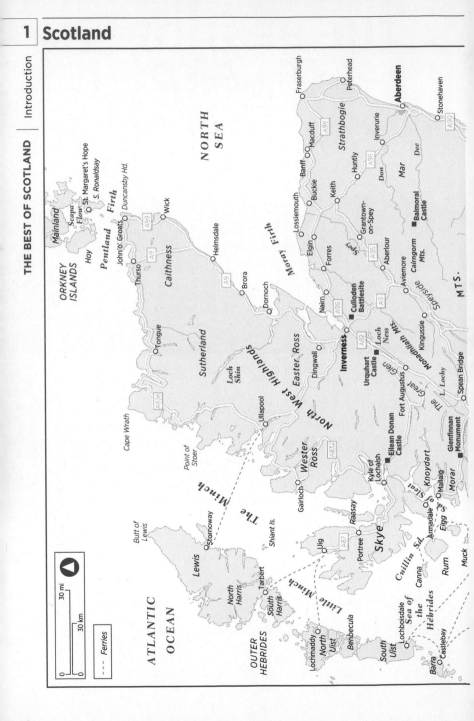

NORTH SEA

ORKNEY ISLANDS

Mainland
Scapa Flow
Hoy
St. Margaret's Hope
S. Ronaldsay
Duncansby Hd.
Pentland Firth

Fraserburgh
Peterhead
Aberdeen
Stonehaven
Strathbogie
Macduff
Banff
Inverurie
Buckie
Keith
Huntly
Mar
Dee
Balmoral Castle
Lossiemouth
Grantown-on-Spey
Elgin
Forres
Aberlour
Cairngorm Mts.
Nairn
Aviemore
Culloden Battlesite
Kingussie
Inverness
Urquhart Castle
Loch Ness
Spean Bridge
L. Lochy
Fort Augustus
Glenfinnan Monument
Eilean Donan Castle
Kyle of Lochalsh
Knoydart
Mallaig
Morar
Armadale
Eigg
Rum
Muck

Wick
John O'Groats
Thurso
Caithness
Helmsdale
Brora
Dornoch
Moray Firth
Tongue
Sutherland
Loch Shin
Dingwall
Easter Ross
Ullapool
Wester Ross
Gairloch
Raasay
Uig
Portree
Skye
Cuillin
Canna
Sea of the Hebrides

Cape Wrath
Point of Stoer
The Minch
Butt of Lewis
Stornoway
Shiant Is.
Lewis
North Harris
Tarbert
South Harris
Little Minch
Benbecula
North Uist
Lochmaddy
South Uist
Lochboisdale
Barra
Castlebay

ATLANTIC OCEAN
OUTER HEBRIDES

North West Highlands
Monadhliath Mts.
MTS.
Spey
The Great Glen

30 mi
30 km
Ferries

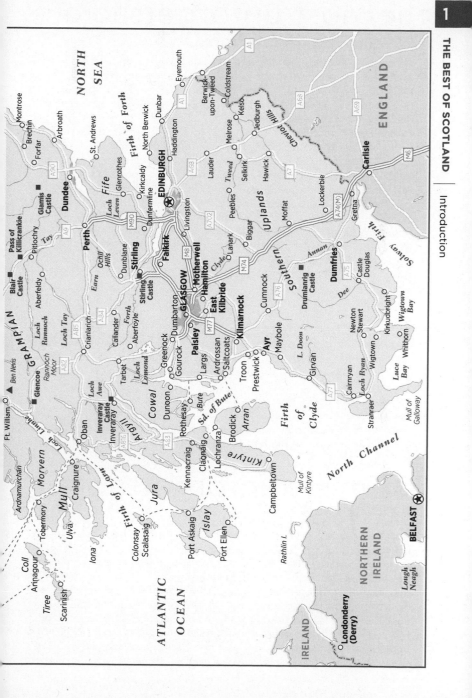

THE most unforgettable
TRAVEL EXPERIENCES

o **Edinburgh at Festival Time:** Every August Edinburgh erupts into a spectacular celebration of culture, art, dance, politics, music, and street performance as a clutch of festivals—headed by the Edinburgh International Festival, the unstoppable Fringe, and the heart-stirring Military Tattoo—sweep across every venue and public space in the city. See p. 102.

o **Haunting the Castles:** Scotland is littered with ancient castles. Many—such as **Urquhart** (p. 326) on the banks of Loch Ness and the cliff-top **Tantallon** (p. 122)—stand in ruined splendor. Others such as Macbeth's very own **Cawdor** are luxurious, legendary family homes. See p. 338

o **Horseback Riding Through the Highlands:** Travel the romantic way through fragrant heather and over lichen-covered rocks on an equestrian excursion into the Highlands. One of Scotland's biggest stables, the **Highland Riding Centre** in Drumnadrochit (p. 325), stands close to the brooding northern shores of Loch Ness.

o **Cruising the Caledonian Canal:** Connecting three of the Highlands' longest lochs (Ness, Lochy, and Oich), the Caledonian Canal once transported goods between Scotland's east and west coasts. Today you can take in spectacular waterborne views of the Scottish countryside from the decks of the cabin cruisers that ply these calm waters. See p. 327.

o **Exploring the Heart of Neolithic Orkney:** Discover some of Europe's most mysterious and best-preserved prehistoric sites on the western edges of mainland Orkney. The huge Ring of Brodgar stone circle and imposing Stones of Stenness stand close to Maeshowe chambered cairn and the Neolithic village of Skara Brae. See p. 399.

o **Getting in Touch with Your Inner Viking:** Join the thousand-strong horde of "Vikings" who march through Lerwick, Shetland, every January as part of **Up Helly Aa,** Europe's largest fire festival. In a pagan-like desire to light up the seemingly endless winter night, they set fire to a replica longboat in the harbor. See p. 412.

THE most unforgettable
CITY EXPERIENCES

o **Walk the Royal Mile** (Edinburgh): Stunning views, narrow closes, and dark *wynds* (alleys) spread out in all directions along this street, which forms the backbone of Edinburgh's medieval Old Town. Take in the many free museums and some of Scotland's most well-known attractions along the way. See p. 73.

o **National Museum of Scotland** (Edinburgh): Fresh faced from a major renovation, this transformed museum is crammed with national icons from the 12th-century Lewis Chessmen to Dolly the sheep, the first mammal cloned from an adult cell. Follow the story of Scotland to the top floor and stunning city views. See p. 80.

o **Underground Edinburgh:** Journey deep into Edinburgh's dark side via a tour through its spooky underground vaults and long-buried city streets. Listen to tales of grim goings-on as you travel through this subterranean realm, home to many of the city's most notorious ghosts. See p. 76.

o **The Burrell Collection** (Glasgow): Sir William Burrell (1861–1958), a wealthy industrialist who devoted much of his life to accumulating art, is responsible for this fabulous collection. Set in parkland on Glasgow's southside, it's one of Scotland's most admired collections. See p. 175.

o **Cathedral of St. Kentigern** (Glasgow): St. Kentigern's is mainland Scotland's only complete medieval cathedral. Striking contemporary stained glass adds a modern touch to the heritage of this ancient building, which was cleared of all but a few icons of idolatry in the 1600s. Leave time to lose yourself in the adjacent sprawling Necropolis cemetery. See p. 171.

o **Aberdeen Art Gallery:** A treasure trove of art from across the globe, this prestigious gallery showcases exhibits from the 1700s to the present, from Hogarth to Reynolds to Picasso. It's also the place to catch the most important temporary exhibits in northeast Scotland. See p. 277.

THE best FOOD & DRINK EXPERIENCES

o **Whisky Tasting:** Take a behind-the-scenes tour of one of Scotland's many whisky distilleries where the angels are said to sneak a share from each cask. Or join the **Scotch Malt Whisky Society** for a day and sample as many as you please at their **Vaults** bar. See p. 105.

o **Edinburgh's Fine Dining:** Scotland's capital claims five Michelin-starred chefs whose restaurants are among the best places to eat in the country. Three chefs, including top Scottish chef Martin Wishart, are based in Leith, while the sumptuous 21212 is the latest top-rated addition to Edinburgh's restaurant scene. See p. 90.

o **Afternoon Tea:** This famed meal is one of the most refined ways to while away an afternoon in Scotland. Recommended spots include **Greywalls Hotel** in East Lothian (p. 123) and **Duisdale Hotel** on the Isle of Skye (p. 364). Alternatively make a day of it on an **Afternoon Tea Tour** (p. 35).

o **Tucking into the U.K.'s Best Fish & Chips** (Anstruther): No place in the United Kingdom makes better fish and chips than the Anstruther Fish Bar & Restaurant. Enjoy a portion of the nation's favorite dish along with views of fishing boats and the North Sea at this busy harborfront restaurant. See p. 246.

o **Real Ale and Traditional Music** (Lerwick, Shetland): Enjoy a pint of real ale and a taste of traditional music in one of Lerwick's friendly pubs. Many of Shetland's excellent fiddle and accordion players start their careers in these laid-back harborside bars, where visitors can sample some of Scotland's best local brews. See p. 414.

o **Scottish Smokehouses:** Freshly caught seafood is transformed by Scotland's traditional smokehouses. The smoldering fires of the **Marrbury Smokehouse** on the banks of the Solway Firth add pungent flavors to hand-caught wild salmon, Kirkcudbright scallops, and succulent mussels. See p. 153.

THE best LOCAL EXPERIENCES

o **Six Nations Rugby Match** (Edinburgh): Join the whole of Scotland in cheering its national rugby team on home ground at a Six Nations Championship match in Edinburgh's Murrayfield stadium. If you can't snag a ticket, head to a local pub and watch the action unfold on a big screen. See p. 107.

o **An Afternoon in Cramond** (Edinburgh): This old waterfront village is a locals' favorite on sunny afternoons. Explore a tiny offshore island, the scant remains of a Roman fort, and Lauriston Castle; and walk the banks of the River Almond, site of the first known human habitation in Scotland. See p. 86.

o **The Prince of Wales** (Aberdeen): Featuring Aberdeen's longest bar counter (with an old spittoon trough) and a collection of whisky and brewing memorabilia on the walls, this characterful establishment is a perennial favorite with locals and visitors alike. Given the quality of the beer and the hearty lunches, it's no wonder. See p. 280.

o **A Highland Game:** Held throughout the year, these family-friendly sporting days celebrate Scottish culture like no other event. Highlights include men in kilts tossing cabers (small tree trunks) and local Scottish dancing. The best known is Braemar's late August **Royal Highland Gathering,** near Balmoral Castle. See p. 305.

o **Hootananny** (Inverness): This city-center nightspot offers the remarkable combination of traditional Scottish music, a Thai restaurant, and large screens for the latest music videos. Still, it's undeniably popular, and never more so than on Fridays, when local singers and songwriters showcase their talents, or on Saturday afternoons when there's a *ceilidh* (an evening of traditional music and dance). See p. 333.

o **A Boat Trip to Foula** (Shetland): Journey across the water to Foula, one of Britain's most isolated and windswept islands. The handful of hardy inhabitants living on this wild but beautiful lump of rock off the west coast of Shetland still follow the old Julian calendar, celebrating Christmas Day on January 6. See p. 418.

THE best ACTIVITIES FOR FAMILIES

o **Our Dynamic Earth** (Edinburgh): Take your family on a trip through the physical landscapes of the Earth from the Big Bang, through erupting volcanoes to lush rain forests. Leave time for a planetarium show at Future Dome. See p. 85.

o **Glasgow Science Centre:** Housed in a titanium clad pod-like building on the south bank of the River Clyde, this leading family-focused attraction inspires and informs all ages on the concepts behind science and technology. Learning is fun and interactive and an adjacent IMAX cinema wows every time. See p. 174.

o **Blair Drummond Safari & Adventure Park** (near Stirling): Visit the wild side of Scotland and get up close to animals from across the globe at this top family-friendly attraction. Admission includes a journey through wildlife reserves, a sea lion show, and a boat trip around chimp island. See p. 258.

o **Loch of Lowes Wildlife Reserve** (Dunkeld): Children can view some of Scotland's rarest birds at the hides perched on the shores of this small loch. Or watch a live link of nesting ospreys that migrate from Africa to breed here every year. A visitor center provides interactive information and retail therapy. See p. 293.

o **Boat Trips from Mull:** Take your family on a sea safari and hop aboard one of the several boats that depart from Tobermory's harbor for the surrounding waters. Tours range from two-hour jaunts to the local seal colony to all-day whale-watching adventures. See p. 371.

o **Old Scatness** (Shetland): History is brought to fun-filled life at Old Scatness, near Sumburgh Head, Shetland. While archaeologists continue unearthing an Iron Age broch, Pictish homes, and Norse dwellings at this amazing site, children can dress up as Vikings and join in a variety of activities. See p. 416.

THE best OF CONTEMPORARY SCOTLAND

o **The Scottish Parliament** (Edinburgh): Love it or loath it, there's no denying Scotland's extraordinary new parliament building embodies a thoroughly modern Scotland. Spreading out below Salisbury Crags, this architectural masterpiece cost a cool £414 million and is best experienced via a free tour that includes the hallowed debating chamber. See p. 79.

o **Striding Arches** (near Moniaive, Dumfries, and Galloway): Contemporary site-specific art and stunning Scottish countryside combine in this memorable piece by landscape artist Andy Goldsworthy. Walk the route between this collection of striking arches that blaze a trail and make a bold artistic statement across Cairnhead. See p. 148.

o **Glasgow's Theatre Scene:** Be inspired by the best in European contemporary theatre, presented by cutting-edge Scottish artists at Glasgow's hippest performing arts venues including the Tramway, the Arches, and the Tron. See p. 188.

o **The Falkirk Wheel:** A triumph of ambitious Scottish engineering, this gleaming claw-like structure is the world's first and only rotating boatlift. The Wheel effortlessly swings boats the 35m (115 ft.) between the Union and Forth and Clyde canals using only a fraction of power and Archimedes' Principle. See p. 120.

o **Ben Cruachan Power Station:** A mountain towering above Loch Awe in Argyll harbors the world's second-largest hydroelectric power station. Enormous turbines pump water from the loch to a reservoir high up above. You can take a guided tour and learn more in an exhibition center. See p. 229.

o **Aberdeen Arts Centre:** On the outside it's a traditional granite Victorian institution, but inside it's a lively arts complex offering a contemporary and extraordinarily broad program. Catch the latest plays, arthouse films, and exhibitions. If that's not enough, enjoy a drink at the bright cafe-bar. See p. 279.

THE best HISTORIC EXPERIENCES

o **The Borders' Abbeys:** Spend a day exploring gentle countryside and the four great ruined abbeys—Kelso, Dryburgh, Jedburgh, and Melrose—that cluster around the heart of the Scottish Borders. Brought to their knees by the English and the

Reformation, these former ecclesiastical powerhouses remain magnificent even in ruins. See chapter 6.

o **Alloway, Birthplace of Burns:** Visit the tiny cottage where Scotland's much-loved national poet, Robert "Rabbie" Burns was born and the auld Brig o' Doon immortalized in his epic poem *Tam O'Shanter*. A swish new museum and grand monument and gardens complete a Burns day out. See p. 200.

o **Stirling Castle:** One of the most formidable fortresses in the British Isles, Stirling Castle boasts views of the Wallace Monument and played a pivotal role in the battle for an independent Scotland. Its fully restored Renaissance palace is a must-see triumph of its era. See p. 256.

o **Innerpeffray Library** (Crieff): One of Scotland's hidden historical gems, this Georgian library attached to an old church is lined with the precious leather-bound volumes that once formed one of Scotland's earliest book-lending services. Take a guided tour or don a pair of white gloves to leaf through these old tomes. See p. 291.

o **Hugh Miller's Cottage** (Cromarty): This ancient thatched cottage is the former home of Cromarty's most famous son, Hugh Miller. Born here in 1802 and largely self-taught, Miller became a pioneer in the field of geology and a celebrated man of letters. Inside his cottage are collections of personal belongings and geological specimens. See p. 342.

o **Maeshowe** (the Orkney Islands): The enigmatic Maeshowe is one of Europe's largest and best-preserved chambered cairns. Visit at sunset on the winter solstice as the sun's last rays shine down the narrow passageways, lighting the back wall of the 5,000-year-old chamber. See p. 399.

THE best OF THE GREAT OUTDOORS

o **Fishing the Salmon-Rich Tweed:** The River Tweed is one of the world's great salmon rivers and an angler's paradise. These scenic waters, which strike a gentle course through the best of the Scottish Borders, are also famous for brown and sea trout as well as grayling. See p. 58.

o **Teeing off on the St. Andrews Links:** Known as the "home of golf," St. Andrews claims a collection of prime links courses, including the world-famous **Old Course.** Book a tee time well in advance of your trip to enjoy a round at this golf shrine, where the courses are shaped by nature and undiminished by time. See p. 248.

o **Cycling Through Glencoe:** Site of a famous 1692 massacre, Glencoe is a brooding landscape of stark and grandiose mountain scenery. Many consider Glencoe to be at its most mystical when wet. It's a dramatic ride and cyclists should come prepared for rain because around 250cm (100 in.) are recorded here every year. See p. 317.

o **Climbing Ben Nevis:** Britain's highest mountain looms 3¾ miles southeast of Fort William. At 1,342m (4,403 ft.), the snow-capped granite mass dominates this entire region of Scotland and a trip to its summit can be done in a day. See p. 318.

o **Bird Watching on Fair Isle:** Take your binoculars to the cliffs of Fair Isle, home to some of Europe's largest colonies of seabirds, including guillemots, Arctic skuas, and the comical puffin. More than 340 species have been recorded by the famous observatory at this important staging post for migrating birds. See p. 412.

o **Walking Across Papa Stour:** For some of the most dramatic and unusual coastal scenery in the British Isles, walk around the island of Papa Stour, Shetland. As well as jagged cliffs, stacks, and arches, you'll see *gloups* (caves), *geos* (gulleys), and mysterious subterranean passages that cut right through the land. See chapter 13.

THE best COUNTRYSIDE DRIVES

o **The A708 from Selkirk to Moffat:** This 34-mile route between the Borders and Dumfries and Galloway strikes a scenic course between two very different landscapes of southern Scotland. The road clings to river valley and loch side as it passes Grey Mare's Tail waterfall and old Tibbie Shiels inn. See p. 145.

o **The Isle of Arran:** Arran combines radically different climates and topographies in a relatively small space. Prehistoric monuments and sweeping vistas of Northern Ireland await along the 56-mile circumnavigation of the island's coastal road which, excluding stopover times, should take half a day to drive. See chapter 8.

o **The Lochs & Mountains South of Oban:** Encounter Scotland's longest freshwater loch (Awe), some of the country's most historic buildings (Kilchurn and Carnasserie castles), and one of its most notorious battlefields (the slopes of Ben Cruachan) on the 87-mile route that follows an excellent network of highways along the jagged coast. See chapter 8.

o **The Trossachs:** Ruled for generations by the MacGregor clan, the Trossachs combine mist-shrouded lochs with legends of Rob Roy. Spend half a day following the A821 from Callander to Aberfoyle as it threads through dramatic terrain and include detours to Loch Katrine and the Brig o' Turk. See chapter 9.

o **The Isle of Skye:** Follow the A87 west from the Kyle of Lochalsh as it skims past the brooding Cuillin Hills. From Portree loop 20 miles around the Trotternish Peninsula. Known for its odd rock formations, this coastal road travels through rocky seascapes before opening onto Loch Snizort. See chapter 12.

o **The Road to the Isles (the A830):** Leading northwest from Fort William to Mallaig and ferries to the islands, the A830 passes mountains and lochs plus a Victorian engineering triumph—Neptune's Staircase, a network of eight locks that raise the Caledonian Canal 19m (62 ft.). See chapters 11 and 12.

THE best CASTLES & PALACES

o **Edinburgh Castle:** One of the country's most famous attractions, Edinburgh Castle embodies a proud, independent Scotland. The ancient volcanic plug it crowns has been occupied since at least 900 B.C. and over the past 3,000 years this historic site has witnessed some of the bloodiest events in Scottish history. See p. 73.

o **Palace of Holyroodhouse** (Edinburgh): Sealing the foot of Edinburgh's famous Royal Mile and facing Scotland's new parliament building, the Palace of Holyroodhouse is the Queen's official residence in Scotland. Dripping with tales of murder, pomp, fine art, and antique furniture, palaces don't come much finer than this distinguished royal stronghold. See p. 78.

o **Linlithgow Palace** (West Lothian): Once one of the nation's most glamorous royal residences, Linlithgow is today one of Scotland's most poignant ruins. Mary Queen of Scots was born at this loch-side palace, which despite being roofless and badly damaged in places retains all its ability to impress. See p. 118.

o **Scone Palace** (Scone): Ancient Scottish kings were crowned here upon the legendary Stone of Scone (now on display in Edinburgh Castle). The palace you see today was rebuilt in 1802 from ruins that incorporated a 1580 structure with stones laid during the dim early days of Scottish and Pictish union. See p. 288.

o **Glamis Castle** (Glamis): The core of this Scottish Baronial masterpiece was built as a defense against rival clans during the 1400s. As conflicts eased, however, Glamis evolved into a luxurious ancestral home. Haunted by Lady Glamis, who was burned as a witch, the castle also featured in the ambitions of Macbeth. See p. 301.

o **Balmoral Castle** (Ballater): Queen Victoria's beloved Scottish residence remains a popular retreat for the British monarchy and draws hordes of visitors seeking a glimpse into royal life Highland style. Limited public access is allowed to the castle itself, but the glorious surrounding estate is worth a visit alone. See p. 303.

SCOTLAND IN DEPTH

A small and dynamic nation, Scotland is only 275 miles long and some 150 miles wide at its broadest. Owing to its mountainous interior and deep penetration by sea lochs, no Scot lives more than 40 miles from saltwater. But despite the small size of their country, the Scots have extended their influence around the world, by virtue of their indomitable spirit, distinctive culture, and constant curiosity.

Inventor Alexander Graham Bell and explorers Mungo Park and David Livingstone came from Scotland. This country gave the world entrepreneur Andrew Carnegie, poet Robert Burns, novelist Sir Walter Scott, actor Sean Connery, singer Annie Lennox, and comedian/actor Billy Connolly. But, curiously, for a long time, its most famous resident has been neither man nor woman but Nessie, the Loch Ness Monster.

The border is just a line on a map; you're hardly aware of crossing from England to Scotland. Yet even though the two countries have been joined constitutionally since 1707, Scotland is quite different from England and is very much its own country. In fact, on July 1, 1999, Scotland was granted greater independence when British Prime Minister Tony Blair restored regional government, and a new Scottish Parliament was opened by Queen Elizabeth in Edinburgh.

Much of Scottish history has been shaped by the country's location in a remote corner of northwestern Europe. Amazingly, Scotland encompasses 787 islands (although only about a quarter are inhabited). Its 6,158 miles of coastline are deeply penetrated by the Atlantic Ocean on the west and the often-turbulent North Sea on the east. In fact, the sea has shaped Scotland's destiny more than any other element, and bred a nation of seafarers, many of whom still earn their living on the water.

SCOTLAND TODAY

Throughout Scotland, there's a mood of change in the air. One reason for this is that expatriate Scots are returning from abroad, because there are now far more opportunities in Scotland despite the recent downturn in the economy. Today, even the population of the Highlands is the highest it's been in a century. The migrations of the 19th century—when Scots people went overseas in order to find a better life—are now slowly starting to reverse. Slowly but surely, some of the estimated 20 million Scots who live outside the country are making the long trip home.

Part of this increased optimism is generated by the prospect of eventual Scottish independence from England. Scotland has had its own Parliament since 1999, but even a Parliament of its own may not satisfy the rising tide of Scottish separatism. Under the present arrangement, the Queen is still the head of state and the British prime minister the head of government. At sporting events, Scots can be heard singing "Flower of Scotland" instead of "God Save the Queen."

Scotland is once again starting to turn a strong face to the world, with a powerful combination of innovation and tradition. Its high-tech industries are playing an important role in the technological revolution, and today the country produces 13% of Europe's personal computers, 45% of Europe's workstations, and 50% of Europe's automated banking machines. The country is also at the forefront of the renewable energy industry, tapping into its considerable potential for wind and tidal power generation. Meanwhile, exports of Scotland's time-tested crafts (woolen tweeds and knitwear) are thriving, the market for Scotch whisky has burgeoned all around the world, and tourists are visiting in record numbers.

One of Scotland's biggest challenges is that half of the country still belongs to just 350 people—the "lairds," who include English aristocrats, reclusive foreign investors, pop stars, desert sheiks, offshore companies, and investment bankers. Dating from the 12th century and reinforced by the infamous Highland Clearances of the early 1800s, the ancient system is coming under review. In 2002, the islanders of **Gigha** won the fight to own their own land even though they weren't the top bidder for its sale, and their 1,375-hectare (3,400-acre) island has been handed over to a community trust. Something similar happened on **South Uist** in 2006. As a result, the islands are gradually undergoing a process of social and economic regeneration.

THE MAKING OF SCOTLAND

Beyond this brief introduction, readers interested in Scottish history can't do better than Rab Houston's *Scotland: A Very Short Introduction* (Oxford University Press, 2008) as a first port of call. Concise, informative, unpretentious, and highly readable,

DATELINE

6000 B.C. The earliest known residents of Scotland establish settlements on the Argyll Peninsula.

3000 B.C. Celtic tribes invade, bringing the Gaelic language with them.

A.D. 82 Roman armies directed by Agricola push into southern Scotland; the Roman incursion is, however, short-lived.

A.D. 90 Romans abandon all plans of conquering Scotland, retreating to England and the relative safety of Hadrian's Wall.

500 Newcomers from Ireland, known as "Scots," invade; their bloodlines are soon mingled with Norse, Pictish, Celtic, and Teutonic tribes.

563 St. Columba establishes a mission on Iona, accelerating the movement established by earlier ecclesiastics to Christianize Scotland.

843 Kenneth MacAlpin unifies the Picts and the Scots.

1005–34 Malcolm II unites the four major tribes of Scotland into one broadly cohesive unit.

this little book provides much food for thought, as it outlines all the main currents in Scottish history and draws out the reasons why the country is the way it is today. The book also benefits from interesting illustrations, a useful chronology at the back, and a handy list of Scottish monarchs.

For more in-depth discussion of places and people, ideas and events, turn to *The Oxford Companion to Scottish History* edited by Michael Lynch (Oxford University Press, 2011). It's well worth keeping a copy in your car as you drive round the country, so you can consult it as you visit particular historical sites. Compiled from the contributions of over 180 experts, this volume offers the latest research in easily digestible gobbets of text on a wealth of issues, from the historical background to Macbeth to the facts about climate change over the centuries.

Early History

Although little is known about the early tribes and invaders of Scotland, their impact on the landscape is strikingly apparent. Visit the **Callanish Stones,** which still stand erect on the windswept Isle of Lewis almost 4,000 years later, and you can't fail to be impressed. But by the time the Romans decided to invade in A.D. 82, we do know that the land was occupied by a people known as the Picts (Painted Ones). Despite spectacular bloodletting, the Romans failed to conquer the country, and the building of **Hadrian's Wall** marked the northern limits of their influence. Today, however, the remains of Hadrian's Wall (at Housesteads in Northumberland, for example), lie firmly in England, with the Scottish border farther north.

By A.D. 500, the Picts were again attacked, this time by the Dalriada Irish, known as the Scots, who were successful. Ramblers who visit **Kilmartin Glen** in Argyll today can't help but stumble across some of the 800 forts, *cromlechs* (stone circles), and burial mounds that litter the region that formed the center of their kingdom. Over time, the Scots intermarried with the Picts, and as Britons emigrated from the south and Norsemen from the northeast, new bloodlines were established and linguistic influences introduced (from Celtic and Norse dialects to Low German and Saxon English).

1124–53	David I builds monasteries, consolidates royal power and prestige, and imports Norman values.		1314	The victory of the Scots over the English armies at Bannockburn leads to the Treaty of Northampton (1328), formally recognizing Scotland's independence from England.
1266	The Hebrides and the coast of western Scotland are released from Norse control; the Donald clan consolidates power here into a semi-autonomous state within Scotland.		1468	The Orkney and Shetland Islands are given to Scotland as part of the marriage dowry of a Norse princess to a Scottish king.
1272	Edward I of England embarks on an aggressive campaign to conquer both Wales and Scotland, but is deflected by Robert the Bruce, among others.		Late 1400s	The Auld Alliance with France, a cynical arrangement based mostly on mutual distrust of England, is born.

continues

The next chapter in Scottish—and indeed European—history was played out on the small Hebridean island of **Iona.** The **abbey** you see there today (and can even stay in—see chapter 12) is the legacy of the Christian community established by **St. Columba** when he arrived from Ireland in 563. The remoteness of this haven of Christianity ensured that the culture and learning of Columba and his followers survives the plundering and barbarism of the Dark Ages.

Among the earliest surviving buildings in Scotland today are the *brochs* (circular towers), dating back to the Iron Age. Examples such as the **Broch of Mousa** (p. 415) in the Shetland Islands are among the most sophisticated drystone structures ever built. Their function is the subject of ongoing debate; many archaeologists believe that rather than being defensive in nature, they were the stately homes of their time.

The Middle Ages

The Scots and the Picts were united in 843 under the kingship of a chieftain named Kenneth MacAlpin, in the face of invasive pressures from England and Scandinavia and by virtue of the unifying force of Christianity. Under Malcolm II (1005–34), the British and the Angles, who occupied the southwest and southeast of the Scottish mainland, merged with the Scots and the Picts. Malcolm's son and heir, Duncan, was murdered by Macbeth of Moray—an event that would later provide the plotline for Shakespeare's "Scottish play." Visit **Glamis Castle** (p. 301), north of Dundee, and you can stroll around "Duncan's Hall," where the Victorians imagined Macbeth killed Duncan.

Malcolm III's marriage to an English princess, Margaret (later St. Margaret), furthered the Anglicization of the Scottish Lowlands. A determined woman of strong ideas, she imported English priests into Scotland and carried out Church reforms that soon replaced St. Columba's Gaelic form of Christianity. Her introduction of the English language laid the groundwork for making Scotland a potential English kingdom.

Cultural assimilation with England continued under David I (1081–1153), who made land grants to many Anglo-Norman families, providing Scotland with a feudal aristocracy and bringing in ancient names such as Bruce, Fraser, and Lindsay. He also embarked on a lavish building spree. The now-ruined **abbeys of Jedburgh, Kelso,**

1535 At the urging of Henry VIII of England, Parliament officially severs all ties with the Catholic Church, legally sanctioning the Reformation.	**1603** Mary's son, James VI of Scotland, accedes to the throne of England as James I, and unifies the two countries.
1559–64 John Knox lays out the basic outline of the Scottish Presbyterian Church.	**1689** The English Parliament strips the uncompromising Catholic James II of his crowns (England, Scotland and Ireland) and imports the Protestant William and Mary from Holland to replace him. The Union of Parliaments takes place in 1707.
1561 Queen Mary returns to Scotland from France.	
1568 Mary is defeated and flees to England.	**1746** Bonnie Prince Charlie's attempt to reclaim his grandfather's throne ends in defeat by English forces at the Battle of Culloden, destroying any hope of a Stuart revival.
1572 John Knox dies; his work is continued by Andrew Melville.	
1587 Mary Queen of Scots is executed.	

Melrose, and **Dryburgh** are his legacy. Parish churches at Dalmeny and Leuchars, and the church of David I in Dunfermline (p. 238), are other particularly fine examples of ecclesiastical architecture that survive from this period; the Vikings left few Celtic churches intact.

In 1266, after about a century of Norse control, the foggy and windswept Western Isles were returned to Scotland following the Battle of Largs. Despite nominal allegiance to the Scottish monarch, this region's inhabitants quickly organized themselves around the Donald (or MacDonald) clan. The numerous castles you see in the area today—including **Dunaverty** off the coast of Kintyre, **Kildonan** on Arran, and **Knock** on Skye—bear testimony to the fact that MacDonald territory was ruled almost as an independent state. The honorary title of their chief, Lord of the Isles, is still one of the formal titles used on state occasions by Britain's Prince of Wales. To learn more about perhaps the most important clan in Scottish history, visit the Clan Donald Visitor Centre, at **Armadale** on the Isle of Skye (chapter 12).

In the meantime, real trouble was brewing in the south. Edward I, the ambitious Plantagenet king of England, yearned to conquer the entire island. Successful at first, he set up John de Balliol as a vassal king to rule Scotland for him. Many of Scotland's legendary heroes lived during this period: Sir William Wallace (1270–1305), who drove the English out of Perth and Stirling; Sir James Douglas, the Black Douglas (1286–1330), who terrorized the English borders; and Robert the Bruce (1274–1329), who finally succeeded in freeing Scotland from England. You can still visit the scene of his coronation (in 1306, in defiance of the English) at **Scone,** just outside Perth (see chapter 10), and it's well worth making the journey to **Bannockburn** near Stirling to see where he finally defeated Edward II of England at the Battle of Bannockburn in 1314. Scotland's independence was formally recognized in the 1328 Treaty of Northampton, inaugurating a heady but short-lived separation from England.

The **Orkneys** and the **Shetlands,** Norse to the core, were finally brought into the Scottish web of power as part of the marriage dowry of the Norse princess Margaret to James III in 1468. It was at this time that the Scots entered into an alliance with the French that would later have far-reaching effects. The line of Stuart (or Stewart)

1750–1850 England and Scotland experience rapid industrialization; the Clearances strip many crofters of their farms, creating great bitterness and forcing new patterns of Scottish migrations.

1789 The French Revolution begins; British monarchists tighten their grip on civil unrest in Scotland.

Late 19th century Great successes in science and engineering propel Scotland into the forefront of industrial know-how around the globe.

Mid-20th century The decline of traditional industries, especially shipbuilding, painfully redefines the nature of Scottish society.

1970 The discovery of North Sea oil deposits brings new prosperity to Scotland.

1973 Scotland, as part of the United Kingdom, becomes a member of the Common Market, forerunner of the European Union.

1974 The old counties or shires are reorganized; many regions are renamed.

continues

kings—so named because the family had become powerful as stewards of the English king—were generally accepted as the least troublesome of a troublesome bunch. Real power, however, lay with Scotland's great lords, patriarchs of the famous clans. Jealous of their bloodlines and territories, they could rarely agree on anything other than their common distrust of England.

The medieval period brought numerous Norman-influenced motte and bailey castles such as Bothwell Castle in Lanarkshire. Many of these were originally built of wood, and were only gradually replaced by more permanent stone structures, with long curtain walls and cylindrical towers. Under the influence of the European Renaissance, castle architecture was adapted to the formation of elaborate fortified palaces. Famous examples include those at Linlithgow, Falkland, and Stirling.

With the building of monasteries and cathedrals came a turn to the Gothic style, which was better suited to larger structures. In Glasgow, Elgin, and Dunblane, you can see pointed Gothic arches, vaulting, and lancet windows. On St. Giles in Edinburgh is one of the few remaining crown spires used in late Gothic ecclesiastical construction. When the barons built churches other than cathedrals, however, they continued to use the traditional Scottish formula of stepped buttresses, crenellated towers, and roofs of stone slab. The Reformation later prompted the stripping of ornamentation from Scotland's churches. Examples of pre-Reformation woodwork does, however, survive at King's College and St. Machar's in Aberdeen (p. 276).

In the 15th century, Scottish literature really started to make its mark through the poetry of the so-called Scottish Chaucerians Robert Henryson, William Dunbar, Gavin Douglas, Sir David Lyndsay, and King James I (*The King's Quair*).

The Reformation

The passions of the Reformation burst on an already turbulent Scottish scene in the person of John Knox, a devoted disciple of the Geneva Protestant John Calvin and a bitter enemy of both the Catholic Church and the Anglican Church. His polemics were famous; in his struggle against the ardently Catholic Queen Mary, he wrote his *First Blast of the Trumpet Against the Monstrous Regiment of Women*. His was a

1981 The largest oil terminal in Europe is launched at Sullom Voe in the Shetland Islands.

1988 Pan Am Flight 103 from London crashes at Lockerbie, killing all passengers, as well as some locals.

1997 Scotland votes to establish a legislature of its own for the first time since 1707.

1999 On July 1, Queen Elizabeth opens a new Scottish Parliament for the first time in 300 years.

2003 Scotland joins England in sending troops to fight in Iraq.

2004-5 Scotland grapples with long-overdue land reform.

2007 Scotland marks 300 years of union with England.

2011 Scotland holds its fourth general election since the opening of the new Scottish Parliament.

2014 Glasgow hosts the Commonwealth Games.

CLANS, tartans & KILTS

To the outsider, Scotland's deepest traditions appear to be based on the clan system of old with all the familiar paraphernalia of tartans and bagpipes. This is, however, a romantic memory, and in fact, a good part of the Scots—the 75% of the population who live in the central Lowlands, for example—have little or no connection with the clansmen of earlier times.

The clan tradition dates from the tribal units of the country's earliest Celtic history. Power was organized around a number of chieftains, who commanded loyalty from the inhabitants of a particular region in exchange for protection against exterior invasions. The position of chieftain wasn't hereditary, and land was owned by the clan, not by the chieftain. Clan members had both rights and duties. Rigidly militaristic and paternalistic—the stuff with which Scottish legend is imbued—the clan tradition is still emphasized today, albeit in a much friendlier fashion than when claymores and crossbows threatened a bloody death or dismemberment for alleged slights on a clan's honor.

Chieftains were absolute potentates, with life and death power over members and interlopers, although they were usually viewed as patriarchs actively engaged in the perpetuation of the clan's bloodlines, traditions, and honor. The entourage of a chieftain always included bodyguards, musicians (harpers and pipers), a spokesman (known as a tatler), and—perhaps most important to latter-day students of clan traditions—a bard. The bard's role was to sing, to exalt the role of the clan and its heroes, to keep a genealogical record of births and deaths, and to compose or recite epic poems relating to the clan's history.

The clan system had broken down long before Sir Walter Scott wrote his romantic novels about them and long before Queen Victoria made Scotland socially fashionable. The clans today represent a cultural rather than a political power. The best place to see the remnants of their tradition in action is at any traditional Highland gathering, although battalions of bagpipers seem to show up at everything from weddings and funerals to political rallies and parades throughout Scotland.

SCOTLAND IN DEPTH | The Making of Scotland

peculiar mixture of piety, conservatism, strict morality, and intellectual independence, all of which are still pronounced features of the Scottish character. Knox was the writer who probably had most influence during this period; he also authored *History of the Reformation.*

Knox's teachings also helped shape the democratic form of Scottish government and set the Scottish Church's austere moral tone for generations to come. Later, the Church of Scotland's almost obsessive insistence on self-government would lead to endless conflicts, first with the Scottish and then, after unification, with the British monarchs. In Edinburgh, you can still visit the **John Knox House** (p. 76), where the fiery reformer once lived.

Mary Queen of Scots

When Mary Stuart, Queen of Scots (1542–87), took up her rule, she was a Roman Catholic of French upbringing trying to govern an unruly land to which she was a relative newcomer. Daughter of Scotland's James V and France's Mary of Guise, she became queen at only 6 days of age. She lived at **Stirling Castle** (p. 256) as an infant

17

TARTAN splendor

Although not every visitor to Scotland is descended from a clan, almost all are familiar with plaids and the traditions associated with them. Over the centuries, each clan developed a distinctive pattern to be worn by its members, presumably to better identify its soldiers in the heat of battle. (Today, *tartan* is used interchangeably with *plaid,* but the word *plaid* originally referred specifically to a mantle of cloth draped over the back and shoulders.)

Kilts enjoy an ancient history. Checkered tartans are first mentioned in a 1471 English inventory. The clans developed special dyeing and weaving techniques: for example, Alder bark steeped in hot water produces a black dye; gorse, broom, and knapweed produce shades of green; cup moss produces purple; dandelion leaves produce magenta; bracken and heather produce yellow; white lichens produce red; and indigo had to be imported for blue.

When Bonnie Prince Charlie launched his rebellion in 1745, he used tartans as a symbol of his army. As a consequence, the public display of tartans was banned for a period after his defeat. During Queen Victoria's reign, however, tartans came into high fashion, as she and her kilt-wearing German consort, Albert, made all things Scottish popular.

Today, the Scottish Tartans Authority has registered over 5,000 different tartans, each subtly different from the others. All are available for sale somewhere in Scotland's shops and markets. If you're not fortunate enough to be of Scottish extraction, don't worry: Queen Victoria long ago authorized two Lowland designs as suitable garb for Sassenachs (the English and, more remotely, the Americans). By contrast, though, you should only wear the Balmoral tartan if you're a member of the Royal Family.

On a purely decorative and symbolic level, and with rich interest for anyone tracing genealogical roots, is Robert Bain's *The Clans and Tartans of Scotland,* enlarged and re-edited by Margaret MacDouglass, with heraldic advice supplied by P. E. Stewart-Blacker and with dozens of illustrations (Collins, 1959).

monarch before being sent to be educated in France. At the age of 15, she married the heir to the French throne, but returned to Scotland after his death. Mary then set out on two roads that were anathema to the Scots: to make herself absolute monarch in the French style and to impose Roman Catholicism. The first alienated the Scottish nobles, and the second made her the enemy of John Knox and the Calvinists. After a series of disastrous political and romantic alliances, her life was ended by the executioner's axe in England. The execution order was reluctantly issued by her cousin Elizabeth I, who considered Mary's presence an incitement to civil unrest and a threat to the stability of the English throne. You can follow the dramatic story of her life at the string of palaces where she once lived. In the Borders there's **Mary Queen of Scots' Visitor Centre** (p. 127), while in Edinburgh, at **Holyroodhouse** (p. 78), you can see where her Italian secretary, David Rizzio, was stabbed 56 times in front of her. The Queen also used to stay at **Falkland Palace** for hunting and hawking.

For the court of such culture-conscious monarchs as Mary Stuart, music was imported from both England and France. The madrigals and choral compositions of the Scottish 16th century can be found in a collection of songs by the Scottish Early Music Consortium, *Mary's Music.* During the same era, a Scottish-born composer,

Robert Carver (1490–1546), created a remarkable body of polyphonic vocal music whose allure grew increasingly fashionable among British early music buffs in the 1990s. Carver's music can be appreciated on *Scottish Renaissance Polyphony Vols. 1 & 2*, as performed by the Scottish choral group Capella Nova.

Union with England

Mary's son succeeded where his unfortunate mother had failed. In 1603, James VI of Scotland also assumed the throne of England as James I, Elizabeth's heir. His coronation united England and Scotland and finally broke the power of the Scottish lords.

Despite the hopes for peace that accompanied the union, religion soon became the source of discontent. James, and his heir, Charles I, attempted to promote a Church of Scotland governed by bishops, in opposition to the Presbyterian Church's self-ruling organization. So incensed were the Scots that in 1638 they signed the **National Covenant,** which not only reasserted the Reformation's principles but also questioned the King's right to make laws, a role the Covenanters believed should be filled by Parliament.

Yet Charles I, king of England from 1625 to 1649, believed strongly in the divine right of kings. When the English Parliament stripped away much of his authority in 1642, Charles went north to organize an army against the Parliamentary forces centered in London. A civil war ensued, with the forces of Parliament being led to victory by Oliver Cromwell (1599–1658). Charles fled to Scotland, but the Scots turned him over to Parliament, and in 1649 he was convicted of treason and beheaded. Under the ensuing Commonwealth, Cromwell assumed a dominant political role and became Lord Protector in 1653. King in all but name, he ruled England until his death.

But trouble brewed in Scotland. The death of Charles I led to deep divisions in the country, which eventually led to open defiance of Cromwell, and proclamation of Charles II as king. The Scots even launched abortive invasions of England. Cromwell's forces finally defeated the Scots at **Dunbar,** to the east of Edinburgh, in 1650. For nearly 9 years (1651–60), Scotland was under Commonwealth military occupation, and the garrisons the English built left a lasting legacy with the founding of the town of **Fort William** and the building of ramparts at Inverness, among other places. Religious friction continued, however, after the restoration of Charles II to the English throne.

In the arts, decorative painting became popular in houses and public buildings in the late 16th and early 17th centuries. Most of this was the work of local artisans, who used bright colors to produce designs of fruit and flowers, scenes from the Bible, and patterns using conventional idioms. Tempera painting on ceilings and paneling can still be seen in such places as Gladstone's Land in Edinburgh and Provost Skene's House in Aberdeen, though the fashion later changed in favor of ornamental plasterwork such as can be seen in Old Moray House on the south side of Canongate on the Royal Mile in Edinburgh.

Whereas baronial mansions of the late 16th and early 17th centuries draw on the Scottish architectural heritage of gables, garrets, turrets, towers, and facade adornments, country houses thereafter looked to foreign exemplars. Sir William Bruce (1630–1710) adopted the Classical style exhibited by Kinross House and the courtyard at the Palace of Holyroodhouse (p. 78). James Smith (1644–1731) developed a more specifically Palladian version that is perhaps best seen today at Dalkeith Palace.

TRADITIONAL SCOTTISH music

The earliest characteristics of Scottish music are found in the folk tradition. Two traditions exist—the Lowland, where the Scottish version of English is spoken, and the Gaelic music of the Highlands and Hebrides. The first Lowland songs and ballads were written down in the Skene Manuscript (now in the National Library of Scotland) around 1615, and in about 1650 numerous published editions of Lowland tunes began to appear. Gaelic songs were not collected until the 19th century, and because the Highland ballads often differed from clan to clan, you may still hear today a version that has never been written down or recorded.

The folk music of the Orkney and Shetland islands has Scandinavian origins. The ancient Norn language was spoken in Orkney until the late 17th century and in Shetland until the mid-18th century, but was allowed to die out; and since folksongs were in that language, those tunes have also almost disappeared.

A feature of Scottish music is the Scotch snap, a form of syncopation consisting of two notes, the second of which is three times as long as the first. The Scotch snap apparently originated in the 18th century and is found in many authentic Scottish tunes as well as in the 18th century's pseudo-Scottish melodies.

The three national musical instruments of Scotland are the harp, the bagpipe, and the fiddle. The most ancient of these is the harp, which is of Irish origin. It lost its popularity by the 18th century, as the fiddle, flute, and lute took precedence; some harp music even passed to the bagpipes. Interest in the harp has revived, however. The fiddle (derived from the early *fedyl*) edged out two former competitors, the *rebec* and the *croud* (the Welsh *crwth*), for predominance in the bowed-string instrument category. Today, especially in Strathspey and Shetland, you can hear the fiddle in both solo and concert form.

The bagpipe originated in the Near East. It may have been introduced into Britain by the conquering Romans, who found Scotland too tough to tame. The great Highland bagpipe survived the defeat at Culloden, at which time it was

In the literature of the times, most notable were the poets William Drummond—whose work shows the heavy influence of Spenser—and Sir Thomas Urquhart of Cromarty, who was best known as the translator of Rabelais.

The Jacobites

In 1689, when the English Parliament stripped Catholic James II of his crown and imported Protestant monarchs William and Mary from Holland, the exiled ex-king and then his son James Edward (the Old Pretender) became focal points for Scottish unrest. The Jacobites (the name comes from *Jacobus*, the Latin form of James) attempted unsuccessfully in 1715 to place the Old Pretender on the English throne and restore the Stuart line. Although James died in exile, his son Charles Edward (the Young Pretender), better known as Bonnie Prince Charlie, carried on his father's dream. Charismatic but with an alcohol-induced instability, he was the central figure of the 1745 Jacobite uprising. Today, the **Glenfinnan Monument** at the head of Loch Shiel (west of Fort William; p. 320) marks the spot where he raised his standard; the grandeur of the memorial is testimony to the inspiration his story would provide to later generations of Scottish patriots.

outlawed, partly because it was prized as a military instrument; the dread sound of the piper often sent terror through enemy ranks. Later on, piping was encouraged in new Highland regiments, and the Scots became feared throughout the world for their prowess as soldiers and for the brave skirl of the pipes. The bagpipe is known now chiefly through its use by the pipe bands of Scottish regiments.

Church, court, and concert music also flourished in Scotland. Before the Reformation, most towns of any size had active song schools, mainly under church direction. A major change in church music was brought about by Calvinist reformers who, in the 17th century, denigrated the organ as a "popish instrument" and destroyed them wherever they could. None of this, however, interfered with the Gaelic "long psalms" of Celtic Scotland, in which each line is intoned musically by the leader, with the congregation then singing the line.

Choral and orchestral music are widespread today, and universities have thriving music departments. There is a Scottish National Orchestra as well as the BBC Scottish Symphony Orchestra, and a Scottish Opera, plus various ensembles and musical guilds. For an excellent introduction to the glories of Gaelic song, try the Glasgow Gaelic Musical Association's album *Gaelic Galore,* or the Glasgow Phoenix Choir's album *With Voices Rising.* Alison Kinnaird has been acclaimed as Scotland's finest harpist; on *The Quiet Tradition,* she teams up with Christine Primrose to produce subtle interpretations of traditional songs. The stirring performances of Hamish Moore, frequently named as one of Scotland's finest pipers, can be appreciated on *Cauld Wind Pipes* and on a companion recording called *Open Ended.* A different piper, known as either Pibroch or Piobaireachd (depending on whether you endorse the English or Gaelic spelling of his name), can be heard on a recording entitled *The Classical Music of the Great Highland Bagpipe.*

Although the revolt was initially promising, the many Scottish adherents who crossed religious lines to rally to the cause led to the Jacobite forces being crushed at the **Battle of Culloden.** You can still walk this battlefield near Inverness today, and a visitor center fills in the background (see chapter 11). Fearing a rebirth of similar types of Scottish nationalism, the clan system was rigorously suppressed; clans that supported the Jacobite cause lost their lands, and, until 1782, the wearing of Highland dress was made illegal.

The Young Pretender himself was smuggled unglamorously out of Scotland, assisted by Flora MacDonald, one of the era's most romantic heroines. Her birthplace near the **Kildonan Museum** on South Uist is now marked by a monument. The Bonnie Prince himself went on to lead a life of dissipation in Paris and Rome, and the hopes of an independent Scotland were buried forever.

The Industrial Revolution

During the 18th century, the Scottish economy underwent a radical transformation of growth and diversification. The British government, fearing civil unrest, commissioned the highly capable General George Wade to build barracks (hence **Fort**

RETURN OF THE stone OF DESTINY

After a rocky journey, the Stone of Scone, or Stone of Destiny, has finally been returned to Scotland. Physically, the stone is a somewhat unprepossessing block of sandstone, measuring 66cm (26 in.) long and 40cm (16 in.) wide and weighing 152kg (336 lbs.). But it's not just a stone: Revered for centuries as a holy relic, it allegedly came from the Middle East, and in biblical times Jacob is said to have used the stone as a pillow.

The stone was used at Dunadd, Iona, and Dunstaffnage for enthroning the Dalriada Irish Monarchs, called Scots. Later it was moved to Scone, and in 1292 John Balliol became the last king to be crowned on the stone in Scotland. So powerful was its legend that Edward I took it to England in 1296, believing possession of the stone gave him sovereignty over Scotland. There it stayed, positioned under the coronation chair in Westminster Abbey in London. In 1328, the Treaty of Northampton, recognizing Scotland's independence, returned the stone to Scotland, but the English reneged on the promise and the stone never moved from Westminster Abbey.

On Christmas Day 1950, however, the stone was stolen from the abbey by a group of Scottish Nationalists. It was found about 4 months later in Arbroath Abbey and returned to Westminster. A rumor spread that the found stone was actually a replica, but this has never been proved.

In 1996, the Stone of Destiny was officially returned to Scotland. It left Westminster Abbey by Land Rover, crossing from England into Scotland at the border town of Coldstream, where a small but moving ceremony was held. On November 30 of that year, the stone proceeded with all due ceremony up the Royal Mile in Edinburgh to its permanent home beside the Scottish Crown Jewels in Edinburgh Castle, where you can see it today (p. 73).

Although Scots in general hailed the return of the stone after 700 years in English captivity, not all are pleased. Some have denounced it as a "cheap political ploy," especially as technically the Queen is merely "lending" it to her Scottish subjects and can call it back to London for a future coronation. Some Scots also want to see the stone returned to Scone. "Edinburgh has no claim, legally, morally, or whatever, to the Stone of Scone," said Andrew R. Robinson, administrator of Scone Castle. "It's not called the Stone of Edinburgh, is it?"

Augustus), roads (from Dunkeld to Inverness, for example), and bridges (notably the **Tay Bridge** at Aberfeldy), presumably to increase military access from London in the event of a revolt. Their unintended effect, however, was to encourage business and commerce.

As trade with British overseas colonies, England, and Europe increased, the great ports of Aberdeen, Glasgow, and Leith (near Edinburgh) flourished. The merchants of Glasgow grew rich on a nearly monopolistic tobacco trade with Virginia and the Carolinas, until the outbreak of the Revolution sent American tobacco elsewhere. Other forms of commerce continued to enrich a battalion of shrewd Scots.

In the 18th century Scottish literature really started to blossom, with a spate of lucid and powerful prose written in English: novelist Tobias Smollett (*Roderick Random* and *Humphrey Clinker*), economist Adam Smith (*The Wealth of Nations*), philosopher David Hume (*Treatise on Human Nature*), and James Boswell, friend and biographer of Dr. Samuel Johnson. It was also in the 18th century that Robert Burns (1759–96) produced his famous verses combining the humor and vigor of Scottish speech with the lilt of Scottish songs. Burns, known especially for love lyrics and satires, is Scotland's national bard, though is revered throughout the world. *Burns: A Biography of Robert Burns,* by James MacKay, is one of the best works devoted to him. MacKay defends the author of *Tam O'Shanter* and *Auld Lang Syne* against previously published charges that he was a drunkard and a rake.

The history of native-Scottish portrait painting began with George Jamesone of Aberdeen (1589/90–1644), whose self-portrait can be seen in the Scottish National Portrait Gallery (p. 81). In the early 18th century, a school of portraitists developed in Scotland, following the rich tradition in England. Chief among such artists was Allan Ramsay (1718–84), who is widely held to have influenced England's Sir Joshua Reynolds. Perhaps his best work is a picture of his wife, which hangs in the National Gallery in Edinburgh (p. 80). Ramsay eventually moved to London, leaving the field for his major successor, Sir Henry Raeburn (1756–1823).

At about this time, a taste for romantic landscapes, historical, and genre painting developed. Perhaps the most famous exponent was Sir David Wilkie (1785–1841), who did much to establish a wider market for Scottish art. Testament to his and his colleagues' efforts was the founding of the Royal Scottish Academy of Art in 1826, through which professional painters could exhibit and sell their works. The most important recent book on the artist is *David Wilkie: The People's Painter* by Nicholas Tromans (Edinburgh University Press, 2007). This scholarly work presents the latest research on Wilkie, and shows how his visions of Scottish history reached beyond elite patrons to influence popular consciousness. The book also reproduces and discusses the artist's major pictures.

Also in the 18th century, architect William Adam, and his more famous sons, Robert (1728–92) and James (1730–94), continued where James Smith left off. They evolved the so-called Adam style of design, characterized by light, decorative reworkings of Greek and Roman classical motifs. For fine examples of Robert Adam's work, visit Mellerstain near Kelso (p. 131) or Culzean Castle on the Ayrshire coast (p. 205).

The infamous Clearances between 1750 and 1850 changed Scotland's demographics forever. Small farmers, or crofters, were expelled from their ancestral lands to make way for sheep grazing. Increased industrialization, continued civil unrest, migration to urban centers, and a massive wave of immigration to the United States, Canada, Australia, South Africa, and New Zealand all contributed to depopulation of the countryside and a dispersal of the Scottish ethic throughout the world. You can still see the ruins of deserted crofts, farmsteads, and villages all over the Highlands.

Meanwhile, rapid progress in the arts, sciences, and education, coupled with the arrival of the Industrial Age, meshed productively with the Scottish genius for thrift, hard work, shrewdness, and conservatism. The 19th century produced large numbers of Scots who made important contributions to nearly all fields of endeavor. Witness the engineering feats of Telford (such as the **Caledonian Canal**), the lighthouses of the Stevenson family (at **Cape Wrath** and on the **Isle of May,** for example), and the architecture of the Adam brothers (at **Mellerstain House** near Kelso or **Culzean Castle** in Ayrshire). You will find that the country's Victorian past remains much in evidence; to see what this environment really looked like when it was peopled by its creators, pick up a copy of *Victorian Scotland* by James Crawford, Lesley Ferguson, and Kristina Watson (Royal Commission on the Ancient and Historical Monuments of Scotland, 2010). This large-format volume presents a fascinating collection of old photographs that show the rich at leisure in their mansions and poor village children with no shoes. It's a smartly produced volume that would make a good present to take home at the end of your stay in Scotland.

In architecture, the 19th century brought the Baronial Revival, pioneered at Sir Walter Scott's Abbotsford House near Melrose (p. 135). Following the construction of Balmoral Castle (p. 303) for Queen Victoria, the style became a popular export throughout the dominions of the British Empire. Examples can be seen today from New Zealand to Canada. By the end of the century, Charles Rennie Mackintosh (1868–1928), combined the revival's more specifically Scottish vernacular idioms with Art Nouveau and Arts and Crafts elements to develop a style notable for its strength of form and ornamental restraint. Among his finest creations are the Glasgow School of Art (p. 170) and Hill House, Helensburgh (now owned by the National Trust for Scotland; see p. 186). Sir Robert Lorimer (1864–1929) adapted Mackintosh's ideas in pursuit of the new fashion for restoring old castles.

One of the great Scottish writers of the era was Sir Walter Scott, novelist and poet, known for Medieval Romanticism (*Ivanhoe*) and perceptive description of character and locales (*The Heart of Midlothian*). Notable historian and essayist Thomas Carlyle was Scotland-born (*Sartor Resartus* and *The French Revolution*). An acclaimed poet, James Hogg, also wrote a famous prose work, *The Private Memoirs and Confessions of a Justified Sinner*. And in the middle of the century, a lion of the literary world was born in Edinburgh: Robert Louis Stevenson (1850–94), who penned such classics as *Treasure Island*, *Kidnapped*, and *The Strange Case of Dr. Jekyll and Mr. Hyde*, as well as poems, especially for children.

At the end of the 19th century, the so-called Kailyard (or "cabbage patch") school of writing developed. Kailyard writing used Scots dialect and idealized village life. J.M. Barrie was perhaps the most famous name associated with the genre, though he is more famous as the dramatist who wrote *Peter Pan*.

Other notable men of letters who lived and worked in the late Victorian and Edwardian eras were Andrew Lang, poet, essayist, and historian, also known for his collections of fairy tales; John Buchan, who wrote perhaps the first espionage thriller, *The Thirty-Nine Steps*; and Douglas Brown, author of *The House with the Green Shutters*, an anti-Kailyard novel. Few people associate that quintessential Londoner, Sherlock Holmes, with Scotland, but the great detective's creator, Sir Arthur Conan Doyle, was born in Edinburgh and studied medicine at the city's university.

One of the most important artists of the later 19th century was William MacTaggart (1835–1910), who brought an Impressionist sensibility to his rugged landscapes and seascapes. In turn, it was French naturalism and symbolism that influenced the so-called Glasgow Boys, a group of anti-academic artists whose number included Sir James Guthrie (1859–1930), Sir John Lavery (1856–1941), Sir George Pirie (1863–1946), and William George Macgregor (1855–1923). A large collection of their work can be seen at Kelvingrove Art Museum and Gallery in Glasgow (p. 173). The definitive book on the subject is *The Glasgow Boys* by Roger Billcliffe (Frances Lincoln, 2008), a former museum curator and now the owner of his own gallery in Glasgow. Billcliffe presents an authoritative, lavishly illustrated survey of the artists, styles, subjects, and themes of this fascinating art movement.

Queen Victoria, who had a deep love for Scotland (memorably dramatized in the 1997 film *Mrs. Brown*), popularized the Highland Games, which for many decades had been suppressed after the failure of the 1745 rebellion. Highland Gatherings or Games have their origins in the fairs organized by the tribes or clans for the exchange of goods. The first were held perhaps as long as 1,000 years ago. Such gatherings often featured trials of strength among the men, with the strongest being selected for the chief's army. In 1848, the Queen and her consort, Prince Albert, attended the Braemar Gathering and, as recorded in her journal, saw Duncan, her *ghillie*, win the race up the hill of Craig Choinnich. (*Ghillie* originally meant a male attendant or Scottish Highland chief, though today it's used to refer to a hunting or fishing guide; Duncan, incidentally, was rumored to have been the Queen's lover.) The same tradition continues today: throwing hammers, putting rounded stones found in the rivers, tossing the caber (tree trunk), and running in flat races and up steep hillsides, as well as bagpipe playing and dance performances. The Heavies, a breed of gigantic men, draw the most attention for their prowess. Braemar is nowadays the most famous gathering; it is held in late August or early September and is still patronized by the royal family. Other major games are held at Ballater (Grampian), Aberdeen, Elgin, and Newtonmore.

The 20th Century to Present

Scotland endured bitter privations during the Great Depression and the two world wars. Following World War I, a "Scottish Renaissance" tried to reinforce the national identity through the use of a synthetic language called Lallans, a name once applied to Lowland Scots but now consisting of a mix of dialects. Despite these efforts, English remained the language of literature in Scotland, though novelists and poets still often use Scots vernacular.

Twentieth-century writers of note include Edwin Muir, an anti-Renaissance Orkney Islander known for his great metaphysical poetry and his translations of Kafka; James Bridie, playwright and cofounder of the Glasgow Citizens' Theatre; and Eric Linklater, Orkney-born writer of satirical and comic novels. Perhaps the most influential novelists were Lewis Grassic Gibbon, who was most famous for his trilogy, *A Scots Quair,* and Neil Gunn, author of *Morning Tide*. Another important writer—though of a very different kind—is Muriel Spark, best known for *The Prime of Miss Jean Brodie* that draws on the experiences of her own school days in Edinburgh.

An early 20th-century loose grouping of artists was the Scottish Colourists, whose work took inspiration from the French Fauvists and looked to cafe culture, glamorous women, picturesque scenes, and still lives for their subject matter. *The Scottish Colourists: 1900–1930* by Philip Long and Elizabeth Cumming (National Galleries of Scotland, 2000) presents many of their most famous works in glossy reproductions. It also contains useful introductions to each of the figures belonging to the group, and highly readable essays on the art historical background. The work of J.D. Fergusson (1874–1961) can best be seen at the museum dedicated to him in Perth (p. 286), that of Samuel Peploe (1871–1935) in Kirkcaldy Museum and Art Gallery, and there are good examples of the paintings of Francis Cadell (1883–1937) and Leslie Hunter (1877–1931) in the Scottish National Gallery of Modern Art in Edinburgh (p. 79) and the Kelvingrove Art Museum in Glasgow.

Important figures in post-war Scottish art include Edinburgh artist Anne Redpath (1895–1965) and Leith-born Eduardo Paolozzi (1924–2005), who toward the end of his life donated the contents of his studio to the Dean Gallery in Edinburgh (p. 79). *Scottish Art 1460–1990,* by Duncan Macmillan (Mainstream Publishing, 2000), provides a good overview of Scottish art from the royal miniatures of James IV's court to the post-modern experiments of recent decades. In more recent times, architecture in Scotland has increasingly followed international trends. By far the most important new building is the Scottish Parliament. Designed by Catalan architect Enric Miralles, the complex has won architectural prizes for its dramatic forms and structures and has quickly become a major tourist attraction (p. 79).

In the 1960s and 1970s, Scotland found that, like the rest of Britain, its aging industrial plants couldn't compete with more modern commercial competition from abroad. The most visible decline occurred in the shipbuilding industries; the vast Glasgow shipyards that had once produced some of the world's great ocean liners went bankrupt. The companies that produced automobiles were wiped out during the 1930s. Many commercial enterprises once controlled by Scots had been merged into English or multinational conglomerates.

However, in 1970, the discovery of North Sea oil by British Petroleum boosted the economy considerably and provided jobs for thousands of workers. Oil has continued to play a prominent role in the Scottish economy. In 1981, the largest oil terminal in Europe opened at **Sullom Voe** in the remote Shetland Islands.

As part of the United Kingdom, Scotland became a member of the European Common Market in 1973, although many Scots—perhaps owing to their longtime isolationism—opposed entry. Some voters expressed a fear that membership would take away some of their rights of self-government and determination. In 1974, Scotland underwent a drastic revision of its counties, and many regions were renamed. Tayside, for example, was carved out of the old counties of Perth and Angus.

In 1999, under Prime Minister Tony Blair's devolution reforms, Scotland was allowed to elect its own legislature for the first time since its 1707 union with England. A total of 129 Scots were elected to this newly formed Parliament. Unlike the Welsh Parliament, the Scottish version, centered at Edinburgh, has the power to tax and make laws, as well as to pursue such matters as healthcare, education, public transportation, and public housing. Scotland is still represented in the main British Parliament in London, and must bow to the greater will of London in matters of foreign policy.

The Scottish Parliament got off to a bad start in 2000, with Scotland's 21 robustly competitive newspapers writing of "the silly season." The press noted that members of Parliament awarded lawmakers with commemorative medals before they had done anything, granted bonuses, and fretted about parking spaces and vacation grants instead of tackling the country's problems. Comedian Billy Connolly dismissed the body "as a wee pretendy Parliament." The ridicule was compounded by the fact that the new Scottish Parliament Building in Edinburgh cost more than 10 times the original budget, in excess of £400 million.

In music, Scottish traditionalists continued to be popular in the 20th century, playing versions of time-tested Scottish melodies, sometimes in Gaelic. A handful of the more reliable favorites included the Alexander Brothers, the Shotts and Dykehead Band, and—perhaps most famous and influential of all (credited with keeping Scottish spirits aloft during and just after World War II)—the inimitable Harry Lauder. One of the most visible of the modern Scottish folk groups was the Corries, whose spirited music was popular in the early 1970s even before its foremost composer, Roy Williamson, composed "Flower of Scotland." The best insight into both their poetry and their patriotism can be gleaned from *The Complete Corries* or *The Best of the Corries*.

Many Scottish musicians have found success in the rock and pop scene of the English-speaking world, even if they haven't developed a distinctively Scottish sound of their own or formed an easily recognizable "scene." Among the bands and singers who have achieved commercial success are Primal Scream, Annie Lennox, The Jesus

& Mary Chain, Simple Minds, Texas, The Proclaimers, Belle & Sebastian and Franz Ferdinand. Most recently, Scotland has exported the *Britain's Got Talent* phenomenon Susan Boyle, whose rags-to-riches story has touched millions across the world.

Twentieth-century Scotland has been captured effectively in a number of highly recommended films. *The 39 Steps,* a novel by John Buchan, has been adapted for film at least four times. By far the best version is also the earliest, made in 1935 by Alfred Hitchcock. The plot is based on the now-familiar thriller archetype of a man on the run—in this case, reluctant secret-agent Richard Hannay, who tries to stay one step ahead of German spies pursuing him over the Highlands of Scotland. *I Know Where I'm Going* (1945) is a romance set at the end of World War II, made by the famous film-making duo, Powell and Pressburger. The setting is the Hebrides, with lots of scenic backdrops. One reviewer claimed he'd never seen a picture that "smelled of the wind and rain of Scotland in quite this way." Martin Scorsese has hailed it as a hidden masterpiece.

Also set in the Hebrides is *Whisky Galore!* (1949), a classic Ealing comedy, adapted from Compton Mackenzie's novel. The plot concerns a cargo vessel at the end of World War II, which—with a cargo of 50,000 cases of whisky—is wrecked off the coast of a small Scottish island. *Ring of Bright Water* (1969) is based loosely on a memoir by wayward Scottish aristocrat, Gavin Maxwell. Set on the rugged west coast of Scotland, it is the humorous yet touching story of a tame otter and his bemused carers (played by Bill Travers and Virginia McKenna).

By contrast, *The Wicker Man* from 1973 is sometimes described as "the *Citizen Kane* of horror movies." It follows the misadventures of a police officer who comes to a Scottish island in search of a missing girl whom the locals claim never existed.

A coming-of-age romantic comedy film from 1981, *Gregory's Girl* was written and directed by Bill Forsyth. Set in Cumbernauld, not far from Glasgow, it centers around an awkward teenager (played by Gordon John Sinclair) and his problems finding love. In spite of its low budget, the film is frequently listed among critics' top 100 British films ever made. Another of Forsyth's films, *Local Hero* (1983), was filmed near Mallaig and features an American oil company executive sent to a Scottish fishing village on a mission. *My Name is Joe* from 1988 is a gritty realist drama directed by Ken Loach. Peter Mullan stars as an unemployed recovering alcoholic who meets and falls for a health worker. The film was shot mainly in the council estates of Glasgow, and many members of the cast were actual drug addicts. Continuing the theme of addiction but switching the action to Edinburgh, Danny Boyle's 1996 movie, *Trainspotting,* follows a motley group of heroine addicts led by Ewan McGregor.

Braveheart (1995) has been around long enough to be hailed as a classic in Scotland, resonating with viewers as a stirring call for independence from England. Mel Gibson stars as William Wallace, the 13th-century patriot. It must be noted, however, that the movie is less than faithful to historical fact. *Breaking the Waves* (1996) directed by Lars von Trier offers an emotional rollercoaster of a far more troubling kind. Set in the 1970s, it follows the relationships of an oil-rig worker (Stellan Skarsgård) and his young wife (Emily Watson) in a remote community in northern Scotland. The acting performances are often considered among the best ever committed to film.

In current literature, Ian Rankin has won well-deserved success for his Inspector Rebus novels, while Alan Warner has fostered a growing readership with novels such as *The Worms Can Carry Me to Heaven* (2006). Meanwhile, a tradition of representing local speech and urban living runs through the work of James Kelman and Irvine Welsh.

EATING & drinking

FROM ANGUS BEEF TO HAGGIS The Scottish restaurant scene has undergone a revolution during the last 20 years or so. No longer is the diner subjected to plates of overcooked meat with vegetables boiled for several hours. The emphasis of the new cuisine is on fresh, locally produced food, cooked with a lighter touch and served with presentational finesse. The type of venue has changed too in recent times. Whereas in the past a Scot going out for dinner would head for the nearest hotel, today you have many more options; independent restaurants seem to be opening everywhere, often by newly arrived immigrants, along with bistros and wine bars and gastropubs. Scotland's culinary strength resides in the quality and variety of its raw ingredients, ranging from seafood and freshwater fish to beef and game. One of Scotland's best-known exports is pedigree **Aberdeen Angus beef.** Scottish **lamb** is also an important product, renowned for its tender, tasty meat. A true connoisseur can taste the difference in lamb by its grazing grounds, ranging from the coarse pastureland and seaweed of the Shetlands to the heather-clad hills of the mainland.

Game forms an important part of Scotland's food heritage, in all its variety: from woodcock, red deer, and grouse to the rabbit and hare in the crofter's kitchen. And **fish** in this land of seas, rivers, and lochs is a mainstay, from salmon to the pink-fleshed brown trout to the modest herring that's transformed into the kipper (the best are the Loch Fyne kippers). Scottish **smoked salmon** is, of course, a delicacy known worldwide. While many restaurants adopt an eclectic approach to cooking, it takes a wise chef to leave well alone. There's nothing to beat **Lismore oysters** or **Loch Etive mussels** prepared with the minimum of fuss.

Scotland also produces some excellent **cheeses.** A particularly good hard cheese is Dunlop, which comes from the Orkney Islands as well as Arran and Islay. From the Highlands, one of the most-acclaimed cheeses is Caboc, creamy and rich, formed into cork shapes and rolled in pinhead oatmeal. Many varieties of cottage cheese are flavored with herbs, chives, or garlic.

Last, but by no means least, is **haggis,** still Scotland's national dish. One wit described it as a "castrated bagpipe." Traditionally cooked in a sheep's stomach, it's made with bits and pieces of the lung, liver, and heart of sheep mixed with suet and spices, along with onions and oatmeal. Haggis is often accompanied by a shot or two of single-malt whisky.

For an overview of Scottish cuisine, start by consulting *Caledonian Feast: Scottish Cuisine Through the Ages* by Annette Hope (Mainstream Publishing, 1987). To then try and cook some classic dishes yourself, turn to *Traditional Scottish Recipes* by Eleanor Cowan (Waverley Books, 2009).

WHEN TO GO
Weather

You need to give careful consideration to the seasonal weather when you're planning a trip to Scotland. The Lowlands usually have a moderate temperature all year-round. In spring, the average high temperature is 53°F (12°C), rising to about 65°F (18°C) in summer. By the time autumn has arrived, the temperatures have dropped back to

SINGLE MALT OR BLEND?

"It's the only liquor fit for a gentleman to drink in the morning if he can have the good fortune to come by it . . . or after dinner either." Thus wrote Sir Walter Scott of the drink of his country—**Scotch whisky.** Of course, if you're here or almost anywhere in Britain or Europe, you don't have to identify it as *Scotch* whisky when you order. That's what you'll get. In fact, in Britain generally, they look at you oddly if you order Scotch as you would in the States.

An important distinction among whiskies is whether they're blends or single malt. Many connoisseurs prefer single malts, whose tastes depend on their points of origin: Highlands, Lowlands, Islay, or Campbeltown on Kintyre. These are usually seen as sipping whiskies, not to be mixed with water (well, maybe soda) and not to be served with ice. Many have come to be used as after-dinner drinks, perhaps served in a snifter, like cognac.

Blended Scotches came into being because the single malts were for a long time too harsh for delicate palates and they were expensive and time-consuming to produce. A shortcut was developed: The clear and almost tasteless alcohol produced in the traditional way could be mixed with such ingredients as American corn, Finnish barley, Glasgow city tap water, and caramel coloring, with a certain percentage of malt whiskies that flavored the entire bottle. Whichever you prefer, both the single malts and the blends must be made within the borders of Scotland and then aged for at least 3 years before they can legally be called Scotch whisky.

When it comes to whisky, the leading writer on the subject for several decades has been Charles MacLean, who is also a consultant to the whisky industry and advises a top auction house on sales of rare whiskies. His latest book *Great Whiskies* (Dorling Kindersley, 2011) is an A to Z of 500 fine bottles that will make an enthusiast of even the most casual drinker. This beautifully designed and fully illustrated book includes several useful whisky tour itineraries.

The making of Scottish **beer**—the ales drunk by the common folk in earlier days—almost died out when palates became more adapted to Scotch whisky and when a malt tax was levied in the 18th century, followed in the 19th century by beer duty. The brewing industry has made a comeback in the past 30 years, however, and Scottish beer, or Scotch ale, is being produced in quantity once again. **Real ale** is beer made from malted barley, hop flowers, yeast, and water, with a fining process (using an extract from the swim bladders of certain fish, vegetarians take note) to complete the brewing. Ales are fermented in casks in a series of steps. Scottish ale, either dark or light, is malty and full of flavor.

spring levels. In winter, the average temperature is 43°F (6°C). Temperatures in the north of Scotland are lower, especially in winter, and you should dress accordingly. It rains a lot in Scotland, but perhaps not as much as age-old myths would have it; the amount of rainfall in Edinburgh is exactly the same as in London. The west of Scotland, however, is subject to the rain-filled clouds that blow in from the Atlantic. September is often the sunniest month.

Average Temperature & Rainfall in Scotland

EDINBURGH	JAN	FEB	MAR	APR	MAY	JUNE	JULY	AUG	SEPT	OCT	NOV	DEC
Temp. (°F)	38	39	42	45	50	55	59	58	54	49	42	40
Temp. (°C)	3	3	5	7	10	12	15	14	12	9	5	4
Rainfall (in.)	2.2	1.6	1.9	1.5	2.0	2.0	2.5	2.7	2.5	2.4	2.5	2.4
ABERDEEN	JAN	FEB	MAR	APR	MAY	JUNE	JULY	AUG	SEPT	OCT	NOV	DEC
Temp. (°F)	38	38	41	44	49	54	58	57	53	48	42	39
Temp. (°C)	3	3	5	6	9	12	14	13	11	8	5	3
Rainfall (in.)	2.5	2.0	2.1	1.9	2.1	2.0	2.8	2.8	2.5	3.0	3.1	2.9

When You Find Bargains

The cheapest time to travel to Scotland is off-season: **November 1 to December 12** and **early January to March 14.** In the past few years, airlines have been offering heavily discounted fares during these periods, with weekday flights even cheaper than weekend ones.

Rates generally increase between **March 14 and June 5** and in **October,** and hit their peak in the high seasons from **June 6 to September 30** and **December 13 to the end of December.** July and August are when most British people take their holidays, and so in addition to the higher prices, you have to deal with crowds and limited availability of accommodation.

In winter, Scotland is usually rainy and cold—but it doesn't shut down when the tourists leave. In fact, the winter season gives visitors a more honest view of Scottish life. Additionally, many hotel prices drop by 20%, and cheaper accommodation offers weekly rates (unheard of during peak travel times).

Scotland Calendar of Events

You can get details of specific events at many of the festivals below by going to **www.edinburgh-festivals.com**.

For an exhaustive list of events beyond those listed here, check **http://events.frommers.com**, where you'll find a searchable, up-to-the-minute roster of what's happening in cities all over the world.

JANUARY

Celtic Connections, Glasgow. Beginning with a torchlit parade that lights up the wintry streets, the city comes to life with a fortnight of concerts celebrating Celtic music and dance. There are venues throughout the city, but most notably the Old Fruit Market, on Albion Street. For tickets and details, call 𝄞 **0141/353-8000,** or visit www.celticconnections.com. Mid-January to late February.

Burns Night, Ayr (near his birthplace) and Dumfries. Naturally, during the celebrations to honor Robert Burns, there's much toasting with Scotch and eating of haggis. For details, call 𝄞 **01292/443-700** in Ayr or 𝄞 **01387/253-862** in Dumfries. See also www.burnsmuseum.org.uk for information. January 25.

Up Helly Aa, Lerwick, in the Shetland Islands. The most northerly town in Great Britain still clings to tradition by staging an ancient Norse fire festival, the aim of which is to encourage the return of the sun after the pitch-dark days of winter. Its highlight is the burning of a replica of a Norse longboat. See www.visitshetland.com. Last Tuesday in January.

FEBRUARY

Aberdeen Angus Cattle Show, Perth. This show draws the finest cattle raised in Scotland. Sales are lively. Call 𝄞 **01738/622-477** or visit www.aberdeen-angus.co.uk. Early February.

Six Nations Rugby Championship, Edinburgh. Sixty-seven thousand cram into the Murrayfield stadium for each of Scotland's home matches. Visit www.scottishrugby. org. Early February.

Fort William Mountain Festival. Films, lectures, music, and exhibitions are staged in Fort William, at the foot of Ben Nevis. See www.mountainfilmfestival.co.uk. Mid-February.

MARCH

Whuppity Scourie, Lanark. Residents of the Strathclyde get so tired of winter that they stage this traditional ceremony to chase it away. Call 🕐 **01555/661-661.** March 1.

Glasgow Comedy Festival. Glaswegians are certainly not shy in heckling some of comedy's biggest names. Call 🕐 **141/552-2070** or see www.glasgowcomedyfestival. com. Mid-March to early April.

APRIL

Ceilidh Culture, at various venues, Edinburgh. For details about this traditional Scottish music and dancing festival, call 🕐 **0131/228-1155** or visit www.ceilidh culture.co.uk. Early April.

Kate Kennedy Procession & Pageant, St. Andrews. A historic pageant is staged annually at this ancient university. See www.katekennedyclub.org.uk. Second Saturday in April.

Beltane Fire Festival, Edinburgh. Join the costumed revelers as they dance around the Calton hill accompanied by drummers and musicians in this modern take on an ancient Celtic fertility ceremony. It's also a good excuse for a party. See www.beltane. org. End of April.

Spirit of Speyside Whisky Festival. Special tours and tastings are laid on at various Speyside distilleries. Call 🕐 **07876/414-046** or see www.spiritofspeyside.com. Late April and early May.

MAY

Scottish Motorcycle Trials, Fort William. The trials run for 6 days at the beginning of the month, drawing enthusiasts from all over Europe. Visit www.ssdt.org. Early May.

Royal Scottish Academy Annual Exhibition, Edinburgh. Showcase of the best of the academicians' works. Call 🕐 **0131/225-**

6671 or see www.royalscottishacademy. org. Early May to late June.

Pitlochry Festival Theatre, Pitlochry. Scotland's "theatre in the hills" launches its season in mid-May. Call 🕐 **01796/484-626** or visit www.pitlochry.org.uk. Mid-May to October.

Gay Pride, Edinburgh or Glasgow. Scotland's annual gay-pride celebration alternates between Edinburgh and Glasgow. Contact Pride Scotia (🕐 **0131/556-9471;** www.pride-scotia.org). One Saturday in May or June.

JUNE

Lanimer Day, Lanark. A week of festivities features a procession around the town's boundaries, the election of a Lanimer Queen and a Cornet King, a parade with floats, and Highland dances and bagpipe playing. Call 🕐 **01555/663-251** or visit www.lanarklanimers.co.uk. The Thursday between June 6 and 12.

Guid Nychburris (Good Neighbors), Dumfries. This age-old festival is an event similar to (but less impressive than) the Selkirk Common Riding (see below). Visit www. guidnychburris.co.uk. Mid-June.

Royal Highland Show, at the Ingliston Showground, outskirts of Edinburgh. This show is devoted to agriculture and country pursuits. Call 🕐 **0131/335-6200** or visit www.royal highlandshow.org. Mid- to late June.

Selkirk Common Riding, Selkirk. Commemorating Selkirk's losses in the 1513 Battle of Flodden—only one Selkirk soldier returned alive from the battle to warn the town before dropping dead in the marketplace—some 400 horses and riders parade through the streets, and a young unmarried male is crowned at the sound of the cornet, representing the soldier who sounded the alarm. Call 🕐 **01835/825-060** or visit www.returntotheridings.co.uk. Mid-June.

Peebles Beltane Festival. A town "Cornet" rides around to see if the boundaries are safe from the "invading" English, a young girl is elected Festival Queen, and her court is filled with courtiers, sword bearers, guards, and attendants. Children of the town dress in costumes for parade floats through the streets. See www.peebles beltanefestival.co.uk. Mid-June.

RockNess, Loch Ness. For one weekend in June, music lovers descend on the shores of Loch Ness to see great bands, and some comedy acts as well. See www.rockness. co.uk. Mid-June.

Glasgow International Jazz Festival. Jazz musicians from all over the world come together to perform at various venues around the city. Call ☎ **0141/552-3552** or visit www. jazzfest.co.uk. Late June to early July.

JULY

Fèis An Eilein Summer Events, Isle of Skye. This series of concerts, ceilidhs, theatre performances, and children's events helps to maintain the vibrancy of Skye's culture. See www.feisaneilein.com. Throughout July and August.

Hebridean Celtic Festival, Isles of Lewis and Harris. This music festival attracts the biggest names in the Scottish folk world. See www.hebceltfest.com. Mid-July.

Wickerman Festival, near Kirkcudbright. Inspired by Robin Hardy's 1973 cinematic cult thriller-chiller of the same name, this is Scotland's best alternative festival. Don't miss the climactic burning of the wickerman on Saturday night. See www.thewickerman festival.co.uk. Late July.

AUGUST

Lammas Fair, St. Andrews. Ferris wheels and whirligigs are hauled in, cotton candy (candy floss) and popcorn are sold, and palm readers read your future. There's even an opportunity for bungee jumping. Visit www. standrews.co.uk. Five days in early August.

World Pipe Band Championships: Piping Live!, Glasgow. This weeklong festival of bagpiping takes place on Glasgow Green in the city's East End. Contact ☎ **0141/221-5414** and visit www.rspba.org or www. pipinglive.co.uk. Mid-August.

Edinburgh International Festival. Scotland's best-known festival is held for 3 weeks (see chapter 5 for more information). More than 1,000 shows are hosted and 1,000,000 tickets sold. Numerous other festivals are also held in Edinburgh at this time, celebrating everything from books to

jazz. Nothing, however, tops the Military Tattoo against the backdrop of the floodlit Edinburgh Castle. Call ☎ **0131/473-2099** or visit www.eif.co.uk. Three weeks in August.

SEPTEMBER

Ben Nevis Mountain Race, Fort William. A tradition since 1895, as many as 500 runners compete for the coveted MacFarlane Cup by running up the footpaths to the summit and back. Bagpipes rise in crescendos at the beginning and end of the race. See www.bennevisrace.co.uk. First Saturday in September.

Braemar Gathering. The Queen and other members of the royal family often show up for this annual event, with its massed bands, dancing competitions, and trials of great strength by a tribe of gigantic men. Contact ☎ **01339/755-377** or visit www. braemargathering.org. First Saturday in September.

Hamilton Flat Races, Hamilton, near Glasgow. This horseracing festival takes place over 2 to 3 days. Call ☎ **01698/283-806** or visit www.hamilton-park.co.uk. Mid-September.

Camanachd Cup Final, different venue each year. The finale of the season's games of shinty (a sometimes-brutal hockey variant) is an extraordinary spectacle. Call ☎ **01463/226-551** or visit www.shinty. com. Mid-October.

OCTOBER

Highland Autumn Cattle Show, Oban. Since the days of Rob Roy, Oban has been a marketplace for the distinctive Highland Cattle. Buyers and sellers descend on Oban to buy and sell at the industrial-looking Caledonian Auction Mart, 3 miles south of Oban. Call ☎ **01631/563-122** or see www. highlandcattlesociety.com. Mid-October.

Sound Festival, Aberdeen. This festival draws aficionados of avant-garde music. See www.sound-scotland.co.uk. Late October to early November.

NOVEMBER

Dundee Jazz Festival. Jazz musicians from around the world converge on venues across Dundee. See www.jazzdundee. co.uk. Throughout November.

St. Andrews Week, St. Andrews. An annual festival of exhibitions, concerts, sporting events, and fireworks displays. See www.standrewsfestival.co.uk. The week ending November 30.

DECEMBER

Flambeaux Procession, Comrie, Tayside. This torchlight parade takes place on New Year's Eve. For details, call ✆ **01764/652-578** in Crieff. December 31.

Hogmanay, Edinburgh. Hogmanay begins on New Year's Eve and merges into New Year's Day festivities. Events include a torchlight procession, a fire festival along Princes Street, a carnival, and a street-theatre spectacular. See www.edinburghs hogmanay.org. December 31.

RESPONSIBLE TOURISM

There are many ways to experience the attractions of Scotland without burning liters of petrol or indulging in an orgy of consumerism. A popular way is to see the Scottish landscape from the saddle of a bike. Touring by bike can be challenging in the Highlands, but the ride is smoother in the Kingdom of Fife, and around Glasgow and Edinburgh, as the countryside is criss-crossed with scenic lanes. Of course, you have to stop for sheep crossings, but that's part of the fun. Most of the Western Isles, and Shetland and Orkney, can also be traversed by bike. Bikes can be rented in most major towns and cities. Transporting them on Scotland's many ferries is easy and inexpensive.

Many visitors come to Scotland just to explore its parks, in particular, the Loch Lomond and the Trossachs National Park, and the Cairngorms. The **Association of National Park Authorities** (✆ **029/2049-9966;** www.nationalparks.gov.uk) provides information on all the U.K.'s national parks, and provides hiking advice.

Other useful organizations worth bearing in mind are the **Royal Society for the Protection of Birds** (✆ **01767/680-551;** www.rspb.org.uk), which manages numerous bird reserves in Scotland, and the **Scottish Mountaineering Club,** whose website offers useful information for hill walkers and climbers (www.smc.org.uk). If you live in the United States, you can get information before you go from **The Mountaineers Books** (✆ **206/223-6303;** www.mountaineersbooks.org), which has an extensive collection of titles on hiking, biking, and mountaineering in Britain, and especially Scotland.

TOURS & SPECIAL INTEREST TRIPS

Escorted tours are structured group tours, with a group leader. The price usually includes everything from airfare to hotels, meals, tours, admission costs, and local transportation.

Reputable companies offering general tours of Scotland include **Abercrombie & Kent** (✆ **800/554-7016;** www.abercrombiekent.com), **Maupintour** (✆ **800/255-4266;** www.maupintour.com), and **Tauck World Discovery** (✆ **800/788-7885;** www.tauck.com), who all offer luxury escorted tours with prices to match. For less expensive holidays, try **Wallace Arnold Worldchoice** (✆ **0845/365-6747;** www.waworldchoice.com), which is particularly popular with o **The Southern Upland Way:** Rivaling the West Highland Way, this is the second of Scotland's great walks. The footpath begins at Portpatrick and runs 212 miles along the southwest coast to Cockburnspath, on the east coast. It passes through some of the most dramatic scenery in the Borders, including Galloway Forest Park. See p. 156.

o **East Neuk:** Directly south of St. Andrews lie some of Scotland's loveliest fishing villages, collectively known as East Neuk. The most enchanting walk is between the villages of Pittenweem and Anstruther. It's often breezy here, with wind from the sea, so dress accordingly. The path begins at the bottom of West Braes, a cul-de-sac off the main road in Anstruther. See p. 243.

o **The Trossachs:** The Trossachs Trail extends from Loch Lomond, in the west, to Callander, in the east, and also from Doune to Aberfoyle and the Lord Ard Forest, to the south. In the north, it's bounded by the Crianlarich Hills and Balquhidder, the site of Rob Roy's grave. Ever since Sir Walter Scott published *The Lady of the Lake* and *Rob Roy,* the area has attracted hikers in search of unspoiled natural beauty.

Our favorite start for walks is the village of Brig o' Turk, between lochs Achray and Venachar, at the foot of Glen Finglas. From here you can set out in any direction, including one signposted toward the Achray Forest. There's also the Glen Finglas circular walk; and many hikers leave Brig o' Turk heading for Balquhidder via Glen Finglas. See "Callander & a Trio of Lochs," in chapter 9.

o **The West Highland Way:** Unquestionably one of Scotland's great walks, the West Highland Way begins north of Glasgow, in Milngavie. The footpath stretches 95 miles northward along Loch Lomond, going through Glencoe to Fort William and eventually to Ben Nevis, Britain's highest mountain. Even if you want to walk only part of this path, you need to make plans in advance. See p. 269.

o **Ben Nevis:** 33/4 miles southeast of the town of Fort William looms Ben Nevis, Britain's highest mountain. At 1,342m (4,403 ft.), the snow-capped granite mass dominates this entire region of Scotland. This trip can be done in a day, but you'll need to massage your feet in the evening at a local pub. See p. 318.

older travelers, and the U.S.-based **Trafalgar Tours** (© 866/544-4434; www.trafalgartours.com). Also worth considering is **Globus & Cosmos Tours** (© 866/755-8581; www.globusandcosmos.com). For more information on escorted general-interest tours, including questions to ask before booking your trip, see www.frommers.com/planning. See also the sections on tours in Edinburgh on p. 71 and in Glasgow on p. 164.

Many visitors come to Scotland to walk amidst the spectacular mountain scenery. **Mountain Innovations** (© 01479/831-331; www.scotmountain.co.uk) is among the best, offering vacations year-round as well as "skills" courses on navigation and tackling the mountains in the snow. **Wilderness Scotland** (© 0131/625-6635; www.wildernessscotland.com) organizes walking trips at all levels of difficulty, and also offers canoeing, mountain-biking, and sailing breaks.

Those who are interested in observing Scotland's extraordinary wildlife should check out the **Grant Arms Hotel** (© 0800/043-8585; www.grantarmshotel.com), which operates as a base for a variety of guided safaris, taking in rare birds, mammals, and flora. A much-loved but all too rare resident of Scotland is the otter; consult the websites of the **International Otter Survival Fund** (© **01471/822-487;** www. otter.org or www.ottershop.co.uk) for remarkably good-value trips that allow you a privileged glimpse of this elusive species.

If, on the other hand, your enthusiasm is for cooking, consider a residential course at **Kinloch Lodge** on the Isle of Skye (© **01471/833-333;** www.claire-macdonald. com) or at **Knowle B&B** on Loch Ness (© **01456/450-646;** www.lochnessguest house.co.uk). One-day courses are available at the **Port of Menteith Cook School,** run by TV chef Nick Nairn (© **01877/389-900;** www.nicknairncookschool.com).

A good way for aficionados of Scotch whisky to see Scotland is to undertake a tour of distilleries. There are numerous companies that organize tours on this theme. Try **Whisky Tours Scotland** (www.whisky-tours-scotland.com) or **Distillery Destinations** (© **0141/429-0762;** www.whisky-tours.com).

Two reputable companies that offer a range of special interest tours (as well as some general interest ones) are **McKinlay Kidd** (© **0844/804-0020;** www. seescotlanddifferently.co.uk), which offers visits to whisky distilleries, a "Scottish seafood trail," whale- and shark-watching breaks, and classic- and sports-car tours; and **McLean Scotland** (© **01738/560-435;** www.mcleanscotland.com), who can take you on Scottish cuisine and golfing holidays, clan tours, and circuits of the country's great castles.

Alternatively, for a very personal experience of Scotland, book an **Afternoon Tea Tour** (© **07873/211-856;** www.afternoonteatours.com). One of Scotland's top tour operators, this company offers set guided tours taking in historic sites, iconic scenery, and afternoon tea at a country house hotel. It can also organize bespoke tours with itineraries that focus on individual interests and provide a unique glimpse of the more unusual and intimate side of Scotland.

USEFUL TERMS & LANGUAGE

During Scotland's earliest history, the prevailing language was Gaelic, with a smattering of Norse dialects existing alongside. By the 7th century, Northumbrian Old English had established itself in southeastern Scotland, and later, in the medieval period, this was displaced by a variety of northern Middle English, which is often referred to as Early Scots. This language gradually became the dominant language in eastern Scotland until English gained the ascendancy in the 17th and 18th centuries.

In the 15th and 16th centuries, Scotland also had close ties to France, and French—considered a literary language of precision and grace—became the language of the aristocracy. Notably, it was the language of Mary Queen of Scots, who spoke no Gaelic at all.

After the Scottish court moved to England in 1603, English—or the Scottish dialect of the language—spread as the ancient and complex Gaelic language declined in importance. The Reformation in Scotland adopted the 1611 Authorized King James Version of the Bible, and the British government pursued a policy of unifying the whole of Britain linguistically. By the 18th century, many educated Scots (the philosopher David Hume for one) came to consider themselves "Northern British" and took pains to rid themselves of their Scottish speech patterns. However, the old Scots language was adapted to form a new literary language. Its distinctive vocabulary and burr live on in the works of the poet, Robert Burns.

GENERAL RESOURCES FOR responsible TRAVEL

The following websites provide wide-ranging information on responsible travel. For a list of even more tips on the subject, visit www.frommers.com/planning.

o **Responsible Travel** (www.responsibletravel.com) is a good source of sustainable travel ideas; this travel agency is run by a spokesperson for ethical tourism in the travel industry.

o **Sustainable Travel International** (www.sustainabletravelinternational.org) promotes ethical tourism practices, and manages an extensive directory of sustainable properties and tour operators around the world.

o In the U.K., **Tourism Concern** (www.tourismconcern.org.uk) works to reduce social and environmental problems connected to tourism.

o In Canada, **www.greenlivingonline.com** has a useful travel and transport section. The site also profiles of the best green shops and services in Toronto, Vancouver, and Calgary for buying essential kit before your holiday.

o In Australia, the national body that sets guidelines and standards for ecotourism is **Ecotourism Australia** (www.ecotourism.org.au). **The Green Directory** (www.thegreendirectory.com.au), **Green Pages** (www.thegreenpages.com.au), and **Eco Directory** (www.ecodirectory.com.au) offer tips on sustainable travel and directories of green businesses.

o **Carbonfund** (www.carbonfund.org) and **TerraPass** (www.terrapass.org) provide information on "carbon offsetting," or offsetting the greenhouse gas emitted during flights. **Climate Care** (www.

Of course, by the end of the 20th century, the great leveling effects of TV and radio had begun to even out some of the more pronounced lilts of the Scottish tongue. Nowadays, only about 1.2% of the Scottish population—around 60,000 people—speak Gaelic. Most of these people live in the northwestern Highlands or in the Hebridean Islands—especially the Isle of Skye, where about 60% of the population still use Gaelic. All the same, the dialect and speech patterns of the Scots are still rich and evocative, and there is now an increasing pride in the Scottish language. Whereas in, say, the 1950s, school pupils were under constant threat of a whack from the *tawse* (leather strap) if they blurted out a single *aye,* today they might meet with approval from pro-Scots educators when they say, "Whos all comin tae the jiggin?" ("Who's coming to the dance?"). Below is a section of words you might encounter during your travels through Scotland.

aber	river mouth	**ben**	peak, often rugged
ach	field	**birk**	birch tree
aird	promontory	**brae**	hillside, especially along a river
alt	stream		
auch	field	**brig**	bridge
auld	old	**broch**	circular stone tower
baillie	magistrate	**burn**	stream
bal	hamlet or tiny village		

climatecare.org) is also useful, providing an online calculator for determining the carbon emissions associated with your trip.

○ The website **www.ecofriendly tourist.com** offers a useful list of eco-friendly hotels in Scotland as well as a wealth of other useful information for the conscientious traveler.

○ The **Slow Food** movement is thriving in Scotland, championing fresh local food produced and harvested in sustainable ways. See www.slowfood.org.uk and www. slowfoodedinburgh.co.uk.

○ For information on animal-conservation issues throughout the world, visit **Tread Lightly** (www.treadlightly.org). For Scottish-based conservation issues, consult the website of **Scottish National Heritage** (www.snh.gov. uk) and that of the **Scottish Wild-**life **Trust** (www.swt.org.uk). The latter also manages over 120 nature reserves across Scotland. For information about the ethics of swimming with dolphins, visit the **Whale and Dolphin Conservation Society** (www.wdcs.org).

○ For volunteering opportunities in Scotland, visit the websites of the **British Trust for Conservation Volunteers** (www.btcv.org.uk) and the **National Trust for Scotland** (www.nts.org.uk/Volunteering). The following websites also offer lists of volunteering holidays: **www.earthwatch.org**, **www. volunteerabroad.org**, and **www. idealist.org**. Finally, **Volunteer International** (www.volunteer international.org) has a list of questions to help you determine the intentions and the nature of a volunteer program.

---

cairn heap of stones piled up as memorial or landmark

ceilidh Scottish hoedown with singing, music, and tall tales

clach stone

clachan hamlet

close narrow passage leading from the street to a court or tenement

craig rock

creel basket

croft small farm worked by a tenant, often with hereditary rights

cromlech, dolmen prehistoric tomb or monument consisting of a large flat stone laid across upright stones

dram ⅛ fluid ounce

drum ridge

dun fortress, often in a lake, for refuge in times of trouble

eas waterfall

eilean island

factor manager of an estate

fell hill

firth arm of the sea reaching inland

gait street (in proper names)

gil ravine

glen a small valley

haugh water meadow

how burial mound

howff small, cozy room or meeting place

inver mouth of a river

kil, kin, kirk church

kyle narrows of ancient or unknown origin

land house built on a piece of ground considered as property

larig mountain pass

links dunes

loch lake
machair sand dune, sometimes covered with sea grass
mon hill
muir moor
mull cape or promontory
ness headland
neuk nose
pend vaulted passage
provost mayor
reek smoke
ross cape

schist highly compact crystalline rock formation
strath broad valley
tarbert isthmus
tolbooth old town hall (often with prison)
uig sheltered bay
uisge water
uisge beatha water of life, whisky
way bay
wynd alley

SUGGESTED SCOTLAND ITINERARIES

For visitors to Scotland, one of the great pleasures is getting "lost" in the Highlands and islands: wandering, making new discoveries off the beaten track, and finding charming towns and Brigadoon-like villages such as Pittenweem or Crail. Unfortunately, few of us have unlimited time, and so the itineraries in this chapter such as "Scotland in 1 Week" or "Scotland in 2 Weeks" may be helpful for ensuring that you take in the highlights. For those who've been to Scotland and know the major cities of Glasgow and Edinburgh, the "Scottish History and Landscape in a Week" itinerary may be better suited to your needs.

The itineraries that follow take you to some major attractions such as Edinburgh, but also direct you to more secluded spots such as the Trossachs. The pace may seem a little breathless for some visitors, and so skip a town or sight occasionally to include some relaxation time—after all, you're away on a trip, not a military exercise.

All the itineraries below assume the use of a car. If you stick to the main highways, you'll find that Scotland has some of the best-maintained roads in Europe. Off the beaten track, however, you may occasionally find yourself having to open and shut a fence to keep the sheep from wandering astray. Even in the Highlands and on the islands, though, ongoing investment ensures that remote areas generally have good all-weather surfaces. An important precaution before heading out into the wilderness is to make sure you fill up with petrol (gasoline) first. Service stations are few and far between in the Highlands, and when you do find one, prices can be a good 10% higher than in the major conurbations. Of course, also take care in winter: Snow and fog can make driving in remote areas treacherous.

THE REGIONS IN BRIEF

Scotland, Great Britain's oldest geological formation, is divided into three major regions: the **Southern Uplands**—smooth, rolling moorland broken with low crags and threaded with rivers and valleys, between the central plain and the English border; the **Central Lowlands,** where three valleys and the estuaries (firths) of the Clyde, Forth, and Tay rivers make up a fertile belt from the Atlantic Ocean to the North Sea; and the granite **Highlands,** with lochs (lakes), glens (valleys), and mountains, plus the hundreds of islands to the west and north. Each of these regions is then subdivided into smaller regions as detailed below. For reference, see also the map of the whole of Scotland on p. 2.

EDINBURGH & THE LOTHIAN REGION   This area includes not only the country's capital but also West Lothian, most of Midlothian, and East Lothian. Half medieval and half Georgian, **Edinburgh** is at its liveliest every August during the International Arts Festival, but you can visit Edinburgh Castle and Holyroodhouse and walk the Royal Mile year-round. This is one of Europe's most beautiful capitals, and to do it full justice would take a good 3 days. This allows you to take in the highlights of the Old Town and the New Town, which include some of the country's major museums. For your visit to the city, be sure to take advantage of the Edinburgh Pass (available for 1, 2, or 3 days), which provides free access to dozens of major attractions as well as free bus travel within the city (and free transfers to and from the airport).

Edinburgh is surrounded by such major attractions as the village of **Cramond,** the ancient town of **Linlithgow,** and **Dirleton,** the "prettiest village in Scotland." If you take advantage of the many side trips to nearby attractions, you can happily base yourself in Edinburgh for a full week.

THE BORDERS & GALLOWAY REGIONS   Witness to a turbulent history, the Borders and Galloway regions between England and Scotland are rich in castle ruins and Gothic abbeys.

Home of the cashmere sweater and the tweed suit, the **Borders** also proved a rich mine for the fiction of Sir Walter Scott. Highlights are **Kelso,** which Scott found "the most beautiful," and **Melrose,** site of the ruined Melrose Abbey and Scott's former home of Abbotsford. Ancient monuments include Jedburgh Abbey and Dryburgh Abbey, Scott's burial place. At Floors Castle, outside Kelso, you can see one of the great mansions designed by William Adam.

Southwestern Scotland is known as the **Galloway region.** It consists of much of the former stomping ground of Robert Burns and includes towns such as **Dumfries, Castle Douglas,** and **Moffat.** Highlights are the artists' colony of **Kirkcudbright,** the baronial Threave Garden, Sweetheart Abbey outside Dumfries (the ruins of a Cistercian abbey from 1273), and the Burns Mausoleum at Dumfries. The Borders and Galloway Regions cover a large area and, unless you're an enthusiastic cyclist or hiker, a car is really the best way to get around.

GLASGOW & THE STRATHCLYDE REGION   A true renaissance has come to the once-grimy industrial city of **Glasgow,** and you really need to spend at least 2 days in "the greatest surviving example of a Victorian city." As well as the lively street- and nightlife, there are plenty of museums and galleries, notably the Burrell Collection, a wealthy shipowner's gift of more than 8,000 items from the ancient world to the modern; the Hunterian Art Gallery, with its array of masterpieces by everybody from Rembrandt to Whistler; and the Kelvingrove Art Gallery and Museum, home of Britain's finest civic collection of British and European paintings.

Glasgow is at the doorstep of one of the most historic regions of Scotland. You can explore Robert Burns Country in the **Strathclyde region,** especially the district around Ayr and Prestwick, or visit a string of famous seaside resorts (including Turnberry, which boasts some of the country's greatest golf courses). Although Glasgow itself can easily be negotiated on foot and on public buses, a car is useful for exploring the regions beyond the city.

ARGYLL & THE SOUTHERN HEBRIDES   Once the independent kingdom of Dalriada, the **Argyll Peninsula** of western Scotland is centered at **Oban,** a bustling port town and one of Scotland's leading coastal resorts. Important attractions here include **Argyll Forest Park,** actually three forests—Benmore, Ardgartan, and Glenbranter—covering some 24,300 hectares (60,000 acres). You can also visit **Loch Awe,** a natural moat that protected the Campbells of Inveraray from their enemies to the north, and **Kintyre,** the longest peninsula in Scotland—more than 60 miles of beautiful scenery, sleepy villages, and sandy beaches.

The Kintyre coast also provides access to many of the Hebridean Islands. Kennacraig on the Kintyre peninsula is the main departure point for ferries to the islands of **Islay, Jura,** and tiny **Gigha** with its famous gardens. Claonaig, not far away from Kennacraig, is where the boats leave for the short hop over to the **Isle of Arran**—often referred to as "Scotland in miniature." It takes about 2½ hours to drive from Glasgow to Kennacraig or Claonaig. A public bus service operates daily from Glasgow's Buchanan Street Bus Station.

Oban, to the north, is the main ferry port for departures to Mull, Colonsay, Coll, Tiree, and, in the Outer Hebrides, South Uist and Barra. Consult the Caledonian MacBrayne website at www.calmac.co.uk for timetables, fares, and other information. For many routes foot passengers can just turn up and go; for other routes, and if you want to take your car, it's better to book in advance. Special island-hopping, group, and frequent traveler tickets are available. Be aware, though, that ferries are less frequent in winter and may be delayed or cancelled in bad weather. Oban itself can be reached in around 2 hours by car, bus, or train from Glasgow. The train follows the scenic West Highland Line.

FIFE & THE CENTRAL HIGHLANDS   The "kingdom" of **Fife** is one of the most history-rich parts of Scotland, evocative of the era of romance and pageantry during the reign of the early Stuart kings. The most enchanting stretch is a series of fishing villages called **East Neuk.** And **Culross,** renovated by the National Trust, could well be the most beautiful village in Scotland. Opening on to the North Sea, the university town of **St. Andrews,** the "Oxford of Scotland," is the capital of golf and boasts many great courses. The 50-mile drive from Edinburgh can be undertaken by either car or public bus. The area is rich in castles and abbeys, notably Dunfermline Abbey, burial place of 22 royal personages, and Falkland Palace and Gardens, where Mary Queen of Scots came to hunt. You can also visit **Stirling,** dominated by its castle, where she lived as an infant monarch. **Loch Lomond** and the **Trossachs** together form a National Park containing a breathtaking combination of moors, mountains, and lakes.

ABERDEEN & TAYSIDE & GRAMPIAN REGIONS   Carved from the old counties of Perth and Angus, **Tayside** takes its name from the River Tay, which runs for 119 miles and provides prime salmon and trout fishing. Major centers are **Dundee,** an old seaport and royal burgh on the north shore of the Firth of Tay; **Perth,** former capital of Scotland, situated at the point where Highlands and Lowlands meet; and **Pitlochry,** a picturesque Victorian resort that's an ideal base for touring the Valley of the Tummel. The area abounds in castles and palaces, including Glamis, linked to British royalty for 10 centuries, and Scone, an art-filled palace that dates back to 1580. The great city of the north, **Aberdeen,** is called Scotland's "granite city" and ranks third in population. It's the best center for touring "castle country" and is accessible by bus, train, and plane from Edinburgh and Glasgow, as well as from many major English cities. **Braemar,** an easy drive from Aberdeen, is known for its scenery as well as for being the site of every summer's Royal Highland Gathering. Nearby **Balmoral Castle** at Ballater was the "beloved paradise" of Queen Victoria and is still home to the royal family. Finally, you can follow the **Whisky Trail** to check out some of Scotland's most famous distilleries such as Glenlivet and Glenfiddich.

INVERNESS & THE WEST HIGHLANDS   The Highlands' capital is **Inverness,** one of the oldest inhabited areas in Scotland. Top attractions nearby are **Loch Ness,** home of the legendary monster, and **Cawdor Castle,** famously linked with Macbeth. The man-made **Caledonian Canal,** launched in 1803, stretches for 60 miles, joining several natural lochs. As you proceed to the north, you can visit the **Black Isle,** a little-known gem of a peninsula on the east coast, before heading far up north to **Ullapool,** an 18th-century fishing village on the west coast (and the departure point for the ferry to Lewis in the Outer Hebrides), and **John o' Groats,** the closest point accessible by car to **Dunnet Head,** the northernmost point of mainland Britain.

THE HEBRIDEAN ISLANDS   The chain of the Inner Hebrides lies just off the west coast of the mainland. The most visited island is the **Isle of Skye,** a mystical island and subject of the Scottish ballad "Over the Sea to Skye." It's also the only island connected to the mainland by a toll-free bridge. If you're not driving, the Kyle of Lochalsh, at the mainland end of the bridge can be reached by train from Inverness and by coach from most major cities.

The **Isle of Mull,** third largest of the Inner Hebrides, is also rich in legend and folklore, including ghosts, monsters, and the "wee folk." Ferries to Mull leave from Oban daily (see "Argyll and the Southern Hebrides," above). **Iona,** off the coast of Mull, is known as the "Grave of Kings," with an abbey dating from the 13th century. Those with time remaining can also explore the Outer Hebrides, notably **Lewis,** the largest and most northerly (accessible by ferry from Ullapool—see above). Along with the island of **Harris,** Lewis stretches for a combined length of some 95 miles. This is a relatively treeless land of marshy peat bogs and ancient relics.

THE ORKNEY & SHETLAND ISLANDS   These northern outposts of civilization are archipelagos consisting of some 200 islands, about 40 of which are inhabited. With a rich Viking heritage, they reward visitors with remarkable scenery, wildlife, and antiquities. Major centers of the Orkneys are **Kirkwall,** established by Norse invaders and the capital of the Orkneys for 9 centuries, and **Stromness,** the main port of the archipelago and once the last port of call before the New World.

You can fly to Kirkwall from Inverness, Aberdeen, Edinburgh, and Glasgow (see www.flybe.com). Ferries operate from Aberdeen to Kirkwall and from Thurso to Stromness (see www.jogferry.co.uk, www.northlinkferries.com, and www.pentlandferries.co.uk). Bus services connect the ferry terminals with Scotland's major cities.

Lerwick has been the capital of the Shetlands since the 17th century. Many of the Shetland Islands have their own ancient monuments: The most outstanding are Midhower Broch; tombs on Rousay dating from the Iron Age and known as the "great ship of death"; Quoyness Chambered Tomb on Sanday, a spectacular chambered cairn from 2900 B.C.; the Ring of Brodgar between Loch and Stenness, a stone circle of some 36 stones dating from 1560 B.C. and called the "Stonehenge of Scotland"; and Skara Brae, a Neolithic village joined by covered passages, last occupied around 2500 B.C.

Flights to Shetland run from Aberdeen, Edinburgh, Glasgow, Inverness, and Orkney. Flights are also available between some of the Shetland Islands themselves (see www.directflight.co.uk). Northlink Ferries operates services from Aberdeen (www.northlinkferries.com).

SCOTLAND IN 1 WEEK

Although it's impossible to see all of Scotland in 1 week, it should be enough time to see the major sights of Edinburgh and Glasgow, and with the time remaining you can head to the banks of Loch Lomond and to the Highlands beyond.

Days 1 & 2: Edinburgh, Gateway to Scotland ★★★

After checking into your hotel in Scotland's capital, head straight out for the Old Town's **Royal Mile** (p. 73), which runs between two of the city's main attractions, **Edinburgh Castle** (p. 73) and the **Palace of Holyroodhouse** (p. 78). You can probably visit only one of these before lunch, saving the other for the afternoon. If you save Holyroodhouse for the afternoon, you should then also have time to fit in a visit to the **Scottish Parliament** building (p. 79).

As the afternoon wanes, walk down into the New Town for some shopping along the famous **Princes Street.** In the early evening, drop into an Edinburgh pub for a pint or a wee dram—and a sample of local life. Have dinner in one of the New Town's wide variety of restaurants (reviews begin on p. 90).

On **Day 2,** which could turn into a very busy day, check out the artistic masterpieces in the **National Gallery of Scotland** (p. 80) and see some of the historic treasures of the **National Museum of Scotland** (p. 80). You should be able to spend a worthwhile amount of time in both of these museums during a full morning. In the afternoon, though, a change of pace is in order, and so visit the Greek-inspired **Calton Hill** (p. 82) in the east of Edinburgh and the **Royal Botanic Garden** (p. 85), one of Britain's finest. For your final night in Edinburgh, have dinner in one of the historic restaurants of the Old Town, following in the footsteps of Robert Louis Stevenson.

Days 3 & 4: Glasgow, Scotland's Largest City ★★★

On **Day 3,** get an early-morning start and drive to Glasgow, which is only 40 miles west of Edinburgh. You can arrive in time to check into a hotel and see **The Burrell Collection** (p. 175) before lunch. In the afternoon, visit the **Kelvingrove Art Gallery & Museum** (p. 173), and the **Glasgow Science Centre** (p. 174), on the banks of the River Clyde. After a visit to a Glaswegian pub, move on for dinner in one of Glasgow's convivial restaurants (reviews begin on p.178).

On the morning of **Day 4,** visit the **Cathedral of St. Kentigern** (p. 163), which dates back to the Middle Ages. You'll still have time to view the paintings in the **Hunterian Art Gallery** (p. 173) before lunch. In the afternoon, explore Glasgow's fascinating **Museum of Transport** (relocating in 2011) and visit other attractions such as **The Tall Ship at Glasgow Harbour** (p. 174), or take in some shopping along **Sauchiehall Street** or **Argyle Street.** In the evening, you can attend a performance of opera or ballet at the **Theatre Royal** (p. 188).

Day 5: Loch Lomond ★★

From Glasgow, on **Day 5,** take a drive 20 miles northwest to **Balloch** (p. 268), a good center for exploring the landscape around Loch Lomond. The best way to spend a day seeing the area is to take one of **Sweeney's Cruisers** (p. 269). If you return in time, you can also explore **Balloch Castle Country Park** (p. 269). Spend the night in Balloch, situated at the southern end of the Loch.

Day 6: Fort William, Gateway to the Highlands ★

From Glasgow (or Balloch, if you spent the night there), strike out for **Fort William,** 104 miles north of Glasgow. Located on the shores of Loch Linnhe, Fort William is the best stopover for those traveling between Glasgow and Inverness, capital of the Highlands. You can arrive in time for lunch, taking in views of **Ben Nevis,** the highest mountain in Scotland. In the afternoon, visit the ruins of **Old Inverlochy Castle** (p. 319) and **Neptune's Staircase** (p. 319). Spend the night in Fort William.

Day 7: Inverness, Capital of the Highlands ★

Fort William to Inverness is a drive of 68 miles. Before reaching Inverness, drive along the western bank of **Loch Ness** (p. 325), keeping your eye out for the elusive monster. The official **Loch Ness Monster Exhibition** (p. 325) is at Drumnadrochit, and you can also explore the ruins of **Urquhart Castle** (p. 326).

Have lunch in Inverness, and then set out to see the **Culloden Battlefield** (p. 330), with its Graves of the Clans, and also visit the **Fort George/Queen's Own Highlanders Regimental Museum** (p. 330). Spend the rest of the afternoon exploring the historic center of Inverness, nestling around both banks of the Ness River: Overnight in Inverness.

SCOTLAND IN 2 WEEKS

A full 2 weeks for exploring Scotland allows you some breathing space and time to take in some of the more esoteric destinations, soak in the atmosphere, and even visit one of the Hebridean Islands. Towards the end of the fortnight, you'll also have time to explore some of the historic towns of the Borders.

Days 1 to 7

Follow the itinerary outlined above in "Scotland in 1 Week."

Days 8 & 9: Isle of Skye ★★

On **Day 8,** from your last stopover in Inverness (see above), drive the 82 miles southwest along the A832 to the Kyle of Lochalsh, the gateway to the Isle of Skye. You can now drive from Kyle to Skye over a bridge.

Once on Skye, check into a hotel for 2 nights. Although it's the largest of the Hebridean Islands, Skye is relatively small, only 48 miles long, and so you can stay almost anywhere and use the town as your headquarters for exploring the entire island. Some of the best places for lodgings include **Kyleakin** (p. 358), **Sligachan** (p. 359), and **Portree** (p. 360). Portree is the capital of the island. For complete coverage of the Isle of Skye, see p. 356.

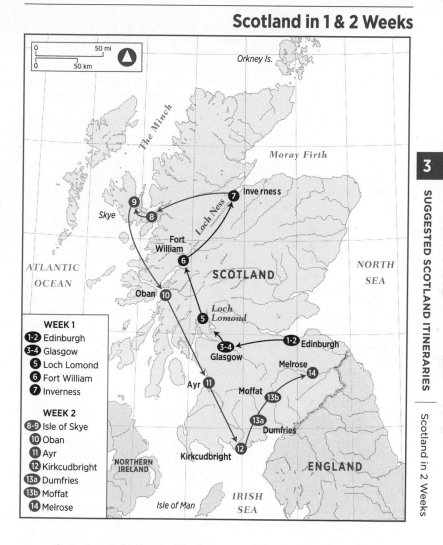

WEEK 1

1-2 Edinburgh
3-4 Glasgow
5 Loch Lomond
6 Fort William
7 Inverness

WEEK 2

8-9 Isle of Skye
10 Oban
11 Ayr
12 Kirkcudbright
13a Dumfries
13b Moffat
14 Melrose

Assuming you base yourself in the center of the island, at the lochside village of Sligachan, you can order lunch and then spend the afternoon driving up the A856 to the north of Skye, taking in the dramatic scenery along the way. You ultimately reach the village of **Uig,** where you can visit the **Skye Museum of Island Life** (p. 361). After leaving Uig, traverse the entire northeastern part of Skye by following the A855 in a half-moon crescent, finally heading back to Sligachan for the night.

On the morning of **Day 9,** set out from Sligachan (or whichever village you've lodged in) to explore the **Sleat Peninsula,** in the south, following the A850 (which becomes the A851). Once at Sleat, visit **Knock Castle** (p. 291), the former stronghold of the MacDonalds, now some of the most evocative ruins in the Hebrides. You can also explore **Armadale Castle Gardens & Museum of the Isles** (p. 363). Allow an hour or so for a visit here. Sleat is known as the garden of Skye, and you can wander at leisure, taking in its woodland glens, cliffs, and waterfalls.

For your afternoon adventure, drive up (via Broadford) to the jagged **Cuillin Hills** (p. 356) or take a 3-hour cruise at Elgol (see **Bella Jane Boat Trips,** on p. 258) to see the hills and other parts of the island from a different angle. Finally, return to your hotel for a well-deserved dinner.

Day 10: Oban ★

On **Day 10,** take the bridge from Skye back to the mainland and head south via Fort William to the coastal resort of **Oban** (p. 231). Oban lies 50 miles to the southwest of Fort William. Check into a hotel here and, after lunch, visit **McCaig's Tower** (p. 234), enjoying the panoramic view across the Firth of Lorn to the Sound of Mull. You should also have time to visit **Dunstaffnage Castle** (p. 231) and walk along the harborfront before dinner.

Day 11: Ayr, Ode to Robert Burns

Leave Oban on the morning of **Day 11,** continuing south to the town of **Ayr** (p. 198), situated 35 miles southeast of Glasgow. The town has many associations with Robert Burns, Scotland's national poet.

Check into a hotel at Ayr and use it as a base for exploring nearby **Alloway,** the birthplace of Burns, which is 1¾ miles to the south. Once there, visit the **Burns Cottage & Museum** (p. 200) and the **Burns Monument & Gardens** (p. 200). Allow at least 2 hours.

You can also make it to **Culzean Castle** (p. 205), 12 miles southwest of Ayr, in the same afternoon. Designed by Scottish architect Robert Adam, this is one of the grandest castles in the west of Scotland. General Eisenhower was a former guest. Return to Ayr for the night.

Day 12: Kirkcudbright, an Artists' Colony ★

On **Day 12,** leave Ayr in the morning and drive into the Borders country, scheduling a stop at the old sheep-market town of **Castle Douglas,** 49 miles southeast of Ayr. Visit the 14th-century ruins of **Threave Castle** (p. 150), and have lunch in town.

In the afternoon, continue for 10 miles to the southwest until you reach the old town of Kirkcudbright, which is the center of a flourishing artists' colony. Here you can stroll around for an hour or two, taking in such attractions as **Broughton House** (p. 152) and the **Tolbooth Art Centre** (p. 152).

Day 13: Dumfries ★ & Moffat

On **Day 13,** head north from Kirkcudbright to join the A75, and continue northeast to the town of Dumfries. At this point, you're 80 miles southwest of Edinburgh and about the same distance from Glasgow.

Like Ayr, Dumfries also has associations with Robert Burns, and you can visit **Burns House** (p. 148) before visiting **Drumlanrig Castle** (p. 149) and the **Dumfries Museum** (p. 148). You might also want to view the ruins of **Sweetheart Abbey** (p. 149) before heading for the town of **Moffat,** a drive of only 22 miles to the northeast. Check into a hotel and spend the rest of the afternoon exploring **Devil's Beef Tub** (p. 145), the **Grey Mare's Tail** (p. 145), and **Annan Water Valley Road** (p. 146) before returning to Moffat for the night.

Day 14: Melrose, Highlight of the Borders ★

Day 14 promises to be busy. Leaving Moffat, head northeast to **Melrose,** which is only 37 miles southeast of Edinburgh. Check into a hotel and use Melrose as a base for exploring nearby attractions. In the town itself, visit **Abbotsford House** (p. 135), former home of Sir Walter Scott; **Melrose Abbey** (p. 135), which has some of the most beautiful ruins in the country; and **Traquair House** (p. 143), Scotland's oldest and most romantic house.

In the afternoon, drive 12 miles east to the town of **Kelso.** From here, take the 6¾-mile jaunt to **Mellerstain,** one of the most famous mansions designed by Robert Adam. Allow 2 hours for a visit. Return to Melrose for the night and plan an early-morning departure for Edinburgh and your return home.

SCOTLAND FOR FAMILIES

Despite Scotland perhaps not being the most child-friendly destination in Europe—many of its pleasures and pastimes, such as playing golf or drinking whisky, are adult-oriented—there are nevertheless many attractions that the entire family can enjoy, especially in Edinburgh and Glasgow. Perhaps the main concern with children in tow is pacing yourselves, particularly in museums. It's advisable, therefore, to spend a good 2 days in Edinburgh and a further 2 days in Glasgow. Thereafter, you can venture out into the countryside, where children will delight in exploring spooky old castles, seeing the mountains, and looking for the Loch Ness Monster.

Days 1 & 2: Edinburgh, Gateway to Scotland ★★★

Try to arrive as early in the day as you can and check into a hotel; this allows you a full day of sightseeing. Start at **Edinburgh Castle** (p. 73) at the beginning of the Royal Mile in the Old Town. Children will delight in the spooky 18th-century prisons and the batteries of cannons that used to protect the fortress. Next, pay a visit to the **Museum of Childhood** (p. 77), on the High Street, and, if you have time, bear in mind also the nearby **Outlook Tower & Camera Obscura** (p. 77).

After lunch in the Old Town, descend on **Princes Street,** the New Town's main shopping street. At the **Scott Monument** (p. 85), it's fun for the whole family to climb the 287 steps for the most panoramic view of the city. Before the afternoon ends, spend an hour or two at **Our Dynamic Earth** (p. 85), which has exhibits where children press buttons to simulate everything from earthquakes to meteor showers. If you're visiting Edinburgh during the month of August, you can also attend the Edinburgh Tattoo in the evening. This colorful and noisy spectacle of soldiers, pipers, and drummers parading takes place nightly Monday through Saturday in Edinburgh Castle.

On **Day 2** in Edinburgh, head first for Leith, where you can go aboard the luxury yacht *Britannia* (p. 86), once owned by Queen Elizabeth II. Next on the schedule is a visit to **Edinburgh Zoo** (p. 83), with its more than 1,500 animals, including some endangered species. Have lunch in the New Town, and then

visit the spectacular **Royal Botanic Garden** (p. 85), one of the best and grandest in Britain, before ending your day by wandering through **The Real Mary
King's Close** (p. 76), which stays open until 9pm in summer. This was the
once-thriving underground part of the Old Town, where the "deepest secrets"
are hidden in a warren of almost buried streets, or "closes."

Day 3: Deep Sea World ★ & Stirling Castle ★★

On **Day 3,** after checking out of your hotel in Edinburgh, drive to **Deep Sea
World** (p. 120), 12 miles west of Edinburgh's center. Allow 90 minutes to visit
this menagerie of water creatures, which includes several sharks.

Afterwards, make your way to **Stirling** (p. 254). This ancient town, lying
between the rivers Forth and Clyde, is famed for its castle. After checking into
a hotel, you'll want to have lunch before exploring the town. In the afternoon,
pay a visit to **Stirling Castle** (p. 256), where Mary Queen of Scots lived as an
infant queen. Children especially enjoy going through the on-site **Museum of
the Argyll and Sutherland Highlanders,** with all the pipe banners and other
paraphernalia. For the rest of the afternoon, you can drive to **Bannockburn**
(p. 257) nearby, where Robert the Bruce once summoned his "Braveheart" army
to defeat Edward II in 1314. The audiovisual presentation of this violent story
at the **Bannockburn Heritage Centre** is as fascinating as Mel Gibson's own
Braveheart movie. Return to Stirling for the night.

Days 4 & 5: Glasgow ★★★

On **Day 4,** drive the 28 miles southwest to Glasgow. Check into a hotel, and
then make your way to the embarkation point for the *Waverley* (p. 174), the
world's last seagoing paddle steamer, which will take you on a trip to see scenic
places along the Firth of Clyde. You can have lunch aboard. Back in Glasgow,
spend 2 hours visiting the **Glasgow Science Centre** (p. 174), a child-friendly
favorite, featuring a Space Theatre and plenty of activities for children to participate in.

On the morning of **Day 5,** pay a visit to the **Kelvingrove Art Gallery &
Museum** (p. 173). Even if your children aren't interested in art, they'll be
intrigued by the collections devoted to ethnography (which includes Eskimo
artifacts) and natural history. Later in the morning, spend an hour or so wandering about the **Museum of Transport** (p. 174). Follow these visits with lunch
at the **Willow Tea Room** (p. 171), where children can indulge in homemade
pastries and ice cream.

In the afternoon, take the family to the **Scottish Maritime Museum**
(p. 206), before descending on **Linn Park** (p. 174), spread across 86 hectares
(213 acres). There are many attractions here, including a children's zoo and
pony rides.

Day 6: Oban ★ & Fort William ★

On the morning of **Day 6,** drive northwest from Glasgow along the western
banks of **Loch Lomond** (p. 268), heading for the coastal resort of **Oban**
(p. 231). The distance between Glasgow and Oban is 56 miles and takes around
2 hours. In Oban, take the children on a tour of **Dunstaffnage Castle** (p. 231)
and up to **McCaig's Tower** (p. 234), an unfinished replica of the Colosseum
of Rome.

After lunch, proceed to the town of Fort William, another 50 miles north from Oban. Check into a hotel in the shadow of Ben Nevis, Scotland's highest mountain. In the afternoon, you can drive through the hauntingly beautiful **Glencoe** (p. 317), scene of the famous massacre of 1692, when the Campbells defeated the MacDonalds. Children are fascinated by the audiovisual presentation at the Glencoe Visitor Center. Return to Fort William for the night.

Day 7: Loch Ness ★★ & Inverness ★

On **Day 7,** leave Fort William and head 68 miles northeast to **Inverness,** the capital of the Highlands. Along the way you can stop at the little village of **Drumnadrochit** to see the official **Loch Ness Monster Exhibition** (p. 325) with its lasers and special effects. Afterwards, explore the nearby ruins of **Urquhart Castle,** which overlooks the loch. It's from here that most sightings of the Loch Ness Monster are reported.

Proceed north, to Inverness, and check into a hotel. After lunch, pay a visit to **Culloden Battlefield** (p. 330), where Bonnie Prince Charlie and his Jacobite army were crushed by the English. Children will also enjoy walking the ramparts at the nearby **Fort George/Queen's Own Highlanders Regimental Museum**

(p. 330). Inverness has many options for a last dinner before a good night's sleep in Inverness and the long journey home the following day.

SCOTTISH HISTORY & LANDSCAPE IN A WEEK

This tour takes in many of the most important historical sights in Scotland. It could also, however, be called "Scotland in a nutshell" because it combines beautiful scenery, historic cities, grand palaces, royal associations, fishing villages, and even a golf course.

Day 1: Stirling ★★ & Its Castle ★★

Set out from Edinburgh on **Day 1** to visit the ancient town of **Stirling,** lying 35 miles to the northwest. Explore **Stirling Castle** (p. 256) in the morning, have lunch and then, in the afternoon, head for the **Bannockburn Heritage Centre** (p. 257) on the site of the battleground where Robert the Bruce's army defeated the English forces of Edward II in 1314. Back in Stirling, if time remains, visit the 15th-century **Church of the Holy Rood** (p. 256). That night, check to see what events are being staged at the **Macrobert Arts Centre** (p. 260), on the campus of Stirling University.

Day 2: Callander ★ & Aberfoyle ★

On the morning of **Day 2,** drive 16 miles northwest of Stirling, to the town of **Callander,** which is set in a thickly wooded valley of lochs. Stop at the Rob Roy & Trossachs Visitor Centre and pick up a map that directs you to the scenic highlights of the area. These include **Leny Park** (p. 262) and **Leny Falls** (p. 262).

After lunch in Callander, drive over to the little town of **Aberfoyle,** 14 miles to the southwest. Check into a hotel, and then stop off at the **Trossachs Discovery Centre** (p. 266) to plan your afternoon's tour of the area's scenic attractions. At Aberfoyle you're on the threshold of the **Trossachs,** arguably the most beautiful natural attraction in Scotland. From here you can explore the **Queen Elizabeth Forest Park** (p. 266), on the eastern shore of Loch Lomond, as well as **Loch Katrine** (p. 266), made famous by Sir Walter Scott's narrative poem *The Lady of the Lake*. After stopping off at **Dukes Pass** (p. 266) for a panoramic view, return to Aberfoyle for the night.

Day 3: Perth ★ & Scone Palace ★★

Leave Aberfoyle on **Day 3,** and drive 57 miles east to the historic Tayside town of **Perth,** the former capital of Scotland. Check into a hotel here and set out to explore the city that's the gateway to the Highlands. For orientation, visit **Kinnoull Hill** (p. 284), which is the geographic dividing point between the Highlands and the Lowlands. You can follow a nature trail here before visiting the 16th-century **Balhousie Castle** (p. 285). Afterwards, you can walk through the **North Inch** (p. 285), a 41-hectare (100-acre) park along the west bank of the Tay River.

Following lunch in Perth, drive 1¾ miles to Old Scone, site of **Scone Palace** (p. 288), with its precious antiques, paintings, and grand architecture. The gardens and woodlands around the palace are also worth seeing before you return to Perth for the night. That evening, check out the program for the **Perth Repertory Theatre** (p. 287).

Scottish History & Landscape in a Week

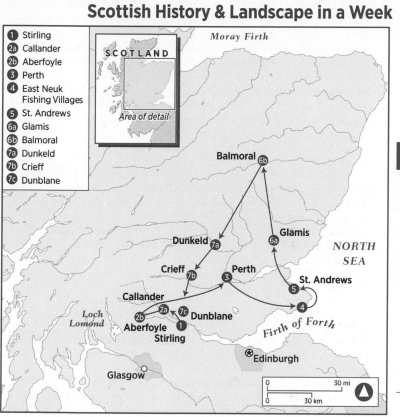

1. Stirling
2a. Callander
2b. Aberfoyle
3. Perth
4. East Neuk Fishing Villages
5. St. Andrews
6a. Glamis
6b. Balmoral
7a. Dunkeld
7b. Crieff
7c. Dunblane

SCOTLAND

Area of detail

Moray Firth

Balmoral 6b

Dunkeld 7a

Glamis 6a

NORTH SEA

Crieff 7b

Perth 3

St. Andrews 5

Callander

2b 2a 7c Dunblane

Aberfoyle

Stirling 1

Loch Lomond

Firth of Forth

⊛Edinburgh

Glasgow

0   30 mi
0   30 km

Day 4: East Neuk Fishing Villages ★★

Leaving Perth in the morning of **Day 4,** drive 54 miles east to East Neuk—a collective name for a series of the most beautiful and unspoiled fishing villages in Scotland. Perhaps begin at **Elie** (p. 244), with its picture-postcard harbor and step-gabled houses. If the weather is warm, you can swim from one of the beaches of golden sand. After a walk around the village for an hour or so, continue north to **Pittenweem** (p. 244), where you can attend a fish auction down by the water (in the mornings Monday through Saturday).

Next, drive north along the A917 to **Anstruther** (p. 245), a fishing port and summer resort. Explore the **Scottish Fisheries Museum** (p. 245), down by the harbor, and later take the picturesque walk over to the tiny hamlet of **Cellardyke** (p. 246). Have lunch at Anstruther.

For the day's final destination, head north again to **Crail** (p. 246). Check into a hotel here and spend the rest of the afternoon strolling around this port with its little fishermen's cottages. Pay a visit to its **Crail Museum & Heritage Centre** (p. 247), marked by an array of fishing memorabilia. Find a local pub and have a dinner of fish and chips with a pint of beer before returning to your hotel.

Day 5: St. Andrews, Birthplace of Golf ★★

On the morning of **Day 5,** leave Crail and drive the short distance of 9⅓ miles north to St. Andrews. Golfers will spend the rest of the day playing on this hallowed turf; others can explore the town's attractions, such as the grounds of the **University of St. Andrews** (p. 249), which Prince William attended, as well as the ruins of the **Castle of St. Andrews** (p. 250). After lunch, you can visit **St. Andrews Cathedral** (p. 250) before descending to the **Secret Bunker** (p. 247), the place from where Britain would have been commanded in the event of a nuclear attack. In the evening you can check out some of the local pubs, or else attend a performance—perhaps a Shakespearean play—at the **Byre Theatre** (p. 251).

Day 6: Royal Castles Glamis ★★ & Balmoral ★

Leave St. Andrews on the morning of **Day 6,** heading north toward Dundee, where you link up with the A90 to Glamis, a distance of 83 miles.

For 600 years, **Glamis Castle** (p. 301) was linked to the British Royal Family, and the late Queen Mother was brought up here. This is also the castle where Macbeth is said to have murdered King Duncan. Allow at least 1½ hours for a look around.

If you have extra time, drive north of Glamis for 4 miles, to the little town of **Kirriemuir.** Here you can visit **Barrie's birthplace** (p. 301): The author of *Peter Pan* is buried in the local cemetery.

After a quick lunch, drive from Kirriemuir to **Ballater,** site of the Queen's **Balmoral Castle** (p. 303). The distance is 61 miles. Built in the Scottish baronial style, this was the summer home of Queen Victoria in the second half of the 19th century, and it's still used today in late summer by Queen Elizabeth and her family. Since it closes at 5pm, you have to time your afternoon carefully. If you're running late, you can skip Kirriemuir.

If Kirriemuir doesn't fit your itinerary, spend your time wandering around the towns of Ballater or Braemar. Overnight in either one and fortify yourself for the next day—your final and perhaps busiest day in Scotland.

Day 7: Dunkeld ★, Crieff ★ & Dunblane

Leave Ballater early on the morning of **Day 7,** heading southwest to **Dunkeld,** a distance of 67 miles. Here, you can visit **Dunkeld Cathedral** (p. 293), one of the most historically important in Britain, and dating back to A.D. 815. You can also wander around the old houses and shops of the pretty town, and stop for coffee in the Royal Dunkeld Hotel, an early 19th-century coaching inn.

After your visit, continue southwest to **Crieff,** a distance of 29 miles. The main attraction here is **Drummond Castle Gardens** (p. 290), which date from the early 17th century. Before lunch, try also to fit in a visit to **The Glenturret Distillery** (Scotland's oldest).

Lunch in Crieff before setting out in the afternoon for **Dunblane,** situated 43 miles to the south. Make sure that you go inside **Dunblane Cathedral** (p. 258), one of the best examples of 13th-century Gothic architecture in Britain. Allow an hour for a visit. When finished, drive southeast to Edinburgh—a distance of 42 miles—for your final night in Scotland.

THE ACTIVE TRIP PLANNER

Scotland's great outdoors is one of the finest destinations in the world in which to get active. No matter which region you choose, you're guaranteed encounters with inspiring landscapes and a rich variety of wildlife.

You don't have to travel far from urban centers to experience lochs, glens, mountains, and coastal regions, many of which are an easy day trip from Scotland's main cities.

TEEING OFF: GOLFING IN SCOTLAND

Scotland is proud to call itself "the home of golf," and although the sport is part of the country's national pride, it hasn't always been so well received. Monks around St. Andrews weren't applauded when they diverted themselves from a schedule of daily chores and praying to play *gowf,* and in 1457 James II churlishly issued edicts prohibiting its practice, preferring the population to hone archery skills instead. The ban was upheld until 1502 when James IV became a golfer himself, and by the mid-1700s the game was firmly entrenched in Scotland and enjoyed by commoners and royalty alike.

Scotland boasts well over 550 golf courses, many of which are among the world's most famous and challenging, and seasoned golfers from across the globe make regular pilgrimages to courses such as the hallowed Old Course in St. Andrews and relative newcomers like The Torrance and The Kittocks at the nearby Fairmont resort. Most of Scotland's courses are municipal and therefore open to everyone and, although they can be found all over the country, many of Scotland's courses are located in the central and southern regions around Fife, Ayrshire, and East Lothian.

You don't need to lug your own set of clubs around, because many courses rent full or half sets. If you're female or plan on playing golf with someone who is, be aware that some courses are restricted to men only, while others limit female players to designated days. Despite this old-fashioned tradition, women's golf thrives in Scotland and the **Scottish Ladies' Golfing Association Ltd** has literally thousands of members. The Association organizes national championships and other tournaments; for full details on these and information on how to find female golfing partners, contact © **01738/442-357** or visit www.slga.co.uk. Another useful organization is the **Scottish Golf Union** (© **01334/466-477;**

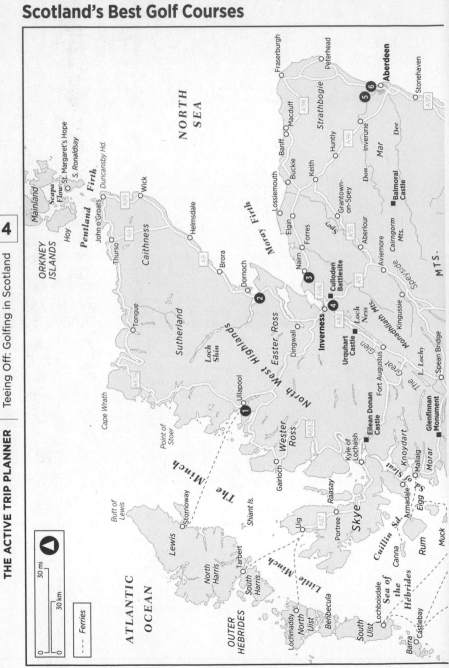

Scotland's Best Golf Courses

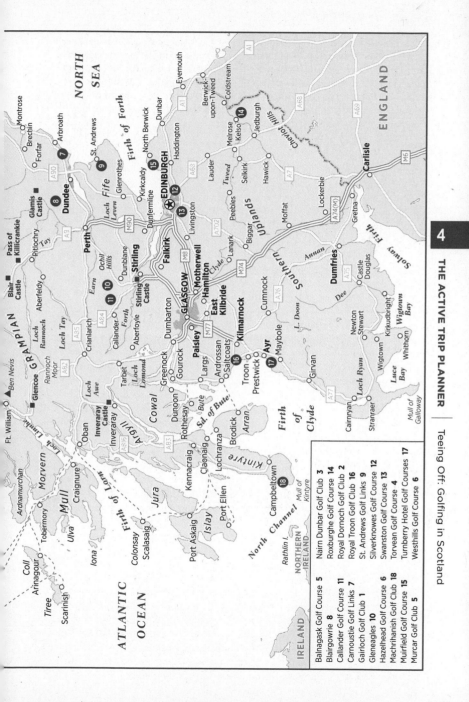

IRELAND

Balnagask Golf Course **5**	Nairn Dunbar Golf Club **3**
Blairgowrie **8**	Roxburghe Golf Course **14**
Callander Golf Course **11**	Royal Dornoch Golf Club **2**
Carnoustie Golf Links **7**	Royal Troon Golf Club **16**
Gairloch Golf Club **1**	St. Andrews Golf Links **9**
Gleneagles **10**	Silverknowes Golf Course **12**
Hazelhead Golf Course **6**	Swanston Golf Course **13**
Machrihanish Golf Club **18**	Torvean Golf Course **4**
Muirfield Golf Course **15**	Turnberry Hotel Golf Courses **17**
Murcar Golf Club **5**	Westhills Golf Course **6**

Visit Scotland provides a wealth of information for anyone planning a golfing trip or the odd round. This organization has a dedicated golf website at http://golf.visitscotland.com and produces an annual, comprehensive, and official *Guide to Golf in Scotland* that you can download from the website or pick up at Tourist Information Centres (TICs) around the country. Another useful website for golfing in Scotland is www.scotlands-golf-courses.com.

www.scottishgolf.org), established in 1920 to foster and maintain a high standard of amateur golf in Scotland. The Union's website is a good source of information on golfing news, clubs, and events across Scotland.

Any serious golfer who's planning to stay in the country for a while should consider joining a local club. Membership makes it easier to bag coveted tee times, and attending or competing in a local club's tournaments can be both fun and sociable. If you're not staying long, you might not bother, but remember to bring a letter from a golf club in your home country—it can open doors otherwise closed to the general public.

Access to many private clubs can be difficult, however, particularly those boasting so much tradition and history that waiting lists for tee-off times stretch on for up to a year in advance. You can always stay in a hotel that has its own course—Gleneagles or Turnberry, for example—thereby guaranteeing the availability of tee times, or you can arrange a golf tour (see below).

Many of Scotland's courses are set among some of the country's most stunning scenery. However, the weather can often be as challenging as the courses and golfers can expect to brace themselves against brisk coastal breezes and sometimes fog, all of which have left their mark on a landscape of gorse and heather that epitomizes Scotland's coastal courses.

Knowing a term or two in advance might help in picking your course. The Scots make a strong distinction between their two types of courses: links and upland. **Links courses** nestle into the sandy terrain of coastal regions and, although years of cultivation have rendered their fairways and putting greens emerald colored, they're still wild around the edges. All links courses are on or near the sea and they include some of the most famous names in Scotland such as St. Andrews, Royal Troon, Turnberry, Prestwick, and Muirfield. In contrast, **upland courses** are based inland and invariably consist of hilly terrain. They're usually drier and less windy than links courses. Nonetheless, it rains a lot in Scotland, especially on the west side of the country, and so a sweater and rain gear are recommended for *all* courses. Examples of upland courses are Gleneagles, Loch Lomond, and Pitlochry.

Golf Tours

Access for non-members to the country's maze of golf courses hasn't always been easy. All that changed, however, with the establishment of **Golf International** (📞 **800/833-1389** or 212/986-9176 in the U.S. and Canada; www.golfinternational.com), which maintains a branch office in St. Andrews. The company caters to golfers from moderate to advanced levels and, against often hitherto impossible odds, will guarantee its clients starting times at 40 or so of Scotland's most sought-after courses, including St. Andrews, Carnoustie, Royal Troon, Prestwick, and Gullane.

Potential clients, in self-organized groups of 2 to 12, produce a wish list of the courses they'd like to play. Starting times are prearranged (sometimes rigidly) with an ease that an individual golfer would find impossible. Packages can be arranged for anywhere from 5 to 14 days (the average is about 7 days) and can include as much or as little golf at as many courses as you want. Weekly prices, including hotels, breakfasts, car rentals, green fees, and the services of a greeter and helpmate at the airport, range from £1,069 to £5,288 per person. Discounted airfares to Scotland can also be arranged.

Some U.S.-based companies specializing in golf tours are **Adventures in Golf,** 22 Greeley St., 7 Medallion Center, Merrimack, NH 03054 (© **877/424-7320** or 603/424-7320; www.adventures-in-golf.com); **Classic Golf & Leisure,** 75–770 McLachlin Circle, Palm Desert, CA 92211 (© **800/283-1619** or 760/772-2560; www.classic-golf.com); **ITC Golf Tours,** 2428 Lewis Ave., Signal Hill, CA 90755 (© **800/257-4981** or 562/595-6905; www.itcgolftours.com); and **Perry Golf,** 1904 Eastwood Rd., Ste. 315, Wilmington, NC 28403 (© **800/344-5257** or 910/795-1048; www.perrygolf.com). A Scottish-based company is **Tayleur Mayde Golf Tours,** 7/9 North St., David St., Edinburgh EH2 1AW (© **800/847-8064** in the U.S., or 0131/524-9554; www.tayleurmayde.com).

The Classic Courses

Scotland is crammed with some of the best golf courses in the world; below are details on merely a few of the most famous. In addition to the big names listed here, many additional courses are detailed in the appropriate destination chapters of this book. Reservations must be made in advance on all these courses.

The **Carnoustie Golf Links,** Links Parade, Carnoustie, Angus (© **01241/802-270;** www.carnoustiegolflinks.co.uk), claims three top courses including the par-72, 6,941-yard Championship Course. The use of a caddy at £40 for 18 holes is required, clubs can be hired for £45 per round, and a trolley costs £12 per round, while green fees are £135.

Golf was first played around 1400 at the par-72 **Old Course, St. Andrews,** Golf Place, St. Andrews, Fife (© **01334/466-666;** www.standrews.org.uk). Many consider this 6,721-yard, 18-hole course to be the real home of golf and this fabled course witnessed yet more history when it hosted the 2000 British Open and Tiger Woods became the youngest golfer to complete a grand slam (and only the fifth golfer ever to perform the feat). The Open returned to St. Andrews for the 28th time in 2010 when South African Louis Oosthuizen won the championship with a 16 under par total of 272. Green fees are £64 to £130, a caddy costs £45 plus tip, and clubs

A Warning for Beginners

Newcomers to golf simply **aren't allowed to play** the country's most legendary courses. Many courses require you to produce evidence of your familiarity with the game and level of competence before you're let loose on the links. Depending on the setting and the season, this could include a letter from your club back home citing your ability and experience, or visual proof that you've mastered a basically sound swing and an understanding of golf-related etiquette.

rent for £30 to £40 per round. Electric carts aren't allowed, and you can rent a trolley on afternoons only, between May and October, for £5 (or £15 for battery powered).

The 18-hole Championship Course at the **Royal Dornoch Golf Club,** Dornoch, Sutherland (© **01862/810-219;** www.royaldornoch.com), 40 miles north of Inverness, has a par of 70. At this 6,514-yard course, the green fees are £44 to £90 Monday through Friday and £50 to £100 on Saturday and Sunday. Caddies cost £35 per round, club rental is £20 to £25 per round, and a trolley rents for £3 per round.

The par-71 Old Course at the **Royal Troon Golf Club,** Craigend Road, Troon, Ayrshire (© **01292/311-555;** www.royaltroon.co.uk), is one of the largest courses in Scotland, with 7,175 yards of playing area. The green fees are £130 for a round or £175 for a round on the Old Course and one of Royal Troon's other two courses. Caddies cost £40 per round, club rental is £40 per round or £55 per day, and a trolley rents for £5 per round, £20 for an electric caddy cart.

The **Turnberry** golf courses, Ayrshire (© **01655/333-000;** www.turnberry.co.uk), give priority at its famous 6,976-yard, par-72 course to guests of the hotel (see "Turnberry Resort" on p. 204). The green fees for this course are £95 to £155 for hotel guests and £115 to £175 for non-guests. Clubs rent for £50 per round and caddy service costs £40 plus tip.

FISHING

Scotland is an angler's paradise. The country's fast-flowing rivers harbor Atlantic salmon and other game fish such as brown trout. These rivers, plus Scotland's many pristine lochs, allow anglers to enjoy some of Europe's most beautiful scenery as well as world-class fishing. Your hotel can often arrange permits, though in some choice spots they can be expensive; for example, a week's permit for one of the grand beats on the River Tay can run into hundreds of pounds. That said, there are many lesser-known rivers where a permit costs a mere few pounds a day.

The **Tweed** and the **Tay** are Scotland's famous salmon-rich rivers. The Tweed flows through the Scottish Borders, while the Tay—Scotland's broadest and longest river—strikes a course through Perthshire. In Aberdeenshire, the **Dee** is fished by Britain's royal family; the Queen herself has been seen casting from these banks. Other anglers prefer the **Spey,** and this region has the added attraction of being home to many of Scotland's whisky distilleries. Some well-heeled anglers prefer the remote lochs and rivers of the **Outer Hebrides.** In general, Scotland's season for salmon fishing runs from late February until late October, but these dates vary from region to region.

Types of Fishing

Here's a breakdown of terms you're likely to hear even before you cast your first line into Scotland's glittering waters:

COARSE FISHING   This means going after any species of freshwater fish except salmon and trout. Especially prized trophies known for putting up a spirited fight are carp, tench, pike, bream, roach, and perch. Because few lochs actually freeze during winter, the sport can be practiced throughout the year. Local Tourist Information Centres all over the country can provide advice.

GAME FISHING   Salmon and trout (brown, rainbow, or sea) are the most desired of the game fish and the ones that have inspired the image of a fly fisherman whipping a lure and line in serpentine arcs above a loch. Many travelers dream of donning bulky rubber waders up to their waists and trying their luck in streams and freshwater lochs. Fly-fishing for salmon and trout is subject to seasonal controls and sometimes requires a permit. For details on game fishing, contact the **Salmon & Trout Association,** which at press time is undergoing reorganization in Scotland. Up-to-date information can be found at www.salmon-trout.org/scotland_who.asp.

SEA FISHING   This term simply refers to fishing from a beach, a rocky shoreline, or a pier. Inshore fishing involves dropping a line into ocean waters within 3 miles of any Scottish coastline; deep-sea fishing is done from a boat, more than 3 miles offshore, in a style made popular by cigar-chomping tycoons and Hemingway clones. Offshore waters are also populated with several species of shark, including porbeagle, thresher, mako, basking, and blue shark. For information on what to expect from offshore waters and fishing in general across Scotland, contact **Visit Scotland** (🕿 **0845/225-5121**) for an annual, comprehensive guide that can be downloaded from www.visitscotland.com/fish.

Fishing Clubs

Getting permits and information on worthwhile places to fish is easier if you join one of the more than 380 fishing clubs headquartered in Scotland. (The oldest angling club in the world, the Ellem Fishing Club, was founded in Scotland in 1829.) Each of its activities is supervised by the **Scottish Anglers National Association** (🕿 **01577/861-116;** www.sana.org.uk), which firmly believes that newcomers should learn at the side of the more experienced. Courses in the fine art of fishing are offered in or around Scotland. For details, contact Visit Scotland at www.visit scotland.com/fish.

BIKING, WALKING & OTHER OUTDOOR ACTIVITIES

Biking

Cycling in Scotland is extremely popular with both locals and visitors, and new routes and cycle ways are springing up all over the country. Once you escape the main urban areas, roads are generally low on traffic and high on scenery although, due to harsh winters, November through March can be an inhospitable time for all but the most seasoned of cyclists. Motorways and some main A roads that are also dual carriageways (divided highways) are out of bounds to cyclists, and a number of the more tourist-trodden routes can be busy with cars during July and August, although it's often possible to find quieter routes or to get off the road altogether.

Your first source of information should be **Cycling Scotland** (🕿 **0141/229-5350;** www.cyclingscotland.org), a government-funded organization dedicated to getting more people on bikes. Although aimed mainly at the local population, this organization's website is rich with cycling tips and information on events and organized rides. Serious cyclists can glean information on mountain biking, cycle speedway, cyclocross, and track racing across Scotland through the Scottish section of the **British Cycling** website at www.britishcycling.org.uk/scotland (or 🕿 **0131/ 317/9704**).

Visit Scotland offers an annual *Active in Scotland* brochure dedicated to adventure and outdoor activities across Scotland. For more information and to download the brochure, visit http:// **active.visitscotland.com**. Another good source of information on walking and biking trails is the **Forestry Commission** in Scotland (℗ **0845/367-3787; www.forestry.gov.uk/scotland**).

Based in England, the U.K.'s national cycling organization is **CTC** (℗ **0131/448-0930** in Scotland). CTC's website is filled with useful information, advice, and news, and membership brings the added benefits of discounts with cycle-related organizations, access to online routes, and insurance. Membership is £37 a year for adults, £12 under-18s, £23 for seniors, and £60 for families. This organization also gives advice on where to rent or buy a bike and offers free legal advice to members involved in cycle-related accidents and information on available medical insurance.

Sustrans (℗ **0845/113-0065;** www.sustrans.org.uk) is a U.K. charity aimed at encouraging cycling, and its online shop at www.sustransshop.co.uk is a good place to purchase route maps and books on cycling in Britain. In addition, all local Tourist Information Centres in Scotland can provide reams of information on routes, off-road trails, and bike rental outfits.

You may take your bike without restrictions on car and passenger ferries in Scotland. It's rarely necessary to make arrangements in advance, but the transport of your bike is likely to cost £2 to £10, plus the cost of your own passage. On trains, there's no charge for bicycles but it's advisable to make a reservation at peak times on commuter routes and on long-distance journeys. Reservations can be made at any staffed train station or when you book your ticket.

A number of organizations offer biking trips in Scotland. These include **Scotland Mountain Biking** (℗ **0141/942-6674;** www.scotlandmountainbiking.com), which leads a 7-day/6-night coast-to-coast bike tour; and **Storybikes** (℗ **07762/000-039;** www.storybikes.co.uk), whose tours uniquely combine tales of Scottish lore and landscape with biking trips around mainly southern Scotland.

Local rental shops offer a wide range of bicycles, from three-speeds to mountain bikes, and accessories such as child seats and tag-a-longs. They can also provide advice on organized trips, ranging from tours of several hours to full-fledged week-long itineraries. Local rental shops with their rates are listed in the appropriate destination chapters of this book.

Bird-Watching

Partly because of their low population density, the moors and Highlands of Scotland attract millions of birds. For reasons not fully understood by ornithologists, the Orkneys shelter absolutely staggering numbers of birds. Bird-watchers cite the Orkneys as even richer in native species than the more isolated Shetlands, with such species as the hen harrier, short-eared owl, and red-throated diver (a form of Arctic loon) not frequently seen in the Shetlands.

Any general tour of the Orkneys will bring you into contact with thousands of birds, as well as with Neolithic burial sites, cromlechs, dolmens, and other ancient sites. A worthy tour operator is **Wildabout Orkney** (✆ **01856/877-737;** www. wildaboutorkney.com), which leads a number of tours and shore excursions taking in the history and bird-rich nature reserves of the region. Tours cost £49 per person and reservations should be made in advance.

A bird-watching specialist is **Orkney Island Wildlife** (✆ **01856/711-373;** www.orkneyislandholidays.com), offering a variety of holidays in the region from April to September that last between 6 and 9 nights and cost £1,150 to £1,850 per person, including full board and exposure to the fields, moors, and wetlands of Shapinsay and Orkney.

During winter and early spring, the entire Solway Firth shoreline in southern Scotland around Loch Ryan, Wigtown Bay, and Auchencairn Bay is an excellent location for observing wintering wildfowl and waders. Inland, Dumfries and Galloway has a rich and varied range of birdlife, including British barn owls, kestrels, tawnies, and merlins. A useful source of information on Scotland's many sea bird colonies is the **National Trust for Scotland,** because around one-fifth of all seabirds in the country nest on land belonging to this organization. For full information on locations and access, visit www.ntsseabirds.org.uk.

Canoeing & Kayaking

Scotland's lochs, seas, and rivers are popular spots for canoeing and kayaking, and several clubs around the country offer instruction and advice. Supervising their activities is the **Scottish Canoe Association** (SCA; ✆ **0131/317-7314;** www.canoe scotland.org). The SCA coordinates all competitive canoeing events in Scotland, including slaloms, polo games, and white-water races, and can provide information on clubs and centers around Scotland. It also offers advice on access and sells books on Scottish canoe touring and white-water through its website. A recommended tour operator for either guided or self-led canoe and kayak tours in Scotland is **Wilderness Scotland** (✆ **0131/625-6635;** www.wildernessscotland.com).

Hiking & Walking

Scotland is unsurpassed for those who love to walk and hikers can expect an abundant choice of terrain including mountain slopes, river valleys, and woodland and coastal paths. Trails for all abilities lie across every region and cater for those who want anything from a short hour-long jaunt to days of hiking.

Scotland boasts some excellent long-distance footpaths, including the **West Highland Way** (www.west-highland-way.co.uk), which begins north of Glasgow in the town of Milngavie and stretches 96 miles to the foot of Ben Nevis, and the **Southern Upland Way** (www.southernuplandway.gov.uk), with a starting point in Portpatrick in Dumfries and Galloway and an end point a mere 212 miles away in Cockburnspath on the southeast coast.

The **Scottish Borders** is one of the finest areas for walking, with ranges such as the Pentland Hills and the Tweed Valley promising rolling terrain and scenic trails. The haunting coastline of **Dumfries and Galloway** around the Solway Firth is ideal for gentle walks, or head north into the Galloway National Forest for more challenging trails. Another excellent spot for coastal walking is the **Fife coastal path,** which leads around the southeast corner of the region taking in old fishing harbors and artists' communities.

In central Scotland, the **Cairngorms National Park** is located close to Scotland's main area for skiing, and rangers offer guided walks through forested land to skilled and beginner hikers alike. In the west of the country, some of Scotland's most memorable walks are found along **Loch Lomond** and in the **Trossachs.**

Whichever region of Scotland you choose to walk in, local Tourist Information Centres and the visitor centers of national parks and forests are filled with leaflets and books on trails and routes. **Visit Scotland** (✆ **0845/225-5121**) has also produced its own comprehensive brochure on *Walking in Scotland* and a resource-rich website from which it can be downloaded at http://walking.visitscotland.com. The **Ramblers Association** (✆ **01577/861-222**; www.ramblers.org.uk/scotland) can put you in touch with local walking groups.

Self-led walking tours of the Highlands and Islands that include accommodation are offered by **Bespoke Highland Tours** (✆ **01854/612-628**; www.highland-tours.co.uk). Choose from a series of treks, lasting from 5 to 12 days, including the **West Highland Way** and the **Great Glen Way.** The tours are reasonably priced, ranging from £350 to £470.

Walkers can arrange accommodation and luggage transfer, and obtain detailed advice on routes from **Easyways** (✆ **01324/714-132**; www.easyways.com), who can manage your treks along long-distance walks including the West Highland Way, the Great Glen Way, Rob Roy Way, and St. Cuthbert's Way. **North-West Frontiers** (✆ **01997/421-474**; www.nwfrontiers.com), specializes in both guided and self-guided walking holidays in Scotland that lead hikers through remote glens, magnificent mountains and lochs, and isolated islands and beaches where you're likely to encounter seals, deer, and many species of birds, including divers and golden eagles. **Walkabout Scotland** (✆ **0845/686-1344**; www.walkaboutscotland.com) specializes in walking holidays in the Highlands as well as day-long hiking tours. **C-N-Do Scotland** (✆ **01786/445-703**; www.cndoscotland.com) has been organizing hiking tours since 1984 and hooks up its patrons with the best in hiking, good Scottish food, and wildlife viewings on its tours, which can be just for a day or stretch over a week.

And based in Montclair, Virginia, the **English Lakeland Ramblers** (✆ **800/724-8801** or 703/680-4276; www.ramblers.com) can book you on one of their tours of Skye, Lewis, and Harris.

Horseback Riding & Pony Trekking

Horseback riding and trekking through Scotland's panoramic countryside across both the Lowlands and the Highlands can be enjoyed by everyone, from novices to experienced riders.

Although more adventurous riders prefer the hillier terrain of the Highlands, the Scottish Borders in the southeast (chapter 6) is the best for horseback riding—in fact, it's often called Scotland's horse country. (The equivalent in the United States is Kentucky.) On the western coastline, Argyll (chapter 8) is another recommended center for riding amongst dramatic scenery. The Argyll Forest Park, stretching almost to Loch Fyne, encompasses 24,300 hectares (60,000 acres) and contains some of the finest scenery in Scotland. Its trails lead through forests to sea lochs that cut deep into the park.

Pony trekking is popular across both moorland and glen and is reason enough to visit Scotland. Highland ponies have been trekking tourists for years and most centers lead treks from 2½ hours to a full day, and have ponies suitable for nearly all age

THE ACTIVE TRIP PLANNER — Biking, Walking & Other Outdoor Activities groups. You'll find operators in Kirkudbright and around Stirling as well as on Shetland, plus several in the Hebrides. Local Tourist Information Centres and **Visit Scotland** (✆ **0845/859-1006**; www.visitscotland.com) can provide full information on regional equestrian centers.

Mountaineering

Mountain climbing in Scotland ranges from moderate treks over heather-clad hilltops to demanding rock face climbs that bear the brunt of the country's harsh winter weather.

The **Southern Uplands,** the **offshore islands,** and the **Highlands** of Scotland contain the best mountaineering sites. Regardless of your abilities, treat the landscape with respect. The weather can turn foul during any season with almost no advance notice, creating dangerous conditions. If you're climbing rock faces, you should be familiar with basic techniques and the use of such specialized equipment as carabiners, crampons, ice axes, and ropes. Don't even consider climbing without proper instruction and equipment.

Ben Nevis is the highest (but by no means the most remote) peak in Scotland. Despite its loftiness at 1,336m (4,383 ft.), it has attracted some daredevils who have driven cars and motorcycles to points near its top; one eccentric even arranged the transport of a dining table with formal dinner service and a grand piano.

If you want to improve your rock-climbing skills, consider joining a club or signing on for a mountaineering course at a climbing center. **Sport Scotland** (✆ **0141/534-6500;** www.sportscotland.org.uk) can provide advice on reputable centers, while the **Mountaineering Council of Scotland** (✆ **01738/493-942;** www.mcofs.org.uk) is also a mine of useful information and contacts. Membership of the Council allows overnight stays at the club's climbing huts located around the country. True rock-climbing aficionados looking to earn certification should consider Mountain Leader Training. The **Scottish Mountain Leader Training Board** (✆ **01479/861-248;** www.mltuk.org) is based at Aviemore and organizes a range of training schemes and qualifications.

Sailing & Watersports

Scotland has a rich maritime heritage and so you have plenty of opportunities to get afloat. There are sailing schools and charter operations all round the coast, as well as on inland lakes and rivers. **The Royal Yachting Association,** RYA House, Ensign Way, Hamble, Hants, SO31 4YA (✆ **023/8060-4100;** www.rya.org.uk) can provide a list of suitable companies. There's also a wealth of advice and instruction among the books published by Wiley Nautical (www.wileynautical.com).

Wherever you travel in Scotland, you're never far from the water. Windsurfing, canoeing, water-skiing, and sailing are just some of the activities available at a number of sailing centers and holiday parks. You'll find it easy to rent boats and equipment at any of the major resorts along Scotland's famous lochs. Scotland's **National Water-sports Centre** is based at the Isle of Cumbrae in Ayrshire (© **01475/530-757;** www.nationalcentrecumbrae.org.uk) and local Tourist Information Centres and **Visit Scotland** (© **0845/859-1006;** www.visitscotland.com) can provide full information on regional operators.

EDINBURGH & THE LOTHIANS

As Scotland's capital since the 15th century, Edinburgh is famous for its split personality. On the city's south side the dark, narrow cobbled streets of its medieval Old Town close in over a vast plug of volcanic rock crowned with the brooding Edinburgh Castle and sealed with the Palace of Holyroodhouse. To the north, Edinburgh's New Town spreads out into a vista of neoclassical town planning framed by the Firth of Forth and dotted with an array of parks, gardens, and leafy public squares.

SIGHTSEEING   Every inch of Edinburgh is stuffed with history. Visitors of all ages are invited to get up close with the past at Edinburgh's prestigious museums, crowned by the **National Museum of Scotland.** Art lovers will revel in the **Scottish National Galleries,** which celebrate a spectrum of work from the medieval to the contemporary. Escape the city streets for the wild volcanic heights of **Arthur's Seat** or the windswept maritime shores of the Port of **Leith.**

EATING & DRINKING   World-class dining awaits you at Edinburgh's impressive collection of award-winning restaurants, which crown the city's ever-diversifying dining scene. Scotland's capital boasts some of the country's best places to sample its national cuisine, but the scene is far from parochial and diners can expect to indulge in dishes from around the world. Leith has surged forward as the best place to eat out in Edinburgh and here fresh seafood can be sampled to perfection at its many top restaurants.

SHOPPING   Edinburgh's famous **Princes Street** forms the city's backbone of high street brands and department stores, topped by the much-loved **Jenners.** A block north, the far more chic **George Street** is lined with designer names; however, the discerning Edinburgh shopper favors the **West End Village,** where exclusive brands flourish at its many independent stores. More eclectic shopping defines **Old Town,** where vintage clothing stores and fine tartan outlets gather around Grassmarket and the Royal Mile.

ARTS & CULTURE   Famous for its explosion of festivals that dominate summer time in the city, Edinburgh is a cultural world leader. Revelers can expect to enjoy a host of other festivities, including the iconic **Hogmanay** and Bacchanalian **Beltane** celebrations, all underpinned by a year-round calendar of enviable theatre, music, film, and comedy. Clubbers are well served by nightlife that flourishes during the university academic year.

THE best TRAVEL EXPERIENCES IN EDINBURGH

o **Exploring Edinburgh Castle:** This stunning castle is Edinburgh's most iconic landmark and must-see tourist destination for good reason. Amazing views, unstoppable history, and a swath of Scotland's treasures are waiting to be experienced behind its mighty battlements. See p. 73.

o **Tucking into fresh seafood at Leith:** Edinburgh's old port is famous for top-notch fresh seafood and a rich choice of restaurants in which to enjoy it cooked to perfection, from the traditional way to Indian style. See p. 95.

o **Climbing Arthur's Seat:** Take a walk on the wild side of Scotland's capital and hike the well-trodden path to the summit of this brooding 251m (823-ft.) high natural landmark. The easy climb is a small price to pay for the views waiting at the top. See p. 73.

o **Descending into the underground vaults:** Come face to face with the dark side of Edinburgh's history and many of its prominent ghosts on a tour into the long buried vaults of Old Town, which some claim are the most haunted place in Britain. See p. 76.

o **Taking a boat trip to Inchcolm:** Escape to the sea onboard a boat bound for Inchcolm island in the heart of the Firth of Forth, home to Scotland's finest medieval abbey and a host of playful wildlife. See p. 116.

ESSENTIALS
Getting There

BY PLANE   Edinburgh is an hour's flying time from London. **Edinburgh International Airport** (© **0844/481-8989;** www.edinburghairport.com) is 7½ miles west of the city center, receiving flights from within the British Isles, the rest of Europe, and New York (Newark). For more information, see chapter 14. Double-decker Airlink buses make the round-trip from the airport to Edinburgh city center every 10 minutes, letting you on and off at Haymarket or Waverley train stations. The fare is £3.50 one-way or £6 round-trip, and the ride takes about 25 minutes. For more information, call © **0131/555-6363** or visit www.flybybus.com. There's a busy taxi rank at the airport and a ride into town costs around £25, depending on traffic.

BY TRAIN   Edinburgh has two train stations—Haymarket in the West End, which receives trains that travel up the west coast of England before terminating at Waverley, the city's main station in the city center at the east end of Princes Street. The **East Coast** trains that link London's King's Cross with Waverley station are fast and efficient and include a buffet bar. Trains depart London every hour or so, taking about 4½ hours and costing £115 to £200 round-trip. Considerable savings can be made if you reserve in advance and commit to traveling on specific trains; see www.eastcoast. co.uk for details or © **08457/225-111.** Scotrail (© **0845/601-5929;** www. scotrail.co.uk) operates the Caledonian Sleeper service—overnight trains from London with sleeper berths. One-way fares cost around £94. There's a taxi rank in Waverley station and Edinburgh's bus station (see below) is only a short walk away.

Greater Edinburgh

BY BUS The least expensive way to travel between London and Edinburgh is by bus, but it's a 9½ hour journey. **MegaBus** (✆ **0871 266-3333;** www.megabus.com) is the cheapest option with one-way fares costing from £14. **National Express** (✆ **08717/818-178;** www.nationalexpress.com) also runs a regular service and one-way fares cost anywhere between £17 and £68. Coaches depart from London's Victoria Coach Station, delivering you to Edinburgh's **St. Andrews Square Bus Station,** St. Andrews Square.

BY CAR Edinburgh is 46 miles east of Glasgow and 105 miles north of Newcastle-upon-Tyne in England. No express motorway links Edinburgh with London, which lies 393 miles to the south. The M1 from London takes you part of the way north, and then becomes the A1—otherwise known as the "Great North Road"—leading drivers along the coast to enter Edinburgh from the east. Allow 8 hours or more if you're driving from London. A city bypass, the A720, circles Edinburgh and routes from all other directions meet this road, making it easy to enter the city from whichever point suits you. The M8 links Edinburgh with Glasgow and connects with the city on the west side of the bypass, while the M90/A90 travels down from the north over the Forth Road Bridge.

WORLD heritage EDINBURGH

Although Edinburgh's Old and New Towns are very different regions of the city, they are united as a single UNESCO World Heritage site, in recognition of their historical and architectural importance. Most visitors stay, eat, and spend the majority of their time in Edinburgh within this site, which contains the lion's share of the city's museums, galleries, monuments, and attractions. **Edinburgh World Heritage** (✆ 0131/220-7720; www.ewht.org.uk) provides a wealth of information and resources all aimed at helping visitors make the most of their time in the Old and New Towns. You can follow a range of thematic trails, such as *Walk in the Footsteps of Robert Louis Stevenson,* around the Heritage Site; pick these up at the Tourist Information (p. 68) or download from Edinburgh World Heritage's website, along with a series of accompanying podcasts.

Visitor Information

Edinburgh's main **Tourist Information Centre** (✆ 0845/225-5121; www.edinburgh.org) is located at the street level of Princes Street Mall, which is adjacent to Waverley train station and the Balmoral Hotel. Here you can gather tons of information; staff can also help book a place to stay and sightseeing tickets. The office is open from 9am Monday through Saturday and 10am on Sunday until between 5pm in winter and 7pm or 8pm in summer. There's also an information desk at Edinburgh Airport (✆ 0870/040-0007).

Orientation

The center of Edinburgh is divided between its Old and New Towns. The renowned **Royal Mile** forms the spine of **Old Town** leading downhill from Edinburgh Castle to the Palace of Holyroodhouse. A labyrinth of ancient wynds, closes, and steep stone stairways spread out on either side of the Royal Mile, and on the south side of the castle Old Town opens out into the **Grassmarket,** a wide medieval street where the city's convicted criminals were once hung until dead on the dreaded gallows. Today cafes, pubs, and shops line this historic thoroughfare, spilling out onto its pavements in summer.

To the north of Old Town, joined by the high vaulted North Bridge, is Edinburgh's **New Town.** Still hailed as a masterpiece of city planning, its wide neoclassical streets, squares, crescents, and gardens were created between 1765 and 1850 in response to the cramped, claustrophobic, dark Old Town.

New Town is flanked by **Princes Street,** whose shop-lined north side gazes across the wide expanse of Princes Street Gardens to Old Town. North of, and running parallel to, Princes Street is New Town's second great street, **George Street,** which begins at Charlotte Square and extends east to St. Andrews Square and is lined with upmarket shops and restaurants. Directly north of George Street lies New Town's third main thoroughfare **Queen Street,** which opens out onto Queen Street Gardens and is a main traffic route through the city. Nestled between Princes Street and George Street is **Rose Street**—a narrow pedestrianized lane lined with pubs, shops, and restaurants. The equally narrow **Thistle Street** between George Street and Queen Street is a secret haven of boutique shopping and fine dining.

The Neighborhoods in Brief

Old Town   This area is the ancient heart of Edinburgh and the place where the city began. Its backbone is the **Royal Mile,** a medieval thoroughfare stretching along the spine of the volcanic crag that supports Edinburgh Castle to the flat land of Holyrood Park—an untamed landscape in the heart of the city that's home to the Palace of Holyroodhouse and the imposing Arthur's Seat. English author Daniel Defoe described the Royal Mile as "the largest, longest, and finest street for buildings and number of inhabitants in the world." Many argue that little has changed and today no one has truly experienced Edinburgh until they take time to explore Old Town's dark, cobbled, history-soaked streets, as vibrant today as they were when Defoe visited.

New Town   Lying to the north and below Old Town, Edinburgh's New Town is one of the largest Georgian developments in the world and its wide streets and architecture stand in direct contrast to the labyrinth of Old Town. New Town is planned around a network of squares, streets, terraces, and circuses, reaching from Haymarket in the west to Abbeyhill in the east and from Canonmills at its northern perimeter uphill to Princes Street, its main artery, along the southern tier. Within New Town lies the **West End Village,** an area north of Shandwick Place known for contemporary shops and pubs. While technically outside of New Town, Edinburgh's **West End** leads along Lothian Road and is home to many of the city's theatres, cinemas, and nightclubs, some more salubrious than others.

Marchmont   About 1 mile south of the west end of the Royal Mile, this suburb was constructed between 1869 and 1914 as a massive building program of new housing for people who could no longer afford to live in New Town. It borders a large public park, the Meadows, which links this area with Old Town. Marchmont is busy with students and while there's nothing to draw tourists here, this area is popular for festival-time sublets (see "Festival Accommodation" box, p. 108).

Bruntsfield   This suburb to the southwest of Old Town is fringed by Bruntsfield Links, a landscaped area of park land where James IV gathered his Scottish army before marching to their devastating defeat at Flodden in 1513. It's also the site of the mass graves of the city's plague victims. Today the main thoroughfare, Bruntsfield Place, is lined with unusual shops and trendy cafes, as well as some accommodation options.

Stockbridge   Spreading out to the northwest of New Town, Stockbridge is one of Edinburgh's hidden gems. Once a village on the outskirts of the city, this region was incorporated into Edinburgh in the 19th-century yet still maintains a village feel. This is an upmarket area with a bohemian edge and is a known for its unusual shops, rustic cafes, and proximity to the Water of Leith and Edinburgh's Botanical Gardens.

Leith   Standing proud a few miles north of Princes Street is the Port of Leith, the city's major harbor, which opens onto the Firth of Forth. The port might not flex the maritime muscle it used to, but it's still a region to be reckoned with; it only reluctantly became part of the city of Edinburgh in 1920. Today cruise ships dock at Leith's Ocean Terminal and the whole area has undergone significant regeneration. Although this isn't an area in which many visitors stay, it's the best place in the city to eat and a must-see for anyone wanting to glimpse the often overlooked maritime side of Edinburgh past and present.

Newhaven   Newhaven is an old fishing village west of Leith. Founded in the 1400s, this tiny harbor was once a bustling fish market which has, like Leith, undergone significant restoration. There's not that much to see today, apart from sweeping views of the Firth of Forth and Kingdom of Fife to the north. Newhaven's old harbor is now a focus for a number of restaurants and a base for trips out onto the surrounding waters.

Getting Around

Many of Edinburgh's attractions are located within a small area along or around the Royal Mile, Princes Street, or one of the major streets in New Town. As such it's easy to explore on foot and, because of its narrow lanes, wynds, and closes, you can only explore Old Town in any depth by walking.

BY BUS   Edinburgh's bus system is operated by **Lothian Buses** (*©* 0131/555-6363; www.lothianbuses.com), whose frequent, inexpensive service covers every corner of the city. The fare for a one-way journey of any distance is £1.20 for adults, 70p for children aged 5 to 15, free for children under 4. A **Day Saver Ticket** allows 1 day of unlimited travel on city buses at a cost of £3 for adults and £2 for children. A network of night buses runs throughout the night and a one-way fare on any of these services is £3. Exact change is required to purchase any ticket. Route maps and timetables can be downloaded from Lothian Buses' website or call into one their travel shops on either Waverley Bridge or Hanover Street for more information. Both offices are open Monday through Friday 9am to 6pm and Saturday 10am to 6pm. The Waverley Bridge Travel shop also opens on Sunday from 10am to 5:15pm.

BY TAXI   You can hail a taxi or pick one up at any of Edinburgh's numerous taxi stands. Meters begin at £2 and increase £2 every ⅔ mile. Taxi ranks are at Hanover Street, North St. Andrews Street, Waverley Station, Haymarket Station, Lothian Road, and Lauriston Place. Fares are displayed in the front of the taxi, including extra charges for night drivers or destinations outside the city limits. You can also call a taxi: Try **City Cabs** (*©* 0131/228-1211) or **Central Radio Taxis** (*©* 0131/229-2468).

BY CAR   Most residents don't drive around the center of Edinburgh; public transport is very good, the city's traffic system is tricky, and parking is expensive and difficult to find. Metered parking is available (exact change required) but some zones are only for permit holders; vehicles with no permit are towed away and Edinburgh's traffic wardens are notoriously active in handing out tickets. A yellow line along the curb indicates no parking. Major car parks (parking lots) are at Castle Terrace, convenient for Edinburgh Castle, Lothian Road, and the West End; and St. John Hill, convenient for the Royal Mile and St. James Centre (entrance from York Place), close to the east end of Princes Street.

If you want to rent a car for touring outside of the city or for heading onward, it makes sense to reserve in advance (see chapter 14 for more information). Most of the major companies have offices both at Edinburgh Airport and in the city center. Options include **Enterprise** (*©* 0800/800-227; www.enterprise.co.uk) and **Hertz** (*©* 0843/309-3026; www.hertz.co.uk).

BY BICYCLE   Edinburgh is relatively tolerant toward cyclists and an increasing number of locals choose to bike as their main form of transport. That said, the many cobbled roads both in New and Old Towns make for difficult terrain on two wheels and, because the city is constructed around a series of hills, don't expect a flat ride. There's a network of bike paths round the city, especially on the north side, and athletic types wanting to explore areas such as Cramond and South Queensferry will find cycling a good option. Bike rental companies include **Leith Cycles'** Abbeyhill branch on Cadzow Place (*©* 0131/652-1760; www.leithcycleco.com); rentals start at £10 for a half-day and include a helmet, lock, map, and puncture repair kit. Children's bikes, trailers, and tag-alongs can also be rented.

Essentials

EDINBURGH & THE LOTHIANS

BY TRAM Edinburgh is in the process of installing a tram system. The proposed route will run from Newhaven, via Leith Walk, Princes Street, and Haymarket train station to the airport. At the time of writing the tram system is still under construction. Updates are available at **www.edinburghtrams.com**.

Organized Tours

If your time in Edinburgh is limited, an organized tour can provide a quick introduction to the city's main sights. One of the most popular tours is via an open top bus. These trips run daily throughout the year and depart from Waverley Bridge every 15 minutes in summer and every 30 minutes in winter from 9:35am; the last tour of the day departs just after 4pm. You can hop on and off at stops along the way, and you can choose your commentary by theme and language. Tickets cost £12 for adults, £11 for seniors and students, and £5 for children aged 5 to 15. A number of different companies provide these tours; for more information, call ✆ **0131/220-0779,** see www.edinburghtour.com, or just turn up at Waverley Bridge.

One of the more unusual ways to see the city is via a rickshaw. **B-spokes** (✆ **0131/656-6499;** www.b-spokes.com) operates a selection of rickshaw tours, including a Photography Tour that takes you to the best views Edinburgh has to offer and a **Kids' Tour,** which is full of tales of wizards and ghosts; or you can create a tour of your own. Rates start at £25 per person and waterproof screens and blankets are provided if needs be. These rickshaws also operate as **Pedicabs** at night. They can be hailed in the same way as a regular taxi and operate throughout the city center.

Mercat Tours (✆ 0131/225-5445; www.mercattours.com) run the city's most highly rated walking tours. All Mercat's trained guides hold history degrees and their many tours are as entertaining as they are informative. Choose from tours such as "Secrets of the Royal Mile" and the popular "Ghosts and Ghouls," all of which run daily throughout the year and meet outside the Mercat Cross by St. Giles cathedral on the Royal Mile. Tickets start at £8 for adults and £4 for children 5 to 15 (no children under age 5) and can be bought on the day at the start of a tour or booked in advance at Tourist Information (p. 68), Mercat's office on Blair Street, online, or by phone. Mercat also runs regular tours in Spanish.

Many other tour companies offer an increasing range of ways to navigate Edinburgh and learn about its past, literary heritage, and many ghosts. Details of some of these companies are included in relevant sections throughout this chapter. Alternatively call into **Tourist Information** (✆ 0845/225-5121) to find out what's on offer.

[Fast FACTS] EDINBURGH

American Express A branch of American Express can be found at 69 George St. (✆ **0131/718-2505**). It's open Monday through Friday 9am to 5:30pm and Saturday 9am to 4pm.

Babysitters A reliable service is provided by Super Mums, 6 Glencairn

Crescent (✆ **0131/225-1744;** www.supermums.co.uk).

Business Hours In Edinburgh, banks are usually open Monday through Friday 9am to 5pm; some also open on Saturdays from 10am to 3pm. Shops are generally open Monday

through Saturday 10am to 6pm; on Thursday some stores open until 8pm. Offices generally open Monday through Friday 9am to 5pm.

Currency Exchange There are currency exchanges at Edinburgh Airport and Waverley train station.

Dentists If you have a dental emergency, go to the **Chalmers Dental Centre,** 3 Chalmers St. (📞 **0131/536-4800**), which delivers a walk in clinical service for adults aged 16 and over; open Monday through Thursday 9am to 4:45pm. Children under 16 will be treated at the Children's Department of the **Edinburgh Dental Institute** on Lauriston Place (📞 **0131/536-4970**), which is open Monday through Friday 9am to 11am and 2 to 3pm. On evenings and weekends, call the **Lothian Dental Advice Line** 📞 0131/536-4800 or **NHS 24** on 📞 **08454/24-24-24.**

Doctors You can seek advice from NHS Lothian's Lauriston Building, 1 Lauriston Place (📞 **0131/536-1000**). However, the city's 24-hour Accident and Emergency Department is located at the **Royal Infirmary of Edinburgh,** 51 Little France Crescent, Old Dalkeith Road (📞 **0131/536-1000;** www.nhslothian.scot.nhs.uk). This hospital is approximately 3 miles south of the city center and served by numerous buses including nos. 24, 48, and 33. A taxi to the Infirmary from the city center costs around £10 to £15.

Embassies & Consulates See "Fast Facts: Scotland," p. 436.

Emergencies Call 📞 **999** in an emergency to summon the police, an ambulance, or firefighters.

Hospitals See "Doctors" above.

Internet Access The **Internet Café** (📞 **0131/226-5400**) on West Bow in the heart of Old Town provides access on a ticket basis with tickets starting at £1. Closer to New Town, **Internet Café,** 28 Crighton Place, on Leith Walk (📞 **0131/477-8336;** www.coffeehome.co.uk), is open Monday through Saturday 10am to 10pm, Sunday noon to 10pm. Use of the Internet costs 60p for the first 20 minutes and 3p per minute thereafter.

Laundry & Dry Cleaning **Johnson's Cleaners,** 12 Elm Row (📞 **0131/556-3802**), is open Monday through Friday 8:30am to 5:30pm and Saturday 8:30am to 4pm.

Luggage Storage & Lockers **Waverley Station** has a Left Luggage department (📞 **0131/558-3829**) where items can be left in a secure place. It's open daily from 7am to 11pm. Rates are £7 per item for the first 24 hours, £3.50 per item for every 24 hours thereafter.

Newspapers Published since 1817, *The Scotsman* is a quality daily newspaper. Along with national and international news, it has strong coverage of the arts.

Pharmacies There are no 24-hour pharmacies (also called chemists) in Edinburgh. The major one is **Boots,** 101–103 Princes St. (📞 **0131/225-8331**), open Monday through Friday 8am to 7pm (Thurs till 8pm) and Sunday 10am to 6pm. You can also try a 24-hour supermarket such as **Asda,** 2 Sandpiper Dr., Newhaven (📞 **0131/561-2300**).

Police See "Emergencies," above.

Post Office There are many post offices dotted around the city; a central option is located inside the St. James Centre on Leith Street. It's open Monday through Saturday 9am to 5:30pm. For postal information and customer service, call 📞 **0845/722-3344.**

Safety Edinburgh is generally a safe city to walk around any time of the day or night—in fact, it's one of Europe's safest capitals. However, like any city crimes, such as muggings, do occur, often motivated by Edinburgh's considerable drug problem, and so stay aware of your surroundings.

Toilets Don't hesitate to use Edinburgh's public toilets, often marked wc and located at strategic corners and squares throughout the city. They're perfectly safe and clean, but likely to be closed late in the evening. Toilets can also be found at railway and bus stations as well as in department stores, museums, and art galleries. Many cafes, pubs, and restaurants only allow patrons to use their toilets.

EXPLORING THE CITY
Along the Royal Mile

Old Town's **Royal Mile ★★★** is actually 1 mile and 107 yards long and stretches from Edinburgh Castle all the way to the Palace of Holyroodhouse. It's made up of a chain of linked streets: Castlehill, Lawnmarket, High Street, and Canongate. Walking along you'll see some of the most interesting parts of the old city, including a section of the **Flodden Wall** if you make a short diversion along St. Mary Street. Built in the 16th century, this 1.2m- thick (3ft 11in.) structure used to mark the city limits. The point where a fortified gateway once stood as it crossed the Royal Mile was known as the World's End. Today a pub of the same name now stands near the spot.

Holyrood Park, which opens out at the east end of the Royal Mile, is a dramatic landscape in the heart of the city, characterized by rocky crags, a loch, sweeping meadows, and a tiny ruined chapel. The 250m-high (820-ft.) peak of **Arthur's Seat ★★★** is the park's crowning glory, rewarding all who climb with a breathtaking panorama over Edinburgh and the countryside beyond.

Edinburgh Castle ★★★ CASTLE   Few places in Scotland are filled with as much history, legend, and lore as Edinburgh Castle, which is in fact a complex of buildings spread over the summit of an ancient plug of volcanic rock. Evidence suggests its settlement dates back at least 3,000 years, with the first fortification referred to around A.D. 600. In the 12th century, David I built a royal castle here that included a chapel dedicated to his mother Queen Margaret. This tiny Norman chapel still stands and is the oldest building in Edinburgh. After centuries of invasions, demolitions, and upheavals, the remaining buildings are a result of the castle's role as a military garrison and include the National War Museum of Scotland. Visitors can view the Royal Palace, home to the bedchamber where Mary Queen of Scots gave birth to James VI of Scotland (later James I of England). Other highlights include the mighty Great Hall, the Honours of Scotland (Scottish Crown Jewels), and the Stone of Destiny upon which generations of Scottish and British monarchs have been, and continue to be, inaugurated. Take time to seek out Mons Meg, a 15th-century cannon weighing more than 5 tons that stands guard on the castle battlements, and enjoy unbeatable views over the city and beyond.

Castlehill. ℂ **0131/225-9846.** www.edinburghcastle.gov.uk. Admission £14 adults, £11 seniors, £8.20 children 5–15. Apr–Sept daily 9:30am–5pm; Oct–Mar daily 9:30am–6pm.

Gladstone's Land ★ HISTORIC SITE   This 17th-century merchant's house is one of the few surviving examples of a typical Old Town tenement and provides a tangible flavor of the living conditions for those with money at this time. A reconstructed shop at street level displays replicas of goods from the period, but the best part is an upstairs apartment, which is decorated in keeping with its original style and

---

📎   **Edinburgh Pass**

If you're planning to visit a number of Edinburgh attractions, the Edinburgh Pass (www.edinburghpass.com) could save you money. This pass allows the holder entry to over 30 attractions in and around the city and prices range from £27 adults and £17 children for 1 day to £52 adults and £33 children for 3 days.

Edinburgh Attractions

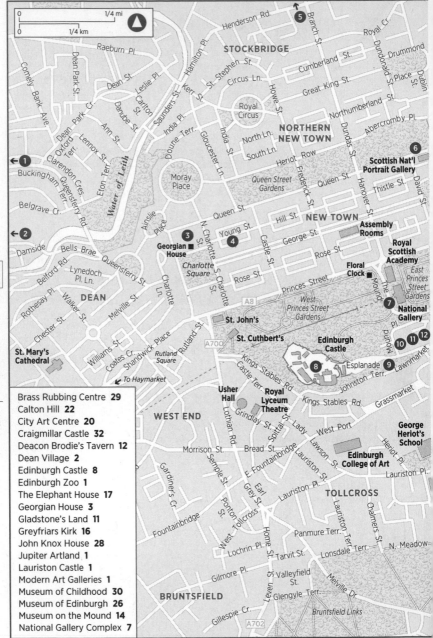

Brass Rubbing Centre **29**
Calton Hill **22**
City Art Centre **20**
Craigmillar Castle **32**
Deacon Brodie's Tavern **12**
Dean Village **2**
Edinburgh Castle **8**
Edinburgh Zoo **1**
The Elephant House **17**
Georgian House **3**
Gladstone's Land **11**
Greyfriars Kirk **16**
John Knox House **28**
Jupiter Artland **1**
Lauriston Castle **1**
Modern Art Galleries **1**
Museum of Childhood **30**
Museum of Edinburgh **26**
Museum on the Mound **14**
National Gallery Complex **7**

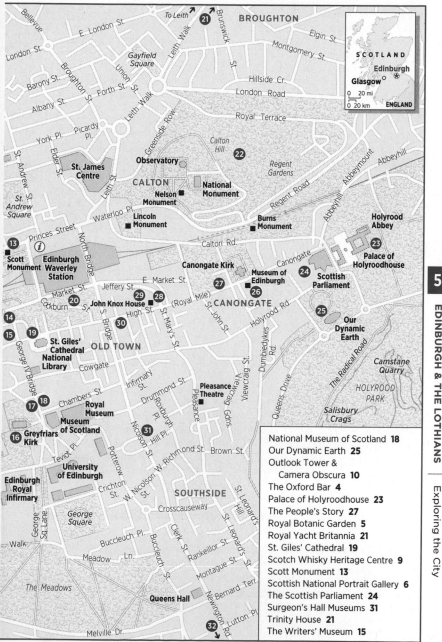

SCOTLAND

Edinburgh

Glasgow

0   20 mi
0   20 km   ENGLAND

BROUGHTON

To Leith **21**

E. London St.

Bellevue

London St.

Brunswick St.

Elgin St.

Montgomery St.

Hillside Cr.

London Road

Gayfield Square

Barony St.

Broughton St.

Forth St.

Union St.

Albany St.

York Pl.

Picardy Pl.

Leith Walk

Royal Terrace

St. Andrew St.

Elder St.

St. James Centre

Leith St.

Greenside Row

Calton Hill **22**

Regent Gardens

Abbeymount

Abbeyhill

St. Andrew Square

Observatory

CALTON

Nelson Monument

National Monument

Regent Road

Abbeyhill

Holyrood Abbey

Princes Street

ⓘ

Waterloo Pl.

Lincoln Monument

Burns Monument

Calton Rd.

Palace of Holyroodhouse **23**

13

Scott Monument

Edinburgh Waverley Station

North Bridge

Market St.

Jeffery St.

E. Market St.

Canongate Kirk

Canongate

Museum of Edinburgh

Scottish Parliament **24**

Cockburn St.

20

John Knox House

29 **28**

High St.

(Royal Mile)

CANONGATE

27

26

25

Our Dynamic Earth

14

15

19

St. Giles' Cathedral National Library

30

S. Bridge

St. Mary's St.

OLD TOWN

Cowgate

St. John St.

Holyrood Rd.

Dumbiedykes Rd.

Camstane Quarry

George IV Bridge

Chambers St.

Infirmary St.

Drummond St.

Pleasance Theatre

Viewcraig Gdns.

The Radical Road

HOLYROOD PARK

17 **18**

Royal Museum

Roxburgh Pl.

Pleasance

Salisbury Crags

16

Greyfriars Kirk

Museum of Scotland

31

Nicolson St.

Hill Pl.

W. Richmond St.

Brown St.

Queens Drive

Teviot Pl.

Potterow

University of Edinburgh

Crichton St.

W. Nicolson St.

SOUTHSIDE

St. Leonard's Hill

Edinburgh Royal Infirmary

George Sq. Lane

George Square

Crosscauseway

St. Leonard's St.

Walk

Buccleuch Pl.

Meadow Ln.

Clerk St.

Rankeillor St.

Montague St.

Bernard Terr.

Newington Rd.

Lutton Pl.

The Meadows

Queens Hall

32

Melville Dr.

5

EDINBURGH & THE LOTHIANS | Exploring the City

75

underground EDINBURGH

Edinburgh folklore is rich with tales of an underground city, not all of which are unfounded. Abandoned railway tunnels lead under New Town, a legacy of old train lines that once linked the ports along Edinburgh's coast with Waverley station. However, it's in Old Town that tales of underground Edinburgh take on a mythical status. It's long been rumored that a network of secret tunnels spread out from Edinburgh Castle, one of which leads under the Royal Mile to the Palace of Holyroodhouse. However, more grounded in the real world are stories of bricked over streets. In the late 18th and early 19th centuries as the fortunes of Old Town declined, anyone with the funds to do so fled its cramped unhygienic closes for the wide-open streets of the blossoming New Town. Most of the dilapidated housing around the Royal Mile was demolished, and in the case of streets such as Mary King's Close, the lower levels were simply built over and tales of underground streets with resident ghosts passed into urban legend.

In the late 1990s, the old street level sections of Mary King's Close were rediscovered and today form one of Edinburgh's spookiest tourist attractions. Located beneath the City Chambers, **The Real Mary King's Close** (☎ **08702/430-160;** www.realmary kingsclose.com) is accessed via Warriston's Close off the Royal Mile and transports visitors back to the 17th century. Expect to be led through a hidden and haunted underground warren of old houses where people lived and worked for centuries. Learn about Mary King herself and the last man to leave her close, whose ghost is believed to still occupy his old house. This attraction is open November to March Sunday through Thursday 10am to 5pm and Friday and Saturday 10am to 9pm, and April to October daily 10am to 9pm. Admission is £12 for adults and £6 for children 5 to 15.

Dubbed as the most haunted place in Britain, the layers of vaults that lie beneath South Bridge are no place for the fainthearted. When the bridge was built in the late 18th century, a complex of vaults was built into its enormous arches. Some of these dark spaces were used for storage while various tradesmen occupied others, but the damp drove them out and the city's destitute and often criminally inclined moved in, transforming the complex into a slum that was soon closed down. Today **Mercat Tours** (☎ **0131/225-5445;** www.mercattours.com) takes visitors deep into these forgotten vaults via a series of tours, some of which focus on the history of these hidden spaces; others introduce those who dare to descend to the many ghosts who call this place home. Tours run on various days at set times and tickets start at £8 for adults and £4 for children.

filled with period furnishings and a glorious painted ceiling dating back to 1620. The top two floors date back to the same period and can be rented through the National Trust for Scotland as a holiday apartment.

477B Lawnmarket. ☎ **0131/226-5856.** www.nts.org.uk. Admission £6 adults, £5 seniors and children. Apr–June and Sept–Oct daily 10am–5pm; July–Aug daily 10am–6:30pm.

John Knox House HISTORIC HOME This distinctive medieval building was the final home of hard-line Protestant reformer John Knox. Founder of the Scottish Presbyterian Church, which ousted Catholicism to become Scotland's dominant religion, Knox is famous for his inflammatory, chauvinistic treatise *The First Blast of the Trumpet Against the Monstrous Regiment of Women,* largely inspired by his opposition to the Catholic queens of Europe including Mary Queen of Scots. Even if you're not interested in Knox this late-15th-century house is well worth a visit; its three floors showcase medieval craftsmanship, including a frescoed ceiling in The Oak Room. Today Knox's house is joined with the Scottish Storytelling Centre, whose award-winning modern headquarters seamlessly integrates with the adjacent 15th-century building, containing a bright cafe and performance space.

43–45 High St. ✆ **0131/556-9579.** www.scottishstorytellingcentre.co.uk. Admission £4 adults, £3.50 seniors, £1 children 7 and up, under-7s free. July–Aug Mon–Sat 10am–6pm, also Sun noon–6pm.

Museum of Childhood ☺ MUSEUM This small but fascinating museum devoted solely to the history of childhood takes visitors on a journey through the toys and games that children have grown up with from the 18th to 21st centuries. Exhibits include child-sized pedal cars, magnificent dollhouses, and toy soldiers as well as books and clothes. Hands-on areas keep young children occupied while parents take a walk down memory lane.

42 High St. ✆ **0131/529-4142.** www.edinburghmuseums.org.uk. Free admission. Mon–Sat 10am–5pm; Sun noon–5pm.

Museum of Edinburgh MUSEUM Across from the Canongate Tolbooth, the Museum of Edinburgh is housed in Huntly House, a fine example of a restored 16th-century mansion, whose builders preferred a bulky, relatively simple design that suited its role as a secular building. Today, this warren-like museum is dedicated to the history of Edinburgh and features faithfully crafted reproductions of rooms inspired by the city's traditional industries, including glassmaking and pottery. Original plans for New Town are also on display along with the National Covenant, a petition for religious freedom created in 1638.

142 Canongate. ✆ **0131/529-4143.** www.edinburghmuseums.org.uk. Free admission. Mon–Sat 10am–5pm; Aug Sun noon–5pm.

Outlook Tower & Camera Obscura ☺ OBSERVATION POINT Housed in the top chamber of this white Victorian Outlook Tower is an 1853 periscope which throws a revolving image of Edinburgh's streets and buildings onto a circular table. Visitors are invited to interact with these images while guides share stories of the city's landmarks and history. Additional attractions include a Magic Gallery crammed with optical illusions and the Electric Room complete with a giant plasmasphere.

Castlehill. ✆ **0131/226-3709.** www.camera-obscura.co.uk. Admission £10 adults, £8 seniors and students, £7 children 5–15. July–Aug daily 9:30am–7:30pm; Sept–Oct and Apr–June daily 9:30am–6pm; Nov–Mar daily 10am–5pm.

〰️ **Old Town Adventure**

The Old Town Adventure pack is a family guide to exploring aimed at those with children aged 7 to 12. The pack contains a foldout map, child-friendly guides, and a set of stickers. It costs £3.50 and can be picked up at the Storytelling Centre next to John Knox House as well as at a number of museums along the Royal Mile.

Palace of Holyroodhouse ★★ ROYAL BUILDING   Built by James IV in the 16th-century, the Palace of Holyroodhouse is the Queen's official residence in Scotland. This magnificent baroque building, framed by the wild landscape of Holyrood Park, sits adjacent to a now-ruined Augustinian abbey established by David I in the 12th century. The palace has been altered and refurbished by various subsequent monarchs and highlights include the Royal Apartments and the chambers where Mary Queen of Scots lived. Some of the rich tapestries, paneling, massive fireplaces, and antiques from the 1700s are still in place and the Throne Room and other drawing rooms are still used for state occasions. The Great Gallery is lined with portraits of Scottish monarchs by Dutch artist Jacob De Wet, who was commissioned by Charles II in the 17th century to create a series of painting of the royal figures who pre-dated him, some of which are real, others merely legendary. The **Queen's Gallery** stands in front of the palace and displays a changing program of exhibitions of artwork from the Royal Collection.

Canongate. ✆ **0131/556-5100.** www.royalcollection.org.uk. Admission £11 adults, £9.50 seniors, £6.35 children 5-16, £28 families. Joint Palace and Queen's Gallery ticket £15 adults, £14 seniors, £8.50 children 5-16, £39 families. Apr-Oct daily 9:30am-6pm; Nov-Mar daily 9:30am-4:30pm.

The People's Story HISTORIC SITE   Housed in Canongate Tolbooth, which was built in 1591 as a place to collect taxes and serve as a local jail, the People's Story celebrates the social history of Edinburgh residents from the late 18th century to the present day. There's no sniff of royalty here; instead the stories of ordinary folk, how they worked, how they played, the hardships they endured, and the rights they fought for are thoughtfully presented.

163 Canongate. ✆ **0131/529-4057.** www.edinburghmuseums.org.uk. Free admission. Mon-Sat 10am-5pm; Sun in Aug noon-5pm.

St. Giles' Cathedral ★★ CATHEDRAL   Also known as the High Kirk of Edinburgh, St. Giles' is one of the most important churches in Scotland and a key architectural landmark along the Royal Mile. The oldest parts date back to 1124, but following a fire in 1385 many sections were rebuilt and altered during a large-scale restoration in the 19th century. The brooding stone exterior features a distinctive crowned spire and graceful flying buttresses and one of the outstanding features of the large vaulted interior is the Thistle Chapel. Built in 1911 and dedicated to the Knights of the Thistle, Scotland's order of chivalry, this intricate space houses beautiful stalls and detailed heraldic stained-glass windows.

High St. ✆ **0131/225-9442.** www.stgilescathedral.org.uk. Free admission (£3 donation suggested). May-Sept Mon-Fri 9am-7pm, Sat 9am-5pm and Sun 1-5pm; Oct-April Mon-Sat 9am-5pm and Sun 1-5pm.

Scotch Whisky Heritage Centre MUSEUM/ENTERTAINMENT COMPLEX   Visitors to this entertaining and informative attraction are whisked through a whisky barrel ride dedicated to the making of Scotland's favorite tipple before being taught how to sample a wee dram of choice. You're then invited to view the world's largest whisky collection before a tour concludes in a whisky bar where long views of Edinburgh complement the many malts available to sample.

354 Castlehill. ✆ **0131/220-0441.** www.scotchwhiskyexperience.co.uk. Admission £12 adults, £9.50 seniors and students, £6.25 children 6-17, £28 families. Daily Sept-May 10am-6pm; June-Aug 10am-6:30pm.

GREYFRIARS kirk & BOBBY

A short detour along George IV Bridge from the Royal Mile leads to Greyfriars Kirk (www.greyfriarskirk.com), an old Edinburgh church built in 1620 whose 17th-century churchyard, crammed with gravestones and mausoleums, is a favorite stop for local ghost tours and the place where many signed the National Covenant in 1638 in commitment to Scottish Presbyterianism. The most famous graves here are that of John Gray, a member of the Edinburgh City Police and night watchman who died in 1858, and his faithful dog Bobby who guarded his owner's grave for 14 years until he too passed away in 1867. A statue of the loyal Bobby stands close to the main entrance of Greyfriars Kirkyard and a number of books and films retelling the story of this faithful hound have since been created. This remarkable dog was awarded Freedom of the City status and his collar and bowl are now on display in the Museum of Edinburgh (p. 77).

The Scottish Parliament ★★ ARCHITECTURE   This bold and controversial modern building stands opposite and in contrast to the Palace of Holyroodhouse at the east end of the Royal Mile and, like it or loath it, embodies a strong statement of Scotland's past, present, and future. Designed by the late Spanish architect Enric Miralles, who died before his vision was completed, this unique building cost a cool US$893 million and the first debate finally took place in its chambers in 2004. The facade is amazing enough in itself, but to truly understand the philosophy behind the architecture and to enter the hallowed debating chamber, a guided tour is a must.

Canongate. ℂ **0131/348-5200.** www.scottish.parliament.uk. Free admission. April-Sept Mon-Fri 10am-5:30pm; Oct-Mar 10am-4pm; Sat year-round 11am-5:30pm.

Museums & Art Galleries

City Art Centre GALLERY   Spread out over six floors of an imposing former warehouse behind Waverley station, the City Art Centre boasts an impressive collection of Scottish art from the 17th century to the present day. A changing program of exhibitions showcase paintings, drawing, photographs, sculpture, and installations from subjects as broad as Highland Art to human anatomy, alongside new work from local and international artists.

2 Market St. ℂ **0131/529-3993.** www.edinburghmuseums.org.uk. Free admission. Mon-Sat 10am-5pm; Sun noon-5pm.

Modern Art Galleries ★★ GALLERY   The two galleries that make up the Modern Art Galleries—the Gallery of Modern Art and Dean Gallery—house Scotland's best collection of modern and contemporary art. The Modern Art Gallery sits in 4.8 hectares (12 acres) of landscaped grounds featuring sculptures from Henry Moore and Barbara Hepworth. The gallery itself contains a large collection of international post-war work from artists including Francis Bacon, Andy Warhol, and Damien Hirst and work from the early 20th century such as cubist paintings and pieces by Matisse and Picasso. Across the road the Dean Gallery displays a wide collection of Dada and Surrealism, including work by Salvador Dalí, Max Ernst, Joan Miró, and Edinburgh-born

THE national MUSEUM OF SCOTLAND REOPENING

In July 2011 the National Museum of Scotland triumphantly reopened the original Victorian section of this magnificent attraction following an ambitious refurbishment which cost nearly £48millon and closed the galleries for three years.

The museum originally opened in 1866, hot on the heels of the Great Exhibition and infused with the same sense of adventure and discovery that inspired 18th- and 19th-century travelers and explorers. As well as restoring the actual building to its dazzling Victorian elegance, the refurbishment process has also dusted off and revitalized the museum's founding spirit and a journey through its wide, high ceiling galleries feels like a stroll through a living encyclopedia.

Collections showcase a huge range of objects and artifacts from around the world all of which embody Scotland's achievements and journeys across the globe. And, just as travelers of old brought-back stories as well as objects, so the exhibits are presented and explained through the stories behind them.

Today visitors enter the building through its large sandstone vaults, originally used for storage and now housing a shop and atmospheric brasserie, which serves locally-sourced food. You'll then journey up a level to enter the Grand Gallery, the building's impressive focal point which was modeled after London's Crystal Palace and houses the museum's largest and most impressive exhibit—the

sculptor Sir Eduardo Paolozzi, who gave an extensive body of his private collection to the National Galleries of Scotland, including prints, drawings, plaster maquettes, and molds. This gallery also hosts a number of temporary or traveling exhibitions. Both galleries are a 15-minute walk from the west end of Princes Street.

75 Belford Rd. © 0131/624-6200. www.nationalgalleries.org. Free admission; a charge for some temporary exhibitions. Daily 10am–5pm. Bus: 13.

Museum on the Mound MUSEUM   This is one of Edinburgh's newest museums and is dedicated to the subject of money. Detailed displays bring visitors face to face with a million pounds and Scotland's oldest banknote, and chart the history of the Bank of Scotland, the rise of building societies, and much more. The Mound on which the museum stands is a manmade structure and a glass display shows just what this city center hill is made of.

The Mound. © 0131/243-5464. www.museumonthemound.com. Free admission. Tues–Fri 10am–5pm; Sat–Sun 1–5pm.

National Gallery Complex ★★★ GALLERY   Located in the center of Princes Street Gardens, this imposing complex is made up of three connected buildings dedicated to displaying Scotland's national collection of fine art from the early Renaissance to the end of the 19th century. The main building is the National Gallery itself whose wide galleries house the main collection and contain masterpieces from around the world from artists such as Raphael, Rubens, Van Gogh, and Cézanne, as well as a collection dedicated to the history of Scottish painting. The Royal Scottish Academy Building displays a program of temporary world-class exhibitions and is joined with the National Gallery via the Weston Link, which contains a cafe and IT gallery.

The Mound. © 0131/624-6200. www.nationalgalleries.org. Free admission; a charge for some temporary exhibitions. Fri–Wed 10am–5pm; Thurs 10am–7pm.

Window on the World. This incredible installation is four stories high and contains over 800 objects including a girder from the original Tay bridge, the jaws of an enormous sperm whale and a 14th-century knight's helmet. Numerous galleries lead off this impressive focal point and themes to explore and interact with include Discoveries, where you'll find the oldest surviving color TV, and Facing the Sea, the only permanent gallery in the U.K. devoted to the island cultures of the Pacific. The museum also celebrates Scotland's own history and some of the key Scottish exhibits to seek out include Bonnie Prince Charlie's traveling canteen, believed to have been a 21st birthday present for the young prince, and a 16th-century necklace that once graced the neck of Mary Queen of Scots.

Young visitors were well catered for in the museum's refurbishment making this one of the best attractions in Edinburgh for families. Alongside reams of interactive exhibits there's a super fun large learning center dedicated to inspiring children, while the Natural World galleries will keep all ages wide eyed and entertained for hours.

The grand reopening, which coincided with an impressive election victory of the Scottish National Party and was attended by thousands, reflects a rising wave of confidence in Scotland's cultural identity and embodies a strong message of pride in the nation's past, present and future. See also below.

National Museum of Scotland ★★★ MUSEUM Consisting of two distinctive buildings, one dating back to 1866 and a second modern build which opened in 1998, this national treasure house is the place to delve deep into Scotland's rich history from its geological origins to the present day. The Victorian part of the building has just reopened after an impressive refurbishment (see box above) and contains 16 new exhibition galleries making this the largest museum in the UK outside of London. Also make time to explore the equally impressive contemporary section of the museum where a multitude of objects tell the story of Scotland and its accessible roof top claims sweeping views over the city and beyond.

Chambers St. ℂ **0300/123-6789.** www.nms.ac.uk. Free admission. Daily 10am-5pm.

Scottish National Portrait Gallery ★★ GALLERY Housed in a grand red sandstone Arts & Crafts building, the Scottish National Portrait Gallery was the first of its kind in the world and is filled with images, from paintings to photographs, of famous and not so famous Scots. The gallery has undergone a large-scale restoration aimed at restoring and revealing more of this neo-gothic building, whose best bits include a detailed frieze of famous Scots in chronological order and external decorative statues of Scottish poets and monarchs. The gallery will continue to present historical and thematic exhibitions of sitters and artists alike.

George St. ℂ **0131/624-6200.** www.nationalgalleries.org. Free admission. Check the website for latest opening hours.

Surgeon's Hall Museums MUSEUM Edinburgh's rich medical history make this unusual museum, which houses one of the most important surgical collections in the world, well worth a visit. On the upper floors you can chart the development of surgery from 1505 to the 20th century and the downstairs Dental Museum is crammed with every conceivable dentistry tool alongside 3,000-year-old dentures.

Jupiter Artland ★★

A recent addition to Edinburgh arts scene, **Jupiter Artland** (✆ 01506/889-900; www.jupiterartland.org) describes itself as a garden of discovery and is a contemporary sculpture garden in the city's western outskirts. The garden sits in the grounds of Bonnington House and contains a growing number of specially commissioned pieces created in situ. Maps are provided and imaginations are teased in this unique haven of hidden landscapes. Jupiter Artland is open mid-May to mid-September Thursday through Sunday 10am to 5pm. Admission is £8.50 for adults and £4.50 for children aged 6 to 16. **First** (✆ 01324/602-200; www.firstgroup.com) bus services nos. 27 and X27 depart from Regent Road and Haymarket train station in Edinburgh and drop off close to the entrance of Bonnington House.

The Sherlock Holmes section of the Pathology Museum brings a dose of light relief to the myriad of specimens on display. However, the must-see of the museum's more macabre objects are a plaster cast of William Burke's head taken moments after his execution—you can still see the mark of the hangman's rope on his neck—and a small pocket notebook bound with a section of this notorious body snatcher's skin. Due to the medically graphic nature of some of the exhibits this museum isn't for the squeamish and not recommended for children under 10. Anyone under age 16 must be accompanied by an adult.

Nicolson St., opposite the Festival Theatre. ✆ **0131/527-1649.** www.museum.rcsed.ac.uk. Admission £5 adults, £3 seniors. Mon–Fri noon–4pm.

Additional Attractions

Brass Rubbing Centre ARTS & CRAFTS One of Edinburgh's more unusual and hands on attractions, the Brass Rubbing Centre is a collection of replica monumental brasses depicting mediaeval knights and ladies and Celtic patterns—those commemorating Robert the Bruce are particularly impressive. Visitors are invited into this lofty building, which stands on the site of a 15th-century church, to view the collection and take detailed rubbing of the brasses on black or white paper and using silver wax.

Trinity Apse, Chalmers Close, off the Royal Mile. ✆ **0131/556-4364.** www.edinburghmuseums.org.uk. Admission is free and costs to take a rubbing range from £2 to £20. Apr–Sept Mon–Sat 10am-4.30pm closed noon-1pm for lunch.

Calton Hill ★★★ MONUMENT Rising 106m (350 ft.) off Regent Road, Calton Hill and its assortment of monuments have helped Edinburgh earn the sobriquet "Athens of the North." Construction began on the large **Scottish Monument,** which dominates the summit, in 1826 and although this ambitious structure was intended to replicate the Parthenon, funds dried up and the building was never completed. Other (completed) buildings include the 32m (106-ft.) high **Nelson Monument** (✆ 0131/556-2716; www.edinburgharchitecture.co.uk), which contains relics of the man himself and is crowned by a large time ball that enables vessels on the Firth of Forth to set their chronometers accurately. Modeled after the Tower of the Winds in Athens, the **Dugald Stewart Monument** is one of the best vantage points in Edinburgh and a choice spot from which to be buffeted by panoramic views of the city as they spread out below. Calton Hill is best entered via Waterloo Place, which is also where you'll find the entrance to **Calton Old Cemetery.** Dating from the 1700s, this old burial ground is the final resting place of a number of famous Scots including the philosopher David Hume. American's should look out for the **Scottish-American Soldiers Monument** opposite Hume's Robert Adam designed tomb. Crowned with a statue of Abraham Lincoln, this unusual monument remembers all those Scots who fought for the Union during the American Civil War.

Calton Hill can be entered via Waterloo Place and Royal Terrace. Entrance is free except for the Nelson Monument that costs £3. Oct–Mar Mon–Sat 10am–3pm; April–Sept Mon 1–6pm, Tues–Sat 10am–6pm.

Craigmillar Castle ★ ☺ CASTLE   Dubbed Edinburgh's other castle, Craigmillar stands close to the Royal Infirmary of Edinburgh and is one of Scotland's best preserved medieval castles. At its heart stands a late 14th-century tower whose labyrinthine interior is filled with a complex of rooms including a Great Hall and Queen Mary's Room where the Queen of Scots is said to have stayed. A large complex of buildings grew around the tower, however, much of these are now merely picturesque ruins. This is a great attraction for families because there are plenty of creepy nooks and crannies to explore and the large lawns make for a perfect picnic spot.

Craigmillar Castle Rd. ✆ **0131/661-4445.** www.historicscotland.gov.uk. Admission £4.20 adults, £2.50 children. Apr–Sept daily 9:30am–5:30pm; Oct daily 9:30am–4:30pm; Nov–Mar Sun–Wed 9:30am–4:30pm. By public transport take any bus to the Royal Infirmary, it is a ½ mile walk to the castle.

Dean Village ★ HISTORIC SITE   Beautiful Dean Village is one of the city's most photographed sights. Dating from the 12th century, this former grain-milling center occupies a valley about 30m (100 ft.) below the rest of Edinburgh on the edge of the Water of Leith. It's a few minutes from the West End at the end of Bells Brae off Queensferry Street, and you can enjoy a celebrated view by looking downstream, under the high arches of Dean Bridge (1833), designed by Telford. The village's old buildings have been restored and converted into apartments and houses. You don't come here for any one particular site but to stroll around, people-watch, and enjoy the village.

Edinburgh Zoo ★★ ☺ ZOO   Scotland's largest animal collection is located on the western edges of the city and spreads over 32 hectares (79 acres) of hillside parkland with unrivaled views towards the Pentland Hills. The zoo is home to over 1,000 animals including many endangered species and best-loved creatures include the sun bears, Sumatran tigers, koala bears, and Malayan tapirs. A recent addition is the Bungo Trail, a state-of-the-art chimpanzee facility that allows visitors close up viewings and opportunities to learn about their links with humans. The zoo also boasts a large penguin population who leave their enclosure every day at 2:15pm to

National Galleries Bus

If you plan to visit the various branches of the Scottish National Galleries, from the Dean to the Portrait, a good way to get around is by using the free shuttle bus service that stops near or right at the entrances of them all. The buses run at 45-minute intervals from about 11am to 5pm daily, although you should check with gallery staff at each branch to confirm they're running on their regular schedule.

EDINBURGH UNESCO CITY OF literature

Scottish author Ian Rankin is famous for claiming of Edinburgh that "the stories are in the stones," and there's no denying that the streets of Scotland's capitol are a potent place for aspiring and established writers alike. In recognition of the city's distinguished literary history, Edinburgh was hailed as the world's first UNESCO City of Literature (www.cityofliterature.com) in 2004. However, this honorable status isn't only concerned with celebrating the city's long-dead literary greats, it's also firmly dedicated to the development of Edinburgh's literary culture in the present, thus ensuring its long and vibrant future.

The main focus of the city's literary scene is the **Edinburgh International Book Festival** (www.edbookfest.co.uk), the largest public celebration of books in the world, that takes place every August in Charlotte Square during the main festival period (see box p. 102). But at any time of year, here are Edinburgh's top five literary places to visit.

IN OLD TOWN
The Writers' Museum (*© 0131/529-4901; www.edinburghmuseums.org.uk), in Lady Stair's Close off the Lawnmarket, is a free treasure trove of portraits, relics, and manuscripts relating to three of Scotland's greatest men of letters: Robert Burns (1759–96), Sir Walter Scott (1771–1832), and Robert Louis Stevenson (1850–94). Collections include Burns' writing desk, Sir Walter Scott's pipe and chess set, and a number of Stevenson's early editions. The house itself dates backs to 1622. The museum is open Monday through Saturday 10am to 5pm, and on Sundays in August noon–5pm.

The Elephant House (*© 0131/220-5355;** www.elephanthouse.biz) cafe on George IV Bridge is where J.K. Rowling penned her early Harry Potter books. This popular spot opens daily from 8am until 11pm and dishes up picture-postcard views of Edinburgh Castle in rustic, elephant-themed surroundings along with a broader-than-average selection of cafe-style food.

Deacon Brodie's Tavern (*© 0131/225-6531**), on Lawnmarket opposite George IV Bridge, is named after William Brodie, a respected citizen by day and thief by

take a stroll. An agreement has been signed between China to Scotland to bring two giant pandas, the breeding pair Tian Tian and Yangguang, to the zoo.

134 Corstorphine Rd. *© **0131/334-9171.** www.edinburghzoo.org.uk. Admission £16 adults, £13 seniors and students, £11 children 3-14, £48 family ticket. Apr–Sept daily 9am–6pm; Oct and Mar daily 9am–5pm; Nov–Feb daily 9am–4:30pm. Parking £4. Bus: 12, 26, or 31 from Princes St.

Georgian House ARCHITECTURE   This National Trust for Scotland property is the place to find out just what life was like for the well-to-do of Edinburgh 200 years ago. The house stands at the heart of Charlotte Square, one of the most magnificent areas in New Town. Designed by Robert Adam this classical masterpiece surrounds a large garden at the center of which stands a statue of Queen Victoria's beloved Prince Albert. The Georgian House dates back to 1796 and is filled with period furnishings, china, and artwork all capturing the elegance of the era and a sense of the below-stairs life of the servants.

7 Charlotte Sq. *© **0844/493-2117.** www.nts.org.uk. Admission £6 adults, £6 children, students, and seniors, £16 family ticket. Mar daily 11am–4pm; Apr–June and Sept–Oct daily 10am–5pm; July–Aug daily 10am–6pm; Nov daily 11am–3pm.

night who was eventually caught and hung in 1788. His notorious double life inspired Robert Louis Stevenson's *The Strange Case of Dr. Jekyll and Mr. Hyde,* and the fictional protagonist of Muriel Spark's *The Prime of Miss Jean Brodie* was created as a direct descendant of Deacon Brodie himself.

IN NEW TOWN

The Oxford Bar (© 0131/539-7119; www.oxfordbar.com) on Young Street is famous the world over as Ian Rankin's Detective Inspector John Rebus' pub of choice. However, Scottish writers have favored this venerable bar since the 19th century, and it remains a popular locals' pub.

The Gothic-inspired **Scott Monument ★** (© 0131/529-4068; www.edinburgh architecture.co.uk), on the east end of Princes Street, is a more-than-60m-high (200-ft.) elaborate spire at the center of which sits a large statue of Sir Walter Scott and his dog. Visitors can pay £2.50 to climb the spire's 287 steps to enjoy spectacular views of the city. The Monument is open April to September Monday through Saturday 9am to 6pm and Sunday 10am to 6pm; and October to March Monday through Saturday 9am to 3pm and Sunday 10am to 3pm.

Those seeking to tap into Edinburgh's prodigious literary inspiration by walking the city's streets have a number of tour choices. Ian Rankin has created a free iPhone app that leads walkers around his favored Edinburgh haunts and can be downloaded from his website www. ianrankin.net. Other options include **Edinburgh Literary Tours** (www. edinburghbookloverstour.com), which leads a daytime Edinburgh Book Lovers' tour (£10 full price/£8 concessions) and an evening Lost World Literary Pub Crawl (£8 full price/£7 concessions); reserve via the website. **Leith Walks** (© 0131/555-2500; www.leithwalks. co.uk) specialize in 2-hour walking tours taking in the locations featured in Irvine's Welsh's *Trainspotting* (£8 per person).

Our Dynamic Earth ★ ☺ THEME PARK   This family-friendly attraction is as close to Disney as Edinburgh gets. Visitors are led on an entertaining journey through the physical earth and natural diversity from the Big Bang to a tropical rainforest where skies darken at 15-minute intervals and torrents of rain cascade onto the recreated landscape. En route you're transported to different terrains via a 4D experience, encounter a simulated volcano, and a real (if small) iceberg. A multitude of opportunities to interact and learn are provided along the way. A visit also includes a show in the Future Dome digital planetarium.

Holyrood Rd. © 0131/550-7800. www.dynamicearth.co.uk. Admission £12 adults, £11 seniors, £8 children 3-15, children 2 and under free. Nov–Mar Wed–Sun 10am–5:30pm; Apr–June and Sept–Oct daily 10am–5:30pm; Jul–Aug daily 10am–6pm.

Royal Botanic Garden ★★ GARDEN   One of the grandest outdoor spaces in Britain, the "Botanics" as these gardens are affectionately known, cover over 28 landscaped hectares (70 acres) 1 mile north of Princes Street. The gardens date back to the late 17th century when they were used for medical studies and now form an exquisite tranquil haven loved by visitors and residents alike. The many areas to stroll through include a Chinese Garden, a Scottish Heath Garden, and a glorious Victorian Temperate Palm House. The brand-new visitor center by the western entrance features plenty of child-friendly displays, a very popular cafe, and a changing program of exhibitions. In spring, the rhododendrons alone are reason enough to visit Scotland.

Inverleith Row. ℂ **0131/552-7171.** www.rbge.org.uk. Admission to the gardens free; to the Glasshouse £4 adults, £3 seniors, £1 children aged 9 and under. Feb–Oct daily 10am–6pm; Nov–Jan daily 10am–4pm. From Princes St. take bus no 8, 17, 23, or 27.

5 Leith

Leith is an essential visit for anyone interested in Edinburgh's maritime history. Archaeological excavations of this area have revealed medieval wharfs dating back to the 12th century and today cruise ships still dock at Ocean Terminal. Areas such as The Shore have benefited from considerable regeneration and manage to retain much of their historical charms, aided by interpretive boards depicting harbor life of old. Those who want to dig deeper should take time to explore a couple of maritime attractions. The biggest tourist draw is the **Royal Yacht Britannia** ★ (ℂ **0131/555-5566;** www.royalyachtbritannia.co.uk) moored at Ocean Terminal. Launched on April 16, 1953, this 125m (410-ft.) luxury yacht sailed more than a million miles before she was decommissioned on December 11, 1997. Onboard, you're guided around all five levels by an audio tour and can walk the decks where Prince Charles and Princess Diana strolled on their honeymoon. A visit also includes a trip to the Royal Apartments, engine room, and captain's cabin. The yacht is open daily November to March from 10am with the last tour at 3:30pm; April to June and October from 10am, with the last tour at 4pm; and July to September from 9:30am, with the last tour at 4.30pm. On Kirkgate, **Trinity House** (ℂ **0131/554-3289;** www.trinity houseleith.org.uk) maritime museum is for the real enthusiast and is filled with a host of memorabilia, model ships, and navigational instruments. This museum is free and tours can be joined every Saturday at 1, 2, or 3pm. Lothian bus nos. 36 and 22 link The Shore and Ocean Terminal with the city center.

Cramond

The small, village-like district of Cramond lies 4 miles west of the center of Edinburgh and is rarely discovered by visitors. Its edges push against the mouth of the River Almond as it tumbles into the Firth of Forth, and the pretty waterfront and riverside walkways are popular with Edinburgh families at weekends. The earliest evidence of human habitation in Scotland dates back to 8500 B.C. and was unearthed

TRACING YOUR ancestral ROOTS

There are a number of avenues to explore if you want to trace the Scottish side of your family tree. In addition to the many books on clan histories, a number have their own museums throughout Scotland and local tourist offices can provide details on where to find them. Staff at Historic Scotland properties are also well briefed on the most popular Scottish names related to their sites and are more than happy to share information.

For anyone wanting to dig deeper, the **Scotlands People Centre** at General Register House, 2 Princes St.

(✆ **0131/314-4300**; www.scotlands peoplehub.gov.uk), helps researchers gain access to records held by the General Register Office and the National Archives of Scotland (www.nas.gov.uk). The center is open Monday through Friday from 9am to 4:30pm. Free introductory sessions run most days, otherwise a day's research costs £10 and should be reserved in advance by phone or on the website. Also in Edinburgh on Victoria Place, the **Scottish Genealogical Society** (✆ **0131/220-3677**; www.scots genealogy.com) can assist with research into Scottish family history.

at this tranquil spot, which also boasts the scant remains of a Roman fort. Today a cozy waterfront cafe sells ice creams and teas, and you can stroll 1½ miles along the banks of the Almond to the **Cramond Brig** (✆ **0131/339-4350**; www.cramond brig.com) pub standing beside an old bridge across the river. This area is rich with bird life and species such as curlews and oystercatchers can be spied along this shore. When the tide is out, you can cross an old causeway to explore the tiny Cramond Island, which lies 1 mile offshore.

Lauriston Castle (✆ **0131/336-2060**; www.edinburghmuseums.org.uk) stands inland on Cramond Road South and is one of the city's finest historical houses. The oldest section dates back to the 1600s and, following redecoration in the early 19th century, Lauriston shines with Edwardian elegance. Also take time to enjoy the castle's serene gardens, which include an award-winning Japanese Friendship Garden. Tours of the castle are scheduled at 2pm Saturday through Thursday April to October and 2pm on Saturdays and Sundays only November to March, and cost £5 for adults and £3 for children. Lothian bus no. 41 links Cramond with the city center.

WHERE TO EAT

Edinburgh's dining scene has changed dramatically over the past few years and the options, styles, and types of cuisine on offer are more diverse than ever before. At the top end of the dining scale Edinburgh boasts five Michelin-starred restaurants, the most of any U.K. city outside of London. A host of new vibrant eateries have sprung up all over the city, perfectly complementing Edinburgh's longstanding top tables. Many establishments specialize in Scottish cuisine and local seafood, but you can also expect to choose from dishes celebrating food from all over the world. Leith has rapidly established itself as the best region in the city for eating out; in New Town, George Street is the place to be seen dining out, but the parallel Thistle Street is lined with many of Edinburgh's finest and most intimate dining experiences. In Old Town, some of the city's most established restaurants still pack a considerable culinary punch.

Edinburgh Hotels & Restaurants

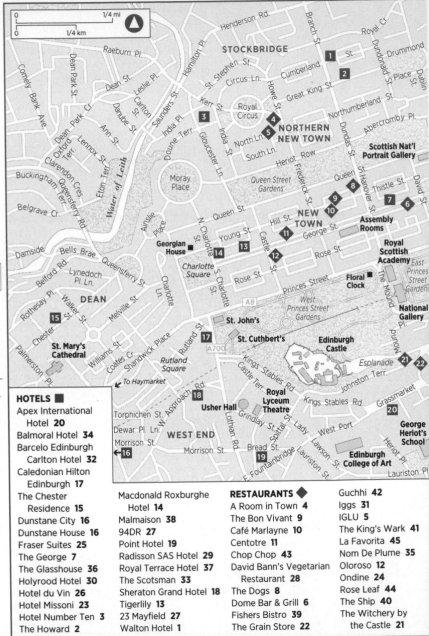

HOTELS ■

Apex International Hotel **20**
Balmoral Hotel **34**
Barcelo Edinburgh Carlton Hotel **32**
Caledonian Hilton Edinburgh **17**
The Chester Residence **15**
Dunstane City **16**
Dunstane House **16**
Fraser Suites **25**
The George **7**
The Glasshouse **36**
Holyrood Hotel **30**
Hotel du Vin **26**
Hotel Missoni **23**
Hotel Number Ten **3**
The Howard **2**

Macdonald Roxburghe Hotel **14**
Malmaison **38**
94DR **27**
Point Hotel **19**
Radisson SAS Hotel **29**
Royal Terrace Hotel **37**
The Scotsman **33**
Sheraton Grand Hotel **18**
Tigerlily **13**
23 Mayfield **27**
Walton Hotel **1**

RESTAURANTS ◆

A Room in Town **4**
The Bon Vivant **9**
Café Marlayne **10**
Centotre **11**
Chop Chop **43**
David Bann's Vegetarian Restaurant **28**
The Dogs **8**
Dome Bar & Grill **6**
Fishers Bistro **39**
The Grain Store **22**

Guchhi **42**
Iggs **31**
IGLU **5**
The King's Wark **41**
La Favorita **45**
Nom De Plume **35**
Oloroso **12**
Ondine **24**
Rose Leaf **44**
The Ship **40**
The Witchery by the Castle **21**

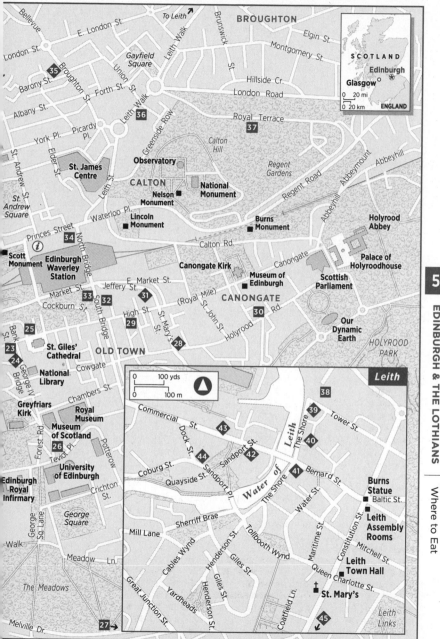

BROUGHTON

E. London St.

Brunswick St.

Elgin St.

Montgomery St.

Bellevue

London St.

Broughton St.

Barony St.

Albany St.

York Pl.

Picardy Pl.

St. Andrew St.

Elder St.

Gayfield Square

Union St.

Forth St.

Leith Walk

To Leith

Hillside Cr.

London Road

Royal Terrace

Royal Terrace

Greenside Row

SCOTLAND

Edinburgh

Glasgow

20 mi

20 km

ENGLAND

35

36

37

St. James Centre

St. Andrew Square

Observatory

Calton Hill

CALTON

Nelson Monument

National Monument

Regent Gardens

Regent Road

Abbeyhill

Abbeyhill

Abbeyhill

Waterloo Pl.

Lincoln Monument

Burns Monument

Holyrood Abbey

Princes Street

Scott Monument

Edinburgh Waverley Station

North Bridge

Calton Rd.

Calton Rd.

Canongate

Palace of Holyroodhouse

34

Jeffery St.

E. Market St.

Canongate Kirk

Museum of Edinburgh

Scottish Parliament

Market St.

Cockburn St.

South Bridge

High St.

St. Mary's St.

(Royal Mile)

St. John St.

Holyrood Rd.

CANONGATE

Our Dynamic Earth

HOLYROOD PARK

33

32

31

30

29

28

25

Bank St.

23

24

George IV Bridge

St. Giles' Cathedral

OLD TOWN

Cowgate

National Library

Chambers St.

Greyfriars Kirk

Royal Museum

Forrest Rd.

Museum of Scotland

Teviot Pl.

Potterow

University of Edinburgh

Edinburgh Royal Infirmary

Crichton St.

George Square

George Sq. Lane

Meadow Ln.

The Meadows

Melville Dr.

26

27

Leith

100 yds

100 m

38

39

40

Commercial St.

Dock St.

Coburg St.

Quayside St.

Sandport Pl.

Sandport St.

Water of Leith

The Shore

The Shore

Tower St.

Bernard St.

Water St.

Maritime St.

Constitution St.

Burns Statue

Baltic St.

Leith Assembly Rooms

Mitchell St.

43

44

42

41

Mill Lane

Sherriff Brae

Cables Wynd

Henderson St.

Giles St.

Tollbooth Wynd

Leith Town Hall

Queen Charlotte St.

St. Mary's

Walk

Great Junction St.

Yardheads

Henderson St.

Giles St.

Coatfield Ln.

Leith Links

45

89

Edinburgh has a grand total of five Michelin-starred restaurants, and reservations are recommended at all of them. In New Town, **number one** (© 0131/557-6727; www.restaurant numberone.com) at the Balmoral Hotel (p. 108) is renowned for its innovative Scottish- and French-influenced cuisine presented in a traditional setting. Open daily, a fixed-price, three-course dinner costs £62, and vegetarian and tasting menus are also available. Also in New Town, the new Michelin star on the block is the sumptuous **21212** (© 0130/ 523-1030; www.21212restaurant.co.uk) on Royal Terrace. Housed in a listed Georgian building, 21212's flamboyant decor and modern French cuisine has wowed critics. Open Tuesday through Saturday, lunch costs between £26 for two courses and £46 for four; a five-course dinner is £69. 21212 also features four grand designer bedrooms with rates starting from £175 per night.

In Leith, **The Plumed Horse** (© 0131/ 554-5556; www.plumedhorse.co.uk) on Henderson Street is led by chef Tony Borthwick. Fine Scottish-influenced cuisine is complemented by the work of local artists gracing the restaurant walls. Open Tuesday through Saturday, a four-course lunch costs £26 and a three-course dinner £55. Nearby on The Shore, top Scottish chef Martin Wishart opened his Leith restaurant in 1999 and snagged Edinburgh's first Michelin star in 2001. Still one of the top tables in the city, restaurant **Martin Wishart** (© 0131/553-3557; www.martin-wishart.co.uk) is epitomized by simple, refined style and creative French-styled cuisine. Open Tuesday through Saturday, lunch costs £29 and a three-course dinner is £65. Leith's third Michelin star belongs to **The Kitchin** (© 0131/555-1755; www.thekitchin.com) on Commercial Quay. Scottish chef Tom Kitchin creates seasonally inspired menus from the best produce Scotland has to offer. Open Tuesday through Saturday, the atmosphere is warm and relaxed. A three-course lunch costs £25, while main courses at dinner are about £30 to £33. Kitchin has recently opened a second restaurant, **Castle Terrace** (© 0131/229-1222; www.castle terrarestaurant.com), and transported his winning combination of modern British cuisine and laid-back ambience to Edinburgh's Old Town.

By law all restaurants are nonsmoking and reservations are recommended for Friday and Saturday evenings and on any night of the week during the Festival period (p. 102) and Hogmanay.

Note: For the locations of the restaurants below, see the "Edinburgh Hotels & Restaurants" map on p. 88.

New Town
EXPENSIVE

Dome Bar & Grill ★ INTERNATIONAL Located in a restored Georgian building with an elaborate domed ceiling and amazing classical interior, the Dome is a complex of eating and dining spaces including The Grill, The Club Room, and the more informal Garden Café. The interior is a feast of elaborate columns, sculptures, and marble mosaic floors and the accompanying menus support meat-heavy dishes such as roast breast of Barbary duck, peppered pork steak, and Scottish beef all accompanied by a good wine and champagne menu. At Christmas, larger-than-life decorations transform this already decadent building.

5

Where to Eat

EDINBURGH & THE LOTHIANS

14 George St. ℭ **0131/624-8624.** www.thedomeedinburgh.com. Main courses lunch £12–£25; dinner £13–£29. AE, MC, V. The Grill Room open daily noon–late, The Club Room open Mon–Wed 10am–5pm and Thurs–Sat 10am–late.

MODERATE

A Room in Town ★★ SCOTTISH   Deliberately downbeat, A Room in Town is characterized by wooden floors, loud artwork, excellent food, and a lively atmosphere. This is a real taste of New Town at its most untouristy. Expect melt-in-the-mouth Scottish food such as Isle of Gigha halibut and Highland venison topped with Orkney dark island gravy, all of which can be rounded off with a selection of Scottish and Irish cheeses. If you can't bag a table here, try one of the other restaurants belonging to this small chain including A Room in the West End on William Street and A Room in Leith on Dock Place.

18 Howe St. ℭ **0131/225-8204.** www.aroomin.co.uk. Lunch main courses £9 or 2 courses £13, dinner main courses £13–£19. AE, MC, V. Sun–Thurs noon–2:30pm and 5:30–9:30pm, Fri–Sat noon–3pm and 5:30–10:30pm.

Centotre ★ ITALIAN   Housed in one of George Street's divine classical Georgian masterpieces, Centotre combines beautiful surroundings with first-class Italian cuisine and is one of the finest places to dine in New Town. The interior combines historical gravitas with contemporary modern decor and in doing so creates an upbeat downtown vibe. By day this is a busy cafe, in the evening fine dining prevails and diners can choose from a menu filled with homemade pastas and top-quality pizzas.

103 George St. ℭ **0131/225-1550.** www.centotre.com. Lunch and dinner main courses £12–£18. AE, MC, V. Mon–Sat 7:30am–midnight; Sun 10am–10pm.

IGLU ★ SCOTTISH   Tucked away off a main New Town street, IGLU is a down-to-earth, friendly, simple restaurant that champions wild, organic, and local produce. This fine Edinburgh eatery prides itself on sourcing ethically produced meat and other ingredients and cultivates strong links with local producers in order to guarantee a firsthand knowledge of how and where the food they serve was reared or grown. Menus include dishes such as MacLeod black pudding, wild boar burger, and hare terrine all creatively prepared and accompanied by a strong wine list.

2b Jamaica St. ℭ **0131/476-5333.** www.theiglu.com. Lunch 2 courses £10, dinner main courses £10–£20. AE, MC, V. Tues–Sat 6–10pm, Fri–Sat noon–3pm, Sun 11am–8pm.

Oloroso MODERN BRITISH   Oloroso is known for its rooftop terrace commanding long views of Edinburgh Castle and Fife in the distance—a choice spot for alfresco dining in summer. Veteran chef Tony Singh favors Scottish produce that's served with minimal fuss. A hint of Indian influence sneaks onto the menu with dishes such as Uttapam—South Indian-style sour rice flour pancakes—complementing the likes of smoked salmon with sherry and aged rum.

33 Castle St. ℭ **0131/226-7614.** www.oloroso.co.uk. Lunch 2 courses £20, 3 courses £25; dinner 2 courses £35, 3 courses £40. AE, MC, V. Daily noon–2:30pm and 7–10:30pm.

INEXPENSIVE

The Bon Vivant ★★ 🎁 CONTINENTAL   Discreet and intimate yet rustic around the edges, the Bon Vivant is a warm, inviting, candlelit haven of good food and fine wine. The relatively small menu changes daily and represents exceptional value for money. All main courses hover around the £9 to £10 mark, and options may include wild garlic, artichoke and basil risotto, or braised lamb shank, but it's the before and afters that make this place stand out. As well as normal-sized appetizers and desserts for around £4, diners can choose bite-sized amounts for £1 and sample as many different dishes as they like. Starter bites could include broccoli and sun-dried tomato quiche or duck liver pate, and desserts includes such treats as winter-berry pancakes or rhubarb tart. The accompanying wine list also changes on a regular basis and includes over 30 that you can sample by the glass.

55 Thistle St. ℭ **0131/225-3275.** www.bonvivantedinburgh.co.uk. Main courses £8–£10. AE, MC, V. Daily noon–10pm.

Café Marlayne ★ 🍴 FRENCH For lovers of French food, this bistro-style restaurant is the place to savor superb cuisine in elegant surroundings. This intimate, wood-floored restaurant is busy with business folk during the day and transforms itself into a more romantic candlelit experience at night. Lunch options feature grilled mackerel fillets with watercress, crushed potatoes, and mustard sauce, while dinner main courses include rose veal chops or whole baked sea bass. Vegetarian options are available on request. Café Marlayne recently opened a more contemporary branch on Antigua Street at the top of Leith Walk, thus transporting its fine French cuisine to a larger restaurant close to all the nightlife at this end of New Town.

76 Thistle St. ℭ **0131/226-2230.** www.cafemarlayne.com. Lunch main courses £7–£8, dinner courses £12–£15. AE, MC, V. Daily noon–2:30pm and 6–10pm.

The Dogs SCOTTISH/MODERN BRITISH Simple with a twist is the selling point of this recently expanded, popular New Town eatery. As the name suggests, dogs are the theme of the relatively basic bistro-style interior that's enhanced with pictures and cushions with unusual canine images. Both the lunch and dinner menus take simple ingredients and prepare them with flair into imaginative dishes such as braised lamb heart stuffed with prunes and bacon, and winter vegetable pie topped with oat crumble. The company has opened two further Dog restaurants in New Town: The Seadogs seafood restaurant on Rose Street, and Amore Dogs Italian restaurant above The Dogs on Hanover Street. Both stay faithful to the good food with no-frills theme.

110 Hanover St. ℭ **0131/220-1208.** www.thedogsonline.co.uk. Lunch main courses £4–£6, dinner main courses £8–£12. AE, MC, V. Daily noon–4pm and 5–10pm.

Nom De Plume ★★ CONTINENTAL Set high up on Broughton Street, the bistro-style Non De Plume is the kind of place you'll pop in for a quick coffee and end up staying for hours. Pine tables and floors blend with comfy sofas, bookshelves, soft jazz, and the aroma of good food, all of which makes for one of the friendliest, most relaxed, and least pretentious of New Town's many dining options. The long menu includes a wide range of choices for meat and fish eaters as well as vegetarians and champions basic, filling, freshly made food such as hearty stews, fish pies, hot chilies, and nachos.

60 Broughton St. ℭ **0131/478-1372.** Main courses £6–12. MC, V. Mon–Thurs 11am–10:30pm, Fri–Sat 11am–midnight, Sun noon–10pm.

Old Town
EXPENSIVE
The Witchery by the Castle ★ SCOTTISH/FRENCH This iconic Edinburgh eatery has been linked with witchcraft for years and bills itself as the oldest, most haunted restaurant in town; the Hellfire Club supposedly met here during the

Edinburgh's cafe culture is prolific and in summer spreads out across the cobbled streets of both Old and New Town. Just off the Royal Mile in Old Town, **Captain Taylor's Coffee House** (© 0131/556-9756) on South Bridge is a friendly spot to tuck into inexpensive, teas, coffees, cakes, and sandwiches daily from 9am until 5pm; all profits are used by a local charity to help the city's homeless. **Peter's Yard,** on the southern outskirts of Old Town at Quartermile leading from Lauriston Place to the Meadows (© 0131/228-5876; www.petersyard.com), is a coffeehouse and bakery that's popular with Edinburgh students. It's the best place to buy and try artisan breads, pastries, and cookies from 7am weekdays and 9am weekends until 6pm. Also on the south side of the city, **Falko & Konditormeister,** on Bruntsfield Place (© 0131/656-9763; www.falko.co.uk), is famous for its German breads, cakes, and pretzels, which can be sampled Wednesday through Sunday until 6pm at this popular cafe or picked up at their bakery in Gullane or Edinburgh's Farmer's Market (p. 97).

In New Town, tea lovers must take time to sample a cup or two at **Eteaket,** on Fredrick Street (© 0131/226-2982; www.eteaket.co.uk), where the tea menu is as long as your arm and tea accessories can be picked up as the perfect gift. Over a block on Hanover Street, locals queue out of the door on Sunday mornings for breakfast at **Urban Angel** (© 0131/225-6215; www.urban-angel.co.uk), a legend among Edinburgh's cafe aficionados where fresh, local, organic produce is transformed into sandwiches, salads, and tapas. And if you're looking for the best coffee Edinburgh has to offer, head to **Artisan Roast** on Broughton Street (© 0759/059-0667; www.artisanroast.co.uk), where ethically sourced beans from around the world are roasted on-site in "Fatima," a Turkish coffee roaster. Passionate staff will advise on the coffee that's right for you, and you can either linger over a cup inside or grab takeout anytime between 8am weekdays and 10am weekends until 7:30pm.

Middle Ages. When it comes to food, the menu demonstrates creative flair. Fine Scottish meats and seafood are used to create memorable dishes such as Witchery haggis and roast hot-smoked Loch Duart salmon. If you want to take more time to relish the spooky atmosphere, The Witchery has a selection of eight theatrically decorated, Gothic-style suites that start from £295 a night.

352 Castlehill, Royal Mile. © **0131/225-5613.** www.thewitchery.com. Reservations recommended. Fixed-price lunch and pre-theatre menu £30 for 3 courses; dinner main courses £16–£50. AE, DC, MC, V. Daily noon–4pm and 5:30–11:30pm.

MODERATE

The Grain Store ★★ SCOTTISH A local favorite serving some of the best food based on regional produce. The decor is rustic, with exposed stonework and polished wooden floors and each dish from the regularly changing menu is individually prepared to order. From field and stream comes an array of market-fresh ingredients, including game birds in the autumn, forest-fresh mushrooms, lamb from the Borders, Scottish salmon from the rivers, Angus beef, and Perthshire venison. Many dishes such as wild halibut with spinach, almonds, and fennel and mussel veloute are

5

EDINBURGH & THE LOTHIANS | Where to Eat

Edinburgh is full of places to tuck into a quick and inexpensive meal that packs a far higher nutritional punch than the average burger joint. In Old Town, **Always Sunday** (© 0131/662-0667; www.alwayssunday.co.uk) is a light-filled cafe near St. Giles' cathedral on the Royal Mile that dishes up instant, hearty meals such as stuffed baby peppers throughout the day. Nearby on Holyrood Road, **The Holyrood 9A** (© 0131/556-5044; www.fullerthomson.com) is famous for its very long menu of filling gourmet burgers. Also in Old Town at the top of Cockburn Street, **The Baked Potato Shop** (© 0131/225-72) is a local favorite and serves inexpensive soups, haggis samosas, and hot baked potatoes with a wide choice of fillings.

In New Town, **Henderson's** (© 0131/225-6694; www.hendersonsofedinburgh.co.uk) vegetarian bistro/deli on Hanover Street has been selling a full range of hot vegetarian food and take-away sandwiches for 50 years. And **Wannaburger** (© 0131/220-0036; www.wannaburger.com) on Queensferry Street in the West End is an ever-popular burger bar where the burgers are made from pure Aberdeen Scotch beef and free-range Scottish chicken. **Illegal Jacks** (© 0131/662-7499; www.illegaljacks.co.uk) on Lothian Road is a Tex-Mex joint that rolls out burritos, tacos, and quesadillas stuffed with a choice of fillings. Also on Lothian Road, the cafe bars of both the **Filmhouse** cinema (© 0131/228-2688; www.filmhousecinema.com) and **Traverse** theatre (© 0131/228-1404; www.traverse.co.uk) both serve a good selection of quick meals such as large plates of nachos until late into the evening.

prepared simply to preserve their natural flavors. Starters are complemented with homemade bread baked every morning, and you can round off the night with a choice of homemade desserts such as vanilla panna cotta with honey-roasted figs.

30 Victoria St. © **0131/225-7635.** www.grainstore-restaurant.co.uk. Fixed-price lunch £13 for 2 courses, £15 for 3 courses; dinner main courses £14–£28. AE, MC, V. Daily noon–2pm and 6–10pm.

Iggs ★ SPANISH/SCOTTISH   For well over 2 decades, Iggs has attracted a loyal Edinburgh following who keep coming back to enjoy modern Spanish cuisine all created with fine Scottish ingredients and served in intimate surroundings. Lunch and pre-theatre choices could include braised chicory with romesco, goat's cheese, and piquillo peppers; and evening main courses feature dishes such as seared loin of peppered tuna, steamed mussels, and flash-fried razor clams. If you can, bag a table by the window because these feature wide views north over Princes Street and New Town. If you fancy tapas instead, Iggs sister restaurant Barioja serves traditional Spanish tapas all day and is located next door.

15 Jeffrey St. © **0131/557-8184.** www.iggs.co.uk. Fixed price lunch £13, fixed-price pre-theatre £19, dinner main courses £14–£19. AE, DC, MC, V. Mon–Sat noon–2:30pm and 6–10:30pm. Pre-theatre menu served 6–6:45pm.

Ondine ★★ 🎁 SEAFOOD   One of Edinburgh's most heralded new restaurants, Ondine butts up against Hotel Missoni (p. 113) and serves seafood with flair in a cool, contemporary setting. At the heart of the restaurant is the Crustacean Bar, where oysters from all over Britain can be shucked individually or in plates of six.

Menus include a lunch and pre-theatre option as well as the full dinner experience, with dishes such as scallop curry or fruits of the sea served over crushed ice sitting alongside dear old British favorites like fish and chips and mushy peas. A small selection of meat dishes such as age-dried sirloin complement a menu that champions sustainably sourced ingredients.

2 George IV Bridge. ℂ **0131/226-1888.** www.ondinerestaurant.co.uk. Lunch and pre-theatre £16 for 2 courses, £19 for 3 courses, dinner main courses £14–£25. MC, V. Daily noon–3pm and 5:30–10pm.

INEXPENSIVE

David Bann's Vegetarian Restaurant ★ 🍴 VEGETARIAN   Hailed as Edinburgh's best vegetarian restaurant, the food is so good here that even carnivores come to savor the well-flavored dishes whipped up with market-fresh ingredients, often shipped in that day from the fertile fields of Scotland. The atmosphere exudes a relaxed ambience encased in a warm and minimalist decor. The man himself—chef Bann—roams the world for inspiration for his meat-free recipes. Sample dishes include Thai fritter of spiced broccoli with smoked tofu, or organic Udon noodles with ginger red pepper sauce. Leave room for dessert so you can round off the night with ginger and lime ice cream or malt whisky panna cotta.

56-58 St Mary's St. ℂ **0131/556-5888.** www.davidbann.com. Main courses £9–£13; fixed-price brunch £6.25. AE, MC, V. Sun–Thurs noon–10pm, Fri noon–10:30pm, Sat 11am–10:30pm, Sun 11am–10pm.

Leith

MODERATE

Fishers Bistro ★★ INTERNATIONAL/SEAFOOD   Some Edinburgh food writers rate this longstanding seafood restaurant as their favorite in the city, and Fishers is certainly renown for its outstanding seafood both in terms of selection and quality. Fishers sits at the end of Leith's old harbor, and a suitably nautical aura prevails with fishnets, pictures of the sea, and various marine memorabilia spilling out over the restaurant walls. The Miller family founded the restaurant in the early 1990s, and their chefs offer such enticing appetizers as braised baby octopus or some of Scotland's best fish such as grey sole or salmon from Shetland as main courses. Vegetarian and some meat choices are available, such as Aberdeen Angus beef reared on the Scottish Borders. Fishers also owns sister New Town restaurant Fishers in the City on Thistle Street, whose reputation is no less impressive.

1 The Shore. ℂ **0131/554-5666.** www.fishersbistros.co.uk. Main courses £10–£17. AE, MC, V. Mon–Sat noon–4pm and 5–10pm, Sun noon–4pm and 5–10:30pm.

The Ship ★ SEAFOOD   Also known as "The Ship on the Shore" in recognition of its top spot on Leith's old harbor, The Ship is one of the more refined dining experiences this side of town and takes eating seafood up a notch in terms of the ambience of the surroundings and quality of the food. In addition to a lunch and dinner menu, The Ship also prepares a Crustacean and Mollusk menu that includes such regional delights as crab from North Berwick, steamed mussels, and Loch Creran oysters, all of which can be washed down with a glass or two of champagne. A specials board makes the most of the catch of the day. No visit is complete with sampling The Ship's Bloody Mary Oyster Shot, a snip at only £2.50.

24-26 The Shore. ℂ **0131/ 555-0409.** www.theshipontheshore.co.uk. Main courses £17–£22. AE, MC, V. Daily noon–10pm.

INEXPENSIVE

Chop Chop ★ CHINESE   Chop Chop opened this, its second Edinburgh restaurant, in 2010; the first can be found on Morrison Street near Haymarket station, and both are among the city's most popular places to eat. Endorsed by Gordon Ramsey's *F-Word*, Chop Chop's award-winning northern Chinese cuisine keeps locals coming back again and again to tuck into an impressive range of meat and fish dishes and its famous Jiao Zi (boiled dumplings) and Guo Tie (fried dumplings)—small parcels of wheat flour pastry stuffed with all manner of ingredients such as pork and green pepper and beef and chili, all served with the ingredients for you to create your own accompanying sauce. Set meals and banquets are also served in informal, minimalist surrounding looking out over a cobbled, landscaped section of the old port.

76 Commercial Quay. ℰ **0131/553-1818.** www.chop-chop.co.uk. Main courses £8–£10. Wed–Sat and Mon noon–2pm, Sun 12:30–2:30pm, Wed–Fri and Mon 6–10pm, Sat–Sun 5–10pm.

Guchhi ★★ 🍴 INDIAN/SEAFOOD   A newcomer on Leith's growing culinary scene, Guchhi takes the freshest of Scottish seafood and prepares it Indian style, using only the best herbs and spices. The owners and head chefs Vishart Das and Sachin Dhanola trained in restaurants in Goa and seafood restaurants throughout the U.K. before finally creating Guchhi, where they celebrate the food and flavors they know so well. Guchhi takes Indian cooking to a different level and presents clean, unexpected tastes that zing around the mouth. Dishes such as tandoori-smoked mackerel and oven-baked scallops in Bombay duck sauce are just two samples from the sizable menu, which also includes a range of Indian tapas. The cool and contemporary decor is an appealing combination of traditional-styled Indian furnishings set against light blue and white.

9-10 Commercial St. ℰ **0131/555-5604.** www.guchhi.com. Main courses £10–£17. AE, MC, V. Daily noon–11pm.

The King's Wark ★★ SCOTTISH/SEAFOOD   This centuries-old building stands on one of oldest spots in Leith and is a winning combination of traditional pub—complete with thick stone walls, flagstone floors, and crackling open fires—and outstanding, reasonably priced food. This long-time Edinburgh favorite is steeped in a tradition dating back to the days when this patch was a busy port and maintains all the laid-back informality of a local pub. Atmosphere aside, the food is consistently first class. Simple and inventive dishes such as whole roasted sea bream stuffed with herbs alongside the inevitable haggis characterize a changing menu, which is also complemented by a specials board. There's also a good selection of Scottish beers.

36 The Shore. ℰ **0131/554-9260.** www.thekingswark.co.uk. Main courses £9–£16. MC, V. Mon–Sat noon–3pm and 6–10pm, Sun 11am–3pm and 6–10pm.

La Favorita ★ ☺ ITALIAN   La Favorita is simply the best pizza restaurant in Edinburgh and is consistently busy every day. Thin-crust pizzas and calzone are cooked in a huge wood-fired oven fueled with logs from sustainable Scottish forests. Many other Italian favorites fill the menu, including a long list of pasta dishes and starters meant for sharing, and large dishes of Italian ice cream to finish. This is a good choice for families, because kids eat for just £1 and Beano the Clown makes an appearance on Sundays. Service is swift and friendly, and they deliver all over the city.

325-331 Leith Walk. ℰ **0131/554-2430.** www.la-favorita.com. Reservations recommended. Main courses £10–£20. MC, V. Daily noon–11pm.

EDINBURGH & THE LOTHIANS   Where to Eat

Rose Leaf ★★ ☺ SCOTTISH/SEAFOOD   Tucked firmly off Leith's main drag, the Rose Leaf is one of Edinburgh's much-loved gems and one rarely discovered by visitors. This famed and friendly cafe/bar is open from breakfast to dinner, and has the ambience and decor of a quirky, traditional pub and the reputation of being one of the nicest places in the city to eat. Hearty and homemade sums up the style of cuisine, with menus featuring large bowls of creamy *Cullen skink* (smoked fish soup), Aberdeen Angus burgers with Scottish cheddar, and rainbow trout cooked with almonds. A brunch menu is served from 10am to 5pm, and a Mini Me children's menu is filled with healthy options for small appetites. Have one of the Rose Leaf's famous Pot Tails—cocktails for two served in old-fashioned teapots.

23-24 Sandport Place. ℂ **0131/476-5268.** www.roseleaf.co.uk. Reservations for dinner strongly recommended. Main courses £7–£13. MC, V. Daily 10am–10pm.

SHOPPING

In New Town, **Princes Street** is the main shopping area lined with big-name chain stores. At the east end sits **Jenners** (www.houseoffraser.co.uk), Edinburgh's much-loved department store that has been trading since 1838. Head a block north to George Street for more exclusive stores, crowned at its east end off St. Andrews Square with a large branch of **Harvey Nichols** and a cluster of chic shops along Multrees Walk.

In Old Town, the **Royal Mile** is dedicated to tourists and soaked with tartan-focused gift shops, but there are many unusual stores to be discovered along **Cockburn Street** and **Victoria Street.** The **Grassmarket** is the place to shop for vintage clothes. Bargain hunters should take time to explore the many thrift stores in Stockbridge, and food lovers will delight in the weekly **farmers market** (www.edinburghfarmersmarket.co.uk) that gathers on Castle Terrace every Saturday morning. Edinburgh has a couple of small malls, including **Ocean Terminal** (www.oceanterminal.com) in Leith and the **St. James Shopping Centre** (www.stjamesshopping.com) off the east end of Princes Street. Shopping hours are generally Monday through Saturday from 9am to 6pm, and Sunday from 11am to 5pm. On Thursdays, many stores remain open until 7 or 8pm.

Accessories & Jewelry

Alistir Tait   This charming old Edinburgh jewelry shop has a reputation for Scottish minerals such as agates; Scottish gold; and garnets, sapphires, and freshwater pearls. It also sells a superb selection of antique pieces. Of particular interest are pieces made with the rare Scottish cairngorm—quartz drawn from the country's mountains. 116A Rose St. ℂ **0131/225-4105.** www.alistirtaitgem.co.uk.

📎 West End Village

The West End Village (www.westendvillage.org) sits at the far western edge of New Town to the north of Shandwick Place. It's a small, picturesque patch dedicated to the finer things in life and little discovered by visitors. An impressive cluster of independent, upmarket clothes, accessories, and home furnishing stores line these small Georgian streets all interspersed with a selection of fine cafes, pubs, and restaurants.

Fabhatrix Hat lovers can browse through 300 innovative styles of every conceivable type of head ware, all fashioned by local designers and milliners from farther afield. Accompanying accessories include scarves, wraps, hatpins, and jewelry created by textile artists and jewelers. 13 Cowgatehead, off Grassmarket. ✆ **0131/225-9222.** www.fabhatrix.com.

Children

Helios Fountain The children's section of this much-loved, quirky Edinburgh store is one of the best in the city. Here you can pick up old-fashioned and traditional toys such as Kaleidoscopes, spinning tops, and marbles as well as cute soft toys and magic wands. There's also a varied selection of children's books and plenty of unusual adult gifts to keep the grownups happy. 7 Grassmarket. ✆ **0131/229-7884.** www.helios-fountain.co.uk.

Nippers This local children's clothing company creates designer clothes for children at affordable prices. There's a range of styles for newborns to children aged 6. Accessories including shoes, blankets, and toiletries are also on sale alongside a wide choice of fancy dress costumes. 131 Bruntsfield Place. ✆ **0131/228-5086.** www.nippersforkids.com.

Clothes

Bill Baber The shop may be called Bill Baber, but his wife Helen is the fashion designer powerhouse behind this longstanding bastion of Scottish designer clothing. Traditional patterns are adapted into modern designs that include jackets, tops, and dresses fashioned from wool and linen, suitable for both relaxation and formal occasions. 66 Grassmarket. ✆ **0131/225-3249.** www.billbaber.com.

Harwick: Cashmere of Scotland With seasonal collections for both men and women, Harwick is the best place in Edinburgh to buy soft and stylish cashmere. Subtle and bright colors blend into both formal and smart jumpers, dresses, and cardigans, and you can pick up soft cashmere socks, scarves, and gloves. 71 Grassmarket. ✆ **0131/225-8634.** www.hawickcashmere.com.

Joyce Forsyth From this small studio/shop off the Grassmarket, Joyce Forsyth creates and sells her colorful collection of Scottish designer knitwear. Each item is unique and collections include box jackets, flared coats, and hats, all made from completely natural fibers. 42 Candlemaker Row. ✆ **0131/220-4112.** www.joyceforsyth.co.uk.

Totty Rocks A breath of contemporary fresh air, Totty Rocks is a chic women's boutique. Two local female designers create and hand-make a unique collection of stylish and highly wearable clothes that are proudly Scottish yet make a very definite statement of their own. 40 Victoria St. ✆ **0131/226-3232.** www.tottyrocks.co.uk.

Walker Slater Specialists in Scottish tweed, Walker Slater is a good choice for men seeking traditionally inclined but far-from-stuffy clothing. The company originated in the Highlands, and its collections of suits, coats, and linens remain faithful to these roots. There's a limited selection for women, but this is primarily a store for men to indulge in fine clothing Scottish style. 20 Victoria St. ✆ **0131/220-2636.** www.walkerslater.com.

Food & Drink

Demijohn ★★ A cross between a liquor store and an apothecary, this shop is lined with bottles (called demijohns) filled with various spirits, including artisan wines and

Thanks in part to a large student population, Edinburgh is rather rich in vintage clothes outlets. Among the best is the **Rusty Zip** (14 Teviot Pl. ✆ **0131/226 4634**). This retro clothing outlet packs a lot in, whether cool vintage items or cheesy retro accessories. Larger sister outlet is **Armstrong's** at 80 Grassmarket (✆ **0131/220-5557**). Also consider **Elaine's Vintage Clothes** in Stockbridge, where the owner is often on hand to advise shoppers (55 St. Stephen St. ✆ 0131/225-5783), or **Herman Brown,** which specializes in women's and gent's togs from the 1940s to present (151 West Port ✆ **0131/228-2589**). A newcomer to the city is **The Frayed Hem** (45 Cockburn St. ✆ **0131/225-9831**), with furs, tuxes, and silk shirts. Just outside the city in the coastal town of Portobello is newcomer **Urban Igloo** (240a High St., Portobello ✆ **0788/271-3641**), which specializes in 'upcycled' (adapted) clothing alongside the usual retro goods.

meads. Top picks include Bramble whisky liqueur, gooseberry gin, and elderflower vodka, all of which are decanted into the bottle of your choice. Other products include oils and vinegars, and baskets can be delivered anywhere in the world. 32 Victoria St. ✆ **0131/225-3265**. www.demijohn.co.uk.

Iain J Mellis   Follow your nose to this specialist cheese monger to discover a world of delicious Scottish, Irish, French, and other top-quality cheeses. There are often queues out of the door of the Old Town branch, where locals also pick up accompanying products including breads, olives, pickles, cold meats, and coffees. 30A Victoria St. ✆ **0131/226-6215**. www.mellischeese.co.uk.

Valvona & Crolla   This legendary Italian delicatessen is Scotland's oldest and has been selling specialist European foods and fine Italian wine since 1934. Floor-to-ceiling shelves are stocked with pastas, coffees, chocolates, and much more, and large cool counters are lined with continental cheeses, cold meats, and cakes. The store also runs a program of cookery demonstrations and wine-tasting events, and has a food hall in Jenners department store on Princes Street. Elm Row. ✆ **0131/556-6066**. www.valvonacrolla.co.uk.

The Whisky Shop   All branches of this small chain sell whisky and whisky alone. There's a fine range of both single malts and blends to deliberate over with a selection of price tags to match. Scottish products dominate the shelves, but there are also Irish, Japanese, and American whiskies plus a large range of miniatures. 28 Victoria St. ✆ **0131/225-4666**. www.whiskyshop.com.

Gifts

Paper Tiger   This well-established independent stationers is known for its large selection of cards, notebooks, journals, pens, and unusual gifts. Many cards feature Edinburgh scenes or images created by Scottish artists, and the small but eclectic book selection covers subjects from cupcakes to walking in the Cairngorms. 53 Lothian Rd. and 6A-8 Stafford St. ✆ **0131/226-2390**. www.shoppapertiger.com.

Red Door Gallery   Championing artisan jewelry, paintings, prints, and other pieces of art, Red Door is well stocked with gift ideas. There's also a range of quirky cards by local artists. 42 Victoria St. ✆ **0131/477-3255**. www.edinburghart.com.

Studio One   Sister store to Paper Tiger, Studio One is a labyrinth of small basement spaces crammed with all kinds of delightful gifts for the home including soft furnishing and kitchenware. There's also shelf upon shelf of personal gifts including jewelry, toiletries, and toys. 10-14 Stafford St. © **0131/226-5812.** www.shopstudio1.co.uk.

Maps & Prints

The Royal Mile Gallery   The long shelves of this comfortable old gallery are brimming with antique prints of all sizes depicting Edinburgh scenes as well as views from across Scotland and farther afield. Make time to rummage through a table or two piled high with old maps of Scotland and the world; they're all surprisingly reasonably priced. 272 Canongate. © **0131/558-1702.** www.royalmilegallery.com.

Music

Bagpipes Galore   This friendly store is the place for all those who always wanted a set of bagpipes but didn't know where to buy them. Prices start at £250 and go over £1,000. Individual instruction is also available starting at £12 for 30 minutes. Also stop in for CDs of pipe music including marching pipe bands and Scottish favorite the Red Hot Chili Pipers. 82 Canongate. © **0131/556-4073.** www.bagpipe.co.uk.

Coda Music   Coda stocks a blistering selection of both traditional and contemporary folk music. There's a world of Scottish music to choose from, including pipers and Scottish dance and ceilidh. Racks also features CDs of blues, country, and jazz music. 12 Bank St. © **0131/662-7246.** www.codamusic.co.uk.

Tartans & Kilts

Anta   Some of the most stylish tartans are found at Anta. The Victoria Street branch focuses on clothing and stocks fine-quality, often unusual items such as tartan corsets, as well as more traditional skirts and scarves, plus kilts for men. Nearby on Grassmarket a second, much larger branch sells home furnishing including rugs, cushions, and throws. (1) Crockett's Land, Victoria St. © **0131/225-4616.** (2) 73 Grassmarket. © **0131/225-9096.** www.anta.co.uk.

Geoffrey (Tailor) Kiltmakers & Weavers ★   This is the most famous kiltmaker in Edinburgh and past customers have included Sean Connery, Charlton Heston, and Mel Gibson (who favors the tartan design Hunting Buchanan and wore his outfit when he received an award from the Scottish government after filming *Braveheart*). Traditional ladies and gentlemen's kilts are hand-sewn and made to measure, and time should be allowed for the process to be completed. An accompanying array of accessories such as sporrans, kilt pins, Celtic-patterned buckles, and brochures can also be purchased. 57-59 High St. © **0131/557-0256.** www.geoffreykilts.co.uk.

Ness Scotland   There are two branches of this fun store along the Royal Mile selling a range of women's clothes and accessories, some of which are tartan inspired, others in colors to match. The soft tartan rugs, hats, and handbags are popular with locals as well as tourists. (1) 367 High St. © **0131/226-5227.** (2) 336-340 Lawnmarket. © **0131/225-8815.** www.nessbypost.com.

Tartan Weaving Mill & Exhibition   This shopping venue and attraction is run by Geoffrey Tailor Kiltmaker (see above) and introduces visitors to all aspects of the wonderful world of tartan. You can view working looms and learn the history behind

Scotland's national dress as well as being fitted and photographed in full Highland Dress. Whether it's a rug, scarf, or kilt you're after, the knowledgeable staff will help you decide which tartan is right for you. 555 Castlehill, Royal Mile. ℂ **0131/226-1555.** www. geoffreykilts.co.uk.

SPECIAL EVENTS & FESTIVALS

Edinburgh's event and festival year begins with the New Year itself and the city's world-famous **Hogmanay** celebrations, which now spread over 4 days from December 30 to January 2. The celebrations include a thousands-strong torchlight procession and burning of a Viking longboat, and events such as the 1pm run down the Royal Mile and "The Loony Dook" dip in the Firth of Forth at South Queensferry on New Year's Day. New Year's Eve, however, is the big night during which Princes Street is sectioned off for a ticket-only street party featuring big-name bands. If want a ticket to this sell-out event, keep an eye on the Hogmanay website (ℂ **0844/894-2011;** www.edinburghshogmanay.com) and buy early. However, be assured that the spectacular midnight fireworks that explode from Edinburgh's castle can be seen all over the city. Hogmanay is now part of a wider event called **Edinburgh Sparkles** (www. edinburghsparkels.com), which celebrates 6 weeks of winter in the city including Christmas and New Year and features a fairground, ice-skating rink, and continental market in Princes Street Gardens.

January 25 is **Burns Night,** *the* night when Scots the world over gather to consume the traditional supper of haggis, *neeps* (turnips), and *tatties* (potatoes), accompanied by a wee dram of whisky, while listening to recitals of the works of Scotland's Bard, Robert "Rabbie" Burns, whose birthday is being celebrated. Burns suppers are held in restaurants all over town.

Beltane is an age-old celebration marking the mid-point between the spring equinox and summer solstice, and in Edinburgh every April 30 the **Betlane Fire Society** (www.beltane.org) takes to the summit of Carlton Hill to reenact in spectacular style the mythical union of the May Queen and the Green Man. Around 10,000 people hike up the hill to see the event, and tickets can be bought in advance via the Fire Society's website (see above) or at the box office on Regent Road at the foot of Carlton Hill on the night. The Beltane Fire Society also performs an equally fire-infused **Samhuinn** celebration every October 31. Part street theatre, part carnival, part pagan ritual, this colorful event is free and starts with a procession leading down the Royal Mile from Edinburgh Castle to Parliament Square where the last celebration of summer is re-enacted before winter takes over the land.

Science takes over the city in April when the **Edinburgh International Science Festival** (ℂ **0131/553-0320;** www.sciencefestival.co.uk) encourages all ages to explore, learn, and be amazed by the wonderful world of science and technology.

In June, it's Leith's turn to celebrate its heritage and culture via the **Leith Festival** (ℂ **0131/555-4104;** www.leithfestival.com), which spreads over 10 days in the middle of the month. In the second half of June, the **Edinburgh International Film Festival** (ℂ **0131/228-4051;** www.edfilmfest.org.uk) burns bright across cinema screens around the city. At the end of July, just before Edinburgh's festival season kicks off in earnest, the **Edinburgh Jazz and Blues Festival** (ℂ **0131/467-5200;** www. edinburghjazzfestival.com), the largest of its kind in Britain, hosts around 120 concerts around the city.

EDINBURGH'S famous FESTIVALS

August is the jewel in the crown of Edinburgh's festival year, and throughout this month the city is transformed by a clutch of world-class festivals celebrating theatre, music, opera, dance, comedy, street theatre, literature, art, politics, and diversity, to name but a few. This can be a confusing time because many people think that just one festival is taking place when in fact there are many, and navigating your way through the increasing number of brochures and websites promoting the literally thousands of events that take place during this period can be mind-boggling for the first time visitor.

The festival that started it all is the **Edinburgh International Festival** (✆ **0131/473-2000;** www.eif.co.uk), which has been running since 1947 and brings internationally renowned performers from across the worlds of theatre, opera, music, and dance to the city's prominent venues. You can get information from the festival's offices and box office at **The Hub,** an old church on Castle Hill at the junction between the Royal Mile and Johnston Terrace; it's open daily year-round.

The **Edinburgh Festival Fringe** (✆ **0131/226-0026;** www.edfringe. com), commonly known as merely "the Fringe," was created alongside the International Festival in 1947 as an opportunity for anybody—professional or amateur—to put on a show wherever they can find an empty stage or street corner. The Fringe has grown to become the biggest arts festival in the world and is an outpouring of creativity from around the world, encompassing street performers, comedy, offbeat theatre, late-night cabaret, and much more. The Fringe's box office and shop is located on 180 High St. (the Royal Mile).

One of the most exciting August spectacles is the **Royal Edinburgh Military Tattoo** (✆ **0131/225-1188;** www. edintattoo.co.uk), which takes place over 3 weeks every night except Sundays on the floodlit esplanade in front of Edinburgh Castle. First performed in 1950, the Tattoo features the precision marching of the Massed Band of Her

ENTERTAINMENT & NIGHTLIFE

Edinburgh is justifiably proud of its thriving year-round, world-class cultural scene that spreads a rich array of theatre, film, dance, and music events across the city's many venues. The West End around Lothian Road is the focus of a number of theatres and cinemas plus some clubs, while in Old Town the area around Cowgate and Grassmarket boasts a lively, mainly student-focused nightlife scene. In New Town, a number of trendy bars have blossomed along George Street, but there are many more traditional pubs to be enjoyed along Rose Street and West Register Street just off the east end of Princes Street. The heart of Edinburgh's gay community beats around the **Broughton Street** area towards the top of Leith Walk. For detailed, up-to-date information on all entertainment options, pick up a copy of *The List* (£2.20), or check listings online at **www.list.co.uk**.

The Performing Arts

THEATRE Edinburgh has many theatres. At the mainstream end of the market, options include the **Edinburgh Playhouse,** 18–22 Greenside Place (✆ **0844/847-1660;** www.edinburghplayhouse.org.uk), the city's largest theatre whose program

Majesties Royal Marines and other regiments from around the world, along with Highland dancing, motorcycle displays, and the heart-stirring massed pipes and drums bands, all concluding by the poignant spectacle of the Lone Piper playing high up on the castle ramparts. The Tattoo Office and Shop is at 32 Market St. behind Waverley station.

The other major festivals that take place during August include the **Edinburgh International Book Festival** (℡ 0845/373-5888; www.edbookfest. co.uk; see the box on p. 84); the **Edinburgh Art Festival** (℡ 0131/226-6558; www.edinburghartfestival.com), which presents the best in Scottish and international art in galleries across the city; and the **Edinburgh Comedy Festival** (www.edcomfest.com). Less well known is the family-friendly **Edinburgh Mela Festival** (℡ 0131/332-2888; www. edinburgh-mela.co.uk), which showcases the creativity of the city's ethnic minority communities; the **Festival of Spirituality and Peace** (℡ 0131/221-2277; www.festivalofspirituality.org.uk), organized by the Edinburgh Inter-Faith Association; and the **Festival of Politics** (℡ 0131/348-5200; www.festivalof politics.org.uk), which is hosted by the Scottish Parliament.

Tickets to most festivals go on sale well before August and can be bought in advance via the individual festivals' websites, telephone reservation lines, or in person at their box offices. Be warned that tickets for many shows at the International Festival and Military Tattoo sell out months in advance, and so book early to avoid being disappointed.

There are many ways to save money on tickets, such as booking for the lower-priced preview shows at the start of the festival season and making the most of the Fringe's 2-for-1 ticket deals that can be bagged on the first Monday and Tuesday of the festival. The Fringe also operates a Half Price Hut by the National Gallery Complex on the Mound, selling a limited number of cheap tickets for shows on the day of purchase. Also look out for discount coupons in newspapers such as *The Scotsman* and make the most of the hundreds of free shows that take place across most of the festivals.

focuses on large-scale touring musicals, comedy, and dance; and the **Festival Theatre**, 13–29 Nicolson St., and **King's Theatre,** 2 Leven St., both managed by the same company and tickets for their wide repertoire of classical entertainment can be booked by phone or online (℡ 0131/529-6000; www.fctt.org.uk). The resident company of **Royal Lyceum Theatre,** Grindlay Street (℡ 0131/248-4848; www.lyceum.org.uk), produces a strong program of work from major and establishing playwrights. The **Traverse Theatre,** Cambridge Street (℡ 0131/228-1404; www.traverse.co.uk), is funded to present new work by contemporary Scottish writers. The **Scottish Story Telling Centre,** 43 High St. (℡ 0131/556-9579; www.scottishstorytellingcentre. co.uk), presents a regular program of storytelling and music events in its small performance space.

BALLET, OPERA & CLASSICAL MUSIC   Performances by the **Scottish Ballet** and the **Scottish Opera** can be enjoyed at the **Edinburgh Playhouse** (see above). The **Scottish Chamber Orchestra** perform at the **Queen's Hall,** Clerk Street (℡ 0131/668-2019; www.thequeenshall.net). Edinburgh's other major music venue is the **Usher Hall** (℡ 0131/228-1155; www.usherhall.co.uk), which presents mainly classical concerts but also some jazz, rock, and pop.

FOLK MUSIC Folk music is performed in a number of pubs around the city such as **Sandy Bells** (℃ **0131/2252-751**), 25 Forrest Rd. Some hotels regularly feature traditional Scottish music in the evenings, including **King James Hotel,** 107 Leith St. (℃ **0871/376-9016;** www.thistle.com), whose **Jamie's Scottish Evening** is presented daily at 7pm from April to October and includes dinner and a show. Also look out for information on the **Scots Music Group** (℃ **0131/555-7668;** www. scotsmusic.org), who organize regular ceilidhs in the city.

FILM Edinburgh's Lothian Road area is filled with choices for the dedicated cinemagoer. At the Princes Street end, the **Filmhouse,** 88 Lothian Rd. (℃ **0131/228-2688;** www.filmhousecinema.com), is Scotland's premiere specialist cinema and shows a diverse range of mainstream, independent, and repertory titles. At the far south end of this area, the Art Deco **Cameo,** 38 Home St. (℃ **0871/902-5723;** www.picturehouses.co.uk), is one of Edinburgh's best-loved cinemas and the place to catch new, mainly mainstream releases. Midway between the two is a multiscreened **Odeon,** 18 Lothian Rd. (℃ **0871/2244-007;** www.odeon.co.uk).

COMEDY Open 7 nights a week, **The Stand** (℃ **0131/558-7272;** www.the stand.co.uk) on York Place in New Town is hailed by many as one of the world's best comedy clubs and is the place to catch both raw talent and established acts.

The Club & Music Scene

Bongo Club · Tucked away in a quiet corner close to Our Dynamic Earth (p. 85), Bongo is one of the coolest clubs in town and hosts a varied program of club nights. The no-nonsense dance floor regularly rocks to the beat of hip-hop, dub, funk, reggae, ceilidhs, and much more. Those who need to rest their dancing feet can escape to an upstairs bar and exhibition space. 37 Holyrood Rd. ℃ **0131/558-7604.** www.thebongoclub. co.uk. Hours vary. Cover £3–£6.

Cabaret Voltaire A thriving, atmospheric club, housed in some of Old Town's underground vaults, Cabaret Voltaire is one of the best to be found around the Cowgate area. Dance music characterizes this multi-floor, cave-like venue, which is open every night of the week and hosts a strong program of live gigs alongside regular club nights such as Killer Kitsch on Sundays. 36 Blair St. ℃ **0131/220-6176.** www.thecabaret voltaire.com. Cover free–£8.

Ghillie-Dhu In no time at all Ghillie-Dhu has established itself as one of Edinburgh's most popular drinking and entertainment spots. This large venue maintains all the history and tradition of the old building it's housed in, and yet is also a thoroughly modern pub, restaurant, and performance venue. Live music takes to the stage every night alongside regular ceilidhs and tea dances. 2 Rutland Place. ℃**0131/222-9930.** www.ghillie-dhu.co.uk. Daily noon–3pm.

HMV Picturehouse HMV Picturehouse took over this old Art Deco cinema a few years ago and in transforming it into a mainstream music venue retained many of the building's attractive old features. The auditorium still has all the feel of the movies, but today the stage where the screen once stood hosts a range of gigs from new bands to those still going strong, alongside club nights. This is a popular venue with all ages and has the added advantage of cheaper drinks than many of the city's other clubs. 31 Lothian Rd. ℃ **0131/221-2280** or ℃ **0843/221-0100.** http://venues.meanfiddler.com/hmv-picture-house. Tickets £4–£20.

Leslies Bar (☏ 0131/667-7205; www.lesliesbar.com), with its wood paneling and thistle wallpaper, is a traditional old pub on Ratcliffe Terrace on the south side of town with a long whisky menu featuring malts from across Scotland. In New Town, whisky fans should aim for **Dirty Dicks** (☏ 0131/260-9920), an old flagstone-floored pub at the west end of Rose Street established in 1859 and crammed with eclectic memorabilia and 150 different malts in racks above the bar. While in Edinburgh, serious whisky aficionados are encouraged to make the pilgrimage to the Scotch Malt Whisky Society (☏ 0131/554-3451; www.smws.co.uk), tucked away on Giles Street in Leith. A £10 day membership to the society has to be purchased to enter their **Vaults** bar, which sits in a centuries-old warehouse and stocks around 1,300 single malts that can be sampled by the dram. The Vaults opens daily from 10am (11am on Sun) until late, and the adjacent **Vintners Rooms** (☏ 0131/554-6767; www.vintnersrooms.com) restaurant opens for lunch and dinner Tuesday through Saturday.

The Jazz Bar   Soak up some jazz at this smooth and intimate subterranean club dedicated to jazz and jazz alone. Top names play its small stage as the audience relaxes at candlelit tables or in alcove seating. Take time to view the photographs of previous gigs that line the stairwell. Teatime gigs kick off Tuesdays through Saturdays at 6pm, early and late evenings gigs occur daily at 9pm and midnight respectively, and there's an extra session on Saturday afternoons at 3pm. 1A Chambers St. ☏ 0131/220-4298. www.thejazzbar.co.uk. Covers vary from donations to the musicians to £10 for special events.

Voodoo Rooms   This lavish bar, club, and restaurant fills a classical New Town property and has quickly established itself as one of the chicest venues in the city. The Voodoo Rooms spreads out over three bars and two entertainment spaces—the Ballroom and Speakeasy—which host an eclectic mix of events including dance, live music, cabaret, and club nights. 19a West Register St. ☏ 0131/556-7060. www.thevoodoorooms.com. Bar open Mon–Thurs 4pm–1am, Fri–Sat noon–1am. Event tickets £3–£10.

Pubs & Bars

Bow Bar   A long established bar in the heart of Old Town, the Bow Bar is a slice of traditional Edinburgh hospitality and a firm favorite with locals. Choose from a strong selection of real ales that are still drawn through tall founts, and a superb selection of 150 single-malt whiskies from virtually every corner of Scotland. Antique phonographs, pendulum clocks, and an assortment of other old fixtures and fittings add to the suitably ambient atmosphere. 80 West Bow. ☏ 0131/226-7667. Mon-Sat noon-11:30pm, Sun 12:30-11pm.

Café Royal Circle Bar ★   This historic establishment opened the doors of its present location in 1863 and is one of Edinburgh's most famous bars. Café Royal is also renowned for its opulent oyster bar now serving a wider selection of Scottish fare and haunted by its very own ghost. 19 W. Register St. ☏ 0131/556-1884. www.caferoyal.org.uk. Mon-Wed 11am-11pm, Thurs 11am-midnight, Fri-Sat 11am-1am, Sun 12:30pm-11pm.

5

EDINBURGH & THE LOTHIANS | Entertainment & Nightlife

Divino ★   Thanks to Enomatic technology that hermetically seals a bottle of wine once it has been opened, this sleek new Italian wine bar sells around 40 wines by the glass. Soak up the new ambiance of this solid Old Town building while sampling as many different vinos as you like, all of which can be accompanied by Italian antipasti. Regular wine-tasting nights allow customers to educate their palettes and make new friends. 5 Merchant St. ℂ **0131/225-1770.** www.divinoedinburgh.com. Sun–Fri 3pm–midnight, Sat noon–1am.

Kenilworth   For anyone wanting to glean a sense of fine old Edinburgh pubs, the Kenilworth is a must. This glorious old establishment is situated in the heart of Rose Street, which was the city's traditional drinking alley in the days before the trendy new bars of George Street burst onto Edinburgh's nightlife. Characterized by an old-fashioned central bar, the Kenilworth shines with wood and brass and cozy nooks and remains one of the finest spots in New Town to down a pint of real ale. 152-154 Rose St. ℂ **0131/226-1773.** Sun–Thurs 10am–11pm, Fri–Sat 10am–1am.

Queens Arms 🎁   The Queens Arms is a recent addition to the New Town pub scene but feels like an establishment that's been around for a long time. There's a good mix of tradition and gleaming new pub frequented by a wide age range. Drinks include a fine selection of wines, whiskies (including a Japanese whisky), ales, and cocktails. 49 Fredrick St. ℂ **0131/225-1045.** www.queensarmsedinburgh.com. Mon–Sat 11am–1am, Sun 12:30pm–1am.

5 Gay Bars & Clubs

C. C. Bloom's   Named after Bette Midler's character in *Beaches*, C. C. Bloom's is one of Edinburgh's most enduring gay spots. The upstairs bar offers drink deals and events including karaoke and DJ nights, while the dance floor of the downstairs club champions a wide range of music. The next-door bar **Café Habana** is also one of Scotland's most popular gay bars and a good spot for a round or two of pre-club drinks. 23-24 Greenside Place. ℂ **0131/556-9331.** Mon–Sat 6pm–3am, Sun 3pm–3am.

New Town Bar   Adjacent to the corner of Queen Street, this New Town street-level pub is a laid-back, friendly spot for a drink. Regular events include quiz nights and songs around the piano on Sunday afternoons. The basement club with its resident DJ opens 10pm to 2am on Friday and Saturday nights and hosts regular men-only events such as *Bears in the Basement*. 26B Dublin St. ℂ **0131/538-7775.** www.newtown bar.co.uk. Mon–Thurs noon–1am, Fri–Sat noon–2am, Sun 12:30pm–1am.

Regent Bar   The Regent straddles a corner of a crossroads in the Abbeyhill suburb to the north of the Palace of Holyroodhouse and is one of Edinburgh's best-loved gay bars. The atmosphere is relaxed and friendly and a good range of beer and wines can be enjoyed while sinking into comfy sofas. A menu of basic, hearty food such as nachos and lasagna is also on offer (main courses £6–£9). 2 Montrose Terrace. ℂ **0131/6618-198.** Mon–Sat 11am–1am, Sun noon–1am.

SPECTATOR SPORTS & OUTDOOR ACTIVITIES

Spectator Sports

FOOTBALL   Like many Europeans, Edinburghers have a real zeal for football (soccer). There are two local teams—the Heart of Midlothian (www.heartsfc.co.uk), otherwise known as "Hearts," and Hibernian (www.hibernianfc.co.uk), also known as "Hibs"—who battle each other and other national and European teams. Hearts' home ground is **Tynecastle Park,** Gorgie Road (© 0131/337-7200), and Hibs' home ground is **Easter Road Stadium,** Albion Place (© 0131/661-2159). Games are traditionally played on Saturday afternoons and often televised in pubs throughout Scotland. Tickets are around £22 for adults, £12 for under-18s.

HORSE RACING   Place your bets at the **Musselburgh Racecourse,** Linkfield Road (© 0131/665-2859; www.musselburgh-racecourse.co.uk), about 4 miles east of Edinburgh. In summer, the races are on a flat circular track, but in winter, the more elaborate National Hunt format challenges horses and riders to a series of jumps and obstacle courses. Admission is £15 to £25 for adults, and free for under-16s.

RUGBY   Home of the Scottish Rugby Union, **Murrayfield Stadium,** Murrayfield (© 0131/346-5000; www.scottishrugby.org), is about 1 mile west of Edinburgh. Matches mainly take place from September to April, usually on Saturdays. The top fixtures are those of the Six Nations Championship between Scotland, Wales, England, Ireland, Italy, and France. Other matches are usually between Edinburgh or Glasgow and other U.K. teams. Ticket prices range from £15 for adults and £5 for under-18s to £30 for adults and £15 for under-18s.

Outdoor Activities

GOLF   Edinburgh Leisure (www.edinburghleisuregolf.co.uk) manages six golf courses around the city. Fees per 18 holes are £18 to £20 on weekdays and £21 to £24 at weekends, plus club rental. Courses include the par-71, 6,300-yard **Silverknowes,** Silverknowes Parkway (© 0131/336-3843; www.silverknowesgc.com), 3 miles west of the city center; the par-67, 5,418-yard **Craigentinny,** Fillyside Road (© 0131/554-7501), 3 miles east of Edinburgh; the par-71, 5,731-yard **Braid Hills,** Braid Hills Approach (© 0131/447-666; www.braids-united.co.uk), 3 miles south of Edinburgh's city center; and the par-70, 5,697-yard **Carrick Knowe,** Glen Devon Park (© 0131/554-1096; www.carrickknowegolfclub.co.uk), which is 5 miles west of Edinburgh.

SAILING/KAYAKING   Experience the waters of the Firth of Forth firsthand by contacting the **Port Edgar Sailing Centre,** Port Edgar, South Queensferry (© 0131/331-3330; www.portedgar.co.uk), about 9 miles west of the city center. Between Easter and mid-October, it offers instruction in small-craft sailing, powerboating, and sea and river kayaking and rents dinghies for £20 an hour. April to September, the center is open daily 9am to 7:30pm, in winter daily 9am to 4:30pm.

SNOWBOARDING/SKIING   The **Midlothian Snowsports Centre** (© 0131/445-4433; www.midlothian.gov.uk) in the Pentland Hill Regional Park on Biggar Road, manages two main and two nursery artificial slopes. Prices for the first hour are £12 adults and £8 children, including equipment rental. The center is open Monday through Friday 9:30am to 9pm and weekends from 9:30am to 7pm.

TENNIS   Edinburgh Leisure (© 0131/458-2100; www.edinburghleisure.co.uk) manages a number of tennis courts around the city including **Craiglockhart Tennis Centre,** 177 Colinton Rd. (© 0131/443-0101), who have a number of indoor and outdoor courts. Reservations are required; indoor courts cost £23 per hour, outdoor courts cost £8.50 per hour. The center is open Monday through Friday 9am to 10:30pm, Saturday 9am to 6pm, and Sunday 9am to 10pm. Edinburgh Leisure also manages a number of outdoor public courts behind George Square, on the north side

FESTIVAL accommodation

It should come as no surprise that throughout August and early September when Edinburgh's festivals (see box p. 102) are in full swing, demand and rates for accommodation in the city both increase dramatically. If you're planning to stay in Edinburgh at this time it pays to shop around and book well in advance. Many visitors choose to rent an apartment during the festival period as it often makes economic sense and a large number of sublets are available to choose from—many are the homes of Edinburgh residents seeking to escape the city at its busiest. In addition to the vacation rental companies listed above, these companies manage festival rentals: **Edinburgh Festival Rentals** (© 0131/ 221-1646; www.edinburghfestivalrentals. com), **Festival Flats** (© 01620/810-620; www.festivalflat.net), and **The Festival Partnership** (© 0131/478-1294; http://edinburghfestival.net).

of the public park known as the Meadows. These are staffed daily from noon to 8pm April to September and cost £8.50 per hour.

WHERE TO STAY

Edinburgh boasts a dizzying array of accommodation from iconic opulent hotels to a plethora of inexpensive hostels and seemingly limitless guesthouses. The city has upped its game over the past few years, particularly at the luxury end of the market where bold new boutique hotels rub shoulders with more traditional, long established options. The majority of Edinburgh's hotels are gathered in New Town and within easy walking distance of the city's main attractions and nightlife. Old Town is popular with hostelling students but is also home to some of Edinburgh's more unusual luxury hotels. Many of Edinburgh's guesthouses and B&Bs are to be found south of Old Town around Edinburgh University and to the west of New Town around Haymarket train station and Murrayfield Stadium (p. 107). All vary in quality and cost, and many are within walking distance of the city center. Those looking to rent a vacation apartment will find plenty to choose from; companies to try include **Edinburgh Holiday Lets** (© 07711/921-903; www.edinburghholidaylets.co.uk), **Dickins** (© 0131/ 558-1108; www.dickins.co.uk), and **Edinburgh Self-Catering** (© 0131/478-0934; www.edinburghselfcatering.co.uk).

If you're visiting Edinburgh during the festival period (see box below), for Hogmanay, and anytime an international rugby match is scheduled at Murrayfield Stadium (check the "Fixtures" section of the Scottish Rugby website at www. scottishrugby.org), reserving a place to stay well in advance is essential.

New Town

VERY EXPENSIVE

Balmoral Hotel ★★★ When this legendary hotel opened in 1902 it was the grandest in northern Britain and today, thanks to a US$35-million restoration and continued refurbishment, it remains top of the luxury options for those seeking a traditional Scottish experience. The Balmoral commands the east end of Princes Street and is famous for its soaring clock tower—one of Edinburgh's landmarks. Kilted doormen welcome visitors and epitomize the formal yet friendly approach adopted by hotel staff. All the Balmoral's sophisticated rooms and suites are influenced by Scottish heritage and incorporate generous-sized marble finished bathrooms, and some claim romantic views of the castle and Old Town. Dining options include the opulent **Number One** (see the "Michelin-Starred Edinburgh" box on p. 90) and the more convivial brasserie **Hadrian's.** Piano-accompanied afternoon tea is served in the **Palm Court,** which in the evenings is a choice spot for a glass of chilled vintage champagne. The exclusive **Balmoral Spa** is one of Scotland's best urban spas and a haven of relaxation and fitness in the heart of the city.

1 Princes St., EH2 2EQ. www.thebalmoralhotel.com. © **888/667-9477** in the U.S., or 0131/556-2414. Fax 0131/557-3747. 188 units. £360–£555 double; from £670 suite. AE, DC, MC, V. Valet parking £25 per overnight. **Amenities:** 2 restaurants; 2 bars; pool (indoor); health club and spa; concierge; room service. *In room:* A/C, TV, fax, hair dryer, Internet (£15 per day).

Caledonian Hilton Edinburgh ★ The imposing Caledonian is one of Edinburgh's landmark hotels and combines all the luxury you'd expect of a Hilton hotel with a prime central location. Public areas are reminiscent of Edwardian splendor, while the bedrooms (many of which are exceptionally spacious) are conservatively styled with reproduction furniture. The rooms on the upper floors are the smallest, and those at the front and east side of the hotel boast commanding views of Edinburgh Castle and Princes Street Gardens. Nestled among the Edwardian decor is **Henry J Beans** an American-style diner; other dining options include the rather more formal **Pompadour Restaurant.** Guests can work off any indulgence at the on-site **LivingWell Health Club,** which includes an indoor pool and spa.

Princes St., EH1 2AB. www.hilton.co.uk/caledonian. © **0131/222-8888.** Fax 0131/222-8889. 249 units. £159–£339 double; £259–£1,009 suite. Children 15 and under stay free in parent's room. AE, DC, MC, V. Parking £15. **Amenities:** 5 restaurants; 5 bars; pool (indoor); gym; concierge. *In room:* TV, minibar, hair dryer, Wi-Fi (£15 per day).

The Chester Residence ★★★ ☺ Tucked away in a quiet corner of the West End, the Chester Residence is a collection of well-appointed suites spread over four immaculate Georgian townhouses and offers an appealing combination of an apartment of your own alongside all the services you'd expect of a top-rated hotel. These award-winning suites come with well-equipped kitchens and sitting rooms and are fully decked out with modern technology, including enormous plasma TVs. Mews suites at street level also have their own private gardens, while the rooftop penthouses claim magnificent views and roll-top baths. The main reception area includes a bar and the many services that can be arranged for guests include in-room dining and spa treatments.

9 Rothesay Place, EH3 7SL. www.chester-residence.com. © **0131/226-2075.** Fax 0131/226-2191. 19 units. £205–£425 suite. AE, MC, V. Parking £25 for 24 hours. **Amenities:** Bar; concierge; room service; babysitting. *In room:* TV/DVD, kitchen, hair dryer, iPod docking station, Wi-Fi (free).

The George ★★ The George commands a prime and prominent spot near St. Andrews Square and is a cocoon of elegant luxury in the heart of an area busy with shops and restaurants. Designed by famed architect Robert Adam, the George opened in 1755, was transformed into a hotel in 1972, and has recently emerged from a £20-million restoration looking better than ever. Public areas exhibit all the style and gentility of a country house, while the various-sized bedrooms, which have undergone frequent refurbishments, have a distinctly more modern feel; the best units are those with views and the quietest are those at the back of the hotel. The **Tempus** restaurant and bar epitomizes New Town at its most chic and is popular with guests and non-guests.

19–21 George St., EH2 2PB. www.principal-hayley.com. ☎ **0131/225-1251.** Fax 0131/226-5644. 249 units. £189–£212 double; £297–£356 suite. AE, DC, MC, V. **Amenities:** Restaurant; bar; concierge; baby-sitting. *In room:* A/C, TV, minibar, hair dryer, Wi-Fi (free).

The Glasshouse ★   This striking hotel is an appealing combination of old and new. Guests enter through the impressive surviving facade of Lady Glenorchy church that once stood on this spot behind which the contemporary hotel opens out. Despite stiff competition in recent years, it remains one of the most stylish places to stay in town. Modern, well-furnished bedrooms and suites lie behind floor-to-ceiling windows opening to panoramic views of Edinburgh. The hotel's rooftop garden is reason enough to stay.

2 Greenside Place, EH1 3AA. www.glasshouse-hotel.co.uk. ☎ **0131/525-8200.** Fax 0131/525-8205. 65 units. £355 double; £510 suite. AE, DC, MC, V. Parking £18. **Amenities:** Restaurant; bar; health club; room service; babysitting. *In room:* A/C, TV, CD player, minibar, hair dryer, Wi-Fi (free).

The Howard ★★   Dubbed the most discreet luxury hotel in the city, The Howard comprises a trio of Georgian-terraced houses that have been transformed from private homes into a small collection of refined rooms and suites, all of which make for a more intimate experience than many of the city's larger high-end hotels. The Howard embodies the classical elegance of the era when the houses were originally conceived and managed to maintain the aura of a private home. Individually decorated rooms are mid-size to spacious and come with some of the best bathrooms in town, featuring power and double showers and, in some, a Jacuzzi. Breakfast can be enjoyed in bed or in the hotel's **Atholl** restaurant, which is also an extremely popular spot for afternoon tea.

34 Great King St. EH3 6QH. www.townhousecompany.com. ☎ **0131/557-3500.** Fax 0131/557-6515. 18 units. £185–£350 double; £255–£475 suite. AE, DC, MC, V. **Amenities:** Restaurant; room service. *In room:* TV, hair dryer, Wi-Fi (free).

Sheraton Grand Hotel ★★   A six-story modern hotel and oasis of glamour in the heart of Edinburgh's West End. Set back from the busy Lothian Road at the far end of Festival Square, this sumptuous hotel welcomes guests into soaring public rooms, while the various-sized guest rooms and suites are all recently renovated and exude comfort, style, and mood lighting. The castle-view rooms on the top three floors are the best. A rooftop hydro pool is the star of the hotel's leisure facilities. Dining options include **Santini,** a contemporary Italian restaurant, and **The Terrace,** a choice spot to enjoy a carvery meal and views of Edinburgh Castle.

1 Festival Sq., EH3 9SR. www.sheraton.com. ☎ **800/325-3535** in the U.S. and Canada, or 0131/229-9131. Fax 0131/228-4510. 269 units. £170–£265 double; £305–£500 suite. AE, DC, MC, V. **Amenities:** 3 restaurants; 2 bars; 2 pools (indoor/outdoor); health club and spa; concierge; room service; babysitting. *In room:* A/C, TV, minibar, hair dryer, Wi-Fi (£10).

EXPENSIVE

Hotel Number Ten ★ 👜   This relatively small hotel housed in a restored Georgian townhouse offers visitors a more intimate, but no less stylish stay than many of New Town's larger hotels. Individually decorated rooms vary in size and price from relatively small doubles to spacious suites; all come with polished hardwood floors, slate-tiled bathrooms, and Chinese antiques, and some sport floor-to-ceiling windows looking out over New Town at its best. The hotel's restaurant **Bacchus** champions local produce. For an extra £6 a day, guests can make use of the leisure facilities at the nearby Caledonian hotel (see review above).

10 Gloucester Place, EH3 6EF. www.hotelnumberten.com. ☏ **0131/225-2720.** Fax 0131/220-4706. 17 units. £80–£210 double; £160–£260 suite. AE, MC, V. **Amenities:** Restaurant; bar; room service. *In room:* TV, DVD/CD players, fridge, safe, iron, hair dryer, Wi-Fi (free).

Macdonald Roxburghe Hotel ★   Overlooking the large, neoclassical, tree-lined Charlotte Square, the Roxburghe embodies understated tradition and is well placed for the shops along Princes and George Streets, Edinburgh's theatres, and Old Town. Recent refurbishment has remained faithful to the hotel's Georgian architecture and modern luxuries blend seamlessly with a period feel in the guestrooms. The largest rooms are in the original building and maintain original features such as imposing fireplaces. The on-site **Vital Health, Fitness and Beauty** club contains good leisure facilities and offers spa treatments and fitness classes. The **Melrose** restaurant overlooks Charlotte Square and sources many ingredients from Scottish suppliers; the Melrose lounge is a choice spot for afternoon tea.

38 Charlotte St. EH2 4HQ. www.macdonaldhotels.co.uk. ☏ **0844/879-9063.** Fax 0131/240-5555. 198 units. £85–£210 double; £269–£600 suite. AE, DC, MC, V. **Amenities:** Restaurant; bar; pool (indoor); fitness center; spa; concierge; room service. *In room:* TV, minibar, hair dryer, Wi-Fi (£10 per day).

Tigerlily ★★ 🎁   One of the newest and coolest Edinburgh hotels, Tigerlily has swiftly built a reputation as the best boutique hotel in town. Lavish comfort, contemporary fabrics, polished wooden floors, and bold colors epitomize the spacious rooms and suites, which are topped off with modern facilities such as flatscreen TVs, preloaded iPods, and extra touches such as fruit and flowers. Suites come complete with modern fireplaces and en-suite wet rooms with extra large baths. The on-site restaurant and bar is extremely popular, and contemporary Scottish food alongside a menu of cocktails is served in a maze of individually decorated areas exuding a different atmosphere and style.

125 George St., EH2 4JN. www.tigerlilyedinburgh.co.uk. ☏ **0131/225-5005.** 33 units. £130–£180 double; £310–£360 suite. AE, MC, V. **Amenities:** Restaurant; bar; room service. *In room:* TV/DVD, iron, hair dryer, DVD library, Wi-Fi (free).

MODERATE

Royal Terrace Hotel ★   A large contemporary hotel at the east end of New Town, the Royal Terrace is one of the best of New Town's limited moderately priced accommodation options. Royal Terrace looks out over long views towards the Firth of Forth and is close to the entertainment, dining options, and shops towards the top of Leith Walk and Princes Street. The bedrooms are smart and well sized and include a collection of 10 luxury rooms that come with added extras such as a food and drink basket. During the summer, the restaurant spreads outside onto a garden terrace.

18 Royal Terrace, EH7 5AQ. www.royalterrace.co.uk. ☏ **0131/557-3222.** Fax 0131/557-5334. 107 units. £70–£180 double. AE, MC, V. **Amenities:** Restaurant; bar; pool (indoor), fitness center, sauna, steam room; room service. *In room:* TV, hair dryer, Wi-Fi (free).

Walton Hotel   This little hotel, a well-restored 200-year-old townhouse, provides basic, cozy accommodation right in the heart of New Town with Princes Street only a few blocks north. Triple and a family-sized room are on offer as well as doubles, most of which come with showers only in the en-suite bathrooms, except for double deluxe rooms that also have a tub. Breakfast is served in an airy dining room and the full cooked Scottish option is a fulfilling way to start a day's sightseeing.

79 Dundas St., EH3 6SD. www.waltonhotel.com. ☏ **0131/556-1137.** Fax 0131/557-8367. 10 units. £90–£150 double. MC, V. Free parking. *In room:* TV, hair dryer, Wi-Fi (free).

Hotels belonging to all the big chains are dotted throughout Edinburgh and on its outskirts in areas such as Newhaven and Leith. They're often the cheapest, if blandest, accommodation options. Favorites in New Town include the **Holiday Inn Express** on Picardy Place (www.hieedinburgh.co.uk; ✆ 0131/558-2300), with doubles from £60 to £160; and the **Premier Inn** on Morrison Link near Haymarket train station (www.premierinn.com; ✆ 0871/527-8368), with doubles from £50 to £80. Good options in Old Town include the hotel **IBIS** on Hunter Square off the Royal Mile (www.ibishotel.com; ✆ 0131/240-7000), with doubles from £50 to £140; and the **Novotel** on Lauriston Place (www.novotel.com; ✆ 0131/656-3500), with doubles from £70 to £230. Hotel options convenient for Edinburgh Airport include the **Hilton Edinburgh Airport,** situated within the airport boundaries (www.hilton.co.uk; ✆ 0131/519-4400), offering doubles for £140 to £195 and complementary shuttle bus to the airport terminal.

West of New Town
EXPENSIVE

Dunstane City ★   Housed in a solid 19th-century villa, Dunstane City is a small, friendly contemporary hotel that perfectly complements its more traditional sister hotel Dunstane House (see below). Rooms are modern and well furnished with rates lower than you'd pay for this level of comfort in the city center. Larger suites contain super king-sized beds, CD/DVD players, and loads of space in which to spread out. Bathrooms come with power showers and Molton Brown toiletries. Day passes for nearby leisure facilities can be organized.

5 Hampton Terrace, EH12 5JD. www.dunstanehotels.co.uk. ✆ **0131/337-6169.** Fax 0131/337-6060. 18 units. £100–£180 double; £140–£250 suite. AE, MC, V. **Amenities:** Cafe/bar. *In room:* TV, hair dryer, Wi-Fi (free).

Dunstane House ★   Set high up and back from a main route into the city, Dunstane House (sister hotel to the Dunstane City (above)) is a large grand property built in the 19th century that cultivates all the feel of an old country house hotel, and yet is only a short distance from Haymarket train station. A string of guesthouses line this road and this is one of the more expensive but more indulgent options. The bedrooms are well sized and richly furnished, with the more deluxe options featuring four-poster beds. The hotel's **Skerries** Scottish restaurant champions Orkney seafood, and the well-stocked **Stane Bar** is staffed by trained whisky ambassadors who can help choose the wee dram that's right for you.

4 West Coates, EH12 5JQ. www.dunstanehotels.co.uk. ✆ **0131/337-6169.** Fax 0131/337-6060. 16 units. £100–£240 double; £170–£280 suite. AE, MC, V. **Amenities:** Restaurant; bar; room service. *In room:* TV, hair dryer, Wi-Fi (free).

Old Town
VERY EXPENSIVE

Fraser Suites ★★   One of the plethora of new contemporary luxury accommodation that's sprung up in Edinburgh over recent years, Fraser Suites is tucked off the Royal Mile on a small, discreet street overlooking the Mound and New Town beyond and is a complex of boutique rooms and suites that offers visitors space, style, and location, location, location. All rooms have the added advantage of kitchenettes with fridges and microwaves (larger rooms contain full kitchens and dining areas), while super-sized suites come with obligatory stunning views and walk in wardrobes. Breakfast is served in the adjacent **Glasshouse** restaurant, which is also a choice spot for evening dining.

12-26 St Giles St., EH1 1PT. www.edinburgh.frasershospitality.com. ℂ **0131/221-7200.** Fax 0131/221-7201. 75 units. £290–£365 double; £400–£745 suite. AE, MC, V. **Amenities:** Restaurant; bar; gym; concierge; room service. *In room:* TV, kitchenette, fridge, microwave, safe, iron, hair dryer, iPod docking station, Wi-Fi (free).

Hotel Missoni ★★★   Hugging a prime Old Town spot at the corner of George IV Bridge and the Royal Mile, this hotel is the epitome of style, having been developed in collaboration with the renowned fashion dynasty, Missoni, in Italy. With its distinctive yet minimalist design of gray, black, and brown, Missoni blends fashion with function, form with design, and is one of the most exclusive places to stay in the city. This cool and contemporary hotel is spread over six floors and filled with unexpected splashes of color and even iconic pieces of design, some of which Rosita Missoni once had in her own home. Many of the fabulously chic bedrooms and suites open onto the panoramic views of the city and come complete with designer bathrooms. Missoni's **Cucina** restaurant is a feast of light, geometric design, specialty Italian food, and fine wine.

1 George IV Bridge, EH1 1AD. www.hotelmissoni.com. ℂ **0131/220-6666.** Fax 0131/226-6660. 136 units. £135–£210 double; £400–£950 suite. AE, MC, V. **Amenities:** Restaurant; bar; exercise room; concierge; room service. *In room:* A/C, TV, minibar, safe, hair dryer, iPod docking station, Wi-Fi (free).

The Scotsman ★★★   Standing proud on North Bridge, the main route between Edinburgh's New and Old Towns, the Scotsman is one of the city's most iconic luxury hotels and a good choice for those seeking a sense of history and tradition alongside first-class facilities and a prime location. The hotel's name honors the famous Scottish national newspaper that was published in this building for nearly a century. Traditional styling and cutting-edge design are harmoniously wed in the spacious bedrooms, all with names like Editor or Publisher's Suite and remaining faithful to the building's history. They include state-of-the-art bathrooms and such extras as an Edinburgh monopoly board. The Scotsman's lower levels house a well-equipped modern gym that occupies the space where printing presses used to steam out the latest news.

20 N. Bridge, EH1 1DF. www.thescotsmanhotel.co.uk. ℂ **0131/556-5565.** Fax 0131/652-3652. 68 units. £350 double; from £400 suite. AE, DC, MC, V. **Amenities:** Restaurant; bar; pool (indoor); gym and spa; room service; babysitting. *In room:* TV, DVD player, minibar, hair dryer, Wi-Fi (free).

EXPENSIVE

Barcelo Edinburgh Carlton Hotel ★   Standing on the Old Town end of North Bridge, this upmarket option is convenient for both New and Old Towns and is an appealing combination of tradition and plush hotel. The building itself was once one of Edinburgh's leading department stores and much of the architectural charm of 1900 remains including Victorian turrets and Flemish gables. Bedrooms are spacious, comfortable, and furnished with subdued modern simplicity, and private bathrooms feature tubs and showers. The Carlton is known for its top-notch service at it brasserie-style **Bridge Restaurant,** or guests can take time to relax in the modern cocktail lounge. If spas are your thing, the hotel's leisure club features all the facilities you'd expect along with an ample choice of spa treatments for those in need of pampering and rejuvenating.

19 North Bridge, EH1 1SD. www.barcelo-hotels.co.uk. ☎ **0131/472-3000.** Fax 0131/556-2691. 189 units. £110–£250 double. AE, DC, MC, V. **Amenities:** Restaurant; bar; pool (indoor); health club w/Jacuzzi; concierge; room service; babysitting. *In room:* TV, hair dryer, Wi-Fi (free).

Holyrood Hotel ★★   Holyrood is an impressive and exceedingly stylish, modern hotel in the shadow of the Palace of Holyroodhouse. This deluxe charmer stands in contrast to some of Edinburgh's older, grander hotels but is no less luxurious for it. Bedrooms come with marble en-suite bathrooms, while suites with their extra space are a good choice for families. Excellent dining and leisure facilities include a piano lounge and **Vital Health and Wellbeing Club.** This end of the Royal Mile has spruced itself up dramatically over recent years and the arrival of the Scottish Parliament and Our Dynamic Earth has attracted new restaurants and cafes to the area.

81 Holyrood Rd., EH8 8AU. www.macdonaldhotels.co.uk/holyrood. ☎ **0131/550-4500.** Fax 0131/550-4545. 156 units. £100–£270 double. AE, MC, V. **Amenities:** Restaurant; bar; pool (indoor); health club w/ sauna; room service. *In room:* A/C, TV, hair dryer, Wi-Fi (£9 per hour).

Hotel du Vin ★★   The Hotel du Vin group has taken over the site of a former lunatic asylum on the south side of Old Town and transformed it into one of Edinburgh's most enticing boutique hotels. This patch of Old Town is tucked away from the main tourist drag but close to the heart of the action during festival time. Richly styled rooms are embellished with added elements such as drench showers and luxurious Egyptian cotton sheets. Eating and drinking facilities are top rate and include the French styles **Bistro du Vin** and outdoor terrace seating in summer. There's even a cigar shack, a whisky "snug" (cozy bar), and a tasting room where you can sample wine from some of the world's finest vineyards.

11 Bristo Place, EH1 1EZ. www.hotelduvin.com. ☎ **0131/247-4900.** Fax 0131/247-4901. 47 units. £100–£210 double; £210–£445 suite. AE, MC, V. **Amenities:** Restaurant; bar; room service. *In room:* A/C, TV/DVD, hair dryer, Internet (free).

Radisson SAS Hotel ★ ☺   Housed in a restored brick medieval-style building midway along the Royal Mile, the Radisson is a haven of modern luxury in a bustling patch of Old Town, though triple-glazed windows keep out the noise. In spite of the antique geography, the hotel is thoroughly modernized and offers first-class facilities, though it lacks the old-world charm of some of Edinburgh's grande dame hotels. It's also one of the best-equipped hotels in the area, with such luxuries as a leisure club and a jet-stream pool. Most of the bedrooms are spacious and well decorated, and large family rooms sleep up to five. Bathrooms contain heated floors for those chilly Scottish mornings.

80 High St., EH1 1TH. www.radissonblu.co.uk/hotel-edinburgh. ☎ **800/395-7046** in the U.S. and Canada, or 0131/557-9797. Fax 0131/557-9789. 238 units. £115–£180 double; £170–£215 family rooms. AE, DC, MC, V. **Amenities:** Restaurant; bar; pool (indoor); concierge; room service. *In room:* TV, minibar, safe, hair dryer, Wi-Fi (free).

MODERATE

Apex International Hotel ★ ☺   A modern European-styled hotel on the edge of Grassmarket, the Apex is an appealing combination of central location, simple style, modern conveniences, and good facilities. Families are well catered for here because children can stay and eat for free as long as they're sharing a room with an adult. There's a host of toys for children to enjoy in public areas, and all guests leave with a complimentary red Apex duck. Rooms at the front have wide views over the hustle of Grassmarket and Edinburgh Castle, and larger rooms come with added extras such as a fridge and bathrobes; DVD/CD players are available from reception. **Yu Time,** the Japanese-influenced leisure facilities, include a sleek stainless steel ozone pool and tropicarium, and the rooftop **Heights** restaurant is a spectacular spot to indulge in some fine Scottish cuisine. A second Apex is situated practically next door and other hotels in this small chain are also located on Waterloo Place in New Town and on Haymarket Terrace close to the train station.

31–35 Grassmarket, EH1 2HS. www.apexhotels.co.uk. ✆ **0845/365-0000,** or +44 (0)131/441-0440 from outside the U.K. Fax 0871/221-1353. 171 units. £90–£160 double; £100–£160 family rooms. AE, DC, MC, V. **Amenities:** Restaurant; bar; pool (indoor); gym; spa; room service. *In room:* TV, iron, hair dryer, Wi-Fi (free).

Point Hotel　　This modern hotel, in the shadow of Edinburgh Castle, has one of the most dramatic contemporary interiors of any Edinburgh hotel and is a surprising moderate option in the heart of the city. The minimalist decor emphasizes color and innovation, and the bedrooms are spacious and attractively furnished (premium units are more comfortable and roomier than standard units). Sweeping views of the castle are one of the hotel's best selling points and a feature of most of the guest rooms, except for those in the rear. The Point is very convenient for all the nightlife of Edinburgh's West End; if you prefer to stay in, the hotel's bistro-style restaurant serves international cuisine with a focus on Scottish seafood and meats, and the **Monbooddo** bar is a relaxing spot for a cocktail or wee dram.

34 Bread St., EH3 9AF. www.pointhoteledinburgh.co.uk. ✆ **0131/221-5555.** Fax 0131/221-9929. 139 units. £70–£160 double. AE, DC, MC, V. **Amenities:** Restaurant; bar; room service. *In room:* TV, hair dryer, Wi-Fi (£15 per day).

South of Old Town
MODERATE

94DR ★★★ ☺　　Standing opposite Edinburgh's Commonwealth swimming pool, 94DR takes guesthouses to a new level of boutique style and service and is a refreshing contemporary option on the city's moderately priced accommodation scene. Modern style infused with a sense of tradition reigns supreme, and each well-appointed room comes with walk-in power shower—a deluxe room also features a roll-top bath—and luxury toiletries. The freshly prepared breakfasts are a highlight, and guests who want a long lie-in can choose to have a breakfast box delivered to their room. The owners bend over backwards to provide whatever extras any guest may require, from airport transfers to in-room massages and bike rental. Kids are made to feel more than welcome and a small children's room adjoining one of the top-floor bedrooms includes bunk beds, a toy chest, and Xbox.

94 Dalkeith Rd., EH16 5AF. www.94dr.com. ✆ **0131/662-9265.** 7 units. £80–£150 double. MC, V. *In room:* TV/DVD, hair dryer, iPod dock, Wi-Fi (free).

23 Mayfield ★★★ ☺ 🎁　　Simply the best guesthouse in town, 23 Mayfield combines comfort with tradition—look out for the framed copy of the Scottish Declaration of Independence—and first-class service with award-winning breakfasts. This solid Victorian house was built in 1868 by a tea and coffee merchant, and today bedrooms are decorated in a Tudor style; the highlights are the Jacobean Rooms complete with four-poster beds. Modern luxuries include music systems with surround sound, mood lighting, raindrop showers, and Scottish sea kelp toiletries. The top-floor family room features a Nintendo Wii and telescope for peering into the night sky. The very long breakfast menu sources as much local produce as possible, and in the evening guests can relax into deep couches in the book-lined drawing room. The owners can also organize bike rental, complete with packed lunches and backpacks.

23 Mayfield Gardens, EH7 2BX. www.23mayfield.co.uk. ⓒ **0131/667-5806.** Fax 0131/667-6833. 9 units. £40–£65 per person per night. MC, V. *In room:* TV, music system, hair dryer, Wi-Fi (free).

Leith

EXPENSIVE

Malmaison ★★   This stylish boutique hotel perched on the edge of Leith's old harbor is a good choice for those wanting a slice of luxury outside the bustle of the city center, plus an array of fine dining options on the doorstep. Like all buildings in Leith, Malmaison has history. This baronial-style Victorian building complete with a stately stone clock tower served as a seamen's mission before being converted to a swish hotel in the mid-1990s. Malmaison is hip and unpretentious, boasting a minimalist decor and low-key elegance. Rooms are individually designed and well equipped; suites come complete with tartan roll-top baths and views over the Firth of Forth. The facilities include a **Brasserie** with a menu of French and British cuisine (main courses £10–£25), a cafe and wine bar favored by locals, and a state-of-the-art gym.

1 Tower Place, Leith, EH6 7DB. www.malmaison.com. ⓒ **0131/468-5000.** Fax 0131/468-5002. 100 units. £100–£220 double; from £240 suite. AE, DC, MC, V. Free parking. Bus: 16 or 35. **Amenities:** Restaurant; bar; gym. *In room:* TV, minibar, CD player/music library, hair dryer, Wi-Fi (free).

SIDE TRIPS FROM EDINBURGH

Armed with a good map, and a selection of train timetables if you don't want to drive, there are many historic towns, major attractions, and seaside communities waiting to be explored in a day. In addition to the places detailed below, Glasgow, Stirling, and Dunfermline are also all very easy day trips from Scotland's capital.

South Queensferry

Officially part of the City of Edinburgh, the small burgh South Queensferry lies 10 miles west of the city center on the banks of the Firth of Forth where the world-famous Forth road and rail bridges steam across the water. The town, and North Queensferry its counterpart across the Firth, are named in honor of Saint Margaret, Queen of King Malcolm III, who used to cross the water here in the "Queen's Ferry." A tiny High Street is a delight of quirky shops and quaint cafes, and a highlight of a visit is a trip to **Inchcolm Island ★★**, home to the ruins of a 13th-century abbey and a host of wildlife. Trips aboard *The Maid of the Forth* (ⓒ **0131/331-5000;** www.maidoftheforth.co.uk) depart from Howes Pier for Inchcolm from April to October (check the website for a detailed schedule); tickets cost £10 for adults, £3 for children. There's a fine range of dining options to choose from; one of the most celebrated is the **Hawes Inn** (ⓒ **01313/311-990;** www.vintageinn.co.uk), which features in Robert Louis Stevenson's *Kidnapped.*

First bus no. 43 connects Edinburgh's St. Andrews bus station with South Queensferry, and a regular train service connects Edinburgh Waverley with Dalmeny station, which is a short walk from the High Street.

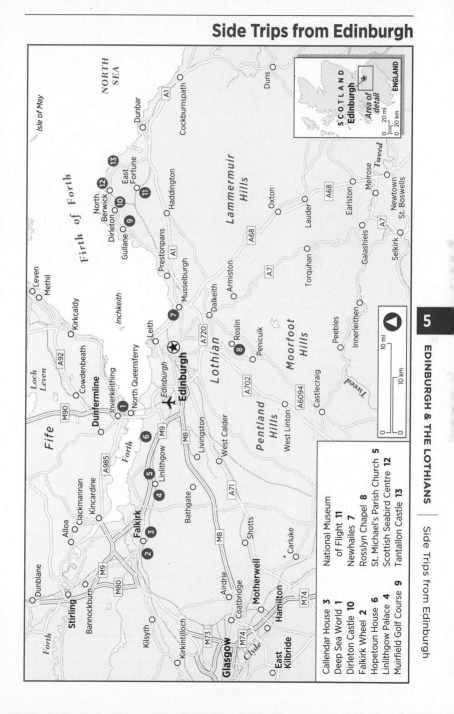

NORTH SEA

Isle of May

Firth of Forth

NORTH SEA

Dunbar

A1

Cockburnspath

Duns

Area of detail

SCOTLAND

Edinburgh

ENGLAND

20 mi

0 20 km

13

12 North Berwick

East Fortune

11

10 Dirleton

9 Gullane

Haddington

Lammermuir Hills

Oxton

A68

Melrose

Tweed

Earlston

Newtown St. Boswells

Lauder

A7

Galashiels

Selkirk

Prestonpans

A1

Musselburgh

Armiston

A7

Torquhan

Innerleithen

Leven

Methil

Kirkcaldy

Inchkeith

Cowdenbeath

Dalkeith

A720

Roslin

8 Penicuik

Moorfoot Hills

Peebles

Innerleithen

Leith

7

Edinburgh ✈

Lothian

Castlecraig

A702

A6094

Castlecraig

West Linton

Tweed

10 mi

10 km

Loch Leven

A92

Dunfermline

Inverkeithing

North Queensferry

1

Forth

A985

Kincardine

Fife

M90

6

M9

Linlithgow

M8

Livingston

West Calder

A71

Pentland Hills

5

4 Bathgate

Shotts

Carluke

Clackmannan

Alloa

Falkirk

3

2

M9

M8

Motherwell

Dunblane

Bannockburn

Stirling

M9

M80

Kilsyth

Airdrie

Coatbridge

Hamilton

East Kilbride

M73

M74

M74

Glasgow

Clyde

Kirkintilloch

Forth

Callendar House **3**	National Museum
Deep Sea World **1**	of Flight **11**
Dirleton Castle **10**	Newhailes **7**
Falkirk Wheel **2**	Rosslyn Chapel **8**
Hopetoun House **6**	St. Michael's Parish Church **5**
Linlithgow Palace **4**	Scottish Seabird Centre **12**
Muirfield Golf Course **9**	Tantallon Castle **13**

Tours from Edinburgh

A large number of tour operators based in Edinburgh offer a wide choice of trips into the rest of Scotland from the city center. These trips range from day tours around Rosslyn Chapel and the Scottish Borders to 5-day excursions into the Highlands and Islands. The pick of the larger tour operators include **Highland Experience** (✆ 0131/226-1414; www.highlandexperience.com) and **Rabbie's** (✆ 0131/226-3133; www.rabbies.com). For a very personal experience of Scotland, book an **Afternoon Tea Tour** (✆ 07873/211-856; www.afternoonteatours.com); one of Scotland's top tour operators, this Edinburgh-based company offers set guided tours or will create bespoke itineraries focusing on individual interests and providing a unique glimpse at the more unusual and intimate side of Scotland. **Wild Green Travel** (✆ 0131/478-6500; www.wildgreentravel.com) leads small groups on walking and whisky tasting tours, taking in a few local pubs along the way.

WHERE TO EAT & STAY

Orocco Pier ★   Views from hotel bedrooms don't come more sweeping than the ones across the Firth of Forth offered by this modern, comfortable hotel situated right on the edge of the waterfront. Eating here is of equal quality as two levels of balconies offer excellent al fresco dining in summer, or you can snuggle into warm booths or around a glowing open fire on chilly days. Menus start with excellent breakfasts including a champagne option and conclude with a dinner menu that favors seafood and imaginative meat dishes such as suckling pig (main courses £13–£20).

17 High St., EH30 9PP. www.oroccopier.co.uk. ✆ **0870/118-1664.** Fax 0870/288-9060. 17 units. From £110 double. AE, DC, MC, V. **Amenities:** Restaurant; bar. *In room:* TV, DVD and CD players, minibar, safe, hair dryer, Wi-Fi (free).

Linlithgow

Linlithgow is one of West Lothian's loveliest historic towns and an easy and popular day trip from Edinburgh, which is 18 miles to the east. In 1542, Mary Queen of Scots was born into this royal burgh and the site of her birth, **Linlithgow Palace,** is one of Scotland's most evocative ruins. Those who choose not to pay to enter the Palace can still walk and picnic in the surrounding parkland that encompasses a small loch and claims imposing views of the ruins. A number of eating options, from cafes to upmarket restaurants, are dotted along Linlithgow's High Street. **The Four Marys** (✆ 01506/842-171; www.thefourmarys.co.uk) is by far the best pub for food and friendlessness. A regular train service runs every half-hour between Edinburgh and Linlithgow; the journey takes 20 minutes, and a round-trip fare costs £7.40 adults and £3.70 children.

Linlithgow Palace ★★ RUINS   External views of this ruined palace are impressive, but the only real way to appreciate its historical gravitas is to head inside and explore. Visitors enter via a grand courtyard at the center of which stands a large restored 16th-century three-tiered fountain. Although the palace is roofless, its pink-ocher walls climb five floors and are supported on the lower edge by flying buttresses.

Many of the former royal rooms are still remarkably preserved and the Great Hall remains impressive. The palace began its decline when James VI moved his court to London in 1603, and a devastating fire in 1745 sealed its tragic fate.

Off High St., Linlithgow. © **01506/842-896.** www.historic-scotland.gov.uk. Admission £5.20 adults, £4.20 seniors, £3 children 16 and under. Apr–Sept daily 9:30am–5:30pm; Oct–Mar daily 9:30am–4:30pm.

St. Michael's Parish Church CHURCH   South of the palace stands the medieval kirk of St. Michael the Archangel, site of worship of many a Scottish monarch since its consecration in 1242. Despite being ravaged by the disciples of John Knox (who then chided his followers for their "excesses") and temporarily transformed into a stable by Cromwell, this remains one of Scotland's best examples of a parish church and features a striking contemporary "crown" on top of the church's tower.

Adjacent to Linlithgow Palace. © **01506/842-188.** www.stmichaelsparish.org.uk. Free admission. May–Sept Mon–Sat 10:30am–4pm, Sun noon–4pm; Oct–Apr Mon–Sat 10:30am–1pm.

WHERE TO EAT

Livingston's ★ MODERN SCOTTISH/FRENCH   Tucked away off Linlithgow's High Street, this cottage-like restaurant sits in converted stables and has been a mainstay of West Lothian's eating out scene for over 20 years. Diners can pick to eat in either the original stone building or a newer conservatory overlooking a neat little garden. Candlelight creates a warm and romantic atmosphere in which to enjoy acclaimed food. The chef is inventive and imaginatively uses quality ingredients. Lunch and dinner menus are both fixed price and heavy with local meats such as venison and seafood such as roast fillet of halibut served with crab, crushed potatoes, and a shellfish and saffron broth. The ample wine list includes a host of champagnes.

52 High St. (opposite the post office), Linlithgow. © **01506/846-565.** www.livingstons-restaurant. co.uk. Fixed-price 2-course lunch £18, 3-course lunch £21; fixed-price dinner £33 for 2 courses, £39 for 3 courses. MC, V. Tues–Sat noon–2pm and 6–9pm.

North Berwick

This royal burgh dating from the 14th century is an upmarket holiday resort on the edge of the Firth of Forth, 24 miles east of Edinburgh, and the place where city residents head when the sun shines. Visitors are drawn here for the golf and wide-open beaches with views of **Bass Rock,** a steep-sided plug of volcanic rock just offshore that once served as a prison and today is the breeding ground of about 10,000 gannets. The gannets return from Africa in the spring, usually around April, to nest here until fall. You can discover more about these birds and others along this coastline at the **Scottish Seabird Centre** ★ ☺ (© **01620/890-202;** www.seabird.org), which sits at the center of North Berwick's harbor. Here you can also spy on dolphins and seals in the surrounding waters and take a boat trip to Bass Rock. The center opens daily year-round from 10am closing at 6pm in the summer and between 4 and 5:30pm in winter. Admission costs £8 for adults and £4.50 for children aged 4 to 15. Boat trips to Bass Rock run from March to October and cost extra. The Sea Bird Centre takes part in ScotRail's "Kids Go Free" program (see p. 428 for details), and direct trains between North Berwick and Edinburgh run roughly every 30 minutes. The journey takes a half-hour and a round-trip ticket costs £6 for adults, £3 for children.

East Lothian is a golfer's heaven and boasts the highest number of links courses in close proximity in the world. You can choose from 22 courses including the par-70, 6,801-yard **Muirfield Golf Course** (✆ 01620/842-123; www. muirfield.org.uk), one of the greatest courses in the world, which has hosted 15 Open Championships and is due to host the 2013 tournament. Comprehensive information on all the courses in the region can be found at **www. golfeastlothian.com**, where you can also find out more about accommodation and the East Lothian Visitor Golf Pass, which can save money on where to play and stay in the region.

WHERE TO STAY

The Glebe House   This dignified 1780 home belongs to Gwen and Jake Scott, who've worked hard to preserve its original character as the residence of the pastor for the nearby Presbyterian Church. This friendly bed-and-breakfast is near many golf courses and is just a minute's walk south of the town's main street, near the edge of the sea. Each cozy guest room boasts part of Mrs. Scott's collection of hand-painted porcelain, artfully arranged on tabletops, in wall niches, and on hanging shelves. Views include 1.6 hectares (4 acres) of field, garden, and horse paddock. Hearty Scottish breakfasts are served in a formal, high-ceilinged dining room.

4 Law Rd., North Berwick, EH39 4PL. www.glebehouse-nb.co.uk. ✆**01620/892-608.** Fax 01620/893-586. 4 units. £100 double. No credit cards. *In room:* TV, hair dryer.

Additional Attractions

Deep Sea World ★ ☺AQUARIUM   Scotland's most comprehensive aquarium, Deep Sea World, is stocked with a menagerie of water-dwelling creatures from seals to seahorses. Visitors take a trip through underwater microclimates featuring views of a kelp forest; sandy flats that shelter bottom-dwelling schools of stingray, turbot, and sole; murky caves favored by conger eels and small sharks; and a scary trench whose sponge-encrusted bottom careens abruptly away from view. Schools of shark and battalions of as many as 5,000 fish stare back at you. Allow at least 90 minutes for your visit, and try to avoid the weekend crowds.

Battery Quarry, North Queensferry. ✆01383/411-880. www.deepseaworld.com. Admission £13 adults, £8.25 children 3-14, £40 family ticket. Mon–Fri 10am–5pm; Sat–Sun 10am–6pm. North Queensferry is 12 miles northwest of Edinburgh and connected by a regular train service.

Falkirk Wheel ★★★ ☺ ARCHITECTURE   When an ambitious project was proposed to re-link the Union and Forth & Clyde canals, the major obstacle to overcome was the fact that one canal lay 35m (115 ft.) below the other and the flight of 11 locks that once joined them had been demolished. The solution, the Falkirk Wheel, is an impressive genius of modern engineering. Boats enter from one canal and the wheel, which operates according the Archimedes' principle of water displacement, rotates using a fraction of power and discharges them into the other canal. Visitors can hop aboard a boat trip to experience this, the world's only rotating boat wheel, or spend time in the visitor center to find out how it was created and how it works.

Lime Road, Tamfourhill, Falkirk. ✆ 0870/500-208. www.thefalkirkwheel.co.uk. Boat trips £8 adults, £5 children 3-15. Mar–Oct daily 10am–5:30pm; Nov–Mar Wed–Sun 11am–4pm. The Falkirk Wheel is approximately 23 miles from Edinburgh. There's a frequent train service between Edinburgh and Falkirk and regular buses connect the town center with the Wheel.

Hopetoun House ★ HISTORIC SITE   Set amid beautifully landscaped grounds, *a la* Versailles, Hopetoun is Scotland's greatest Robert Adam mansion and a fine example of 18th-century architecture (note its resemblance to Buckingham Palace). Seven bays extend across the slightly recessed center, and the classical style includes a complicated tympanum, as well as hood molds, quoins, and straight-headed windows. A rooftop balustrade with urns completes the ensemble. You can wander through splendid reception rooms, filled with 18th-century furniture, paintings, statuary, and other artwork, and check out the panoramic view of the Firth of Forth from the roof. After touring the house, take the nature trail, explore the deer parks, see the Stables Museum, or stroll through the formal gardens.

1¾ miles from the Forth Road Bridge near South Queensferry, 10 miles from Edinburgh off the A904. ⓒ **0131/331-2451.** www.hopetoun.co.uk. Admission £9.20 adults, £8 seniors, £4.90 children 16 and under, £25 families. Easter–Sept daily 10:30am–5pm (last admission 4pm).

National Museum of Flight ★ ☺ MUSEUM   Discover the history of aviation from WWI to the present day at this national museum set deep inside East Fortune Airfield, which was built in 1915 to help protect the U.K. from attacking German zeppelins. Visitors can learn everything here from how planes fly to the technology that took Concorde through the sound barrier. There are around 50 aircraft to view, including such classics as the Spitfire and Tiger Moth, as well as the chance to view their restoration process in action. There are plenty of opportunities for children to get hands on with history and an annual air show in July.

East Fortune Airfield is 20 miles east of Edinburgh off the B1347. ⓒ **0131/225-7534.** www.nms.ac.uk/flight. Admission £9 adults, £7 seniors, children 12 and under free. Apr–Oct daily 10am–5pm; Nov–Mar Sat–Sun 10am–4pm.

Newhailes HISTORIC SITE   Often called "The Sleeping Beauty," this impressive late-17th-century mansion has largely survived intact thanks to the fact that it lay dormant for years. The house is a testament to early 18th-century decorative Rococo interiors which, as a National Trust official explained, is because "nobody in this house earned a penny after 1790 and subsequent owners couldn't afford to change anything." Expect a feast of ornate decoration including rich furnishings, gilding, antique wallpaper, damask, and needlepoint as well as such unique features as a

---

The Final Frontier

The Falkirk Wheel lies close to the remains of a section of the **Antonine Wall** (www.antoninewall.org), a stone-and earth-fortified rampart that once stretched 37 miles across central Scotland. The wall was built by the Romans in A.D. 142 and represented the far northwestern frontier of their empire until it was abandoned in around A.D. 160 and they retreated south to Hadrian's Wall. To find out more about the Antonine Wall, walk through a section of it, and delve into 600 years of history of the area, visit **Callender House** in Callender Park, Falkirk ⓒ **01324/503-779**; www.falkirk.gov.uk/cultural). Callender House is free to enter and open Monday through Saturday 10am to 5pm, and on Sundays from April to September from 2 to 5pm.

East Lothian is home to two impressive castles that make for a fascinating day trip from Edinburgh. Midway between North Berwick and Gullane is Dirleton, often cited as one of the prettiest villages in Scotland. At the center of the village is a 13th-century castle (📞 01620/850-330; www.historic-scotland.gov.uk). Abandoned by its residents in 1663, **Dirleton Castle** looks like a fairy-tale fortification with its towers, arched entries, and oak ramp similar to the drawbridge that used to protect it. The castle was partially destroyed by Cromwell in 1650, and surviving highlights include the remains of the Great Hall and kitchen, as well as what's left of the Lord's Chamber. The surrounding gardens date from the late 19th and early 20th century and are one of the highlights of a visit. Dirleton Castle is open April to September daily 9:30am to 5:30pm and October to March daily 9:30am to 4:30pm. Admission is £4.70 adults and £2.80 children.

Some 1¾ miles east of North Berwick and 25 miles east of Edinburgh on the A198 stand the formidable ruins of the 14th-century **Tantallon Castle** (📞 01620/892-727; www.historic-scotland.gov.uk). This ancient stronghold has been described as the last great castle to be built in Scotland; construction began in the 1350s. Its location high on the top of a sheer cliff face is stunning. The castle has endured a number of sieges, and the sturdy gun in the east tower is an exact replica of the kind of weapon used to defend Tantallon in both the 15th and 16th centuries. Tantallon is open April to September daily 9:30am to 5:30pm, October daily 9:30am to 4:30pm, and November to March Sunday through Wednesday 9:30am to 4:30pm. Admission is £4.70 adults and £2.80 children.

7,000-volume library hailed by Samuel Johnson as "the most learned room in Europe." Make time to explore the surrounding parkland with its woodland walks, summerhouse, and grotto.

Newhailes Road, Musselburgh. 📞 **0844/493-2125.** www.nts.org.uk. Tours of the house take 1¼ hours. Admission £11 for adults, £8 seniors and children 5–15, £27 families. May–Sept Thurs–Mon noon–5pm. Musselburgh is 4 miles to the east of Edinburgh. Bus no. 44.

Rosslyn Chapel ★★★ CHAPEL   Sir William St. Clair founded Rosslyn Chapel in 1446 and this intricate holy site has been the subject of legend and lore ever since. Rosslyn is one of the alleged sites of the Holy Grail and shot to fame through its pivotal role in Dan Brown's international bestseller *The Da Vinci Code* and the subsequent movie. Every inch of this historic masterpiece is adorned with elaborate stonework, depicting everything from devils to dragons, knights to farmer's wives, and angels playing the bagpipes. By far the most celebrated piece is the Apprentice Pillar, which an apprentice mason carved after being inspired by a dream.

Chapel Loan, Roslin. 📞 **0131/440-2159.** www.rosslyn-chapel.com. Admission £7.50 adults, £6 seniors, children 15 and under free. Oct–Mar Mon–Sat 9:30am–5pm, Sun noon–4:45pm; Apr–Sept Mon–Sat 9:30am–6pm, Sun noon–4:45pm. Roslin is 6 miles south of Edinburgh. Bus no. 15.

Where to Eat & Stay

Ducks ★★   A few years ago, restaurateur Malcolm Duck moved his successful business from Edinburgh into this old 16th-century hotel in the village of Aberlady and in doing so transported his acclaimed fine dining from the city to the countryside. There are two dining experiences on offer. The first Ducks is a formal white linen affair whose regularly changing menu transforms local East Lothian produce into memorably exquisite food (main courses £10–£22). The second is the bar/bistro called Donald's (named after Malcolm's father), where inexpensive bar food such as fish and chips and steak and ale pies are served for around £10, all complemented by a selection of over 50 single malts and a choice of real ales. Ducks is also a restaurant with rooms and all the en-suite guest rooms have been refreshed and refurbished, with the Butler Suite offering a four-poster experience.

Kilspindle House, Main St., Aberlady, EH32 0RE. www.ducks.co.uk. *(C)* **01875/870-682.** 23 units. £80–£115 double. AE, MC, V. **Amenities:** Restaurant; bar. *In room:* TV, hair dryer, Wi-Fi (free).

The Golf Inn Gullane is popular with golfers and this ivy-clad hotel, restaurant, and bar off Main Street provides decent accommodation alongside hearty Scottish cuisine (main courses £10–£20). The fairly standard rooms are clean and comfortable; all are connected to the golf channel, and those in Hazel Cottage come with floor to ceiling garden views. Larger parties can opt for the Muirfield Suite, which sleeps four. The cozy Niblick bar is decked out in golf memorabilia galore and serves a lighter menu (main courses £6–£12) for those who don't want a full restaurant meal.

Main St., Gullane, EH31 2AB. www.golfinn.co.uk. *(C)* **01620/843-259.** Fax 01620/842-066. 14 units. £45–£60 per person per night. MC, V. **Amenities:** Restaurant; bar; Wi-Fi in public areas (free). *In room:* TV, hair dryer.

Greywalls Hotel ★★ Built in 1901, this elegant, Edwardian country house retreat stands in 2.4 hectares (6 acres) of beautiful formal gardens and within a 5-mile radius of 12 golf courses. The property was visited from time to time by Edward VII, who admired the views across the Firth of Forth and south to the Lammermuir Hills. In the paneled library, guests relax on comfortable sofas before a blazing log fire. The guest rooms vary in size; some smaller ones are simply decorated, while the more spacious units are furnished with period pieces. Each comes with a beautifully kept bathroom. The light French-style dishes served in the Chex Roux restaurant are as appealing to the eye as to the palate; specialties include fresh seafood.

Muirfield, Duncur Rd., Gullane, EH31 2EG. www.greywalls.co.uk. *(C)* **01620/842-144.** Fax 01620/842-241. 23 units. £230–£320 double. AE, DC, MC, V. Follow signs from the A198 about 5 miles from North Berwick. **Amenities:** Restaurant; bar; 2 tennis courts; putting green; croquet lawn; room service; baby-sitting. *In room:* TV, hair dryer, Wi-Fi (free).

The Old Club House ★★ 🎁 SCOTTISH/CONTINENTAL Brimming with tradition and warm hospitality, this lovely old half-timbered pub/restaurant claims wide views over a children's golf course and is well known by locals for its home-cooked food and convivial atmosphere. The decor remains faithful to the building's history and is a feast of old wooden floors and golfing memorabilia. The menu is a mix of Scottish favorites including local seafood and haggis, alongside pastas and curries. Lighter bites such as filled focaccia and a children's menu are also available. The outside terrace is a pretty spot for dining al fresco in warm weather.

East Links Rd., Gullane. *(C)* **01620/842-008.** www.oldclubhouse.com. Main courses £9–£17. MC, V. Food served daily 12:15–9:30pm.

THE BORDERS & DUMFRIES & GALLOWAY

S outhern Scotland is an appealing fusion of the gentle rolling landscape of the Scottish Borders to the east and more rugged Dumfries and Galloway to the west. The Borders bore the brunt of the centuries-old conflict between Scotland and England, and the ruins of its battered ancient abbeys are reason enough to visit. Less well known are the historic estates and haunting coastline of Dumfries and Galloway, where poet Robert Burns lived out his last years and wrote his best work.

SIGHTSEEING Get up close and personal with the Scotland that Sir Walter Scott loved best at his former home **Abbotsford,** on the outskirts of Melrose and one of the Borders' many historic houses and estates. Sights associated with Robert Burns are scattered throughout Dumfries, but travel farther to discover fine gardens at **Threave** and **Port Logan.** Writers and artists gravitate to the towns of **Kirkcudbright** and **Wigtown,** and spread out over the landscape near Moniaive and Glenkiln.

EATING & DRINKING Most of the best dining in southern Scotland is to be experienced in the restaurants of the region's many **fine country house hotels.** Here top chefs work culinary wonders with produce sourced from local farms, rivers, and smokehouses; Borders lamb and freshly caught salmon and seafood from the Solway Firth take pride of place on imaginative menus. **Regional breweries** are far more prevalent than whisky distilleries, and the discerning real ale drinker will find a rich variety of choice in the area's fine country pubs.

HISTORY The evocative ruins of the Borders' four great 12th-century abbeys—**Dryburgh, Melrose, Jedburgh,** and **Kelso**—are testimony to the region's turbulent past. Equally stirring is the history waiting to be discovered at southern Scotland's many fine castles such as **Floors** near Kelso and the medieval stronghold of **Caerlaverock** south of Dumfries. Shadows of Mary Queen of Scots lie across the land, and sights including **Traquair House** on the edges of Peebles and the remote **Hermitage Castle** are steeped in stories and secrets of Scotland's most bewitching monarch.

NATURE City dwellers escape the nearby urban centers of Edinburgh and Glasgow to enjoy the many outdoor activities southern Scotland's

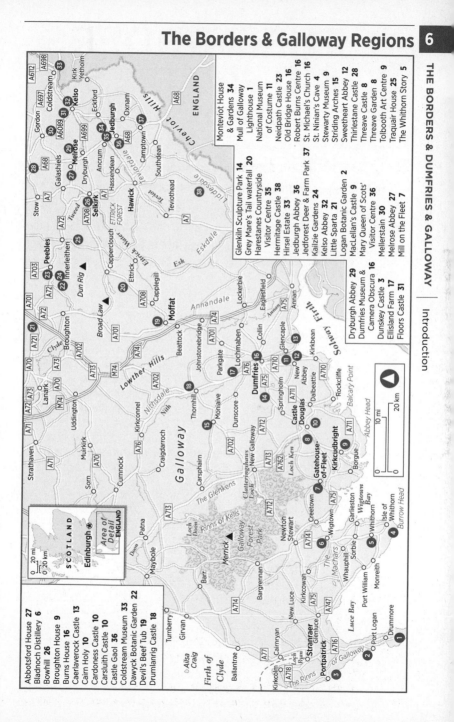

Monteviot House
& Gardens **34**
Mull of Galloway
Lighthouse **1**
National Museum
of Costume **11**
Neidpath Castle **23**
Old Bridge House **16**
Robert Burns Centre **16**
St. Michael's Church **16**
St. Ninian's Cave **4**
Stewarty Museum **9**
Striding Arches **15**
Sweetheart Abbey **12**
Thirlestane Castle **28**
Threave Garden **8**
Threave Castle **8**
Tolbooth Art Centre **9**
Traquair House **25**
The Whithorn Story **5**

Glenkiln Sculpture Park **14**
Grey Mare's Tail waterfall **20**
Harestanes Countryside
Visitor Centre **35**
Hermitage Castle **38**
Hirsel Estate **33**
Jedburgh Abbey **36**
Jedforest Deer & Farm Park **37**
Kailzie Gardens **24**
Kelso Abbey **32**
Little Sparta **21**
Logan Botanic Garden **2**
MacLellan's Castle **9**
Mary Queen of Scots'
Visitor Centre **36**
Mellerstain **30**
Melrose Abbey **27**
Mill on the Fleet **7**

Dryburgh Abbey **29**
Dumfries Museum &
Camera Obscura **16**
Dunskey Castle **3**
Ellisland Farm **17**
Floors Castle **31**

Abbotsford House **27**
Bladnoch Distillery **6**
Bowhill **26**
Broughton House **9**
Burns House **16**
Caerlaverock Castle **13**
Cairn Holy **10**
Cardoness Castle **10**
Carsluith Castle **10**
Castle Gaol **36**
Coldstream Museum **33**
Dawyck Botanic Garden **22**
Devil's Beef Tub **19**
Drumlanrig Castle **18**

natural landscapes offer. Walkers will enjoy the challenge of the **Southern Upland Way** or the infinite number of trails winding through the Pentland Hills south of Edinburgh or the Galloway Forest Park to the west. An altogether more tranquil natural environment awaits along the **Solway coast,** where wide tidal estuaries form wildlife rich nature reserves.

THE best TRAVEL EXPERIENCES IN THE BORDERS & DUMFRIES & GALLOWAY

- **Step back in time at Traquair House:** This oldest continuously inhabited house in Scotland was once a favored destination of royal hunting parties. Spend a day discovering its tangled history, soaking up its romance, and sampling Traquair's very own ale. See p. 143.

- **Explore the still-splendid ruins of Melrose Abbey:** Be beguiled by the glowing rose-colored remains of this once great abbey, where the heart of Robert the Bruce rests in peace. See p. 135.

- **Drive the A708 from Selkirk to Moffat:** Take the scenic route between the Borders and Dumfries and Galloway and experience the haunting land and water-scapes of St. Mary's Loch, pausing along the way at the spectacular Grey Mare's Tail waterfall. See p. 145.

- **Browse through the historic streets and artists' studios of Kirkcudbright:** Be inspired by some of the region's finest artists who live and exhibit their work in this charming waterfront town. See p. 151.

- **Be wowed by words at Wigtown's annual book festival:** Scotland's National Book Town comes alive with literature during its September festival. Join the host of readers and writers sharing their secrets and plundering the town's miles of bookshelves. See p. 154.

JEDBURGH: GATEWAY TO THE BORDERS

48 miles SE of Edinburgh; 57 miles N of Newcastle-upon-Tyne; 13 miles S of Melrose

The small town of Jedburgh is divided by the River Jed and developed around its 12th-century Augustinian abbey close to Dere Street, an old Roman road that used to link the city of York in England with the Antontine Wall. Jedburgh is a typical Borders market town, and evidence of the region's turbulent past can be found in its now peaceful streets, dominated by the evocative ruins of its once mighty abbey and crowned by the still formidable Castle Gaol. A highlight of any visit is the fortified townhouse once inhabited by Mary Queen of Scots, but if you have time, head into the region's famously gentle rolling countryside.

Essentials

GETTING THERE   There's no direct rail link to Jedburgh. The nearest **train station** is at Berwick-upon-Tweed (© **08457/484-950;** www.nationalrail.co.uk for information and tickets), from which it's a time-consuming two-bus trip to Jedburgh, the first from Berwick-upon-Tweed to Kelso, the second from Kelso to Jedburgh.

Contact **Traveline Scotland** for timetables and fares (✆ **0871/200-2233;** www. travelinescotland.com). There are daily **buses** from Edinburgh operated by **National Express** (✆ **08717/818-178;** www.nationalexpress.com); the journey takes 1 hour 40 minutes, and the fare is £9 one-way, £18 round-trip. If you're **driving,** at Corbridge (England), continue north into Scotland along the A68 and from Edinburgh join the A68 at the east side of the city bypass (A720). From the center of Edinburgh, expect a driving time of around 75 minutes.

VISITOR INFORMATION The **Tourist Information Centre (TIC)** (✆ **01835/ 863-170;** www.visitscottishborders.com) is at Murray's Green, adjacent to the town's main car park and across the road from the abbey ruins. It's open year-round daily from 10am to 5pm.

Exploring the Town

Castle Gaol HISTORIC SITE   Crowning a prime elevated spot on the edge of town, Jedburgh's Georgian prison stands on the site of the town's former castle, which was torn down in the 15th century to keep it from falling under English control. The prison built to replace it in 1820 was, in its day, a model of good practice and modern conveniences; its cells even had central heating and were a far cry from the typical dungeons of the time. A tangible sense of life for those once locked up here can be gleaned today along with the history of the Royal Burgh of Jedburgh.

Castle Gate. ✆ **01835/864-750.** Free admission. Mon–Sat 10am–4:30pm; Sun 1–4pm.

Jedburgh Abbey ★★ ABBEY   This famous ruined abbey, founded by David I in 1138, is one of Scotland's finest. Under the Augustinian canons from Beauvais, France, it achieved abbey status in 1152; in its heyday it was regaled in all the royal pageantry of the coronation of the founder's grandson, Malcolm IV (1153–65), and the marriage of Alexander III (1249–86) to his second wife, Yolande de Dreux. The abbey was sacked by the English in 1544 and 1545, which along with the Protestant Reformation brought about this impressive building's demise. For about 300 years, a small section of the abbey was used as the town's parish church, but in 1875 other premises were found and the ruins lay empty. Teams of architects have since restored the original medieval design and, although roofless, the abbey is otherwise fairly complete. Highlights of a visit include the late-12th-century west front, the still-magnificent nave, and almost complete cloister. The adjacent visitor center displays a host of fascinating artifacts from the abbey including the "Jedburgh Comb," which used to form part of an 8th-century shrine.

Abbey Place. ✆ **01835/863-925.** www.historic-scotland.gov.uk. Admission £5.50 adults, £4.40 seniors, £3.30 children 15 and under. Apr–Sept daily 9:30am–5:30pm; Oct–Mar daily 9:30am–4:30pm.

Mary Queen of Scots' Visitor Centre ★ HISTORIC HOME   In 1566 Mary Stuart spent a month in Jedburgh, where she almost died of a mysterious ailment after a tiring 23-mile return ride from a visit to the Earl of Bothwell at Hermitage Castle (see below). In a later lament—commenting on the emotional agonies of the last 20 years of her life—she wrote, "Would that I had died at Jedburgh." The dignified house where she lived during this time is a well-presented showcase of paintings, engravings, and articles related to Mary's life and death, including a lock of her hair and death mask. Visitors are also invited to stroll in Mary's footsteps in the pear tree garden that joins the house—a reminder of the days when Jedburgh was famous for its fruit.

Queen St. ✆ **01835/863-331.** Free admission. Mar–Nov Mon–Sat 10am–4:30pm; Sun 11am–4:30pm.

Exploring the Area

Harestanes Countryside Visitor Centre NATURE RESERVE   For a family-friendly experience of nature, head north of Jedburgh to this visitor center. Here all ages can follow marked trails or take guided walks through one of the most beautiful spots in the Borders. The center also features a Discovery Room complete with wild-life displays and a gift shop specializing in local crafts and tearoom. A program of fun activities from Easter treasure trails to photography and basket-weaving workshops take place throughout the year.

At the junction of the A68 and B6400, Monteviot. ℭ **01835/830-306.** www.scotborders.gov.uk/harestanes. Free admission. Apr–Oct daily 10am–5pm.

Hermitage Castle CASTLE   Take the same journey south of Jedburgh as Mary Queen of Scots made in 1566 to the bedside of her lover, the Earl of Bothwell (1535–78), who lay wounded by English troops at this moody castle. Still mired in the misty gloom of the 1300s, this isolated riverside medieval castle close to the Anglo-Scottish border is steeped in stories of murder, intrigue, and all kinds of ghastly goings-on. Its original owner, Lord Soulis, was accused of devil worship and boiled alive by the angry townspeople. The castle was restored in the early 1800s and is a choice spot to revel in some of the region's most turbulent history and finest countryside.

On an unclassified road (the castle is signposted) between the A7 and B6399, 10 miles south of Hawick. ℭ **01387/376-222.** www.historic-scotland.gov.uk. Admission £4 adults, £3.20 seniors, £2.40 children 15 and under. Apr–Sept daily 9:30am–5:30pm.

Jedforest Deer & Farm Park ★ ☺ PARK/FARM   You'll find some of the area's best walks and nature experiences at this child-friendly park. Around 32 hectares (79 acres) of this 405-hectare (1,000-acre) farm are open to the public and filled with rare breeds of farm animals including pigs and chickens. However, deer are the stars of the show as the park prides itself on herds of red fallow and Asian Sitka deer, which either nuzzle or flee from visitors. Grab a bag of special deer food and follow one of the two trails along the softly undulating, partially forested terrain. One of Scotland's top falconers is also based here at **Falconry Scotland** where demonstrations and sessions for handling falcons, hawks, owls, and eagles take place at lunchtime and mid-afternoon.

Camptown, 5 miles south of Jedburgh along the A68. ℭ **01835/840-364.** www.jedforestdeerpark.co.uk. Admission £5 adults, £3 children 3–16 and seniors. Easter–Aug daily 10am–5:30pm; Sept–Oct daily 11am–4:30pm.

Monteviot House & Gardens GARDEN   This magnificent Borders country house and landscaped gardens stand on both the ancient Roman road Deer Street and the curving banks of the River Teviot. The rambling house is an appealing blend of architectural styles charting its growth from the early 18th-century, and a visit leads though a number of rooms noted for their fine art and antique furniture. Of particular interest is the new chapel created in 1962 and dedicated to the Borders saints. The surrounding 12-hectares (30 acres) of peaceful grounds are made up of gardens and woodland all seen at their best at different times of the year and all a tranquil haven of Borders countryside at its most picturesque.

Off the B6400, which leads east off the A68 north of Jedburgh. ℭ **01835/830-380.** www.monteviot.com. Admission garden £3.50 adult, under-16s free; house £3.50 adult, under-16s free. Garden open Apr–Oct daily noon–5pm; house July only daily 1–5pm.

Where to Eat & Stay

Situated across the road from the abbey ruins on Abbey Place, the **Clock Tower Bistro** (✆ **01835/869-788;** www.clocktowerbistro.co.uk) is the best place in the center of Jedburgh for lunch or dinner, and the **Abbey View Café Bookshop** (✆ **01835/863-873**) next door is a charming spot for coffee and cakes.

Ancrum Craig   The oldest section of this delightful property dates back to 1722 when it was constructed as a farmhouse. From this simple beginning the house expanded into the large, warm Victorian home it is today. Surrounded by landscaped gardens, with views stretching out over the valley of the Teviot, Ancrum Craig is a fine example of a baronial Scottish house. The guest rooms are cozy, one with a tub and the other two with a shower-only bathroom. The largest is the Gold Room, with a bay window boasting sweeping views; the smallest, the Heather Room, overlooks the original farmhouse. Generous breakfasts are served in a light-filled dining room, and in the evening guests are invited to relax in the grand drawing room, which is warmed by an open fire on chilly nights.

Ancrum, Jedburgh, TD8 6UN. www.ancrumcraig.co.uk. ✆ **01835/830-280.** Fax 01835/830-259. 3 units. £60–£80 double. MC, V. Call for directions. **Amenities:** Wi-Fi (free). *In room:* TV, hair dryer.

Ferniehirst Mill Lodge   This chalet-inspired modern guesthouse sits in a peaceful neighborhood away from the town center and attracts those (including hunters and anglers) seeking quiet and rural charm. A haven for wild fowl on 10 hectares (25 acres) of private land, it stands in a secluded valley beside the fast-moving Jed Water. Its pine-paneled guest rooms are functional but comfortable, each with a private bathroom. The guest lounge includes a bar and TV, and horse-riding excursions can also be arranged. For an extra £18, you can add a home-cooked three-course dinner to your stay; picnics can also be prepared for an extra £6.

Off the A68, 2½ miles south of Jedburgh, TD8 6PQ. www.ferniehirstmill.co.uk. ✆/fax **01835/863-279.** 8 units. £30 per person per night. MC, V. **Amenities:** Bar. *In room:* Hair dryer.

Jedforest Hotel ★   Originally a shooting lodge, this 19th-century hotel has been extended over the years into the rambling property it is today on 14 hectares (35 acres) of peaceful grounds that offer private fishing on the River Tweed—known for the largest average size of its fish. Shooting can also be organized through a local agent, and a spread of golf courses lie all around. Bedrooms come in a wide range of sizes and styles, from standard to king size, even a four-poster suite. Four rooms, as comfortable as those in the main house, lie in the river cottage adjacent to the hotel. A team of skilled chefs prepare a menu of Scottish and international cuisine all served in the Scottish-themed **bistro,** which is also open to non-guests who call to reserve a table. Only children over 12 are welcomed.

Camptown, Jedburgh, TD8 6PJ. www.jedforesthotel.com. ✆ **01835/840-222.** Fax 01835/840-226. 12 units. £110–£165 double; £180 suite. AE, DC, MC, V. 3 miles south of Jedburgh. **Amenities:** Restaurant; bar; room service. *In room:* TV, Wi-Fi (free).

The Spinney Guest House & Lodges ★   This small complex provides guests with a choice of bedrooms in the main house offering B&B accommodation or two self-catering pinewood lodges in the surrounding grounds. Leather and wood furnishings feature throughout the well-maintained, good-sized guest rooms, and hearty breakfasts are served in the comfortable dining room. The fully equipped lodges in the surrounding grounds come with either one or two bedrooms plus their own bathrooms, sitting rooms, and kitchens along with a private balcony on which to soak up the best of the Borders sunshine and views of the Cheviot hills.

Langlee, off the A68 1¾ miles south of Jedburgh, TD8 6PB. www.thespinney-jedburgh.co.uk. **① 01835/863-525.** Fax 01835/864-883. 5 units. £64 double; 1-bedroom lodge £180–£200; 2-bedroom lodge £260–£300 for 3 nights midweek or the weekend. MC, V. *In room:* TV, hair dryer.

KELSO: ABBEY RUINS & ADAM ARCHITECTURE ★

44 miles SE of Edinburgh; 12 miles NE of Jedburgh; 15 miles E of Melrose

Sir Walter Scott hailed Kelso as "the most beautiful, if not the most romantic, village in Scotland," and it remains one of the best of the Borders' historic towns. The town lies at the point where the River Teviot meets the River Tweed and developed around its once thriving, now very ruined abbey. Kelso is one of the best places in the Borders for shopping, but the main reasons to visit are its poignant abbey ruins and the two great historic properties of Floors Castle and the Mellerstain House, both of which were partially designed by the great architect William Adam. Kelso's central position within the region makes this flourishing market town a good base from which to also explore the surrounding towns.

Essentials

GETTING THERE   The nearest train station is Berwick-upon-Tweed, from which **Perryman's Bus** (① 01289/308-719; www.perrymansbuses.co.uk) service no. 67 links with Kelso. Buses depart roughly every 2 hours and take 50 minutes to reach Kelso. The one-way fare is £5. **Munro's of Jedburgh** (① 01835/862-253; www. munrosofjedburgh.co.uk) operates a direct bus service between Edinburgh and Jedburgh, which also stops at Kelso. This service, the no. 51/52, departs hourly from Edinburgh bus station and takes just under 2 hours to reach Kelso. The fare is £6.50 one-way, £11 round-trip.

If driving from Edinburgh, join the A68 at the east side of the city bypass (A720), and then fork left north of Lauder onto the A697. At Whiteburn fork right onto the A6089, which leads to Kelso.

Exploring the Area

Floors Castle ★★ CASTLE   Standing high upon the banks of the Tweed, Floors Castle is the magnificent home of the 10th Duke of Roxburghe and Scotland's largest inhabited castle. The castle was created in 1721 when William Adam was invited to extend an older original building. In the mid-19th century leading Scottish architect William Playfair was then commissioned to remodel Floors into the romantic masterpiece it is today. Both interior and exterior still command the grandeur they were designed to evoke, all thoroughly embellished by an outstanding fine art collection brought to Floors in the early 20th century by Mary Goelet, the American wife of the eighth duke. A guided tour leads visitors through a succession of rooms including the Drawing Room, complete with 17th-century tapestries, and the sweeping ballroom, which claims long views of the Roxburghe estate. Riverside walks, a children's play area, and the holly tree that marks the spot where Scottish King James II was killed in 1460 all await in the surrounding grounds.

Off the A697, 1¾ miles north of Kelso. © **01573/223-333.** www.floorscastle.com. Admission £8 adults, £7 seniors, £4 children 5–16, under-5s free. Easter weekend and May-Oct daily 11am–5pm.

Kelso Abbey ABBEY   Once a great ecclesiastical center, Kelso Abbey has lain in ruins since the late 16th-century, when it suffered its last and most devastating attack by the English, who ripped off its roofs and reduced large sections to rubble. Although the remains of Kelso's abbey may not be as impressive as others in this region, it is the oldest (1128) and was probably the largest and richest. What remains of the west transept tower suggests the abbey's original massive construction, and it, along with the west front are flanked by buttresses crowned with rounded turrets. Sir Walter Scott knew Kelso Abbey well; he spent time here studying at Waverley Cottage, which can be seen from the abbey's parking area and was once Kelso's Grammar School, where the famous author learned how to read and write.

Bridge St. No phone. www.historic-scotland.gov.uk. Free admission. Open 24 hr.

Mellerstain ★★ HISTORIC SITE   Seat of the earls of Haddington, Mellerstain is one of the most famous William and Robert Adam-designed mansions and one of Scotland's greatest Georgian residences. William built two wings in 1725 and the main building was designed by his son Robert 40 years later. One of Mellerstain's enduring legacies is the "Household Book" of Lady Grisell Baillie (1665–1746), the estate's most famous resident, whose book is a detailed account of 18th-century customs and social life. An impressive library is a highlight of Mellerstain's opulent interior, which is richly embellished with antique furniture. The surrounding wildlife-filled parkland was laid out in 1725 by William Adam, and the garden terrace offers panoramic views south towards the Cheviot Hills.

5 miles northwest of Kelso off the A6089. © **01573/410-225.** www.mellerstain.com. Admission £8.50 adults, £4 children, under-5s free. Easter weekend, May–June and Sept Sun, Wed, and bank holidays 12:30–5pm; July–Aug Sun-Mon and Wed–Thurs 12:30–5pm; Oct Sun 12:30–5pm.

Outdoor Activities

Designed by Dave Thomas, one of Britain's leading golf-course architects, the par-72, 7,111-yard **Roxburghe Golf Course** (© **01573/450-331;** www.roxburghegolf club.co.uk) is the only championship course in the region. Guests of the Roxburghe Hotel (see "Where to Eat & Stay," below) can most easily get tee times, but the course is also open to non-members. Greens fees are £35 to £70 for 18 holes, less for hotel guests.

Favorite spots for walkers in the region include the village of **Kirk Yeetholm,** 8 miles southeast of Kelso on the B6352 whose Border Hotel is the official end of the **Pennine Way,** a 266-mile hike that begins at Edale in Yorkshire, England. Excellent walking can also be found around **Smailholm Tower** (© **01573/460-365;** www. historic-scotland.gov.uk), which stands on a ridge 7 miles west of Kelso and is sign-posted off the B6404. This restored medieval peel tower (fortified tower) rises 18m (59 ft.) above a loch and commands outstanding Borders' views. Smailholm Tower is open April to September daily 9:30am to 5:30pm and October to March weekends only 9:30am to 4:30pm. Admission is £4.50 for adults, £3.60 for seniors and £2.70 for children aged 5 to 15.

6 | ROBERT ADAM: architect TO THE KING

In the field of architecture, one Scottish name towers over all the rest: **Robert Adam** (1728–92), whose adaptations of the Italian Palladian style have been admired and duplicated in public and private buildings around the world. He has emerged as Britain's most prestigious neoclassical architect in a century that produced many talented competitors. Today owning an Adam-designed building is a considered an honor.

Adam's genius derived from his synthesis of the decorative traditions of the French and Italian Renaissance with those of ancient Greece and Rome. His designs are notable for their lavish use of color, inspired by Grecian vase paintings and artifacts uncovered from archaeological digs such as Pompeii. Adam also demonstrated a well-developed business sense and had the knack of decorating the right house at the right time for rich clients who helped propel him into the spotlight.

Throughout much of his career Robert collaborated with his capable but less talented younger brother, **James** (1730–94), who handled many of the everyday details of the commissions they executed together, which in many cases also included every aspect of a property's interior decoration and furnishings. The brothers' education in the visual arts began early thanks to their father **William Adam** (1689–1748), who was the leading Scottish architect of his day and designed a host of manor houses in what's been described as a crude but vigorous Palladian style.

Robert was born in Kirkcaldy, in Fife, but soon moved to London, the source of most of his large commissions. He laboriously studied the architecture of imperial Rome under the supervision of then-famous French antiquarian C.L. Clérisseau, with whom he toured widely in Italy and Dalmatia (a region which now lies mainly in Croatia). In 1764, Adam compiled the information he gleamed on these tours in his acclaimed *The Ruins of the Palace of the Emperor Diocletian at Spalatro.* In 1761, Robert, along with architect William Chambers, was appointed architect of the king's works, at the time one of the most prestigious posts in Britain. In 1773, an illustrated volume, *The Works of Robert and James Adam,* documented the brothers' vision which they justifiably claimed revolutionized the principles of English aesthetics.

The Adam style, a richly detailed yet airy interpretation of neoclassicism, was a radical departure from the more ponderous and sometimes ecclesiastical forms that preceded it. Almost immediately, the Adam style of ceiling decorations and mantelpieces was widely copied throughout Britain, and within less than a generation this vision radically influenced furniture styles throughout Europe and North America, most notably France's Louis XVI style. Adam buildings in Scotland include the **Old Quad** at the University of Edinburgh and **Mellerstain** in the Borders (see review above).

Where to Eat & Stay

In addition to the listings below, the **Ivy Neuk** B&B (www.ivyneuk.com; ✆ **01573/226-270**) at 62 Horsemarket offers good quality, inexpensive accommodation; and the **Cobbles Inn** restaurant and bar (www.thecobblesinn.co.uk; ✆ **01757/223-548**) at 7 Bowmont St. and the **Pharlanne** delicatessen (www.pharlanne.co.uk; ✆ **01573/229-745**) at 13 Bridge St. are recommended places to eat.

The Cross Keys Hotel   Previous guests at this stately Georgian hotel, built in 1769 on the site of an old Scottish coaching inn, include Bonnie Prince Charlie and Beatrix Potter. The hotel commands a central position on the edge of Kelso's French-style cobbled main square, and its mid-size guest rooms are well appointed. Rooms at the back are quieter. The on-site **Oak Room** restaurant is busy with both residents and locals from morning coffee to dinner and serves a menu of modern Scottish and Mediterranean cuisine, while the cozy bar boasts an impressive collection of single-malt whiskies, local ales, and fine wine.

36 The Square, Kelso, TD5 7HL. www.cross-keys-hotel.co.uk. ✆ **01573/223-303.** Fax 01573/225-792. 28 units. £77–£137 double. AE, MC, V. **Amenities:** Restaurant; bar. *In room:* TV, hair dryer.

Ednam House Hotel ★★   The Ednam is tucked away in a quiet spot close to the center of Kelso and is a careful conversion of a mid-18th-century Georgian house often referred to as "that lovely place beside the river." The house maintains the comfortable feel of a much-loved home and is filled with an unusual collection of antiques. Ednam's Principal Rooms—the original master bedrooms of the old manor—overlook the River Tweed and other doubles with scenic river views have slightly higher rates attached. For a real treat, book a 2-night stay in the adjacent Georgian-style Orangerie, which features two elegantly furnished and comfortable bedrooms and a large private river facing the sitting room. Food here is as magnificent as the rooms, and the riverside restaurant serves a daily changing menu of traditional and modern Scottish cuisine that makes full use of local seasonal produce.

Bridge St., Kelso, TD5 7HT. www.ednamhouse.com. ✆ **01573/224-168.** Fax 01573/226-319. 32 units. £120–£150 double; £167 Principal Room; £226 the Orangerie. MC, V. **Amenities:** Restaurant; bar. *In room:* TV, hair dryer.

The Roxburghe Hotel & Golf Course ★★   This late-19th-century country house nestles amongst 81 hectares (200 acres) of woodland, lawns, and gardens. It

COLDSTREAM

The small town of Coldstream sits on the banks of the River Tweed at a point where it forms part of the boundary between Scotland and England, 9 miles northeast of Kelso, and is famous for giving its name to the British army's oldest continually existing Corps—the Coldstream Guards. Part of the Queen's personal troops, the Coldstream regiment was founded over 360 years ago and was the only one to survive the disbanding of Cromwell's New Model Army in 1661; it still undertakes active service. Learn all about this iconic regiment at the **Coldstream Museum** (✆ **01890/ 882-630**) on Market Square. The museum is free to enter and open March to September Monday through Saturday 10am to 4pm and Sunday 2 to 4pm, and October Monday through Saturday 1 to 4pm.

Other places to visit in the town include **Henderson Park,** which stands high above the banks of the Tweed and features a stone monument commemorating Coldstream's connection with the guards. Or take time to follow riverside walks along the Tweed to the tiny old village of **Lennel,** 1 mile northeast of Coldstream, or the **Hirsel Estate** (✆ **01555/851-536;** www.dandaestates. co.uk), which stands off the A697 as it leads into Coldstream. The estate is open year-round and features a small museum, woodland walks, a tearoom, and craft center.

was built as the Roxburghes' family home who valued its location on the banks of the trout-filled River Teviot, and in 1982 the property was converted into a splendid country house hotel. The old stable block contains six guest rooms and an additional 16 rooms are located in the main house. Many guest rooms and suites are individually designed; some include four-poster beds, and all are well appointed and infused with classical elegance. Public areas are traditional and informal and warmed by a series of open fires. The Roxburghe can arrange numerous leisure activities from archery to fishing, and the hotel's restaurant makes full use of produce grown on the surrounding estate.

Off the A698 at Heiton near Kelso, TD5 8JZ. www.roxburghe-hotel.com. ℂ **01573/450-331.** Fax 01573/450-611. 22 units. £125–£185 double; from £245 suite. AE, DC, MC, V. **Amenities:** Restaurant; bar; golf course; croquet lawn; salon; room service . *In room:* TV, hair dryer, iPod docking stations, Wi-Fi (free).

MELROSE ★

37 miles SE of Edinburgh; 70 miles NW of Newcastle-upon-Tyne; 40 miles W of Berwick-upon-Tweed

The small town of Melrose is one of the highlights of the Borders. Most people travel here to be awed by the beguiling ruins of its once-powerful abbey where the heart of Robert the Bruce lies in a sealed casket, and then make the short trip west to Dryburgh, one of the Borders' other great ruined abbeys. Dryburgh is the burial place of Sir Walter Scott and the author's presence can be felt all around this region; his former home Abbotsford House lies only 1¾ miles west. Melrose also stands close to the Southern Upland Way (p. 156), which passes through town, and a day's hike on the section along the River Tweed outside Melrose is one of the most delightful and scenic walks in Scotland.

Essentials

GETTING THERE The nearest train station is at Berwick-upon-Tweed from which **Perryman's Bus** (ℂ 01289/308-719; www.perrymansbuses.co.uk) service no. 67 links with Melrose. Buses depart roughly every 2 hours and take 90 minutes to reach Melrose. Fares are about £5 one-way and £10 round-trip. Contact **National Rail Enquiries** for train timetables and fares (ℂ 8457/484-950; www.nationalrail. co.uk). **First** (ℂ 08708/727-271; www.firstgroup.com) operates bus no. 62, a direct service from Edinburgh to Melrose that runs roughly every hour, with the journey taking around 2 hours. Contact First for up-to-date timetables and fares, or **Traveline Scotland** (ℂ 0871/200-2233; www.travelinescotland.com).

If driving from Edinburgh, join the A68 at the east side of the city bypass (A720) and follow this road until the junction with the A6091, which leads west into Melrose.

VISITOR INFORMATION **Melrose Tourist Information Centre** is at **Abbey House,** Abbey Street (ℂ 0870/608-0404; www.melrose.bordernet.co.uk). It's open April to June and September to October Monday through Saturday 10am to 4:30pm and Sunday noon to 4pm; July and August Monday through Saturday 10am to 5:30pm and Sunday noon to 5pm; and November to March Friday and Saturday 10am to 2pm.

Exploring the Area

If you have the time, it's worth exploring around the edges of Melrose's small center. Take a stroll across the **Gattonside Suspension Bridge,** an old iron bridge built in 1826 that spans the Tweed, and seek out the town's abandoned train station off Palma Place where advertising boards from the 1960s (when the train line was closed) still line the canopy of the deserted old platform. Other historic attractions include the **Trimontium Heritage Centre,** on The Square (℃ **01896/822-651;** www.trimontium.org.uk/wb), which reveals the history of a large Roman frontier post once located near Melrose. The center is open from April to October daily 10:30am to 4:30pm, and admission is £2 for adults, £1.50 for seniors and children, and £5 for families. Adjacent to the abbey on St. Mary's Road, **The Harmony Garden** (℃ **0844/493-2251;** www.nts.org.uk) is an old-fashioned walled garden rich with herbaceous borders and pristine lawns. The garden is open April to October Monday through Saturday 10am to 5pm and Sunday 1 to 5pm; admission is £6 adults, £5 seniors and children, and £16 families. For evening entertainment in the region, check out what's on at the **Wynd** (℃ **01896/820-028;** www.thewyndmelrose.com), a small independent arts center that programs an eclectic range of theatre, film, and live music performances.

Abbotsford House ★★ HISTORIC HOME   This grand former home of Sir Walter Scott was designed by the author himself and epitomizes all the Scottish romance and chivalry for which Scott was famous. After Scott's literary works, the Scottish baronial Abbotsford, built on the banks of the Tweed in 1822, is considered to be his most enduring achievement. The house is stuffed with the huge collection of relics Scott collected during his lifetime including artifacts associated with the historical characters he re-created in his novels including a gun, sword, and dagger owned by the cattle herder come outlaw Rob Roy. The most fascinating part of the tour is Scott's old study, lined with rare books and showcasing the author's old writing desk, chair, and death mask. You can also see Scott's library complete with 9,000 rare volumes and the dining room overlooking the Tweed where Scott died on September 21, 1832.

Off the B6360, 2 miles west of Melrose. ℃ **01896/752-043.** www.scottsabbotsford.co.uk. Admission £7 adults, £3.50 under-15s, £18 families. Mid-Mar to mid-Sept Mon–Sat 9:30am–5pm; also Sun mid-March to May 11am–4pm, June to mid-Sept 9:30am–5pm.

Melrose Abbey ★★ ABBEY   These lichen-covered ruins, among the most evocative in Europe, are all that's left of the ecclesiastical community established here by Cistercian monks in 1136. The romantic pull of this ruined abbey was immortalized by Sir Walter Scott, who was instrumental in getting the decayed remains repaired and restored in the early 19th century. Scott wrote, "If thou would'st view fair Melrose aright, go visit in the pale moonlight" and in daylight hours the abbey's red-sandstone shell almost glows in the sun. Many elongated windows, carvings, and delicate tracery still exist along with the ground plans of two large cloisters that once lay to the north and west of the abbey. A stone plague marks the spot where it's believed the heart of the Bruce lies buried and an adjoining museum is filled with medieval artifacts unearthed in the abbey's grounds.

Abbey St. ℃ **01896/822-562.** www.historic-scotland.gov.uk. Admission £5.50 adults, £4.40 seniors, £3.30 children 5-15. Apr–Sept daily 9:30am–5:30pm; Oct–Mar daily 9:30am–4:30pm.

A walk along THE BORDERS: ST. CUTHBERT'S WAY

Follow in the footsteps of 7th-century St. Cuthbert along the Scotland–England border by walking all or part of the 62½-mile St. Cuthbert's Way, which stretches from Melrose across the border into England to the Holy Island of Lindisfarne on the Northumberland coast. St. Cuthbert began his ministry in Melrose in about A.D. 650 and was later appointed Bishop of Lindisfarne where he died and was buried in 687. Following Cuthbert's death, the community he created on the island produced one of the greatest legacies of the Anglo-Saxon period, the Lindisfarne Gospels. This marked walk starts at Melrose Abbey and passes many places linked to Cuthbert's life and legend including prehistoric relics, Roman ruins, and historic castles. The complete walk takes around 4 to 5 days to complete, or you can meander along the first part from the abbey into the nearby Eildon Hills. Visit the Melrose Tourist Information Centre for more details or see www.stcuthbertsway.fsnet.co.uk.

Thirlestane Castle ★ CASTLE   One of Scotland's most imposing country houses, Thirlestane has been owned by the Maitland family since 1218. Over the centuries the castle has been added to and altered and strikes a fairytale pose of pink sandstone baronial towers and turrets against the backdrop the Leader valley. The interior is festooned with ornamental plaster ceilings—some of the country's finest from the Restoration period—and portraits of the Maitland's family ancestry line the walls of the State Dining Room. Children will enjoy the old nurseries where collections of Georgian, Edwardian, and Victorian toys are housed, and a taste of life below stairs can be gleaned among the cast-iron ranges of the old kitchen. A castle tour also includes a visit to Bonnie Prince Charlie's room where the man himself slept in 1745 and the chance to explore surrounding formal gardens and parklands.

10 miles north of Melrose off the A68. ℂ **01578/722-430.** www.thirlestanecastle.co.uk. Admission £10 adults, £7 seniors, £6 children 5–15, £25 families. Easter weekend, May–June and Sept Sun, Wed–Thurs and bank holidays 10am–5pm; July–Aug Sun–Thurs 10am–5pm.

Shopping

Melrose is one of the best destinations for shopping in the Borders. Most stores open Monday through Saturday from 9:30am to 5pm and some open on Sundays from 11am to around 4pm.

Mason's of Melrose, 9 Market Square (ℂ **01896/822-196**), is an old-fashioned bookshop whose shelves are filled with books on subjects from local history to gardening alongside adult and children's fiction and a wide choice of greetings cards. Also on Market Square, **The Country Kitchen** (ℂ **01896/822-586**) displays a comprehensive selection of English, French, and Scottish cheeses, along with pâtés, meat products, and fresh-ground coffee. For gifts including jewelry and stationary, visit **Tracey M** on the Wynd (ℂ **01896/820-532**). The **Abbey Mill** (ℂ **01896/822-138**), close to the abbey ruins on Annay Road, is the best place for all things tartan and Scottish knitwear. The **George and Abbotsford** hotel and real ale pub on High Street (ℂ **01896/822-308**) features a small beer shop stocked with bottles of real ale from breweries across the Borders and beyond.

Where to Eat & Stay

A local favorite for food, coffee, and cakes throughout the day is **Russell's** on Market Square (℡ **01896/822-335**). Two of the town's most likable pubs are the **King's Arms,** High Street (℡ **01896/823-998**), and the **George and Abbotsford,** also on High Street (℡ **01896/822-308**).

Buccleuch Arms Hotel ★★   Standing off a main route between Melrose and Dryburgh, this inviting hotel-cum-pub began life as an inn back in 1836 and is one of the best places to stay and dine in the Borders. Buccleuch was voted Scottish Inn of the Year in 2011 and all its en-suite guest rooms are individually designed and fuse bright modern touches and splashes of color with a traditional style. Public areas are warmed by open fires and ooze all the panache and comfort an old inn should. Homemade food created from the best Border produce is a step above normal pub food and served for most of the day and into the evening in the main bar, where you can also linger over a choice of single malts, real ales, and select wines. A family suite is available and the hotel can help organize local activities and beauty treatments.

The Green, St. Boswells, TD6 0EW. 5 miles south of Melrose off A68. www.buccleucharms.com. ℡ **01835/822-243.** 19 units. £100–£115 double. MC, V. **Amenities:** Restaurant; bar. *In room:* TV, hair dryer, Wi-Fi (free).

Burts Hotel   One of Melrose's most attractive old buildings, the black-and-white Burts Hotel is festooned with frothing window boxes in summer and commands a central spot on the town's Market Square. This family-run inn dates back to 1722 and its decor has a rich traditional feel with tartan touches throughout. Guest rooms are modern, comfortable, and individually decorated, and attractive public areas sport Windsor chairs and an old fireplace. Informal lunches and suppers are served in the bistro bar as well as 90 different single-malt whiskies. The award-winning restaurant champions the best in Scottish cuisine and features dishes prepared with local game and fish all rounded off with sinfully good deserts.

Market Square, Melrose, TD6 9PN. www.burtshotel.co.uk. ℡ **01896/822-285.** Fax 01896/822-870. 20 units. £133 double. AE, DC, MC, V. **Amenities:** Restaurant; bar; room service; Wi-Fi (free). *In room:* TV, hair dryer.

King's Arms Hotel ☺   One of Melrose's oldest commercial buildings still in use, this 17th-century coaching inn overlooks the center of town. Inside is a series of basic public rooms and a number of simple but comfortably furnished small guest rooms plus a family suite with three double beds. The restaurant serves a mix of seafood, meat dishes, pastas, and pies at reasonable prices alongside a light bites menu of baked potatoes, sandwiches, and omelets.

High St., Melrose, TD6 9PB. www.kingsarms-melrose.co.uk. ℡ **01896/823-998.** Fax 01896/823-812. 7 units. £90 double; £150 family suite. MC, V. **Amenities:** Restaurant; bar. *In room:* TV, hair dryer.

Marmion's Brasserie MODERN SCOTTISH   This tasteful child-friendly restaurant is a cross between a brasserie and a coffee shop and is housed in a 150-year-old building close to the abbey ruins. Its kitchen favors Scottish ingredients that are transformed into frequently changing menus of modern flavors such as sea bass with smoked bacon and mushroom stuffing and garlic crushed potatoes for dinner, or steak and ale pie with mustard mash for lunch. Marmion's is also a relaxing place to start the day with coffee, homemade scones, and the morning papers.

2 Buccleuch St., Melrose TD6 9LB. ℡ **01896/822-245.** www.marmionsbrasserie.co.uk. Reservations recommended for dinner. Main courses lunch £9–£12; dinner £12–£20, 3-course set dinner menu £20–£22. MC, V. Daily 10am–9pm.

Townhouse Hotel   This well-maintained family-owned hotel in the heart of Melrose is the sister property of Burt's Hotel (see above). Sporting an equally pristine black-and-white exterior as its partner hotel, the Townhouse offers guests a choice of plush recently refurbished rooms that range from standard to superior and one family suite. The room quality is high and all are individually designed and comfortable. The modern brasserie is open for informal lunches and dinners of salads, seafood, and steaks, and more formal dining of first-class Scottish fare is served in the restaurant. Staff can also help organize activities including golf, cycling, and fishing.

Market Square, Melrose TD6 9PQ. www.thetownhousemelrose.co.uk. ✆ **01896/822-645.** Fax 01896/823-474. 11 units. £124–£136 double; £136 family room. MC, V. **Amenities:** Restaurant; bar. *In room:* TV, hair dryer, Wi-Fi (free).

A Side Trip to Dryburgh Abbey

Six miles southeast of Melrose off the B6356 stands the remains of the Border's fourth great ruined abbey, Dryburgh. En route you can choose to take a short detour to **Scott's View** ★. Signposted off the B6356, this famous vantage point high above the Tweed Valley overlooks Sir Walter's beloved Eildon Hills.

Dryburgh Abbey ★★ ABBEY   The most secluded of all the ruined Borders abbeys, Dryburgh stands in haunting Gothic isolation surrounded by gnarled yew trees and cedars of Lebanon, said to have been planted by knights returning from the Crusades. The ravaged remains of this once-splendid building stand in peace on a wide loop of the River Tweed and its natural surrounds all serve to enhance the remaining fragments' haunting sense of beauty. In its heyday Dryburgh was never as powerful as its three neighboring abbeys—Kelso, Jedburgh, and Melrose—and its gentle ruins are more the place to appreciate the peace and solitude that epitomized a monk's life rather than be wowed by the wealth and influence these ecclesiastical power houses wielded. Sir Walter Scott was buried in Dryburgh's north transept after he died in 1832.

Off the B6356, Dryburgh, ✆ **01835/822-381.** Admission £5 adults, £4 seniors, £3 children 5–15. Apr-Sept daily 9:30am–5:30pm; Oct-Mar daily 9:30am–4:30pm.

Where to Eat & Stay

Clint Lodge Country House ★   This grand country house is owned by the Duke of Sutherland and has been carefully converted into a small guesthouse filled with charm and grace. In the 18th century the building served as a sporting lodge, and its tranquil setting is surrounded by panoramic views over the Tweed Valley. The mid-size bedrooms are comfortable and traditionally furnished, often with a treasure-trove of family heirlooms. Dinner is served in the dining room whose traditional ambiance perfectly complements home-cooked fresh Scottish fare. Other public areas include a sun lounge and drawing room, and guests are more than welcome to make the most of the lodge's pretty gardens.

Off the B6356 at St. Boswells, Melrose TD6 0DZ. www.clintlodge.co.uk. ✆ **01835/822-027.** Fax 01835/822-656. 5 units. £100–£110 double. MC, V. **Amenities:** Restaurant. *In room:* TV.

Dryburgh Abbey Hotel ★   Located right next to the abbey ruins and on the banks of the Tweed, this country house hotel is a good choice for those seeking a tranquil rural setting and slice of traditional Scottish hospitality along with good leisure facilities. It was built in 1845 as the home of Lady Grisell Baillie and haunted by the "gray lady," who had an ill-fated affair with a monk leading to his execution and her suicide. Rooms come in a choice of standard and deluxe doubles and some suites, which boast plenty of room and wide views of the abbey and river. Food is served in the Abbey Bistro and Tweed Restaurant, and afternoon tea can be taken in the lounge or better still in the adjacent gardens overlooking the abbey ruins.

Off the B6404 next to Dryburgh Abbey and close to St. Boswells, TD6 0RQ. www.dryburgh.co.uk. © **01835/822-261.** Fax 01835/823-945. 38 units. £80–£115 double; £128–£160 suite. AE, MC, V. **Amenities:** Restaurant; bar; pool (indoor); sauna; room service; Wi-Fi (free). *In room:* TV, hair dryer.

SELKIRK

40 miles SE of Edinburgh; 73 miles SE of Glasgow.

Selkirk is one of Scotland's oldest Royal Burghs and commands an elevated position above the Ettrick Valley, one of the Borders' most bewitching landscapes. The surrounding countryside is Selkirk's greatest attraction because there's a limited amount to see and do in the town itself. Connections with Sir Walter Scott and William Wallace are strong and Bowhill, one of the region's finest country houses, stands on the western fringes of town. The great African explorer Mungo Park was born near Selkirk in 1771. Park was a doctor who won fame exploring the River Niger where he drowned in 1806 while escaping from hostile natives. A gleaming white statue of the explorer stands atop a tall white plinth at the east end of High Street opposite the old surgeon's hall where Park trained.

Essentials

GETTING THERE   Berwick-upon-Tweed is the nearest train station, but there's no direct bus service between the two towns. Those wishing to travel by bus must first catch a service to Galashiels 6 miles north of Selkirk, and then catch a connecting service. **First** bus no. X95 connects Edinburgh with Selkirk; buses depart every half an hour and the journey takes just under 2 hours. Details of fares and timetables for all these routes can be obtained from **Traveline Scotland** (© **0871/200-2233;** www.travelinescotland.com).

If driving from Edinburgh, join the A68 at the east side of the city bypass (A720) and follow this road until the junction with the A6091, which heads west into Melrose and then becomes the A7 as it swings south to Selkirk.

VISITOR INFORMATION   The **Tourist Information Centre** is located in **Halliwell's House Museum** (see below) on Market Place (© **01750/720-054;** www.visitscottishborders.com). April to June and September, it's open Monday through Saturday 10am to 5pm and Sunday 10am to noon; July and August Monday through Saturday 10am to 5pm and Sunday 10am to 1pm, and October Monday through Saturday 10am to 4pm and Sunday 10am to noon.

Exploring the Area

Standing in the center of Selkirk on Market Place, **Halliwell's House Museum** (© **01750/200-96**) is the place to unearth the town's history and view a careful reconstruction of the former ironmonger's shop that once occupied this old building. Admission is free, and a visit also includes a tour of the **Robson Gallery,** which exhibits contemporary art and local crafts. The museum is open April to October Monday through Saturday 11am to 4pm and Sunday noon to 3pm. A small abandoned graveyard surrounding the ruined **Kirk o' the Forest** stands adjacent to this museum. According to legend this poignant kirkyard with its commanding views of the surroundings forests and valleys is the place where William Wallace was declared Guardian of Scotland in around 1297 in the aftermath of his glorious victory at the Battle of Stirling Bridge (p. 257).

Sir Walter Scott's Courtroom (ⓒ **01750/207-61**) on Market Place is a final stop on a tour of town. Now a museum, this imposing old building is the place where the man himself, as Sheriff of Selkirk from 1803 to 1332, dished out justice to the local population. The museum is free to enter, and a visit includes a peek into the old courtroom as well as finding out more about Scott's time as sheriff and the lives of Mungo Park and the region's other great writer James Hogg, otherwise known as the "Ettrick Shepard," who penned the classic *Confessions of a Justified Sinner*. The museum is open April to September Monday through Friday 10am to 4pm and Saturday 11am to 3pm plus Sunday May to August 11am to 3pm, and October Monday through Saturday noon to 3pm.

From Selkirk the A708 winds a spectacular route southwest past **St. Mary's Loch ★★** and the **Grey Mare's Tail waterfall ★** to **Moffat** (p. 144), or head northwest for the gentler countryside of the Tweed Valley Forest Park and **Traquair House** (p. 143).

Bowhill ★★ ☺ HISTORIC SITE Set against some of the Borders' most mysterious scenery, the magnificent 18th-century Bowhill estate is the family home of the Scotts of Buccleuch. Bowhill's rare-art collection includes works by Canaletto, Claude, Gainsborough, and Reynolds and is as grand as the house itself. These paintings, along with fine French furniture, porcelain, silverware, tapestries and mementos of Sir Walter Scott, are all encountered on a tour of the house. The surrounding country estate features a fabulous children's adventure playground and five waymarked trails that range from a gentle stroll around the loch to a 7-mile woodland hike. Details of Bowhill's ranger-led activities can be found in the Visitor Centre and the estate also includes a small theatre created inside a converted Victorian Game Larder, which hosts a program of small-scale productions.

Off the A708, 3 miles west of Selkirk. ⓒ **01750/222-04**. www.bowhill.org. Admission to house £8 adults, £7 seniors, £3.50 children 3–15; admission to Country Estate £3.50 adults, £2.50 seniors and children. House July–Aug daily 1–4:30pm; Country Estate Apr daily 11am–4pm; May–June Sat–Sun 11am–4pm; July–Aug daily 10am–5pm.

Where to Eat & Stay

Recommended places to eat in the center of Selkirk include the **Selkirk Deli** (ⓒ **07851/997-747**) on High Street, and the **Willow Brasserie** inside **The County** hotel (www.countyhotelselkirk.co.uk; ⓒ **01750/721-233**), also on High Street.

Best Western Philipburn Country House Hotel ★ Surrounded by 1.6 peaceful hectares (4 acres) of gardens and woodlands, this country house hotel occupies an elevated position on the outskirts of Selkirk towards the Ettrick Valley and Bowhill (see above). The main house contains 12 high-quality guest rooms, all comfortable and modern and some with balconies, garden views, and spa baths. Alternatively guests can choose to stay in one of four cozy wooden lodges that sleep between two and five people and each contain their own kitchen and lounge. Dining options are a choice between the Bistro or more formal and fine-dining-focused 1745 Restaurant—both favor local produce and Scottish dishes—and pre-dinner drinks are served in the hotel bar.

Linglie Rd., Selkirk, TD7 5LS. www.philipburnhousehotel.co.uk. ©**01750/207-47.** Fax 01750/216-90. 16 units. £120–£170 double. Lodges £50 per person per night. AE, MC, V. **Amenities:** 2 restaurants; bar. *In room:* TV, hair dryer, Wi-Fi (free).

Heatherlie House Hotel An imposing stone-and-slate Victorian mansion with steep gables and turrets, this fine and friendly hotel is set on .8 hectares (2 acres) of woodlands and mature gardens close to the center of Selkirk. The guest rooms are all immaculately maintained and furnished in a traditional style in keeping with the era of the house. All rooms are en-suite except for one single room. An open fire adds warmth to the lounge, where reasonably priced bar meals are available daily or dinner may be served in the high-ceilinged "Heather" room. The hotel bar is well stocked with real ales and single malts, and shooting trips can be arranged.

Heatherlie Park, Selkirk, TD7 5AL. www.heatherliehouse.co.uk. © **01750/721-200.** Fax 01750/720-005. 7 units, 6 with private bathroom. £74 double. MC, V. **Amenities:** Restaurant; bar. *In room:* TV, hair dryer.

PEEBLES

23 miles S of Edinburgh; 53 miles SE of Glasgow; 20 miles W of Melrose

The royal burgh of Peebles stands on the banks of the River Tweed, one of Scotland's major salmon fishing rivers. This county town is surrounded on all sides by a diversity of natural landscapes including the Pentland Hills, Glentress Forest, and the Tweed Valley. Outdoor enthusiasts can choose from activities including walking, mountain biking, fishing, shooting, and golf. This countryside is also home to ancient estates such as Traquair, whose roots reach back to the times when royal hunting parties plundered the region's great forests.

Peebles is known as a writer's town. Robert Louis Stevenson lived here for a while and the town was also home to Sir John Buchan (Baron Tweedsmuir, 1875–1940), a Scottish author who was appointed Governor-General of Canada and is remembered chiefly for his adventure story *The 39 Steps,* which Hitchcock made into a film in 1935.

Essentials

GETTING THERE The nearest train station is Edinburgh Waverley 23 miles away; contact **National Rail Enquiries** for train timetables and fares (© **8457/484-950;** www.nationalrail.co.uk). **First** (© **08708/727-271;** www.firstgroup.com) operates bus no. 62, a direct service from Edinburgh to Peebles that runs roughly every half-hour; the journey takes about an hour. Contact First for up-to-date timetables and fares, or **Traveline Scotland** (© **0871/200-2233;** www.travelinescotland.com).

If you're driving from Edinburgh, join the A702 from the city bypass (A720); shortly thereafter take a sharp left onto the A703, which leads into the A701 until Leadburn, where the road goes back to the A703 and heads directly south to Peebles.

VISITOR INFORMATION The **Tourist Information Centre** (© **01721/723-159;** www.visitscottishborders.com) is on High Street. It's open April to September, Monday through Saturday 9am to 5pm and Sunday 11am to 4pm; July to August, Monday through Friday 9am to 6pm and Sunday 10am to 4pm; November to December, Monday through Saturday 9:30am to 5pm and Sunday 11am to 3pm; January to March, Monday through Saturday 9:30am to 4pm.

Exploring the Area

A typical Borders market town, Peebles is characterized by the wide attractive High Street lined with mainly Victorian buildings and small, independent stores selling souvenirs and gifts. The Chambers Institute just off High Street houses the small **Tweeddale Museum and Gallery** (✆ **01721/724-820**). Peebles' striking war memorial stands in the courtyard opposite the Institute and its sparkling Celtic cross is housed in an open shrine-like building of bronze panels and marble and surrounded by the names of the 225 men from Peebles who lost their lives in World War I.

Riverside walks leading into the surrounding countryside start on the banks of the Tweed as it flows through the center of town. Follow the river west for 1 mile to reach the 12th-century **Neidpath Castle** (✆ **01875/870-201;** www.neidpathcastle. co.uk). Standing proud above the river, this romantic old building is still privately owned and tours can be organized; check with the Tourist Information Centre (above) for more details. Tourist Information can also provide details on the many other walks in and around the town.

Peebles is close to some of southern Scotland's most picturesque countryside including the **Pentland Hills** to the northwest (✆ **0131/445-3383;** www. pentlandhills.org), featuring over 60 miles of signposted trails with visitor centers, off the A702 north of Penicuik and east off the A70 near Balerno. **Glentress Forest** (www.glentressforest.com) immediately northeast of Pebbles is laced with mountain bike trails for all abilities and accessible off the A72 east of town. For details on the forest and bike rentals, contact **The Hub in the Forest** (✆ **01721/721-736;** http:// thehubintheforest.co.uk).

Dawyck Botanic Garden GARDEN   This stunning botanical garden is owned and run by the Royal Botanic Garden Edinburgh (p. 85) and provides visitors with a year-round feast of seasonal color from carpets of springtime snowdrops to the vibrant blaze of fall. The garden is divided into a blending array of landscapes, including an Azalea Terrace that bursts into life in late spring and the Beech Walk that leads to views of Dawyck House. A program of guided walks around Dawyck runs throughout the season; contact the garden for details on dates and times.

Off the B712 near Bellspool, 8 miles southwest of Peebles. ✆ **01721/760-254.** www.rbge.org.uk. Admission £5 adults, £4 seniors, £1 children 5–16, £10 families. Feb and Nov 10am–4pm; Mar and Oct 10am–5pm; April–Sept 10am–6pm.

Kailzie Gardens GARDEN   Restored during the past 20 years, Kailzie Gardens provides a stunning array of plants from early spring to late autumn and boasts a collection of waterfowl, chickens, and owls. The beautifully kept 6.8 hectares (17 acres) include a formal Walled Garden of shrubs and roses as well as greenhouses showcasing fuchsias, geraniums, and other conservatory plants. Old pathways lead through woodland and around a scenic duck pond rich in bird life and countryside views. From Easter until the end of August, Kailzie also provides live viewings of the ospreys that nest in the surrounding Tweed Valley Forest Park. The on-site restaurant, located inside an old stable building, is a recommend place to eat in the area even if you aren't visiting the gardens.

Kailzie on the B7062, 2½ miles southeast of Peebles. ✆ **01721/720-007.** www.kailziegardens.com. Admission £3 adults, £1 children 5–16; gardens only £1. Apr–Oct daily 11am–5:30pm; Nov–Mar daily daylight hours.

Little Sparta ★★ GARDEN   For his inspiration for this garden in the Pentland Hills, Ian Hamilton Finlay turned to the gardens created by great poet-philosophers from Epicurus to William Shenstone. Finlay died in 2006, but Little Sparta, with its metaphors ranging from the French Revolution to Scottish fishing fleets, is his legacy to the world. His creation is hailed as the "only original garden" created in Britain since 1945, and it blends poetic and sculptural elements with a perfectly manicured landscape. The garden is itself a major work of art, containing some 275 pieces made mostly of stone, wood, and metal. Little Sparta is not suitable for children under 10.

Stonypath, near Dunsyre (off the A702), 17 miles northwest of Peebles. ℭ **01899/810-252.** www. littlesparta.co.uk. Admission £10. June–Sept Wed, Fri, and Sun 2:30–5pm.

Traquair House ★★ HISTORIC HOME   Dating from the 10th century, Traquair is one of Scotland's most romantic old houses. Once surrounded by ancient forests, this staunchly Stuart household claims rich associations with Mary Queen of Scots and the Jacobite uprisings. One of the most poignant exhibits is an ornately carved oak cradle in the King's Room, in which Mary rocked the infant James VI. Following the demise of the Jacobite cause, the Earl of Traquair sealed the main gates to his great house vowing they would not open again until a Stuart king was crowned in London.

Tours of the house lead visitors through a remarkable property rich with history and collections of portraits, books, and furniture, while treasures in the museum include a letter signed by Mary Queen of Scots and a wall painting dating from the early 16th century. The surrounding grounds are an informal 40-hectare (100-acre) spread of woodland walks, a maze, craft workshops, and walled gardens rich with wildlife and activities for children. Also take time to sample a glass of Traquair ale brewed in the old-fashioned way in original oak vessels. If you'd like to stay overnight at Scotland's oldest inhabited house, rent one of the three elegant rooms, each of which costs £180 per couple for bed and breakfast.

Off the A72 at Innerleithen, 6 miles east of Peebles. ℭ **01896/830-323.** www.traquair.co.uk. Admission £7.60 adults, £6.90 seniors, £4.10 children 3-16, £21 families. Apr–May and Sept daily 11am–5pm; June–July and Aug daily 10:30am–5pm; Oct daily 11am–4pm; Nov daily 11am–3pm.

Where to Eat & Stay

Cringletie House Hotel ★★★   This imposing 1861 red-sandstone Victorian mansion with towers and turrets is one of the most delightful country-house hotels in the Borders. Known for its charming setting and luxurious rooms, the hotel stands on 11 hectares (27 acres) of well-manicured grounds, which are awash with snowdrops in spring and feature a 17th-century walled garden. The house is the epitome of traditional luxury and maintains all the feel of an intimate Scottish country home. Each of the spacious individually decorated guest rooms and suites are named after a Border town and look out over views of the extensive grounds. Dinner is served in the elegant Sutherland Restaurant, which is open to both guests and non-guests, features a spectacular painted ceiling, and serves gourmet cuisine. Cringletie is the best place in the Borders for afternoon tea enjoyed in the bar, library, or Maguire lounge.

Off the A703 at Eddleston, 2½ miles north of Peebles, EH45 8PL. www.cringletie.com. ℭ **01721/725-750.** Fax 01721/725-751. 13 units. £160–£215 double; £220–£285 suite. AE, MC, V. **Amenities:** Restaurant; bar; croquet lawn; pitch and put course (putting green course). *In room:* TV, hair dryer, robes, Wi-Fi (free).

The Horseshoe Inn ★★ FRENCH/SCOTTISH   At this award-winning inn, diners can choose between the informal Bistro or formal Bardoulet's restaurant (named after the Horseshoe's acclaimed chef). Both are warmly decorated in a traditional style and serve menus of mainly French cuisine with some Scottish influences and plenty of local produce. Main courses on the regularly changing bistro menu can include Dover sole, rump of lamb, or haggis bonbon. In the restaurant, diners choose between a la carte and tasting menus; dishes might be fricassee of wild mushroom risotto with soubise, spinach and truffle salad, or roasted saddle and shoulder of roe deer. The accompanying wine list is extensive and features many options by the glass. The Horseshoe Inn also has eight well-appointed guest rooms that cost £100 to £150 per night. Reservations are recommended.

Off the A703 at Eddleston, 5 miles north of Peebles. ✆ **01721/730-225.** www.horseshoeinn.co.uk. Bistro main courses £9–£23, restaurant main courses lunch £6–£10, dinner £17–£24, tasting menu £50 per person. MC, V. Tues–Thurs noon–2:30pm & 7–9pm, Fri–Sat noon–2:30pm & 7:15pm–9:30pm, Sun noon–2:30pm.

Osso ★ MEDITERRANEAN/SCOTTISH   Although this contemporary restaurant hasn't been open for long, it's already earned a strong reputation for first-class gourmet food. This is a popular local choice for coffees and homemade cakes throughout the day, and along with a selection of inventive sandwiches, the lunchtime menu also features tapas and main courses such as homemade burgers and pasta of the day. Fine dining prevails from 6pm onwards with an a la carte menu of seafood and unusual meats such as braised hare leg alongside Scottish sirloin. Tasting menus of dishes that make the best use of local seasonal produce can also be served, but these must be requested when booking a table.

Innerleithen Rd., Peebles. ✆ **01721/724-477.** Main courses lunch £5–£10, dinner £10–£18. MC, V. Mon–Sat 10am–4:30pm, Thurs–Sat 6–9pm, Sun 11am–4:30pm.

Windlestraw Lodge ★★   This amiable, secluded Edwardian country house on the banks of the Tweed is a haven of simple luxury and fine countryside. The house features six very comfortable rooms all subtly decorated and featuring luxury bathrooms. The restaurant prides itself on homemade dishes created with seasonal produce sourced from farms all over the Borders as well as homegrown herbs. Large peaceful gardens look out over the Tweed Valley, which offers an abundance of walking, fishing, and cycling.

Off the A72 (Galashiels Road), Walkerburn, 8½ miles east of Peebles, EH43 6AA. www.windlestraw.co. uk. ✆ **01896/870-636.** Fax 01896/870-404. 6 units. £140–£210 double. MC, V. **Amenities:** Restaurant, bar. *In room:* TV, hair dryer.

Entertainment & Nightlife

The **Eastgate Theatre & Arts Centre** (✆ **01721/725-777;** www.eastgatearts. com) on Eastgate, which is the A72 as it leads through town, is a buzzing regional arts venue whose program includes music, theatre, film, and dance and whose foyer cafe is a pleasant spot for a drink. Other options for drinking in the town include the bar at the **Tontine Hotel,** High Street (✆ **01721/720-892;** www.tontinehotel.com), which also has a pleasant bistro area.

MOFFAT

61 miles S of Edinburgh; 22 miles NE of Dumfries; 60 miles SE of Glasgow

A small town at the head of the Annandale Valley, Moffat stands on the cusp between the Borders and Dumfries and Galloway. The town grew as a holiday resort from the mid-17th century onwards thanks to the curative properties of its waters, which earned Moffat the status of spa town. Robert Burns visited to sample both the waters and the beer served in Moffat's pubs and it was here that the poet composed the drinking song "O Willie Brewd a Peck o' Maut." The surrounding hills and valleys are sheep farming land and contain some of the finest walking in southern Scotland. People also visit this charming town on the banks of the Annan River for its abundance of fishing and golf.

Essentials

GETTING THERE   The nearest train station is in Lockerbie, 15 miles south of Moffat (© 08457/484-950; www.nationalrail.co.uk for information and tickets). **Stagecoach** (© 01292/613-500; www.stagecoachbus.com) operates the frequent bus service no. 380 between Lockerbie and Moffat; the journey takes around 35 minutes and contact Stagecoach for timetables and fares. There's also a train station at Dumfries, which is connected to Moffat by the Stagecoach bus service no. X74. Contact **Traveline Scotland** for timetables and fares (© 0871/200-2233; www.travelinescotland.com).

If you're driving from Dumfries, head northeast along the A701. From Edinburgh join the A702 from the city bypass (A720) and follow this road south until it meets the A/M74; travel south along this road and exit at junction 15 for Moffat. The A/M74 is also the main route from Glasgow.

VISITOR INFORMATION   The **Tourist Information Centre** (© 01683/220-620; www.visitdumfriesandgalloway.co.uk) is on Churchgate. Opening hours are April to June Monday through Saturday 10am to 5pm, Sunday noon to 4pm; June to September Monday through Saturday 9:30am to 5:30pm, Sunday 11am to 5pm; October Monday through Saturday 10am to 4:30pm, Sunday 11am to 4pm.

Exploring the Area

The countryside surrounding Moffat is a walkers' paradise. To the northeast the Moffat Water, Yarrow, and Ettrick valleys spread out on either side of the A708, the main route to Selkirk. Ten miles into this route the **Grey Mare's Tail ★**, one of Britain's highest waterfalls, cascades 60m (200 ft.) from Loch Skeen in the hills, down a spectacular rock face before tumbling past the Tail Burn, site of a prehistoric bank and ditch, and finally emptying into Moffat Water. From the car park (£2 fee) at the foot of the waterfall off the A708, a well-trodden 2½-mile trail leads up the valley to Loch Skeen, which at 500m (1,640 ft.) is Scotland's highest upland loch—look out for nesting peregrine falcons along the way.

Farther north and halfway between Moffat and Selkirk lies **St. Mary's Loch ★**, a large bucolic body of water popular with anglers and inspirational to writers, which, according to local legend, has no bottom. Tibbie Shiels Inn (see "Where to Eat & Stay" below) stands at the southern end of the loch and is overlooked by a large statue of the Scottish poet and novelist James Hogg, who worked these valleys as a shepherd and whose grandfather Will o' Phaup is credited with being the last man who could speak with fairies. A day's angling can be arranged through **St Mary's Angling Club** (© 07980/350-031; http://sites.google.com/site/stmarysloch) or ask at Tibbie Shiels. The Southern Upland Way (p. 156) skirts the east shore of St Mary's Loch from where it heads towards Moffat and then west into the Lowther Hills.

A sheer-sided 152m-deep (500-ft.), 1¾-mile-wide hollow known as the **Devil's Beef Tub** lies in the hills 5 miles northwest of town. Formed at the point where four hills meet, this dramatic natural hollow derives its name from the cattle thieves who once hid their stolen livestock here. The Devil's Beef Tub can be viewed from the A701, a main road leading north from Moffat; to reach it on foot from town, head along the **Annan Water Valley Road,** a rural route with virtually no traffic.

Moffat is also a prime spot for golfers with 11 courses lying within a 25-mile radius. For more information, visit the Tourist Information Centre (see above) or see the town's website (www.visitmoffat.co.uk).

Where to Eat & Stay

Annandale Arms Hotel ★ This recently refurbished former coaching inn stands in the center of Moffat off the town's large tree-lined square. Public areas exude traditional hospitality and decor and are characterized by an intimate oak-paneled bar and old suit of armor standing guard over reception. Guest rooms are modern and comfortable; most of the gleaming en-suite bathrooms come with a tub and shower (some are shower only) and family rooms are available. This is also the best place in town to eat because the food is exceptional, award-winning, and served with style in an intimate small dining room open to both guests and non-guests. Local produce dominates a menu of fine Scottish cuisine and diners can expect to choose from dishes including matured Scotch beef steak, organic lamb, or wild salmon. Packed lunches can also be prepared.

High St., Moffat. www.annandalearmshotel.co.uk. ✆ **01683/220-013.** Fax 01683/221-395. 16 units. £110 double. AE, MC, V. **Amenities:** Restaurant; bar. *In room:* TV, hair dryer, Wi-Fi (free).

Tibbie Shiels ★ This legendary inn on the southern banks of St Mary's Loch is a perfect spot for anyone wanting to experience the solitude and beauty of the Yarrow Valley. The inn was created by Tibbie Shiels herself, a friend of James Hogg whose statue overlooks this spot; other former friends and famous guests include Sir Walter Scott and Robert Louis Stevenson. The rooms are basic, comfortable, and en-suite; many come with loch views and all are popular with walkers, and although none have TVs, there's one in the resident's lounge. A family room is available and a caravan in the surrounding grounds that sleeps six can also be hired—although this is often booked well in advance. The on-site bar is flag-stoned, warmed by a wood-burning stove, and often packed with locals. Hearty homemade food created with local ingredients is served from noon until 8pm in the loch-facing restaurant and on outside tables in summer. This place is not for those who prefer modern conveniences and luxury, but it's perfect for anyone seeking a slice of authentic hospitality, rich local history, and the Scottish countryside at its best.

Off the A708 approximately 15 miles from Moffat, TD7 5LH. www.tibbieshiels.com. ✆ **01750/42231.** 6 units. £80 double; £300 for 3 nights in the caravan. AE, MC, V. **Amenities:** Restaurant; bar.

DUMFRIES: AN ODE TO BURNS ★

80 miles SW of Edinburgh; 79 miles SE of Glasgow; 34 miles NW of Carlisle

Southwest Scotland's largest town, Dumfries grew around the banks of the River Nith just north of the point where its estuary joins the Solway Firth. The town and its surrounds have strong associations with Robert Burns, who lived in Dumfries from 1791 until his death in 1796 and in Ellisland Farm to the north of the town for 3 years previously. It was here that Burns wrote some of his best-known songs including "Auld Lang Syne." A statue of Scotland's national poet stands proud on Dumfries'

High Street and you can visit his former house, favorite pub, and mausoleum as well as Ellisland Farm.

The center of Dumfries is mainly pedestrianized making it easy to walk to the various scattered sights that will take little more than a morning to visit. There is, however, far more to do and see in the surrounding countryside.

Essentials

GETTING THERE Scotrail (© 0845/601-5929; www.scotrail.co.uk) operates a rail service between Glasgow's Central Station and Dumfries. The journey takes 1¾ hours; a one-way ticket costs £13.70, while a same-day round-trip ticket is £18.

Stagecoach (© 01292/613-500; www.stagecoachbus.com) bus service X74 connects Glasgow's Buchanan Street station with the bus station on Buccleuch Street in Dumfries. The journey takes 2 hours and costs £7.70 one-way or £11 round-trip. The easiest way to travel by public transport from Edinburgh is to catch a train from Waverley to Lockerbie, which is 12½ miles south of Dumfries, and then catch Stagecoach bus service no. 81 to Dumfries. There's no direct train link to Dumfries from either Edinburgh or Lockerbie. Contact **Traveline Scotland** (© 0871/200-2233;** www.travelinescotland.com) for more details and timetables for this journey.

If you're driving from Edinburgh, follow directions to Moffat (p. 144) and then follow the A701 southwest to Dumfries. From Glasgow follow the M74/A74 to Moffat and then see directions above. To park in the center of Dumfries, you need to obtain a disc for your dashboard that notes your time of arrival. Discs are free and can be picked up at the Tourist Information Centre (see below) or from most stores.

VISITOR INFORMATION The **Tourist Information Centre** is at 64 Whitesands (© 01387/253-862; www.visitdumfriesandgalloway.co.uk). It's open December to June and October Monday through Friday 9:30am to 5pm, plus Saturday April to June and Sunday in October 10:30am to 4pm; and September and November Monday through Saturday 9am to 5pm and Sunday 10:30am to 4pm.

Exploring the Town

In the center of town, **Whitesands** is a wide riverside esplanade that used to be the setting for horse and hiring fairs and today is the main visitor car park. At Whitesands four bridges span the river; the earliest was built by Devorgilla Balliol, whose son was appointed Scotland's "vassal king" by Edward I of England in an attempt to control the country through this puppet monarch. Devorgilla Bridge is still used as a footbridge, and at its far end on Mill Road stands **Old Bridge House** (© 01387/256-904;** www.dumfriesmuseum.demon.co.uk). Built in 1660, it's Dumfries' oldest building and now a free museum dedicated to everyday life through the centuries; it's open April to September Monday through Saturday from 10am to 5pm and Sunday 2pm to 5pm. The **Robert Burns Centre** (© 01387/264-808; www.dumfriesmuseum.demon.co.uk) stands farther along Mill Road in a converted 18th-century water mill and features exhibits and a presentation about the poet and Dumfries at the time Burns lived here. The center is free to enter and open April to September Monday through Saturday from 10am to 5pm and Sunday 2 to 5pm, and October to March Tuesday through Saturday from 10am to 1pm and 2 to 5pm.

In addition to **Burns House** (see below), the final stop on a Burns tour of Dumfries is his mausoleum in the churchyard of **St. Michael's Church,** on St. Michael's Street. This large neo-Grecian shrine-like monument is built of local sandstone and drips with nostalgia. Burns died in 1796, but his remains weren't moved here until 1815 where they now rest in peace along with those of his wife, Jean Armour, and five of their children.

Those looking for things to do in Dumfries in the evening can follow in Burn's footsteps and savor a wee dram at the town's most famous pub the **Globe Inn,** 56 High St. (© **01387/252-335;** www.globeinndumfries.co.uk), where the poet's favorite seat still survives. Alternatively head for the **Robert Burns Centre** (see above), which is an art-house cinema in the evenings (for details of what's on, see www.rbcft.co.uk) and whose **Hullabaloo** restaurant (© **01387/259-679;** www.hullabaloo restaurant.co.uk) is a pretty riverside spot for an informal meal.

Burns House HISTORIC HOME   In 1796, Scotland's national poet died in this unpretentious, terraced stone house off St. Michael's Street. Although Burns only lived here for the last 3 years of his life, his old house contains many personal relics and mementos as well as much of the original furniture used by Burns during his creative years—including the chair he sat on to write the last of his poems.

Burns St. © **01387/255-297.** www.dumfriesmuseum.demon.co.uk. Free admission. Apr–Sept Mon–Sat 10am–5pm, Sun 2–5pm; Oct–Mar Tues–Sat 10am–1pm and 2–5pm.

Dumfries Museum & Camera Obscura MUSEUM   Southwestern Scotland's largest museum occupies a converted 18th-century windmill atop Corbelly Hill. The museum is rich with collections relating to the region's early geology and history ranging from early Christian stones to artifacts of 18th-century country life. Here visitors can also learn more about the wildlife to be found along the Solway Firth, while some exhibits relate to the site's role as a 19th-century astronomical observatory. The museum's top floor is occupied by a camera obscura that provides panoramic views of town and countryside.

Church St. © **01387/253-374.** www.dumfriesmuseum.demon.co.uk. Museum free admission; camera obscura £2.30 adults, £1.15 children 5–16 and seniors. Apr–Sept Mon–Sat 10am–5pm; Oct–Mar Tues–Sat 10am–1pm and 2–5pm. Camera obscura closed Oct–Mar.

Exploring the Area

Rich in Covenanter history and home to writers and artists, the small village of **Moniaive** (www.moniaive.org.uk), 23 miles northwest of Dumfries, is one of southern Scotland's most attractive small communities. In the surrounding hills of this little discovered part of Dumfries and Galloway, landscape artist Andy Goldsworthy has created **Striding Arches** ★ (www.stridingarches.com), a series of striking red sandstones arches that "stride" across the landscape. The road leading to this dramatic piece of landscape art is signposted from the center of Moniaive.

Also close to Dumfries, the **Glenkiln Sculpture Park** is a collection of six sculptures including work by Moore and Rodin set in a glen around Glenkiln reservoir. To reach the park, turn north off the A75 (signposted to Shawhead) 6 miles west of Dumfries.

Caerlaverock Castle ★ ☺ CASTLE   Medieval castles don't come more dramatic and romantic than the imposing Caerlaverock, whose moat-surrounded battlements have withstood many a border conflict between England and Scotland. The castle opens out into a triangular shape behind its twin-towered gatehouse and here visitors can view exhibitions on siege warfare while exploring the red sandstone ruins of the remaining battlements. The land around Caerlaverock is a National Nature Reserve and filled with walks through woods and wetlands.

8 miles southeast of Dumfries off the B725. ℂ**01387/770-244.** www.historic-scotland.gov.uk. Admission £5.20 adults, £3.10 children, £4.20 seniors. Apr–Sept daily 9:30am–5:30pm, Oct–Mar daily 9:30am–4:30pm.

Drumlanrig Castle ★ ☺ CASTLE   This pink castle, built between 1679 and 1689 in a parkland ringed by wild hills, is one of the family seats of the Duke and Duchess of Buccleuch and Queensberry. The building itself is one of Scotland's finest examples of late Renaissance architecture and behind its pink sandstone walls lies an outstanding collection of old masters including work by Rembrandt, Holbein, and Reynolds, although da Vinci's *Madonna with the Yarnwinder,* valued at US$50 million, was famously stolen in 2004 by two thieves posing as sightseers. The castle also features the Scottish Cycle Museum dedicated to Drumlanrig's former blacksmith Kirkpatrick Macmillian, who invented the rear-wheel-driven bicycle. Bikes can be rented to explore the trails winding through the surrounding estate, and a large adventure playground will keep children occupied for hours.

3 miles north of Thornhill off the A76. ℂ**01848/331-555.** www.drumlanrig.com. Admission £9 adults, £7.50 seniors, £5 children 3–16, £26 families. Apr–Aug daily 11am–4pm.

Ellisland Farm ★ FARM/MUSEUM   From 1788 to 1791, Robert Burns made his last attempt at farming at Ellisland Farm, which he claimed was the "poet's choice" of the farms he was offered to rent from landlord Patrick Miller. Although Burns wrote some of his most famous work and two of his children were born here, the farm itself proved infertile for the poet and he soon moved his family to Dumfries. Ellisland is still a working farm as well as a museum dedicated to Burns. One of the best things to do here is retrace the poet's steps along scenic trails to the banks for the River Nith where Burns often walked when taking a break from his writing.

6 miles north of Dumfries off the A76. ℂ **01387/740-426.** www.ellislandfarm.co.uk. Admission £4 adults, £3 seniors, under-15s free. Apr–Sept Mon–Sat 10am–1pm and 2–5pm, Sun 2–5pm; Oct–Mar Tues–Sat 2–4pm.

National Museum of Costume MUSEUM   Explore a century of style at this country house museum, which leads visitors on a journey through fashion from the late Victorian era to the present day. Changing displays take a peek at what people wore and why over the past 200 years and show off many of the fashions that have come and gone. The house itself—set in rambling wooded grounds—is also a delight, and displays reveal stories of the family who lived here and the man who gave his vast costume collection to the National Museums of Scotland.

Shambellie House, New Abbey off the A710 6 miles south of Dumfries. ℂ**0300/123-6789.** www.nms. ac.uk. Admission £4.50 adults, £3.50 seniors, £2 children, £11 families. Apr–Oct daily 10am–5pm.

Sweetheart Abbey ABBEY   The red sandstone ruins of this formerly awe-inspiring 13th-century abbey dominate the tiny village of New Abbey. The abbey was founded in 1273 by Devorgilla Balliol, who following the death of her husband John Balliol the Elder became one of Europe's richest women; most of Galloway, as well as estates and castles in England and Normandy once belonged to her. Although the roof and monk's cloister are almost entirely gone, much of the abbey remains intact. An effigy of Lady Devorgilla can be found in the ruined south transept, and the grave of the lady herself is located in the former high altar where she lies buried along with her beloved husband's embalmed heart.

Off the A710 at New Abbey 6¾ miles south of Dumfries. ℂ **01387/850-397.** www.historic-scotland. gov.uk. Admission £3 adults, £2.50 seniors, £1.80 children 15 and under. Apr–Sept daily 9:30am–5:30pm; Oct daily 9:30am–4:30pm; Nov–Mar Sat–Wed 9:30am–4:30pm.

Threave Castle ★ CASTLE   This ruined 14th-century stronghold of the Black Douglases built by Archibald the Grim, Lord of Galloway, stands on a small island in the River Dee. Over the doorway of this massive five-story tower is the gallows knob from which the Douglases, once one of the most powerful families in Scotland, hanged their enemies. For James II this formidable family proved too powerful for comfort, and the almost impregnable Threave Castle was the last Douglas stronghold to surrender to royal hands in 1455. The castle is only accessible via a small boat that sails throughout the day in season; it's a short walk through farmlands to reach the dock from the car park.

Off the A75 19 miles southwest of Dumfries. ℂ **07711/223-101.** www.historic-scotland.gov.uk. Admission (including ferry ride) £4.20 adults, £3.40 seniors, £2.50 children 15 and under. Apr–Sept daily 9:30am (last sailing at 4:30pm), Oct 9:30am (last sailing at 3:30pm).

Threave Garden ★ GARDEN   About 1 mile southeast of Threave Castle, these gardens are built around Threave House, a Scottish baronial mansion constructed during the Victorian era. The garden is at its best in April when nearly 200 different varieties of daffodil burst into bloom, and in June, when rhododendrons provide a riot of color. There is, however, plenty to see year-round as the estate also features a Countryside Centre and large wildfowl sanctuary. Parts of the house are also open to visitors.

Off the A75 17 miles southwest of Dumfries. ℂ **0844/493-2245.** www.nts.org.uk. Admission £11 adults, £8 seniors and children 15 and under, £27 families. Garden, visitor, and countryside centers Feb–Mar and Nov–Dec Fri–Sun 10am–5pm, Apr–Oct daily 10am–5pm; house Apr–Oct Wed–Fri and Sun 11am–3:30pm.

Where to Eat & Stay

Ashton Hotel   Located on the south side of town close to the university, this contemporary hotel is the best place to stay for those wanting to be in Dumfries. Guest rooms are spacious and modern, with power showers and large beds that make them the most comfortable accommodation option in town. Food is served throughout the day from breakfast to dinner at the modern on-site Brasserie & Bar 59, which is also a chilled-out spot for a relaxing drink after a hard day's sightseeing.

Bankend Rd., Dumfries, DG1 4ZZ. www.astonhotels.co.uk. ℂ **01387/272-410.** Fax 01387/267-303. 71 units. £70–£110 double. MC, V. **Amenities:** Restaurant; bar; room service. *In room:* TV, hair dryer, Wi-Fi (free).

The Auld Alliance SCOTTISH/FRENCH   With a name that tips its hat to the "auld alliance" between France and Scotland—who joined forces many times over the centuries in united support against the English—this chic restaurant adds a distinctly Scottish twist to classical French food. Chef Patron Thierry worked in restaurants across both France and the U.K. before settling in Dumfries and bringing his culinary expertise to this new venture, where diners choose from either a bistro or set menu. Bistro dishes may include beef bourguignon or curried mussels with clams and French fries, and the fine dining set menu is characterized by dishes such as herb-stuffed free-range chicken with boulangére potato and mushroom and tarragon sauce. A children's menu is also available.

60 Moffat Rd., Dumfries. ℂ **01387/256-800.** www.auldalliancedumfries.com. Reservations recommended. Main courses £7–£16; fixed-price menu 2 courses £19, 3 courses £24. MC, V. Daily 11:30am–9:30pm.

Cavens Country House Hotel ★   Breathe in the tranquility of the Solway Firth at this comfortable country house hotel near the coast south of Dumfries. The hotel stands within 2.4 hectares (6 acres) of landscaped gardens and is a haven of traditional comforts and first-class food. All the individually designed rooms feature long views of the surrounding grounds, with the larger Estate bedrooms providing that bit more space to relax. Expect to enjoy the best of the region's produce in the hotel's respected restaurant. An array of local attractions and outdoor activities lie on the doorstep.

Kirkbean, 13 miles south of Dumfries off the A710, DG2 8AA. www.cavens.com. © **01387/880-234.** Fax 01387/880-467. 8 units. £110–£190 double. MC, V. **Amenities:** Restaurant; bar; Wi-Fi (free). *In room:* TV, hair dryer.

Trigony House Hotel ★★   Built around 1895 as a shooting lodge for a nearby castle, this relaxed country house hotel stands in 1.6 hectares (4 acres) of tranquil landscaped gardens. The hotel has the feel of a warm family home, and its guest rooms offer unpretentious comfort and countryside views. Open to both guests and non-guests, the hotel's restaurant is one of the best in the region for both quality of food and informal, friendly service. Choose between a la carte dining, an inexpensive bar menu, or a combination of the two, all of which are characterized by homemade dishes created from as much free-range and organic produce as possible. The hotel can help organize many outdoor activities from biking to falconry and pony trekking to fishing, and offer an amiable guest lounge warmed by a log-burning stove to relax in afterwards.

Off the A76 just south of Thornhill, 12miles north of Dumfries, DG3 5EZ. www.trigonyhotel.co.uk. © **01848/331-211.** Fax 01848/331-303. 10 units. £105–£155 double. MC, V. **Amenities:** Restaurant; bar. *In room:* TV, hair dryer, Wi-Fi (free).

KIRKCUDBRIGHT: AN ARTISTS' COLONY ★

108 miles SW of Edinburgh; 28 miles SW of Dumfries; 103 miles S of Glasgow; 50 miles E of Stranraer

The ancient burgh of Kirkcudbright (Kir-*coo*-bree) sits at the head of Kirkcudbright Bay on the Dee estuary and is one of the most attractive towns in the region. For generations many of its old color-washed houses have belonged to weavers, potters, and painters all attracted by the bohemian ambiance of Kirkcudbright's 18th-century streets and harbor and the light that pours across the water. There are several attractions to discover in the town, and plenty of festivities take place throughout the year of which highlights include art exhibitions, a September jazz festival, and a host of summer festivities. Also take time to explore farther afield and discover some of the region's delightful small communities such as the Gatehouse of Fleet to the northwest of Kirkcudbright.

Essentials

GETTING THERE   The nearest train station is at Dumfries. **Stagecoach** (© **01292/613-500;** www.stagecoachbus.com) bus service no. 501/502 departs from Whitesands in Dumfries to Kirkcudbright throughout the day; the journey takes around an hour. The latest fares and timetables can be obtained from Stagecoach or **Traveline Scotland** (© **0871/200-2233;** www.travelinescotland.com).

If you're driving from Dumfries, continue southwest along the A75 past Castle Douglas until you come to the junction with the A711, which takes you into Kirkcudbright.

VISITOR INFORMATION The **Tourist Information Centre** is at Harbour Square (℡ **01557/330-494;** www.kirkcudbright.co.uk). It's open February to March and November Monday through Saturday 10am to 4pm and Sunday 11am to 4pm; April to June and September to October Monday through Saturday 10am to 5pm and Sunday 11am to 4pm; and July to August Monday through Saturday 9:30am to 6pm and Sunday 11am to 5pm.

Exploring the Area

Kirkcudbright's wide streets huddle around the east bank of the River Dee, and its clutch of historical sights along with an eclectic collection of art galleries and shops are the town's biggest draw. Once the town's court and prison, the **Tolbooth Art Centre** (℡ **01557/331-556;** www.dumfriesmuseum.demon.co.uk) on High Street is the place to discover the history of Kirkcudbright's artist colony and view some its best work. Gathered close to the center are a number of artist's shops selling original textiles, jewelry, ceramics, and paintings. Nearby on St. Mary Street, the **Stewarty Museum** (℡ **01557/331-556;** www.dumfriesmuseum.demon.co.uk) is a showcase of the distinctive culture, history, traditions, and sociology of this part of Dumfries and Galloway; admission is free.

Head 8½ miles northwest of Kirkcudbright to **Gatehouse of Fleet,** a small town that lies north of the A75 and whose western boundary is marked by Cardoness Castle (p. 153). In the center of town a former 18th-century cotton mill on the banks of the Water of Fleet has been converted into a history and heritage center, and its displays are stuffed with information about the surrounding area. The **Mill on the Fleet** (℡ **01557/814-099;** www.millonthefleet.co.uk) also contains a pretty riverside cafe and book and gift shops; it's free to enter and open from April to October daily.

Broughton House HISTORIC HOME This 18th-century mansion once belonged to artist Edward Atkinson Hornel (1864–1933). Known for his bold and colorful style, Hornel was one of the "Glasgow Boys," a series of major figures who emerged from the Glasgow School of Art, and whose work depicted life in his native Dumfries and Galloway. Hornel's portrait (painted by Bessie McNicol) is displayed in the dining room of the artist's former home where visitors can also view pictures by the man himself as well as his large reference library and Burns collection. One of Broughton House's most appealing aspects is its small but charming Japanese-style garden, whose plantings sometimes appeared in Hornel's paintings.

12 High St. ℡ **0844/493-2246.** www.nts.org.uk. Admission £6 adults, £5 seniors and children 15 and under, £16 families. Apr–Oct daily noon–5pm; Feb–Mar Mon–Fri 11am–4pm.

MacLellan's Castle CASTLE Dominating the center of Kirkcudbright, this stirring castle was built in 1582 for the town's provost, Sir Thomas MacLellan. Successive generations lost the family fortune and their prosperous home fell into the impressive ruin it is today. Many sections, however, are still intact, including a large staircase that leads to a Banqueting Hall with a massive fireplace containing a "lairds lug"—a secret spy hole through which the laird could eavesdrop on his guests. Visitors can also explore the castle's old vaults where a team of servants toiled away.

Off High St. ℡ **01557/331-856.** www.historic-scotland.gov.uk. Admission £4 adults, £3.20 seniors, £2.40 children 5-15. Apr–Sept daily 9:30am–5:30pm.

The short stretch of the A75 that hugs the coast as it curls around Wigtown Bay from Creetown to Gatehouse of Fleet is a superb short road trip for history lovers. The first stop just south of Creetown is the roadside ruins of **Carsluith Castle.** This ruined tower house dates back to the 16th century, commands long views across Wigtown Bay nature reserve, and stands adjacent to the **Marrbury Smokehouse** (℃ 01671/ 820-476; www.visitmarrbury.co.uk), where you can pick up such delicacies as smoked Kirkcudbright scallops and wild Cree smoked salmon. Continue southeast to reach **Cairn Holy,** two haunting Neolithic burial chambers that lie at the top of a narrow track off the A75 and still maintain a peaceful aura of mystery. The final stop, **Cardoness Castle,** lies southwest of Gatehouse of Fleet just off the A75 at the junction with the B727 and is a well preserved, 15th-century six-story tower house. All three properties are managed by **Historic Scotland** (℃ 0131/668-8600; www.historic-scotland.gov.uk); both Carsluith Castle and Cairn Holy are free to enter and always open, whereas Cardoness Castle is open April to September daily 9:30am to 5:30pm and October to March weekends only 9:30am to 4:30pm, and admission costs £5 adults, £3 children, and £4 seniors.

Where to Eat & Stay

The Castle Restaurant SCOTTISH/CONTINENTAL   Located directly opposite MacLellan's Castle (see above), this restaurant serves freshly prepared imaginative food from as much organic Dumfries and Galloway produce as possible. Small menus cater for carnivores, fish lovers, and vegetarians, and the children's menu always promises something healthier than fries. Service is friendly and dishes such as prosciutto-wrapped monkfish with a saffron-infused roasted red pepper sauce are well presented. Leave room and time to linger over deserts such as cinnamon filo baskets with Bramley apple fool and calvados fudge sauce or Cream of Galloway ice cream.

5 Castle St. ℃ **01557/330-569.** www.thecastlerestaurant.net. Main courses £9–£18. MC, V. Daily noon–3pm and 6:30–9:30pm.

Gladstone House ★ 🔥   The best value accommodation in town, Gladstone House is a carefully restored Georgian townhouse that maintains all of the gentility and grandeur of the era in which it was built, seamlessly merged with all modern comforts. Guests are encouraged to make themselves at home and make full use of the large peaceful lounge and sheltered gardens. Guest rooms are well appointed and come with town views. Hearty breakfasts with homemade bread and preserves and three-course dinners of first-class Scottish food are served in an elegant dining room.

48 High St., Kirkcudbright, DG6 4JX. www.kirkcudbrightgladstone.com. ℃ **01557/331-734.** 3 units. £75 double. MC, V. **Amenities:** Restaurant; bar. *In room:* TV, hair dryer, Wi-Fi (free).

WIGTOWN: SCOTLAND'S NATIONAL BOOK TOWN

54 miles SW of Dumfries; 133 miles SW of Edinburgh; 93 miles S of Glasgow

With its wide open Main Street flanked by a grand town square and string of independent bookstores, Wigtown is proud to be Scotland's National Book Town. During the 10 days in late September when its vibrant book festival (www.wigtownbook festival.com) takes over the town, this small community is transformed by the presence of some of the U.K.'s top authors and the sea of visitors who come to hear them speak. At other times people visit for the peace of a large nature reserve, the outdoor activities of the Galloway Forest Park, and to follow in the footsteps of St. Ninian who first brought Christianity to Scottish soil at nearby Whithorn.

Essentials

GETTING THERE   If traveling from the south, the nearest train station is in Dumfries; for anyone heading down from the north, the best train station to aim for is at Barrhill, 25½ miles northwest of Wigtown. There's no direct bus service between Dumfries and Wigtown. You need to first catch Stagecoach bus service no. 500 to Newton Stewart, and then service no. 415 from Newton Stewart to Dumfries. Stagecoach service no. 57 connects Barrhill with Wigtown. Contact **Traveline Scotland** (© **0871/200-2233;** www.travelinescotland.com) for more details and timetables for these journeys.

If you're driving from Dumfries, head southwest along the A75 until Newton Stewart and then turn south along the A714, which leads directly to Wigtown.

VISITOR INFORMATION   There's no dedicated **Tourist Information Centre** in Wigtown, but you can pick up information at the County Buildings adjacent to the main square that also houses the town's library.

Exploring the Area

It won't take long to explore this tiny town unless you're a book lover, in which case its plethora of bookstores will detain you for hours. Wigtown buts up against a large nature reserve which spreads out over tidal flats on the east side of town. This evocative, silent landscape is a haven for bird-watchers, and visitors can expect to spy at various times of the year pink-footed geese, ducks, and wading birds from two public hides. Scotland's most southerly whisky distillery occupies a riverside location at Bladnoch, 0.7 miles south of Wigtown, and is open daily. Tours of **Bladnoch Distillery** (© **0198-840-2605;** www.bladnoch.co.uk) run throughout the day and cost £3 per person.

North of Wigtown, the **Galloway Forest Park** (www.gallowayforestpark.com), Britain's largest forest park, occupies 300 square miles of untamed landscape. Three visitor centers are dotted throughout the park and the nearest to Wigtown is Kirroughtree to the east off the A75 just past Newton Stewart, from where a string of way-marked trails for all abilities leads into the woods. Galloway Forest Park is also the U.K.'s only **Dark Sky Park ★**, which means that all measures are taken to ensure no light pollution dulls the exceptionally dark night sky here and stargazers can feast on blankets of star-studded darkness.

South of Wigtown, the remote **Isle of Whithorn** pushes deep into the Solway Firth and was once an important center for pilgrims traveling to pay homage to St.

Ninian, an early Christian missionary who brought the faith to Scotland in the 5th century. Trace the pilgrim's route to St. Ninian's tiny ruined **chapel** on the outskirts of the Isle of Whithorn village and see the inlet where the ancient boats were pulled ashore. Then head across the peninsula to **St. Ninian's Cave** where, according to legend, this holy man lived a life of windswept retreat and solitude. Both of these sights are always open and free to enter.

The Whithorn Story MUSEUM/RUINS   Trace the history of this ancient region at this intriguing visitor center, which reveals the story of the area's early Christian past and much more. Fragments of history detail life at this once-thriving cultural crossroads and displays provide unusual snapshots of the past such as a Viking cat farm. Head out behind the center to explore the ruins of a small medieval cathedral that once stood here, as well as a collection of early Christian stones.

George St., Whithorn. ✆ **01988/500-508.** www.whithorn.com. Admission £4.50 adults, £3 seniors, £3 children 5–16, £12 families. Apr–Oct daily 10:30am–5pm.

Where to Eat & Stay

In Wigtown, **Readinglasses** (✆ 01988/403-266; www.reading-lasses.com) on South Main Street is a bookshop dedicated to books by and about women and an award-winning bistro/cafe that serves deeply delicious soups, sandwiches, cakes, and deli platters throughout the day. In Bladnoch, the family-friendly **Bladnoch Inn** (✆ www.the-bladnoch-inn.com; 01988/402-200) opens daily for lunch and dinner and serves a good menu of traditional pub food as well as providing clean and comfortable B&B accommodation. **The Steam Packet Inn,** on the water's edge at Harbour Row in the Isle of Whithorn (www.steampacketinn.biz; ✆ 01988/500-334), serves a basic lunch and dinner menu that champions local seafood and Scottish produce and has a number of large harbor-facing rooms available on a bed-and-breakfast basis.

Hillcrest House ★ 👔   With many rooms overlooking Wigtown's large nature reserve, visitors can expect serene views and nights of complete peace and quiet at this first-class B&B. Hillcrest has all the feel of a family home and welcomes guests into six individually decorated rooms, each featuring its own chandelier and all named after a different Scottish firth. Some of the en-suite guest rooms come with a shower and a tub, some are shower only; the grand Moray Firth rooms feature four-poster beds and binoculars to peer into the adjacent nature reserve. Both guests and non-guests can choose to dine here in the evening, and Hillcrest's food has consistently won awards for its quality and dedication to all ingredients real and local. This is a good choice for families because Hillcrest has one double room with an additional set of bunk beds and a large garden for young guests to let off steam.

Maidland Place, Station Rd., Wigtown, DG8 9EU. www.hillcrest-wigtown.co.uk. ✆ **01988/402-018.** 6 units. £78 double. AE, MC, V. **Amenities:** Restaurant. *In room:* TV/DVD, CD player, hair dryer, robes, Wi-Fi (free).

PORTPATRICK

141 miles SW of Edinburgh; 8 miles SW of Stranraer; 97 miles SW of Glasgow; 80 miles W of Dumfries

The tiny harbor town of Portpatrick clutches the extreme edge of southwest Scotland and exudes all the flavor of an old Scottish fishing port. Once a thriving coastal port between Scotland and Ireland, Portpatrick was known as the "Gretna Green for

Ireland" and couples who wanted to marry quickly would land on Saturday, have the banns called on Sunday, and marry on Monday.

Today visitors head for this small, picturesque harbor for its rugged seascapes, handful of quirky craft stores, and to breath in the sea air. Portpatrick's cliffs are also the starting point of the **Southern Upland Way,** one of Scotland's greatest long-distance footpaths. From Portpatrick the route leads hikers on a 212-mile journey through much of southern Scotland's most memorable landscapes, including the Galloway Forest Park (p. 154), to Cockburnspath on the east coast. Most walkers have neither the time nor the stamina for the entire hike, but many travel here to enjoy one of the least-challenging stretches, which leads from Portpatrick's cliffs to Castle Kennedy, 13 miles east.

Portpatrick is also a recommended stop for those traveling to the Mull of Galloway, Scotland's most southerly point at the end of the peninsula, which is guarded by a remote lighthouse. The Mull of Galloway Lighthouse, along with the Logan Botanic Garden that you pass en-route, are both open to the public.

Essentials

GETTING THERE The nearest train station is at Stranraer. **Stagecoach** (℗ 01292/613-500; www.stagecoachbus.com) bus service no. 367 connects Stranraer with Portpatrick. The service runs regularly throughout the day and the journey takes around 20 minutes. Contact Stagecoach or **Traveline Scotland** (℗ 0871/200-2233; www.travelinescotland.com) for up to date timetables and fares.

If you're driving from Stranraer, join the A77, which heads southwest to Portpatrick.

Exploring the Area

It won't take long to explore Portpatrick's small harbor front with its gift shops and sea-facing pubs and cafes. The **Lighthouse Pottery** (℗ 01776/810-284; www.lighthousepottery.co.uk) on the south side of the harbor is an emporium of handmade ceramics, glassware, and gifts, and shoppers will also want to browse around **Smugglers Cove** (℗ 01776/810-513) on the harborfront, an Aladdin's cave of unusual jewelry, accessories, ornaments, and crafts.

The ruins of **Dunskey Castle** command a cliff-top location half a mile south of Portpatrick. Built in 1510, this grim keep rises abruptly from the cliff top and its dramatic remains can easily be reached via car or on foot. These cliffs are also a haven for bird-watchers who can expect to be bombarded with black guillemots, herring gulls, and fulmers.

Some 10 miles south of Portpatrick is the little hamlet of Port Logan and **Logan House** (not open to the public), the seat of the ancient McDougall family who laid out the **Logan Botanic Garden** (℗ 01776/860-231; www.rbge.org.uk), north of Port Logan off the B7065. These remarkable gardens are part of the Royal Botanic Garden Edinburgh (p. 85), and thanks to the warm touch of the Gulf Stream they're an unexpected pocket of exotic paradise right in the middle of Scotland's southern-most tip. The gardens overflow with displays of plants gathered from the southern hemisphere including eucalyptus groves, cordylines, palms, tree ferns, and flowering shrubs, and are open mid-March to October daily from 10am to 5pm. Admission is £5 for adults, £4 for seniors, £1 for children 5 to 16, and £10 for families.

Farther south, still at the very tip of the peninsular, stands the **Mull of Galloway Lighthouse** (℗ 01776/830-682; www.mull-of-galloway.co.uk). First lit in 1830, this working lighthouse shoots out a powerful beam that on a clear night can be spied

28 miles away. The lighthouse opens its doors to the public from Easter until October on weekends from 10am to 4pm, and visitors are invited to climb its 26m (85-ft.) high tower. Admission is £4 adults and £1 children under 14.

Where to Eat & Stay

In the center of Portpatrick's harborfront on North Crescent, the **Crown Hotel** (www.crownportpatrick.com; ✆ **01776/810-261**) is a good local pub serving a seafood-heavy pub food menu and also rents rooms on a bed-and-breakfast basis. And standing above the village on Heugh Road, the **Fernhill Hotel** (www.mcmillan hotels.co.uk; ✆ **01776/810-220**) is also a recommended place to stay and eat.

Campbells MEDITERRANEAN/SEAFOOD   This small family-run restaurant is a favorite with both locals and visitors and occupies a prime spot on the edge of Portpatrick's harborfront. The elegant interior combines white linen with sea views and a relaxed atmosphere and makes for a fine setting to enjoy the seafood for which Campbells is known. Starters might include grilled Solway king scallops or Mediterranean fish soup, and although fish dishes also feature primarily on the main-course menu, meat dishes such as Barbarie duck breast and rack of lamb are always available. Round off a meal with a simple dessert of local Galloway ice cream or almond tart.

1 South Crescent, Portpatrick. ✆ **01776/810-314.** www.campbellsrestaurant.co.uk. Main courses £11–£33, 2-course lunch £11. MC, V. Tues–Sat noon–2:30pm and 6–9:30pm, Sun 12:30–2:30pm and 6:30–9:30pm.

Knockinaam Lodge ★★   Built in 1869, this three-story Victorian hunting lodge faces its own private beach and sits among towering cliffs 5 miles southwest of Portpatrick. The hotel embodies all the charm and romance of its coastal setting and all the ambiance of Scottish manorial living with its oak-paneled bar, classically luxurious guest rooms, and striking sea views. It was in the 12 hectares (30 acres) of Knockinaam's private woodland that Sir Winston Churchill met General Eisenhower during World War II, and guests can stay in the Churchill room where the man himself slept. Dining at Knockinaam is exquisite, informal, and candlelit, and you can choose from lunch and dinner menus that show off the best of modern Scottish cooking.

Portpatrick, DG9 9AD, signposted off the A77 west of Portpatrick. www.knockinaamlodge.com. ✆ **01776/810-471.** Fax 01776/810-435. 10 units. £220–£400 double. AE, DC, MC, V. **Amenities:** Restaurant; bar; Wi-Fi (free). *In room:* TV/DVD, hair dryer.

GLASGOW & THE AYRSHIRE COAST

Glasgow is Scotland's largest city and home to much of its population. Sprawling around the banks of the river Clyde as city merchants grew rich on the transatlantic trade in tobacco and then cotton in the 18th and 19th centuries, Glasgow was once famous for its formidable shipbuilding industry. From the embers of an industrial past that shaped the British Empire, the ever-resourceful Glasgow forged a new identity in the latter years of the 20th century and now stands proud as one of Europe's most vibrant cultural capitals.

SIGHTSEEING   Glasgow began life as a medieval ecclesiastical center and its powerful cathedral, a rare surviving pre-Reformation beauty, is reason enough to visit. Lose yourself for days in the vast collections of Glasgow's art galleries and museums, some of the U.K.'s finest, where the work of Charles Rennie Macintosh is celebrated alongside treasures from around the world. Don't leave without paying homage to the Clyde, where shining new attractions such as the Glasgow Science Centre have rejuvenated historic riverbanks.

EATING & DRINKING   With a culinary scene that has diversified and improved over many years, Glasgow's restaurants impress visitors with their high quality and range of options. The center of the city along with Merchant City and the West End prickle with long-established favorites who've perfected the art of Scottish food and stand beside a growing number of eateries specializing in cuisine from around the world.

SHOPPING   Glasgow's shopping experience is one of the best in Britain and is unmatched by any other Scottish city. The city's eminent Style Mile has it all for the discerning shopper seeking the latest look, the best bargains, and a mind-blowing number of choices. The West End's independent shops pride themselves on vintage, quirky, and all things offbeat.

ARTS & CULTURE   Once the sun goes down Glasgow knows how to party. The city's many theatres champion a spectrum of work from the classics to some of Europe's edgiest performances, and its legendary music scene spans the iconic Barrowland to concerts by national orchestras. All complemented by the coolest clubs in Scotland.

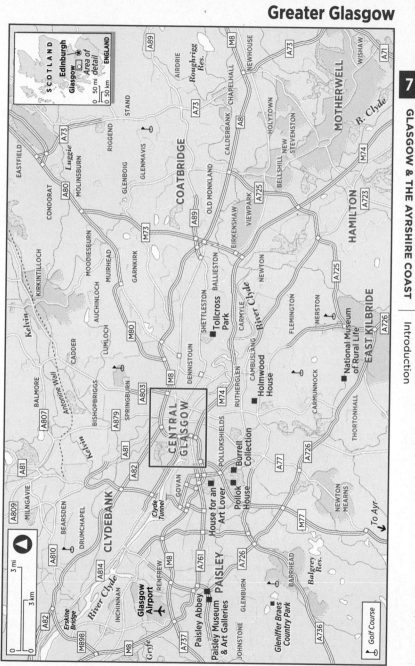

SCOTLAND

Edinburgh

Glasgow

Area of detail

ENGLAND

0 50 mi
0 50 km

A89

A73

A8

A71

WISHAW

NEWHOUSE

MOTHERWELL

R. Clyde

M74

A723

HAMILTON

A725

EAST KILBRIDE

A726

National Museum of Rural Life

NERSTON

NEWTON MEARNS

THORTONHALL

To Ayr

A736

Golf Course

AIRDRIE

Roughrigg Res.

CHAPELHALL

CALDERBANK

HOLYTOWN

STEVENSTON

BELLSHILL NEW

VIEWPARK

BIRKENSHAW

NEWTON

CARMYLE

FLEMINGTON

CARMUNNOCK

A726

A77

A726

M77

Balgrey Res.

BARRHEAD

Glenburn

STAND

RIGGEND

GLENMAVIS

GLENBOIG

OLD MONKLAND

COATBRIDGE

A89

A73

M73

GARNKIRK

BALLIESTON

SHETTLESTON

Tollcross Park

DENNISTOUN

M8

RUTHERGLEN

CAMBUSLANG

Holmwood House

River Clyde

CENTRAL GLASGOW

A803

A879

SPRINGBURN

BISHOPBRIGGS

CADDER

M80

LUMLOCH

AUCHINLOCH

MUIRHEAD

MOODIESBURN

KIRKINTILLOCH

Kelvin

CONDORAT

MOLINSBURN

Luggie

A80

A73

EASTFIELD

BALMORE

Antonine Wall

Kelvin

A807

A81

MILNGAVIE

A809

BEARSDEN

DRUMCHAPEL

CLYDEBANK

River Clyde

INCHINNAN

Erskine Bridge

A82

M898

M8

Gryfe

A737

JOHNSTONE

A814

RENFREW

M8

Clyde Tunnel

GOVAN

House for an Art Lover

Pollok House

Burrell Collection

POLLOKSHIELDS

M74

A82

A81

Glasgow Airport

Paisley Abbey

PAISLEY

A761

A726

Paisley Museum & Art Galleries

Gleniffer Braes Country Park

A810

3 mi
3 km

159

THE best TRAVEL EXPERIENCES IN GLASGOW

○ **Delve deep into the Burrell Collection:** This vast and eclectic collection symbolizes shipping magnate William Burrell's lifelong love affair with art. He bought for the love of it and donated his 9,000-piece treasure trove to the wider public. See p. 175.

○ **Discover Glasgow's Mackintosh heritage:** The vision and pure style of Glasgow-born artist/architect Charles Rennie Mackintosh blazed across the early 20th century. Discover the school that trained him and some of the finest buildings he created on a Mackintosh tour of Glasgow. See p. 170.

○ **Soak up the might of the Clyde:** The legendary Clyde estuary formed the gateway to the New World and constructed and launched a thousand ships. Soak up the river that built the city and an empire at the rejuvenated riverbank around the Glasgow Science Centre. See p. 172.

○ **Step back in time at Glasgow cathedral:** Take time to unearth Glasgow's ecclesiastical roots at its stunning medieval cathedral and lose yourself among the crumbling gothic splendor and whispers of immortality at its adjacent Necropolis. See p. 171.

○ **Shop your socks off on the Style Mile:** Only London claims more square footage of shopping space than Glasgow in the U.K. Dedicated shoppers can choose between high street brands, top designer stores, or independent outlets flaunting a style all their own on Glasgow's famed Style Mile. See p. 184.

ESSENTIALS

Arriving

BY PLANE **Glasgow Airport** is at Abbotsinch (© **0870/040-0008;** www. glasgowairport.com), 10 miles west of the city via the M8, and receives flights from London Heathrow and Gatwick and various other U.K. airports, plus a number of U.S. destinations. For more information, see chapter 14. **First** (© **0141/423-6600;** www.firstgroup.com) operates service no. 500, a shuttle bus between the airport and Glasgow city center. This 24-hour service runs up to every 10 minutes; the ride takes 25 minutes and costs £4.50 one way or £7 round-trip for adults, £3.30 one way or £5.50 round-trip for children. Alternatively First's 747 service connects the airport with Buchanan Street bus station (see below) and the West End. This service runs every 20 minutes and takes around 50 minutes to reach the bus station; a one-way fare costs £3.90 and a round-trip fare is £5. Alternatively a taxi to the city center costs £20 to £22.

Glasgow's second airport, **Prestwick** (© **0871/223-0700;** www.glasgow prestwick.com) receives flights from destinations across Europe and stands on the Ayrshire coast 33 miles southwest of the city center. This airport is connected with Glasgow by **ScotRail** trains from Central Station (© **0845/601-5929;** www. scotrail.co.uk) and the X77 **Stagecoach** bus (© **01292/613-500;** www.stagecoach bus.com) from Buchanan Street bus station.

BY TRAIN Glasgow's main train station is **Central Station** on Gordon Street. **Virgin Trains** (© **08719/744-222;** www.virgintrains.co.uk) operates a regular service between London Euston and Glasgow Central. The journey time is approximately

4½ hours and an advance one-way ticket costs between £65 and £150. You can also travel from London King's Cross on some **East Coast** trains (© **08457/225-111; www.eastcoast.co.uk**) via Edinburgh. The journey is an hour longer and a one-way fare costs between £40 and £135. **ScotRail** (© **0845/601-5929;** www.scotrail.co.uk) operates the Caledonian Sleeper service—overnight trains to London with sleeper berths. One-way fares cost around £94. Central Station also serves southern Scotland.

Glasgow's **Queen Street Station** stands on the north side of George Square and serves the north and east of Scotland, with trains arriving from and departing to Edinburgh every 15 minutes throughout the day until 11:30pm. The journey between the two cities takes 50 minutes and a round-trip fare costs £11 off peak or £20 to travel in peak hours, which are before 9:15am and between 4:30 and 6:30pm. You can also travel to Highland destinations from this station as well as Aberdeen and Stirling.

BY BUS **Buchanan Street Bus Station** is 2 blocks north of Queen Street Station on Killermont Street. **National Express** (© **08717/818-178;** www.national express.com) operates a regular service from London's Victoria coach station. Coaches take between 8½ and 11 hours to reach Glasgow, depending on the number of stops, and a one-way fare is between £13 and £68. **Megabus** (© **0871-266-3333;** www.megabus.com) also operates a coach service between London Victoria and Buchanan Street. The journey takes between 8 and 10 hours and a one-way fare is £11. **Scottish Citylink** (© **08705/505-050;** www.citylink.co.uk) operates a frequent bus service between Glasgow and Edinburgh, a round-trip ticket costs £9.40; the journey time is around 1 hour 20 minutes but can be much longer in rush hour.

BY CAR Glasgow is 47 miles west of Edinburgh, 216 miles north of Manchester, and 404 miles north of London. From England, Glasgow is reached via the M74, which becomes the A74 as it leads into the city center. From Edinburgh, the M8 joins the two cities and travels directly through the heart of Glasgow. Other major routes into the city are the A77 from Prestwick and Ayr, which becomes the M77 as it enters the city, and the A8 from the west, which becomes the M8 around the port of Glasgow. The A82 leads from the northwest (the Highlands) on the north bank of the Clyde, and from the northeast the M80 joins the M8 east of the city center.

Visitor Information

The **Greater Glasgow and Clyde Valley Tourist Board,** 11 George Sq. (© **0141/204-4400;** www.seeglasgow.com), is open October to May Monday through Saturday 9am to 6pm; June to September Monday through Saturday 9am to 7pm; and also on Sunday April to September 10am to 6pm. There's also a Tourist Information desk at Glasgow airport.

Orientation

It's hard to identify the center of Glasgow, because the city's focus shifted west over the centuries from its medieval heart. At the core of this ancient area, which is now in the northeast corner of the city, stands the great Cathedral of St. Kentigern, a perfect example of pre-Reformation Gothic architecture that dates in part to the 12th century. Behind the cathedral is the Necropolis burial ground, while across the square is Provand's Lordship, the city's oldest house, built in 1471. South of the cathedral on High Street is the Tolbooth Steeple (from 1626) at Glasgow Cross, and

Finding an Address

Glasgow is a sometimes sprawling city whose various districts have built up at different times over the years. Large sections have been demolished—some for slum clearance, others to make way for new highways. The city center is built on a grid system and is easy to navigate; some say it reminds them of New York. Outside of this area following a consistent street plan is tough, as squares or terraces can suddenly interrupt your route. House numbers can run in odds or evens and clockwise or counterclockwise, and sometimes numbers aren't used at all. So don't be surprised to see something like "Black-friars Street," without a number, given as an address. Grab a detailed map before setting out and if in doubt find the nearest cross street, and then look for your location from there. If it's a hotel or restaurant, the sign for the establishment is likely to be more prominent than the number anyway.

farther south still on the banks of the River Clyde is **Glasgow Green,** which has been common land since 1178 and was Britain's first public park. The area is known as Glasgow's **East End** and while it's interesting to explore during the day, this is an area to avoid at night.

From the East End, the area west of High Street marks Glasgow's growth away from its medieval roots in the same way Edinburgh's New Town grew away from its ancient Old Town. From High Street, Ingram Street leads through Merchant City into the monumental heart of modern Glasgow around George Square which, along with the area west until the M8 and south to the banks of the River Clyde, is considered to be the center of the modern city.

Apart from the Gallery of Modern Art in Royal Exchange Square, there are few attractions in Glasgow's city center because this area is mainly dedicated to shopping, dining, and nightlife. The **Merchant City** is a compact area of streets that developed into a working area of warehouses, housing, and markets as Glasgow and the British Empire expanded. Thanks to recent renovation Merchant City has been reinvigorated into a district dedicated to upmarket shopping and dining, all of which perfectly complements the area's historic buildings such as Hutcheson's Hall (from 1802). West again the broad pedestrian thoroughfares of **Buchanan, Argyle,** and **Sauchiehall streets** form the heart of Glasgow's main shopping district.

The city's Victorian **West End** spreads out past the M8 and is easily reachable from the city center via public transport—both buses and subway. Here **Kelvingrove Park** grows around the River Kelvin as it flows through the city. Glasgow University and its students dominate this area, which also contains the Kelvingrove and Hunterian museums and art galleries, some of the finest in the U.K. Just a few strides away is Byres Road, a street lined with bars, shops, and restaurants, while Glasgow's **Botanic Gardens** lie to the north off the Great Western Road.

Although the River Clyde has played a formative role in Glasgow's development, until recent years there have been few reasons for visitors to seek it out, yet alone cross over to its south side. Redevelopment has altered this status with modern attractions such as the **Glasgow Science Centre** directly south of the West End drawing tourists to this area. Farther south still at around 3 miles southwest of the city center is the heavily wooded **Pollok Country Park,** home to the **Burrell**

Collection Gallery, one of Glasgow's best attractions. Both of these areas are well connected with the city center by public transport.

The Neighborhoods in Brief

To locate the following neighborhoods, see the "Glasgow Attractions" map, on p. 168.

Medieval Glasgow Also referred to as Old Glasgow, this is where St. Mungo arrived in A.D. 543 and built his church in what's now the northeastern part of the city. At the top of High Street stands the **Cathedral of St. Kentigern** and the **Necropolis,** one of Britain's largest Victorian cemeteries. You enter the **Necropolis** by crossing the Bridge of Sighs, styled after the famous bridge of the same name in Venice. Old Glasgow's major terminal is High Street Station. South of the cathedral, **Glasgow Green,** opening onto the River Clyde, has been a public park since 1662. This East End of Glasgow has many interesting attractions that are fine to explore in daylight hours, but this is not a region to walk through alone at night or a recommended place to stay.

Along the River Clyde It was once said that "The Clyde made Glasgow; Glasgow made the Clyde." Although the city is no longer so dependent on the river, you can still enjoy a stroll along the **Clyde Walkway ★,** which stretches from King Albert Bridge, at the western end of Glasgow Green, for 1¾ miles downstream to Stobcross, now the site of the **Scottish Exhibition and Conference Centre.** This is one of the city's grandest walks; on these waters, Glasgow once shipped its manufactured goods around the world. However, if time is limited, you may want to concentrate instead on the major museums and historic Glasgow.

The Merchant City Glasgow spread west of High Street in the 18th century, largely because of profits made from sugar, cotton, and tobacco in trade with the Americas. The Merchant City extends from Trongate and Argyle Street in the south to George Street in the north. Its major terminal is Queen Street Station and it boasts some of Britain's most elegant **Georgian and Victorian buildings,** as well as **Greek Revival churches.** Tobacco barons once occupied much of the area, but their buildings have been recycled for other uses.

Glasgow Center Continuing its western progression, the city center of Glasgow is dominated by George Square and Central Station. This is the major shopping district, including such venues as Buchanan Galleries. Also here are many of Glasgow's major theatres and other entertainment venues as well as Buchanan Street Bus Station.

The West End Beyond the M8 lies the West End home to the University of Glasgow and several major galleries and museums, most of which gather around **Kelvingrove Park.** The West End mixes culture, art, and parks, and is dominated by university students. Also in the West are the city's **Botanic Gardens.**

The South Side of the River Clyde to the west of the center is growing in popularity thanks to new attractions such as the Glasgow Science Centre and old time favorites including the Burrell Collection.

Getting Around

The best way to explore the center of Glasgow is on foot. Its grid system makes getting around a logical process, but in places there are some punishingly steep streets to navigate. That said, most of the city's attractions are outside of the center and to see these you need to rely on public transport.

BY BUS   Glasgow is serviced by **First** buses (© **0141/423-6600**; www.first group.com). Services run frequently throughout the day, but are greatly curtailed after 11pm. Schedules can be picked up at **Buchanan Street Bus Station** on Killermont Street or downloaded from the Glasgow section of First's website at www.firstgroup. com/ukbus/glasgow. One-way fares start from £1 for short journeys and exact change is required. Alternatively, day passes cost £3.75 for adults and £2.25 for children.

BY UNDERGROUND   Called the "Clockwork Orange" (from the vivid orange of the trains), Glasgow's subway is a fast and efficient way for traveling around the city. The circular route contains 15 stops and trains run every 5 to 12 minutes including Sunday. The service operates Monday through Saturday 6:30am to 11:30pm and Sunday 10am to 6pm. Tickets can be bought at any subway station and the fare for a one-way journey is £1.20 adults and 60p children, or a day **Discovery Ticket** costs £3.50. Full information on public transport can be obtained at the information desk at Buchanan bus station or the **Travel Centre** at St. Enoch Square subway station (© **0141/333-3708**), which is open Monday through Saturday 8:30am to 5:30pm.

BY TAXI   Taxis in Glasgow are excellent. You can hail them on the street or call **Glasgow Taxis** (© **0141/429-7070**; www.glasgowtaxis.co.uk). Fares are displayed on a meter next to the driver. When a taxi is available on the street, a "TAXI" sign on the roof is lit a bright yellow. Most taxi trips within the city cost £5 to £9. The taxi meter starts at £2 and increases by 25p every 61m (200 ft.).

BY CAR   Driving around Glasgow is tricky business, even for locals. You're better off with public transport. The city is a warren of one-way streets, and parking is expensive and difficult to find. Metered parking is available at 10p for half an hour or 30p per hour, exact change required. And you must watch out for zealous traffic wardens issuing tickets: Some zones are marked PERMIT HOLDERS ONLY—your vehicle will be towed if you have no permit. A yellow line along the curb indicates no parking. Multistory car parks (parking lots), open 24 hours a day, are found at Anderston Cross, Cambridge, George, Mitchell, Oswald, and Waterloo streets.

If you want to rent a car to explore the countryside, it's best to make a reservation before leaving home (see chapter 14). But you can rent a car upon arrival as all the major rental agencies are represented at Glasgow airport. In addition, **Enterprise** has a branch on Oswald Street (© **0141/221-2124**; www.enterprise.co.uk), which is close to Central Station, and further west there's a branch of **Avis** at 70 Lancefield St. (© **0844/581-0147**; www.avis.co.uk).

BY BICYCLE   Parts of Glasgow are fine for biking, and you might want to rent a bike to explore the surrounding countryside. Bikes can be rented at **Gear of Glasgow,** 19 Gibson St. in the West End (© **0141/339-1179**; http://gearbikes.com). Rates range from £10 for a half-day or £15 for a full day to £60 for a week, and a driver's license or passport must be left as a deposit. Bikes come with a lock and baskets can be rented for an extra £5 and car racks for £10. The store is open daily 10am to 6pm and Sunday noon until 5pm.

Organized Tours

City Sightseeing Glasgow (© **0141/204-0444**; www.citysightseeingglasgow. co.uk) operates frequent open-top bus tours around the city throughout the year. A complete tour takes about 1 hour and 15 minutes, but you're free to hop off and on at any of the 15 stops along the way and a ticket is valid for 2 days. Buses depart from stop no. 1 at George Square from 9:30am until 4:30pm and run every 15 minutes

Glasgow Underground

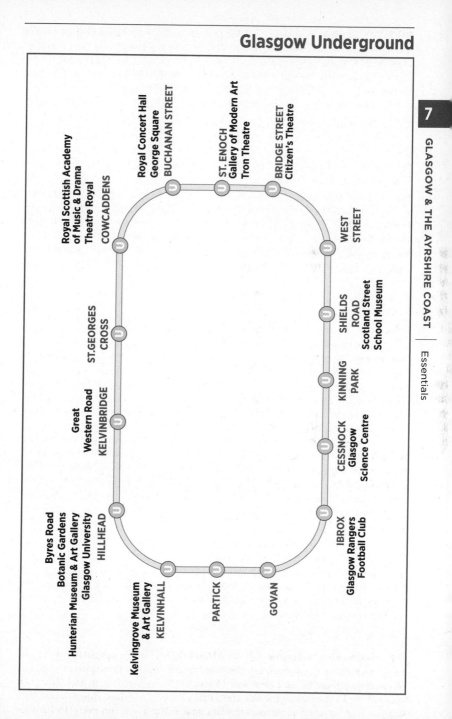

from April to October and every half-hour November to March. Tickets can be bought from the driver and cost £11 for adults and £5 for children 5 to 15, or £25 for families.

If you prefer to stay on terra firma, **GreetinGlasgow** (© **07751/976-935;** www. greetinglasgow.com) leads walking tours around Merchant City and the East End, taking in the main sights and some hidden history. Tours last 1 hour and 20 minutes, cost £8 per person (under-14s free), and depart daily at 10am and 2pm but must be reserved in advance.

[Fast FACTS] GLASGOW

Business Hours Most **offices** and **banks** are open Monday through Friday 9am to 5pm; some banks also open on Saturday when opening times vary from bank to bank. **Shops** are generally open Monday through Saturday 9:30am to 6pm. On Thursday stores remain open until 8pm; many also open on Sundays from 11am to 5 or 6pm.

Currency Exchange Most city center banks operate a *bureaux de change,* and nearly all will cash traveler's checks if you have the proper ID. There are also currency exchanges at Glasgow Airport and Central Station.

Dentists If you have an emergency, go to the Accident and Emergency Department of **Glasgow Dental Hospital & School,** 378 Sauchiehall St. (© **0141/ 232-6323;** www.gla.ac.uk/ schools/dental). It's not a walk-in facility and appointments need to be made by telephone first. Hours are Monday through Friday 8:30am to 5:15pm; at other times, call **NHS 24** © **08454/242-424.** You can also call NHS 24 in an emergency (© 08454 242424; www.nhs24.com.

Doctors The major hospital is the **Glasgow Royal Infirmary,** 82–86 Castle St. (© **0141/211-4000**).

Embassies & Consulates See "Fast Facts: Scotland" (p. 436).

Emergencies Call © **999** in an emergency to summon the police, an ambulance, or firefighters.

Hospitals See "Doctors," above.

Hot Lines Women in crisis can call **Women's Aid** (© **0141/553-2022;** www. glasgowwomensaid.org.uk). Gays and lesbians can contact the **Gay and Lesbian Switchboard** ((© **0141/847-0447;** www.sgls.co.uk). The **Rape Crisis Centre** is at © **0141/552-3200** or visit www.rapecrisiscentre-glasgow.co.uk.

Internet Access You can get online at the **iCafe** on Great Western Road (© **0141/572-0788;** www. icafe.uk.com). Wi-Fi is free with the purchase of food or coffee; otherwise free Internet access is available at the Mitchell Library on North Street.

Laundry & Dry Cleaning Try the **Park Laundrette,** 14 Park Rd. ((© **0141/ 334-3433;** www.majestic laundrette.co.uk), open Monday and Wednesday to Saturday 8am to 6pm, Thursday 8am to 9pm, and Sunday 10am to 4pm.

Luggage Storage & Lockers **Buchanan Bus Station** has a number of left luggage lockers. There's also a Left Luggage Department on platform 1 at **Central Station,** open Monday through Saturday 6am to midnight and Sunday 7am to midnight. Rates are £7 per item for the first 24 hours, £3.50 per item for every 24 hours thereafter.

Newspapers & Magazines Published since 1783, the *Herald* (www. heraldscotland.com) is the major newspaper with national, international, and financial news, sports, and cultural listings; the *Evening Times* (www.evening times.co.uk) offers local news.

Pharmacies There are branches of Boots (www. boots.com) in most of the main shopping malls and at 200 Sauchiehall St.

(© 0141/332-1925), open Monday through Wednesday and Friday and Saturday 8am to 7pm, Thursday 8am to 8pm, and Sunday 10:30am to 5:30pm.

Police   In an emergency, call © **999.** For other inquiries, contact police headquarters at © **0141/532-2000.**

Post Office   The main branch is at 47 St. Vincent's St. (© **0845/722-3344**). It's open Monday through Saturday 9:30am to 5:30pm.

Safety   Glasgow is the most dangerous city in Scotland, but it's relatively safe when compared with cities of its size in the United States. Muggings do occur, and often they're related to Glasgow's rather large drug problem. The famed razor gangs of Calton, Bridgeton, and the Gorbals are no longer around to earn the city a reputation for violence, but you still should stay alert.

Toilets   They can be found at train stations, bus stations, museums, and some department stores. Toilets in restaurants, hotels, and pubs are often for the use of their patrons only. Glasgow also has a system of public toilets, often marked wc. Don't hesitate to use them, but they're likely to be closed late in the evening.

EXPLORING THE CITY

Glasgow's attractions are scattered all around the city. In order to make the most efficient use of time, it's useful to think of the city in terms of its different districts and what each has to offer.

City Center & Merchant City

Glasgow's vast **George Square** was laid out in 1781 and is considered to be the center of the city. This Georgian creation is the focus of Glasgow's many celebrations and is dominated on its east side by the huge **City Chambers.** Opened in 1888 by Queen Victoria, this elaborate building is a testament to the city's wealth during the empire-building Victorian era and its lavish interior is a feast of mosaics, grand marble staircases, and large carved statues. Free tours run every Monday through Friday at 10:30am and 3:30pm and even if you miss a tour, take time to wander in and simply marvel. An imposing representation of Sir Walter Scott sits atop a 24m (80-ft.) column in the center of the square, and of the numerous statues that are scattered around the circumference, Victoria and her beloved Albert and Robert Burns are among the most significant. The last monument to be constructed here was the Cenotaph war memorial that stands opposite the City Chambers.

Glasgow's center is dominated by shopping and there's little to detain visitors other than the **Glasgow School of Art** (see box p. 170), **Tenement House,** and the **National Piping Centre** (© **0141/353-0220;** www.thepipingcentre.co.uk) on McPhater Street—whose small museum traces the history of this iconic Scottish musical instrument.

Immediately east of Glasgow's center lies the area now called Merchant City, which grew into a region of warehouses, markets, and houses as trade prospered in the 19th century and whose streets are named after the most prosperous merchants and the regions they traded in. Significant buildings here include **Hutcheson's Hall** on Ingram Street; **Merchant's House,** one of the few surviving merchant's homes at 42 Miller St.; and **Ramshorn Church** on Ingram Street, now used as a theatre by the University of Strathclyde and whose surrounding churchyard is the city's oldest. (Glasgow's wealthy once paid to be buried in the walled section known as "paradise.") This area is fascinating to walk around and its main attraction is the **Gallery of Modern Art** (GOMA).

Glasgow Attractions

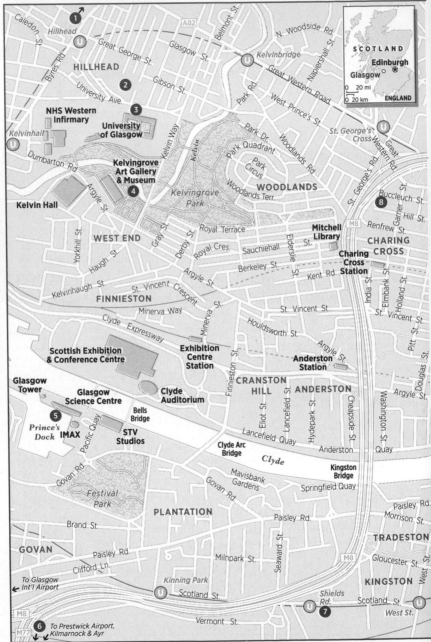

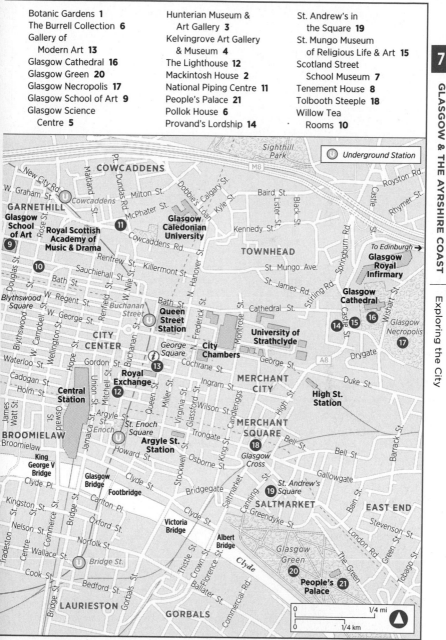

Botanic Gardens **1**
The Burrell Collection **6**
Gallery of
  Modern Art **13**
Glasgow Cathedral **16**
Glasgow Green **20**
Glasgow Necropolis **17**
Glasgow School of Art **9**
Glasgow Science
  Centre **5**

Hunterian Museum &
  Art Gallery **3**
Kelvingrove Art Gallery
  & Museum **4**
The Lighthouse **12**
Mackintosh House **2**
National Piping Centre **11**
People's Palace **21**
Pollok House **6**
Provand's Lordship **14**

St. Andrew's in
  the Square **19**
St. Mungo Museum
  of Religious Life & Art **15**
Scotland Street
  School Museum **7**
Tenement House **8**
Tolbooth Steeple **18**
Willow Tea
  Rooms **10**

CHARLES rennie MACKINTOSH (1868–1928)

The internationally celebrated artist, architect, and designer Charles Rennie Mackintosh was born in Glasgow in 1868. Mackintosh believed that architects and designers should be allowed more artistic freedom and many of his most important buildings can be found in and around the city. The place to start any Mackintosh tour is the **Glasgow School of Art** (℗ 0141/353-4526; www.gsa.ac.uk) on Renfrew Street where Mackintosh studied before designing the magnificent building that houses the school today. Tours of the building lead visitors through this influential architectural masterpiece and depart daily on the hour between 11am and 5pm from April to September and daily at 11am and 3pm from October to March (£8.75 adults, £7 seniors, £4 under-18s). Also in the city center is **The Lighthouse** (℗ 0141/276-5360; www.glasgow.gov.uk) on Mitchell Lane, a modern center for architecture and design housed in the old *Glasgow Herald* building, which

was Mackintosh's first public commission and completed in 1895. The Lighthouse is free to enter and contains the **Mackintosh Interpretation Centre,** the first facility to provide an overview of Mackintosh's art, design, and architecture, which is open Monday, Wednesday, and Saturday 10:30am to 5pm and Tuesday 11am to 5pm.

Two very different Mackintosh-designed buildings can be found in the Southside. **House for an Art Lover,** in Bellahouston Park on Dumbreck Road (℗ 0141/353-4770; www.houseforanartlover.co.uk), was built from designs by Macintosh entered into a competition whose purpose was to design "a grand house in a thoroughly modern style." Although admired, his plans didn't win and this house wasn't built until after Mackintosh's death. Completed in 1996 this elegant, light-infused contemporary sensation stands beside an Art Park filled with outdoor art installations. The house is generally open daily 10am to

Gallery of Modern Art ★★ GALLERY   Housed in an elaborate neoclassical building that was built in 1778 as a townhouse for one of Glasgow's notoriously wealthy tobacco lords, this thoroughly modern gallery makes full use of its elegant interior to showcase the work of the U.K.'s top contemporary artists. Its permanent collection includes pieces by major modern Scots artists such as Douglas Gordon and Ken Currie, and despite promoting work that's not always the most easily accessible, this magnificent much-loved gallery is one of the most visited contemporary art galleries in the U.K.

Royal Exchange Sq. ℗ **0141/287-3005.** www.glasgowlife.org.uk. Free admission. Mon–Wed and Sat 10am–5pm; Thurs 10am–8pm; Fri and Sun 11am–5pm.

Tenement House HISTORIC HOME   For a taste of early 20th-century life for Glasgow's working class who lived in the city's many tenements, head to this authentic 19th-century property. Tenements are small apartments and this one was occupied for 50 years from 1911 by a Miss Agnes Toward, who worked as a shorthand typist until she retired in her 70s. Miss Toward never married, did little to alter her tiny four-room tenement, and kept many household items such as wartime leaflets that most people threw away. Her diligence and unwillingness to alter her long time home now allow visitors the opportunity to step back in time at this fascinating property.

145 Buccleuch St. ℗ **0844/493-2197.** www.nts.org.uk. £6 adults, £5 seniors and children, £16 families. Mar–Oct 1–5pm.

4pm, although it sometimes closes for private functions so call ahead before visiting. Admission costs £4.50 for adults, £3 for seniors and children over 10, under-10s free. Also on the Southside, **Scotland Street School Museum** (*0141/287-0513*; www.glasgowlife.org.uk) on Scotland Street is a Mackintosh-designed building that was a school until 1979 and now serves as a museum, which recreates Glasgow school life over the last century. The museum also contains Mackintosh's architectural plans for the building and is open Tuesday through Thursday and Saturday 10am to 5pm and Friday and Sunday 11am to 5pm. Admission is free.

There are two further stops on any Mackintosh tour of the city in the West End, most notably **Mackintosh House,** the artist's old Glasgow home adjacent to the **Hunterian Art Gallery** (p. 172), and the **Kelvingrove Art Gallery & Museum** (p. 172), which displays samples of Mackintosh's work.

To conclude a tour, head back to the city center and take tea at the famed **Willow Tea Rooms** (*0141/332-0521*; www.willowtearooms.co.uk) at 217 Sauchiehall Street. When they opened in 1904, the tearooms were a sensation thanks to their Mackintosh design, which has since been restored to its original glory. The tearooms are open Monday through Saturday 9am to 5pm and Sunday 11am to 4:15pm and afternoon teas cost £12 per person—reservations recommended.

A 1-day **Macintosh Trail Ticket** is the cheapest way to view all these properties. Tickets cost £16 per person and include admission to all attractions plus subway or bus travel between them. Tickets can be bought in person at the Tourist Information Centre on George Square (p. 167), at any of the participating venues, or in advance via the Charles Rennie Mackintosh Society website www.crmsociety.com, which also includes full information on other Mackintosh related properties.

The East End & Medieval Glasgow

Glasgow grew from its east side and this region is a must for history lovers and anyone wanting to really get underneath the city's skin. Glasgow's medieval heart burns in the northeast where visitors will discover its mighty **cathedral** and **Provand's Lordship** (*0141/552-8819*; www.glasgowlife.org.uk), the city's oldest house. This free attraction was built in 1471 and sits in the Cathedral Precinct across from **St. Mungo's Museum** (both share the same opening hours). The **Glasgow Necropolis** ★ (www.glasgow.gov.uk/parks) is a great rambling, crumbling cemetery stuffed with grand urns, old gravestones, creepy catacombs, and soaring monuments dating back to the 1800s and rising behind the cathedral. Park rangers give free tours of the Necropolis; call *0141/287-5064* to book a place.

From this region the High Street runs south to the **East End,** which extends away from the city center at the **Glasgow Cross,** a large junction of five main thoroughfares marked by the seven-story **Tolbooth Steeple,** which was once part of a larger 17th-century building. Highlights of the East End include **Glasgow Green,** Britain's oldest public space, which was gifted to the people of Glasgow in the 15th century and lines the north side of the Clyde. Today this land is home to the **People's Palace. St. Andrew's in the Square** (*0141/559-5902*; www.standrewsinthesquare.com) is an often overlooked gem of an 18th-century church that stands in St. Andrews Square and has been fully restored to its shining glory. The church is also

Glasgow's Centre for Scottish Culture and can be viewed for free on Thursday mornings between 10:30am and 1pm.

Glasgow Cathedral ★★★ CATHEDRAL   One of Glasgow's most memorable buildings, this early medieval Gothic-style structure dates back to the 12th century and is mainland Scotland's only complete medieval cathedral. Once a place of pilgrimage, before 16th-century zeal purged it of all monuments of idolatry, Glasgow's cathedral is dedicated to St. Mungo (also known as St. Kentigern), whose tomb lies in the Laigh Kirk (lower church), a vaulted crypt said to be the finest in Europe. Other highlights include the nave that dates from the 1400s and is crowned by an open timber roof. A fine collection of modern stained glass throws stunning dashes of light across the dark interior and the most celebrated pieces are *The Creation* by Francis Spear in the Great West Window and the deep blue Millennium Window created by glass painter John K. Clark.

Cathedral Square, Castle St. ✆ **0141/552-6891.** www.glasgowcathedral.org.uk. Free admission. Apr–Sept Mon–Sat 9:30am–6pm, Sun 1–5:30pm; Oct–Mar Mon–Sat 9:30am–4pm, Sun 1–4pm.

People's Palace HISTORIC SITE   Housed in a rich sandstone building opposite the grand 19th-century Doulton Fountain, the People's Palace tells the story of both the city of Glasgow and its residents from 1750 to the end of the 20th century. Glimpses into how Glaswegians lived, worked, and played are brought to life via photographs, films, old artifacts, and new interactive computer displays. Most memorable is the adjoining Winter Gardens, a large, delicate glasshouse filled with exotic plants and a buzzing cafe.

Glasgow Green. ✆ **0141/276-1625.** www.glasgowlife.org.uk. Free admission. Tues–Thurs and Sat 10am–5pm; Fri and Sun 11am–5pm.

St. Mungo Museum of Religious Life & Art ★ MUSEUM   Opened in 1993, this eclectic, award-winning museum explores the role and importance of religion in people's lives and across all cultures and ages. Its collections span the centuries and highlight the various religious groups that have lived in Glasgow and the west of Scotland. The museum is also hailed as unique for its representation of Buddha, Ganesha, Shiva, and others; its chilled-out cafe opens out onto Britain's first Zen garden.

2 Castle St. ✆ **0141/276-1625.** www.glasgowlife.org.uk. Free admission. Mon–Thurs and Sat 10am–5pm; Fri and Sun 11am–5pm.

The West End

Glasgow's West End is the region where the city's rich 18th-century merchants built their fine homes, away from the busy city center, and the place where the city's university moved in 1870. The district remains popular with students and academic staff and the university's splendidly Gothic campus contains the **Hunterian Museum & Art Gallery**—Scotland's oldest public museum—and the **Mackintosh House.** The River Kelvin winds through the West End and the vast **Kelvingrove Park** was created around its banks in the mid-19th century as a recreation space for well-to-do Victorian residents. This popular green space is home to the **Kelvingrove Art Gallery & Museum** and a number of children's play areas. Glasgow's tranquil **Botanic Gardens** (✆ **0141/276-1614**) can also be found here, spreading north off the Great Western Road for 16 hectares (40 acres) and showcasing an extensive collection of tropical plants and herb gardens as well as the magnificently restored Victorian Kibble Palace glasshouse.

Unappreciated Genius: Alexander 'Greek' Thomson

Perhaps even more important than Mackintosh, Alexander 'Greek' Thomson (1817–75) brought an unrivaled vision to Glasgow. While the influence of classical Greece was nothing new to Victorian architects, Thomson honed it to essentials and then mixed in Egyptian, Assyrian, and other Eastern-influenced motifs. Like Mackintosh, he increasingly found himself out of step with (and well ahead of) others. While a number of his structures have been tragically lost to the wrecker's ball, some key works remain: for example, terraced houses such as Moray Place (where he lived on the city's Southside) or Eton Terrace near Glasgow University campus.

Hunterian Museum & Art Gallery ★★ MUSEUM   This attraction is divided into two parts. Its museum, which opened in 1807, sits on one side of University Avenue and displays many fascinating items from the private collections of its early benefactor William Hunter, including dinosaur fossils and Viking plunder. Across the avenue is the more popular art gallery exhibiting 17th- and 18th-century paintings (Rembrandt to Rubens) and 19th- and 20th-century Scottish work, and the **Macintosh House,** once the architect's own home, that today contains the Mackintosh Collection, the largest single holding of his work. The museum has had a new roof installed and this space will feature a new permanent collection devoted to the Romans in Scotland.

University of Glasgow, University Avenue. ✆ **0141/330-5431** or **0141/330-4221.** www.hunterian.gla. ac.uk. Free admission to the gallery and museum; admission to Mackintosh House is £3 adults, £2 seniors and children. Mon–Sat 9:30am–5pm. The university is 1¾ miles west of the city center and the nearest subway station is Hillhead.

Kelvingrove Art Gallery & Museum ★★ MUSEUM   Hailed as one of Glasgow's landmark attractions, Kelvingrove is one of the U.K.'s most visited museums outside London. Following extensive restoration the Kelvingrove reopened its doors in 2006 to show off its 22 themed galleries displaying around 8,000 objects from its internationally significant collections. Exhibits include sections covering ancient Egypt, 300-million-year-old marine-life fossils, and one of the world's greatest collections of arms and armor. The galleries also contain a superb collection from Dutch and Italian Old Masters, including Giorgione's *Adulteress Brought Before Christ,* Rembrandt's *Man in Armor,* and Millet's *Going to Work.* Scottish painting is well represented from the 17th century to the present. Expect plenty of interactive exhibits to keep young visitors engaged.

Argyle St. ✆ **0141/276-9599.** www.glasgowlife.org.uk. Free admission. Mon–Thurs and Sat 10am–5pm; Fri and Sun 11am–5pm. The Kelvingrove is 1¾ miles west of the city center and the nearest subway station is Kelvinhall.

Clydeside

The legendary Clyde made Glasgow and its banks were once the focus of a world dominating shipbuilding industry—the *QE2* was launched here in 1967. The section of the Clyde directly south of the West End has undergone significant regeneration and now boasts a number of new features, namely the **Glasgow Science Centre,** the **Clyde Auditorium**—an iconic concert venue nicknamed "The Armadillo"—and

The Riverside Museum

Glasgow recently opened the doors of its brand-new **Riverside Museum**, 100 PointHouse Place, Glasgow, G3 8RS. (© **0141 2872720**; www.glasgowlife. org.uk, Mon-Thurs, Sat: 10am-5pm, Fri & Sat: 11am-5pm) which is located on the Clyde's north bank about ½ mile downstream (west) of the Science Centre. This free, state-of-the-art new attraction houses collections from the now-closed Museum of Transport. One of the last remaining Clyde-built tall ships, the SV *Glenlee* (© **0141/222-2513**; www.glenlee.co.uk) is moored in a new berth beside the museum.

the headquarters of BBC Scotland. However, remnants of the river's past life can be detected such as **Finnieston Crane,** a giant-cantilever crane dating back to the 1920s.

To truly appreciate the might of the Clyde and take in what were once vast shipyards turning out more than half the earth's tonnage of oceangoing liners, hop aboard the *Waverley,* the world's last seagoing paddle steamer, which spends the summer months plying the waters around the Firth of Clyde and Ayrshire coast. Day trips to destinations including Tobermory, the Isle of Staffa, and Iona from the Waverley's moorings in Anderson Quay adjacent to the Glasgow Science Centre should be reserved in advance (© **0845/130-4647**; www.waverleyexcursions.co.uk) and cost around £43 for adults, £39 for seniors, and £21 for children.

Alternatively take to the skies and indulge in a bird's eye view of Scotland's west coast on a **Loch Lomond Seaplane** ride (© **01436/675-030**; www.lochlomond seaplanes.com), which departs from the waters by the Science Centre and costs around £139 per person or £449 for an exclusive family trip.

Glasgow Science Centre ★★★ ☺ PLANETARIUM Housed in a gleaming titanium-clad landmark new build on the south banks of the Clyde, this modern family-friendly attraction showcases Glasgow's contribution to science and technology over the past, present, and future. The main part of this attraction is its Science Mall, which spreads over three floors and features tons of imaginative and fun interactive exhibits as well as a changing program of exhibitions. For an extra £2.50 you can tag a Planetarium show onto a visit and sit back and enjoy a trip around the night sky. A ride in the Glasgow Tower transporting visitors 100m (328ft) into the air to take in wide views the city and surrounding countryside costs a further £2.50. This site also features an IMAX cinema that screens films in both 2D and 3D. The IMAX charges separate admission: £9 for adults or £7 seniors and children.

50 Pacific Quay. © **0141/540-5000.** www.gsc.org.uk. Admission £10 adults, £8 students and seniors. Daily 10am-5pm. Hours are sometimes restricted in the winter.

Southside

Although the area of Glasgow that spreads out south from the Clyde is generally called Southside, in fact it consists of a number of different districts, some more salubrious than others. This region is littered with large parks and golf courses, most notably **Pollok Country Park,** home to the **Burrell Collection,** and **Pollok House,** while **Linn Park,** on Clarkston Road, an 86-hectare (213-acre) spread of pine and woodland, offers scenic river walks and children's playgrounds. The attractions in this region are scattered but all easily reached via public transport from the city center and include two of interest to Mackintosh fans: **House for an Art Lover** and the **Scotland Street School Museum** (see box on p. 170).

The Burrell Collection ★★★ MUSEUM   This museum houses the mind-boggling treasures left to Glasgow by Sir William Burrell, a wealthy ship owner who had a lifelong passion for art. Burrell started collecting art when he was 14, and his passion continued until he died aged 96 in 1958. His tastes were eclectic: Chinese ceramics, French paintings from the 1800s, tapestries, stained-glass windows from churches, even stone doorways from the Middle Ages. It's said that the collector "liked about everything," including one of the very few original bronze casts of Rodin's *Thinker*. He did, however, find some art distasteful, including avant-garde works ("Monet was just too impressionistic"). You can see a vast aggregation of furniture, textiles, ceramics, stained glass, silver, art objects, and pictures in the dining room, hall, and drawing room, which were reconstructed from Sir William's home, Hutton Castle at Berwick-upon-Tweed. Ancient artifacts, Asian art, and European decorative arts and paintings are featured.

Pollok Country Park, 2060 Pollokshaws Rd. ✆ **0141/287-2550.** www.glasgowlife.org.uk. Free admission. Mon-Thurs and Sat 10am-5pm; Fri and Sun 11am-5pm. Pollok Country Park is 3 miles south of the city center and can be reached via First bus services: 45, 48, or 57.

Pollok House HISTORIC HOME/GALLERY   Head south of the Burrell Collection through Pollok Country Park and you discover this lofty Georgian country house that once served as the manor house of the Pollok estate. The house is presented as a living home and admission to the vast basement level servant's quarters where around 48 indoor staff toiled is free. This warren-like level features the Kitchen restaurant, housed in the original old kitchen and complete with lines of copper pans and a strong reputation for traditional home baking. For a taste of life "above stairs," head to the upper floors—entrance to this part of the house is also free from November to March (entry fees apply Apr–Oct). Here visitors can take in a superb art collection that includes paintings by William Blake and Spanish masters such as Goya and El Greco and round off a visit with a stroll through the surrounding formal gardens.

Pollok Country Park, 2060 Pollokshaws Rd. ✆ **0844/493-2202.** www.nts.org.uk. Admission to the upper part of the house from Apr-Oct £9 adults, £6.50 seniors and children, £22 families. Open daily 10am-5pm. Pollok Country Park is 3 miles south of the city center and can be reached via First bus services: 45, 48, or 57.

WHERE TO EAT

Merchant City has developed into a strong focal point for dining out. Here streets such as Candleriggs and Royal Exchange Square are lined with bars, cafes, and restaurants. In the West End, Bryes Road—particularly at the south end near Dumbarton Road and the north end close to the Great Western Road—are awash with any array of restaurants serving every kind of cuisine imaginable. Some higher-end restaurants close on Sunday and from 2:30pm until their pre-theatre menus kick in around 5:30pm the rest of the week. Reservations are recommended at all the restaurants listed below, especially at weekends. *Note:* For the locations of the restaurants below, see the "Glasgow Hotels & Restaurants" map on p. 174.

Glasgow Hotels & Restaurants

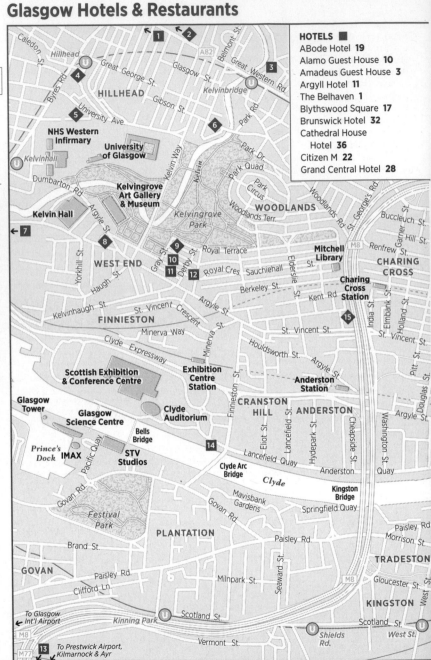

ABode Hotel **19**
Alamo Guest House **10**
Amadeus Guest House **3**
Argyll Hotel **11**
The Belhaven **1**
Blythswood Square **17**
Brunswick Hotel **32**
Cathedral House
   Hotel **36**
Citizen M **22**
Grand Central Hotel **28**

Hotel du Vin **1**
Lorne Hotel **12**
Malmaison **16**
Manor Park Hotel **7**
Marks Hotel **21**
Mint **14**
Park Inn Glasgow **23**
Radisson SAS **26**
Sherbrooke
   Castle Hotel **13**
Ten Queens
   Drive **27**

RESTAURANTS ◆
The Bistro **2**
Brian Maule at
   Chardon d'Or **18**
Cafe Gandolfi **34**
Cail Bruich **2**
City Merchant **33**
The Corinthian Club **29**
Gamba **25**
Ingram Wynd **35**
Jamie's Italian **30**
La Vallée Blanche **5**

Michael Caines at
   ABode Glasgow **19**
Mother India's Cafe **8**
Mussel Inn **24**
No. Sixteen **9**
Russian Café-Gallery
   Cossachok **31**
Stravaigin **6**
Two Fat Ladies at
   The Buttery **15**
Two Fat Ladies City Centre **20**
Ubiquitous Chip **4**

City Center

EXPENSIVE

Brian Maule at Chardon d'Or ★★★ FRENCH/SCOTTISH Ayr-born Brian Maule is hailed as one of Scotland's finest chefs. After a stint as head chef of Le Gavroche, one of London's best restaurants, he brought his culinary skill and finesse back to native turf. Maule's cuisine is prepared with passion, commitment, and the best possible regional ingredients, and each dish is a creation of his own original style. Starters include such delights as roulade of rabbit, foie gras, and pistachio nuts, while light, full-flavored, inventive main courses feature the likes of oven-roasted cod with squid ink pasta and tempura of squid. Leave room for sumptuous deserts, which could include homemade ice cream or star anis blancmange with griottinne cherries, or simply round off the night with a selection of French and Scottish cheeses.

176 W. Regent St. ✆ **0141/248-3801.** www.brianmaule.com. Main courses £24–£28. AE, MC, V. Mon–Fri noon–2:30pm, Mon–Thurs 5–10pm.

MODERATE

Gamba ★★★ SEAFOOD Gamba not only serves some of the best seafood in Glasgow, but is also one of the city's finest restaurants having earned a raft of awards since it opened around a decade ago. Inside a chic modern setting, diners are treated to top customer service and dazzled by the repertoire of dishes. Although the specialty is fish and seafood, Gamba treats carnivores to first-class Scottish meats such as Dunalastair red deer and tempts vegetarians with roast pepper, pesto, and goat's cheese tart. However, seafood rules the menu and in addition to main courses of lemon sole and Barra monkfish, there's a whole section of flavorsome crustacean and mollusks to choose from. Desserts sound simple but are marvelous in both taste and texture. Try the warm cherry bakewell with vanilla ice cream or chocolate tart with honey crème fraiche.

225A W. George St. ✆ **0141/572-0899.** www.gamba.co.uk. Lunch 2 courses £17, 3 courses £20; dinner main courses £14–£22. AE, MC, V. Mon–Sat noon–2:30pm and 5–10:30pm.

Michael Caines at ABode Glasgow ★★★ SCOTTISH/CONTINEN-TAL Michael Caines is one of the U.K.'s most acclaimed chefs and his chic restaurant at one of Glasgow's most fashionable hotels (p. 193) serves some of the city's finest cuisine in a relaxed yet efficient style. The team is led by chef Craig Dunn, who was crowned Scottish Hotel Awards' Chef of the Year in 2010. Expert use is made of Scottish regional produce to create award-winning meals, which start with particularly sublime appetizers—try the signature crab and ginger cannelloni. Main courses are equally impressive and could include herb-crusted loin of Borders lamb or fillet and shin of Highland beef. Polish off the night with desserts such as pistachio soufflé or a selection of fine cheeses. Alternatively choose the seven-course tasting menu (£68 per person). "Amazing Graze" lunches are popular with the city's business community, but at night the place takes on a more romantic ambience. A temperature-controlled wine room is a special feature of the restaurant, and it's supervised by perhaps the finest sommelier in Glasgow.

In the ABode Hotel, 129 Bath St. ✆ **0141/572-6011.** www.michaelcaines.com. Lunch 3 courses £13.50, 4 courses £18, 5 courses £22.50; dinner main courses £20–£26. AE, MC, V. Tues–Sat noon–2:30pm and 6–10pm.

Two Fat Ladies City Centre ★ MODERN SCOTTISH/SEAFOOD This relatively new city center eatery is part of the Two Fat Ladies chain, the original of which sits at 88 Dumbarton Road in the West End—two fat ladies is the nickname for the number 88 in bingo and there's no connection to the "Two Fat Ladies" of TV's Food Network fame. This is a real intimate charmer of a restaurant, decked out with fairy lights and soft beech wood and is, like the whole chain, known for exceptional customer service and superb seafood. This city center branch is popular with business folk at lunchtime, but the ambience changes after dark and gains a more romantic feel. Shellfish is particularly prominent on the menu with dishes such as steamed Loch Etive mussels in white wine and garlic cream available as both starters and main courses, while meat options feature top-notch Scottish produce such as McDuff of Lanarkshire fillet of beef. Round off the evening with memorable desserts such as Cranachan meringue nest.

118a Blythswood St. ✆ **0141/847-0088.** www.twofatladiesrestaurant.com. Fixed-price lunch/pre-theatre £16 for 2 courses, £18 for 3 courses; main courses £15–£25. MC, V. Mon–Sat noon–3pm and 5:30–10:30pm.

INEXPENSIVE

Jamie's Italian ☺ ITALIAN   Ever since TV chef Jamie Oliver opened the doors of his much-anticipated Glasgow restaurant, lines of eager diners have regularly formed to sample his rustic-themed Italian cuisine inspired by dishes supposedly preferred by everyday Italian folk. The location on the edge of George Square couldn't be more central and its lofty, multilevel interior remains faithful to the building's grand architecture but is graced with deli counters, trays of pasta, wooden tables, and all things simply Italian. Quick-to-prepare dishes are the order of the day such as Burger Italiano complete with melted fontina cheese and crispy salami or grilled chicken topped with a warm tomato, olive, chili, and caper sauce. A menu of homemade pastas ranges from good old spaghetti bolognese to scallop and squid ink angel hair and wild truffle tagliatelle. A sorbet with fresh fruit makes for a light ending; alternatively the chocolate and espresso tart will fill any remaining hole in your appetite.

1 George Sq. ✆ **0141/404-2690.** www.jamiesitalian.com. Main courses £7–£16. AE, MC, V. Mon–Sat noon–11pm, Sun noon–10:30pm.

Mussel Inn ☺ SEAFOOD   Shellfish harvesters in western Scotland own this distinctive eatery, which serves some of the freshest and most succulent mussels, oysters, scallops, and other shellfish in Glasgow. The chefs are known for their "kilo pots" of mussels, which feed in plankton-rich cold waters and can be served cooked in their own juices or in a choice of flavors from white wine, garlic, shallots, and cream to refried beans, jalapenos, salsa, and lime crème fraiche. Other dishes include grilled platters of queen scallops, hot seafood platters, and shellfish pasta. Finish with warm sticky date pudding or apple and cinnamon strudel.

157 Hope St. ✆ **0141/572-1405.** www.mussel-inn.com. Main courses £7–£23. MC, V. Mon–Fri noon–2:30pm and 5–10pm, Sat noon–10pm, Sun 12:30–10pm.

Merchant City

MODERATE

City Merchant SCOTTISH   This cozy restaurant in the heart of Merchant City offers friendly service and a strong menu of Scottish flavors. The reliably good cuisine delivers an array of well-prepared fresh food at a reasonable price. Seafood choices come from both coastal waters and river and are all well prepared; expect to choose from Shetland salmon and West Coast shellfish. Meats are similarly sourced across Scotland; sample a starter of Dingwall haggis followed by a prime Scottish steak topped with a whisky and peppercorn or Arran and mustard sauce. Top off a Scottish-themed dinner with a traditional clootie dumpling, made with flour, spices, and dried fruit and served with custard.

97–99 Candleriggs. ℂ **0141/553-1577.** www.citymerchant.co.uk. Main courses £18–£28. AE, DC, MC, V. Mon–Sat noon–10:30pm, Sun 4:30–9:30pm.

The Corinthian Club ★★ INTERNATIONAL   One of Glasgow's most opulent venues and Merchant City's finest Victorian building, the Corinthian Club is a five-floored extravaganza. It was built in 1842 and served as the Glasgow Ship Bank before having its former glory thoroughly restored. A resplendent decor of crystal chandeliers and rococo friezes make for a luxurious atmosphere all crowned with a 7.5m (25-ft.) illuminated glass dome as its stunning centerpiece. Menus are created around the freshest products available and for lunch you might feast on a Corinthian club sandwich or for dinner herb-crusted three-bone rack of Shetland lamb or vegetable bouillabaisse. This is a choice spot to indulge in afternoon tea served daily from 2:30pm until 5pm, or to start the day with a breakfast of toasted soda bread with smoked salmon and scrambled eggs. This is also a late-night gaming venue, and so food is served until the early hours.

191 Ingram St. ℂ **0141/552-1101.** www.thecorinthianclub.co.uk. Main courses £10–£24. Afternoon tea £15–£22. AE, MC, V. Mon–Fri 7:30am–6am, Sat–Sun 11pm–6am.

Ingram Wynd ★ SCOTTISH/CONTINENTAL   A surprisingly refreshing slice of Victorian-style dining in the midst of Merchant City's many trendy restaurants, Ingram Wynd serves mainly traditional Scottish dishes in equally traditional surrounds. Polished wood, leather, and gold-framed mirrors are overlooked by a stuffed stag's head, which graces the walls and watches diners linger over whisky and beetroot cured salmon, chicken stuffed with haggis all rounded off with Amaretto crème brulee. Take time to peruse the local memorabilia adorning the walls, including old maps and photographs.

58 Ingram St. ℂ **0141/553/2470.** Lunch 2 courses £11, 3 courses £14; dinner main courses £13–£19. AE, MC, V. Mon–Fri noon–2:30pm and 5pm until late, Sat and Sun noon until late.

Russian Café-Gallery Cossachok RUSSIAN   If you're a fan of Russian cuisine, this is one of the few places in Scotland to indulge. Owners Lev and Julia Atlas have created a haven of Russian food and art at this restaurant/gallery where both emerging and established artists exhibit their work and regular concerts of Russian folk, gypsy, and klezmer music complement menus of dishes from Russia, Moldavia, Armenia, and Georgia. Diners come here to feast on *borscht*, stroganoffs, *blintzes* (stuffed pancakes), and Siberian *pelmeni* (Russian ravioli stuffed with a spicy beef and pork mince). Winnie the Pooh con Miel is a favorite desert consisting of a honey pot of vanilla ice cream and almonds, all glazed with honey. The vibrancy of the menu is reflected in the warm authentic decor created in collaboration with Estonian artist Denis Boyar.

10 King St. ℂ **0141/553-0733.** Main courses £9–£15; pre-theatre £14 for 2 courses. MC, V. Mon–Sat noon–11pm, Sun 4–10pm.

INEXPENSIVE

Cafe Gandolfi ☺ SCOTTISH/FRENCH   This gastronomically delightful cafe is many people's favorite in the city and was a mainstay of Merchant City's dining scene before this slice of town transformed itself into a dining hot spot. A remake of a Victorian pub, it boasts rustic wooden floors, benches, and stools and if you don't fill up on breakfast dishes such as eggs Alba with peat smoked salmon, head straight for the main menu, which caters very well for vegetarians and also includes meat dishes such as smoked venison with gratin dauphinois. The amiable atmosphere and willingness to create smaller portions for children make this a good family choice.

Bar Gandolfi occupies the attic space above the cafe and is a stylish spot to sample some of the many wines on offer, while farther along Albion Street, **Gandolfi Fish** is the latest addition to the Gandolfi chain and specializes in serving sustainably sourced Scottish seafood cooked to perfection.

64 Albion St. ✆ **0141/552-6813.** www.cafegandolfi.com. Main courses £7.50–£16. MC, V. Daily 9am–11:30pm.

West End
EXPENSIVE
The Bistro ★★ SCOTTISH/FRENCH   The Bistro is Hotel du Vin's renowned restaurant. The decor and ambiance is in keeping with the era of the building and oozes with intimate, oak-paneled elegance. Head chef Paul Tamburrini creates daily changing menus from the finest ingredients sourced from regional and local producers including the Queen's meat supplier. True foodies craving regional flavors might select 28-day dry-aged steaks served with chateaubriand, pommes sauté, spinach a la crème, tomato salad and lettuce hearts, or grilled native lobster with garlic butter. Choose a classic dessert of pear and almond tart or an assiette de fromages with homemade breads and pear and raison chutney. In summer guests can dine al fresco in the hotel's hidden garden.

In Hotel du Vin (p. 195), 1 Devonshire Gardens. ✆ **0141/339-2001.** www.hotelduvin.com. Main courses £18–£27. AE, MC, V. Mon–Fri noon–2:15pm, Sun 12:30–2:45pm, and daily 6–10pm.

Ubiquitous Chip ★ SCOTTISH   Despite being an old timer of Glasgow's dining scene—this restaurant opened its doors in 1971—Ubiquitous Chip still managed to bag a Scottish Restaurant of the Year award in 2010. Like the ambience, the decor is unpretentious and appealingly rustic, characterized by rough-textured stone walls and a glass-covered courtyard with reams of climbing vines and a fish pond. The diverse clientele includes everyone from trendy couples to celebrating families who come to enjoy imaginative Scottish food created with the best local ingredients. Set menus and cheaper dishes served in the brasserie area include Orkney organic salmon, Perthshire wood pigeon, venison haggis, and Dumfriesshire lamb. If you don't want a full meal, guests can pop into one of the bar areas and snack on nibbles for around £4.

12 Ashton Lane, off Byres Rd. ✆ **0141/334-5007.** www.ubiquitouschip.co.uk. Restaurant fixed-price lunch £25 for 2 courses, £30 for 3 courses; fixed-price dinner £35 for 2 courses, £40 for 3 courses; brasserie meals bar meals £2.95–£6.75. AE, DC, MC, V. Restaurant Mon–Sat noon–2:30pm and 5:30–11pm, Sun 12:30–3pm and 6:30–11pm. Bar Mon–Sat 11–1am, Sun 12:30pm–1am.

MODERATE
Cail Bruich ★ SCOTTISH   Voted New Scottish Restaurant of the Year in 2010, Cail Bruich is a small family-run restaurant close to Glasgow's Botanical Gardens that's swiftly established a strong reputation for refined seasonal Scottish cuisine. Seasonal and fresh prevail on the relatively short but imaginative menu all served in classical, sophisticated surroundings. Start the evening with melt in mouth Parmesan and white truffle tortellini or terrine of pheasant, pigeon, and hare, before picking from North Sea cod or Perthshire venison. Beef lovers be assured that the 100% Scottish steaks are hung for a minimum of 28 days before being served with a sauce of

choice. Desserts of quince, vanilla panna cotta, or dark chocolate fondant with salted caramel, nut crumble, and milk ice cream will leave a final zing in your mouth.

725 Great Western Rd. ℂ **0141/334-6265.** www.cailbruich.co.uk. Main courses £15–£25; lunch and pre-theatre menus £14 for 2 courses, £17 for 3 courses. MC, V. Mon–Sat noon–2:30pm and 5:30–9:30pm, Sun 12:30–3pm and 5–10pm.

La Vallée Blanche FRENCH   A welcome addition to the Bryes Road area of fine restaurants, La Vallée Blanche's light yet warm and inviting dining room styles itself (as the name suggests) after the architecture of the French alpine valley—think wood panels, lanterns, and reams of wine racks. The service and food are both of an equally high standard and evening diners can expect to choose from such main courses as roast breast of guinea fowl and red wine-poached tarbert halibut, while desserts made to savor include dark chocolate tart or Seville orange, almond, and olive oil cake. This is also a fine spot for lunch or a pre-theatre meal whose shared menu displays a good choice of main courses including options such as zucchini, watercress, and horserad-ish risotto with aged Parmesan and rosemary cream to please vegetarian palettes.

360 Bryes Rd. ℂ **0141/334/333.** www.lavalleeblanche.com. Lunch £6–£14, Dinner 2 courses £14, 3 courses £17. MC, V. Tues–Fri noon–2:15pm, Sat–Sun noon–3:30pm, daily 5:30–10pm.

No. Sixteen ★ MODERN SCOTTISH   The restaurant itself may be small but the reputation and quality of the cuisine served here since 1991 is massive. Old Scottish and European recipes are turned on their heads with innovative dishes such as slow-braised ox cheeks with baked squash, pesto, celeriac mash, and red wine sauce, or thyme and oregano gnocchi with cauliflower cream, Parmesan, and mixed leaves. Prices are surprisingly reasonable for the quality of the cuisine; desserts such as vanilla panna cotta with caramelized figs and honey are a steal at under £6 and one of the many reasons this wee restaurant is consistently busy.

16 Byres Rd. ℂ **0141/339-2544.** www.number16.co.uk. Reservations recommended. Fixed-price lunch £10 for 2 courses, £13 for 3 courses; dinner main courses £14–£18. MC, V. Mon–Sat noon–2:30pm and 5:30–10pm, Sun 12:30–2:30pm and 5:30–9pm.

Two Fat Ladies at The Buttery ★★ SCOTTISH/SEAFOOD   Traditional Scot-tish reigns supreme here at one of Glasgow's longest serving restaurants. The decor is a feast of oak panels, rich tartans, and stained glass crowned by a regal marble topped bar. Imaginative menus demonstrate all the culinary finesse and talent around which the small but renowned Two Fat Ladies chain have built their reputation. The seafood-dominated menu contains some meat options, including pan-fried supreme of Gressingham duck. Be tempted by the selection of desserts and round off the evening with warm treacle steamed pudding, caramel poached pears with Drambuie chantilly cream, or a Two Fats grand dessert that includes a taste of all the sweets on the menu that evening and is made for sharing.

The Shandon Belles, another Two Fat Ladies restaurant, is located in the base-ment and serves signature first-class Scottish cuisine in distinctly cozy surrounds.

652–654 Argyle St. ℂ **0141/221-8188.** www.twofatladiesrestaurant.com. Main courses £17–£26; fixed-price lunch and pre-theatre menu £16–£19. Mon–Sat noon–3pm and 5:30–10:30pm, Sun 12:30–9pm. AE, MC, V.

INEXPENSIVE

Mother India's Cafe ★ INDIAN   A very popular Indian tapas restaurant and spin off from the excellent Mother India restaurant on nearby Westminster Terrace, this

Glasgow is stuffed with options for anyone seeking to fill up on a quick panini, hearty soup, or inexpensive bar meal. Recommended in Merchant City are **Peckham's** (✆ 0141/553-0666; www.peckhams.co.uk), housed in an old Art Deco building on Glassford Street and serving deli-style food until 10pm Sundays through Thursdays and until midnight on Fridays and Saturdays; and **Bar 91** on Candleriggs (✆ 0141/552-5211; www.bar91.co.uk), where you can pull up a chair at one of their scrubbed wooden tables and tuck into burgers, sandwiches, and salads from noon daily until 9pm Monday through Thursday and 5pm on Saturday and Sunday. Favorites in the West End include **Òran Mór** ★, at the top of Bryes Road (✆ 0141/357-6200; www. oran-mor.co.uk), whose inexpensive Scottish-themed bar menu includes traditional favorites such as fish and chips,

all served daily from noon until 9pm Sunday through Wednesday and until 10pm Thursday through Saturday. Also on Bryes Road, **Heart Buchanan** (✆ 0141/334-7626; www.heart buchanan.co.uk) is a top delicatessen and serves hearty and healthy food all day until 9:30pm on Mondays through Saturdays and 7pm on Sundays; and **Naked Soup,** on Kersland Street off the Great Western Road near the Botanic Gardens (✆ 0141/334-8999; www. nakedsoup.com), is a family-run cafe that sells the best soup in the city daily until 5pm. In the city center, the Mackintosh-designed **Willow Tea Rooms** on Sauchiehall Street (✆ 0141/332-0521; www.willowtearooms.co.uk) serves sandwiches, baked potatoes, salads and, of course, afternoon tea Monday through Saturday 9am to 5pm and Sunday 11am to 4:15pm.

ambient, laid-back eatery opposite the Kelvingrove art gallery is a gem of fine India cuisine and efficient service. The tapas-style menu enables diners to try many different dishes from staples of vegetable, chicken, and fish pakoras to more unusual house specialties including butter chicken topped with almonds and lamb cooked with coconut, cream, and yogurt. If casual dining and the chance to mix and match small portions sound appealing, this local favorite won't let you down.

1355 Argyle St. ✆ **0141/339-9145.** www.motherindiascafeglasgow.co.uk. Tapas £3–£10. MC, V. Mon-Thurs noon–10:30pm, Fri-Sat noon–11pm, Sun noon–10pm.

Stravaigin ★★ SCOTTISH/INTERNATIONAL   Stravaigin is old Scots for "to wander" and under the philosophy of "think global eat local," this long-time Glasgow favorite eatery creates memorable cuisine inspired by trips across the globe. Although ideas are sourced globally, ingredients are very much sourced locally and the finest regional Scottish produce is used to create wild seafood dinners, or a la carte dishes including spice route curries or mustard and thyme pork belly with Brussels sprout and ham hough spiked barley risotto. A comprehensive selection of Scottish cheeses perfectly complements a strong dessert menu and a regular program of events such as Plantagenet wine tasting are worth booking in advance. Equally worthy of a visit is Stravaigin 2 on Ruthven Lane.

28 Gibson St. ✆ **0141/334-2665.** www.stravaigin.com. Main courses £13–£23, fixed-price menus (lunch or pre-theatre) £13–£16. AE, DC, MC, V. Mon-Fri 5–10:30pm, Sat-Sun 11am–10:30pm.

SHOPPING

When it comes to shopping in the U.K., Glasgow is surpassed only by London. Dedicated shoppers will discover an impressive amount of choice from large glitzy malls to small independent stores. Most of Glasgow's shopping focuses around its **Style Mile** (www.glasgowstylemile.com), who's southern edge stretches east from Central Station along Argyle Street and into Merchant City; to the north, Sauchiehall Street and **Buchanan Galleries** shopping mall conclude the mile.

This area features a number of distinct sections. In addition to the Buchanan Galleries, which includes an enormous branch of the **John Lewis** department store, there are two other large indoor shopping complexes in the region. **Princes Square** lies behind an early 19th-century blonde sandstone facade and its many levels are a feast of specialty shops, including stores dedicated to designers such as Vivienne Westwood, along with a choice of restaurants and cafes. Princes Square can be entered from **Buchanan Street,** a long pedestrian thoroughfare running north to south that's lined with many stores including the famed **Fraser's** department store. The third and newest shopping complex is the **St. Enoch Shopping Centre** on St. Enoch Square off Argyle Street to the east of Central Station. Here visitors can spend all day shopping under the biggest glass roof in Europe, and its many shops include a branch of Debenhams department store. **Argyle Street** itself is one of Glasgow's major shopping arteries, which along with the pedestrianized **Sauchiehall Street** to the north form the well-trodden bargain-hunting ground for mainstream shopping.

The **Argyll Arcade** at 30 Buchanan Street was built in 1827 and is Europe's oldest covered shopping arcade. Architectural highlights of this little-altered early Victorian arcade include a high vaulted glass roof underneath which lies the largest collection of retail **jewelers,** both antique and modern, in Scotland. This is the place to shop for high quality diamond jewelry, watches, and wedding rings—some even say it's lucky to buy a wedding ring here.

Further upmarket shopping lies on the east side of the Style Mile at **Merchant City,** where those with an eye for fashion can browse through the latest seasonal collections of designers such as Versace, Prada, Gucci, and Armani. Here a cluster of women's clothing and accessories stores in **Royal Exchange Square** gather around the Gallery of Modern Art (p. 170), which has a store stocking a range of gifts inspired by the collection. However, the main designer thoroughfare in Merchant City is **Ingram Street,** which leads east from Royal Exchange Square to High Street. Here

---

Food & Wine on the Run

Glasgow rather excels in its modern delicatessens. **Heart Buchanan Fine Food and Wine** (380 Byres Rd., © 0141/334-7626) is perfect for picnic nosh to take to the nearby Botanic Gardens. If you're a cheese lover, then a stop by the tiny **IJ Mellis Cheesemonger** ★★ (492 Great Western Rd., © 0141/339-8998) is necessary for an outstanding selection of British and Irish cheeses. Nearby is the Glasgow branch of **Lupe Pintos,** (313 Great Western Rd., © 0141/334-5444): It's the perfect stop for Mexican and American foodstuffs.

On Glasgow's Southside, in the Shawlands district near Queens Park, the **1901 Deli** (11 Skirving St., © 0141/632-1630) has a plentiful supply of treats for any outdoor feast.

Bring That Passport!

Visitors from outside the European Union should take along their passports when they go shopping, in case they make a purchase that entitles them to a VAT (value-added tax) refund. See "Getting Your VAT Refund" on p. 441.

many grand buildings built by Glasgow's merchants in the 18th and 19th centuries, including a lofty former banking hall, now house exclusive clothing stores. Highlights in this area include the **Italian Centre,** a small complex in a courtyard off Ingram Street and nicknamed "mini-Milan," with exclusive stores that are honey pots for designer-label shoppers.

Outside of the Style Mile, the West End is the place to potter around more independent, quirkier shops, most of which are located along or close to Bryes Road and Great Western Road. This is also a good spot for vintage clothing, arts and crafts, and specialty food shops. Prime shopping spots here include **De Courcy's Arcade** on Cresswell Lane off Bryes Road, a veritable heaven for vintage clothing buffs.

And for a real slice of Glaswegian market life, take time to experience **The Barras,** held every Saturday and Sunday 10am to 5pm on a large patch of ground between London Road and Gallowgate in the East End about ⅓ mile east of Glasgow Cross. This much-loved legendary market has been formally trading for nearly a century and attracts hundred of traders who ply their many wares, from clothes to collectables, in lines of stalls.

Antiques

Victorian Village This warren of tiny shops stands in a slightly claustrophobic cluster, and although much of the merchandise isn't particularly noteworthy, you can find many exceptional pieces if you're willing to go hunting. Several store owners stock reasonably priced 19th-century articles; others sell old jewelry and clothing alongside a helter skelter of artifacts. 93 W. Regent St. © **0141/332-0808.** http://victorianvillageglasgow.com.

Art & Crafts

Boxwood The creation of interior designer and stylist Jill Stewart, the "Boxwood Look" is inspired by New England and Scandinavian style with a dash of rustic simplicity. Ranges include artwork, vintage-inspired home furnishings, and gifts for all ages. 388 Bryes Rd. © **0141/357-6642.** www.boxwood.net.

Compass Gallery The curators of this refreshing gallery concentrate on new local young artists, who are often university graduates. Prices are reasonable and you can find something special for as little as £25, depending on the exhibition. 178 W. Regent St. © **0141/221-6370.** www.compassgallery.co.uk.

Cyril Gerber Fine Art One of Glasgow's most respected art galleries veers away from the avant garde, specializing in British paintings, sculptures, and ceramics crafted between 1880 and the present day, as well as the work of Scottish artists. Cyril Gerber is a respected art authority with lots of contacts in art circles throughout Britain and has supplied work to many major galleries. Pieces begin at around £200. 148 W. Regent St. © **0141/221-3095.** www.gerberfineart.co.uk.

Ahead of His Time: Charles Rennie Mackintosh

Although legendary today and his works recognized the world over, Charles Rennie Mackintosh (1868–1928) was largely forgotten in Scotland at the end of his life. Forms of nature, especially plants, inspired his elegant motifs, which were far from the fashion of the day. Most of his work is in Glasgow but about 40 kilometers (25 miles) west of Glasgow, in Helensburgh, is his greatest achievement in residential design: Hill House. For more information on all his buildings, visit the website of the **Charles Rennie Mackintosh Society** at www.crmsociety.com, or call ✆ **0141/946-6600**. See also p. 170.

Glasgow Print Studio   This contemporary studio is part of the wider **Trongate 103** center for arts and creativity (www.trongate103.com), and sells and exhibits a diverse selection of original work by local print artists. Knowledgeable staff can advise on framing requirements for each piece at this very accessible new gallery. Trongate 103, King St. ✆ **0141/552-0704**. www.gpsart.co.uk.

Glasgow School of Art Shop ★   This small store prides itself on its award-winning range of products inspired by the work of Charles Rennie Mackintosh. Products include books, cards, stationery, coffee and beer mugs, glassware, and sterling-and-enamel jewelry all created from original designs. Although the shop doesn't sell furniture, the staff will refer you to **Bruce Hamilton, Furnituremaker,** based in the Lindwood district (✆ **01505/322-550**; www.brucehamilton.co.uk), a craftsman whose work they recommend and who produces high-quality reproductions of Mackintosh-designed furniture. Enter via the east entrance of the building at 11 Dalhousie St. ✆ **0141/353-4526**. www.gsa.ac.uk.

Gifts & Home Furnishing

Designworks   A plush choice of stylish home furnishing items fill this light, contemporary West End store. Displayed alongside individual and unusual furniture items, you'll find a cornucopia of soft fabrics, ornaments, cushions, and china in a range of designs from the ornate to the rustic. 38 Gibson St. ✆ **0141/339-9520**.

Papyrus   A favorite with student shoppers seeking quirky gifts or funky wares to brighten up the kitchen, Papyrus is a good hunting ground for unusual cards, gifts, and housewares. 374 Bryes Rd. ✆ **0141/334-6514**. http://papyrusgifts.co.uk.

Jewelry

Henderson   Occupying the street level of Glasgow's famous Willow Tea Rooms, this well-known jeweler stocks a range of delicate sliver pieces created in Mackintosh style. Other similarly themed gift items are also for sale. 217 Sauchiehall St. ✆ **0141/331-2569**. www.hendersonjewellers.co.uk.

Jodie's   This fun and quirky jewelry boutique is a treasure trove of cute and unusual pieces that appeal to younger shoppers. Many trendy brands fill the shelves including *Me and Zena* and *Disney Couture*, whose items are fashioned around Disney's most iconic characters. There's also a good choice of watches, including a selection from *Ice Watch*. Jodie's also has a branch in Argyll Arcade (see above). 24 Gordon St. © **0141/204-4762.**

Kilts & Tartans

Geoffrey Tailor   The fine-quality kilts this family business has been crafting for four decades are among the best in Scotland. Its main office and best-known branch are located on Edinburgh's Royal Mile (p. 100), but this Glasgow branch is also well worth visiting for anyone serious about purchasing Scottish attire at its finest. 309 Sauchiehall St. © **0141/331-2388.** www.geoffreykilts.co.uk.

Hector Russell ★★   Founded in 1881, Hector Russell is one of Scotland's oldest and most prestigious kiltmakers. Crystal and gift items can be picked up here, but the real heart and soul of the store is the selection of impeccably crafted and reasonably priced tweed jackets, tartan-patterned accessories, waistcoats, and sweaters made from top-quality wool for both men and women. Hand-stitched kilts for men, women, and children are also for sale and an experienced sales staff is on hand to help you choose. 110 Buchanan St. © **0141/221-0217.** www.hector-russell.com.

Toys

The Sentry Box   This small store tucked off Bryes Road is an Aladdin's cave of traditional handcrafted toys. This fascinating old-fashioned shopping experience is a good stop for children and adults wanting a quick trip down memory lane. 175 Great George St. © **0141/334-6070.**

SPECIAL EVENTS & FESTIVALS

Following Glasgow's **Hogmanay** celebrations, which sees thousands of revelers gather in George Square to cheer in the new year, **Celtic Connections** (© **0141/ 353-8000;** www.celticconnections.com), the city's annual festival of contemporary and traditional Celtic music, lights up venues and stages around Glasgow during January. In February the **Glasgow Film Festival** (© **0141/332-6535;** www. glasgowfilm.org) takes over the city's cinemas, swiftly followed in March by the **Aye Write!** (© **0141/287-2999;** www.ayewrite.com) book festival and the **Glasgow International Comedy Festival** (© **0141/552-2070;** www.glasgowcomedy festival.com). Art lovers gather in city during April for the **Glasgow International Festival of Visual Art** (© **0141/276-8383;** www.glasgowinternational.org.uk), and in June the **Glasgow International Jazz Festival** (© **0141/552-3552;** www. jazzfest.co.uk) attracts top names from the world of jazz to venues around the city. In August over 50,000 people gather on Glasgow Green for the **World Pipe Band Championships** (© **0141/353-8000;** www.theworlds.co.uk) before the year turns once again and the **Glasgow Loves Christmas** (http://glasgowloveschristmas.com) celebrations take to the streets, transforming George Square into an outdoor ice skating rink and hosting a program of family events, including a Santa Dash.

Two of the city's districts host very different festivals during the year. In June, the **West End Festival** (© **0141/341-0844;** www.westendfestival.co.uk) kicks off with a large opening parade and features all kinds of music, theatre, and family-friendly events, and **Merchant City** celebrates in September with a program of theatre, music, comedy, and dance events (www.merchantcityfestival.com).

ENTERTAINMENT & NIGHTLIFE

Glasgow is one of the most culturally vibrant cities in the U.K. Although it doesn't boast the festivals for which Edinburgh is famous, Glasgow's year-round program of theatre, music, dance, and film is second to none and complemented by an excellent clubbing scene, which some claim is the best in Scotland. For detailed information on all entertainment options, pick up a copy of *The List* (£2.20), which is published every four weeks, or check listings online at **www.list.co.uk**.

The Performing Arts

THEATRE Glasgow has an enviable selection of theatres whose stages are filled with performances that range from the best of mainstream productions to internationally acclaimed experimental work. At the mainstream end of the market, the **King's Theatre,** 297 Bath St. (✆ **0844/871-7648;** www.ambassadortickets.com), offers a wide range of productions, including straight plays, musicals, and comedies and in winter an annual fun-filled pantomime; and the **Theatre Royal,** 282 Hope St. (✆ **0844/871-7647;** www.ambassadortickets.com) is resplendent with Victorian Italian Renaissance plasterwork and glittering chandeliers and hosts touring productions by national theatre companies from across the U.K. One of Glasgow's best-loved theatres is the **Citizens Theatre,** 119 Gorbals St. (✆ **0141/429-0022;** www.citz.co.uk). Fondly known as "the Citz," this glorious Victorian theatre has been through a number of incarnations until it became the Citizens Theatre in 1945. Today its program is a mix of its own productions and touring companies and favors both emerging and established playwrights and theatre companies. The ornate **Pavilion Theatre,** 121 Renfield St. (✆ **0141/332-1846;** www.paviliontheatre.co.uk), specializes in mainstream music concerts, comedy, and nostalgic shows.

The **Tron Theatre,** 63 Trongate (✆ **0141/552-4267;** www.tron.co.uk), occupies one of the three oldest buildings in Glasgow, the former Tron Church. The church, with its famous Adam dome and checkered history, was transformed into a small theatre in the 1980s and now presents the best contemporary drama, dance, and music events. On the Southside, the **Tramway,** 25 Albert Dr. (✆ **0845/330-3501;** www.tramway.org), offers a vibrant and innovative mix of contemporary theatre and dance in an auditorium that once served as one of the city's tram sheds. This venue also boasts a delightful Hidden Garden. In the West End, **Òran Mór,** Bryes Road (✆ **0141/357-6200;** www.oran-mor.co.uk), which means "great melody of life," occupies a former parish church and is known for its music, comedy, and theatre events, including its lunchtime "A Play, a Pie and a Pint" performances.

For a real slice of bygone Glasgow nightlife, catch a show at the **Britannia Panopticion,** 113–117 Trongate (✆ **0141/553-0840;** www.britanniapanopticon.org), the oldest surviving music hall in the U.K. where Stan Laurel first trod the boards in 1906. Even though the building is in need of restoration, it still plays host to a number of cabaret, comedy, music, and film events—be warned that this charming old building has no heating so wrap up warmly if you're visiting in winter.

BALLET, OPERA, CLASSICAL MUSIC & CONTEMPORARY The **Theatre Royal** and **Tron Theatre** (see above) both host performances by **Scottish Opera** (✆ **0141/248-4567;** www.scottishopera.org.uk), while **Scottish Ballet** (✆ **0141/331-2931;** www.scottishballet.co.uk) is based at the **Tramway** (see above), although most of its Glasgow performances are held at the **Theatre Royal.** The **Glasgow Royal**

Concert Hall, 2 Sauchiehall St., is home to the **Royal Scottish National Orchestra** (© 0141/226-3868; www.rsno.org.uk), and alongside its performances you can catch folk, world, country, and rock and pop concerts in its 2,475-seat auditorium. **City Halls,** Candleriggs, is home to the **BBC Scottish Symphony Orchestra** (© 0141/552-0909; www.bbc.co.uk/orchestras/bbcsso), and the **Scottish Chamber Orchestra** (© 0131/557-6800; www.sco.org.uk) also regularly performs at this elegant Victorian venue. Adjacent to City Halls on Candleriggs is the **Old Fruitmarket** where jazz, pop, and world music gigs regularly rock the roof of this charming old building. These three venues are run by **Glasgow Concert Halls** and tickets can be bought, or information obtained, from © 0141/353-8000 or www.glasgowconcerthalls.com.

FILM The **Glasgow Film Theatre,** 12 Rose St. (© 0141/332-6535; www.glasgowfilm.org), is a fabulous two-screen Art Deco cinema that screens the best in specialized and world cinema and includes **Café Cosmo,** a very chic cafe/bar. In the West End, the **Grosvenor,** Ashton Lane (© 0845/116-6002; www.grosvenorcafe.co.uk), is a cinema and cafe/bar that screens mainstream and more unusual films as well as a number of eclectic film-related events. For the big-screen multiplex movie experience, head to the **CiniWorld,** 7 Renfrew St. (© 0871/200-2000; www.cineworld.co.uk).

COMEDY The **Stand,** 333 Woodlands (© 0844/335-8879; www.thestand.co.uk), is Glasgow's premiere comedy club. In March, Glasgow's Comedy Festival (p. 102) blazes across many of the city's venues.

The Club & Music Scene

The Arches ★ This top arts venue occupies a prime spot underneath Central Station and although it's known for experimental theatre and boundary-pushing visual arts, it's the legendary club nights that have earned this trendy venue its super-cool reputation. Discovering and promoting new talent is the underlying aim of club nights, which are generally held on Wednesday, Friday, and Saturday. 253 Argyle St. © 0141/565-1035. www.thearches.co.uk. Tickets £7–£20.

Barrowland ★★ This legendary hall is one of Europe's top small venues. Its 1,900-seat hall is known for its excellent acoustics and has played host to many top acts including David Bowie, Macy Gray, and Sheryl Crow, and continues to draw big names that would usually be attracted to bigger stages. It's also a good place to catch Glasgow's emerging talent on the music scene. The cover runs highest for the most popular bands, whose shows must be booked well in advance. Gallowgate. © 0141/552-4601. www.glasgow-barrowland.com. Cover £11–£26.

King Tut's Wah-Wah Hut ★ This sweaty, crowded rock bar borrowed its name from a New York venture and is one of Glasgow's longest-standing leading concert venues. Numerous top bands including Blur and Travis played here before they hit the big time, and King Tut's continues to promote a mix of new and established bands. The capacity is a mere 300 and this venue remains a good place to check out local bands and the occasional international act. 272-A St. Vincent St. © 0141/221-5279. www.kingtuts.co.uk. Cover £5–£18.

Nice 'n' Sleazy One of Glasgow's most unpretentious, down-to-earth clubs, Nice 'n' Sleazy is intimate and friendly and boasts reasonable cover charges, except on nights when more well-known bands are playing. Entertainment is a vibrant mix of club nights and gigs, plus free open mic acoustic events on quieter nights such as Mondays. 421 Sauchiehall St. © 0141/333-0900. www.nicensleazy.com. Cover from £3.

Òran Mór   Although many know this spirited venue for its theatre, music events here are just as good. Regular **Club O** nights are laid-back affairs and focus on indie music on Thursdays and chart-topping R&B and electro on Friday and Saturday. For an altogether more refined experience, catch live jazz and funk in the main bar on Sundays from 4pm. Bryes Rd.ⓒ **0141/357-6200.** www.oran-mor.co.uk. Cover free–£6.

Sub Club   One of Glasgow's best club venues, the Sub Club sits underground near Central Station and has, since its opening in 1987, built a strong reputation for excellent dance nights. The sound system is first class and the DJs who pump out the music through it are a good mix of much-loved residents and new local talent. 22 Jamaica St.ⓒ **0141/248-4600.** www.subclub.co.uk. Cover £3–£10.

The 13th Note   If you don't mind rough-around-the-edges in terms of decor, this long-serving basement bar/club is a recommended place to catch local gigs. Indie, rock, punk, new wave, and experimental bands all play here over the course of a week. The vegan cafe is also a winner and serves top-notch, hearty bar food until late. 50-60 King St.ⓒ **0141/553-1638.** www.13thnote.co.uk. Cover free–£5.

Pubs & Bars

Bon Accord   This amiably weathered pub is one of the finest places in the city to sip a pint of hand-pumped real ale. An incredible array of new and established cask ales fill these cellars, so many that the Bon Accord organizes cellar tours to explain more about the beers they champion, all of which are managed by Russell Burt, Bon Accord's cellarman for the past 27 years. Whisky lovers will also find a large selection of malts from across Scotland and live music and quiz nights ensure a lively atmosphere. Open Monday through Saturday noon to midnight, Sunday noon to 11pm with food served daily 12:30 to 8pm. 153 North St.ⓒ **0141/248-4427.** www.bonaccordweb.co.uk.

Curler's Rest   Occupying a prime spot in the middle of Bryes Road, the Curler's Rest is a laid-back bar in the middle of the West End. Polished wooden floors and furniture and deep sofas help create a warm atmosphere, where you can enjoy a wide choice of regional and imported beers, including five cask ales, and a long wine list. Food leans towards the gastropub end of the market but still includes favorites such as fish and chips (main courses £8-£13). Tuesday nights are quiz nights. Open daily noon to midnight. 256-260 Bryes Rd.ⓒ **0141/341-0737.** www.curlersrestglasgow.co.uk.

Moskito   This city center basement bar has proved itself enduringly popular and is often busy with an after-work or late-night drinking crowd. Flagstone floors, stone walls, and large wooden tables and booths provide a cool, laid-back setting. Live DJ sets kick off after 10pm. Good bar meals are served from noon (12:30pm on Sundays) until 9pm. The bar itself opens daily from noon (12:30pm on Sundays) until 2am Sunday through Thursday and until 3am Fridays and Saturdays. 200 Bath St.ⓒ **0141/331-1777.** www.moskitoglasgow.com.

The Pot Still   Whisky lovers will travel a long way to sample a wee dram or two at this fabulous old city center pub, which lies close to many of Glasgow's theatres and currently sells an incredible 483 whiskies (and the list keeps growing). The bar itself has all the feel of a good mellow whisky, and knowledgeable owners advise on the malt that's right for you. Open Monday through Thursday noon to 11pm, Friday and Saturday noon to midnight. 154 Hope St.ⓒ **0141/333-0980.** www.thepotstill.co.uk.

The Scotia Bar ★ Established in 1762, The Scotia Bar is the oldest pub in Glasgow and claims a long and colorful history. The dark interior has changed little since 1920 and gleams with brass pumps, red leather, and old pictures, while ales include Belhaven Best, which is brewed in Dunbar. This pub is also renowned for its live music and support of local writers; singers, musicians, and writers perform almost nightly and if you stay long enough you'll be encouraged to perform yourself. Food is served at lunchtime. Make sure you keep an eye open for one of the many ghosts that are said to haunt this bar. Open Monday through Saturday noon to midnight, Sunday noon to 11pm. 112-114 Stockwell St. ② **0141/552-8681.** www.scotiabar.net.

WEST ★ This brewery-cum-bar occupies the former wool-winding room of Glasgow's iconic Templeton Carpet Factory, which lies in the East End of Glasgow Green near the People's Palace (p. 172)—when in business, the factory supplied carpets for the Taj Mahal and Houses of Parliament. Today the beer that's brewed here is among the finest in Scotland and is created in accordance with the Reinheits-gebot, known as the German Purity Law that ensures no artificial additives make their way into the beers. The range of brews includes refreshing lagers and full-flavored wheat beers, which can be sampled in the grand beer hall that looks down onto the brewhouse below. The restaurant serves a full menu of German/Scottish dishes including both regional seafood and schnitzel sandwiches (main dishes £7-£12). The beer hall and restaurant open daily 11am to 9pm; bar opens daily 11am to 11pm (to midnight Fri–Sat). Glasgow Green. ② **0141/550-0135.** www.westbeer.com.

Gay Bars & Clubs

Bennets, 90 Glassford St. (② **0141/552-5761;** www.bennetsnightclub.co.uk), is one of the major gay/lesbian nightclubs in town and features three bars and two dance floors, one of which is dedicated to cheesy pop while the other focuses on dance music. Attracting a slightly older crowd, **Waterloo Bar,** 306 Argyle St. (② **0141/248-7216;** www.waterloobar.co.uk), is the oldest gay bar in Glasgow and each night of the week celebrates the music of a different decade, while Sunday afternoons is time for a game of bingo. In Merchant City, **Delmonicas,** 68 Virginia St. (② **0141/552-4803**), is a stylish pre-club bar that hosts a number of events including quiz and DJ nights and karaoke. Glasgow also plays hosts to **Glasgay!** (② **0141/552-7575;** www.glasgay.com) in October, Scotland's annual celebration of queer culture.

Spectator Sports & Outdoor Activities

GOLF **Glasgow Life** (② **0141/287-4350;** www.glasgowlife.org.uk) manage six golf courses around the city and charge £10 for a round of 18 holes at all of them, with youths under 18 playing for free. Courses include **Lethamhill,** 1240 Cumbernauld Rd. (② **0141/276-0810**), which is set in mature parkland and is 3 miles northeast of the city center; and **Linn Park,** Simshill Rd. (② **0141/276-0702**), which boasts wide views of the city alongside good facilities. Two 9-hole courses are **Alexandra Park,** Alexandra Parade (② **0141/276-0600**), and **Knightswood,** Lincoln Avenue (② **0141/276-0700**). Visitors are advised to call 24 hours in advance to arrange tee times. Open daily from 10am to 5pm in winter, daily from 7am to 8pm in summer.

FOOTBALL (SOCCER) Glasgow has two main football teams: **Rangers** and **Celtic.** Rangers home ground is Ibrox Stadium (*C* **0871 702 1972;** www.rangers. co.uk) and Celtic's home ground is Celtic Park (*C* **0871 226 1888;** www.celticfc.net).

SPORTS COMPLEXES **Glasgow Life** (*C* 0141/287-4350; www.glasgowlife. org.uk) also manages the city's many sports centers, which all have comprehensive programs of fitness classes and good facilities. In the West End, the **Kelvin Hall International Sports Arena** on Argyle Street (*C* 0141/357-2525) offers a well-equipped fitness suite with over 50 gym machines and free weights, plus volleyball and basketball courts, an indoor track, and a climbing wall. It's open daily Monday through Friday 7:15am (10am on Wednesday) to 10pm, and 9am to 5pm Saturday (to 8pm Sunday). Facilities at the **Scotstoun Leisure Centre,** 72 Danes Dr., Scotstoun (*C* 0141/959-4000), which is about 1¾ miles from the center of Glasgow, include a swimming pool, outdoor tennis courts, and gym. It's open Monday through Friday from 7am (10am on Thursday) until 10pm, Saturday 9am to 5pm, and Sunday 9am to 9pm. Fees are consistent across these sport centers with fitness classes costing £4.60, the climbing wall £3.65, a gym session £5.20, and swimming £2.25.

WATERSPORTS & ICE-SKATING The **Lagoon Leisure Centre,** Mill Street, Paisley (*C* 0141/889-4000; www.renfrewshireleisure.com), offers indoor facilities that include a free-form pool with a wave machine and flume. You'll also find sauna suites with sun beds, Jacuzzis, and a Finnish steam room. The center is open Monday through Friday from 7am to 10pm and Saturday and Sunday from 9:30am to 5pm. A session in the pool costs £3.60 adults, £1.90 children 16 and under. There are frequent trains throughout the day from Glasgow Central Station to Paisley. **Braehead Arena,** King's Inch Rd. (*C* 0141/885-4600; www.braehead.co.uk), 6 miles west of the center of Glasgow, converts to an Olympic-sized ice skating rink at weekends during the winter and school holidays. A session costs £6 for adults and £5 for children, and skate rental is £2. It's advisable to check in advance before heading out because this venue converts back to an arena when large concerts are scheduled.

WHERE TO STAY

Most places to stay in Glasgow are to be found in the city center or West End; visitors will find few options on the east side of the city. In the city center, large hotels and big chains dominate, targeting business as well as leisure travelers. In the West End, a string of guesthouses and smaller hotels cluster around the Sauchiehall Street and Kelvingrove Park area. All vary in quality, style, and price, and most offer family-sized rooms; however, many don't have elevators due to the age and era of the buildings. It's a good idea to reserve in advance for high season (late July and August) and New Year and to take time seeking out discount package deals. If your preference is for serviced apartments, try **The Spires** (www.thespires.co.uk; *C* 0845/270-0090), 77 Glassford St. in Merchant City.

City Center & Merchant City

VERY EXPENSIVE

Blythswood Square ★★★ Blythswood opened in fall 2009 and swiftly established a reputation as Glasgow's best luxury hotel, securing the converted Scottish Hotel of the Year award the following year. It occupies the old Royal Scottish Automobile Club in the center of the city, a building dating from 1823 that the hoteliers restored to its former glory. Deluxe hotel rooms and state-of-the-art bathrooms are elegant, supremely comfortable, and the epitome of good taste, while public areas maintain many of the building's original features including wood paneling, grand staircases, marble floors, and Art Deco flourishes. The restaurant occupies the RSAC's former ballroom and is grand in both dimensions and cuisine and the famous Rally Bar, named after the Monte Carlo Rally, which once started from Blythswood Square, is known for sublime cocktails. The hotel's leisure club and spa is simply the city's finest.

11 Blythswood Square, G2 4AD. www.townhousecompany.com. © **0141/208-2458.** 88 units. £110–£285 double; £450 suite. AE, DC, MC, V. **Amenities:** Restaurant; bar; 2 pools (indoor); health club and spa; concierge; room service. *In room:* A/C, TV/DVD, CD player, minibar, hair dryer, robes, Wi-Fi (free).

EXPENSIVE

ABode Hotel ★ This appealingly restored Edwardian charmer, 6 blocks north-west of Central Station, is one of central Glasgow's most loved hotels. The public spaces celebrate the building's civic history and feature a grand staircase, listed wall-paper, and best of all, an old-fashioned original cage elevator. All the rooms have high ceilings and are very spacious, and some have the added appeal of original stained glass. Rates are dependent on the size and style of the rooms, which are ranked in four categories: "comfortable," "desirable," "enviable," and the truly fab "fabulous." The hotel's best asset, however, is its restaurant, one of Glasgow's most sophisticated (**Michael Caines;** see p. 178). The downstairs Bar MC is also recommended for its reasonably priced high-end bar meals and moody atmosphere.

129 Bath St., G2 2SY. www.abodehotels.co.uk. © **0141/221-6789.** Fax 0141/221-6777. 59 units. £80–£165 double. AE, DC, MC, V. **Amenities:** Restaurant; bar; room service. *In room:* TV/DVD, minibar, hair dryer, Wi-Fi (free).

Grand Central Hotel ★★★ Few restored hotels have created so much buzz and generated so much recognition so quickly. Once Glasgow's most prestigious hotel, this historic property is joined with the city's Central Station and its restoration remains faithful to all the romance of the bygone age of travel it was originally created to serve. Archive images of past guests including Frank Sinatra and Roy Rogers and Trigger line walls and the stunning Champagne Bar overlooks the station concourse where J.F. Kennedy made his first public speech aged 17. Other past claims to fame include being the site from which John Logie Baird transmitted the world's first long distance television pictures in 1927. History aside guests can expect first-class cus-tomer service, bedrooms and suites epitomized by contemporary style and comfort, sweeping public areas, and superb dining at the Tempus restaurant.

99 Gordon St., G1 3SF. www.principal-hayley.com. © **0141/240-3700.** Fax 0141/240-3701. 186 units. £80–£165 double. AE, MC, V. **Amenities:** Restaurant; bar; concierge; room service. *In room:* TV, hair dryer, Wi-Fi.

Malmaison ★★ The Malmaison chain has transformed this former Greek Ortho-dox church built in the 1830s into one of Glasgow's hippest hotels. Behind the suit-ably imposing exterior, few original details remain as the contemporary interior exemplifies ultramodern. Bedrooms vary in size from smallish to average, but are chic and appointed with such extras as specially commissioned art and top-of-the-line toiletries. Suites range from one-bedroomed deluxe affairs to the deeply luxurious Big Yin. A popular brasserie lies in a vaulted basement or guests can relax in the former crypt—now a sleek modern bar. Other facilities include a well-equipped gym.

278 W. George St., G2 4LL. www.malmaison.com. © **0141/572-1000.** Fax 0141/572-1002. 72 units. £120–£160 double; £170–£320 suite. AE, DC, MC, V. **Amenities:** Restaurant; bar; gym; room service; Wi-Fi in public areas. *In room:* A/C, TV, CD player, hair dryer, Internet (fee).

Park Inn Glasgow ★   If you're looking for Victorian Glasgow, head elsewhere. But if you gravitate to a minimalist Japanese style, check in at this trendy and exceedingly contemporary hotel, close to Buchanan bus station and the Glasgow Royal Concert Hall. The hotel has a diverse medley of bedrooms in various shapes, sizes, and configurations, each with a certain flair. Nothing is overly adorned here, and yet comfort and style, along with different colors and textures, make every unit a winner. The smallest are the studios, but you can also rent a theme suite, or a very large suite. The beautifully kept bathrooms contain such extras as power showers with body jets and the on-site Oshi restaurant specializes in modern Scottish cuisine.

2 Port Dundas Place, G2 3LD. www.glasgow.parkinn.co.uk. ✆ **0141/333-1500.** Fax 0141/333-5700. 100 units. £79–£89 double; £139–£159 suite. AE, DC, MC, V. **Amenities:** Restaurant; bar; room service. *In room:* TV, minibar, hair dryer, Wi-Fi (free).

Radisson SAS ★   Across from Central Station, this chain hotel with its sleek modern edges is almost Scandinavian in its minimalist design. Blond wood furnishings and access to state-of-the-art leisure facilities make this place appealing to travelers who prefer the big hotel experience. Standard rooms are a little on the small side, but each unit is simple and stylish and many feature floor-to-ceiling windows. Bathrooms come with heated floors for those chilly Glasgow mornings. The on-site Collage restaurant celebrates modern art and Mediterranean food with a Scottish touch.

301 Argyle St., G2 8DL. www.radissonblu.co.uk. ✆ **0141/204-3333.** Fax 0141/204-3344. 250 units. £100–£190 double; £165–£240 suite. AE, DC, MC, V. **Amenities:** Restaurant; 2 bars; pool (indoor); gym; concierge; room service. *In room:* TV, minibar, safe, robes, hair dryer, Internet (free).

MODERATE

Marks Hotel ☺   Easily identifiable by its stepped, angular glass frontage, this contemporary hotel is a decent, affordable central option. Floor-to-ceiling windows are the winning feature of some rooms, and city views get better and longer the higher the floor. In addition to standard and executive choices, family rooms are also available with a double and two single beds, plus plenty of space to unwind. Bold design extends to the hotel's informal One Ten bar and grill, where the menu is an appealing mix of traditional Scottish and international cuisine.

110 Bath St., G2 2EN. www.markshotels.com. ✆ **0141/353-0800.** Fax 0141/353-0900. 103 units. £75–£85 double. AE, MC, V. **Amenities:** Restaurant; bar; room service. *In room:* A/C, TV, hair dryer, Wi-Fi (free).

INEXPENSIVE

Brunswick Hotel ✦   One of Merchant City's few accommodation options, the Brunswick is a stylish boutique hotel that occupies a choice spot in this historic part of the city. The interior decor is simple, bold, modern, and comes without frills. The bedrooms continue the comfortable yet minimalist style. The on-site cafe/bar Brutti Ma Buoni (translated as "ugly but good") stays open until in the early hours and serves a big menu of moderately priced Italian-themed cuisine from 11am to 10pm.

106-108 Brunswick St., G1 ITF. www.brunswickhotel.co.uk. ✆ **0141/552-0001.** Fax 0141/552-1551. 18 units. £50–£95 double. AE, DC, MC, V. **Amenities:** Restaurant; bar. *In room:* TV, Wi-Fi (free).

Citizen M ★   A relative newcomer on Glasgow's diversifying accommodation scene, Citizen M is big, bold, trendy, and a rare bargain. This large, very square hotel sits bang in the middle of town, and its 198 rooms spread out over eight floors. Rooms are small in size but big in functional luxury. The beds are large and uber-comfortable, but its

Chain Hotels

For the pick of Glasgow's big chain hotel options in the city center, try the **IBIS,** 222 West Register St. (www.ibis hotel.com; © 0141/225-6000), with doubles from £50 to £85; the **Premier Inn,** 187 George St. (www.premierinn. com; © 0871/527-8440), with doubles from £70; or the **Holiday Inn Express,** 165 West Nile St. (www.hiexpress glasgow.co.uk; © 0141/331-6800), with doubles from £70 to £100. In Merchant City, a good choice is the **Ramada,** 201 Ingram St. (www.ramadajarvis.co.uk; © 0844/815-9103), with doubles from £60 to £100. At Glasgow Airport, a double room at the **Holiday Inn Express** (www.expressglasgowairport.co.uk; © 0141/842-1100) costs £65 to £75.

features such as touch-screen controllable blinds, temperature, and mood lighting that make this place remarkable. Bathrooms are shower only, but they're powerful and rainfall; the large windows are nice and soundproof. Canteen M, the on-site grab-and-go restaurant, continues the clean and contemporary theme and stocks sandwiches and sushi. Reservations can be made only online, not via telephone.

60 Renfrew St., G2 3BW. www.citizenmglasgow.com. © 0141/404-9485. 198 units. £70–£100 double. AE, MC, V. **Amenities:** Restaurant; bar; room service. *In room:* TV, hair dryer, Wi-Fi (free).

West End

VERY EXPENSIVE

Hotel du Vin ★★★ ☺ Despite stiff competition from a sprinkle of new luxury accommodation options in the city center, this glamorous and tranquil hotel continues to very definitely hold its own. Set back behind a line of trees at the exclusive One Devonshire Gardens, Hotel du Vin spreads out over three Victorian properties each now even more elegant than in their heyday. The various-sized rooms and suites are furnished in period style and feature lots of luxurious accessories, including drench showers. The public spaces are the place to sink into a deep sofa and relax. Hotel du Vin's **Bistro** restaurant serves excellent cuisine (p. 181) and often creates some winning special offers. Although there's no in-house spa, a large selection of beauty and body treatments for both sexes can be arranged in-room. Despite the antiques, Hotel du Vin is more than happy to cater to children by providing toys, cots, and highchairs. There are also interconnecting bedrooms, and the restaurant can prepare meals for smaller appetites.

1 Devonshire Gardens, G12 0UX. www.hotelduvin.com. © 0141/339-2001. Fax 0141/337-1663. 49 units. £160–£335 double; £425–£975 suite. AE, DC, MC, V. Free parking. **Amenities:** 2 restaurants; bar; exercise room; room service. *In room:* TV/DVD, CD player, minibar, hair dryer, Wi-Fi (free).

MODERATE

Argyll Hotel Small but friendly, this traditional hotel housed in a Georgian building is well placed for the art galleries and museums around Glasgow University and West End restaurants. The modernized guest rooms are basic but clean and comfortable, and the breakfasts are superb. The Scottish-themed Sutherlands restaurant is also open for evening meals and often hosts events including live music and murder mystery nights.

973 Sauchiehall St., G3 7TQ. www.argyllhotelglasgow.co.uk. © 0141/337-3313. Fax 0141/337-3283. 38 units. £90–£160 double. AE, MC, V. **Amenities:** Restaurant; bar; room service. *In room:* TV, hair dryer, Wi-Fi (free).

Lorne Hotel   A stylish, large boutique hotel in an area known for its smaller guest-houses, the Lorne is a contemporary alternative close to Kelvingrove Park. Public spaces are characterized by dark wood and leather sofas. Refreshingly, the restaurant Bukharah specializes in India cuisine—it won the 2010 Scottish Curry Award—and is lead by Mahrukh, the U.K.'s first female Asian head chef. Accommodation range from classic doubles to self-contained apartments aimed at guests who want more space or to stay for a while. The on-site bar prides itself on its cocktails, and the rest of the West End, Clydeside, and even the city center are within easy reach.

923 Sauchiehall St., G3 7TQ. www.lornehotelglasgow.com. © **0141/330-1555.** Fax 0141/330-1550. 102 units. £80–£85 double; from £95 suite. AE, MC, V. **Amenities:** Restaurant; bar; room service Wi-Fi (free). *In room:* A/C, TV, hair dryer, Internet.

INEXPENSIVE

Alamo Guest House ★★ 🖋   This warm, welcoming, family-run guesthouse offers some of the best accommodation of its type in the city, and is a real must for those preferring a smaller and more intimate place to stay. This large Victorian building is tucked away in a quiet cul-de-sac on the edge of Kelvingrove Park and is very convenient for all West End attractions and restaurants. Classically decorated rooms come in various shapes and sizes; the largest boasts a king-sized Louis XV bed and luxury bath, plus two large bay windows overlooking the park. Smaller doubles still feature period furniture but aren't all en-suite. Breakfasts are served in a park-facing dining room and those wanting a night in can choose from an enormous DVD collection.

46 Gray St., G3 7SE. www.alamoguesthouse.com. © **0141/339-2395.** 12 units. £52–£105 double. MC, V. *In room:* TV/DVD player, hair dryer, Wi-Fi (free).

Amadeus Guest House   This restored Victorian townhouse lies in a cul-de-sac overlooking the River Kelvin. Bedrooms are basic and small to medium in size, each with a contemporary, bright decor that adds to the cozy and comfortable feel. Breakfast comes in the form of a large continental buffet and is served by candlelight and accompanied by Mozart. Rooms spread out over three levels (no elevator) and large family options are available alongside standard doubles and twins.

411 N. Woodside Rd., G20 6NN. www.amadeusguesthouse.co.uk. © **0141/339-8257.** Fax 0141/339-8859. 9 units. £48–£58 double. AE, MC, V. *In room:* TV, hair dryer.

The Belhaven   A few minutes walk from the Botanical Gardens and Bryes Road, the Belhaven is a modern guesthouse located inside a well-restored Victorian terrace house. Guestrooms offer plenty of space and good basic facilities and sizes include large family rooms and a king suite whose winning feature is a two-person spa bath. Unusually for a guesthouse, the Belhaven has its own guests-only bar that stays open until late and serves snack-style food such as toasted sandwiches between 6pm and 8pm.

15 Belhaven Terrace, G12 0TG. www.belhavenhotel.com. © **0141/339-3222.** Fax 0141/339-2212. 16 units. £75–£95 double. MC, V. **Amenities:** Bar. *In room:* TV, hair dryer on request.

Manor Park Hotel   This impressive West End townhouse was a private home when built in 1895 and converted into a hotel in 1947. The property has been much improved and upgraded since then and the owners Angus and Catherine MacDonald—true Scots to the core, both speak Gaelic—offer grand Scottish hospitality. The guest rooms, all named after Scottish islands, are grand in a traditional style and feature beechwood pieces set against a background of floral wallpaper. Ample Scottish breakfasts are served in equally traditional style.

28 Balshagray Dr., G11 7DD. www.manorparkhotel.com. *0141/339-2143.* Fax 0141/339-5842. 10 units. £60–£75 double. AE, MC, V. Free parking. **Amenities:** Wi-Fi (free). *In room:* TV, hair dryer.

East End
INEXPENSIVE
Cathedral House Hotel The panoramic views of Glasgow cathedral and the Necropolis are reason enough to stay at this well-run, affordable hotel. The building itself is a restored Glaswegian baronial-style house dating back to the 1800s and stands on a tree-lined square adjacent to the cathedral. It's a small but choice hotel that's packed with atmosphere and history and within walking distance of the city center. All the comfortable bedrooms are individually designed in an attractive minimalist style. This simple style extends into the restaurant and bar where a reasonably priced menu of bar food is supported by a choice of draft ales and short cocktail menu.

29–32 Cathedral Sq., G4 0XA. www.cathedralhousehotel.org. *0141/552-3515.* Fax 0141/552-2444. 7 units. £80 double. MC, V. Free parking. **Amenities:** Restaurant; bar; room service. *In room:* TV, hair dryer.

Clydeside
MODERATE
Mint Breath in wide views of the Clyde and the scent of maritime Glasgow at this ultra modern riverside hotel. This is definitely the accommodation of choice for anyone preferring the contemporary over the traditional as clean, functional design and new technology shine throughout. Each of the spacious guestrooms feature an iMac multimedia entertainment system and super-fast free Wi-Fi; many also have long views of the river. Mint is more central than you might think with the city center around 1½ miles east and the West End a short walk north. However, the on-site cafe and restaurant make staying in worthwhile, not least for the al fresco dining on the banks of the Clyde in summer.

Finnieston Quay, G3 8HN. www.minthotel.com. *0141/240-1002.* Fax 0141/248-2754. 164 units. £75–£130 double. AE, MC, V. Free parking. **Amenities:** Restaurant; bar; room service. *In room:* Hair dryer, Wi-Fi (free).

Southside
EXPENSIVE
Sherbrooke Castle Hotel ★★ If staying in the city center isn't a priority, this splendid Scottish baronial hotel set deep inside landscaped gardens on Glasgow's leafy southside is an excellent getaway choice. Traditional touches and modern efficiencies are the hallmarks of this architectural delight, built in 1896 as the private residence of a rich contractor. He designed it around three sides of a large hall and staircase; its facade is festooned with towers and turrets. During World War II, the building was used by the Royal Navy, but was converted into a hotel afterwards. Bedrooms are the epitome of luxury and comfort and a large romantic suite occupies the castle's "Sleeping Beauty" tower. Local produce is a mainstay of the carefully crafted Scottish and international dishes served at the on-site restaurant.

11 Sherbrooke Ave., Pollokshields G41 4PG. www.sherbrooke.co.uk. *0141/427-4227.* Fax 0141/427-5685. 25 units. £150 double; £175–£225 suite. AE, DC, MC, V. **Amenities:** Restaurant; bar; room service. *In room:* TV, hair dryer, Wi-Fi (free).

Ten Queens Drive ★★ 🎒 One of a growing number of guesthouses that cater for the luxury end of the market, Ten Queens Drive occupies a choice spot on the edge of a large park in a tree-lined spot of the city's southside. This property has undergone significant refurbishment and glows with an appealing combination of Victorian glory and contemporary luxury. Individually designed elegant guest rooms come in a number of sizes each with first-class bathrooms, some with corner baths; the Club rooms and suites are particularly spacious. The two-bedroom townhouse suite is good for families wanting extra space. Discounted packages are available for longer stays. Fresh and local is the order of the day on both the restaurant menu and choice of smaller bar snacks.

10-16 Queens Dr., G42 8BS. www.tenqueensdrive.co.uk.🕿 **0141/424-0160.** 21 units. £120–£150 double, £175–£250 suite. AE, MC, V. Free parking. **Amenities:** Restaurant; bar; concierge; room service. *In room:* TV, hair dryer, Wi-Fi (free).

SIDE TRIPS FROM GLASGOW

Famous for its world-class golf courses, a string of seaside resorts that stretch from Largs to Girvan, and as the birthplace of **Robert Burns,** the rugged Ayrshire coast to the west of Glasgow is framed by views of the Isle of Arran, Scotland's most southerly island. Both coast and Isle are easy day trips from Glasgow either by car or public transport. A host of attractions including **New Lanark,** one of Scotland's UNECSO World Heritage Sites, and the bonny banks of **Loch Lomond** (p. 268) are also within striking distance.

Ayr

The royal burgh of Ayr braces itself against the breezy Firth of Clyde and is the largest and most popular resort on Scotland's west coast. Standing at the point where the River Ayr empties into the Firth, the town is 35 miles southwest of Glasgow and offers beach and riverside walks, fishing, and golf, plus Scotland's top racecourse. The main draw however, is the village of **Alloway,** 1¾ miles south of Ayr, where Scotland's national poet was born on January 25, 1759, and a clutch of Burns-related sights wait to be explored.

ScotRail trains from Glasgow's Central Station (🕿 **08457/484-950;** www. scotrail.co.uk) whisk you to Ayr in 50 minutes; the round-trip fare is £9.40. A number of bus services including no. 57 connect Ayr with Alloway; contact **Stagecoach** (🕿 **01292/613-500;** www.stagecoachbus.com) for timetables and fares.

Ayr's **Tourist Information Centre** is at 22 Sandgate (🕿 **0845/225-5121;** www. ayrshire-arran.com). It's open April to June, Monday through Saturday 9am to 5pm; July and August, Monday through Saturday 9am to 6pm, Sunday 10am to 5pm; September, Monday through Saturday 9am to 5pm, Sunday 11am to 5pm; and October to March, Monday through Friday 9am to 5pm.

EXPLORING THE TOWN

Ayr claims two main draws: its bracing seaside and Burns associations. Day-trippers arrive via the car park on the seafront where a wide expanse of sand is dominated by a children's adventure playground and mini golf course. The Scots always claimed that their mile differed in length to the English mile, and even after the Union of the Crowns in 1701 they continued to measure their own miles in their own way until the end of this century. Ayr seafront still upholds the historic "lang Scots mile," partly in honor of Burns who pays reference to it in his famous poem *Tam o' Shanter,* and

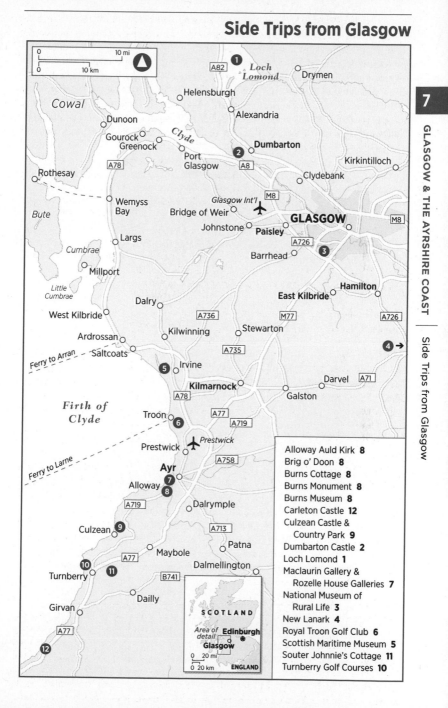

Side Trips from Glasgow

Map labels:

0 10 mi
0 10 km

Cowal

Loch Lomond ❶ A82 Drymen

Helensburgh

Dunoon

Gourock Greenock Clyde Alexandria

Port Glasgow Dumbarton ❷ A8

Rothesay A78 Kirkintilloch

Clydebank

Bute Wemyss Bay Glasgow Int'l

Bridge of Weir ✈ M8

Johnstone Paisley GLASGOW M8

Largs A726

Cumbrae Barrhead ❸

Millport

Little Cumbrae Hamilton

Dalry East Kilbride A726

West Kilbride A736 Stewarton M77

Kilwinning A735 ❹ →

Ardrossan Saltcoats Darvel A71

Ferry to Arran Irvine ❺ A77 Galston

Kilmarnock A78 A719

Firth of Clyde Troon ❻

Prestwick ✈ Prestwick

Prestwick A758

Ferry to Larne Ayr ❼ Alloway ❽ Dalrymple

A719 A713 Patna

Culzean ❾ Maybole

Turnberry ❿ ⓫ Dalmellington B741

Girvan Dailly A77

⓬

SCOTLAND

Area of detail Edinburgh Glasgow ✷

0 20 mi
0 20 km ENGLAND

Legend:

Alloway Auld Kirk **8**
Brig o' Doon **8**
Burns Cottage **8**
Burns Monument **8**
Burns Museum **8**
Carleton Castle **12**
Culzean Castle & Country Park **9**
Dumbarton Castle **2**
Loch Lomond **1**
Maclaurin Gallery & Rozelle House Galleries **7**
National Museum of Rural Life **3**
New Lanark **4**
Royal Troon Golf Club **6**
Scottish Maritime Museum **5**
Souter Johnnie's Cottage **11**
Turnberry Golf Courses **10**

199

visitors are invited to blow away the cobwebs and stroll their unofficial mile, which leads south along the coast.

In the town itself riverside walks lead past the **Auld Brig o' Ayr** and the **Auld Kirk of Ayr** (www.auldkirk.org), where Burns' father William served as an Elder. In the center of town on the High Street, the **Wallace Tower** rises 34m (112 ft.) and was constructed in 1828 on the site where the Scottish hero's father is thought to have lived.

Located about 1½ miles south of Ayr, on Monument Road in Rozelle Park, the **Maclaurin Gallery** and **Rozelle House Galleries** (✆ 01292/443-708; www. south-ayrshire.gov.uk/galleries) exhibits a significant amount of work by Scottish artist Alexander Goudie alongside a major collection of contemporary art. The surrounding 37 hectares (90 acres) of woodland are laced with nature trails and feature a craft shop and tearooms. The park leads off the B7024 (Monument Road) to Alloway and is open Monday and Wednesday through Saturday from 10am to 5pm and Sunday 2 to 5pm. Admission is free.

The **Ayr Racecourse** (✆ 0870/850-5666; www.ayr-racecourse.co.uk), about 1½ miles north of the town center (follow signs on the A77), is open year-round. Races are usually held Friday, Saturday, and Monday, generally at 2:15pm. Peak racing season is May to October, with jumping events held in November, January, and April. The Scottish Grand National is held mid-April.

ALLOWAY ★: birthplace OF RABBIE BURNS

Some 1¾ miles south of Ayr, Alloway is one of the region's prettiest villages and the place where Robert Burns was born into a gardener's cottage—the "auld clay biggin"—built by his father William Burns in 1757.

The tiny **Burns Cottage** stands on the edge of the B7024, the main road that leads through Alloway, and still contains some of its original furniture including the bed in which the poet was born. The cottage is part of wider attraction that encompasses a nearby new **Burns Museum** (✆ 0844/493-2601; www. burnsmuseum.org.uk) on Murdoch's Lane, which houses the world's largest Burns collection consisting of some of the poet's personal belongings and handwritten manuscripts—including the original manuscript of *Auld Lang Syne*—along with a host of ways to learn about and interact with Rabbie's life and work. The Museum includes an airy cafe overlooking peaceful gardens featuring environmental art and is joined with Burns Cottage via a landscaped walkway adjacent to the main road. Parking is free at either site and joint entry to both costs £8 adults, £5.25 children and seniors, and £20 families. Opening times are daily April 1 to September 30, 10am to 5:30pm, and October 1 to March 31, 10am to 5pm.

Close to the museum stands the **Burns Monument,** a grand Grecian-style building erected in 1823 amid landscaped gardens and housing a statue of the poet. There are more Burns statues around the world than of any other writer and they're all mapped out within the monument. The **Brig o' Doon** immortalized in Burn's *Tam o' Shanter* spans the river adjacent to the monument, and the final stop on the Burns tour of Alloway is the haunted ruins of **Alloway Auld Kirk,** where the poet's father is buried and Tam o' Shanter stumbled upon the fearful witches.

Three golf courses are nearby; the best is the municipal **Belleisle Golf Course,** Doonfoot Road, Alloway (© **01292/441-258;** www.ayrbelleislegolfclub.com), but there are some three dozen courses in the surrounding area.

WHERE TO EAT & STAY

The Beresford ★ MEDITERRANEAN   An appealing combination of restaurant, wine bar, and art gallery, the Beresford is a popular and stylish spot to dine and drink. Food is served from 9am until 9pm, and its morning, lunch, and evening menus are all infused with French and Mediterranean influences from the fresh pastries that are served all day to evening choices including Italian fish stew and mushroom risotto with white truffle oil. An eclectic array of artwork lines the walls and much of the work in the top-floor gallery is for sale. The Beresford is also a good choice for an evening drink.

22 Beresford Terrace. © **01292/280-820.** Lunch main courses £7–£10; dinner main courses £10–£17. MC, V. Daily 9am until late, food served until 9pm.

Brig o' Doon House Hotel ★★   Stay in style at this grand oasis of traditional luxury in the shadow of the Burns memorial. The hotel's peaceful gardens spread out along the banks of the River Doon at the point where it's crossed by the Brig o' Doon—the famous medieval footbridge Tam o'Shanter rode across to escape Nannie the witch. The hotel boasts five spacious deluxe rooms plus a further five at the adjacent Doonbrae House, or choose one of the two super comfortable suites, Rose Cottage and The Gables. The hotel's fine restaurant champions traditional Scottish cuisine created with locally sourced produce and accompanied by garden views.

High Maybole Rd., Alloway, KA7 4PQ. 1¾ miles south of Ayr on B7024. www.costley-hotels.co.uk. © **01292/442-466.** Fax 01292/441-999. 12 units. £120–£140 double. AE, MC, V. **Amenities:** 2 restaurants; bar. In room: TV, hair dryer.

The Chestnuts Hotel   Situated close to two golf courses and Ayr's seafront, this relaxed hotel might not be the most luxurious choice in town, but it is one of the friendliest. All rooms are clean and comfortable and options include two set up for families. The on-site lounge bar and restaurant are frequently packed with locals who flock here to choose from a long menu favoring traditional pub food and real ales.

52 Racecourse Rd., Ayr KA7 2UZ. www.chestnutshotel.com. © **01292/264-393.** Fax 01292/880-754. 14 units. £75–£85 double. MC, V. **Amenities:** Restaurant; bar. In room: TV, hair dryer.

Fairfield House   This grand Victorian hotel on the southern edges of Ayr's seafront gleams with fully restored elegance. Its facilities are some of the best in town and include a well-equipped leisure club complete with indoor pool, sauna, and steam room. Large and luxurious guest rooms come in a mix of traditional and contemporary designs; those with sweeping sea views cost more per night. Dining at Fairfield is a particularly fine experience, complemented by a strong wine list and recognized with a clutch of awards.

12 Fairfield Rd., Ayr, KA7 2AR. www.fairfieldhotel.co.uk. © **01292/267-461.** Fax 01292/261-456. 44 units. £140–£200 double; £185–£250 suite. AE, DC, MC, V. **Amenities:** Restaurant; bar; pool (indoor); health club and spa; room service. In room: A/C (some rooms), TV, hair dryer, Wi-Fi.

Troon & the Royal Troon Golf Club ★

The resort town of **Troon,** 6¾ miles north of Ayr and 31 miles southwest of Glasgow, looks out across the Firth of Clyde and takes its name from the curiously shaped promontory jutting out into the Clyde estuary, on which the old town and the harbor stand. The promontory was called Trwyn, the Cymric word for "nose," which later became Trone and finally Troon. The town's wide streets are swept by an often enthusiastic sea breeze, and an imposing statue of *Britannia* stands on the seafront as a memorial to the dead of two world wars. In summer, visitors find plenty of room on Troon's 1¾ miles of **sandy beaches** that stretch along both sides of its harbor. However, Troon's famed golf links are the main draw.

The **Royal Troon Golf Club** on Craigends Road (© **01292/311-555**; www.royaltroon.co.uk) is one of the world's finest championship courses; The Open has been played off and on here since 1923. The 7,175-yard, par-71 **Old Course** is the more famous and has an SSS (Standard Scratch Score) of 75. A newer addition, the 6,289-yard, par-71 **Portland,** with an SSS of 71 is, by some estimates, even more challenging. The nine par-3 holes of the **Craigend** course attract mainly junior players and family golfers. Visitors are only invited to play between mid-April and mid-October and greens fees are £175 for a day tariff that includes a round on both the Old Course and Portland or £130 for just a round on the Old Course. Caddies should be booked in advance and cost £40 per round; club rental is £40 to £50, a trolley rents for £5, and an electric caddy cart costs £20 per round.

ScotRail trains from Glasgow's Central Station (© **08457/484-950**; www.scotrail.co.uk) bound for Ayr stop at Troon en route. The journey from Glasgow takes around 40 minutes and a round-trip fare costs £8.30. The same service also connects Ayr with Troon, a 10-minute ride and £3.20 fare away.

WHERE TO EAT & STAY

Barceló Troon Marine Hotel ★   This grand landmark 1890s hotel stands proud on the Ayrshire coast, overlooking the Royal Troon golf course. Views across the water to the Isle of Arran are suitably stunning, with many guest rooms facing seaward—a lucky few look down upon the Royal's 18th hole. Accommodation includes both basic and deluxe doubles plus a limited number of luxurious suites all named after famous golfers who have stayed here. The on-site **Fairways** restaurant serves first-class modern Scottish cuisine in style and the Arran bar is a choice spot to mull over a wee dram and the day's play.

8 Crosbie Rd., KA10 6HE. www.barcelo-hotels.co.uk. © **01292/314-444.** Fax 01292/316-922. 89 units. £75–£165 double. AE, MC, V. **Amenities:** Restaurant; bar; pool (indoor); spa; gym; steam room; sauna; Jacuzzi; room service. *In room:* TV, hair dryer, Wi-Fi.

The Highgrove ★ TRADITIONAL SCOTTISH   This charming white-painted, red-roofed brick building sits on a hillside north of Troon and feasts on terrific sea views. Traditional Scottish reigns supreme and diners can expect a decor rich with tartan carpets and wood paneling in the restaurant and coffee lounge. Food is served from 9am and starts with breakfast rolls and fresh scones and, although Scottish food is championed, dishes such as Thai lamb curry and Provencal vegetables with Brie de Meaux wrapped in a herb pancake spice up both lunch and dinner menus. Leave room for suitably indulgent deserts such as pink meringue chantilly with pistachio ice cream.

Upstairs are nine simple but comfortable guest rooms with TVs, phones, and hair dryers, renting for £110 bed-and-breakfast or £145 dinner and bed-and-breakfast.

Old Loan's Rd., Troon, KA10 7HL. © **01292/312-511.** www.highgrovehouse.co.uk. Lunch main courses £8–£12, dinner main courses £11–£17. AE, MC, V. Daily coffee shop menu served 9am–5pm, lunch noon–2:30pm, dinner 6–9:30pm. Drive 1¾ miles north of Troon on A78.

Lochgreen House Hotel ★★ Adjacent to the fairways of the Royal Troon golf course is one of Scotland's loveliest country-house hotels, set on 12 lush hectares (30 acres) of forest and landscaped gardens. The property opens onto views of the Firth of Clyde and the tiny island of Ailsa Craig and its interior evokes all the opulence of the late Victorian era. Guests meet and mingle in two luxurious sitting rooms with log fires, or take long walks around landscaped grounds. Spacious bedrooms come in either traditional or more contemporary styles, with premier accommodation boasting balconies all their own and glorious bathrooms. Be tempted by the blend of Scottish and French cuisine served at the hotel's restaurant, where views of woodland and gardens complement seafood, game, and Scottish beef.

Monktonhill Rd., Southwood, Troon, KA10 7EN. www.lochgreenhouse.com. ℂ **01192/313-343.** Fax 01292/317-661. 38 units. £123–£240 double. AE, MC, V. **Amenities:** 2 restaurants; 2 bars; concierge; room service. *In room:* TV, hair dryer, Wi-Fi (free).

South Beach Hotel This large Victorian sparkling white hotel sits bang on Troon's seafront and is a solid, friendly place to stay. Well-appointed rooms offer clean and comfortable accommodation to the south of Troon's harbor close to both the Royal Troon and municipal golf courses and the beach. An airy conservatory restaurant overlooks the sands, or guests can dine on good-quality pub food—including large sharing platters—in Millar's bar.

73 South Beach, Troon, KA10 6EG. www.southbeach.co.uk. ℂ **01292-312-033.** Fax 01292/318-438. 32 units. £70–£120 double. MC, V. **Amenities:** Restaurant; bar. *In room:* TV, hair dryer, Wi-Fi (free).

Turnberry: World-Class Golf ★

South of Culzean Castle (p. 205), the little town of Turnberry is one of Scotland's best golfing resorts. It began to flourish early in the 20th century and following service during both world wars as an airbase and hospital, the courses and its grand hotel were restored to their former glory.

From the original two 13-hole golf courses, the complex has developed into the two 18-hole courses, Ailsa and Kintyre, known worldwide as the **Turnberry Golf Courses,** alongside the nine-hole Arran course plus a golf academy. The 7,204-yard, par-70 Ailsa has a SSS of 72 and is one of the most exacting courses yet devised. This demanding course has been the scene of numerous championship tournaments and PGA events and golfers come here for the prestige and the challenge of a course often buffeted by less than favorable weather. Redesigned in 2001, the par-72 Kintyre course is framed with glorious views of the Ailsa Craig island and offers golfers an invigorating links experience. Guests at the Turnberry Resort (see below) are given priority for the Ailsa course and for details on how to book a round on this, or the Kintyre course, call ℂ **01655/334-032** or visit www.turnberry.co.uk for details.

Greens fees for resort guests start at £55 for a round on Kintyre and £77 for Ailsa; for non-guests, £75 for 18 holes on Kintyre or £95 on Ailsa. Clubs rent for £50 per round or £70 per day, and a caddy service is £40 plus tip. If you're not staying at the resort, give them a call in the morning to check on any unclaimed tee times—but it's a long shot.

A short drive east of Turnberry is **Souter Johnnie's Cottage,** Main Road, in Kirkoswald (ℂ **0844/493-2147;** www.nts.org.uk), 4 miles west of Maybole on the A77. This was the 18th-century home of the village cobbler, John Davidson (Souter Johnnie), who, with his friend Douglas Graham of Shanter Farm, was immortalized by Burns in *Tam o' Shanter*. The cottage is furnished in the style of Souter Johnnie's time and contains a set of old cobbler's tools. It's open April to September Friday through Tuesday 11:30am to 5pm; admission is £6 for adults, £5 for children and seniors, and £15.50 for a family ticket.

A final sight along the Ayrshire coast is **Carleton Castle,** along the A77 some 6 miles southwest of the compact seaside town of Girvan. Once owned by the Cathcart family, in its heyday the castle was a watchtower, built to guard the coastline against invaders. According to local legend one laird, Sir John Cathcart married and murdered a succession of wives in order to gain their money; however, his canny eighth wife May, inspiration of the "The Ballad of May Colvin," realized what her murdering husband was up to and pushed him off the cliff to his death. Cathcart's desperate screams are said to still haunt the ruins of his castle.

WHERE TO EAT & STAY

Glenapp Castle ★★★ ☺ This superbly restored and sumptuously decorated Scottish baronial castle stands high above a tiny village overlooking the Irish Sea around 20 miles southwest of Turnberry. Built in 1870, Glenapp stands within 14½ hectares (36 acres) of stunning gardens and woodlands riddled with walks and wildlife. Elegant lounges and dining rooms await you inside this vast Victorian mansion along with 17 spacious and individually furnished bedrooms and suites. Antiques and oil paintings spread through every room and high Victorian windows allow the sun to stream through. Dining at Glenapp, which has some of the finest wine cellars in the area, is a gourmet experience and the kitchen makes full use of produce grown in its own gardens. Glenapp is also very family friendly and lays on books, games, and DVDs for its young visitors.

Ballantrae, Ayrshire on the A77 KA26 0NZ. www.glenappcastle.com. ✆ **01465/831-212.** Fax 01465/831-000. 17 units. £415–£505 double; £485–£620 suite; Rates include all meals. AE, MC, V. **Amenities:** Restaurant; bar; tennis court, croquet lawn; room service. *In room:* TV/DVD, CD player, Wi-Fi.

Malin Court Hotel On one of the most scenic strips of the Ayrshire coast, this well-run hotel fronts the Firth of Clyde and the Turnberry golf courses. Housed in a relatively modern building, Malin Court cultivates a casual atmosphere and has created a welcoming retreat that offers guests a blend of informality and comfort. Bedrooms are mostly medium size and modern in decor and claim either views over the coast or adjacent golf courses. The hotel's Cotters restaurant typifies the same winning combination of scenic location and relaxed service, and creates both modern and traditional Scottish fare from the finest local ingredients. In addition to the obligatory round of golf, staff can also arrange hunting, fishing, riding, and sailing.

Off the A719 between Turnberry and Middens, KA26 9PB. www.malincourt.co.uk. ✆ **01655/331-457.** Fax 01655/331-706. 18 units. £128–£148 double. AE, DC, MC, V. **Amenities:** Restaurant; bar; room service. *In room:* TV, hair dryer, robes, Wi-Fi (free).

Turnberry Resort ★★★ ☺ The Turnberry is a remarkable and opulent Edwardian property, built in 1908. You can spot the hotel's wide white facade, red-tile roof, and dozens of gables from afar as it commands a striking, coast-facing pose. Public areas are awash with Waterford crystal chandeliers, Ionic columns, molded ceilings, and oak paneling, and each guest room is furnished in a classical style and has a marble-sheathed bathroom. The rooms, which vary in size, open onto views of the lawns, forests, and (in some cases) the Scottish coastline. Many gravitate here to make full use of the resort's championship golf courses, but other leisure facilities such as its large sea-facing indoor pool and serene spa are equally first class. Children are more than welcome; they receive a special package on arrival and are well catered for with a range of activities.

Maidens Rd., Turnberry, KA26 9LT. www.turnberry.co.uk. ⓒ **01655/331-000.** Fax 01655/331-706. 221 units. £167–£480 double; £267–£760 suite. AE, DC, MC, V. 50 miles south of Glasgow off the A77. **Amenities:** 3 restaurants; 3 bars; pool (indoor); 2 tennis courts; health club and spa; bike rental; concierge; room service; babysitting. *In room:* TV, hair dryer, minibar, Wi-Fi.

Other Attractions

Culzean Castle & Country Park ★★★ ☺ CASTLE

Built by the famous Scottish architect Robert Adam in the late 18th century, to integrate with an old medieval tower house, this cliff-top castle was the seat of the powerful Kennedy clan and is a fine example of a grand country house. A dramatic oval staircase forms the centerpiece of the castle around which the whole house radiates. Visitors are allowed entry into a string of grand rooms including Lady Allsa's Boudoir and the State Bedroom, as well as the not so grand but equally fascinating kitchens. The castle is one of the numerous experiences on offer at Culzean (pronounced "Cul-*lane*"). Other highlights include an 18th-century walled garden that forms the basis of a 228-hectare (563-acre) country park. Here visitors can bird-watch at the enormous swan pond and explore numerous other old buildings in the estate grounds such as an old pagoda and the grand Camellia House orangery. Young visitors can enjoy a large adventure playground and miles of woodland paths and beaches.

12 miles south of Ayr, off A719 near Maybole. ⓒ **0844/493-2149.** www.culzeanexperience.org. Admission castle and country park £14 adults, £10 seniors and children 5–15, £34 families; country park only £9 adults, £6.50 seniors and children 5–15, £22 families. Castle open Apr–Oct daily 10:30am–5pm; country park open year-round daily 9:30am–sunset. Bus no. 57 from Ayr.

Dumbarton Castle CASTLE

From the 5th century until 1018, Dumbarton was the center of the ancient kingdom of Strathclyde and its castle was the kingdom's mighty fortress. This historic building hangs on a volcanic rock perched beside the Firth of Clyde and offers stunning views and, surprisingly for a building whose history stretches back 1,500 years, fine examples of Georgian military architecture. The castle's Dark Age history is never far away and legends of Merlin and Viking raids run deep. Mary Queen of Scots also sought royal refuge at this dramatic site in 1548 while waiting to be whisked to safety in France.

Off the A814 at Dumbarton. ⓒ **01389/732-167.** www.historic-scotland.gov.uk. Admission £4.20 adults, £3.40 seniors, £2.50 children. Apr–Sept daily 9:30am–5:30pm; Oct daily 9:30am–4:30pm; Nov–Mar Sat–Wed 9:30am–4:30pm. 20 miles northwest of Glasgow. A regular train service links Glasgow Queen Street with Dumbarton East.

National Museum of Rural Life ★ ☺ MUSEUM

Get a firsthand experience of life in the Scottish countryside at this museum and working farm, which still uses many traditional 1950s farming methods. This is a winning attraction for children as you can get close up to Tamworth pigs, Scots Dumpys chickens, Ayrshire cows, and best of all Mari the Clydesdale horse. Young visitors are invited to become garden detectives and discover which creatures live in sheds, hedges, and flower beds. The farm also features a Georgian farmhouse while the museum itself tells the story of the landscape and the folk who have worked it over the generations.

Wester Kittochside, Philipshill Rd., East Kilbride. ⓒ **0300/123-6789.** www.nms.ac.uk. Admission £6 adults, £5 seniors, under-12s free. Daily 10am–5pm. 11 miles south of Glasgow. First bus no. 31 connects Glasgow city center with the museum.

New Lanark ★★★ HISTORIC SITE   This small restored 18th-century cotton mill village set within a deep gorge on the banks of the river Clyde is a UNESCO World Heritage Site. It's not just the bricks and mortar of the old mills and workers' housing that makes this place so significant, but the philosophy of social reform that underpinned its industry. Under the enlightened management of social pioneer Robert Owen, at a time when conditions for the working class teetered on cruelty, he introduced a system of providing decent housing, fair wages, free healthcare and education, and the world's first nursery school. This fascinating attraction details the full history of this pioneering industrial center and the people who lived and worked here.

25 miles southeast of Glasgow, New Lanark Rd, off the A73. © **01555/662-322.** www.newlanark.org. Admission £8.50 adults, £7 seniors, £6 children, £24.50 families. Apr–Sept daily 10am–5pm; Oct–Mar daily 11am–5pm. A regular train service connects Glasgow Central with Lanark train station, which is connected by bus with New Lanark.

Scottish Maritime Museum MUSEUM   Irvine harbor outside Glasgow was once a major trading port, and its maritime history lives on at this restoration, which is the main site of the Scottish Maritime Museum. Here you can tour through an old engine shop and a shipyard worker's tenement flat all restored to how it would have looked pre-1920s. Visitors can also view a collection of vessels moored at the harbor including the SY *Carola*, built on the Clyde in 1898 as a private family yacht and the oldest seagoing steam yacht in Great Britain. Test your own shipbuilding skills by building a model boat and see if it floats.

Linthouse Building, Harbour Rd., Irvine. © **01294/278-283.** www.scottishmaritimemuseum.org. Admission £3.50 adults, £2.50 seniors and children 5–14, £9.50 families. Apr–Oct daily 10am–5pm. A regular train service connects Glasgow Central with Irvine train station.

ARGYLL & THE SOUTHERN HEBRIDES

The county of Argyll stretches from the Mull of Kintyre—made famous by Paul McCartney's song—up via Inveraray, seat of the dukes of Argyll, and on to the port of Oban, where ferries depart for the Inner Hebrides. The county also encompasses some of the most beautiful islands, including Islay, renowned for its whisky distilleries; Gigha, with its lush gardens; and Jura, where deer outnumber humans.

SIGHTSEEING **Whisky** aficionados make a beeline to Islay to the distilleries of **Laphroaig, Lagavulin,** and **Bruichladdick,** while children marvel at the hydroelectric power station hidden inside **Ben Cruachan.** Ramblers wander along the picturesque tow path of the **Crinan Canal,** with its 15 locks, and in late spring, plant-lovers flock to **Achamore House Gardens** on Gigha to see the rhododendrons in bloom.

EATING & DRINKING There's nothing to beat sitting in one of the harborfront restaurants in Tarbert as the fishing boats come in to deliver the catch of the day—the freshest scallops, lobster, halibut, and turbot. On Jura, hunters supply the local hotel with venison, and on the estate of Brodick Castle, on the Isle of Arran, Creelers' smokery cures salmon, scallops, and duck. Pubs and hotels throughout Argyll pride themselves on their array of fine single malts, as well as locally brewed beers.

HISTORY There are over 800 ancient sites—from standing stones to burial tombs and forts—in **Knapdale** and **Kilmartin Glen,** which 1,500 years ago was the center of the Gaelic Kingdom of Dalriada. More recent history is dealt with at **Inveraray Castle,** where your imagination is stirred by the armor and weaponry of Clan Campbell. Then in the harbor nearby, children will leap onboard a former lightship, **the Arctic Penguin,** and learn all about Scottish maritime history.

NATURE In the summer, take a guided walk in **Knapdale Forest** to see the **beavers** that have recently been reintroduced. In winter, watch the flocks of geese and swans from the hide at nearby **Moine Mhor Nature Reserve.** On **Loch Long,** in **Argyll Forest Park,** hire a canoe and with luck you'll see gray seals, basking sharks, and perhaps even sea otters. For guaranteed success, take a boat trip from **Oban** harbor to see the **seal colony** on a small island in the bay.

THE best TRAVEL EXPERIENCES IN ARGYLL & THE SOUTHERN HEBRIDES

○ **Enjoy rural Argyll on horseback:** For an idyllic retreat, stay in a cottage on a working farm near Loch Gilphead and explore the surrounding countryside on horseback with the Ardfern Riding Centre. See p. 213.

○ **Become a connoisseur of Islay's famous whiskies:** Argue with the locals over the relative merits of the amber nectars of the Bowmore, Bunnahabhain, Lagavulin, and Laphroaig distilleries on the Isle of Islay. See p. 220.

○ **Escape from civilization by hiking up the Paps of Jura:** These three conical mountains tower dramatically over the Isle of Jura, one of the most sparsely populated and unspoilt islands in the Inner Hebrides. See p. 223.

○ **Amble down the Kintyre Way through spectacular scenery:** Starting from the ruins of the 13th-century Bruce Castle in the pretty fishing village Tarbert, walk all the way down to the Mull of Kintyre through this often-forgotten corner of Scotland. See p. 215.

○ **Lose yourself amid the exotic foliage of the Crarae Glen Gardens:** These extensive gardens bring the lush vegetation of a Himalayan valley to the cooler climes of Loch Fyne. See p. 226

THE ISLE OF ARRAN: SCOTLAND IN MINIATURE ★★

Brodick: 74 miles W of Edinburgh; 29 miles W of Glasgow

At the mouth of the Firth of Clyde is the Isle of Arran, often described as "Scotland in miniature" because of its wild and varied scenery—the glens, moors, lochs, sandy bays, and rocky coasts that have made the country famous. Once you're on Arran, there are local buses to take you from village to village. A coastal road, the A841, runs the 60-mile circuit around the island.

Arran boasts some splendid mountain scenery, notably the conical peak of **Goatfell** in the north (called the "mountain of the winds"), reaching a height of 869m (2,851 ft.). Arran also has plenty of beautiful glens, especially **Glen Sannox,** in the northeast, and **Glen Rosa,** north of Brodick. Students of geology flock to Arran to study igneous rocks of the Tertiary period. Cairns and standing stones at Tormore intrigue archaeologists as well. If you're on a tight schedule, the island, at only 25 miles long and 10 miles wide, can be seen in a single day.

Essentials

GETTING THERE   Express trains operate from Glasgow Central direct to Ardrossan Harbour, taking 1 hour. For 24-hour rail inquiries, call ℂ **08475/484-950;** www.nationalrail.co.uk. If you're driving from Glasgow, head southwest along the A737 until you reach Ardrossan.

From Ardrossan, you make a 30-minute ferry crossing to Arran, arriving in Brodick, Arran's main town, on its east coast. There are up to six boats daily, and the fare is £62 for cars, plus £10 per passenger for a round-trip journey. For information about ferry departures (which change seasonally), check with **Caledonian MacBrayne**

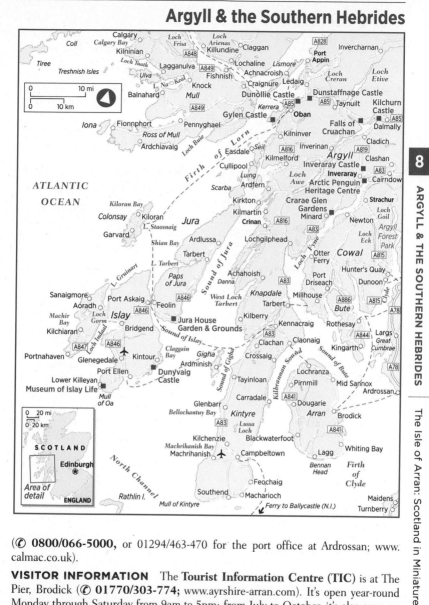

(© **0800/066-5000,** or 01294/463-470 for the port office at Ardrossan; www. calmac.co.uk).

VISITOR INFORMATION The **Tourist Information Centre (TIC)** is at The Pier, Brodick (© **01770/303-774;** www.ayrshire-arran.com). It's open year-round Monday through Saturday from 9am to 5pm; from July to October, it's also open on Sundays from 10am to 5pm.

Exploring the Island

After the ferry docks at Brodick, you may want to head for Arran's major sights, **Brodick Castle** and the **Isle of Arran Heritage Museum** (see below).

The most popular walks on the island are signposted. But if you're really serious about hiking, buy one of two detailed guides at the tourist office—*Seventy Walks in Arran* for £3 and *My Walks in Arran* for £2.50. While at the office, ask about any guided walks the Forestry Commission might be conducting. They're scheduled frequently in summer and range from 2 to 5 hours, costing £5 to £10.

To the south of Brodick is the village of **Lamlash,** on Lamlash Bay. From here, a ferry takes you over to Holy Island with its 303m (994- ft.) peak. A disciple of St. Columba founded a church on this island. In the north, **Lochranza** is a village with unique appeal. It opens onto a bay of pebbles and sand, and in the background lie the ruins of a castle that was reputedly the hunting seat of Robert the Bruce.

Brodick Castle ★★ CASTLE   The historic home of the dukes of Hamilton, this red-sandstone castle dates from the 13th century and contains important collections of silver, antique furniture, portraits, and objets d'art. Some form of a castle has stood on this site since about the 5th century, when the Dalriada Irish, a Celtic tribe, came here and founded their kingdom. The castle is now the property of the National Trust for Scotland and boasts award-winning gardens. Laid out in the 1920s by the Duchess of Montrose, they're filled with shrubs, trees, perennials, and herbs from Tasmania, New Zealand, Chile, and the Himalayas. Especially noteworthy are the rhododendrons, which are one of the special features of the Country Park, a semi-domesticated forest bordering the more formal gardens.

1½ miles north of the Brodick pier head. ℂ **0844/493-2152.** www.nts.org.uk. Admission to both castle and gardens £11 adults, £8 seniors, students, and children aged 6–16, free for children aged 5 and under, £27 families. Car parking £2. Castle: Apr–Oct daily 11am–4pm (till 3pm in Oct); Country Park: year round, daily 9:30am–sunset; Reception Centre, shop: Apr–Sept daily 10am–5pm, Oct daily 10am–4pm, Nov–Dec Fri–Sun 10am–3:30pm. Bus: Any labeled BRODICK CASTLE.

Isle of Arran Heritage Museum MUSEUM   Occupying some old outbuildings for the nearby castle, this museum provides an overview of life on Arran from prehistoric times to the present. The museum includes a cottage filled with 19th-century memorabilia, costumes, and artifacts, including a working kitchen. There's also a blacksmith's shop and forge, and an archive room housing historic records associated with Arran.

Rosaburn, 1½ miles north of the Brodick ferry piers. ℂ **01770/302-636.** www.arranmuseum.co.uk. Admission £3 adults, £2 seniors, £1.50 children aged 5–16, £7 families. Apr–Oct daily 10:30am–4:30pm. Bus: Any labeled BRODICK CASTLE.

Where to Eat

Creelers Seafood Restaurant SCOTTISH   Creelers is located within the small complex of gift shops and cafes created from a 1920s-era farm associated with Brodick Castle, and is about 1 mile north of the center of Brodick Village. This family-run business includes a smokery where salmon, scallops, and duck breast are cured. Many of these products are later served up in the restaurant. Dishes include smoked salmon with capers and horseradish, and mushroom risotto. You can also enjoy some of the freshest seafood in Scotland, much of it pulled in from local fishing boats that day.

Home Farm, Brodick. ℂ **01770/302-810.** www.creelers.co.uk. Reservations recommended. Main courses £12–£18. MC, V. Tues–Sat 12:30–2:30pm and 6–9:30pm.

Shopping

Divided into three businesses, the **Duchess Court Shops,** Home Farm, Brodick, comprises the Island Cheese Company (ℂ **01770/302-595**), Creelers Smokehouse

The Isle of Arran & the Kintyre Pensinsula

Map Legend:
- ✈ Airport
- ⛳ Golf
- 🚨 Lighthouse

Jura
Keillmore
Sound of Jura
Eilean Mor
Point of Knap
Kilmory
Achahoish
Sliabh Gaoil
Loch of Caolisport
A83
Loch Fyne
Cowal
Knapdale
E. Loch Tarbert
Tarbert
W. Tarbert
Bruce Castle
Portavadie
Bute
Glecknabae
Kildavanan
Kilberry Head
Kilberry
W. Loch Tarbert
Kennacraig
Whitehouse
Ardlamont Point
Straad
Inchmarnock
Ardpatrick
Skipness Castle & Chapel
To Colonsay & Islay
Ardpatrick Point
Claonaig
Skipness Point
Ardscalpsie Point
Port Mór
Clachan
Tarbert
Ballochroy
Gigha
Crossaig
Kilbrannan Sound
Lochranza
Sound of Bute
Ardminish
A83
Achamore House Gardens
Catacol
A841
Mid Sannox
Leim
Tayinloan
Sannox Bay
Gigalum
Killean
Grogport
Pirnmill
Goatfell
Corrie
Cara
Carradale Water
Kintyre
Glen Iorsa
Glen Rosa
Brodick Castle
Muasdale
Arnicle
Carradale
Brodick Bay
Glenacardoch Point
Dippen
Dougarie
Carradale Point
Isle of Arran Heritage Museum
Brodick
Glenbarr
Carradale Bay
Arran
Bellochantuy
Margnaheglish
Holy Island
Saddell
Lamlash
Drumadoon Point
Blackwaterfoot
Skeroblingarry
Kilchenzie
Peninver
Brown Head
Whiting Bay
Machrihanish
A83
Campbeltown
Campbeltown Loch
A841
Lagg
Kildonan
Drumlemble
Stewarton
Davaar
Kilmory
Sound of Pladda
Pladda
Knocknaha
Conie Glen
Feochaig
Johnston's Point
SCOTLAND
Area of detail
Firth of Clyde
B842
South Carrine
Macharioch
Edinburgh
Southend
Mull of Kintyre
Dunaverty Rock
Sanda Sound
Sheep Island
Sanda
To Ballycastle (No. Ireland)
ENGLAND

0   5 mi
0   10 km

20 mi
20 km

(© **01770/302-797**), and Arran Aromatics (© **01770/302-595;** www.arran aromatics.com) selling luxury toiletries and cosmetics made on the island.

About 6 miles north of Brodick in Corrie, **Corriecraft & Antiques,** Hotel Square (© **01770/810-661**), sells antiques and pottery. In Lamlash, **Arran Fine Foods,** The Old Mill (© **01770/600-606;** www.paterson-arran.com), offers chutneys, mustards, preserves, bakery items, and other locally produced condiments.

The **Old Byre Showroom,** Auchencar Farm (© **01770/840-227;** www.oldbyre. co.uk), 5 miles north of Blackwaterfoot along the coastal road in Machrie, sells sheepskin, leather, and tweeds, but its biggest draw is the large selection of locally produced woolen sweaters.

Entertainment & Nightlife

Regulars gather in Brodick's pubs to talk, argue, and drink. The **Brodick Bar,** on Alma Road (© **01770/302-169**), is an old pub open Monday through Saturday 11am to midnight. Drop in for some real Scottish ale and a bar meal of local seafood (meals are served Mon–Sat noon–2:30pm and 5:30–10pm). The **Pierhead Tavern** on Shore Road in Lamlash (© **01770/600-418;** www.phtarran.co.uk) is a traditional pub, serving real ales and bar meals. On Sunday evenings at 9:30pm, you can join a general knowledge quiz. Occasionally, on Saturday nights, there's live music. Opening hours are Monday through Saturday from 11am to midnight and Sunday from 12:30pm to midnight.

Where to Stay

IN BRODICK

Auchrannie House Hotel ★★ ☺ Acclaimed as the island's finest hotel and restaurant, this Victorian mansion (once the home of the dowager duchess of Hamilton) stands in pristine glory in 2.4 hectares (6 acres) of landscaped gardens and woods, about 1 mile from the Brodick ferry terminal. Guest rooms in the new wing are the most comfortable, but all the rooms are furnished with taste, in the chic style of a modern boutique hotel. Family suites (two bedrooms) and four-poster rooms are available.

The hotel has two leisure clubs, each with its own pools, sauna, and gym. These include smaller pools for children and a large "playbarn." Guests can choose from three restaurants: a bar-brasserie, a seafood grill, and a more formal restaurant called "eighteen69." Children are well provided for in the first two options, with their own menus and even a soft play and games area. Non-guests should reserve ahead.

Auchrannie Rd., Brodick, Isle of Arran KA27 8BZ. www.auchrannie.co.uk. © **01770/302-234.** Fax 01770/302-812. 64 units. £145–£185 double. AE, MC, V. **Amenities:** 3 restaurants; bar; pools (indoor); health club & spa; sauna; babysitting; Wi-Fi (free). *In room:* TV, hair dryer.

Kilmichael Country House Hotel ★★ Reputedly the island's oldest house, it's certainly the most scenically located. A tasteful combination of the new and antique is used throughout. The guest rooms are beautifully furnished, as are the bathrooms, which are equipped with luxury toiletries. Some rooms have four-poster beds and Jacuzzi tubs. A suite and two other rooms, all with private entrances, are located in a converted 18th-century stable a few yards from the main building.

The food is also noteworthy, made with local produce whenever possible. The fixed-price dinner menu costs £45 per person.

Brodick, Isle of Arran KA27 8BY. www.kilmichael.com. © **01770/302-219.** Fax 01770/302-068. 9 units. £130–£184 double; £164–£205 suite. No children under 12. MC, V. **Amenities:** Restaurant; bar; room service; Wi-Fi (free). *In room:* TV, CD player, hair dryer.

There's no better way to experience the majestic beauty of the moors, Highlands, and headlands of Argyll than on horseback. To arrange an outing, contact the **Ardfern Riding Centre**, Croabh Haven, Loch Gilphead, Argyll (✆ **01852/500-632**). In addition to a stable of around 16 horses, and a working cattle-and-sheep farm between Oban and Loch Gilphead, the center has a cottage that can be rented by groups of up to eight equestrians (from £370 to £650 per week). The center is open all year, but the best times to go are from May to early June and from September to October.

IN WHITING BAY

Royal Hotel   This granite house, located in the center of the village beside the coastal road, was built in 1895, and was one of the first hotels on the island. True to its original function as a temperance hotel, it serves no alcohol, but guests can bring their own wine or beer into the dining room, which serves moderately priced dinners nightly at one sitting. Some of the bedrooms enjoy a vista of the bay and its tidal flats. One room contains a four-poster bed and lots of chintz, while another has a small sitting room.

Shore Rd., Whiting Bay, Isle of Arran KA27 8PZ. www.royalarran.co.uk. ✆/fax **01770/700-286.** 5 units. £95 double. No credit cards. Closed Nov–Mar. Take the Whiting Bay bus from Brodick. **Amenities:** Dining room. *In room:* TV, hair dryer.

IN KILDONAN

Kildonan Hotel   The Kildonan was built as an inn in 1760, just a few steps from the island's best beach. Its location is its great asset, with good views of seabirds and gray seals basking on the rocks of Pladda Island opposite. The rooms are basic, and a little old-fashioned, though all do at least have private bathrooms.

The dining room has enormous windows to make the best of the views. The meals are moderately priced; locally caught seafood is a specialty. Less formal lunches and dinners are served in the lively bar. A crowd of locals is likely to compete in a friendly fashion over the dartboard and billiards tables.

Kildonan, Isle of Arran KA27 8SE. www.kildonanhotel.com. ✆ **01770/820-207.** Fax 01770/820-320. 22 units. £85–£145 double. No credit cards. **Amenities:** Restaurant; bar; room service. *In room:* Hair dryer, no phone.

THE KINTYRE PENINSULA

The longest peninsula in Scotland, Kintyre stretches more than 60 miles, with beautiful scenery, sleepy villages, and miles of sandy beaches. It's one of the country's most unspoiled areas, owing perhaps to its isolation. Kintyre was ancient Dalriada, the first kingdom of the Scots.

If you drive all the way to the tip of Kintyre, you'll be only 12 miles from Ireland. Kintyre is joined to the mainland of Scotland by a narrow neck of land near the old port of Tarbert. The largest town on the peninsula is the port of Campbeltown, on the southeastern coast.

Essentials

GETTING THERE **Loganair** (© 0871/700-2000; www.flybe.com) makes two scheduled 45-minute flights a day from Glasgow Airport to Campbeltown, the chief town of Kintyre.

From Glasgow, you can take buses to the peninsula (schedules vary seasonally). The trip takes about 4 hours one-way. Inquire at **Scottish Citylink,** Buchanan Street Bus Station, Glasgow (© 08705/505050; www.citylink.co.uk).

The most efficient way to travel around Kintyre is by car. From Glasgow, take the A82 up to Loch Lomond and cut across to Arrochar and go over the "Rest and Be Thankful" route to Inveraray (the A83). Then drive down along Loch Fyne to Lochgilphead and continue on the A83 south to Tarbert, which is the gateway to the peninsula. You can take the A83 along the western coast or cut east at the junction of the B8001 and follow it across the peninsula to B842. If your target is Campbeltown, you can reach it by either the western shore (much faster and a better road) or the eastern shore.

Tarbert

A sheltered harbor protects the fishing port and yachting center of Tarbert, located on a narrow neck of land at the northern tip of the Kintyre Peninsula. It's between West Loch Tarbert and the head of herring-filled Loch Fyne and has often been dubbed the "world's prettiest fishing port."

The word *tarbert* derives from a Gaelic word meaning an isthmus, and often denoted a place where Vikings dragged their boats across land on rollers from one sea to another. In 1093, King Malcolm of Scotland and King Magnus Barelegs of Norway agreed the Western Isles were to belong to Norway and the mainland to Scotland. An island was defined as anything a Viking ship could sail around, and so Magnus proclaimed Kintyre an island by having his dragon ship dragged across the 1 mile of dry land from West Loch Tarbert on the Atlantic to East Loch Tarbert on Loch Fyne. After the Vikings gave way, Kintyre came under the control of the MacDonalds, the Lords of the Isles.

EXPLORING THE AREA

The castle at Tarbert dates from the 13th century and was later extended by Robert the Bruce. The castle ruins, **Bruce Castle,** are on a hillock above the village on the south side of the bay. The oldest part still standing is a keep from the 13th century.

One of the major attractions in the area is **Skipness Castle & Chapel,** at Skipness, along the B8001, 10 miles south of Tarbert, opening onto Loch Fyne. The hamlet was once a Norse village. The ruins of the ancient chapel and castle look out onto the Sounds of Kilbrannan and Bute. It was originally built to control shipping along Loch Fyne. A five-story tower remains.

WHERE TO EAT

Anchorage Restaurant ★ 🍴 SCOTTISH/SEAFOOD   The Anchorage remains unpretentious and dependable, despite its many culinary awards. It's housed in a stone harborfront building that was once a customs house. The daily menu includes dishes such as scallops sautéed with lemon-lime butter; halibut with wild mushrooms and a mussel sauce; and brochette of monkfish with saffron rice. Lunches are simpler and very reasonably priced.

Harbour St., Quayside. © **01880/820-881.** www.anchorageargyll.com. Reservations recommended. Main courses £10–£19. MC, V. Tues–Sat noon–2pm and 6–9pm, Sun 6–9pm. Closed Jan.

One of Scotland's Great Walks

The **Kintyre Way** ★★, opened in 2006, is one of Scotland's best long-distance walks. It stretches for 89 miles, beginning at Tarbert in the north of the peninsula and rambling all the way down to the village of Southend in the south. Hikers generally complete the route in 4 to 7 days. Some of the miles are difficult, although nothing to challenge the serious hiker, but miles and miles are filled with gentle rambles along panoramic scenery and rugged coastline, taking in castles, woodland, and wildlife (especially coastal birds) along the way. Pick up a map of the trail at any local tourist office or visit www. kintyreway.com.

WHERE TO STAY

Stonefield Castle Hotel ★★ Stonefield Castle occupies a commanding position in 24 hectares (60 acres) of wooded grounds and gardens 1¾ miles outside Tarbert. It was built in the 19th century in baronial style, with turrets and a steeply pitched roof. The smartly designed guest rooms have plush furnishings in warm colors, and views out over Loch Fyne. Some rooms have four-poster beds; others could be used as family suites. The hotel's gardens are stocked with plants from all over the world; they're particularly renowned for their collection of more than 20 species of tree-size Himalayan rhododendrons, which bloom in April. The formal restaurant serves meals based on produce from the hotel's garden. The hotel also bakes its own bread.

Tarbert, PA29 6YJ. www.oxfordhotelsandinns.com. ✆ **01880/820-836.** Fax 01880/820-929. 32 units. £130–£170 double. AE, MC, V. **Amenities:** Restaurant; bar; room service; Wi-Fi (free). *In room:* TV, hair dryer.

West Loch Hotel This 18th-century coaching inn stands in a rural setting beside the A83, 1 mile southwest of town in low-lying flatlands midway between the forest and the loch. The hotel has two bars, with open fireplaces and wood-burning stoves. The small guest rooms are modestly furnished but are comfortable enough, and many have views of the estuary. The hotel's restaurant serves home-style cooking based on local seafood and game.

Tarbert, PA29 6YF. www.westlochhotel.co.uk. ✆ **01880/820-283.** Fax 01880/820-930. 7 units. £80 double. MC, V. **Amenities:** Restaurant; 2 bars; room service. *In room:* TV, hair dryer.

Campbeltown

Campbeltown is a fishing port and resort at the southern tip of the Kintyre Peninsula, 176 miles northwest of Edinburgh and 135 miles northwest of Glasgow. Popularly known as the "wee toon," Campbeltown has long been linked with fishing and has a **shingle beach.**

The **Tourist Information Centre** is at MacKinnon House, The Pier (✆ **01586/552-056;** www.visitscottishheartlands.com). It's open from late June to mid-September, Monday through Saturday 9am to 6:30pm and Sunday 11am to 5pm; mid-September to late October, Monday through Friday 9am to 5pm and Sunday 11am to 4pm; late October to March, Monday through Friday 10am to 4pm; April, Monday through Saturday 9am to 5:30pm; and May to late June, Monday through Saturday 9am to 5:30pm and Sunday noon to 5pm.

EXPLORING THE AREA

On the quayside, in the heart of town, is the 14th-century **Campbeltown Cross.** This Celtic cross is the finest piece of carving from the Middle Ages left in Kintyre. Nearby, on St. Johns Street, is the **Campbeltown Museum** (① **01586/559-017;** www.museumsgalleriesscotland.org.uk), which has a small but high-quality collection of paintings by Scottish artists, as well as sections on archaeology and local history. The museum is open from Monday to Friday 9am to 5pm. Admission is free.

One of the area's most famous golf courses, the **Machrilhanish Golf Club,** is located nearby (① **01586/810-277;** www.machgolf.com). It's a 6,225-yard, par-70 course. Unfortunately, there's no facility to hire clubs here.

ENTERTAINMENT & NIGHTLIFE

The nightlife in Campbeltown revolves around its pubs, two of which host live music events. They can be found in the center of the village, next door to each other. **The Feathers Inn,** Cross Street (① **01586/554-604**), hosts bands playing a range of musical styles on Thursday nights. It's open daily from 11am to 1am. **The Commercial Inn,** also on Cross Street (① **01586/553-703**), has a variety of live music on Fridays and alternate Saturdays. A specialty here is real ale. It's open Monday to Saturday from 11am to 1am and Sunday from 12:30pm to 1am. You'll find a quieter evening at the **Burnside Bar,** Burnside Street (① **01586/552-306**), open daily from 11am to 1am. Conversation and local single malts are the preferred distractions here.

Cambeltown also has its own cinema, the **Wee Picture House,** 20 Hall St. (① **01586/553-800;** www.weepictures.co.uk). This Art Deco building dates back to 1913, and is believed to be the oldest surviving purpose-built cinema in Scotland.

WHERE TO EAT & STAY

The Argyll Arms   This hotel was originally built as a hunting lodge for the Duke of Argyll; his own suite is now Room 1. The public rooms are now a little dowdy, but the guest rooms have been modernized and, though modest, are quite comfortable. Family rooms are also available. The restaurant specializes in moderately priced dishes based on fish fresh from the quay. There's a lounge bar and a cocktail bar.

Main St., Campbeltown, PA28 6AB. www.argyllarmshotel.co.uk. ① **01586/553-431.** Fax 01586/553-594. 25 units. £65–£90 double. AE, MC, V. **Amenities:** Restaurant; 2 bars; Wi-Fi (free). *In room:* TV, hair dryer.

Craigard House   Built in 1882, this dignified, monastic-looking pile with a bell tower is perched on the northern edge of the loch, about a mile from the town center. The spacious guest rooms are traditionally furnished, and most open onto panoramic

---

📷 Escape to the Isle That Time Forgot

Davaar Island, in Campbeltown Loch, is accessible at low tide to those willing to cross the Dhorlin, a ⅔-mile run of shingle-paved causeway. Boat trips are also possible (ask at the tourist office; see above). Once on the island, you can visit a **crucifixion cave painting,** the work of local Archibald MacKinnon, painted in 1887. It takes about 1½ hours to walk around this tidal island, with its natural rock gardens.

A Journey to Blood Rock

Dunaverty Rock is a jagged hill marking the extreme southern tip of the Kintyre Peninsula. Located 9⅓ miles south of Campbeltown and called "Blood Rock" by the locals, it was once the site of a MacDonald stronghold known as Dunaverty Castle, although nothing remains of it today. In 1647, it was the scene of a great massacre, in which some 300 citizens lost their lives. You can reach it by a local bus (marked SOUTH END) traveling from Campbeltown south about six times a day. Nearby, you'll find a series of isolated, unsupervised beaches and the 18-hole **Dunaverty Golf Course** (✆ 01586/830-677; www.dunavertygolfclub.com).

views of Campbeltown Loch. One of the rooms has a four-poster bed, and five rooms could be used by families. The restaurant's weekly menu may include savory fish crepes, pan-fried duck breast with brandy and pepper-cream sauce, and chicken cacciatore.

Low Askomil, Campbeltown, PA28 6EP. www.craigard-house.co.uk. ✆ **01586/554-242.** Fax 01586/551-137. 13 units. £82–£135 double. AE, MC, V. **Amenities:** Restaurant; bar; room service. *In room:* TV, hair dryer, Wi-Fi (free).

Southend & the Mull of Kintyre

Some 10 miles south of Campbeltown on the B842 is the village of Southend. From Monday to Saturday, three buses a day run here from Campbeltown. Southend has sandy beaches, a golf course, and views across the sea to the Island of Sanda and to Ireland. Legend has it that footprints on a rock near the ruin of an old chapel mark the spot where St. Columba first set foot on Scottish soil. Other historians suggest that the footprints mark the spot where ancient kings were crowned.

About 11 miles from Campbeltown is the Mull of Kintyre, at the southwestern point of the peninsula. Starting at Southend, you take a narrow road until you reach the "gap," from which you can walk down to the lighthouse, a distance of 1½ miles before you reach the final point. Expect to be greeted with westerly gales as you walk. This is one of the wildest and most remote parts of Scotland, and it's this desolation that appeals to visitors. The Mull of Kintyre is only 13 miles from Ireland. When local resident Paul McCartney made it the subject of a song, hundreds of fans flocked to the area.

THE ISLE OF GIGHA & SCOTLAND'S FINEST GARDENS

3 miles W of Kintyre's western coast

The 6-mile long Isle of Gigha boasts Scotland's finest gardens. Often called sacred and legendary, little has changed on the southern Hebridean isle over the centuries. Indeed the island's inhabitants are intent on ensuring that things stay the same, and to this end clubbed together to buy the island in 2002 for £4 million. It is now managed by the Isle of Gigha Heritage Trust (www.gigha.org.uk). March 15, the day when the purchase was completed, is now celebrated by islanders as "Independence Day."

Essentials

GETTING THERE   You can take a **ferry** to Gigha from Tayinloan, halfway up the west coast of Kintyre on the A83. Sailings are daily on the hour during the summer, and take about 20 minutes, depositing you at **Ardminish,** the main hamlet on Gigha. The one-way fare is £12 for cars, plus £3.25 per passenger. For ferry schedules, call ℂ **0800/066-5000** or **01880/730-253** for the port office in Kennacraig, or log on to www.calmac.co.uk or www.gigha.org.uk.

VISITOR INFORMATION   There's no local tourist office, and so ask at Campbeltown on the Kintyre Peninsula (see "The Kintyre Peninsula," above).

GETTING AROUND   Most visitors to Gigha don't take their car, and choose to either walk or take a taxi (call **Oliver's Taxi** at ℂ **01583/505-251**). There's no bus service on the island.

Exploring the Island

The main attraction on Gigha is its famous gardens. Be prepared to spend your entire day walking. The **Achamore House Gardens ★★★** (ℂ **01583/505-400;** www. gigha.org.uk), 1 mile from the ferry dock at Ardminish, overflow with roses, hydrangeas, camellias, rhododendrons, and azaleas. The 20-hectare (49-acre) site was created by the late Sir James Horlick, one of the world's great horticulturalists. The gardens are open year-round, daily 9am to dusk. Admission is £5.

The island has a rich Viking past (the Vikings stored their loot here after plundering the west coast of Scotland), and cairns and ruins still remain. **Creag Bhan,** the highest hill, rises more than 100m (330 ft.). From the top you can look out onto the islands of Islay and Jura as well as Kintyre; on a clear day, you can even see across to Ireland. The **Ogham Stone** is one of only two standing stones in the Hebrides that bears an Ogham inscription, a form of script used in the Scottish kingdom of Dalriada. High on a ridge overlooking the village of Ardminish are the ruins of the **Church of Kilchattan,** dating back to the 13th century.

Where to Eat & Stay

Achamore House ★★   Set in the midst of some of the most beautiful gardens in Scotland, Achamore House is a grand baronial mansion built by a sea captain in 1884. It offers a dozen spacious and simply furnished rooms, with fine views. Each room has its own character, ranging from the Tower Suite, with its antique furnishings, to Col. Horlick's Room with its bay windows opening east over the gardens. There's even the Bridal Suite, with a super-king-size four-poster bed, plus an open fireplace and antiques. Guests can relax in the wooden-paneled library with its fine collection of books or else retreat to the TV lounge with some 500 DVDs to choose from. There's also a grand snooker room with a full-size table.

Isle of Gigha, PA41 7AA. www.achamorehouse.com. ℂ **01583/505-400.** Fax 01583/505-3287. 12 units. £70 double; £130 suite. MC, V. **Amenities:** Dining room. *In room:* No phone.

Gigha Hotel ★   Standing in a lonely, windswept location, this hotel is a 5-minute walk from the island's ferry landing. Built in the 1700s as a farmhouse, it's now owned by the Isle of Gigha Heritage Trust, and contains Gigha's only pub and one of its two restaurants. Each small but cozy room has a private bathroom. Fixed-price dinners are served daily to both guests and non-guests; reasonably priced bar lunches are also available.

Ardminish, Isle of Gigha, PA41 7AA. www.gigha.org.uk. © **01583/505-254.** Fax 01583/505-244. 13 units. £95–£140 double. Rates include half-board. MC, V. Closed Dec 24–26. **Amenities:** Restaurant; bar. *In room:* TV, hair dryer.

THE ISLE OF ISLAY: QUEEN OF THE HEBRIDES ★★

16 miles W of the Kintyre Peninsula; ⅔ mile SW of Jura

Islay (pronounced "*Eye*-lay") is the southernmost island of the Inner Hebrides, separated only by a narrow sound from Jura. The island is only 20 miles at its widest point, and 25 miles long. Often referred to as the "Queen of the Hebrides," it's a peaceful and unspoiled island of moors, salmon-filled lochs, sandy bays, and wild rocky cliffs—an island of great beauty, ideal for long walks.

Essentials

GETTING THERE   Caledonian MacBrayne (© **08705/650-000** or **01880/ 730-253** for the port office at Kennacraig; www.calmac.co.uk) provides a daily ferry service from Kennacraig on the Kintyre peninsula to Port Askaig, on the northeastern coast of Islay. In the summer there are up to four ferries a day. The cost is £51 per car and £9.55 per passenger each way (a 5-day round-trip ticket is more economical). The journey takes about 2 hours.

VISITOR INFORMATION   The Islay Tourist Information Centre can be found at The Square, Bowmore (© **01496/810-254;** www.islayinfo.com). Opening hours are: April to June, Monday through Saturday 10am to 5pm, Sunday 2 to 5pm; July and August, Monday through Saturday 9:30am to 5:30pm, Sunday 2 to 5pm; September and October, Monday through Saturday 10am to 5pm.

Exploring the Island

The island's capital is **Bowmore,** on the opposite coast from Port Askaig, down the A846. Here you can see a fascinating Round Church (no corners for the devil to hide in). But the most important town is **Port Ellen,** on the south coast, a holiday and golfing resort and Islay's principal port. The 18-hole **Machrie golf course** (© **01496/302-310;** www.machrie.com) is 3 miles to the northwest of Port Ellen.

About 7½ miles to the northeast of Port Ellen are the ancient **Kildalton Crosses** in Kildalton churchyard. They're two of the finest Celtic crosses in Scotland. The ruins of the 14th-century fortress, **Dunyvaig Castle,** are just to the south of Kildalton.

In the southwestern part of Islay, in Port Charlotte, the **Museum of Islay Life** (© **01496/850-358;** www.islaymuseum.org) has a large collection of island artifacts dating from prehistory to the present. From Easter to October, the museum is open Monday through Saturday 10am to 4pm. Admission is £3 for adults, £2 for seniors, and £1 for children aged 5 to 16. If traveling without a car, the Portnahaven bus from Bowmore stops here.

Near **Port Charlotte** are the graves of the U.S. seamen and army troops who lost their lives in 1918 when their carriers, the *Tuscania* and the *Otranto,* were torpedoed off the shores of Islay. There's a memorial tower on the **Mull of Oa,** 8 miles from Port Ellen. There's a fine walk to be had by going along the Mull of Oa Road toward the signposted solar-powered Carraig Fhada lighthouse, some 1½ miles away. The Oa peninsula was once the haunt of illicit whisky distillers and smugglers; the area is filled with sheer cliffs that are riddled with caves.

Loch Gruinart cuts into the northern part of Islay, 6¾ miles northeast of Port Charlotte and 8 miles north of Bowmore. As the winter home for wild geese, it has attracted bird-watchers for decades. In 1984, the 1,215 hectares (3,000 acres) of moors and farmland around the loch were turned into the **Loch Gruinart Nature Reserve** (© 01496/850-505; www.rspb.org.uk). The reserve has a hide, nature trails, a visitor center, toilet facilities, and disabled access.

This is another place for great walks. Beaches rise out of the falling tides, but they're too cold and rocky for serious swimming. It's a lonely and bleak coastline, but on a clear day, you can see the Hebridean islands of Oronsay and Colonsay in the distance.

Visiting the Distilleries

The island is noted for its distilleries, which still produce single-malt Highland whiskies by the antiquated pot-still method. Of these, **Laphroaig Distillery,** about a mile along the road from Ardbeg to Port Ellen (© **01496/302-418;** www.laphroaig. com), offers guided tours Monday through Friday at 10 and 2pm. The tour costs £3 per person, but the admission to the visitor center is free. Places on tours can be booked by telephoning or filling in the form on the website. **Lagavulin,** Port Ellen near the south coast of Islay (© **01496/302-749**), is open Monday through Friday from 9:30am to 4:30pm. Tours are by appointment only. Admission is £5 per person and comes with a complementary shot of whisky. A distillery gift shop is open Monday through Friday 8:30am to noon and 1 to 4:30pm.

Bowmore Distillery, School Street, Bowmore (© **01496/810-441;** www. bowmore.com), conducts tours Monday through Saturday at 10 and 11am and 2 and 3pm from Easter to August; during July and August there are also tours at 1pm and 2pm on Sundays; from September to Easter, tours are at 10:30am and 3pm on weekdays, and at 10am on Saturdays. Admission is £5 for adults, and free for children under 18. A whisky tasting is included in the tour (though not for children). You can make purchases without taking the tour by stopping in at the gift shop in the visitor center. It's open Monday through Friday 9am to 5pm, Saturday 9am to 5pm between Easter and mid-September, and Sunday noon until 4pm from July to mid-September.

Port Askaig is home to **Bunnahabhain** (© **01496/840-646;** www. bunnahabhain.com), which is open year-round Monday through Friday. From April to October, hour-long tours are conducted at 10:30am, 1:30pm, and 3:15pm. Tours cost £4. From November to March, tours can be arranged by appointment. Tasting tours (£15) and VIP tours (£25) can also be booked year-round by appointment.

Where to Eat

The Croft Kitchen ★ 🍴 BRITISH   While this single-story cafe-restaurant on the main highway running through Port Charlotte may seem unprepossessing from the outside, it's well worth venturing across the threshold for its homey cooking and welcoming atmosphere. Situated opposite the Museum of Islay Life, it's a handy place to keep in mind for tea and scones in the afternoon or an unpretentious meal of comforting food. The menu changes daily, and includes lots of fresh fish and shellfish, as well as soups, Islay venison with rowanberry jelly, and fresh scampi and chips.

Holding no more than 40 customers at a time, it serves wine, beer, and, of course, whisky, along with generous portions of food.

Port Charlotte, Isle of Islay. ✆ **01496/850-230.** Sandwiches £5–£8.95; lunch main courses £10–£17, dinner main courses £12–£20. MC, V. Daily 10am–8:30pm (last order). Closed mid-Oct to mid-Mar.

Harbour Inn Restaurant ★ SEAFOOD/MODERN BRITISH The fish and seafood at the Harbour Inn is renowned for its freshness and sure-handed preparation. The catch of the day can include lobster and crab, monkfish, scallops, mussels, and oysters. Dishes include scallops with beetroot jam and a lime dressing, and fillet of monkfish wrapped in oak-smoked salmon on a mushroom risotto with a citrus and honey vierge. If seafood is not to your taste, there's pheasant, pigeon, and venison, or Islay beef and lamb. Vegetarians can feast on celeriac tart with sweet peppers and goat's cheese, or wild mushroom risotto. Desserts include jelly and ice cream— though with a little more sophistication than the old-fashioned children's party staple; the homemade ice cream comes in flavors such as rosewater and honey, basil, licorice, and crème de cassis.

The Square, Bowmore, Isle of Islay, Argyll, PA43 7JR. ✆ **01496/810-330.** Reservations recommended on weekends. Lunch main courses £8–£17

Shopping

The **Islay Woollen Mill,** Bridgend (✆ **01496/810-563;** www.islaywoollenmill. co.uk), has been making a wide range of country tweeds and accessories for more than a century. (It made all the tweeds used in Mel Gibson's *Braveheart.*) The mill shop, open Monday through Saturday from 10am to 5pm, sells items made with the *Braveheart* tweeds as well as smart Shetland wool ties, mufflers, Jacob mufflers and ties, flat caps, travel rugs, and scarves.

Entertainment & Nightlife

After work, distillery employees gather at the pub at the **Harbour Inn,** Main Street in Bowmore (✆ **01496/810-330**). This old-fashioned pub, with stone walls, a fireplace, and wooden floors, is open Monday through Saturday from 11am to 1am and on Sunday from noon to 1am. There is, of course, a good selection of single-malt whiskies, some of which have been distilled on Islay itself. Local seafood is served at lunch and dinner. In summer, reservations for meals are recommended.

Where to Stay

Bridgend Hotel ★ This pretty gabled Victorian house has roses creeping up the walls, and one of the most beautiful flower and vegetable gardens on Islay. It's also one of the oldest hotels on the island, with country charm and an informal atmosphere. Guests enjoy drinks beside the open fireplaces in the Victorian cocktail lounge and in the pub, where locals also gather at the end of the day. The mid-size bedrooms are furnished comfortably in muted colors. The hotel restaurant serves up local produce at lunch and dinner to both guests and non-guests. Game—including pheasant, partridge, and woodcock—are specialties.

Bridgend, Isle of Islay PA44 7PJ. www.bridgend-hotel.com. ✆ **01496/810-212.** Fax 01496/810-960. 11 units. £90–£150 double; £160 family room. MC, V. **Amenities:** Restaurant; 2 bars; room service; Wi-Fi (free). *In room:* TV/DVD, hair dryer.

Harbour Inn Although this family-run establishment is better known for its seafood restaurant (see above), it also offers seven bedrooms overlooking Bowmore

Harbour. Each room is bright and airy, with its own individual decoration. Children over the age of 10 are welcome, and two of the guestrooms are suitable for family occupation. The building dates from the 19th century but is completely modernized. The conservatory lounge adjacent to the street-level dining room has fine views of northern Islay and over to the Paps of Jura.

The Square, Bowmore, Isle of Islay, Argyll, PA43 7JR. www.harbour-inn.com. ✆ **01496/810-330.** Fax 01496/810-990. 7 units. £125–£155 double. AE, MC, V. **Amenities:** Restaurant; lounge-bar; babysitting. *In room:* TV, hair dryer.

Port Askaig Hotel   Located on the Sound of Islay overlooking the pier from where ferries depart, this inn dates from the 18th century but was built on the site of an even older inn. It offers island hospitality and Scottish fare and is a favorite of anglers. The bar is popular with locals as well as hotel guests, and you can sit outside in the summer on the front lawn. Bar meals are available for lunch and dinner. The guest rooms are simply decorated with pine furniture.

The A846 at the ferry crossing to Jura, Port Askaig, Isle of Islay, PA46 7RD. www.portaskaig.co.uk. ✆ **01496/840-245.** Fax 01496/840-295. 11 units. £70–£135 double. AE, MC, V. **Amenities:** Restaurant; 2 bars; room service. *In room:* TV, hair dryer.

Port Charlotte Hotel   This 19th-century hotel—actually a trio of cottages joined together—stands next to the small sandy beaches of Port Charlotte with views over Loch Indaal. The guest rooms are immaculately kept, with recently refurbished bathrooms. The hotel's public areas include a bar serving local ales, a comfortable lounge, and a conservatory with views out over the sea.

The Port Charlotte is also the best place to dine in the area. The menu includes lobster, crab, oysters, and scallops, and there's also a good selection of game from the island's estates, including partridge and woodcock. Vegetarians are also catered for, and packed lunches are available on request.

Main St., Port Charlotte, Isle of Islay, PA48 7TU. www.portcharlottehotel.co.uk. ✆ **01496/850-360.** Fax 01496/850-361. 10 units. £170 double; £190 family room. MC, V. **Amenities:** Restaurant; bar; bike rentals; room service. *In room:* TV, hair dryer.

THE ISLE OF JURA: DEER ISLAND ★

⅔ mile E of Islay

Jura is the fourth largest of the Inner Hebrides, 27 miles long and varying from 1¾ to 8 miles in breadth. It takes its name from the Norse *jura*, meaning "deer." The red deer on Jura—Scotland's largest animals, at around 1.2m (4 ft.) in height—outnumber people by about 25 to 1. The hardy islanders themselves number only about 250, and most of them live along the east coast. Jura is relatively unknown, and its mountains, soaring cliffs, snug coves, and moors make it an inviting place for a peaceful holiday.

Essentials

GETTING THERE   Visitors to Jura have to catch the ferry from Kennacraig on the Kintyre peninsula to Port Askaig, on the Isle of Islay; from there, they take a second ferry across the Sound of Islay to Feolin at the southern tip of Jura. **Caledonian MacBrayne** (✆ **08705/650-000** or 01880/730-253 for the port office at Kennacraig; www.calmac.co.uk) operates the ferry for the first leg of the trip. In the summer there are up to four ferries a day. The cost is £51 per car and £9.55 per passenger

> ## The Gloom & Doom of Orwell's *1984*
>
> George Orwell was quite ill when he lived on Jura in the bitter postwar winters of 1946 and 1947, while working on his last novel, *1984*. After a close call when he and his adopted son ventured too close to the whirlpool in the Gulf of Corryvreckan—they were saved by local fishermen—he went on to publish his masterpiece in 1949, only to die in London of tuberculosis in 1950.

each way (a 5-day round-trip ticket is more economical). The ferry for the 5-minute trip from Port Askaig to Feolin on Jura is operated by **ASP Ship Management Ltd** (© **01496/840-681;** see www.islayinfo.com/jura-ferry.html for details). Ferries run daily, approximately every half-hour during the summer. The round-trip fare for passengers is about £4, and for cars £15. Car spaces must be booked in advance for both legs of the journey.

VISITOR INFORMATION The Isle of Islay (see "The Isle of Islay: Queen of the Hebrides," above) has the nearest Tourist Information Centre. Otherwise, for information, visit **www.isleofjura.com**.

Exploring the Island

Jura has only one road, the A846, which begins at Feolin (which is little more than the anchoring place for the ferry) and runs up the east coast of the island as far as the village of Lussagiven. The west of the island is largely uninhabited. Because most of the island is therefore accessible only on foot, visitors should wear sturdy walking shoes and bring rain gear. Most walkers head for the so-called **Paps of Jura,** the three steep conical mountains of quartzite on the western side of the island. The highest of these is Beinn-an-Oir (or "mountain of gold" in Gaelic), which stands at 786m (2,575 ft.) in height.

For those who prefer a gentler stroll, the **Jura House Garden & Grounds** (© **01496/820-315**) at the southern tip of the island is the best place. Situated halfway between Feolin and Craighouse, these gardens were laid out by the Victorians to take advantage of the warmer microclimate on this part of the island. Unfortunately, following the purchase of the property by an Australian hedge-fund manager, the gardens have been temporarily closed; it is expected that they will reopen once suitable arrangements have been made to receive visitors again.

Just off the coast to the southwest of Jura House is Am Fraoch Eilean. This island accommodates the ruins of the square tower of **Claig Castle,** which in centuries past was used by the Lords of the Isles to control sea traffic around the islands.

The island's capital, **Craighouse,** is hardly more than a hamlet. It has the island's only shop, church, and hotel (see below). It also has its own whisky distillery (© **01496/820-385;** www.isleofjura.com). Guided tours are offered to visitors from April to September, Monday through Friday at 11am and 2pm. Advance booking is required.

Where to Eat & Stay

Jura Hotel ★ ⬛ The island's only hotel is a sprawling white-washed building near the center of the hamlet of Craighouse (due east of Feolin along the coast). Parts of the hotel date from the 1600s, but most of what you see today was built in 1956. The mid-size guest rooms are decorated with all modern comforts. In this remote outpost, you'll get a tranquil night's sleep. Affordable meals are served daily at lunch and dinner; the dining room's specialty is Jura-bred venison. The hotel also incorporates the island's only pub; it too serves hearty and tasty meals at both lunch- and dinnertime.

Craighouse, Isle of Jura, PA60 7XU. www.jurahotel.co.uk. © **01496/820-243.** Fax 01496/820-249. 18 units, 12 with private bathroom. £78–112 double; £132–192 family room. AE, DC, MC, V. Closed 2 weeks Dec–Jan. **Amenities:** Restaurant; bar; bikes; room service. *In room:* No phone.

KNAPDALE & THE CRINAN CANAL ★

Knapdale is the area of Argyll between Kintyre in the south and the Crinan Canal to the north. Its main feature is Knapdale Forest, planted in the 1930s as a project by the Ministry of Labour to create work for unemployed men from depressed industrial areas of Britain.

The Crinan Canal starts at Ardrishaig on Loch Fyne, and ends 9 miles away at the village of Crinan on the Sound of Jura. It was built to provide a quick link between the Clyde Estuary and the west coast and islands, avoiding the long voyage around the Kintyre Peninsula. It was designed by John Rennie, and completed in 1801 after 7 years of work. The canal's traffic originally comprised commercial sailing vessels and later Clyde puffers; today it's mostly private yachts. The towpath makes a picturesque walk, past fifteen locks, seven bridges, two lighthouses, and numerous lock-keepers' cottages.

Essentials

GETTING THERE   The most efficient way to travel around Knapdale is by car. From Glasgow, take the A82 up to Loch Lomond and cut across to Arrochar and go over the "Rest and Be Thankful" route to Inveraray (the A83). Then drive down along Loch Fyne to Lochgilphead and continue on the A83 south. If, on the other hand, you're driving from Oban, simply head south along the A816.

For bus and rail connections, see under "Inveraray" below.

VISITOR INFORMATION   The nearest **Tourist Information Centre** is located at Lochnell Street in Lochgilphead (© **01546/602-344;** www.heartofargyll.com). It's open from April to October, Monday through Friday 10am to 5pm, and Saturday and Sunday noon to 5pm.

Exploring the Area

Knapdale is an ancient landscape. It has some of Scotland's best native woodlands—as, for example, at **Taynish National Nature Reserve** (© **01546/603-611;** www.nnr-scotland.org.uk/taynish), where you can follow the nature trails (or cycle paths) and see up to 20 species of butterflies, rare birds, and, if lucky, otters. The reserve is located about 1 mile south of Tayvallich village.

You can see a different natural habitat at **Moine Mhor** or "Great Moss" (© **01546/603-611;** www.nnr-scotland.org.uk/moine-mhor), which is best approached from the tow path of the Crinan Canal, near Bellanoch, where there's a bird hide. The waterlogged system of pools and bogs are home for hen harriers and ospreys in the summer, and geese and swans in winter.

On the B8025 going south from Bellanoch towards Tayvallich is the information center and observation hide of the **Scottish Beaver Trial** at Barnluasgan (✆ **01546/602-518;** www.scottishbeavers.org.uk). A 5-year trial reintroduction of beavers into Knapdale Forest began in 2009. The animals can best be seen at dusk and dawn. Guided beaver walks are offered on Tuesdays at 6pm from June to August.

To the north of the Crinan Canal is **Kilmartin Glen,** which is the location of over 800 ancient sites and monuments, including standing stones, burial tombs, and forts. Around 1,500 years ago, it was the center of the Gaelic Kingdom of Dalriada. The best place to start exploring the area is the **Kilmartin House Museum** (✆ **01546/510-278;** www.kilmartin.org), where you can see archaeological finds and get maps and information for going out to see the most important monuments in the field. Museum opening hours are March to October daily from 10am to 5:30pm, November to December daily from 11am to 4pm; closed from Christmas to the end of February. Admission charges are £5 for adults, £4 for seniors, and £2 for children.

Where to Eat & Stay

Cairnbaan Hotel ★★ Occupying an idyllic spot in the hamlet of Cairnbaan, at Lock 5, about halfway along the Crinan Canal, this is certainly the best hotel in the area. It was built in 1801 to coincide with the opening of the canal, and you can still watch the boats progress through the lock from its front windows. All the guest rooms have recently been refurbished, and offer comfortable and cozy accommodation—perfect for a good night's sleep. (The hotel has played host to the Princess Royal, as well as Bill and Hilary Clinton, and so presumably they thought so, too.)

The hotel's wooden-paneled bar is a warm and jolly affair serving real ale, good wine, a wide selection of malt whiskies, and reasonably priced bar meals (from the daily specials on the blackboard). The restaurant offers an a la carte menu using the best seasonal produce. Beef is supplied by the Ormsary Estate, lamb and pork come from local farmers, fresh game from a local hunter, and fish and seafood from local fishermen. The cooking brings out these ingredients with maximum flavor and minimum fuss. To drink, you can select from the wine list of 50 bins (with particular strength in Bordeaux). Lunch and dinner is served daily to both guests and non-guests.

Cairnbaan, near Lochgilphead, PA31 8SJ. www.cairnbaan.com. ✆ **01546/603-668.** info@cairnbaan. com. 12 units. £98.50–£155 double. AE, MC, V. From Inveraray, drive south on the A83 to Lochgilphead (passing through the villages of Furnace and Minard on the way). At Lochgilphead you come to a small roundabout; follow the signs for Oban and the A816. The Hotel is approximately 2 miles from this roundabout on your left hand side. **Amenities:** Restaurant; bar; room service; Wi-Fi (free). *In room:* TV, hair dryer.

INVERARAY ★★

99 miles NW of Edinburgh; 57 miles NW of Glasgow; 38 miles SE of Oban

The small resort and royal burgh of Inveraray occupies a splendid setting on the upper shores of Loch Fyne. It's particularly attractive when you approach from the east on the A83. Across a little inlet, you can see the white buildings of the town lying peacefully on a piece of land jutting out into the loch.

Essentials

GETTING THERE   The nearest **train station** is at Dumbarton, 45 miles southeast, from where you can take connecting buses to Inveraray. For rail schedules, call ✆ **08457/484-950,** or visit www.nationalrail.co.uk.

The Citylink-926 Service operates **buses** out of Glasgow, heading for Dumbarton, before continuing to Inveraray. The journey takes about 2 hours. From Monday to Saturday, three buses make this run each day (only two on Sun). For bus schedules, call © **08705/505-050,** or visit www.citylink.co.uk.

If you're driving from Oban, head east along the A85 until you reach the junction with the A819, at which point you continue south.

VISITOR INFORMATION The **Tourist Information Centre** is on Front Street (© **01499/302-063;** www.inveraray-argyll.com). It's open from June to mid-September, daily 9am to 6pm; mid-September to October, April, and May, Monday through Saturday 10am to 3pm and Sunday noon to 5pm; and November to March, daily noon to 4pm.

Exploring the Area

At one end of the town's main street is a **Celtic burial cross** from Iona. The parish church is divided by a wall that enables Mass to be held simultaneously in Gaelic and English.

A local beauty spot is the **Ardkinglas Woodland Garden** (© **01499/600-261;** www.ardkinglas.com), 4 miles east of Inveraray, at the head of Loch Fyne. People drive from all over Scotland to see the country's greatest collection of conifers and its masses of rhododendrons bursting into bloom in June. Admission is £4.50 for adults, £3.50 for seniors, and free for under-16s; it's open daily from 9am to 5pm.

Arctic Penguin Heritage Centre MUSEUM   Occupying a former lightship, a three-masted schooner constructed in 1911 called the *Arctic Penguin,* this museum is a mecca for those who love maritime history. Visitors can also see the engine room, the Captain's stateroom, and the Grog Barrels. In stark contrast, there's also the luxurious Lady's Cabin, where the lady of the ship used to spend her time. Exhibits detail the history of Glasgow docks and the launching of the original *Queen Mary* (now in dry dock in California). There's also all manner of maritime memorabilia—even a handcrafted shell valentine made by a mariner for his love. The ship even has its own cinema, where visitors can see a short film on seafaring history.

The Pier, Inveraray. © **01499/302-213.** www.inveraraypier.com. Admission £5 adults, £3 seniors and students, £2.50 children 5–16, £14 families. Daily 10am–5pm.

Crarae Glen Gardens ★ GARDEN   Lying alongside Loch Fyne, these are among Scotland's most beautiful gardens, comprising some 20 hectares (50 acres) of rich woodland with a burn, waterfalls, and fine vistas over the loch. The exoticism of the vegetation, and the gorges and cascades, create the feeling of a Himalayan valley.

8 miles southwest of Inveraray along the A83, near the hamlet of Minard. © **0844/493-2210.** www.nts. org.uk/Property/19. Admission £6 adults, £5 children 5–16, £15.50 families. Gardens open year-round daily 9:30am–sunset; visitor center open Apr–Oct Thurs–Mon 10am–5pm.

Inveraray Castle ★★ CASTLE   The hereditary seat of the dukes of Argyll, Inveraray Castle has been headquarters of Clan Campbell since the early 15th century. The gray-green stone castle is among the earliest examples of the Gothic Revival in Britain, and offers a fine collection of pictures and 18th-century French furniture, old porcelain, and an Armoury Hall, which alone contains 1,300 pieces. In the grounds is a **Combined Operations Museum,** the only one of its kind in the United Kingdom. It illustrates the role No. 1 Combined Training Centre played at Inveraray in World War II. On display are scale models, newspaper reports, campaign

HIKING IN ARGYLL forest PARK

Argyll Forest Park, in the southern Highlands, stretches almost to Loch Fyne and is made up of Benmore, Ardgartan, and Glenbranter. The park covers an area of 24,000 hectares (59,000 acres), contains some of Scotland's most dramatic scenery, and includes a wide variety of habitats, from lush forests to bleak moorlands and mountains. The Clyde sea lochs cut deeply into the forested areas, somewhat in the way fjord "fingers" cut into the Norwegian coast; in the northern part are the Arrochar Alps (so called), where **Ben Arthur** reaches a height of 877m (2,877 ft.).

The park attracts not only those interested in natural history and wildlife but also rock climbers and hill walkers. There are forest walks for all degrees of fitness and experience. Trails leading up to the loftier peaks are strenuous and meant for skilled hikers; others are quite gentle, including paths from the **Younger Botanic Garden** by Loch Eck leading to Puck's Glen.

There's abundant wildlife in the sea lochs: basking sharks, sea otters, gray seals, sea scorpions, crabs, shrimp, sea lemons, and sea slugs, among many other inhabitants. Boats and canoes are available for rent. One of the park's biggest thrills is exploring the underwater caves of Loch Long.

In the early spring and summer, the park trails are at their most beautiful—woodland birds sing out their territorial rights, and the forest is filled with violets, wood anemones, primroses, and bluebells. Sometimes the wildflowers are as thick as carpets. In the rainy climate of the southern Highlands, ferns and mosses also grow in abundance.

To reach the park, take the A83 to connect with the B828 heading for Loch Goll, or follow the A815 to Loch Eck and Loch Long. Both of the Arrochar and Tarbert stops on the Glasgow–Fort William rail line are on the periphery of the park's northeast frontier.

The best place for lodging is **Dunoon,** to the south on the Cowal Peninsula—an easy gateway to the park. Dunoon has been a holiday resort since 1790, created for the "merchant princes" of Glasgow. Recreational facilities abound, including an indoor pool, tennis courts, and an 18-hole golf course. To pick up information about the park and a trail map, go to the **Dunoon Tourist Centre,** 7 Alexandra Parade (© **01369/703-785;** www.visitcowal.co.uk). It's open April to September, Monday through Friday 9am to 5:30pm and Saturday and Sunday 10am to 5pm; October to March, Monday through Thursday 9am to 5pm, Friday 10am to 5pm, and Saturday and Sunday 10am to 4pm.

maps, photographs, wartime posters and cartoons, training scenes, and other mementos. A shop sells souvenirs, and a tearoom serves homemade cakes and scones.

⅔ mile northeast of Inveraray on Loch Fyne. © **01499/302-203.** www.inveraray-castle.com. Admission £9.20 adults, £7.60 seniors and students, £6.20 children 5–16, £25.50 families. Apr–Oct daily 10am–5:45pm.

Where to Eat & Stay

Argyll Hotel   This waterfront inn, built in 1755, boasts views over Loch Fyne and Loch Shira. The comfortable, mid-size guest rooms are decorated in a traditional style with reproduction antique furniture and chintz fabrics. Four so-called executive rooms have either four-poster or Queen Anne beds. The hotel has its own public bar, a guests-only cocktail lounge, and a smart restaurant for evening meals (also open to non-guests). The menu features fish and seafood from Loch Fyne.

Front St., Inveraray, PA32 8XB. www.oxfordhotelsandinns.com. (?) **08444/146-600**. Fax 01499/302-389. 38 units. £100–£160 double. AE, DC, MC, V. **Amenities:** Restaurant; 2 bars; room service. *In room:* TV, hair dryer, Wi-Fi (£12 per day).

The Creggans Inn　This inn commemorates the spot where Mary Queen of Scots is said to have disembarked from her ship in 1563 on her way through the Highlands. Painted white and flanked by gardens, the inn is situated across the road (the A815) from the shores of the loch. It is owned by Sir Charles MacLean and his mother, Lady MacLean, author of several best-selling cookbooks, many of which are for sale here. The well-maintained guest rooms are furnished in a cozy cottage style. Guests also have the use of the upstairs sitting room and the garden-style lounge.

The hotel's formal restaurant serves dinner every evening from 6:30 until 8pm. Specialties include Aberdeen Angus steaks, fresh seafood, and venison. Reservations are required in season. The bar offers pub lunches beside an open fire.

Strachur, PA27 8BX. www.creggans-inn.co.uk. (?) **01369/860-279**. Fax 01369/860-637. 14 units. £100–£180 double. AE, DC, MC, V. **Amenities:** Restaurant; bar; room service. *In room:* TV, hair dryer.

The George Hotel ★　The George is perhaps the most atmospheric hotel in Inveraray. It was formed in 1860 from two private houses that were built in 1770. The street-level welcoming bar was once divided up for use as two churches: one of the Gaelic-speaking congregation and the other for English-speakers. The hotel's public areas are graced with flagstone floors, beamed ceilings, and blazing fireplaces. The guest rooms are cozy, done in old-fashioned Scottish style, some with wooden paneling and tartan carpet. Some also have four-poster beds and claw-foot tubs, full-length Victorian roll-top bathtubs, or Jacuzzis.

The restaurant is among the town's most popular, serving moderately priced lunches and dinners daily. Your options include steaks prepared with pepper or mushroom sauce, grilled halibut, and grilled Loch Fyne salmon with white wine, prawns, and scallops.

Main St. E., Inveraray, PA32 8TT. www.thegeorgehotel.co.uk. (?) **01499/302-111**. Fax 01499/302-098. 17 units. £70–£165 double. AE, DC, MC, V. **Amenities:** Restaurant; 2 bars. *In room:* TV, TV/DVD (in some), Jacuzzi (in some).

LOCH AWE & LOCH ETIVE ★

99 miles NW of Edinburgh; 24 miles E of Oban; 68 miles NW of Glasgow

Only 1 mile wide in most places and 22 miles long, Loch Awe is the longest loch in Scotland. It once served as a natural freshwater moat protecting the Campbells of Inveraray from their enemies to the north; along its banks are the many remains of fortifications from times past. The Forestry Commission has vast forests and signposted trails in this area, and a modern road makes it possible to travel around Loch Awe. It's therefore all the more accessible to walkers, anglers, and bird-watchers.

To the north, the waters of Loch Awe drain via the River Awe through the Brander Pass into Loch Etive, which itself flows into the Atlantic at Connel, a village 3 miles to the north of Oban. A large cantilevered bridge spans the mouth of the loch at the Falls of Lora, a tidal race that's particularly popular with white-water kayakers.

Essentials

GETTING THERE   The nearest train station is in Oban, from where you need to take a connecting bus. **Scottish Citylink,** 1 Queens Park Place, in Oban (call ℂ **01631/562-856** for schedules), has a service from Oban to Glasgow with stopovers at Loch Awe. During the summer season, services from Edinburgh run to Bridge of Orchy and Dalmally. Services from Glasgow run to Dalmally and Lochawe.

If you're driving from Oban, the A85 takes you north, and then east at the village of Connel, where Loch Etive flows into the sea. Staying all the way on the A85, continue via Taynuilt and Bridge of Awe to the northern end of Loch Awe itself.

VISITOR INFORMATION   Consult the **Tourist Information Centre** in Oban (see "Oban," below) and **www.loch-awe.com**.

Exploring the Area

To the east of the top of Loch Awe is **Dalmally,** a small but historically important town. Its unusual 18th-century church is built in an octagonal shape.

For reminders of the days when the Campbells of Inveraray held supreme power in the region of Loch Awe, there's a ruined **castle** at Fincharn, at the southern end of the loch, and another on the island of Fraoch Eilean. The Isle of Inishail has an ancient **chapel and burial ground.**

The bulk of **Ben Cruachan,** rising to 1,119m (3,671 ft.), dominates Loch Awe at its northern end and attracts climbers and hikers. The mountain is also notable as the site of the world's second-largest **hydroelectric power station,** which pumps water from Loch Awe to a reservoir high above. You can join a guided tour of the turbine hall, and there's an exhibition center and cafe (ℂ **01866/822-618;** www.visit cruachan.co.uk). To find it, drive 19 miles east of Oban on the A85. It's open from April to October daily from 9:30am to 4:45pm. From November to March, opening times are Monday through Friday 10am to 3:45pm. The visitor center is usually closed from mid-December until the end of January. The guided tour costs £6 for adults, £5 for seniors and students, and £2.50 for children aged from 6 to 16 years. In order to encourage low-carbon travel, visitors who arrive by bicycle or by public transport gain free admission.

In the shadow of the mountain are the **Falls of Cruachan** and the wild **Pass of Brander,** where Robert the Bruce routed the Clan MacDougall in 1308. The waters of the Awe flow through this pass on their way to Loch Etive. The latter, a sea loch, winds for 19 miles, from Dun Dunstaffnage Bay, at Oban, to Glen Etive and the Moor of Rannoch at the foot of the 910m (3,000-ft.) **Buachaille Etive (the Shepherd of Etive).**

Where to Eat & Stay

Barcaldine House ★★★   This elegant country house was built in 1709 after the local branch of the Campbell family decided that their nearby castle was no longer comfortable enough. Comfort remains the watchword today, and the welcoming atmosphere and luster of the surroundings make you feel that the hotel is your very own country house. The luxurious guest rooms are decorated with antique furniture, warm fabrics, and plush upholstery. Each has its own character and a wealth of 18th- and 19th-century details, from the cornices to the fireplaces. The public rooms are no less stylish. The lounge, where you can have a champagne afternoon tea, has a

Castle of the Once Mighty Campbells

The ruins of **Kilchurn Castle** can be found at the northern tip of Loch Awe, west of Dalmally, and across from the south-bank village of Loch Awe. A stronghold of the Campbells of Glen Orchy in the mid-15th century, it's a spectacular ruin with much of the original structure intact. The ruins have, in recent years, been reinforced and provided with balconies, so you can now explore them when the weather permits.

Kilchurn Castle is owned by Historic Scotland (www.historic-scotland.gov.

uk). It's open from April to September (there's no admission charge). The castle is accessible on foot from the Dalmally roadside (the A85) under the railway viaduct.

You can also see the castle from Loch Awe itself, by taking a steamboat cruise. The **Ardanaiseig Hotel** (✆ **01866/833-333**; www.ardanaiseig. com) runs cruises on a chartered basis, costing £100 to £150 per hour; passengers can share the cost. The trip takes about 30 minutes each way.

---

roaring fire, fine period furniture, and a grand display of malt whiskies on the sideboard. There's also a grand Victorian games room with a full-size snooker table.

Guests and non-guests can enjoy the exquisite cuisine in the dining room. The chef, Oskars Kalnins, trained with Andrew Fairlie at the acclaimed Gleneagles (p. 289), and it shows. The six-course dinner (£50) is a sumptuous affair, with the finest local produce (venison, lamb, scallops, halibut, turbot) and a generous array of luxury ingredients, from foie gras to truffles. All the dishes are executed with refinement and precision. The set lunches are a bargain at about £18 per person.

Barcaldine, on the A828 north of Oban, PA37 1SG. www.barcaldinehouse.co.uk. ✆ **01631/720-219.** Fax 01631/720-540. 11 units. £180–£230 double. AE, DC, MC, V. Drive 3 miles north of Oban on the A85 to the village of Connel, and then cross the bridge over Loch Etive to join the A828. The village of Barcaldine is another 9 miles to the north (going in the direction of Fort William). Look for the signs on the right hand side of the main road. **Amenities:** Restaurant; lounge; snooker room. In room: TV, hair dryer, Wi-Fi (free).

Hotel Ardanaiseig ★★   Although this gray-stone manor house was built in 1834, the architect, William Burn, designed it along 18th-century lines. He also planted what are now some of the rarest trees in Britain—many of them exotic conifers. Clusters of fruit trees stand in a walled garden, and the rhododendrons and azaleas are a wonderful spectacle in May and June. The hotel retains the country-house elegance and period furnishings of its earlier years as a private house. The formal sitting rooms are graced with comfortable sofas, fresh flowers, and polished tables. The guest rooms are named after various local mountains and lochs, and are also furnished with antiques; some have four-poster beds. In the restaurant, the five-course dinner menu offers guests an impressive display of precision cooking.

Kilchrenan by Taynuilt, PA35 1HE. www.ardanaiseig.com. ✆ **01866/833-333.** Fax 01866/833-222. 16 units. £138–£428 double. AE, DC, MC, V. Closed Jan to mid-Feb. Drive 21 miles south of Oban by following the signs to Taynuilt, and then turn onto the B845 toward Kilchrenan. Turn left at the Kilchrenan Pub and continue on for 3¾ miles, following signs into Ardanaiseig. **Amenities:** Restaurant; tennis court. In room: TV, hair dryer, Wi-Fi (free).

OBAN

85 miles NW of Glasgow; 50 miles SW of Fort William

One of Scotland's leading coastal resorts, the bustling port of Oban can be found in a sheltered bay almost enclosed by the island of Kerrera. A busy fishing port in the 18th century, and a fashionable holiday resort during the Victorian period, Oban is now an important ferry port for visitors on their way out to the islands. The town is also often used as a refueling stop for those exploring the west coast of Scotland.

Oban is the gateway to **Mull,** largest of the Inner Hebrides, as well as the island of **Iona.** See chapter 12 for information about these destinations, and details of the ferry service from Oban.

Essentials

GETTING THERE From Glasgow, the West Highland train lines run directly to Oban, with departures from Glasgow's Queen Street Station (call ℂ **08457/484-950** for 24-hr. info). Three trains per day (only two on Sun) make the 3-hour run to Oban.

Frequent coaches depart from Buchanan Station in Glasgow, taking about the same time as the train. Contact **Scottish Citylink** at ℂ **08705/505-050** in Glasgow, or ℂ **01631/563-059** in Oban.

If you're driving from Glasgow, head northwest along the A82 until you reach Tyndrum, and then go west along the A85 until you come to Oban.

VISITOR INFORMATION The **Tourist Information Centre** is on Argyll Square (ℂ **01631/563-122;** www.oban.org.uk). Opening times are April to mid-June and mid-September to October, Monday through Friday 9am to 5pm and Saturday and Sunday 10am to 4pm; mid-June to mid-September, Monday through Saturday 9am to 8pm and Sunday 9am to 7pm; and November to March, Monday through Saturday 9:30am to 5pm and Sunday noon to 4pm.

SPECIAL EVENTS The **Oban Highland Games** are held in August, with massed pipe bands marching through the streets. See www.obangames.com or ask at the tourist office for details. The **Oban Pipe Band** regularly parades on the main street during summer.

Exploring the Area

Near the little granite **Cathedral of the Isles,** 1 mile north of the end of the bay, is the ruin of the 13th-century **Dunollie Castle** (ℂ **01631/570-550;** www.dunollie. org), seat of the lords of Lorn, who once owned a third of Scotland.

You can also visit **Dunstaffnage Castle** ★ (ℂ **01631/562-465;** www. undiscoveredscotland.com), 3½ miles north of Oban, believed to have been the royal seat of the Dalriadic monarchy in the 8th century. It was probably the site of the Scots court until Kenneth MacAlpin's unification of Scotland and the transfer of the seat of government to Scone in the 10th century. The present castle was built around 1263 and it became the castle of the MacDougalls. It's open April to September daily from 9:30am to 5:30pm, in October daily from 9:30am to 4:30pm, and from November to March Saturday through Wednesday from 9:30am to 4:30pm. Admission is £4 adults, £3.20 for seniors and students, and £2.40 for children aged from 5 to 16. You can take a bus from the railway station in Oban to Dunbeg, but it's still a 1½-mile walk to the castle.

Another MacDougall stronghold can be found on the island of Kerrera. **Gylen Castle** dates back to 1587 and is open to the public free of charge all year round.

To explore the coastal scenery of Oban on two wheels, call in at **Oban Cycles,** Barr Bheag, Taynuilt (*©* **01866/822-736;** http://rcscycles.co.uk) or telephone to arrange delivery of a rental bike to your hotel. Alternatively try **Flit Self Drive,** Glencruitten Road, Oban (*©* **01631/566-553;** www.flitselfdrive.co.uk), who also rent bikes by the day or week.

Where to Eat

EXPENSIVE

Knipoch Hotel Restaurant SCOTTISH   Located 6 miles south of town on the shores of Loch Feochan, this whitewashed Georgian house (the oldest part dates from 1592) offers a choice of three dining rooms with a daily five-course menu. The chef relies heavily on Scottish produce, especially fresh fish. Salmon and halibut are smoked on the premises. Try the cock-a-leekie soup, followed by Sound of Luing scallops. There's also an impressive wine list.

The hotel has 20 somewhat old-fashioned guest rooms, priced at £178 to £204 per night for a double, and with a suite costing £236 to £250.

Just off the A816, Kilninver, Knipoch, by Oban, PA34 4QT. *©* 01852/316-251. Fax 01852/316-249. www. knipochhotel.co.uk. Reservations required. Main courses £15–£20. AE, DC, MC, V. Daily 7:30–9pm. Closed mid-Dec to mid-Feb. Drive 6 miles south of Oban on the A816.

The Manor House ★ SCOTTISH   Located in an 18th-century house that now functions as a hotel (see "Where to Stay," below), this restaurant is formal but not stuffy, and is one of the finest dining options in the area. The cuisine is traditional Scottish in style, and the chef uses the highest quality ingredients, many of them sourced locally. Signature dishes include venison, which comes with black pudding, caramelized root vegetables, and a rowanberry glaze; and juliennes of veal, with mushrooms in a Riesling sauce with potato rosti and salsify. The menu always includes several vegetarian options as well. Desserts are of the old-fashioned British variety, with sticky toffee pudding and butterscotch sauce, and marinated brambles with whisky custard among the favorites.

In the Manor House Hotel, Gallanach Rd., Oban, Argyll, PA34 4LS *©* **01631/562-087.** www.manor houseoban.com. Reservations recommended. Main courses £16–£22; fixed-price 5-course meal £38. AE, MC, V. Daily noon–2pm and 6:45–9pm.

MODERATE

The Gathering BRITISH   This imposing building, with verandas all around it, was first opened in 1882 as a private hunting and social club. Today, its street-level func- tions as "O'Donnells Irish Bar" (Mon–Sat 11am–1am, Sun noon–11pm), and its upper floor as a well-managed restaurant. The cooking and presentation is no-non- sense in style, but the food is very tasty. The dishes are based around local produce, with fish, game, lobster, and lamb all featuring regularly on the menu. Especially noteworthy are the saddle of venison with herb-and-port sauce, and local crayfish grilled in garlic butter.

The restaurant-pub also rents out six simply furnished bedrooms, costing from £30 per person, including breakfast and dinner.

Breadalbane St., Oban, Argyll. *©* **01631/564-849.** Reservations recommended. Bar platters £9–£16; fixed-price dinners in restaurant £16–£25. AE, MC, V. June–Sept daily noon–2pm; year-round daily 5–10pm.

Shopping

Many of the crafts items produced by local crofters eventually end up at gift shops in Oban. One of the best outlets is **McCaig's Warehouse,** Argyll Square (© **01631/566-335**), where the tartan patterns of virtually every clan in Scotland are for sale, either by the meter or in the form of kilts, jackets, or more modern interpretations of traditional garb.

Celtic-patterned jewelry, made from gold, silver, or platinum, and sometimes studded with semi-precious gems, is featured at **The Gem Box,** Esplanade (© **01631/562-180**). **Kranenburg Fine Art,** Star Brae, off Argyll Square (© **01631/562-303;** www.kranenburgfineart.com) sells contemporary paintings, sculptures, prints, and jewelry.

If you want to have your own kilt, cape, or a full outfit made, head for one of the town's two best tailors: **Hector Russell, Kiltmaker,** Argyll Square (© **01631/570-240;** www.hector-russell.com), and **Geoffrey Tailors,** 35 Stevenson St. (© **01631/570-557;** www.geoffreykilts.co.uk).

Entertainment & Nightlife

A popular hangout in Oban is **O'Donnells,** an Irish pub on Breadalbane Street (© **01631/566-159**), where you're greeted by a friendly atmosphere. As well as Guinness, the bar's well stocked with a variety of Irish and Scottish whiskies. From Thursday to Saturday, there's entertainment in the form of a live band or a DJ. Over the busy summer period, something is scheduled almost every night. Opening hours are 3pm to 1am daily.

Where to Stay

VERY EXPENSIVE

Isle of Eriska Hotel ★★★ The grandest place to stay in the Greater Oban area is this turreted Victorian mansion at the end of a sweeping drive. In the Middle Ages, this 121-hectare (300-acre) forested island was a church-protected sanctuary. However, in the 19th century, an industrialist purchased it and planted hundreds of beech trees, building a bridge to the mainland. Today you can enjoy a panorama of the surrounding waterways and the forest park with its herds of deer.

Inside the hotel, you encounter a formal sitting room and library/bar. A wide staircase leads up to the baronial bedrooms. Each of the rooms is individually styled, with plush furnishings and chic bathrooms. Families might consider renting the beautifully kitted-out 2-bedroom cottages, which are 100m (328 ft.) from the main building and come with their own private gardens and a hot tub. There is also a 3-bedroom self-catering cottage for rent.

The hotel is known for its refined Scottish cuisine, made primarily from local produce. A fixed-price dinner at the restaurant is available for £44 per person; men are required to wear a jacket and tie. Adjoining the hotel is the Stables Spa with its large heated pool.

Ledaig, by Oban, Argyll, PA37 1SD. www.eriska-hotel.co.uk. © **01631/720-371.** Fax 01631/720-531. 17 units. £297–£970 double; £4,440 cottage for 1 week; 3-bedroom self-catering cottage from £1,000 per week. MC, V. Located 6¼ miles north of Oban. **Amenities:** Restaurant; bar; 6-hole golf course; tennis court; health club & spa; room service; babysitting. *In room:* TV, hair dryer, Wi-Fi (free).

EXPENSIVE

Manor House Hotel Located on the outskirts of town, and opening onto panoramic views of Oban Bay, this stone house was built in 1780, and was once owned by the Duke of Argyll. The good-size guest rooms are decorated in traditional style with floral-patterned curtains and upholstery and reproduction antique furniture. Guests enjoy the use of a beautiful conservatory and the well-kept gardens.

The hotel is well known locally for its restaurant. See "Eating in Oban" above for more details.

Gallanach Rd., Oban, Argyll, PA34 4LS. www.manorhouseoban.com. © **01631/562-087.** Fax 01631/563-053. 11 units. £115–£215 double. No children under 12. AE, MC, V. From the south side of Oban, follow the signs for the car ferry but continue past the ferry entrance for about ⅔ mile. **Amenities:** Restaurant; bar; room service; smoke-free rooms; Wi-Fi (free). *In room:* TV, hair dryer.

MODERATE

Alexandra Hotel   Situated on the promenade 1 mile from the train station, the late-1860s Alexandra evokes Oban in its Victorian heyday. The vast facade with its gables, turreted towers, and Regency front veranda make it something of a landmark in the town. From its public room you can look out onto Oban Bay, and two sun lounges overlook the seafront. The mid-size guest rooms are modestly furnished but pleasant enough, with small bathrooms. About half of the rooms have sea views. Some rooms are specially equipped for those with limited mobility.

Corran Esplanade, Oban, Argyll, PA34 5AA. © **01631/562-381.** Fax 01631/564-497. 78 units. £95–£240 double. AE, MC, V. **Amenities:** Restaurant; bar; pool (indoor); exercise room; room service. *In room:* TV, hair dryer.

Columba Hotel   This red-brick hotel is one of the most impressive Victorian buildings in Oban. It was built in 1870 by the same McCaig who constructed the hilltop "amphitheatre" known as McCaig's Tower. The location is among the best in town, and its "Alba Restaurant" offers views of the port through its large windows. The small guest rooms are unremarkable but have everything you need. Live folk music is sometimes performed in the Harbour Inn Bar (which is also open to non-guests).

The Esplanade, North Pier, Oban, Argyll, PA34 5QD. © **01631/562-183.** Fax 01631/564-683. 50 units. £90–£135 double. AE, MC, V. Free parking. The Scottish Midland Bus Company's Ganavan bus passes by. **Amenities:** Restaurant; bar; car rental; room service; babysitting. *In room:* TV, hair dryer, Wi-Fi (free).

Dungallan House Hotel   One of the town's more upmarket hotels, the Dungallan House was built for the Duke of Argyll as his Oban residence in around 1870. It was used as a hospital during World War I and as a naval office during World War II, but today it's a venerable family-run hotel. The public rooms have high-ceilings and reproduction antique furniture, which evokes the high Victorian style. The guest rooms are bright and comfortable, and most have fine views. Breakfasts are served in the formal dining room; and if you book ahead, dinners can be arranged. Two hectares (5 acres) of woodland and gardens surround the house, and views stretch out over the Bay of Oban. The town center is about 10 minutes' walk away.

Gallanach Rd., Oban, Argyll, PA34 4PD. www.dungallanhotel-oban.co.uk. © **01631/563-799.** Fax 01631/566-711. 13 units, 11 with private bathroom. £156–£174 double. No children under 12. MC, V. Closed Nov–Mar. From Oban's center, drive ⅔ mile, following the signs to Gallanach. **Amenities:** Dining room; bar. *In room:* TV, no phone.

INEXPENSIVE

Dungrianach ★ 👬   This little B&B is one of the best places to stay in Oban. In Gaelic, Dungrianach means "the sunny house on the hill," and the description is apt: the hotel sits in the midst of a wooded area, overlooking Oban Bay and some of the islands of the Inner Hebrides. The location is tranquil and seemingly remote, and yet it's only a few minutes' walk from the ferry terminal. The walk up is, however, a steep one, but that at least enables you to work off all those hearty Scottish breakfasts. The house is furnished with antiques and reproductions. The owners rent a double and a twin-bedded room, each with a little private bathroom. Guests can meet fellow guests in the sitting room, which has a collection of books on Scotland.

Pulpit Hill, Oban, Argyll PA34 4LU. ✆/fax **01631/562-840.** 2 units. £70 double. No credit cards. Free parking. *In room:* TV, no phone.

Foxholes   Far from being a foxhole, this is actually a spacious country house set in a tranquil glen about 3 miles south of Oban. The cozy, tasteful, and comfortable bedrooms are painted in soft pastels and furnished traditionally. All the rooms have panoramic views of the countryside and the hotel's well-maintained gardens. The peace and quiet ensures that guests have a good night's sleep. A five-course fixed-price dinner is available for an additional £21 to £28 per person.

Cologin, Lerags, Oban, Argyll PA34 4SE. www.foxholeshotel.co.uk. ✆ **01631/564-982.** Fax 01631/570-890. 7 units. £102–£110 double. MC, V. Free parking. Closed Nov–Easter. Take the A816 3 miles south of Oban. **Amenities:** Restaurant; bar. *In room:* TV, hair dryer, no phone.

Glenburnie Hotel   This rambling Victorian house on the seafront esplanade is just a 5-minute walk west of the town center. Built in 1897 of granite blocks, it was originally designed as the surgical hospital and home of a prominent doctor. Today, it's a family-run guesthouse, with comfortable furnishings in a traditional style and fine views over the bay, which allow you to watch the ferries coming and going.

The Esplanade, Oban, Argyll PA34 5AQ. www.glenburnie.co.uk. ✆/fax **01631/562-089.** 14 units. £90–£110 double. MC, V. Closed mid-Nov to Easter. *In room:* TV.

FIFE & THE CENTRAL HIGHLANDS

9

The Kingdom of Fife straddles a peninsula squeezed between the Firths of Forth and Tay. The very land of this ancient region is soaked with all the romance and pageantry of the early Stuart kings, and its rolling landscape is littered with royal places and evocative ruins. History and landscape take a dramatic turn in the Central Highlands where the peaks and lochs of the Trossachs and Loch Lomond National Park blend seamlessly with legends of Rob Roy and ballads eulogizing the choice between the high and low roads home.

CITIES　The medieval city of **St. Andrews** stands proud as the home of golf, and players from across the globe make the pilgrimage to its hallowed **Old Course.** History is not to be ignored here as the city's ruined cathedral once protected the bones of St. Andrew himself, Scotland's patron saint. **Stirling,** the region's other main urban center, forms the lynch pin between Scotland's Highlands and Lowlands and is famous for its formidable castle, pivotal battles, and **Wallace Monument.**

COUNTRYSIDE　The legendary **Loch Lomond** is Scotland's largest loch. Its southern edge forms a lowland landscape of gentle hills and islands, but as its waters cross the Highland Boundary Fault to the north, the loch assumes a stark, dramatic character, crammed with moody, rugged hillsides. Part of the same National Park, the **Trossachs** is the collective name given to the wild, loch-strewn Highland area east of Loch Lomond, home to some of Scotland's finest scenery immortalized by the passionate writings of Sir Walter Scott.

EATING & DRINKING　Fife's coastal villages are famous for their working harbors and clutch of seafood restaurants, which include the best fish and chip shop in the U.K. However, St. Andrews stands out as the region's finest place to eat and drink and offers a growing number of city center options alongside rural former coaching inns continuing a long tradition of fine dining and warm hospitality.

COAST　One of Scotland's best-kept secrets is the chain of fishing villages that gather around Fife's southeast tip in a region known as **East Neuk.** There's fine walking to be had along the picturesque coastal path that lines this region, and an eclectic array of art to be discovered in village galleries inspired by East Nuek's landscape and light.

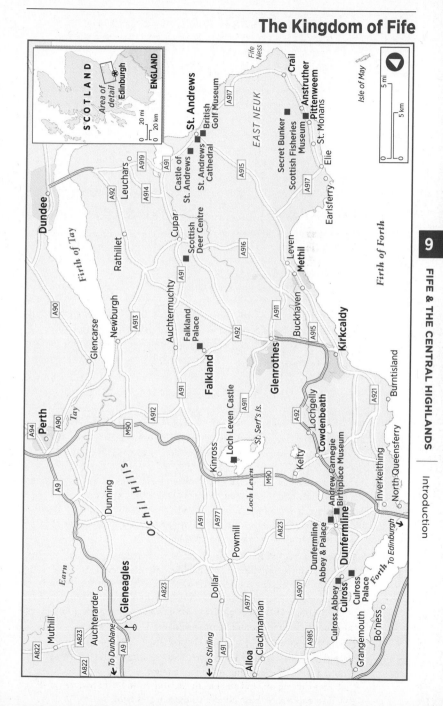

The Kingdom of Fife

THE best TRAVEL EXPERIENCES IN FIFE & THE CENTRAL HIGHLANDS

o **Standing on the battlements of Stirling Castle:** One of the most imposing and impressive castles in Scotland, Stirling is both a military fort and royal Renaissance palace. Take in sweeping views of the surrounding countryside where some of the most pivotal battles in Scottish history were won by some of the country's greatest heroes.

o **Traveling through the Trossachs in the heart of "Rob Roy Country" from Callander to Aberfoyle, via Dukes Pass:** Mountain, loch, and forest close in on all sides on this memorable road that snakes its way through some of Scotland's most fabled and fabulous scenery.

o **Surveying the 18th hole of St. Andrews' historic Old Course from the terrace of the Royal and Ancient clubhouse:** Follow in the footsteps of the world's most famous golfers to this iconic course where many claim the game was born. If you're good enough, and lucky enough, you might even snag a round; otherwise stand back and watch the masters at play.

o **Cruising the waters of the mighty Loch Lomond:** Cruises across Scotland's largest and bonniest loch depart from Loch Lomond Shores in Balloch and the boatyard at Balmaha. Get up close to some of the loch's many islands and view the famous fault line that divides Scotland's lowlands from its highlands.

o **Pottering around East Neuk's picturesque and hard-working fishing harbors:** Numerous fishing fleets still work the waters off East Neuk in the southwest of Fife. Spend a day or two discovering the villages that line this rugged coastline and sampling the U.K.'s best fish and chips.

DUNFERMLINE ★ & ITS GREAT ABBEY

14 miles NW of Edinburgh; 39 miles NE of Glasgow; 52 miles SW of Dundee

An easy day trip from Edinburgh, the ancient town of Dunfermline was Scotland's capital until 1603 and the Union of the Crowns when the royal court departed to London. The Scots call their former capital the "auld grey toun," but its history is colorful and plentiful and forms a major part of any visit. The town's must-see attraction is its magnificent **Abbey** and the adjacent ruins of its former royal palace, which stand at the heart of Dunfermline's Heritage Quarter. Once the center of Scottish linen making, specializing in damask, Dunfermline's most famous son, Andrew Carnegie, was born in one of its tiny weaver's cottages. By World War I, the linen market had largely disappeared and today Dunfermline is a bustling town and excellent first stop in the Kingdom of Fife.

Culross, Fife's most charming village, is within easy reach of Dunfermline and Stirling (p. 241) and is a simple side trip by bus or car.

Essentials

GETTING THERE A regular **ScotRail** service (© **0845/601-5929;** www. scotrail.co.uk) links Edinburgh's Waverley and Haymarket train stations with

Dunfermline. The journey takes around 1 hour and 15 minutes and a same-day round-trip fare is £5.40. **Scottish Citylink** (✆ **0871//266-3333**; www.citylink.co.uk) operates an hourly service between Edinburgh's bus station in St. Andrews Square and Dunfermline. It's a 45-minute bus ride and a same-day round-trip fare is £9.20.

If you're driving from Edinburgh, join the A90 to the west of the city, travel north across the Forth Road Bridge, and merge into the M90. Dunfermline is west of the intersection of the M90 and A92.

VISITOR INFORMATION A **Tourist Information Centre (TIC)** is located at 1 High St. (✆ **01383/720-999**; www.visitdunfermline.com), open Monday through Saturday 9:30am to 5pm plus Sundays 11am to 4pm in August.

It takes no more than a day to explore Dunfermline, whose elevated position allows commanding views of the Firth of Forth. The west side of town is dominated by Pittencrieff Park, also called "the Glen," an enormous, rambling area of public parkland containing the 17th-century Pittencrieff House, an aviary and glasshouse, children's play areas, and roaming peacocks. The park butts up against Dunfermline's Heritage Quarter where you find all the town's main attractions, including the very pink **Abbot House** on Maygate (✆ **01383/733-886**; www.abbothouse.co.uk; open daily 9:30am–4:30pm), which is believed to date to the 15th century and today houses a Heritage Centre. To get to grips with Dunfermline's absorbing history, download the Tourist Information Centre's podcast (www.visitdunfermline.com/podcast.php) and take the tour around town narrated by popular BBC Scottish historian Neil Oliver.

Exploring the Area

Andrew Carnegie Birthplace Museum HISTORIC HOME In 1835, American industrialist and philanthropist Andrew Carnegie was born in a tiny weaver's cottage in the shadow of Dunfermline Abbey. The museum celebrating his birth and life consists of the 18th-century cottage, complete with weaver's loom, and an adjacent memorial hall where you can follow Carnegie's story as he emigrated to the United States and became one of the world's richest men. From the fortune he made in steel, Carnegie gave away more than £244 million before his death in 1919 and Dunfermline received the first of the 2,811 free libraries he provided throughout Britain and the US. *Sesame Street* was produced with a grant from the Carnegie Corporation and children should look out for Bert and Ernie in the memorial hall.

Moodie St. ✆ **01383/724-302.** www.carnegiebirthplace.com. Free admission. March–mid-Dec Mon-Sat 10am-5pm, Sun 2-5pm.

Dunfermline Abbey & Palace ★ ABBEY The first Christian church raised on this site was created by a Culdee (Celtic) community around A.D 800. Nearly 300 years later, Queen Margaret (later St. Margaret), mother of three kings of Scotland, founded a priory here on the spot where she'd married Malcolm III. It was their son David I who turned the priory into a grand abbey of which today only the striking Romanesque nave survives. England's Edward I inflicted severe damage on the abbey in 1303, and its magnificent rebuild was bankrolled by Robert the Bruce in a symbolic display of Scottish resilience. In 1600 the palace witnessed the birth of Charles I, the last monarch to be born in Scotland. Even in ruins, the long and lofty monks' refectory remains a highlight. The complex is owned and managed by Historic Scotland, but the adjoining Abbey Church remains a working church and is free to enter. Numerous Scottish monarchs are buried in this church including Queen Margaret and Robert the Bruce. However, although the Bruce's body rests in peace beneath the church pulpit, his heart was taken on Crusade and finally laid to rest at Melrose Abbey (p. 135).

St. Margaret's St. © **01383/739-026.** www.historicscotland.gov.uk. Admission £3.70 adults, £3 seniors, £2.20 children 5–15. Apr–Sept daily 9:30am–5:30pm; Oct 9:30pm–4:30pm; Nov–March.

Where to Eat

Some of the best places to eat in Dunfermline are on its outskirts such as Keavil House Hotel's Cardoon restaurant (see below). In the town itself, head to **Reuben's Deli** on New Row (© **01383/739-071**) for freshly baked cakes and pastries and a range of light meals, or the **Abbot House** (p. 239), whose landscaped gardens and abbey views make for the perfect spot for afternoon tea.

Room with a View ★ SEAFOOD   Located inside Aberdour's waterfront Forth View Hotel, this small seafood restaurant boasts uninterrupted, sweeping views across the Firth of Forth. Local is the emphasis here in every way, with menus changing on a weekly basis in accordance with stocks at the nearby fish market. Monkfish, halibut, sea bass, oysters, and lobster are all possible dishes and accompanied with ingredients sourced from a range of suppliers close to home. There's always one vegetarian option on the menu and repeat customers even travel from Edinburgh as the dining experience and views make the journey across the Firth of Forth more than worthwhile and reservations essential.

Forth View Hotel, Hawkcraig Point, Aberdour, 8½ miles southeast of Dunfermline. © **01383/860-402.** www.roomwithaviewrestaurant.co.uk. Reservations recommended. Main courses dinner £13–£18, lunch £9–£11. MC, V. Wed–Sun noon–2:30pm, Wed–Sat from 6pm.

The Wee Restaurant ★ 📖 MODERN SCOTTISH   Tucked away beneath the imposing Forth Rail Bridge in nearby North Queensferry, this relative newcomer on the local dining scene may be physically small (capacity 40), but its excellent reputation is large and growing all the time. The interior is sleek, contemporary, and candlelit, and the service is relaxed. However, it's the award-winning cuisine, created around locally sourced ingredients, that secures the Wee Restaurant's place on southwest Scotland's dining map. Simple and tantalizing lunch and dinner menus are filled with the likes of pan-fried Shetland salmon, smoked Orkney beef, and glazed Scottish strawberry crème brûlée, all served with imagination and packed with flavor. Regular wine-tasting nights are a firm local favorite and a place at the table must be booked in advance.

17 Main St., North Queensferry, 6½ miles south of Dunfermline. © **01383/616-263.** www.theweerestaurant.co.uk. 2-course dinner £26, 2-course lunch £16. AE, MC, V. Daily noon–2pm and 6:30–9pm,

Entertainment & Nightlife

Dunfermline is home to two performing arts venues: the **Alhambra Theatre** at the junction of Canmore Street and New Row (© **01383/740-384;** www.alhambra dunfermline.com), whose program includes mainstream comedy, music, and theatre; and the **Carnegie Hall** on East Port (© **01383/602-302;** www.attfife.org.uk/ attfife/index.cfm), where you can catch both music and theatre events and whose Tiffany bar claims wide views over the Firth of Forth. Other popular drinking spots include the **East Port Bar** in the center of town on East Port.

Where to Stay

Best Western Keavil House Hotel ★   This tranquil country hotel on the outskirts of Dunfermline stands in 4.8 hectares (12 acres) of forested land and gardens and features an array of leisure facilities. The bedrooms are generous in size and include amenities such as a writing desk and mid-size bathrooms. Master bedrooms contain four-poster beds. The hotel offers fine formal dining in its **Cardoon** restaurant and less formal food in its bar and lounge.

Main St., Crossford, KY12 8QW. www.keavilhouse.co.uk. © **01383/736-258.** Fax 01383/621-600. 73 units. £85–£125 double; £120 family suite. AE, DC, MC, V. Take the A994, 2 miles west of Dunfermline; the hotel is off the main street at the west end of the village. **Amenities:** Restaurant; bar; pool (indoor); health club w/Jacuzzi; room service; babysitting. *In room:* TV, hair dryer, Wi-Fi (free).

Garvock House Hotel ★   Standing in 0.8 hectares (2 acres) of gardens and woodland, Garvock House was once the private home of a prosperous Victorian family. The house was converted to a small luxury hotel in 1996 and retains many of its original architectural features. Each room remains faithful to the history of the building, and you'll find extra touches such as fluffy bathrobes and books. Although small, the hotel is award winning, and its sophisticated menu supports dishes such as Scottish steaks and seared scallops with Stornoway black pudding. Desserts are exceptional and include warm pear tart tatin and homemade ice cream.

St. John's Dr., Transy, KY12 7TU. www.garvock.co.uk. © **01383/621-067.** Fax 01383/621-168. 26 units. £140–158 double; £280 suite. AE, MC, V. **Amenities:** Restaurant. *In room:* TV, hair dryer, Wi-Fi (free).

A Side Trip from Dunfermline: Culross

Culross ★★★, 6 miles west of Dunfermline, is a charming 17th-century village renovated and preserved by the National Trust for Scotland. This is one of Fife's most atmospheric spots and, strolling around the cobblestone medieval streets lined with whitewashed houses and tiny cottages, it's tempting to believe you've stepped back in time.

Set in tranquil lavender lined gardens at the center of the village stands **Culross Palace ★★** (© **0844/493-2189;** www.nts.org.uk). The palace was built between 1597 and 1611 for prosperous merchant George Bruce. More a grand hall than a palace, this imposing, turmeric yellow building features a beautiful series of painted ceilings, antique furniture, and a tangible sense of life in the late 16th century. It's open April to May Thursday through Monday noon to 5pm; June to August daily noon to 5pm; September Thursday though Monday noon to 5pm; and October Thursday through Monday noon to 4pm. Admission is £8.50 adults, £5.50 children, and £21 per family.

Close to the Palace stands **Culross Pottery & Gallery** (© **01383/882-176;** www.culrosspottery.com), whose shelves are filled with the work of Scottish artists; their **Biscuit Café** serves locally roasted coffee and homemade cakes. Alternatively head to the **Red Lion pub,** next to the village post office (© **01383/880-225;** www.redlionculross.co.uk), for hearty pub food such as steak and mash pie.

The other major attraction here is **Culross Abbey,** a Cistercian monastery founded by Malcolm, Earl of Fife, in 1217. Some of the building is in ruins, while other intact areas still serve as a parish church.

The no. 78 bus operates a frequent service between Dunfermline bus station and Culross; the round-trip fare is £4.50.

LOCH LEVEN & FALKLAND ★

Loch Leven ★ is a large loch and National Nature Reserve on the western outskirts of **Kinross,** 13 miles north of Dunfermline and 27 miles north of Edinburgh. The loch contains seven islands and from Kinross you can catch a small ferry to one of the largest, Castle Island (signposted from the center of town), to see the ruins of **Loch Leven Castle** (🕾 01577/862-670; www.historicscotland.gov.uk). "Those never got luck who came to Loch Leven"—this saying sums up the history of the island's Douglas fortress dating from the late 14th-century. Mary Queen of Scots was the most famous of its ill-fated prisoners, and it was inside its forbidding walls that she signed her abdication on July 24, 1567. Mary subsequently escaped the castle on May 2, 1568 and eventually fled to England and the protection of her cousin Elizabeth I. Around half the original castle still remains and visitors can explore the ruins of a 14th-century tower house and 16th-century curtain wall. It's open April to September daily 9:30am to 5:30pm, and October daily 9:30am to 4:30pm. Admission includes the round-trip ferry ride from Kinross to Castle Island: £4.70 adults, £3.80 seniors, and £2.80 for children 5–15.

Curling on Loch Leven dates back to the 17th century, and large curling "bonspiles" used to take place in winter on its thick frozen waters. You can learn more about the history of the loch via the 8-mile **Heritage Trail** (www.lochlevenheritage trail.co.uk), which leads around its banks and contains prime spots for bird-watching—you'll find two hides en route. Loch Leven is rich with brown trout, and anglers should contact **Loch Leven Fisheries** (🕾 01577/865-386; http://lochlevenfisheries.co.uk) to fish these waters.

The historic village of **Falkland** (12 miles northeast of Kinross) butts up against the eastern slopes of the Lomond Hills, whose forests were once an ancient hunting ground. Falkland's 17th- and 18th-century streets, with their small gift shops and village pubs, gather around its famous palace formerly owned by Scottish royalty and today looked after by the National Trust for Scotland. **Falkland Palace ★** (🕾 0844/493-2186; www.nts.org.uk) dominates the village and is an impressive Renaissance royal hunting lodge once much favored by the Stuart dynasty. Highlights of the Palace's lavishly furnished interior include 17th-century Flemish tapestries and royal portraits, and the magnificent gardens feature a large orchard and the oldest royal tennis court in Britain, built in 1539 for James V. The palace is open March to October Monday through Saturday 11am to 5pm, Sunday 1 to 5pm; admission is £11 adults, £8 children, and £27 families.

Legendary country singer Johnny Cash traced his ancestry back to this region of Fife, and he made the pilgrimage to Falkland and his roots three times over the course of his life. To find out all about Cash's visit, drop into the violin shop on the village square and chat with owner Bob Beveridge, who spent time with the Man in Black and will share his memories with you.

Exploring the Area

Scottish Deer Centre ☺ ZOO   This popular family-friendly attraction is the place to get up close to some of Scotland's best-loved wildlife. Expect to encounter nine different species of deer along with an array of birds of prey and otters. Ranger-led tours run throughout the day and a good time to visit is 3pm—feeding time for the center's resident wolves. There are both indoor and outdoor children's play areas, but best of all for young visitors is the lofty treetop walk. The center also features a shopping area where you can stock up on Scottish woolens and whisky, a cafe, and a picnic area. All of which makes for a good half day's entertainment for all ages.

Off the A91, 3 miles west of Cupar, © **01337/810-391.** www.tsdc.co.uk. Admission £7 adults, £5 children. Summer daily 10am–5pm; winter daily 10am–4pm.

Where to Eat

Ostlers Close ★★ 🍴 MODERN SCOTTISH   Tucked away along a small back lane off Cupar's busy main street, Ostlers Close is an unexpected gem of sublime cuisine in the heart of Fife. Owners Amanda and Jimmy Graham are passionate about Scottish food and source as many fresh local ingredients as possible—Jimmy even grows his own organic vegetables and herbs and forages for fresh mushrooms in surrounding woodlands. The newly refurbished interior exudes warmth and elegance and the daily changing menu includes fresh seafood from nearby Pittenweem and a selection of Scottish cheeses. The accompanying wine list includes a number of fine options for under £20.

25 Bonnygate, Cupar © **01335/655-574.** www.ostlersclose.co.uk. Reservations recommended. Main courses £19–£24. AE, MC, V. Tues–Sat from 7pm; also Sat lunch from 12:15pm.

Where to Stay

Best Western Balgeddie House Hotel   Standing on the northern outskirts of Glenrothes within large landscaped gardens, Balgeddie House was built as a family home in the early 20th century and retains a sense of history and comfort. Balgeddie also boasts all the features and comforts of a modern hotel including a brand new spa, which comes complete with a fitness suite and 17m (55-ft.) indoor swimming pool. Large, comfortable rooms include family options, and the in-house oak-paneled bar and restaurant (main courses £8–£11) overlook a long, formal patio and gardens. The bar is popular with both guests and locals, as is the adjoining **Spencer's Bistro,** reached via a separate entrance on the east side of the hotel.

Balgeddie Way, Glenrothes, KY6 3ET. www.balgeddiehouse.com. © **01592/742-511.** Fax 01592/621-702. 30 units AE, DC, MC, V. **Amenities:** Restaurant; bar; pool; spa. *In room:* TV, hair dryer, Wi-Fi (free).

EAST NEUK'S SCENIC FISHING VILLAGES ★★

"Neuk" is Scots for corner and East Neuk stands on the southeastern corner of a peninsula fringed by the Firth of Forth and North Sea. The region is within half an hour's drive of St. Andrews to the north and easily reached by car from Edinburgh. The string of fishing villages that line this rugged coastline are some of prettiest in all Scotland and a honey pot for local artists. However, their small harbors are both picturesque and hard working and regularly send their fishing fleets out into the North Sea. You can sample their harvest at the region's many fine seafood restaurants.

Each village doesn't take long to explore and the chain from Elie in the west to Crail in the east can be explored in a single day. As much of the accommodation here is self-catering, visitors often find that they have to use larger urban areas as a base from which to explore. However, if possible, book a night or two in one of East Neuk's friendly bed-and-breakfasts or small hotels and take time to truly discover this region.

One of the best ways to achieve this is via the **Fife Coastal Path** (www.fifecoastalpath.co.uk), a well-maintained, clearly marked path that runs from North Queensferry in the south to Newport-on-Tay in the north. The section that leads through East Neuk is one of the best and can easily be joined at any of the villages along this stretch of coastline.

You can't reach East Neuk by rail; the nearest stations are Ladybank, Cupar, and Leuchars, on the ScotRail Edinburgh to Dundee line serving northeast Fife. Buses from St. Andrews connect the villages, but you really need to have your own car here.

Elie ★

With its step-gabled houses and little harbor, Elie, 13 miles south of St. Andrews, is many visitors' favorite village along this coast and makes for a good starting point from which to explore East Neuk. Elie and its close neighbor, Earlsferry, overlook a crescent of gold-sand beach, which is a popular spot with Edinburgh folk in summer as it's only a 25-minute car ride away. The name Elie is believed to come from the *ailie* (island) of Ardross, which now forms part of the harbor and is joined to the mainland by a road. A large stone building, a former granary, at the harbor is a reminder of the days when Elie was a busy trading port.

Earlsferry, to the west, got its name from an ancient ferry crossing, which Macduff, the thane of Fife, is supposed to have used in his escape from Macbeth. East of the harbor stands a stone structure known as the **Lady's Tower,** used by Lady Janet Anstruther, a noted 18th-century beauty, as a bathing cabana.

Elie is an ideal place to experience the Fife Coastal Path as the tiny village of **St. Monans** is only 2½ miles to the east. St. Monans is home to the sister restaurant of **The Seafood Restaurant** in St. Andrew's (p. 251), whose combination of stunning views and fine Scottish seafood is reason enough to visit. East again along the coastal path around another 0.75 miles from the village stands the late 18th-century St. Monans windmill (open July–Aug daily noon–4pm; admission free), Fife's last remaining windmill and testament to the region's salt producing industry.

WHERE TO EAT

Ship Inn ★ SCOTTISH   Standing on the edge of Elie's golden sands, the Ship Inn is a cracking local pub and excellent place to eat or linger over a pint of real ale or dram of whisky from the large selection on offer. The building itself dates back to 1778 and has been a bar since 1830. In summer, you can sit outdoors on the edge of the sands and watch a game of beach cricket organized by the pub, and in winter an open fire burns brightly. The relatively small menu champions pub staples such as steak and Guinness pie and deep fried haddock in beer batter with homemade chips plus a selection of freshly filled baguettes. Owners Richard and Jill Philip also run The Golf Tavern in Earlsferry, known locally as the 19th hole.

The Toft, Elie. ✆ **01333/330-246.** www.ship-elie.com. Main courses £8–£10. MC, V. Lunch Mon–Sat noon–2:30pm, Sun 12:30–3pm; dinner Sun–Thurs 6–9pm, Fri–Sat 6–9:30pm.

Pittenweem ★

A charming and busy fishing village, Pittenweem focuses around its small harbor, one of Fife's best—arrive early to catch the lively fish market that takes place here every morning except Sundays. From its picturesque waterfront, filled with lobster pots, fishing boats, and ice cream shops, the village's narrow streets spread steeply uphill and are peppered with artists' galleries and cozy cafes such as the **Heron Gallery & Bistro,** High Street (✆ **01333/331-014**), where you can view displays of Scottish contemporary art and tuck into homemade scones and steaming cappuccinos. If possible visit in August when an imaginative **Arts Festival** (www.pittenweemartsfes-tival.co.uk) transforms the village into a showcase of Scottish Art.

The *weem* in the village's name means "cave," a reference to **St. Fillan's Cave** (*©* **01333/311-495**) at Cove Wynd just off the harbor. This cave contains the shrine of St. Fillan, an early Christian missionary who lived in the 7th century and who's meant to have resided here as a hermit, writing sermons by the light of his luminous left arm. Admission to the cave is £1 for adults and free for children, and the key can be obtained from the **Little Gallery** or **Cocoa Tree** shop on High Street.

WHERE TO STAY

Rooms@25 ★★ A warm Fife welcome awaits at Rooms@25, one of the loveliest places to stay in East Neuk. A family home and old Victorian cottage, this small bed-and-breakfast contains three contemporary and comfortable rooms, each individually themed and embellished with extras such as luxury toiletries, hot water bottles, and corkscrews. All rooms are located at entrance level, and one room can accommodate families. The breakfasts are particularly outstanding and include the hearty full Scottish with a vegetarian alternative.

25 Charles St., Pittenweem, KY10 2QH. www.roomsat25.co.uk. *©* **01333/313-306.** 3 units. £33 per person per night, £46 single person. MC, V. Closed Sept–Feb. *In room:* TV, hair dryer.

Anstruther

The largest of East Neuk's fishing communities, Anstruther lies 9½ miles south of St. Andrews and 46 miles northeast of Edinburgh and was once an important herring-fishing port. Today this lively community is famous for its scenic harbor and outstanding fish and chips shops—officially the best in Britain. The **Tourist Information Centre** (*©* **01333/311-073**) adjoins the **Scottish Fisheries Museum** (see below) and is open April to September Monday through Saturday 10am to 5pm, and Sunday 11am to 4pm; and October Monday through Saturday 10am to 4pm and Sunday 11am to 4pm.

The **Scottish Fisheries Museum,** St. Ayles, Harbourhead (*©* **01333/310-628;** www.scotfishmuseum.org), at the eastern end of the harbor, is much larger than its entrance suggests and brings to life the history of East Neuk's fishing industry. This fascinating attraction will take a couple of hours to explore and includes a covered boatyard, intricate model ships, a fisherman's cottage, and a 24m (78-ft.) "Zulu" sailing ship, once the backbone of the herring industry. The museum is open April to September Monday through Saturday 10am to 5:30pm, Sunday 11am–5pm; and October to March Monday through Saturday 10am to 4:30pm, Sunday noon to 4:30pm. Admission is £6 adults, £5 seniors, and free for children under 16.

Standing around 5 miles offshore, the **Isle of May ★** is a tiny island and National Nature Reserve and can be visited by boat from Anstruther. On its craggy shores you'll find a bird observatory and a field station, along with the ruins of a 12th-century monastery and the oldest lighthouse in Scotland dating back to 1636.

Most people visit via a day trip on the *May Princess* (*©* **01333/310-103;** www.isleofmayferry.com), a large passenger boat that departs for the Isle of May from the middle pier at Anstruther harbor once a day every day, weather permitting, between April and September. Tickets go on sale from a kiosk 1 hour before departure, or they can be booked in advance by e-mailing through the website. The cost (cash only) is £19 for adults, £17 for seniors and students, and £9.50 for children 3 to 16; departure times vary with the tide. The trip lasts around 4 to 5 hours and includes 2 to 3 hours on the island. Wildlife lovers can expect to encounter hundreds, even thousands, of puffins, which mate on the Isle of May; seals; and possibly whales in July and August. Bird-watching enthusiasts can arrange to stay in the island's observatory for up to a week (see www.isleofmaybirdobs.org for details).

If you're looking for ways to keep children entertained, check out the range of activities on offer at **Neuk Outdoors,** Cellardyke Park (✆ **01333/311-929;** www. eastneukoutdoors.co.uk). Through this company you can book canoeing, rock climbing, abseiling, or coastal scramble trips, or simply rent mountain bikes and explore for yourself.

WHERE TO EAT

Anstruther Fish Bar & Restaurant ★ SEAFOOD   For fish and chip lovers there's simply no finer place to indulge than this award-winning restaurant, which has been the U.K. winner of Fish and Chip Shop of the Year numerous times. Fifers travel from all over the region to feast on the nation's favorite dish inside this immaculate waterfront restaurant or, when the weather permits, grab a takeaway and tuck in while sitting on the harbor wall. Most of the fish is purchased from local fishermen, and nonfish options include venison burgers and chicken curry. Takeaway is also available.

42–44 Shore St., Anstruther. ✆ **01333/310-518.** www.anstrutherfishbar.co.uk. Main courses £5–£8, children's menu £3.40–£5. MC, V. Daily 11:30am–10pm.

The Cellar ★ SEAFOOD   This atmospheric seafood restaurant is the best in town. The building itself dates back to the 17th century and in previous incarnations has been a cooperage and smokery for the town's herring industry. Old stone walls and original beams are still in place and candles provide the light, accompanied in winter by roaring open fires. The menu offers fresh fish caught in nearby waters and prepared with flare, such as seared salmon with crushed olive and mint and garlic new potatoes. There's always a meat option on the menu, and dinner can be rounded off with homemade whisky chocolates.

24 E. Green, Anstruther. ✆ **01333/310-378.** www.cellaranstruther.co.uk. Reservations required. Fixed-price dinner £35 for 2 courses, £40 for 3 courses; fixed-price lunch £20 for 2 courses, £25 for 3 courses. AE, DC, MC, V. Tues–Sat from 6:30pm, Fri–Sat from noon.

WHERE TO STAY

The Waterfront ☺   Located in a prime spot bang in the middle of Anstruther's harborfront, The Waterfront is a popular seafood restaurant with 10 clean and contemporary rooms. Two of the rooms are set up for families, and there's also a family suite offering lots of space for children to spread out. Some rooms have harbor views while others cluster around a small courtyard garden. The breakfast menu is comprehensive and includes a full Scottish and kippers. The street-level, timber-fronted restaurant is also open for lunch and dinner and serves succulent fresh local seafood alongside non-fish options such as haggis-stuffed chicken.

18–20 Shore Rd., Anstruther, KY10 3EA. www.anstruther-waterfront.co.uk. ✆ **01333/312-200.** Fax 01333/312-288. 10 units. £40–£80 double; £65–£85 family room; £100–£130 family suite. MC, V. **Amenities:** Restaurant; Wi-Fi in public areas (free). *In room:* TV, hair dryer.

Crail ★★

Crail, 50 miles northeast of Edinburgh and 9⅓ miles south of St. Andrews, is the easternmost of East Neuk's fishing villages and one of its finest. The village is a favorite with local artists and has grown up around its still-working harbor, where old fishing cottages and lobster creels cluster around the medieval Shoregate. Stop at the **Crail Harbour Gallery and Tearoom** on Shoregate (© **01333/451-896;** www.crailharbourgallery.co.uk), a restored 17th-century fisherman's cottage that's now the gallery of resident artist DS Mackie and a cozy harbor-facing tearoom complete with outdoor patio overlooking the Isle of May. It's open February to November daily from 10:30am.

From Shoregate follow **Castle Walk,** a short walkway that offers panoramic views of the harbor and shoreline and leads to the upper part of the village. At the west end of Marketgate, a tree-lined street flanked by small two- and three-floor houses, stands Crail's **tolbooth** dating from 1598 and formerly the town jail. The **Crail Museum & Heritage Centre,** 62 Marketgate (© **01333/450-869;** www.crailmuseum.org. uk), is adjacent to the tolbooth and its collections provide an insight into the fishing industry and former trading links of these tiny villages. It's open Easter to September Monday through Saturday 10am to 1pm and 2 to 5pm, and Sunday 2 to 5pm; admission is free. Keep heading east from Marketgate to reach the sea-facing **Balcomie Golf Course** (© **01333/450-686;** www.crailgolfingsociety.co.uk), one of the oldest courses in the world and open to visiting golfers.

Shoppers should stop at the **Crail Pottery** (© **01333/451-212;** www.crail pottery.com) on Netherbow. Set in a tranquil courtyard, this long-established pottery sells a mouthwatering range of handcrafted earthenware, ceramics, and pottery. To catch a sample of local folk music, look out for the **Crail Folk Club** (www.crailfolk club.org.uk), whose regular live music nights take place at **The Golf Hotel** (© **01333/450-206;** www.thegolfhotelcrail.com) on the A917 as it passes through town or the **Crail Town Hall** on Marketgate. Check the Folk Club's website for dates and times.

EXPLORING THE AREA

Secret Bunker ★ HISTORIC SITE   Scotland's best-kept secret during 40 years of the Cold War, this amazing labyrinth, built 30m (100 ft.) below ground and encased in 4.5m (15 ft.) of reinforced concrete, is from where government and military officials would have run the country if the U.K. had been involved in a nuclear conflict. It has a guardhouse entrance designed to look like a traditional Scottish farmhouse. You can visit the BBC studio, from where emergency broadcasts would have been made, and the switchboard room, set up to handle 2,800 phone lines. The bunker could allow 300 people to live, work, and sleep in safety while coordinating war efforts. It now contains two cinemas showing authentic Cold War films, an audiovisual theatre, a cafe, and a gift shop.

Crown Buildings, Troywood, 3 miles west of Crail, off the B940. © **01333/310-301.** www.secretbunker. co.uk. Admission £9 adults, £7.50 seniors, £6 children 5–16, £25 families. Easter–October 10am–5pm.

WHERE TO STAY

Selcraig House   This small, super-friendly bed-and-breakfast in the center of Crail brims with old-world charm and warm hospitality. The property dates back to the 1700s and retains many period features such as its ornate fireplaces. The rooms are well maintained and comfortable with one luxury double featuring a four-poster bed and old-fashioned fireplace. Breakfast is served in an Edwardian parlor where guests are invited to listen to music on the old Victorian gramophone, and the menu includes seasonal fish fresh from local suppliers.

47 Nethergate, Crail, KY10 3TX. www.selcraighouse.co.uk. © **01333/450-697.** 5 units. £30–£35 per person per night. Cash only. **Amenities:** Wi-Fi (free). *In room:* TV, hair dryer.

ST. ANDREWS: THE BIRTHPLACE OF GOLF ★★

14 miles SE of Dundee; 51 miles NE of Edinburgh

Golfers consider the medieval royal burgh of St. Andrews to be hallowed ground because the sport was first played here in the 1400s, probably on the site of the Old Course. St. Andrews is dominated by its university, the oldest and most prestigious in Scotland, where royal couple Prince William and Kate Middleton met and studied. The university's buildings are some of the oldest in town; after golf, St. Andrews' ruined great cathedral and castle are its biggest tourist attractions. Part of the pleasure of St. Andrews is to merely explore its medieval streets, which retain much of their sense of history and are framed by the dramatic waters of the North Sea.

Essentials

GETTING THERE ScotRail (**0845/601-5929**; www.scotrail.co.uk) stops 8 miles away, at the town of Leuchars (rhymes with "euchres"), on its Edinburgh–Dundee–Aberdeen run. The service departs roughly every half-hour and it takes an hour from Edinburgh to Leuchars, where a connecting bus makes the 11-minute journey to St. Andrews' bus station on Station Road. A one-way fare is £14 and a round-trip fare is £22.

By car from Edinburgh, head northwest along the A90 and cross the Forth Road Bridge. The A90 becomes the M90 as it leads north and exit at junction 8 to follow the A91 west, which leads through Cupar to St. Andrews.

Dundee airport 15 miles northwest of St. Andrews receives regular flights from London City and Birmingham airports.

VISITOR INFORMATION A **Tourist Information Centre** is located on 70 Market St. (© **01334/472-021;** www.visitfife.co.uk) and opens April to mid-October Monday through Saturday 9:15am to 5pm, Sunday 11am to 4pm, although July to September it closes at 7pm Monday through Saturday and 5pm on Sundays. From mid-October through March, the center is open Monday through Saturday 9:30am to 5pm.

Hitting the St. Andrews Links

St. Andrews Links is made up of six public courses, most famously the 6,721-yard par-72 (ladies 6,032-yard par-76) **Old Course,** established in 1552 and the oldest golf course in the world. This fabled course most recently hosted the British Open in 2010, when Louis Oosthuizen stormed to his first major championship victory.

The other courses here are the 6,625-yard par-71 (ladies 5,992-yard par-75) **New Course,** opened in 1895; the 6,742-yard par-72 (ladies 5,956-yard par-74) **Jubilee Course,** opened in 1897, in honor of Queen Victoria's Diamond Jubilee; the 6,250-yard par-70 (ladies 5,505-yard par-73) **Eden,** opened in 1914; the 5,620-yard par-69 (ladies 4,704 yard par-68) **Strathtyrum,** the newest and most far-flung, opened in 1993; and the 1,520-yard par-30 **Balgove,** a 9-hole course ideal for children, families, and beginners. There's no handicap limit on any of the courses, except the Old Course—max 24 men, 36 ladies, and a handicap certificate is required to play.

All courses are maintained by the **St. Andrews Link Trust** (© **01334/466-666;** www.standrews.org.uk), who also manage a seventh public course, the 6,759-yard par-71 (ladies 5,460-yard par-71) **Castle Course,** which is a mile southeast of town and has its own clubhouse.

Around 42,000 rounds of golf are played on the Old Course each year and applications to play (minimum two golfers) must be submitted by phone (see above) or in person before 2pm on the day before you want to play. There's no play on Sundays, and Saturday's draw is for Monday's play. Applications are entered into a ballot and results are published on the website (see above), and at various places on the Links, by 4pm. Single golfers can chance their luck by arriving at the starter as early as possible on the day they wish to play to see if they can join the first available two or three ball. A current handicap certificate and proof of identity is required for all golfers.

Advance bookings for a round on the New, Jubilee, Eden, Strathtyrun, and Castle courses can be made by calling or e-mailing a minimum of 14 days in advance, though some tee times can be booked online; no booking is required for the Balgove course, just go to the starter.

Greens fees are £64 to £140 for the Old Course, £60 to £120 for the Castle Course, and £12 to £70 for all other courses except Balgove, which is £8 to £12. A caddy costs £45, or £25 for a trainee; they must be paid (and tipped) in cash. Unless you're registered disabled, no golf buggies are allowed on the Old Course and trolleys are only permitted between April and October after noon.

Encircling St. Andrews Links is the world's most prestigious golf club, the **Royal and Ancient** (© **01334/460-000;** www.randa.org). Founded in St. Andrews in 1754 by a group of noblemen, professors, and landowners, it remains more or less rigidly closed as a private-membership men's club and governs the rules of golf everywhere except the U.S.

The Links Clubhouse is located 400 yards from the first tee of the Old Course. It's open year-round to golfers and non-golfers and offers lockers, showers, and changing facilities. There's also a bar and restaurant on site.

For more details on golf associations and golf tours, see "Teeing Off: Golfing in Scotland," in chapter 4.

Exploring St. Andrews

St. Andrews gathers around three main streets: North Street, South Street, and Market Street, which run parallel to each other and lead west from the ruined cathedral. Small cobbled streets link these main thoroughfares, making the town easy and preferable to explore on foot. The historic attractions detailed below form the focus of any visit and also include **Holy Trinity Church,** a restored medieval church dating back to 1410 on South Street.

Even non-golfers should make the pilgrimage to the hallowed **Old Course ★★** and iconic **Royal and Ancient** clubhouse. Close by on Bruce Embankment the **British Golf Museum** (© **01334/460046;** www.britishgolfmuseum.co.uk) leads visitors on a hands-on journey through 500 years of golfing history. It's open November through March daily 10am to 4pm, April through October Monday through Saturday 9:30am to 5pm, Sunday 10am to 5pm. Admission is £6 for adults and £3 children under 16.

It's easy to overlook St. Andrews' fine beaches, including the sweeping **West Sands** leading from the Royal and Ancient clubhouse—the location for the opening scene of *Chariots of Fire*. The smaller, more family-friendly **East Sands** at the old harbor behind the cathedral is a good place to join the Fife Coastal Path (p. 243), and its Long Pier is the setting for red-gowned university students' traditional post-church Sunday walk.

Founded in 1410, the **University of St. Andrews** is the third oldest in Britain. Known as the "Oxbridge" of Scotland, it dominates the town and its grounds stretch west of the castle (see below) between North Street and The Scores. Its best buildings are off North Street and include the tower and church of St. Salvator's College and the courtyard of St. Mary's College, which date back to 1538. An ancient thorn tree, said to have been planted by Mary Queen of Scots, stands near the college's chapel, and St. Leonard's College church also dates from the medieval era. In addition, the university owns the **Gateway Galleries** (© **01344/467-400;** Mon–Fri 9am–5:30pm, Sat 10am–5pm; admission free), a striking round building at North Haugh off the A91 as it leads past the Old Course. Here a rotating program of exhibitions showcases some of the university's finest treasures.

Castle of St. Andrews ★ CASTLE   This ruined 13th-century castle, eerily perched at the edge of the sea, boasts a bottle dungeon and secret passages. Reconstructed several times, it was once a bishop's palace and later a prison for reformers. The bottle dungeon is carved 7m (23 ft.) down into the rock, and both prisoners and food were dropped through it. There's said to be no nastier dungeon in all Scotland. The castle was the scene of the trial and subsequent burning at the stake of religious reformer George Wishart in 1546, watched by the incumbent Cardinal Beaton. Intent on revenge, a group of reformers murdered Beaton 3 months later and retained control of the castle for almost a year. Both attacking Catholic forces and the sieging reformers dug underground passages through which to attack each other, and they remain a unique example of medieval siege warfare. The on-site visitor center and exhibition explains all.

The Scores (273m/900 ft. northwest of the cathedral). © **01334/477-196.** www.historic-scotland.gov. uk. Tickets for the castle only £5.20 adults, £3.10 children. Combined castle and cathedral tickets £7.20 adults, £4.30 children 5–15. Apr–Sept daily 9:30am–5:30pm; Oct–Mar daily 9:30am–4:30pm.

St. Andrews Cathedral ★ CATHEDRAL   Poised on the edge of the coast by the old harbor, the evocative ruins of what was once Scotland's most important cathedral are among the most significant in the country. The cathedral was founded in 1160 and consecrated in 1318 in the presence of Robert the Bruce. The relics of St. Andrew, Scotland's patron saint, were once enshrined in its high altar. Today the remaining ruins strike a dramatic pose against the North Sea, and highlights include the 12th-century St. Rules Tower and cathedral museum.

Off Pends Rd. © **01334/472-563.** www.historic-scotland.gov.uk. Tickets for the cathedral only £4.20 adults, £2.50 children. Combined castle and cathedral tickets £7.20 adults, £4.30 children 5–15. Apr–Sept daily 9:30am–5:30pm; Oct–Mar daily 9:30am–4:30pm.

Where to Eat

St. Andrews is filled with numerous cafes that are busy with students during term time and locals year-round. The bistro at the **Byre Theatre** (see below) is a recommended spot, as is **B. Jannetta** on South Street (© **01334/473-285;** www.jannettas. co.uk), famous for its award-winning ice cream—there are 52 flavors. The tiny **Taste Café** (© **01334/477-959**) on North Street is a good place to grab a takeaway fairtrade coffee and sticky cake. Many of the best restaurants are located within St. Andrews' hotels—see "Where to Stay," below, for detailed listings—and many of the town's bars and pubs serve inexpensive food until late.

The Glass House ★ CONTINENTAL/BRITISH   A relative newcomer in town, this simple, stylish restaurant combines fine continental dining with British favorites in a modern yet warm setting. The building itself is an old Salvation Army church hall now decked out with an open kitchen, modern mezzanine level, and outdoor patio. The menu adds a fresh twist to continental cuisine and includes stone-baked pizza with sauteed leeks and mushrooms and more traditional dishes such as seared Angus rump steak. This company also owns the Grill House restaurant on St. Mary's Place and the Doll's House restaurant on Church Square. Both offer relatively similar styles of food, and both are worthy of a visit.

80 North St., ☏ **013334/473-673.** www.houserestaurants.com. Main courses £8–£11. Daily lunch noon–4pm, early evening menu 4–6:30pm, and dinner from 8:30pm.

The Grange Inn ★ SCOTTISH/SEAFOOD This converted 1700s farmhouse oozes old-fashioned hospitality, fine local food, and long views of the Fife countryside towards St. Andrews. The Grange sits in landscaped gardens and tradition is reflected in both the decor and menu. Scottish favorites grace the menu such as *Cullen skink* (smoked fish soup) and fillet of Scottish salmon, and meat lovers can feast on roasted Fife lamb and a selection of steaks. Vegetarians can choose from dishes such as pumpkin ravioli and butternut squash risotto. Owners Sandy and Bee also own the Nahm-Jim Thai restaurant on Market Street in St. Andrews (www.nahm-jim.co.uk), which recently won the best Thai restaurant category in celebrity chef Gordon Ramsey's search for the best restaurants in Britain.

Grange Rd., at Grange (on the B959). ☏ **01334/472-670.** www.thegrangeatstandrews.com. Reservations recommended. Lunch main courses £9–£13, dinner main courses £14–£22. DC, MC, V. Sat–Sun noon–3pm, Wed–Sat 6–11pm. Drive about 1½ miles from St. Andrews on the B959.

The Seafood Restaurant ★★ SEAFOOD The freshest fish in St. Andrews is served at this top-class restaurant, occupying the site of a former open-air theatre and lying on the banks of West Sands. This was a favorite of Prince William when he attended university in St. Andrews, and the chefs work in full view from the open kitchen—no secrets here. Windows reach from floor to ceiling, allowing diners panoramic sea views. Regularly changing set menus make full use of the products in season at local markets, and you can expect to sample dishes such as lemon sole tempura and stone bass with spiced couscous and pineapple and red pepper chutney. The accompanying extensive wine list features vintage champagne and bottles from around the world.

Bruce Embankment ☏ **01334/479-475.** www.theseafoodrestaurant.com. Reservations required. Fixed-price lunch £14 for 2 courses, £17 for 3 courses; fixed-price dinner £30 for 3 courses. AE, MC, V. Mon–Sat noon–2:30pm, Sun 12:30–3pm, daily 6:30–9pm.

Shopping

St. Andrews' main shopping area clusters around South and Market streets and is a combination of high street chain shops and local independent stores. There's no shortage of places to buy golfing apparel and equipment, and most of these types of stores are located in the west end of town towards the Old Course. Also at this end of town on Albany Place is the **Open View Gallery** (☏ **01334/477-840;** www.openviewgallery.com), which sells a varied selection of fine art, designer jewelry, and photographs including many superb golfing prints. **Bonkers,** 80 Market St. (☏ **01334/473-919;** www.bonkers-standrews.co.uk), is a colorful gift shop selling items for the home and gardens, plenty of pampering products, and a lovely range of children's gifts.

Entertainment & Nightlife

The cultural center of St. Andrews is the **Byre Theatre,** Abbey Street (☏ **01334/475-000;** www.byretheatre.com), which features a varied program of theatre, music, comedy, and dance; tickets cost £10 to £20 for adults, £5 to £12 concessions. The

Byre's bar and bistro is popular with locals and often hosts events such as dinner and ceilidh nights. The **New Picture House** on North Street (© **01334/474-902;** www.nphcinema.co.uk) is a three-screen cinema that shows mainly mainstream films. Tickets cost £6 to £7 for adults and £4.30 to £5 for children 12 and under.

St. Andrews' drinking and nightlife scene focuses on a young crowd and is student dominated. Established drinking spots include **The Victoria Café and Bar,** 1 St. Mary's Place (© **01334/476-964**); this student-filled pub is the place to catch live music and big-screen sports. **The Rule** bar and diner, 116 South St. (© **01334/473-473;** www.the-rule.co.uk), is classically decked out with warm wood and brown leather and features a large beer garden and busy dance area downstairs. This bar also hosts regular quiz and DJ nights. For a game of pool, head to **The Raisin,** 5 Alexandra Place (© **08721/077-077**) which has two tables, a relaxed vibe, and inexpensive drinks.

For dedicated golfers, the bar of choice is **The Dunvegan Hotel's** lounge bar on Pilmour Place (© **01334/473-105;** www.dunvegan-hotel.com). A mere 112 yards from the Old Course, the hotel is owned by golf lovers Jack, a 4th-generation Texan, and his Scottish wife, and their bar is the best "19th hole" in town. Its walls are lined with memorabilia from the many past masters who have enjoyed a pint of ale or one of the 50 whiskies on offer here.

The only nightclub in town is **The Lizard** beneath the Oak Rooms restaurant on North Street (© **01334/473-387**). It's a blend of lounge bar and dance floor, and hosts DJ nights and live music.

Where to Stay

Whatever your preference and budget, you won't struggle to find a place to stay in St. Andrews as both its university and famous golf course ensure a regular and varied stream of year-round visitors. A number of large, upmarket hotels cluster along the west end of The Scores towards the Old Course. North Street, and the quieter Murray Park, are filled with small hotels and bed-and-breakfasts all ranging in price and quality. Some of the more luxurious places to stay are on the outskirts of St. Andrews, whether they're brand-new resorts wanting the room to spread out, or historic coaching inns offering a rural escape within easy reach of town.

EXPENSIVE

Fairmont St. Andrews Bay Golf Resort & Spa ★★★ [green]   Perched on a cliff overlooking the North Sea, Fairmont is a spacious, modern, luxury resort with first-class leisure facilities, including two championship golf courses. The large, well-equipped bedrooms are the finest in the area and combine style, functionality, and comfort with sweeping views of either the ocean or the golf courses. This is famously the place where Prince William reputedly first set eyes on Kate Middleton as she took part in a fashion show hosted by the resort. The spa and fitness club that the Prince once belonged to includes all the facilities you'd expect, such as a large indoor pool and a number of intimate treatment rooms offering pampering galore. The five dining options range from the formal Mediterranean-themed **Esperante** (reservations recommended) to the informal **Rock and Spindle** sports bar. Golf is the main attraction, including the 7,049-yard par-71 Devlin, designed by Australian pro Bruce Devlin, and the 7,037-yard par-72 Torrance, designed by Rider Cup captain Sam Torrance.

St. Andrews Bay, KY16 8PN. www.fairmont.com. © **800/257-7544** in the U.S., or 01334/837-000. Fax 01334/471-115. 209 units. £249–£339 double; £349–£649 suite; from £1,200 Manor home. AE, DC, MC,

V. 3½ miles south of St. Andrews. **Amenities:** 5 restaurants; 2 bars; pool (indoor); health club and spa; children's programs Fri-Sat; concierge; room service babysitting. Free shuttle bus to St. Andrews. *In room:* TV, minibar, hair dryer, Wi-Fi (free).

Peat Inn ★★   Set in a tiny community about 6¾ miles from St. Andrews, the Peat Inn is a luxurious restaurant with rooms offering all the attraction of a rural setting with some of the finest dining in Fife. An inn has occupied this place since the 1700s and today each of the spacious guest rooms and suites are beautifully furnished all with separate bedrooms and living areas. In the award-winning restaurant, top chef Geoffrey Smeddle prepares exceptional cuisine served in an intimate series of small dining rooms. You can choose to have breakfast served in your room.

At the intersection of the A915 and B940, 6¾ miles south of St. Andrews, KY15 5LH. www.thepeatinn.co.uk. ✆**01334/840-206.** Fax 01334/840-530. 8 units. £190 suite for 2. AE, MC, V. **Amenities:** Restaurant; bar; room service; Internet (free). *In room:* TV, hair dryer.

St. Andrews Old Course Hotel ★★★   Many dedicated golfers choose this five-story Old Course Hotel, close to the A91 on the outskirts of town, which overlooks the infamous 17th fairway. Don't let the name mislead you: The hotel isn't related to the links of the same name, and guests here find access to the course just as difficult. (However, the hotel does own the championship The Duke's, a nearby heathland course.) The guest rooms and suites offer traditional wooden furniture and state-of-the-art marble bathrooms, and some come with balconies overlooking the Old Course itself. Extras include robes and slippers, and some suites have their own mini kitchens. The on-site spa includes a gorgeous 20m (65-ft.) pool with waterfall as well as a rooftop hot tub. Various dining experiences are available, including the gourmet Road Hole Restaurant overlooking the Old Course—a perfect spot for afternoon tea.

Old Station Rd., KY16 9SP. www.oldcoursehotel.kohler.com. ✆**01334/474-371.** Fax 01334/477-668. 144 units. £280–£330 double; £612–£1,300 junior suite. Children 11 and under stay free in parent's room. AE, DC, MC, V. **Amenities:** 4 restaurants; 4 bars; pool (indoor); spa w/Jacuzzi; children's activities; concierge; room service; babysitting. *In room:* TV, CD player, hair dryer, whirlpool bath (in some), Hi-Fi (some), Wi-Fi (£15 per day).

MODERATE

Five Pilmour Place ★★   Renovated with an unusual blend of modern design and Indo-Chinese art, this small luxury hotel close to the Old Course offers comfort, style, and convenience. The plush interior also remains faithful to the history of the house, and you can expect a fine restored fireplace and deep sofas in the visitor lounge where guests are encouraged to make themselves at home. The rooms ooze relaxation and include extras such as DVD players—there's also a guest DVD library. Breakfasts are a highlight and options include warm waffles and cream cheese bagels.

5 Pilmour Place, KY16 9HZ. www.5pilmourplace.com. ✆fax **01334/478-665.** 6 units. £85–£150 double. AE, MC, V. *In room:* TV, DVD/CD players, hair dryer, Wi-Fi (free).

Inn at Lathones ★★   Dating back over 400 years, the Inn at Lathones is St. Andrews' oldest coaching inn and famous for both luxury accommodation and fine dining. The Inn is set in rolling countryside on the outskirts of town and guests choose between swish newly refurbished rooms featuring Italian furniture in a converted old blacksmith's house and forge, or deluxe rooms with Jacuzzi baths and log fires in the old inn itself—one of which is reputedly haunted by a gray lady. The award-winning food includes both informal and reasonably priced bar meals and top-notch local dining in the restaurant where dishes such as roasted sea bass and leek and dunsyre blue tart grace the menu. The hotel also offers activity weekends and is one of the best small music venues in the U.K.

By Largoward, KY9 1JE. www.theinn.co.uk. ℂ **01334/840-494.** Fax 01334/840-694. 21 units. £140–£295 double. Children 12 and under stay free in parent's room. AE, MC, V. Take the A915, 5 miles southwest of the center of St. Andrews. **Amenities:** Restaurant; bar; room service; Wi-Fi (free). *In room:* TV, hair dryer.

INEXPENSIVE

Ashlar House ★   One of the best bed-and-breakfast options in town, Aslar House is an appealing combination of elegance and modern comforts combined with warm hospitality and superb breakfasts. This Victorian terrace house contains a number of finely decorated luxury rooms and suites—including one set inside a turret. A downstairs lounge, complete with books and comfy sofas, makes for a pleasant place to relax and the better-than-average breakfasts created from local seasonal fare make for a satisfying way to start the day.

120 North St., KY16 9AF. www.aslar.com. ℂ **01334/473-460.** 6 units. £90–£96 double. MC, V. **Amenities:** Restaurant; bar. *In room:* TV, DVD player, fridge, hair dryer, iPod docking station, Wi-Fi (free).

Ogstons   Popular with a young crowd, Ogstons has a prime central location and a series of comfortable, contemporary bedrooms with a traditional feel combined with modern comforts. Deluxe rooms offer a bit more space and luxury bathrooms, while every bedroom comes with a DVD player. The Oak Rooms, the on-site bar and restaurant, is decked out with soft leather chairs and warm wooden surfaces and the varied menu makes full use of local produce. Food is served from noon to 10pm and reservations are recommended.

North St., KY16 9AG. www.ogstonsonnorthst.com. ℂ **01334/473-387.** 13 units. Doubles from £80. MC, V. **Amenities:** Restaurant; bar. *In room:* TV, DVD player, hair dryer, Wi-Fi (free).

Six Murray Park ★   This boutique bed-and-breakfast in the heart of old St. Andrews is a gem of affordable luxury. The chic individually designed bedrooms are spotless and spacious, and the gleaming bathrooms (showers only) come complete with fluffy robes and thick towels. Old golfing pictures line the staircases and provide a nice touch of the history of St. Andrews and the Victorian vintage of the house. The customer service goes that extra mile and the hearty breakfasts served in the dining room include both cooked and continental options.

6 Murray Park, KY16 9AW. www.sixmurraypark.co.uk. ℂ **01334/473-319.** 6 units. £70–£80 double. MC, V. *In room:* TV, DVD player, hair dryer, Wi-Fi (free).

STIRLING ★★

35 miles NW of Edinburgh; 28 miles NE of Glasgow

Stirling is dominated by its impressive castle, perched on a 76m (250-ft.) basalt rock around which the city grew. This ancient settlement stands on the main east–west route across Scotland and is often described as "the brooch which clasps the Highlands and Lowlands together." Its central location ensured Stirling's strategic importance for anyone wanting to rule Scotland, and the city's history is bloody and turbulent. Two pivotal battles in the fight for Scotland's independence from the English were fought here—Stirling Bridge in 1297, which saw freedom fighter William Wallace lead Scottish troops, and Bannochburn in 1314 when Robert the Bruce took command—both resulting in decisive victories over England.

Stirling, Loch Lomond & the Trossachs

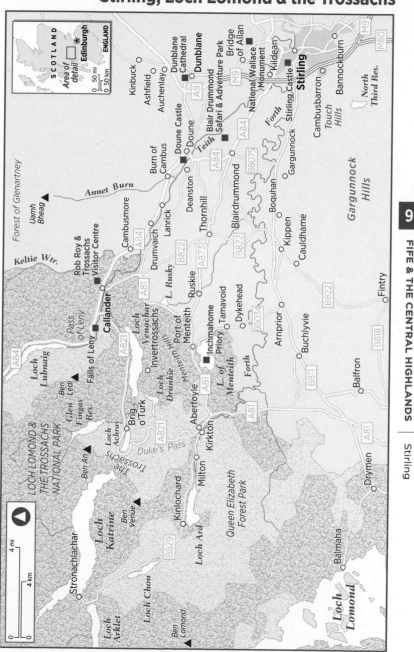

Stirling flourished from the 15th to the 17th centuries when it was much favored by Stuart monarchs. Today the city is busy with university students, and its central location makes Stirling easy to access by both road and rail from Edinburgh and Glasgow.

Essentials

GETTING THERE   Frequent trains run between Glasgow and Stirling (a 40-min. trip) and Edinburgh and Stirling (a 50-min. trip). A 1-day round-trip ticket from Edinburgh is £8 and from Glasgow £6.90. For schedules, contact **National Rail Enquiries** (© 08457/484-950) or visit **ScotRail's** website at www.scotrail.co.uk.

Hourly buses run to Stirling from Glasgow (a 45-min. trip) and Edinburgh (a 60-min. trip). A 1-day round-trip ticket from Glasgow costs £6.60 and from Edinburgh £6.70. Check with **Scottish Citylink** (© 0871//266-3333; www.citylink.co.uk) for details.

If you're driving from Glasgow, head northeast along the A80 to the M80, and then continue north. From Edinburgh, head northwest along the M9.

VISITOR INFORMATION   The **Tourist Information Centre** is at 41 Dumbarton Rd. (© 01786/475-019; www.stirling.co.uk). April to May, it's open Monday through Saturday 9am to 5pm; June to August, Monday through Saturday 9am to 6pm and Sunday 10am to 4pm; September to October Monday through Saturday 9:30am to 5pm; and November to March, Monday through Friday 10am to 5pm and Saturday 10am to 4pm.

Exploring Stirling

Any visit to Stirling should concentrate on its Old Town, the city's ancient center straddling a steep rocky outcrop and crowned with the imposing **Stirling Castle.** This area is filled with historical attractions, some of which are in ruins and many close during the winter. Highlights include the **Old Town Jail** (© 01786/450-050; www.oldtownjail.com), Stirling's Victorian prison on St. John Street, where the harsh squalor of 19th-century justice is revealed in all its grim glory. Also on St. John Street, the **Church of the Holy Rood ★** (© 01786/475-275; http://holyrude.org), which was founded in the 12th century, is memorable for its original oak roof beams and elaborate 19th-century stained glass. Other than London's Westminster Abbey, Holy Rood is the only still-existing church in the U.K. to have hosted a coronation: James VI of Scotland (later James I of England) was crowned here in 1567.

Other sites of historical interest are marked with plaques, and to get a real feel for the history of this area stroll along the **Back Walk,** which leads along the 16th-century city walls from the castle, past an old watchtower, and down into the modern town center.

Here head along Dumbarton Road to the **Stirling Smith Art Gallery & Museum** (© 01786/471/917; www.smithartgallery.demon.co.uk), whose exhibits include *The Stirling Story,* a journey through the city's history, and changing displays of the work of Scottish artists.

Stirling Castle ★★★ CASTLE   One of Scotland's most imposing and important historical sites, Stirling Castle dates from the Middle Ages and sits astride a steep volcanic crag. Stand beside the larger than life statue of Robert the Bruce on the castle forecourt for a king's eye view of the surrounding countryside, the setting of

STIRLING battles

To find out more about the pivotal battles and famous leaders in Scottish history associated with Stirling, you need to explore the city's outskirts. It was at **Bannockburn**, 1¾ miles south of Stirling, that Robert the Bruce and his army defeated the far larger forces of Edward II in June 1314 and in doing so paved the way for Scotland's independence from England. The actual site of the battle is still disputed, but the **Bannockburn Heritage Centre,** Glasgow Road (ⓒ **0844/ 493-2139;** www.nts.org.uk, off the M80/ M9 at Junction 9), stands on **Borestone Brae** where it's believed that the Bruce raised his standard (flag) and commanded his army. Buses 52, X39, and 139 travel from Stirling bus station to this site where you can walk the grounds for free and pay to enter a Heritage Centre to follow an audiovisual presentation detailing the history of the battle.

The site is open daily year-round and the Heritage Centre and shop are open April to September daily 10am to 5:30pm and March and October daily 10am to 5pm. Admission is £5.50 for adults, £4.50 for seniors and children, and £15 per family. The National Trust

for Scotland are currently planning a brand-new, state-of-the-art visitor center for this site, which should be open in 2014 in time for the 700th anniversary of the Battle of Bannockburn.

Seventeen years before Bannockburn, William Wallace also defeated English forces in this area at the Battle of Stirling Bridge on September 11, 1297. The actual battlefield is thought to be a number of miles upstream from the site of the present-day Stirling Bridge, and the place to find out more about this battle and Wallace himself is the **National Wallace Monument** (ⓒ **01786/472-140;** www.national wallacemonument.com), which stands on Abbey Craig 1½ miles north of Stirling. Known to many through Mel Gibson's film *Braveheart,* freedom fighter William Wallace is a Scottish national hero and exhibits on show include his mighty sword. The Monument is open daily November to March 10:30am to 4pm, April to June and September to October 10am to 5pm, and July and August 10am to 6pm. Admission is £7.50 for adults, £4.50 for children 16 and under, and £19.50 per family.

some of the most formative battles in Scottish history. Stirling's impregnable castle was an important seat for Scotland's late medieval monarchs and home of Mary Queen of Scots for the early years of her life. The **Royal Palace** ★★ forms the castle's centerpiece and was built in the 16th century by James V. James married the French Mary of Guise, and masons and craftsmen were brought from France to transform their palace into a royal home of European standing. It remains one of the finest examples of Renaissance architecture in Britain and has recently reopened after a massive restoration project designed to transform it back to its 16th-century glory. Costumed guides are on hand to entertain, inform, and detail every aspect of royal life 500 years ago. Also on display are the **Stirling Heads**—16th-century meter-wide oak medallions, carved by local master craftsmen and detailing the faces of Scottish royalty and Roman emperors. A set of **medieval tapestries** currently being woven at the castle are not to missed and once completed will adorn the walls of the Queen's Inner Hall at the Palace.

The regimental **Museum of the Argyll and Sutherland Highlanders** is also housed inside the castle, and admission includes a tour of **Argyll's Lodging** at the top of Castle Wynd, Scotland's best example of a complete 17th-century Renaissance townhouse.

Upper Castle Hill, ℂ **01786/450-000.** www.historic-scotland.gov.uk. Admission £9 adults, £7.20 seniors, £5.40 children 5-15, free for children 4 and under. Apr–Sept daily 9:30am–6pm; Oct–Mar daily 9:30am–5pm.

Exploring the Area

The **Bridge of Allan** is a small Victorian spa town 3 miles north of Stirling. Its pleasant main street (Henderson Street), lined with shops and cafes, leads towards Allan Water, a large tributary of the River Forth that crashes through the west side of town. Take time to peek behind the scenes and sample a pint of locally brewed ale at the **Bridge of Allan Brewery** on Queens Lane (ℂ **01786/834-555;** www.bridgeof allan.co.uk). A frequent train service runs between Stirling and the Bridge of Allan (£2.30 round-trip) or catch the no. 54 bus from Murray Place in Stirling town center (£3.60 round-trip).

Blair Drummond Safari & Adventure Park ★ ZOO   This large animal park is easily one of the best family-friendly destinations in the region. Visitors cruise through reserves where animals such as lions, bison, and elephant roam, and other attractions include sea lion shows, boat safaris, and lemur land. Younger children are also well catered for with fun fair rides, bouncy castles, and large play areas.

5 miles west of Stirling off the A84. ℂ **01786/841-456.** www.blairdrummond.com. Admission £13 adults, £9.50 children aged 14 and under. Easter to October daily 10am to 5:30pm.

Doune Castle ★★ CASTLE   Setting for the 1975 film *Monty Python and the Holy Grail,* Doune Castle was built around 1400 and used as a royal retreat. Much of the castle is surprisingly intact and it's easy to glean a sense of both bygone domestic and royal life as you wander around a labyrinth of royal apartments, great hall, kitchens, and cellars all built around a defended courtyard. Make sure you pick up an audio tour (included in the admission charge) and let yourself be informed by narrator Monty Python's Terry Jones as he brings to life both the castle's history and the making of the Holy Grail movie. Combine a visit here with a trip to Inchmahome Priory (p. 266), 8½ miles west of Doune, for a history-focused day out.

Doune, 3 miles west of Dunblane off A820. ℂ **01786/841-742.** www.historic-scotland.gov.uk. Admission £4.20 adults, £2.50 children. April–Sept daily 9:30am–5:30pm; Oct daily 9:30am–4:30pm; Nov–March Mon–Wed and Sat-Sun 9:30am–4:30pm.

Dunblane Cathedral ★ CATHEDRAL   Dunblane has been a place of worship since around A.D. 602 when St. Blane first established a Christian site here. The subsequent cathedral is one of the few surviving medieval churches in Scotland and dates back to the 12th century. Most of the glorious Gothic architecture still intact today was built in the 13th century and treated to substantial restoration in the 19th and 20th centuries. Highlights include a magnificent wooden barrel-vaulted roof with colorful armorials and the Barty windows, two stained-glass windows created by artist Louis Davis in the early 20th century featuring scenes from the Song of Simeon. A **Cathedral Museum** (ℂ 01786/825-691; www.dunblanemuseum.org.uk), housed in the 1624 Dean's House opposite the cathedral, is free to enter and displays artifacts, photographs, and papers detailing Dunblane's history.

Cathedral Close. ℂ **01786/823-388.** www.dunblanecathedral.org.uk. Free admission; donation requested. Apr–Sept Mon-Sat 9:30am–6pm, Sun 1:30-6pm; Oct–Mar Mon-Sat 9:30am–4:30pm, Sun 1:30-4pm.

Where to Eat

Some of the finer places to eat in Stirling are located inside its hotels, such as The Heritage inside the Park Lodge Hotel (p. 260) and Adamo (p. 260). On the outskirts of town I recommend **The River House** (© 01786/465-577; www.houserestaurant.com) at Craigforth, sister restaurant to the Glass House in St. Andrews (p. 250), and **The Birds and Bees** (© 01786/473-663; www.thebirdsandthebees-stirling.com), a bistro inside a converted farmhouse at Causewayhead village. Those looking for cafe culture should aim for the comfy sofas or booths inside The Burgh Coffeehouse (http://burghcoffee.com) on King Street, which is open until 8pm every night.

Clives ★ DELI   A popular local choice on the Bridge of Allan's main street, Clive's is a bright and friendly deli restaurant occupying two floors and spreading out continental style onto the outside pavement in summer. Food is served from 8am until late, with breakfasts served until 11:30am and a long lunch menu including sandwiches and hand-cut chips, and meat, fish, and pasta dishes taking over until 6pm. Similar dishes are served into the evening along with a good vegetarian selection such as Thai green curry and veggie fajitas. Hearty cakes, coffees, and a selection of fine teas will fill a gap at any time of day.

26 Henderson St., Bridge of Allan, 3 miles north of Stirling. © **01786/831-616.** www.clives.org. Main courses £6–£13. MC, V. Daily from 8am.

Hermann's Brasserie AUSTRIAN/SCOTTISH   This reliable favorite, housed in an old, traditional townhouse with high-beamed ceilings, lies in the middle of Stirling's atmospheric old town close to the castle. The a la carte menu is an unusual and appealing mix of Scottish dishes and Austrian cuisine. Expect to choose between Austrian cheese spatzle topped with roasted vegetables, Jager Schnitzel, and West coast scallops on Stornoway black pudding. Wine tasting evenings are popular events when chef Hermann Aschaber matches each course to a different wine.

Mar Place House, 58 Broad St., Stirling © **01786/450-632.** www.hermanns.co.uk. Reservations recommended. Main courses lunch £5–£16, dinner £16–£22. AE, MC, V. Daily noon-2:30pm and 6-9:30pm.

Shopping

The focus of Stirling's town center shopping is **The Thistles** (© 01786/470-055; www.thethistles.com), an indoor shopping mall at the junction of Port Street and Murray Place where you'll find a selection of chain stores. One of the better places in town for Scottish gifts such as jewelry and tartans including kilts is **The House of Henderson,** 6–8 Friar St. (© 01786/473-681; www.houseofhenderson.co.uk).

However, some of the best shopping is to be found in outlying areas such as The Bridge of Allan whose Henderson Street is dotted with art, crafts, and gift shops, including **WoodWinters** (© 01786/834-894; www.woodwinters.com), a specialist wine and whisky store.

The area east of Stirling includes a number of former mill towns such as Alva, Alloa, and Tillicoultry. The industry no longer thrives in this region, but visitors can find out all about the history and traditions of woolens, tartan, and tweed making in this part of Scotland at the **Mill Trail Visitor Centre,** West Stirling Street, Alva (© 01259/769-696), 8⅔ miles east of the center of Stirling. September to June it's open daily 10am to 5pm; July and August, it's open daily 9am to 5pm. Information on a trail leading around the former mills of this region and the factory outlets offering bargain prices on cotton, woolens, and cashmere goods can also be picked up here.

Entertainment & Nightlife

Stirling's main arts venue is the **Albert Halls** off Dumbarton Road (© **01786/473-544;** www.stirling.gov.uk/alberthalls), offering a range of mainstream music, theatre, and dance events. It also includes Hendersons restaurant, an excellent spot for pre-theatre food. The **Tolbooth** (© **01786/274-000;** www.stirling.gov.uk/tolbooth) in the heart of the Old Town is a music and arts venue housed in Stirling's renovated medieval jail. On the campus of Stirling University, the **Macrobert Arts Centre** (© **01786/466-666;** www.macrobert.stir.ac.uk) features both mainstream and more unusual plays, music, films, and art exhibits and the no. 54 bus from town stops right outside.

In town head down St. Mary's Wynd for a pint the **Settle Inn** (© **08721/077-077**), which has been serving Scottish ales since the 1700s and is one of the most haunted places in Scotland. **Whistlebinkies** (© **01786/451-256**) also on St. Mary's Wynd is another of Stirling's old pubs and a good place to catch live music.

Where to Stay

EXPENSIVE

Adamo ★★   A boutique hotel in the middle of the Bridge of Allan's main street, Adamo is haven of modern luxury within a traditional setting. Choose from a range of chic rooms and suites whose bathrooms feature jet showers and/or spa baths, or top-floor penthouse apartments. The on-site restaurant and bar are styled in warm woods and soft leather chairs and are a perfect place to relax after a hard day's sight-seeing or a pleasant spot to linger over morning coffee. Adamo's sister hotel stands on Upper Craigs in the center of Stirling and is a similar combination of modern luxury and stylish dining inside a traditional town building.

24 Henderson St., Bridge of Allan 3 miles north of Stirling, FK9 4PH. www.adamohotels.com. © **01786/833-268.** Fax 01786/833-268. 16 units. £160–£180 double, £180–£220 suites, £250–£270 penthouse. AE, MC, V. **Amenities:** Restaurant; bar. *In room:* TV, minibar, hair dryer, Wi-Fi (free).

Stirling Highland Hotel ★★   This is one of Stirling's finest hotels and occupies a former Victorian high school in the heart of the city. The hotel lies within an easy stroll of the castle and its historic atmosphere is treated with respect; many features are still intact, including a working observatory on the top floor. Florals, tartans, and solid-wood furnishings dominate the public and guest rooms and its elevated position allows wide views over the town and surrounding region. The on-site leisure facilities are of a high standard and there's a whole range of pampering, relaxation, and beauty treatments.

A menu of traditional and international cuisine is served at the formal Scholars Restaurant, and the bar—or Headmaster's Study as it's known—stocks a good selection of whisky.

Spittal St., FK8 1DU. www.barcelo-hotels.co.uk. © **0800/652-8413**. Fax 01786/272-829. 96 units. £120–£160 double. AE, DC, MC, V. **Amenities:** Restaurant; pool (indoor); squash court; health club; fitness suite, sauna, steam room, babysitting. *In room:* TV, hair dryer, Wi-Fi (free).

MODERATE

Park Lodge Hotel ★   Built in 1825, this stylish hotel occupies a restored Georgian house and is a good choice for those seeking historically traditional decor and a quiet residential neighborhood. The ivy clad hotel overlooks a park and the Stirling Golf Club, and each bedroom contains antique furnishings faithful to the era in which the house was built—one even contains a four-poster bed. Enjoy a whisky or cocktail in the elegant guest lounge and fine Scottish and French cuisine in The Heritage restaurant. In summer you can take tea in the walled garden, with its widely spaced iron benches and terracotta statues.

32 Park Terrace, FK8 2JS. www.parklodge.net. ©**01786/474-862.** Fax 01786/449-748. 9 units. £90 double. AE, MC, V. **Amenities:** Restaurant; bar. *In room:* TV, hair dryer.

Terraces Hotel 🐾 Built originally as a fine Georgian house, this hotel stands on a raised terrace in a quiet residential neighborhood and combines a central location with good value. The guest rooms are a good size and many have new bathrooms. The on-site Terraces bar and bistro has both formal dining areas and places to chill out, and the outdoor garden terrace is a lovely spot for afternoon tea in summer. The dinner menu features Scottish seafood and dishes made from local meat such as Perthshire lamb with main dishes priced between £10 and £18.

4 Melville Terrace, FK8 2ND. www.terraceshotel.co.uk. ©**01786/472-268.** Fax 01786/450-314. 18 units. £120–£160 double. AE, DC, MC, V. **Amenities:** Restaurant; bar; room service. *In room:* TV, hair dryer.

INEXPENSIVE

Castlecroft ★ Standing in the shadow of Stirling Castle and on the site of the old King's Stables, this modern guesthouse offers a quiet location with sweeping views of the surrounding countryside. All the spacious bedrooms have recently been refurbished and are spread over three levels; two have their own patio area. The welcoming guest lounge has wide views over the Trossachs and a roaring fire in winter. Breakfasts are especially good; expect a wide choice and local produce. The center of Stirling is a 10-minute walk away.

Ballengeich Rd., FK8 1TN. www.castlecroft-uk.com. ©**01786/474933.** 5 units. Double rooms from £55, family rooms from £70. No credit cards. **Amenities:** Bar. *In room:* TV, hair dryer, Wi-Fi (free).

West Plean House 🐾 This working farm south of Stirling is a good choice for those seeking a rural location and value for money. West Plean is surrounded by walking trails and has its own lovely walled garden. The bedrooms are spacious and comfortable and the owners welcoming and helpful. There's also a guest lounge with a TV, board games, books, and Wii console, and the home-cooked breakfasts are first class.

Denny Rd., 3¾ miles south of Stirling on the A872, FK7 8HA. www.westpleanhouse.com. ©**01786/812-208.** Fax 01786/480-550. 3 units. £40 per person per night. No credit cards. Closed 2 weeks in late Dec. *In room:* TV, hair dryer.

CALLANDER & A TRIO OF LOCHS ★★

16 miles NW of Stirling; 43 miles N of Glasgow; 52 miles NW of Edinburgh; 42 miles W of Perth

Callander sits in the eastern edge of **Loch Lomond and the Trossachs National Park** (www.lochlomond-trossachs.org), a 720-square-mile protected area of rural Scotland that includes **Loch Lomond**—Scotland's largest loch—and **the Trossachs,** a spectacularly beautiful area of woodland glens, braes (hills), and smaller lochs.

In 1691, the Rev. Robert Kirk called the Trossachs a commonwealth of "elfs, fawns, and fairies," and the region shot to fame thanks to Sir Walter Scott's 1810 poem *The Lady of the Lake* and novel *Rob Roy,* which romanticized the Scottish outlaw Rob Roy MacGregor (see box p. 263), who lived in the area. Callander and

Aberfoyle (p. 261 and 265, respectively) are good bases from which to explore the Trossachs, whose highlights include lochs Venachar, Achray, and Katrine. There's plenty of good walking to be had with a choice of trails starting at Callander, and the drive along the A821 from this small town through the Trossachs to Aberfoyle via Dukes Pass is one of the best car journeys in Scotland.

Essentials

GETTING THERE   Stirling (p. 254) is the nearest rail link. Once at Stirling, continue the rest of the way to Callander on the C59 First bus route from the Stirling station on Goosecroft Road. Contact **First Buses** (© **08708/727-271;** www.first group.com) for a timetable. A one-way fare is £3.20.

Driving from Stirling, head north along the M9 to junction 10 and then cut northwest along the A84.

Exploring the Area

Callander is an ideal base for exploring the Trossachs, one of Scotland's most fabled and beautiful regions, which lies to the immediate west of the town. The **Rob Roy & Trossachs Visitor Centre** (© **01877/330-342**) located in a converted church in Ancaster Square off Callander's Main Street is an excellent starting point. The center opens daily from 10am, closing at 6pm in July and August, 5pm March to June and September to October and 4pm from November to February. It's packed full of information about the region and what to do. Informative displays include a film about the area narrated by Sean Connery.

Walking is hugely popular with numerous trails leading from the center of Callander, many of which are detailed in the "Callander Paths" leaflet that can be picked up at the visitor center. Details of circular walks from the town center are also displayed on information boards in the Meadow Car Park adjacent to the Riverside Inn on Main Street. Favorite walks include **Bracklin Falls** and the **Falls of Leny,** an impressive sight near the confluence of the River Leny and the River Teith. Or head deeper into the Trossachs to the village of **Brig o'Turk** 6¾ miles from Callander, which lies between lochs Achray and Venachar, at the foot of Glen Finglas. Stunning forested scenery studded with pretty lochs lies in all directions, and favorite walks include the **Glen Finglas** circular one. For more information on walking and other activities including cycling, kayaking, and horse riding in the National Park, head to the **National Park Office** on Callander's Main Street (© **01380/722-600**). The office is open Monday through Friday 9:30am to 12:30pm and 1 to 4:30pm and Saturday 9:30am to 12:30pm. You can also pick up information on the Callander Heritage Trail, a walk around the town via street markers and information boards. Stops include the Old Graveyard, where in the early 1800s "body snatchers" dug up the newly buried to sell to anatomists.

Wildlife is rich and abundant in this region with walkers often spotting grazing deer. Full details of a **Bird of Prey Trail** (www.birdofpreytrail.com) can be found at the **Harbour Café** (p. 263), which also organizes fishing and boat rental on Loch Venachar. Those wanting to explore on two wheels can rent bikes for all ages at **Mounter Bikes** (© **01877/331-052;** www.callandercyclehire.co.uk), next to the Rob Roy and Trossachs Visitor Centre on Ancaster Square. Prices range from £15 for an adult bike full-day rental to £8 for junior bikes; you can also rent tag-a-longs, tandems, and child seats.

A Side Trip to Loch Voil ★—Rob Roy Country

The Trossachs are often referred to as "Rob Roy Country," because the Scottish folk hero and outlaw Rob Roy Mac-Gregor lived and died in this area. Known as the Robin Hood of Scotland, Rob Roy was born in 1671 at Glengyle at the head of Loch Katrine and has been immortalized through the works of Sir Walter Scott and the 1995 film staring Liam Neeson. He died in 1734 and is buried at **Balquhidder Church ★**, 13 miles northwest of Callander off the A84 at the eastern tip of **Loch Voil.** You can go through the churchyard where the Scottish hero is buried up to Kirkton Glen, continuing along through grasslands to a little lake. This signposted footpath leads to the next valley, called Glen Dochart, before it links up once again with A84. Alternatively head west along the banks of this loch to the **Braes o' Balquhidder** where you can enjoy some of the loveliest countryside walks in the Trossachs.

The town has the excellent wooded and scenic **Callander Golf Course,** Aveland Road (✆ **01877/330-090;** www.callandergolfclub.co.uk). At this 5,125-yard par-66 course, greens fees are £25 per round on weekdays and £35 on weekends, or £35 for a day ticket during the week, £45 on weekends. Trolley and equipment rental is available, and the clubhouse serves a good range of food throughout the day. The hilly fairways offer fine views, and the tricky moorland layout demands accurate tee shots.

Where to Eat

Callander Meadows ★ SCOTTISH   Located in the center of town, this acclaimed restaurant with rooms serves top-notch seasonal food and is one of the best places to eat in Callander. The regularly changing menu makes full use of local produce and includes Scottish seafood and meats all served in an intimate and simple setting. Vegetarian options such as roasted root vegetable risotto with olives and Parmesan are also available. Occasions such as Burns Night and Valentine's Day are celebrated with special menus. Callander Meadows' three comfortable en-suite rooms are also recommended (£70– £80 per night).

24 Main St., Callander. ✆ **01877/330-181.** www.callandermeadowsrestaurant.co.uk. Lunch main courses £7–£10, dinner main courses £11–£16. MC, V. Thurs-Sun 10am-2:30pm and 6-9:30pm.

Harbour Café ★★ 🍴 SCOTTISH   Without doubt one of the best cafe/restaurants in Scotland, this modern, comfortable, family-friendly eatery combines good food with outstanding views. Located 4 miles northwest of Callander, Harbour Café is perched on the north bank of Loch Venachar off the A821. A wooden balcony and floor-to-ceiling windows ensure uninterrupted views of the loch and surrounding hills. Menus feature staples such as soups, jacket potatoes, and sandwiches alongside lighter options including oatcakes and Scottish cheeses. Daily specials can be fresh seafood dishes and the homemade cakes are worth the trip alone. Harbour Café also exhibits the work of local artists, and boat rental and fishing can be arranged.

Loch Venachar, off the A821 3 miles west of the junction with the A84. ✆ **01877/330-011.** www.venachar-lochside.co.uk. Main courses £4–£8. MC, V. Daily from 10:30am, last order 7pm (4:30pm in winter).

Lade Inn INTERNATIONAL/SCOTTISH   Surrounded by fields and within earshot of the Leny River, the Lade was built as a teahouse, and then converted after

World War II into a pub and restaurant. This local favorite attracts residents from the surrounding farmlands, as well as visitors from afar, to enjoy the Highland scenery (which includes Ben Ledi, one of the region's most prominent peaks) and to sample the wide range of cask-conditioned ales and cider. Meals make full use of the best local produce and include Scottish flavors such as fresh Trossachs trout and pure breed Highland beef, along with international influences such as the likes of Moroccan lamb tagine spicing up the menu. Children's portions are available for many dishes.

Trossachs Rd. at Kilmahog, 1 mile north of Callander on the A84. ℂ **01877/330-152.** www.theladeinn. com. Reservations recommended. Main courses £9–£17. MC, V. Mon-Fri noon-3pm and 5-9pm, Sat noon-9pm, Sun 12:30-9pm.

Shopping

A good selection of woolens can be found at the **Callander Woollen Mill,** 12–18 Main St. (ℂ **01877/330-273**)—everything from scarves, skirts, and jackets to kilts, trousers, and knitwear. Another outlet for woolen goods (where you can also see local weavers at work) and Scottish foods such as shortbreads, sweets, and jams is the **Trossachs Woollen Mill** (ℂ **01877/330-178;** www.trossachswoollenmill.com), 1 mile north of Callander on the A84 in the hamlet of Kilmahog. Just along the A821 at Kilmahog, the **Lade Inn** (ℂ **01877/330-152;** www.ladeinn.com; see "Where to Eat," above) contains the Scottish Real Ale Shop that sells over 130 Scottish beers brewed at microbreweries across the country.

Entertainment & Nightlife

Callander's Main Street boasts a number of pubs. Whisky lovers are well catered for at the **Old Rectory Inn,** at the west end of Main Street (ℂ **01877/339-215;** www. theoldrectoryincallander.co.uk), where over 100 whiskies line the shelves of the whisky library. You can also sometimes catch local folk bands or join a pub quiz here.

Another local favorite that also occasionally features live music is the **Crown Hotel Pub,** 13 Main St. (ℂ **01877/330-040**). It's another mellow place to sink a pint of ale or lager.

Where to Stay

Annfield House Located away from the center of Callander in a quiet residential area, this late Victorian country house is a high-quality bed-and-breakfast, offering peace and quiet along with all the convenience of being close to town. Spacious guest rooms are clean, comfortable, and beautifully decorated, and the guest lounge is a welcoming retreat at the end of a day of walking. Large and hearty breakfasts make full use of local produce and are served in an elegant dining room where you can choose the substantial "Annfield" full Scottish or smaller options such as cheese omelets. Bike rental and fishing permits can be arranged.

18 North Church St., Callander FK17 8EG. www.annfieldguesthouse.co.uk. ℂ **01877/330-204.** 7 units. £65–£70. MC, V. *In room:* TV, hair dryer.

Arden House ★ This Victorian house, set on a slope above Callander's Main Street, commands glorious views of the surrounding hills and is one of the nicest B&Bs in town. The house was built in 1870 as a vacation home for Lady Willoughby and is instantly recognizable to generations of British TV viewers as the home of Drs. Finlay and Cameron in the BBC TV series, *Dr. Finlay's Casebook.* Today Arden House offers a soothing rest amid gardens at the base of a rocky outcropping known as the Callander Crags, with the popular Bracklinn Falls a 5-minute walk away. The high-ceilinged guest rooms are tasteful and comfortable and public areas boast Victorian antiques. Breakfasts are a highlight and include a dish of the day that could be anything from local smoked haddock to haggis hash or buttermilk pancakes. Children over 14 are welcomed.

Bracklinn Rd., Callander FK17 8EQ. www.ardenhouse.org.uk. © **01877/330-235.** Fax 01877/330-235. 6 units. £70 double; £80 suite. MC, V. From Callander, walk 5 min. north, following the signs to Bracklinn Falls. *In room:* TV, CD player, no phone, Wi-Fi (free).

Roman Camp Country House Hotel ★★   Once a 17th-century hunting lodge, this romantic hotel with its pink walls and small gray-roofed towers was built on the site of a Roman camp. The hotel is set in 8 hectares (20 acres) of glorious gardens that stretch along the banks of the River Teith, whose waters are rich with salmon and sea trout. The rooms have all the feel and comfort of a country house and come complete with antique furniture, while the public areas ooze the elegance of a bygone era. Food is one of Roman Camp's main attractions as the cuisine here is award winning and includes some produce grown in the hotel's own garden. The restaurant is opens for lunch, dinner, and afternoon tea to both guests and non-guests, and staff can prepare packed lunches (starting at £6.50) for guests planning a day's walking in the Trossachs or arrange fishing on the banks of the Teith complete with equipment.

Main St., Callander FK17 8BG. www.roman-camp-hotel.co.uk. © **01877/330-003.** Fax 01877/331-533. 14 units. £145–£185 double; from £215 suite. AE, DC, MC, V. As you approach Callander from the east on the A84, the entrance to the hotel is signposted btw. 2 pink cottages on Callander's Main St. **Amenities:** Restaurant; bar. *In room:* TV, hair dryer.

ABERFOYLE: GATEWAY TO THE TROSSACHS ★

56 miles NW of Edinburgh; 26 miles N of Glasgow

Looking like an alpine village in the heart of Rob Roy country, the small town of Aberfoyle, near Loch Ard, is far smaller than Callander, but still one of the busiest entry points to the Trossachs. Sir Walter Scott's romantic poem *The Lady of the Lake* greatly increased tourism to the area, eventually attracting Queen Victoria, who was enchanted by its beauty. Wordsworth and Coleridge were lured here from their home in England's Lake District and Wordsworth was so inspired he wrote *To a Highland Girl*. Today this region is popular with residents from Glasgow seeking to escape the city, which is only 26 miles south. The creation of the Loch Lomond and Trossachs National Park in 2002 opened this area up to of visitors of all ages and abilities, and you don't have to be an ardent outdoors enthusiast to enjoy some of the best experiences on offer.

Essentials

GETTING THERE   Limited public transport routes serve Aberfoyle. These include bus service AC01, which runs from Monday to Saturday from Glasgow to the center of Aberfoyle and onto the David Marshall Lodge in the National Park (p. 266); and the C29 from Callander to Aberfoyle, which operates Monday through Saturday. Both of these services are run by **Aberfoyle Coaches** (© **0844/567-5670;** www.aberfoylecoaches.com). **First** (© **0871/200-2233;** www.firstgroup.com) operates the 11A service from Glasgow to Balfron, stopping at Aberfoyle on Sundays; and the C11 from Stirling to Aberfoyle, which runs Monday through Sunday. The National

Park has produced a comprehensive booklet detailing public transport options in the region, which you can pick up at visitor information centers or download from the "Visiting" section of their website at www.lochlomond-trossachs.org. However, to really explore the area, a car is useful. From Stirling, take the A84 west until you reach the junction of the A873 and continue west to Aberfoyle.

VISITOR INFORMATION The **Trossachs Discovery Centre** is on Main Street (✆ **01877/382-352**). It's open April to June and September to October daily 10am to 5pm; July to August daily 9:30am to 6pm; November to March Saturday and Sunday 10am to 4pm. Alternatively the visitor center in the **David Marshall Lodge** (see "Exploring the Area," below) is also packed with useful information.

Exploring the Area

The **David Marshall Lodge** (✆ **01877/382-258**) lies around a mile north of Aberfoyle along the A821. The Lodge is open daily July and August from 10am to 6pm, November and December 10am to 4pm, January weekends only 10am to 4pm, and February Thursday through Sunday 10am to 4pm. There's a car parking charge of £3 per day. Here you can pick up leaflets detailing the many walking and cycling trails that snake through moor, woodland, mountain, and loch side starting at either the Lodge, Aberfoyle, or nearby Milton, which lies west of Aberfoyle along the B829. Two of the best walks for families are the **Spling Ring** (2 miles) and **Lochan Loop** (3½ miles) sculpture trails. Another favorite is the **Highland Boundary Fault Trail,** a 4-mile walk leading from the Lodge car park along part of the geological fault that separates the Highlands from the Lowlands.

The Lodge is a recommended place from which to explore the **Queen Elizabeth Forest Park** ★ between the eastern shore of Loch Lomond and the Trossachs. Glorious views can be enjoyed from inside the Lodge, which also houses a cafe and some shops. The grounds outside feature a fabulous play park for young children and **Go Ape** (✆ **0845/643-2035;** www.goape.co.uk), a course of rope ladders, bridges, Tarzan swings, and zip wires that lead through the surrounding treetops. Booking is essential during the summer; prices are £30 for adults and £20 for children aged 10 to 17.

There are places to stop all along the spectacular **Dukes Pass** (A821), which climbs north through the Achray Forest from Aberfoyle. From here you can divert west to **Loch Katrine** ★★, where the small steamer **SS *Sir Walter Scott*** and more modern boat *Lady of the Lake* ply the waters. Regular sailings depart from Easter to late October, between Trossachs Pier and Stronachlachar; a round-trip fare costs around £14 for adults, £13 for seniors and students, and £9 for children 15 and under. Prices vary depending on time of day (morning sailings are more expensive). For information on sailing schedules, call ✆ **01877/332-000** or visit www.lochkatrine.com. Light refreshments and bike rental through **Katrine Wheelz** (✆ **01877/376-366;** www.katrinewheelz.co.uk) are available at Trossachs Pier, and there's a car parking charge of £3 for 4 hours.

Side Trips

About 4 miles east of Aberfoyle off the A81 is **Inchmahome Priory** ★, a ruined Augustinian monastery dating back to 1238 on an island in Lake Menteith. Mary Queen of Scots was sent here as a baby in 1547 and much of this 13th-century place of worship remains intact, while the island itself is a peaceful natural haven. To reach the island, catch a ferry from the Port of Menteith; they run daily April to September from 9:30am with the last sailing at 4:30pm, and daily throughout October from

9:30am with the last sailing at 3:30pm. The fare is £4.70 for adults, £3.80 for seniors, and £2.80 for children 5 to 15. For information call ℂ **01877/385-294,** or see www. historic-scotland.gov.uk.

Shopping

The **Scottish Wool Centre,** Main Street (ℂ **01877/382-850;** www.scottishwool centre.co.uk) sells a varied selection of knitwear and woolens from surrounding mills, including jackets, hats, rugs, sweaters, and cashmere items. You can also pick up Scottish fine food and whiskies at the food hall. In summer several breeds of Scottish sheep can be viewed outside along with birds of prey including falcons and owls. The complex is open daily from 10am to 6pm.

Where to Eat & Stay

There are far fewer places to stay and eat in and around Aberfoyle than Callander. A limited number of bed-and-breakfasts can be found along the B829 as it leads west of Aberfoyle along the edge of Loch Ard: **Creag-Ard House** (www.creag-ard.co.uk; ℂ **01877/382-297**) is a good choice. Alternatively rooms can be found at **The Forth Inn** in the center of Aberfoyle (www.forthinn.com; ℂ **0877/382-372**), which also serves food. This is one of the few places to eat in town and reservations for dinner are essential here, and at any restaurant in the area during high season.

Lake of Menteith ★★ 🏠 Perched on the banks of the Lake of Menteith, this beautiful hotel and waterfront restaurant combines spectacular views with luxurious comfort and fine dining. Built in the 18th century adjacent to a Gothic-style parish church, the hotel served as a manse and ammunitions dump during World War II, before being purchased and refurbished in a Bostonian New England style by the present owners. The setting is hard to beat and the restaurant makes full use of its panoramic views to complement a menu rich with Scottish influences and regional produce such as Perthshire wild game, West Coast salmon, and Buccleuch Estate venison. Guests and non-guests alike can choose between the formal restaurant for lunch and dinner or informal dining in The Port Bar, which in summer makes full use of its outdoor loch facing deck. Accommodation varies from spacious loch facing rooms (by far the best) to smaller ones with country views.

Head south along the B8034 off the A81 (signposted Armprior) and the hotel is 200 meters/yards on the right, FK8 3RA. www.lake-hotel.com. ℂ **01877/385-258.** 16 units. Summer rooms £130–£195, winter £115–£195. **Amenities:** Restaurant; bar. *In room:* TV, hair dryer, Wi-Fi (free).

Macdonald Forest Hills ★★ 😊 This family-friendly country house overlooking Loch Ard is the largest place to stay in the area and a good choice for those wanting top spa facilities, a range of outdoor activities on hand, and on-site fine dining. In the foothills of the Trossachs, the resort stands on 10 hectares (25 acres) of private lands, which are riddled with trails. A haven of tranquility, the house, with its open fires and panoramic views, also has a superb leisure center with a good gym, indoor pool, steam room, and spa bath. The hotel itself contains 49 classically decorated rooms, but families often prefer the loch-facing lodges that come with one to three bedrooms, private balcony or patio, and fully equipped kitchen. Dining options include the Garden Restaurant, which serves a blend of traditional and contemporary Scottish dishes, and the informal and inexpensive Rafters Bar & Bistro.

Kinlochard, Aberfoyle, FK8 3TL. www.macdonaldhotels.co.uk. ℂ **0844/879-9057.** Fax 0870/738-7307. 114 units. Summer £135–£157, winter £64–£157. **Amenities:** 2 restaurants; bar; pool (indoor); health club and spa; kids club; room service. *In room:* TV, hair dryer, Wi-Fi (£7 per day).

THE BONNIE, BONNIE BANKS OF LOCH LOMOND ★★★

Loch Lomond is the largest of Scotland's lochs and lies on the Highland Boundary Fault that cuts through the area and separates the country's low- and highlands; you can literally see the fault as it cuts across both land and water. This region was once dominated by the powerful Lennox clan, but their ancient lands were divided following the execution of the Earl of Lennox in 1425 and much of them possessed by the branch of the Stewart (Stuart) family that spawned Lord Darnley, Mary Queen of Scots' ill-fated second husband. The ruins of **Lennox Castle** stand on Inchmurrin, one of the loch's 30 islands, also noted for its yew trees, planted by Robert the Bruce to ensure a suitable supply of wood for the bows of his archers. The loch is fed from all directions by a plethora of rivers and is around 24 miles long, stretching to 5 miles at its widest point. On the eastern side the imposing Ben Lomond rises to a height of 968m (3,176 ft.).

The famous song "Loch Lomond" was supposedly composed by one of Bonnie Prince Charlie's captured followers on the eve of his execution in Carlisle Jail. The "low road" of the song is the path through the underworld that his spirit will follow to his native land after death, more quickly than his friends can travel to Scotland by the ordinary "high road."

Balloch

Perched on the southern tip of Loch Lomond, Balloch is the largest community in this region and also its busiest thanks to good road, rail, and bus connections with Glasgow. The town grew around the River Leven, where the water drains from Loch Lomond and flows south to the Clyde. Today, the marina forms the heart of the Balloch, although many visitors bypass the town itself and focus a visit on **Loch Lomond Shores,** a large complex that hugs the loch side and is clustered with shops and attractions.

ESSENTIALS
GETTING THERE   A regular train service operated by **ScotRail** (© **0845/601-5929;** www.scotrail.co.uk) runs between Glasgow Queen Street and Balloch stations. The journey takes around 45 minutes and a round-trip fare costs £5.

Scottish Citylink (© **08705/505-050;** www.citylink.co.uk) runs several buses a day to Balloch from Glasgow, costing £5.40 to £7.70 for a round-trip ticket; the trip takes 45 minutes. **First** (© **0871/200-2233;** www.firstgroup.com) also operates a regular bus service between Glasgow and Balloch.

VISITOR INFORMATION   The **National Park Gateway Centre** is located at the Loch Lomond Shores (see "Exploring the Area," below; © **01389/722-600;** www.lochlomond-trossachs.org). The center is open daily from 9:30am to 6pm with extended hours in summer and offers some visitor information. There's also a **Tourist Information Centre** (© **08707/200-607**) in the town center on Ballach Road, open daily from 9:30am in summer and 10am in winter until 6pm except November to March when it closes at 5pm. However, one of the best places to find out more about the region is the **National Park Centre** off the B837 at Balmaha (© **01389/722-100**), which opens daily Easter to October 9:30am to 4pm and weekends only the rest of the year.

One of the great marked footpaths of Scotland, the **West Highland Way** (www.west-highland-way.co.uk) runs along the complete eastern sector of Loch Lomond. The footpath starts at Milngavie, outside Glasgow and ends 96 miles later at Fort William and the foot of Ben Nevis. Serious backpackers often hike the whole route, but you can tackle just sections of it, all of which make for marvelous day hikes through some of Scotland's best scenery.

EXPLORING THE AREA

Balloch's main visitor attraction is **Loch Lomond Shores** (✆ 01389/751-035; www.lochlomondshores.com), a large visitor-focused complex on the eastern edge of town off Ben Lomond Way, containing shops, restaurants, a fabulous sea-life aquarium (✆ 0871/423-2110), loch cruises, and bike, kayak, and canoe rental. **Sweeney's Cruisers** (✆ 01389/752-376; www.sweeney.uk.com) also operates trips onto the water from Sweeney's Shipyard, off Balloch Road in the town center. Choose between 1- or 2-hour cruises, both of which depart regularly in summer and less frequently in winter and sail towards the island of Inchmurrin. Tickets cost between £4 and £6.50.

The 81-hectare (200-acre) **Balloch Castle Country Park** lies on the eastern side of Loch Lomond, ¾ mile north of Balloch train station. The present **Balloch Castle** (✆ 01389/722-600), replacing one that dated from 1238, was constructed in 1808 for John Buchanan of Ardoch in the castle-Gothic style. Its visitor center explains the history of the property. The site has a walled garden, and the trees and shrubs, especially the rhododendrons and azaleas, reach the zenith of their beauty in late May and early June. The park is open year-round daily from 8am to dusk, with free admission. Easter to the end of October, the visitor center is open daily 10am to 6pm.

SIDE TRIPS

A fascinating side trip is the village of **Drymen**, which lies 5 miles northeast of Balloch along the A811. At the edge of the village stands the palatial ruin of **Buchanan Castle ★★**, the ancient fortress of the Duke of Montrose. Hitler's deputy, Rudolf Hess, was imprisoned here in 1941 after he flew to Britain in hopes of ending the war between his country and the Allies. Other illustrious guests have included the Shah of Iran, King George V and Queen Mary, and King Victor Emmanuel of Italy. The roof was removed in 1955 to avoid paying tax, and the castle fell into ruin.

Head west out of Drymen, 4 miles along the B837, to the village of **Balmaha** on the eastern shore of Loch Lomond. Excellent walking trails lead into the surrounding countryside from the National Park Visitor Centre (see "Visitor Information," above), including the Balmaha Millennium Forest Path following a circular route via loch shores and deep forest. You can also hop aboard a loch cruise at the **Balmaha Boatyard** (✆ 01360/ 870-214; www.balmahaboatyard.co.uk).

Both Drymen and Balmaha can be reached via bus no. 309 from Balloch, operated by **McColls Coaches** (✆ 01389/754-321; www.mccolls.org.uk).

WHERE TO EAT & STAY

There are limited places to stay and eat in Balloch itself with more choice to be found along the west bank of Loch Lomond, where options include the **Duck Bay Hotel** and Restaurant (www.duckbay.co.uk; © **01380/751-234**). The village of Drymen is a good base from which to explore the region and options here include the **Winnock Hotel** (www.winnockhotel.com; © **01360/660-245**), a former coaching inn in the center of the village. Alternatively the **Oak Tree Inn** (www.oak-tree-inn.co.uk; © **01360/870-357**) at Balmaha on the eastern shores of Loch Lomond is another cozy local pub offering accommodation, pub food, and choice of local ales and whiskies.

Balloch House   Once called Balloch's grande dame, this was the first hotel built in town and stands beside the river in the center of the village. Today Balloch House offers basic, functionally furnished rooms, each with a shower (some with a tub as well). The large pub and dining area features striped back wood and is a family-friendly spot for either lunch or dinner; the outside decking is particularly nice in summer. The comprehensive menu includes pub favorites such as scampi, burgers, and fish and chips alongside a choice of seafood, meat, and poultry dishes, which you can top off with an array of puddings from treacle tart to spiced poached pears.

Balloch Rd., Balloch G83 8LQ. www.innkeeperslodge.com. © **0845/112-6006.** Fax 01389/755-604. 12 units. From £70 double. AE, DC, MC, V. **Amenities:** Restaurant; bar; room service; Internet (free). *In room:* TV, hair dryer.

Best Western Buchanan Arms Hotel & Spa   Renovated in 2009, the Buchanan Arms is a traditional-style hotel that has grown around a small coaching inn whose old bar still forms the heart of the building. Newly decorated rooms are clean, comfortable, and spacious and the on-site spa, pool, and fitness center are all of a decent size and quality. This is a good base from which to explore both shores of Loch Lomond and blazing open fires welcome guests in winter. The hotel restaurant focuses on traditional Scottish and international fare, and reservations for both guests and non-guests are essential during the summer.

23 Main St., Dryman G63 0BQ. www.buchananarms.co.uk. © **01360/660-588.** Fax 01360/660-943. 53 units. £150–£270 double. AE, MC, V. **Amenities:** Restaurant; bar; pool (indoor); squash court; table tennis; fitness center; spa. *In room:* TV, hair dryer, Wi-Fi (free).

Luss

The village of Luss, 8⅔ miles north of Balloch off the A82 on the western side of Loch Lomond, is one of the loveliest villages in the region. This ancient settlement was rebuilt in the 19th century and is filled with solid sandstone and slate cottages. Park at the **Luss Visitor Centre** (© **01436/860-240**), which is open daily from 10am until 7pm in summer and from 10am until 4pm in winter and is busy with coach tours in summer. The center is fit to burst with information on the village and surrounding area, including details of walks around and in the village. Bus service no. 305 runs between Balloch and Luss and is operated by **Loch Lomond bus services** (© **01389/754-321**).

WHERE TO EAT & STAY

The Lodge on Loch Lomond Hotel   Surrounded by mountain, loch, and woodland, this fine hotel is an attractive blend of traditional and contemporary and offers accessible seclusion along with good leisure facilities and fine dining. Choose between various room styles, many of which boast stunning loch views and others come complete with private saunas. Luxury suites include the Carter Suite named after, and favored by, President Jimmy Carter. The on-site Amberspa features an indoor pool, steam room, sauna, and laconium, and the hotel can help organize numerous outdoor activities including fishing, shooting, and quad biking. The food here is award-winning and guests can choose between the upmarket yet relaxed Colquhoun's restaurant, where the mix of traditional and contemporary is also evident, or the bar area that serves a range of lighter meals. The restaurant is also open to non-guests and reservations are recommended.

Luss G83 8PA. www.loch-lomond.co.uk. © **01436/860-201.** Fax 01436/860-203. 46 units. £95–£160 double; £190–£280 suite. AE, MC, V. Free parking. Take the A82 from Glasgow. **Amenities:** Restaurant; bar; pool (indoor); health club and spa; room service. *In room:* TV, minibar (in some), sauna (in some), hair dryer.

ABERDEEN & THE TAYSIDE & GRAMPIAN REGIONS

The two historic regions of Tayside and Grampian share the North Sea coast between the Firth of Tay in the south and the Firth of Moray farther north. Tayside is named after its major river, the Tay, which offers some of Europe's best salmon and trout fishing, and along its course it flows through the cities of Perth and Dundee. Grampian boasts granite Aberdeen, Scotland's third city, as well as Braemar, site of the most famous of Highland Gatherings, attended by the Queen herself.

CITIES   The port city of **Aberdeen** boasts an ancient university as well as recent prosperity from the North Sea oil industry. Farther south, **Dundee** is now more famous for its fruitcakes and marmalade than its past as a whaling port. Inland, genteel **Perth** is a haven of culture, with two art galleries, a Victorian theatre, and, just outside, the Palace of Scone, where the kings of Scotland were once crowned.

COUNTRYSIDE   **Perthshire** is sporting country, famed for its fishing on the Tay, as well as its shooting estates and golf courses. **Speyside** attracts whisky collectors anxious to taste the single malts at the distilleries that rely on the river's peaty waters. **Aberdeenshire** is Castle Country, harboring, among others, the many-turreted Fyvie Castle, and the Queen's very own Balmoral.

EATING & DRINKING   Look out for salmon on the menu in **Tayside** restaurants—chances are that it's fresh from the water. The fashionable hotels and restaurants of **Aberdeen** are just as likely to serve up the harvest from deep sea fishing; don't forget to try their famous kippers. And if you're happy to blow your budget, there's the exquisite cuisine of Andrew Fairlie's restaurant at **Gleneagles,** often considered Scotland's premier hotel.

COAST   There's more to this stretch of coast than sand and sea. Golfers arrive in droves at the seaside resort of **Carnoustie** for its championship links courses. Farther north, who could fail to marvel at the audacity of the builders of **Dunnottar Castle,** perched improbably on sheer cliffs facing the bleak North Sea. Aberdeen's **Maritime Museum** fills in the backstory to the region's remarkable seafaring history, from the Vikings to oil drilling.

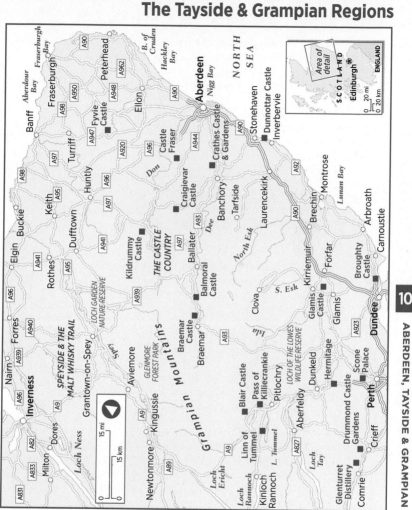

THE best TRAVEL EXPERIENCES IN ABERDEEN & THE TAYSIDE & GRAMPIAN REGIONS

o **Tread in the footsteps of generations of students at the University of Aberdeen:** Soak up the atmosphere of the cobbled streets and weathered stone buildings of this prestigious university, as today's students mill so nonchalantly around you. See p. 276.

- **Delight in the glories of Perth's Branklyn Garden:** Once a private garden, this colorful assemblage of rhododendrons and rare herbaceous plants is fortunately now shared with the public thanks to the National Trust for Scotland. See p. 285.
- **Wander round the medieval center of Elgin:** With its ancient street layout, magnificent ruined cathedral, and fine stone townhouses, Elgin retains the patina of centuries of history. See p. 312.
- **Fortify yourself for a tour of Speyside whisky distilleries:** Although you could visit four or five of the distilleries on the Malt Whisky Trail in 1 day, you may need another day to recover. See p. 306.
- **Wade into the Tay in the hope of hooking a salmon:** Get up for an early breakfast at East Haugh House and then set out for the hotel's own fishing beat. On your return in the evening, the hotel will freeze—or perhaps even cook up—the day's catch for you. See p. 297.

ABERDEEN & CASTLE COUNTRY ★★

130 miles NE of Edinburgh; 67 miles N of Dundee

Bordered by fine sandy beaches—and a very cold sea—the port city of Aberdeen is a vibrant cultural center, with an esteemed university, several important museums, and a lively nightlife. The city is also a good base for exploring the great castles of the Grampian region, as well as fishing in the salmon-filled River Dee, and playing golf at nearby Balgownie.

The cobbled streets of **Old Aberdeen** are the home of the **University of Aberdeen.** Here, you can wander round the ancient buildings of its King's College and Marischal College and also find the **Cathedral of St. Machar,** one of Scotland's most important. Art buffs will enjoy the nearby **Aberdeen Art Gallery,** and on sunny days, the **Cruickshank Botanic Garden** looks spectacular.

The Port of Aberdeen is filled with deep-sea trawlers, so don't be surprised if your hotel breakfast features buttered kippers or smoked haddock with a poached egg. The city also lies on the banks of the salmon- and trout-filled Don and Dee rivers, so smoked salmon and scrambled eggs or pan-fried trout are also local favorites. For those who like a hearty meat dish, you can't do better than an Aberdeen Angus filet steak, cooked nice and rare, preferably with a side order of fries.

Aberdeen's shopping is the best in the northeast. If you're looking for independent boutiques, head straight for **Chapel Street** and **Thistle Street** where you can find gifts, antiques, china, and jewelry. For high-street fashions look for **George Street** and **Union Street,** where all the major chains can be found. If by chance you have Scottish ancestry, it's well worth seeking out the **Aberdeen Family History Shop** on King Street, where you can search through records to find your forebears.

As you might expect with a large student population, Aberdeen has a varied and lively nightlife. The arty crowd heads for **Aberdeen Arts Centre** for its theatre and art-house cinema. The 19th-century **Music Hall**—with pillars, gilding, and plush seats—presents symphony concerts as well as big-name comedy nights. Those looking to let their hair down head take their pick of the city's **nightclubs,** which offer the full spectrum of music, from cheesy pop to garage.

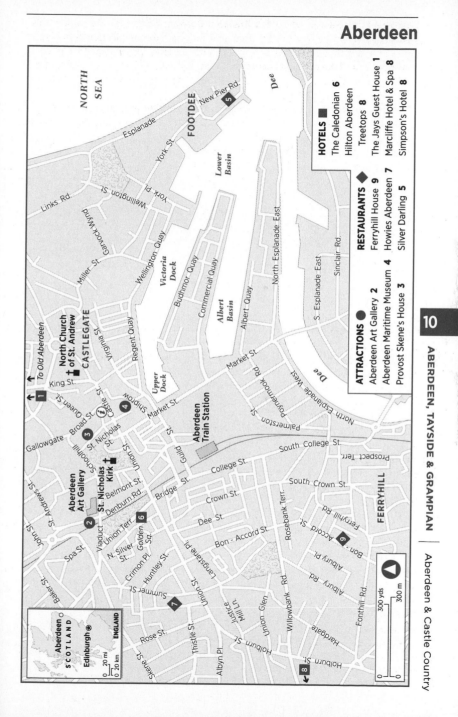

Aberdeen

HOTELS ■
The Caledonian **6**
Hilton Aberdeen
Treetops **8**
The Jays Guest House **1**
Marcliffe Hotel & Spa **8**
Simpson's Hotel **8**

RESTAURANTS ◆
Ferryhill House **9**
Howies Aberdeen **7**
Silver Darling **5**

ATTRACTIONS ●
Aberdeen Art Gallery **2**
Aberdeen Maritime Museum **4**
Provost Skene's House **3**

10

ABERDEEN, TAYSIDE & GRAMPIAN | Aberdeen & Castle Country

Essentials

GETTING THERE Aberdeen is served by a number of airlines, including British Airways, British Midland, easyJet, and KLM. For flight information, contact Aberdeen **Airport** (✆ **0844/481-6666;** www.aberdeenairport.com), which is situated about 6¾ miles from the heart of town and is connected to it by a bus service.

Aberdeen has direct rail links to Britain's major cities. Supersaver fares, available by avoiding travel on Friday and Saturday, make the price difference between a one-way fare and a round-trip ticket negligible. For fares and schedules in Scotland, call **Scotrail** on ✆ **0845/755-0033** with at least a 48-hour notice. For fares from London, call ✆ **08457/225-111** at least 1 week in advance or check www.eastcoast. co.uk. Nineteen trains arrive from Edinburgh on each weekday. Trip time is about 3½ hours. Another 19 trains per day arrive from Glasgow. Some 12 trains per day arrive from London.

Several bus companies have express routes serving Aberdeen, and many offer special round-trip fares to passengers avoiding travel on Friday or Saturday. Frequent buses arrive from both Glasgow and Edinburgh. There are also frequent arrivals from Inverness. For bus schedules in Aberdeen, call **Stagecoach** at ✆ **01224/212-266.**

It's also easy to drive to the northeast. From the south, drive via Edinburgh over the Forth and Tay Road bridges, and take the coastal road. From the north and west, approach the area from the much-improved A9, which links Perth, Inverness, and Wick.

VISITOR INFORMATION The **Aberdeen Tourist Information Centre (TIC)** is at 23 Union St, Aberdeen AB10 1DE (✆ **01224/288-828;** www.aberdeen-grampian.com). In July and August, it's open Monday through Friday 9am to 7pm, Saturday 9am to 5pm, and Sunday 10am to 4pm. All other months, it's open Monday through Friday 9am to 5pm and Saturday 10am to 2pm.

Exploring Aberdeen

In old Aberdeen is the **University of Aberdeen** (✆ **01224/272-000;** www.abdn. ac.uk), a fusion of two colleges. Reached along University Road, **King's College** (✆ **01224/272-137;** bus: 1, 2, 13, and 40) is Great Britain's oldest school of medicine. The college is known for its chapel (from around 1500) with pre-Reformation carved woodwork, the finest of its kind in Scotland; it's open daily 9am to 4:30pm, charging no admission. On Broad Street is **Marischal College** (✆ **01224/272-000**), founded in 1593 by Earl Marischal—it's the world's second-biggest granite structure (El Escorial, outside Madrid, is much larger). The main structure is no longer used for university teaching, but on-site is the Marischal Museum (✆ **01224/274-301;** www.abdn.ac.uk/marischal_museum), displaying exhibits and photos of the university and the Scottish culture of the northeast in general; admission is free, and the museum is open Monday to Friday from 10am to 5pm and Sunday from 2 to 5pm. In 1860, the colleges joined together to form the nucleus of the University of Aberdeen.

Also at the University of Aberdeen, the **Cruickshank Botanic Garden,** St. Machar Drive (✆ **01224/272-704;** www.abdn.ac.uk/botanic-garden; bus: 1, 2, 13, or 40), displays alpines, shrubs, and many herbaceous plants, along with rock and water gardens. May to September it's open Monday through Friday from 9am to 9:30pm and at weekends from 2pm to 9:30pm; October to April, it's open Monday through Friday 9am to 4:30pm. Admission is free.

The **Cathedral of St. Machar,** Chanonry (© **01224/485-988;** www.stmachar. com; bus: 14, 20), was founded in 1131, but the present structure dates from the 15th century. Its splendid heraldic ceiling contains three rows of shields. Look out for the magnificent modern stained-glass windows by Douglas Strachan and the pre-Reformation woodwork. The cathedral is open daily 9am to 5pm.

Aberdeen Art Gallery ★ GALLERY   Built in 1884 to neoclassical designs by A. Marshall MacKenzie, this building houses one of the most important art collections in Great Britain. It contains 18th-century portraits by Raeburn, Hogarth, Ramsay, and Reynolds, as well as acclaimed 20th-century works by Paul Nash, Ben Nicholson, and Francis Bacon. The exhibits also include excellent pieces by Monet, Pissarro, Sisley, and Bonnard, as well as a collection of Scottish domestic silver. There is also a program of special exhibitions and events.

Schoolhill. © **01224/523-700.** www.aagm.co.uk. Free admission. Mon-Sat 10am-5pm; Sun 2-5pm. Buses: 5, 12, 9.

Aberdeen Maritime Museum MUSEUM   Using a unique collection of ship models, paintings, and artifacts, combined with computerized interactive programs, this museum tells the story of the city's long and fascinating relationship with the sea. A major display on the offshore oil industry features a model of the Murchison oil platform. The complex is on four floors, incorporating the 1593 Provost Ross House linked by a modern glass structure to the granite Trinity Church. Windows open onto panoramic views of the harbor.

Shiprow. © **01224/337-700.** www.aagm.co.uk. Free admission. Mon-Sat 10am-5pm; Sun noon-3pm. Buses: 1, 2, 14, 21.

Dunnottar Castle RUINS   The well-preserved ruins of Dunnottar are on a rocky promontory towering 49m (160 ft.) above the surging sea, and the best way to get to them is by a dramatic 30-minute walk from Stonehaven along the cliffs. The ruins include a great square tower and a chapel built in 1292. William Wallace stormed it in 1297, but failed to take it. In 1991, it was the setting for Zeffirelli's film of *Hamlet,* starring Mel Gibson. You can reach Stonehaven from Aberdeen by taking Bluebird Northern bus no. 107, and then walking for 5 minutes. Trains run about every half-hour from Aberdeen to Stonehaven, and the journey time is about 30 minutes.

1¾ miles south of Stonehaven off the A92. © **01569/762-173.** www.dunnottarcastle.co.uk. Admission £5 adults, £2 children 15 and under. Apr-Oct daily 9am-6pm; Nov-Mar Fri-Mon 10am-dusk.

Provost Skene's House HISTORIC HOME   This impressive historic building is named after a rich merchant who was Lord Provost of Aberdeen from 1676 to 1685. It now accommodates a museum with period rooms and artifacts relating to domestic life, including a collection of period costumes. Provost Skene's kitchen has been converted into a cafe.

5 Guestrow, off Broad St. © **01224/641-086.** www.aagm.co.uk. Free admission. Mon-Sat 10am-5pm. Buses: 1, 2, 20.

Where to Eat

Ferryhill House INTERNATIONAL   Located in its own park and garden on the city's southern outskirts, Ferryhill House dates back 250 years. The restaurant boasts one of the region's largest collections of single-malt whiskies—more than 140 types. There's a fireplace for chilly afternoons and a beer garden for midsummer, as well as a conservatory. Though not of a fine-dining caliber, the food is well prepared with market-fresh ingredients, and it's always wholesome, hearty, and filling. Dishes include *Cullen skink* (smoked fish soup), steaks, vegetable tempura, Thai-spiced turbot, chicken fajitas, fried haddock filet, pastas, and beef burgers.

Ferryhill House also rents nine guest rooms. The rate for a double is £70 to £110, with breakfast and Wi-Fi included.

Bon Accord St., Aberdeen AB11 6UA. © **01224/590-867.** Fax 01224/586-947. www.ferryhillhousehotel. co.uk. Reservations recommended Sat–Sun. Main courses £9–£14. MC, V. Free parking. Bus: 16.

Howies Aberdeen ★ SCOTTISH/INTERNATIONAL   This is the latest—and even better—reincarnation of the locally famous Gerard's, which stood here for many years. Specializing in modern Scottish cookery with international influences, the menu includes medallions of Aberdeen Angus filet, pork belly, fish pie, and oven-roasted salmon. The bar stocks a wide range of single malts and ports in addition to a well chosen wine list.

50 Chapel St. © **01224/639-500.** www.howies.uk.com. Reservations recommended. Main courses £12–£15. Two-course lunch menu £9; 3-course dinner menu £22. AE, MC, V. Daily noon–2:30pm and 6–10pm. Located a 15-min. walk southwest of train station.

Silver Darling ★★ FRENCH/SEAFOOD   Silver Darling (a local nickname for herring) is a perennially popular fixture on Aberdeen's restaurant scene. Occupying a former customhouse at the mouth of the harbor, it spins a culinary fantasy around the freshest catch of the day. You might begin with a savory fish soup, almost Mediter-ranean in flavor, and then go on to one of the barbecued fish dishes or pan-fried tuna rolled in crushed peppercorns. Salmon is the invariable favorite.

Pocra Quay, Footdee. © **01224/576-229.** www.silverdarling.co.uk. Reservations recommended. Lunch main courses £10–£16; dinner main courses £18–£20. AE, DC, MC, V. Mon–Fri noon–2pm and 7–10pm, Sat 7–10pm. Closed Dec 23–Jan 8. Bus: 14 or 15.

Shopping

The main shopping districts center on specialty shops on **Chapel** and **Thistle streets,** and on the well-known chains on **George** and **Union streets.**

Of interest to antiques enthusiasts, **Colin Wood,** 25 Rose St. (© **01224/643-019**), stocks furniture, wall clocks, and grandfather clocks from the 17th to the early 20th centuries. Its specialty, however, is maps from the Elizabethan to the Victorian eras. The shop also sells 17th- to early-20th-century prints of northern Scotland. You may also want to browse through the eclectic mix of bric-a-brac and antiques at **Elizabeth Watts Studio,** 69 Thistle St. (© **01224/647-232;** www.elizabethwat-trestoration.co.uk), where items include glass, brass, antique jewelry, china, silver, and a few small furniture pieces. The shop is actually best known for its china and glass restoration studio. **Grandad's Attic,** 12 Marischal St. (© **01224/213-699**), is also worth a browse. It specializes in Art Deco ceramics and antique pine furniture.

For one-stop gift shopping, drop in at **Nova,** 20 Chapel St. (© **01224/641-270;** www.novagifts.co.uk), which stocks china, silver jewelry, rugs, clothing, toys, cards, and gift paper.

To trace your Scottish ancestry, go to the **Aberdeen Family History Shop,** 164 King St. (© **01224/646-323;** www.anesfhs.org.uk), where membership to the Aber-deen and North East Family History Society costs £15. Once you join, you can go through a vast range of publications kept on hand to help members trace their family histories. When you've found out all about your Scottish roots, you can go and have a kilt made up in the appropriate tartan. Perhaps the best kiltmaker in town is **Alex Scott & Co.,** 43 Schoolhill (© **01224/643-924**).

Aberdeen has a good range of golf courses in and around the city, with several notable courses within an easy drive. As always, reservations are advisable at any course. If the two below don't suit you, ask the tourist office for details of other options.

Among the top courses is **Balgownie**, the **Royal Aberdeen Golf Club** (© 01224/702-571; www.royalaberdeen golf.com), created in 1780 in classic links style. An uneven layout, sea breezes, and grassy sand dunes add to the challenge of this 6,415-yard, par-70 course. A letter of introduction is required to play here.

A good alternative is the par-69 **West Hills Golf Course,** West Hill Heights, West Hill Skene (©/fax 01224/740-159; www.westhillgolfclub. co.uk). Situated about 6¾ miles west of Aberdeen, it features 5,849 yards of playing area.

Entertainment & Nightlife

Tickets to events at most venues are available from the **Aberdeen Box Office** (© **01224/641-122;** www.boxofficeaberdeen.com), open Monday through Saturday from 9:30am to 8pm.

THE PERFORMING ARTS The **Aberdeen Arts Centre,** King Street (© **01224/635-208;** www.digifresh.co.uk), has a 350-seat theatre that features professional and amateur groups performing everything from poetry readings and plays to musical concerts and comedy. Ticket prices and performance times vary; call for information. Also on the premises is a 60-seat video projection theatre that screens world cinema features; ticket prices vary depending on what's showing, but start from £8. A large gallery room holds month-long visual-art exhibitions. A cafe/bar, offering light meals and drinks, is open during performance times.

Near Tarves, about 20 miles from Aberdeen, you'll find **Haddo House** (© **01651/ 851-440;** www.nts.org.uk/Property/73), which hosts operas, ballets, and plays from Easter to October in a purpose-built hall on the estate. An early-20th-century hall built of pitch pine, it's based on the Canadian town halls that Lord Aberdeen saw on his travels abroad. The hall was built for the people of the surrounding area on Aberdeen family land (the present Lady Aberdeen still lives in a house on the estate). To find the venue, follow the B9005, 18 miles north to Tarves, and then follow the National Trust and Haddo House signs 1¼ miles east. Tickets for events vary in price according to the production being presented. Admission to the stately home itself costs £9 for adults, £6.50 for seniors and children, and £22 for a family ticket. The house is open only for guided tours, which take place at 11:30am, 1:30pm, and 3:30pm from Easter to June and from September to October, Friday to Monday, and from July to August daily. A stylish cafe offers light meals, tea, and other beverages daily Easter to October from 11am to 5pm.

The 19th-century **Music Hall,** Union Street (© **01224/641-122;** www.box officeaberdeen.com), is an ornately gilded 1,282-seat theatre that stages concerts by the Scottish National Orchestra, the Scottish Chamber Orchestra, visiting international orchestras, and pop bands, as well as occasional comedy performances; it also hosts ceilidhs, crafts fairs, and book sales. Tickets for year-round musical performances average £14 to £35. The **Aberdeen International Youth Festival** is held annually in this hall in August, and features youth orchestras, choirs, and dance and theatre ensembles. Daytime and evening performances are held, and tickets range from £10 to £20.

His Majesty's Theatre, Rosemount Viaduct (② **01224/641-122**), was designed by Frank Matcham in 1906, and is the only theatre in the world built entirely of granite. The interior is late Victorian in style, and the 1,445-seat auditorium hosts operas, dance performances, dramas, classical concerts, musicals, and comedy shows year-round. Tickets range from £10 to £45.

A mixed venue is the **Lemon Tree,** 5 W. North St. (② **01224/642-230**). Its 150-seat theatre stages dance recitals, theatrical productions, and stand-up comedy, with tickets generally priced between £11 and £32. On Saturdays, there's often a matinee at 2 or 3pm, and evening performances are at 7pm. Downstairs, the 500-seat cafe-theatre hosts folk, rock, blues, jazz, and comedy acts, with shows starting between 8 and 10pm. On Sunday afternoon there's free live jazz.

CLUBS Snafu, 1 Union St. (② **01224/596-111;** www.clubsnafu.com), has dancing to house, techno, or disco music from 11pm Wednesday through Sunday. On other nights, there are comedy evenings, and indie and other live music acts. The cover charge depends on the guest DJ, but is usually £3 to £4.

Liquid, 5 Bridge Place (② **01224/595-239;** www.liquidclubs.com/aberdeen), offers a line-up of guest DJs from Wednesday to Saturday 10:30pm to 3am. The cover charges are usually between £3 and £6.50.

PUBS The **Prince of Wales** ★, 7 St. Nicholas Lane (② **01224/640-597**), in the heart of the shopping district, is the best place in the old city center to go for a pint. Furnished with pews in screened booths, it boasts Aberdeen's longest bar counter. At lunch, it's bustling with regulars who devour chicken in cider sauce, Guinness pie, and other hearty fare. On tap are such beers as Buchan Gold and Courage Directors. Orkney Dark Island is also sold here.

Where to Stay

Because of increasing numbers of business travelers to the Granite City—Europe's offshore oil capital—hotels are likely to be heavily booked any time of year. Visitors will also find that room rates are often more expensive during the week than weekends. If you haven't reserved ahead, stop by the **Aberdeen Tourist Information Centre,** Alford Street (② **01224/288-828;** www.aberdeen-grampian.com), where the staff can usually find just the right lodging for you—a family-run B&B, a guesthouse, or a hotel. A £2.50 service fee is charged.

EXPENSIVE

Hilton Aberdeen Treetops ☺ The main selling point of this hotel is its child-friendly amenities. Located about a 10-minute drive west of the center of Aberdeen off the A93, this aesthetically unprepossessing 1960s hotel is a lot better inside than it looks from the outside. The guest rooms are furnished in smart contemporary style and look over landscaped grounds; some rooms even have balconies with lake views. There are numerous family-sized rooms as well. Children are enthusiastically catered for with a playground, a swimming pool, an entertainment program, and a babysitting service.

161 Springfield Rd., Aberdeen AB15 7AQ. www.hilton.com/aberdeen. ② **01224/313-377.** Fax 01224/028-504. 120 units. £60–£150 double. AE, DC, MC, V. Parking £3. Bus: 11. **Amenities:** Restaurant; bar; pool (indoor); health club; children's programs; room service; babysitting. *In room:* TV, minibar, hair dryer, Internet (free).

Marcliffe Hotel & Spa ★★ The Marcliffe is located on the city's western edge, less than a half-hour from the airport, and is a definite cut above other hotels in this part of Aberdeen. The Victorian three-story house is in 3.2 hectares (8 acres) of beautifully landscaped gardens. Inside, the public rooms are decorated with oriental rugs on the stone floors, tartan sofas, and a scattering of antique furniture. The spacious guest rooms are decorated in muted colors, warm fabrics, and reproduction antique furniture. At breakfast you can sample Aberdeen *rowies*, a local specialty, made with butter, that's like a flattened croissant. At dinner, the Conservatory Restaurant offers such regional dishes as Highland lamb and fresh Scottish salmon. Main courses are priced between £20 and £32. In the library lounge, you can choose from more than 130 scotches, 500 wines, and 70 cognacs. Guests also have the use of the spa for a range of health and beauty treatments.

N. Deeside Rd., Aberdeen AB1 9YA. www.marcliffe.com. *✆* **01224/861-000.** Fax 01224/868-860. 42 units. £155–£249 double; £279–£349 suite. AE, DC, MC, V. Free parking. Located on Deeside Rd. out of Aberdeen (well signposted). **Amenities:** Restaurant; bar; room service. *In room:* TV, minibar, hair dryer, Wi-Fi (free).

MODERATE

The Caledonian The Caledonian occupies a grand stone-fronted Victorian building in the center of the city, a 2-minute walk from the train station. Restoration has added a sheen to one of the most elegant series of public rooms in town. The main staircase is particularly grand. The smartly designed guest rooms vary a good deal in size, but all are very comfortable and have well-maintained bathrooms.

10–14 Union Terrace (off Union St.), Aberdeen AB10 1WE. www.thistle.com. *✆* **0870/333-9131.** Fax 0870/333-9251. 77 units. £65–£135 double. Children 11 and under stay free in parent's room. AE, DC, MC, V. Limited free parking. Bus: 17. **Amenities:** Restaurant; bar; room service. *In room:* TV, minibar, hair dryer, Wi-Fi (free).

The Jays Guest House *✦* This is one of the nicest guesthouses in Aberdeen and is conveniently located near the university and the Offshore Survival Centre. The owners are welcoming hosts and attentive in ensuring everything runs smoothly. The recently refurbished guest rooms are bright and airy.

422 King St., Aberdeen AB24 3BR. www.jaysguesthouse.co.uk. *✆* **01224/638-295.** Fax 0122/638-360. 10 units. £90–£110 double. MC, V. Free parking. Lies 3 blocks north of the Civic Centre. Bus: 1, 2, 3, 4, or 7. *In room:* TV, no phone, Wi-Fi (free).

Simpson's Hotel ★ This hotel is formed from two traditional granite townhouses joined together. It offers comfortable rooms decorated with furniture from Spain and painted in rich, bold colors that try to create a warm ambience. The hotel bar and brasserie offer a range of moderately priced Scottish and international dishes prepared with the finest of local ingredients. Guests have complementary use of the health spa.

59 Queens Rd., Aberdeen AB15 4YP. www.simpsonshotel.co.uk. *✆* **01224/327-777.** Fax 01224/327-700. 49 units. £80–£120 double. AE, MC, V. Follow signs for the A96 North, and turn right at Queens Rd. Roundabout. **Amenities:** Restaurant; bar; spa; room service;babysitting. *In room:* A/C, TV, CD player, minibar, hair dryer, Internet (free).

LUXURY HOTELS ON THE OUTSKIRTS OF ABERDEEN

Aberdeen Mercure Ardoe House ★ 🛎 This turreted baronial mansion, built in 1878, sits in the midst of lush gardens and manicured grounds, and offers panoramic views of the River Dee. Though it's close to Aberdeen, it feels a world away from the hustle and bustle of town. Its old-fashioned interior, with wood paneling, ornate fireplaces, and stained-glass windows, reflects the best of the grand Victorian style. The guest rooms are individually decorated and the bathrooms are immaculate. In the formal dining room, Blairs Restaurant, you can order Scottish cuisine made from fresh local ingredients. Soapie's Lounge Bar offers lighter meals. Both are open 7 days a week for lunch and dinner.

S. Deeside Rd. (3 miles south of Aberdeen on the B9077), Blairs, Aberdeen AB12 5YP. www.mercure. com. ⓒ 01224/860-600. Fax 01224/861-283. 109 units. £100–£170 double. AE, DC, MC, V. Pets welcome. **Amenities:** 2 restaurants; 2 bars; health club and spa; room service; babysitting. *In room:* TV, hair dryer, Wi-Fi (free).

Kildrummy Castle Hotel ★   This 19th-century gray-stone mansion, on acres of landscaped gardens, overlooks the ruined castle of Kildrummy. Its guest rooms, many furnished with antiques, vary in size; some of the master rooms have four-poster beds. The grand public rooms have oak-paneled walls and ceilings, mullioned windows, and window seats. The drawing room and bar open onto a flagstone terrace.

Traditional Scottish food, including *Cullen skink* and filet of sole stuffed with smoked Scottish salmon, is served in the dining room. The 6-course tasting menu costs £48. A 4-course Sunday lunch is £29, and lunches on other days (except Monday, when the restaurant is closed) offer main courses that start from about £12.

Kildrummy by Alford AB33 8RA. www.kildrummycastlehotel.co.uk. ⓒ 01975/571-288. Fax 01975/571-345. 16 units. £145–£217 double. AE, MC, V. Closed Jan. From Aberdeen, take the A944 and follow signs to Alford; then take the A97, following signs to Kildrummy. **Amenities:** Restaurant; bar; room service; babysitting; Wi-Fi (free). *In room:* TV, hair dryer.

Thainstone House Hotel ★   This Palladian mansion is one of northeast Scotland's most prestigious country hotels. Set in 16 hectares (40 acres) of grounds, it can serve as both a retreat and a center for exploring this historic part of Scotland or following the Malt Whisky Trail (see "Speyside & the Malt Whisky Trail," later in this chapter). The high ceilings, columns, neoclassical plaster reliefs, and cornices all bear testimony to the Italian sojourns of the architect, Archibald Simpson. The elegantly furnished guest rooms vary in size, but all are well equipped, and the extra touches such as complimentary sherry and shortbread are indicative of the management's attention to detail.

The chef at Simpson's Restaurant offers Continental and Scottish dishes exhibiting imagination and a lightness of touch. For more informal meals, there's also Cammies Lounge.

Inverurie AB51 5NT. www.swallow-hotels.com. ⓒ 01467/621-643. Fax 01467/625-084. 48 units. £120–£200 double; £275 suite. AE, DC, MC, V. From Aberdeen, take the A96, following signs to Inverness; just before Inverurie, turn left and follow signs to the hotel. **Amenities:** Restaurant; bar; pool (indoor); health club and spa; room service; babysitting. *In room:* TV, Jacuzzi, hair dryer, Wi-Fi (free).

Side Trips from Aberdeen: Castle Country

Aberdeen is the center of "castle country"—40 inhabited castles lie within a 40-mile radius. Below is a selection of the best of them.

Castle Fraser ★ CASTLE   One of the most impressive of the fortresslike castles of Mar, Castle Fraser stands on 10 hectares (25 acres) of parkland. The sixth laird, Michael Fraser, began the structure in 1575, and his son finished it in 1636. Visitors can view the spectacular Great Hall and grand apartments, and wander around the grounds, which include an 18th-century walled garden.

Sauchen, Inverurie. ⓒ 0844/4932164. www.nts.org.uk/Property/16. Admission £9 adults, £6.50 seniors, students, and children 5-15; £22 families. Car parking £2. Castle Apr-Jun Wed–Sun noon-5pm; Aug daily 11am-5pm; Sep-Oct Wed–Sun noon-5pm. Gardens year-round daily 9am-sunset. Head 3 miles south of Kemnay, 16 miles west of Aberdeen, off the A944.

Scotland's Castle Trail takes visitors on a tour of fairy-tale castles, imposing stately homes, magnificent ruins, and splendid gardens and parkland. The only signposted route of its kind in Scotland, it guides motorists around rural Aberdeenshire. An accompanying leaflet highlights 11 of the finest properties, from the ruins of the 13th-century Kildrummy Castle and the elegant five-towered Fyvie Castle to two grand examples of the work of the 18th-century architect William Adam—Duff House and Haddo House.

The leaflet also details other noteworthy sites, including Balmoral Castle, a royal home since Queen Victoria's day, and Pitmedden Garden, where the centerpiece Great Garden was laid out in 1675. You can get the leaflet, *Scotland's Castle Trail,* online at www.aberdeen-grampian.com/pdf/Castle-Trail.pdf, or at local tourist offices, or by calling ✆ **0845/225-5121.** Other information related to castles can also be found on the Aberdeen and Grampian Tourist Board website (www.aberdeen-grampian.com).

Craigievar Castle ★ CASTLE   Structurally unchanged since its completion in 1626, Craigievar Castle is an exceptional tower house in the Scottish baronial style. It has 17th-century plaster ceilings in nearly all its rooms. The castle was continuously inhabited by the descendants of the builder, William Forbes, until it came under the care of the National Trust for Scotland in 1963. The family collection of furnishings remains intact.

Some 3¾ miles south of the castle, clearly signposted on a small road leading off the A980, near Lumphanan, is **Macbeth's Cairn,** where the historical Macbeth is believed to have fought his last battle. Originally built of timber in a "motte and bailey" layout, it's now nothing more than a steep-sided hillock marked with a sign and a flag.

On the A980, 6 miles south of Alford. ✆**01339/883-635.** www.nts.org.uk/Property/17. Admission £11 adults, £8 seniors and children 5–16, £27 families. Castle May–June and Sept Fri–Tues 11am–5pm; July–Aug daily 11am–5pm. Gardens year-round daily 9am–sunset. Head west on the A96 to Alford, and then south on A980.

Crathes Castle & Gardens ★ CASTLE   Situated 1¼ miles east of Banchory, Crathes has royal associations dating back to 1323, when the lands of Leys were granted to the Burnett family by King Robert the Bruce. The castle features remarkable late-16th-century painted ceilings and a garden that's a composite of eight separate gardens, giving a display all year. The great yew hedges date from 1702. The grounds are ideal for nature study, and there are five trails, including a long-distance layout with ranger service. Amenities include a licensed restaurant, a visitor center, a souvenir shop, a plant sales area, a wayfaring course, and picnic areas.

Banchory. ✆ **0844/493-2166.** www.nts.org.uk/Property/20. Admission £11 adults, £8 seniors and children 5–16, £27 families. Car parking £2. Nov–Mar Sat–Sun 10:30am–3:45pm (last entry 3pm); Apr–Oct daily 10:30am–4:45pm (last entry 4pm). From Aberdeen, take the A93 15 miles west.

Fyvie Castle ★ CASTLE/ARCHITECTURE   The oldest part of this castle, dating from the 13th century, has been called the grandest existing example of Scottish baronial architecture. There are five towers, named after the families who lived there over 5 centuries. Originally built in a royal hunting forest, Fyvie means "deer hill" in Gaelic. The interior, created by the first Lord Leith of Fyvie, reflects the opulence of

10

ABERDEEN, TAYSIDE & GRAMPIAN

Aberdeen & Castle Country

the Edwardian era. His collections contain arms and armor, 16th-century tapestries, and important artworks by Raeburn, Gainsborough, and Romney. The castle is rich in ghosts, curses, and legends.

Turriff, on the Aberdeen–Banff road. © **0844/493-2182.** www.nts.org.uk/Property/51. Admission £11 adults, £8 seniors and children 5–16, £27 families. Castle Apr–June and Sept–Oct Sat–Wed noon–5pm; July–Aug daily 11am–5pm. Gardens year-round daily 9am–sunset. Take the A947 for 23 miles northwest of Aberdeen.

PERTH ★: GATEWAY TO THE HIGHLANDS

44 miles N of Edinburgh; 22 miles SW of Dundee; 64 miles NE of Glasgow

From its majestic position on the Tay, the ancient city of Perth was the capital of Scotland until the mid-15th century. It's here that the Highlands meet the Lowlands, and Perth makes a good stop if you're heading north. Perth itself has some fine historic buildings, a couple of interesting museums, and also offers some good shopping. The main attraction, **Scone Palace,** lies on the outskirts, and the surrounding countryside is wonderful for gentle strolls or more arduous hikes.

Essentials

GETTING THERE **ScotRail** runs between Edinburgh and Perth (trip time: 90 min.), with continuing a service to Dundee. Call © **08457/484-950,** or visit www.scotrail.co.uk.

Edinburgh and Perth are connected by a frequent bus service (journey time: 1½ hr.). For more information and schedules, check with **Citylink** (© **08705/505-050;** www.citylink.co.uk).

To reach Perth from Edinburgh, take the A90 northwest and go across the Forth Road Bridge, continuing north along the M90 (journey time: 1½ hr.).

VISITOR INFORMATION The **Tourist Information Centre** is at Lower City Mills, West Mill Street (© **01738/450-600;** www.perthshire.co.uk). It's open from April to June daily 9:30am to 6pm, from July to September daily 9am to 7pm, in October daily 9am to 6pm, and from November to March Monday through Saturday 10am to 5pm.

Exploring the Area

For the best view of this scenic part of Scotland, take Bowerswell Road 1 mile to the east of Perth center to reach **Kinnoull Hill,** rising to a height of 240m (787 ft.). After an easy climb, you get a bird's-eye view of the geological Highland Line dividing the Highlands from the Lowlands. A marked nature trail beginning at the Braes Road car

---

Calling All Artists

In May, the 10-day **Perth Festival of the Arts** attracts international orchestras and chamber music societies. There are some dance recitals as well, and a recent trend is to include pop, jazz, and comedy. Concerts are held in churches, the theatre, and concert hall, and even Scone Palace. For information, call © 01739/621-031, or visit www.perth festival.co.uk.

park leads, after a 25-minute walk, to the panoramic view from the top. Here you can see a folly, the **Kinnoull Watch Tower,** and its counterpart, 1 mile to the east, **Binn Hill.** Both structures are imitations of castles along the Rhine.

Perth itself is also noted for its green spaces and picturesque setting beside the river. Just to the northeast of the city center is **North Inch,** a 41-hectare (100-acre) park extending along the west bank of the Tay. Parts of the grounds are given over to sports facilities such as the domed Bells Sports Centre. North Inch, as depicted in Sir Walter Scott's *The Fair Maid of Perth,* was the site of the great 1396 Clan Combat between 30 champions from the clans Kay and Chattan, attended by King Robert III and his queen. To the south of the city center is another park, unsurprisingly called **South Inch.** Both parks were originally granted to the city by King Robert III in 1377.

North of Perth is one of Scotland's acclaimed golf links, the 18-hole **Blairgowrie Golf Club,** Golf Course Road, Rosemont, Blairgowrie (📞 **01250/872-622;** www. theblairgowriegolfclub.co.uk), which comprises 6,229 yards of fairways with a par of 72. This challenging course undulates amid a wild landscape of pine, birch, and fir; you might even spot a deer or two grazing on the course. A pro shop rents clubs and trolleys.

Balhousie Castle CASTLE   In the 16th century, this was the home of the earls of Kinnoull, but today it houses the Black Watch Regimental Museum, with hundreds of weapons, medals, and documents of the Black Watch Regiment from the 18th century to the present day. The regiment was raised in 1739 by General George Wade to help the government pacify rebellious Highlanders, and became famous all over the United Kingdom for its black tartans, which contrasted with the red of government troops.

Hay St., right beyond Rose Terrace on the west side of North Inch. 📞0131/310-8530. www.theblack watch.co.uk/index/balhousie-castle. Admission £4 adults, £3 seniors and students, £2 children aged 5-16, £10 families. Apr–Oct Mon–Sat 9:30am–5pm, Sun 10am–3:30pm; Nov–Mar Mon–Sat 9:30am–5pm.

Branklyn Garden ★GARDEN   Once the finest private garden in Scotland, the Branklyn now belongs to the National Trust for Scotland. It has a superb collection of rhododendrons, alpines, and herbaceous and peat-garden plants from all over the world.

116 Dundee Rd. (A85), in Branklyn. 📞 01738/625-535. www.nts.org.uk/Property/12. Admission £6 adults, £5 students, seniors, and children aged 5-15, £16 families. Apr–Oct daily 10am–5pm. Closed in winter.

Kirk of St. John the Baptist CHURCH   It's believed that the original foundation on this site dates back to Pictish times. The present choir dates from 1440 and the nave from 1490. In 1559, John Knox preached his famous sermon attacking idolatry, causing a turbulent wave of iconoclasm to sweep across the land. In its wake, religious artifacts, stained glass, and organs were destroyed all over Scotland. The church was restored as a World War I memorial in the mid-1920s.

31 St. John Place. 📞01738/622-241. www.st-johns-kirk.co.uk. Free admission (donations suggested). Daily 7am–7pm.

Perth Art Gallery & Museum MUSEUM   The local municipal museum is well worth a visit; the wealth of the town's Victorian era saw to it that the museum received many important bequests of paintings. Among the notable artworks are large Scottish landscapes by John Everett Millais (1829–96). Horatio McCulloch (1805–67) was known as a specialist of Highland scenes, and one of his finest works, *Loch*

Katrine (1866), is also on display. There are numerous other paintings that illustrate the town's history, as well as archaeological artifacts. The growth of the whisky industry and its major role in the area's economy are given particular attention. There are all manner of other artifacts as well: from grandfather clocks to Georgian silver to an effigy of a 29kg (64-lb.) salmon caught by some proud fisherman in 1922.

78 George St., at the intersection of Tay St. and Perth Bridge. ℂ **01738/632-488.** www.pkc.gov.uk. Free admission. Mon–Sat 10am–5pm.

Round House & Fergusson Gallery ★ GALLERY   If you're interested in Scottish art, head for the Fergusson Gallery, which displays some 6,000 works by Scottish artist J.D. Fergusson (1874–1961). He is one of the four painters known collectively as the Scottish Colourists, and is renowned for his gorgeous use of color and vibrant brushwork, which betray the influence of Fauvism. The work of his partner, the dancer Margaret Morris (1891–1980), is also presented in the gallery. There are many photographs of dancers performing her choreography, and her paintings show that she was a talented artist as well.

Marshall Place. ℂ **01738/783-425.** www.pkc.gov.uk. Free admission. Mon–Sat 10am–5pm.

Where to Eat

Dean's @ Let's Eat ★ BRITISH/INTERNATIONAL   The most visually striking restaurant in Perth itself occupies a former theatre built in 1822. There's a cozy lounge, with a log-burning stove and comfy sofas, and a 65-seat restaurant. The menu changes frequently, but might feature a gratin of goat's cheese studded with roasted peppers; grilled brochettes of monkfish with king prawns; and roast Scottish lamb Moroccan-style with minted couscous.

77–79 Kinnoull St. (3 blocks north of High St.). ℂ **01738/643-377.** www.letseatperth.co.uk. Reservations recommended. Lunch main courses £13–£15; dinner main courses £15–£25. AE, MC, V. Tues–Sat noon–2pm and 6:30–9:30pm.

Keracher's Restaurant & Oyster Bar SCOTTISH/SEAFOOD   For five generations, the Kerachers have been serving some of the finest seafood in Perth. Chef Andrew Keracher carries on the family tradition by using the freshest ingredients, cooked to order. Main courses might include Scottish salmon glazed with honey-mustard and served with a leek-and-vermouth cream; and lemon sole with Continental vegetables and a tomato basil dressing. For dessert, try the steamed ginger pudding with vanilla ice cream and vanilla anglaise. The Oyster Bar has a retail counter where you can purchase from the range of Keracher products.

168 South St. (45 min. from Edinburgh on the A90). ℂ **01738/449-777.** www.kerachers-restaurant. co.uk. Reservations recommended. Lunch main courses £8–£11; dinner, 2 courses £22, 3 courses £27. MC, V. Tues–Sat noon–2pm and 6–10pm. Closed 2 weeks in Jan.

The Roost ★★ BRITISH/INTERNATIONAL   The mantra of the chef-patron at the Roost could be "seasonal, local, and, if possible, homemade" (which includes just about everything, from bread to tagliatelle to ice cream). Having worked under big names such as Nick Nairn in Glasgow and Daniel Boulud in New York, Tim Dover has struck out on his own with this unpretentious restaurant, serving innovative but satisfyingly tasty dishes. You could start with foie gras and oxtail balontine with walnut crostini; follow up with lamb loin and braised flank with black olive and rosemary crushed potatoes, ratatouille, and baby spinach; and finish off with chocolate fondant with poached rhubarb and lavender and honeycomb ice cream. Sunday lunches offer traditional British roasts, as well as the options of a fish or vegetarian dish (2 courses £18; 3 courses £20).

Forgandenny Rd, Kintillo, Bridge of Earn, Perth PH2 9AZ. © **01738/812-111.** www.theroostrestaurant. co.uk. Reservations recommended. Lunch main courses £8.50–£9.50; dinner main courses £15–£20. AE, MC, V. Lunch: Tues–Sat noon–2pm and Sun noon–3pm. Dinner: Oct–May Fri–Sat 6:30–9pm; Jun–Sept Thurs–Sat 6:30–9pm. Drive 15 minutes from Perth, south on the A912. At the mini-roundabout between Bridge of Earn and the exits to the M90, follow the signs and turn right, and then right again on to Kintillo Road; the Roost is opposite the arch of Kilgraston School.

Shopping

Cairncross Ltd., 18–20 St. John's St. (© **01738/624-367;** www.cairncross ofperth.co.uk), sells jewelry at a wide range of prices. The specialty is Scottish freshwater pearls. **Timothy Hardie,** 25 St. John's St. (© **01738/633-127;** www.timothyhardie.co.uk), deals in antique jewelry and has a large selection of Victorian pieces. The shop also sells antique silver tea services. **Whispers of the Past,** 15 George St. (© **01738/635-472**), offers an odd mix of items: jewelry, both new and antique, ranging from costume baubles to quality gold and silver pieces; china; pine furniture; and some linens.

   C & C Proudfoot, 112 South St. (© **01738/632-483**), is an eclectic shop whose merchandise includes leather jackets, hand-knitted Arran sweaters, Barbour waxed-cotton jackets, sheepskin jackets and rugs, and wool rugs, as well as a range of handbags, briefcases, scarves, and gloves.

   Perth's main department store is **McEwen's** (© **01738/623-444;** www.mcewens ofperth.co.uk). Established in 1868, it occupies a fine building at 56 St. John St. Inside, you can buy everything from china and glass to cookware, cosmetics, women's clothes, bed linen, and bathroom products. The same store also runs a clothing boutique at 24 St. John St. (© **01738/442-603**).

   Watson of Perth, 163–167 High St. (© **01738/639-861;** www.watsonsofperth. co.uk), has been in business since 1900. It specializes in bone china produced by Royal Doulton, Wedgwood, and others; it also offers cut crystal from Edinburgh, Stuart, and Waterford.

   Perthshire Shop, Lower City Mills, Mill Street (© **01738/627-958**), sells jams, mustards, and oatmeal along with items produced in the neighboring mills. On the shelves are wooden bowls, *spirtles* (wooden stirrers often used in making porridge), and Perthshire tartan scarves and ties, along with a large selection of cookbooks.

Entertainment & Nightlife

The Victorian **Perth Theatre,** 185 High St. (© **01738/621-031;** www.horscross. co.uk), hosts performances of plays and musicals between mid-September and May. From the end of May to early June, it's also a venue for some of the events of the Perth Festival of the Arts. The box office is open Monday through Saturday from 10am to 6pm. Next door to the old theatre is the contemporary, rotund form of **Perth Concert Hall** (contact details the same as for the theatre). It hosts a wide range of events, from classical music to comedy to retro pop acts.

Where to Stay

Huntingtower Hotel ★   This late-Victorian country house is set in 1.4 hectares (3½ acres) of well-manicured gardens. As well as the rooms in the old house, a new wing has recently been added, providing additional accommodation. Taste and care, however, have gone into the design. Rooms vary in size, and each has its own decor. Seven of the rooms offer spa baths. The cottage suites are in a renovated bungalow and have twin beds and a sitting room.

The wooden-paneled restaurant serves fine Scottish and Continental cuisine at reasonable prices (lunch from £10 and three-course dinners at £20). You can also eat in the conservatory and outdoors in the summer.

Crieff Rd., Perth PH1 3JT. www.huntingtowerhotel.co.uk. © **800/780-7234** in the U.S. and Canada, or 01738/583-771. Fax 01738/583-777. 34 units. £99–£125 double; from £150 cottage suite. AE, DC, MC, V. Free parking. Drive 3¾ miles west on the A85. **Amenities:** Restaurant; bar; room service. *In room:* TV, minibar, hair dryer, Wi-Fi (free).

The New County Hotel   This family-run hotel offers attentive service and a wonderful location in the city center of Perth. It's a 5-minute walk from bus and train stations, movie theatres, and other entertainment. The rooms are modern in style, and very comfortable. Adjacent to the reception area is Café 22, the hotel's contemporary coffee and tea bar. The Place Bar and Gavin's Bistro has a real pub atmosphere, and serves gastro-pub style fare at lunchtimes and in the evenings. The more formal Opus One Restaurant serves stylishly executed dishes prepared with market-fresh ingredients. Smoking is discouraged in the hotel, but none of the rooms is specifically designated nonsmoking.

26 County Place, Perth. www.newcountyhotel.com. © **01738/623-355.** Fax 01738/628-969. 23 units. £90–£140 double. MC, V. Free parking. **Amenities:** Restaurant; bar; room service; Wi-Fi (free). *In room:* TV, hair dryer.

Parklands Hotel ★   This hotel near the train station is probably the most fashionable place to stay in Perth itself. The classic Georgian townhouse was the home of the city's Lord Provost from 1867 to 1873. The spacious and smartly decorated guest rooms overlook South Inch Park. The beautiful Victorian conservatory is ideal for afternoon tea, and for main meals there's the choice of the formal 63@Parklands Restaurant (evenings Thurs–Mon) and the more relaxed No.1 The Bank Bistro (lunch and dinner daily).

2 St. Leonard's Bank, Perth PH2 8EB. www.theparklandshotel.com. © **01738/622-451.** Fax 01738/622-046. 14 units. £98–£155 double. AE, DC, MC, V. From the M90 (Edinburgh or Dundee), take junction 10. Take the right-hand fork signed for Perth. At the end of the road, turn left at the traffic lights and follow the edge of South Inch Park. Parklands is the 1st building on the left-hand side. **Amenities:** 2 restaurants; bar; room service. *In room:* TV/DVD, CD player, hair dryer, Wi-Fi (free).

A Side Trip to Scone

Old Scone, located 1¾ miles away from Perth on the River Tay, was the ancient capital of the Picts. The early Scottish monarchs were enthroned here on a slab of sandstone known as the "Stone of Destiny." In 1296, King Edward I of England, the so-called "Hammer of the Scots," moved the stone to Westminster Abbey, and for hundreds of years it rested under the chair on which British monarchs were crowned. The Scots have always bitterly resented this theft, and it was finally returned to Scotland in 1996, to find a permanent home in Edinburgh Castle, where it can now be viewed by the public.

The seat of the earls of Mansfield and birthplace of David Douglas (of fir-tree fame), **Scone Palace** ★★, along the A93 (© **01738/552-300;** www.scone-palace. co.uk), was largely rebuilt in 1802, incorporating the old palace of 1580. Inside is an impressive collection of French furniture, china, ivories, and 16th-century needlework, including bed hangings made by Mary Queen of Scots. A fine collection of rare conifers is found on the grounds in the Pinetum. Rhododendrons and azaleas grow profusely in the gardens and woodlands around the palace. To reach the palace, head northeast of Perth on the A93. It's open from April to October only, daily from 9:30am to 5pm. Admission is £9.60 for adults, £8.60 for seniors, and £6.80 for children 16 and under. A family ticket costs £28. Admission to the grounds only is £5.50 for adults, £4.90 for seniors, and £3.75 for children.

WHERE TO EAT & STAY

Murrayshall House Hotel & Golf Courses ★ This elegant country-house hotel, set on 142 hectares (350 acres) of parkland, is a magnet for golfers, who come to try their hand on its two glorious courses. The hotel also organizes shooting days, and has its own gun cupboard. The hotel chef may even cook up the best specimens from the day's bag.

The hotel's public rooms and guest rooms are all traditionally styled, and many have fine views. The Old Masters Restaurant offers excellent food at reasonable prices: one course for £17, two courses for £22, and three courses for £28.

New Scone, Perthshire PH2 7PH. www.murrayshall.com. **✆ 01738/551-171.** Fax 01738/552-595. 41 units. £100–£170 double; £120–£210 suite; £150–£170 lodge. AE, DC, MC, V. Take the A94 1½ miles east of New Scone. **Amenities:** Restaurant; 2 bars 2 golf courses; 2 tennis courts (lit); exercise room w/ Jacuzzi; room service; babysitting . *In room:* TV, fridge (in some), hair dryer.

GLENEAGLES

56 miles NE of Glasgow Airport; 50 miles NW of Edinburgh Airport

This famous golfing center and sports complex is on a moor between Strathearn and Strath Allan. Gleneagles has three **18-hole golf courses:** the PGA Centenary Course, which is the venue for the 40th Ryder Cup Matches in 2014; the King's Course; and the Queen's Course. There is also the 9-hole PGA National Academy Course, which is ideal for a warm-up round. The resort gets its name from the Gaelic *Gleann-an-Eaglias,* meaning "glen of the church."

Essentials

GETTING THERE The train ride from Perth takes 15 minutes. The trip takes 1 hour and 25 minutes from Edinburgh. For information, call **✆ 08457/484-950.**

The only bus service departs from Glasgow. The trip takes slightly over an hour. For information and schedules, call **✆ 08705/505-050,** or visit www.citylink.co.uk.

Gleneagles is situated just off the A9, about halfway between Perth and Stirling, a short distance from the village of Auchterarder. It lies 55 miles from Edinburgh and 45 miles from Glasgow.

Where to Eat & Stay

The Gleneagles Hotel ★★★ Britain's greatest golf hotel stands on its own 336-hectare (830-acre) estate. When it was built in isolated grandeur in 1924, it was Scotland's only government-rated five-star hotel. It's a true resort and has kept up with the times by offering spa treatments as well as many other activities. There are schools for shooting, fishing, equestrian sports, and falconry, and there are even two off-road driving courses. Public rooms are designed in the grand classic style, with pilasters and fine cornicing. The guest rooms vary greatly in size and degree of luxury.

At the in-house award-winning restaurant, chef **Andrew Fairlie** produces a menu of luxurious food, with ingredients sourced from Rungis Market on the outskirts of

Paris, as well as from local Scottish suppliers. Signature dishes include smoked lobster. The unique flavor comes from smoking lobster shells over old whisky barrels for 12 hours. Quite equally, Aberdeen Angus beef, pheasant, and salmon are all cooked to perfection in beautifully presented dishes.

Auchterarder PH3 1NF. www.gleneagles.com. © 866/881-9525 in the U.S., or 01764/662-231. Fax 01764/662-134. 232 units. £320–£525 double; £740–£2,040 suite. AE, DC, MC, V. Free parking. Take the A9 1½ miles southwest of Auchterarder. **Amenities:** 4 restaurants; 4 bars; pool (indoor); 4 golf courses; tennis courts (lit); health club & spa; bike rental; concierge; hair salon; nail bar; room service; babysitting. *In room:* TV/DVD, CD player (in some), minibar, hair dryer, Internet (free).

CRIEFF & DRUMMOND CASTLE GARDENS ★

18 miles W of Perth; 60 miles NW of Edinburgh; 50 miles NE of Glasgow

From Perth, head west on the A85 for 18 miles to Crieff. At the edge of the Perthshire Highlands, Crieff makes a pleasant stopover, with good fishing and golf. This small burgh was the seat of the court of the earls of Strathearn until 1747. The gallows in its marketplace were once used to execute Highland cattle rustlers.

You can take a "day trail" into **Strathearn,** the valley of the River Earn, the very center of Scotland. Here Highland mountains meet gentle Lowland slopes, and moorland mingles with rich green pastures. North of Crieff, the road to Aberfeldy passes through the narrow pass of the **Sma' Glen,** a famously beautiful spot, with hills rising on either side to 600m (1,970 ft.).

Essentials

GETTING THERE   There's no direct train service. The nearest train stations are at Gleneagles, 8⅔ miles away, and at Perth, 18 miles away. Call © **08457/484-950** for information and schedules.

Once you arrive in Perth, you'll find a regular connecting bus service hourly during the day. For information and schedules, contact **Stagecoach** (© **01738/629-339;** www.stagecoachbus.com).

VISITOR INFORMATION   The year-round **Tourist Information Centre** is in the Town Hall on High Street (© **01764/652-578**). It's open October to April, daily 10am to 4pm; April to June and September to October, Monday through Saturday 9:30am to 5pm and Sunday 10am to 2pm; and July and August, Monday through Saturday 9:30am to 6:30pm and Sunday 10am to 4pm.

Exploring the Area

Drummond Castle Gardens ★★ GARDEN   The gardens of Drummond Castle, first laid out in the early 17th century by John Drummond, second earl of Perth, are among the finest formal gardens in Europe. There's a panoramic view from the upper terrace, overlooking an example of an early Victorian parterre in the form of St. Andrew's Cross. The multifaceted sundial by John Mylne, master mason to Charles I, has been the centerpiece since 1630. Unfortunately, the castle itself isn't open to the public.

Grimsthorpe, Crieff. © **01764/681-433.** www.drummondcastlegardens.co.uk. Admission £5 adults, £4 seniors, £2 children 5–15. May–Oct daily 1–6pm, Easter weekend 1–6pm. Closed Nov–Apr. Take the A822 for 3 miles south of Crieff.

Glenturret Distillery Ltd. DISTILLERY   Scotland's oldest distillery, Glenturret was established in 1775 on the banks of the River Turret. Visitors can see the milling of malt, mashing, fermentation, distillation, and cask filling, followed by a couple of tastings at the end of the tour. This can be followed or preceded by a 20-minute video, *The Water of Life,* and there's also a small museum devoted to the implements of the whisky trade. Real connoisseurs can also take three other tours, costing from £14 to £40, and offering different numbers of tastings and qualities of whisky.

The Hosh, off the A85, Glenturret. ✆ **01764/656-565.** www.thefamousgrouse.com. Guided tours £8.95 adults, £7.50 seniors and children 13–17, free for children aged 12 and under. Jan Mon–Fri 11:30am–4pm; Feb Mon–Sat 11:30am–4pm, Sun noon–4pm; Mar–Dec Mon–Sat 9:30am–6pm, Sun noon–6pm. Take the A85 toward Comrie; ¾ mile from Crieff, turn right at the crossroads; the distillery is ½ mile up the road.

Innerpeffray Library ★★ LIBRARY   This extraordinary Georgian library is improbably situated on open farmland down an unpromising farm lane just to the south of Crieff. Founded in around 1680 by the local landowner, Lord Madertie, who donated his collection of precious leather-bound volumes, it provided a book-lending service to the local population. He also founded a school nearby, and the fruits of his educational zeal can be seen in the borrowers' ledger, where farm workers, students, and artisans of all kinds signed out books in their own, sometimes shaky, hands. Indeed, the Scottish Enlightenment in general saw to it that literacy rates were far higher in Scotland than England up until about 1750, when the latter caught up.

In the 1760s, the library was provided with a purpose-built home, adjoining the old chapel next door (which is also worth a look). As you enter the library (on the first level), you're greeted by a librarian who's happy to give you a guided tour and will provide you with white gloves to leaf through some of the old tomes (which include atlases and books on gardening, natural history, biography, and a host of other subjects). If you find a particularly good read, you can settle into an old armchair and spend the afternoon there. As you leave, a short diversion farther down the farm track by which you came brings you to the ruins of Lord Madertie's stone castle.

Just off the B8062, near Crieff, PH7 3RF. ✆**01764/652-819.** www.innerpeffraylibrary.co.uk. Admission £5 adults, under-15s free. Mar–Oct Wed–Sun 10am–12:45pm and 2pm–4:45pm; Nov–Feb visits by appointment only. Take the B8062 southeast from Crieff in the direction of Auchterarder and look out for Historic Scotland signs about 5 miles from Crieff; the library is situated a few minutes drive down a lane on your right.

Where to Eat & Stay

Knock Castle Hotel ★★   Once the home of Scottish shipping magnate Lady MacBrayne, this Victorian baronial-style mansion is now a luxury hotel and spa complex. The guest rooms in the main house vary in size and degree of luxury; some have four-poster beds, one has a sunken bath with views out of the tower windows; there are also the simpler, but smartly refurbished "Lomond" rooms. A lodge in the grounds offers an additional eight bedrooms.

Lunch and dinner are offered 7 days a week in one or both of the restaurants. The Oak Restaurant at street level is the more formal, while the Stag's View Restaurant on the top floor has panoramic views of the area, and includes a terrace for dining outside in the summer. The chefs serve the finest local produce with elegant presentation; they're also very amenable to special requests. The seven-course taster menu is £45 per person; the table d'hote in the Stag's View is £30 for three courses (or a bargain £18 at lunch).

The gym and pool complex are housed in a large glasshouse looking out over the wooded gardens. There is also a sauna, steam room, and spa bath, and a wealth of health and beauty treatments are available. The hotel has an over 18-years-old policy.

Drummond Terrace, Crieff PH7 4AN. www.knockcastle.com. © **01764/650-088.** Fax 01764/655-659. 22 units; also a lodge with 8 units. £145–£259 double or suite. AE, DC, MC, V. Free parking. A 10-min. walk north of the center of Crieff; turn right off the A85 up Craigard Rd. **Amenities:** 2 restaurants; bar; pool; spa; cinema room. *In room:* TV, hair dryer, Wi-Fi (free).

Murraypark Hotel ☺ This 19th-century stone-fronted house—originally built for a sea captain—lies in a residential neighborhood about a 10-minute walk from Crieff's center. Bedrooms vary in size and layout, but most open onto fine views. Although rooms in the more modern wing are more comfortable, they're hardly as characterful. The hotel's restaurant serves traditional Scottish cuisine in a candle-lit dining room. Main courses range in price from £10 to £22, and include a number of vegetarian options. Guests at the Murraypark also have free use of the leisure facilities in a sister hotel located a 5-minute walk away; these include a swimming pool, sauna, steam room, spa bath, and gym.

Connaught Terrace, Crieff PH7 3DJ. www.murraypark.com. © **01764/658-000.** Fax 01764/655-311. 19 units. £85–£267 double or suite. AE, DC, MC, V. Free parking. A 10-min. walk from the center of Crieff; the hotel lies northwest of Perth St. **Amenities:** Restaurant; bar; babysitting. *In room:* TV, hair dryer, Wi-Fi (£12 per day).

10 DUNKELD ★

58 miles N of Edinburgh; 14 miles N of Perth; 98 miles SW of Aberdeen

Dunkeld lies in a thickly wooded valley of the Tay River at the edge of the Perthshire Highlands. Once a major ecclesiastical center, its history is long and illustrious, stretching right back to the days when it was an important center of the Celtic Church. Today, it remains a pretty and unspoilt town that invites exploration on foot.

The surrounding countryside is beautiful, and you can take long walks and day hikes on both sides of the River Tay going from Dunkeld to Birnam. In all, 36 miles of paths have been joined to create a network of circular routes. Pick up maps and detailed descriptions from the tourist office and set out on a day's adventure, armed, of course, with the makings of a picnic.

Essentials

GETTING THERE Trains from Perth arrive every 2 hours; the journey time is approximately 1½ hours. For information and schedules, call © **08457/484-950.**

Pitlochry-bound buses leaving from Perth make a stopover in Dunkeld, letting you alight at Dunkeld Car Park at the railway station (journey time: 50 min.): Contact **Stagecoach** (© **01738/629-339;** www.stagecoachbus.com).

Driving from Aberfeldy, take the A827 east until you reach the junction of the A9 heading south to Dunkeld.

VISITOR INFORMATION A **Tourist Information Centre** is at no. 11, The Cross (© **01350/727-688;** www.visitdunkeld.com). It's open April to June and September 9 to October 27, Monday to Saturday 9:30am to 5:30pm and Sunday 11am to 4pm; July 1 to September 8, Monday to Saturday 9:30am to 6:30pm and Sunday 11am to 5pm; October 28 to December, Monday to Saturday 9:30am to 5:30pm (closed Jan–Mar).

Exploring the Area

Founded in A.D. 815, **Dunkeld Cathedral** ★ (www.dunkeldcathedral.org.uk) was converted from a church to a cathedral in 1127 by David I. It stands on Cathedral Street in a scenic setting along the River Tay. The cathedral was first restored in 1815, and traces of the 12th-century structure remain today. Admission is free, and the cathedral is open May to September, Monday through Saturday 9:30am to 6:30pm, Sunday 2 to 6:30pm; October to April, Monday through Saturday 9:30am to 4pm. There's no parking at the site.

The National Trust for Scotland has restored many of the old houses and shops around the marketplace and cathedral. The Trust also owns 20 houses on **High Street** and **Cathedral Street** as well. Many of them were constructed in the late 17th century after the rebuilding of the town following the Battle of Dunkeld. The Trust runs the **Ell Shop,** The Cross (✆ **01350/727-460**), which specializes in Scottish handicrafts. Easter weekend to December 24, it's open from Monday to Saturday from 10am to 5:30pm.

Shakespeare fans may want to seek out the oak and sycamore in front of the destroyed **Birnam House,** 1 mile south. This was believed to be a remnant of the Birnam Wood in *Macbeth;* you may recall, "Macbeth shall never vanquished be until great Birnam Wood to high Dunsinane Hill shall come against him."

The **Hermitage,** off the A9 about 1¾ miles west of Dunkeld, was called a folly when it was built in 1758 above the wooded gorge of the River Braan. The Dukes of Atholl (who resided nearby in the long-since demolished Dunkeld House) built the follies, Ossian's Hall of Mirrors and Ossians Cave, to honor the blind bard Ossian. Today, the setting makes for one of the most scenic woodland walks in the area.

Another place of great natural beauty near Dunkeld is the **Loch of the Lowes Wildlife Reserve** ★ (✆ **01350/727-337**; www.swt.org.uk), situated 1¾ miles from the center of town, along the A923 heading northeast. The loch can be approached from the south shore, where there's a visitor center and two bird hides. The 99-hectare (245-acre) reserve is most famous for the rare ospreys, which are on the endangered-species list in Britain. The birds migrate from Africa every summer to breed here, and bird-watchers can enjoy good views of them on nests via a closed-circuit television camera. Telescopes and binoculars are also available to borrow in the hides. The reserve is open year-round from 10am to 5pm. Admission is £4 for adults, £3 for seniors, and £0.50 for children. A family ticket costs £7.50.

If, on the other hand, your interests are of a sporting nature, the **Dunkeld & Birnam Golf Club** at Dunkeld (✆ **01350/727-524**; www.dunkeldandbirnamgolf club.co.uk), is well regarded among aficionados, and offers sweeping views of the surrounding environs. Hours are daily 7am to 11pm April to September. October to March, greens fees are reduced and hours are daily from 8am to 4pm. There's no official dress code; although, if the starter feels you're not dressed "appropriately," you will be asked to "smarten up" the next time you play the course. Jeans and collarless shirts aren't acceptable.

Where to Eat & Stay

Dunkeld offers some very good, but rather pricey, accommodation, unless you avail yourself of dozens of B&Bs, some of which go in and out of business. The tourist office (see above) keeps an up-to-date list.

Hilton Dunkeld House Hotel ★★ This hotel offers the peace and quiet of a Scottish country house with its own estate on the banks of the Tay. It's popular with visitors interested in the sports offered by the area, especially fishing for the salmon and trout in the river that passes through the 113 hectares (280 acres) of parkland. The house is beautifully kept, and rooms come in a wide range of sizes, styles, and furnishings. The formal Garden Room Restaurant is open for dinner nightly, and the Garden Bar is a relaxed place for a lighter lunch.

Dunkeld PH8 0HX. www.hilton.co.uk/dunkeld.© **01350/727-771.** Fax 01350/728-924. 96 units. £80–£265 double. AE, DC, MC, V. Free parking. Follow Atholl St. out of town; the hotel is signposted. **Amenities:** Restaurant; bar; pool (indoor); 2 tennis courts health club w/sauna; babysitting. *In room:* TV, minibar, hair dryer, Internet.

Royal Dunkeld Hotel ★ ☺ This 19th-century coaching inn comes recommended for its prime location right at the heart of Dunkeld, as well as its very moderate prices and friendly atmosphere. It's a particularly good choice if you have children, who can share your room for a very modest surcharge. The food and drink is well worth stopping in for (non-guests are very welcome). The freshest local produce is cooked up in heart-warming dishes, and the portions are very generous. There are special menus for children. The bar is well stocked with real ales and whiskies, and is always popular with locals as well as hotel guests. In the summer there's a beer festival and customers spill out into the garden.

Atholl Street, Dunkeld PH8 0AR. www.royaldunkeld.co.uk.© **01350/727-322.** 25 units. £68–£90 double; £50–£60 in the lodge annex. AE, DC, MC, V. Free parking. **Amenities:** Restaurant; 2 bars; lounge; pool room; snooker room; beer garden. *In room:* TV, hair dryer, Wi-Fi (free).

PITLOCHRY ★

71 miles NW of Edinburgh; 27 miles NW of Perth; 15 miles N of Dunkeld

A popular resort, Pitlochry is a good base for touring the Valley of the Tummel. Ever since Queen Victoria declared it one of the finest resorts in Europe, it has drawn in countless visitors every summer. It's also home to the renowned **Pitlochry Festival Theatre,** Scotland's theatre in the hills.

Pitlochry doesn't exist just to entertain visitors, although it might appear that way in summer—it also produces Scotch whisky. And it's a good overnight stop between Edinburgh and Inverness, 85 miles to the north. You can spend a very busy day in town, visiting its famous distilleries, seeing its dam and fish ladder, and budgeting some time for the beauty spots in the environs, especially **Loch Rannoch** and the **Pass of Killiecrankie,** both ideal for walks. At Blair Atholl stands one of the most visited and intriguing castles in the whole of the country, **Blair Castle.**

Essentials

GETTING THERE Five trains (© 08457/484-950) per day arrive from Edinburgh, and an additional three from Glasgow (trip time from each: 2 hr.). Buses arrive hourly from Perth; contact **Stagecoach** (© 01738/629-339) for schedules. If you're **driving** from Perth, head northwest along the A9.

VISITOR INFORMATION The **Tourist Information Centre** is at 22 Atholl Rd. (© 01796/472-215; www.pitlochry.org). From June to September, it's open daily 9am to 8pm; May and October, hours are daily 9am to 6pm; and November to April, hours are Monday through Friday 9am to 5pm and Saturday 10am to 3pm.

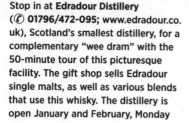

The Wee-est of Wee Drams

Stop in at **Edradour Distillery** (✆ **01796/472-095**; www.edradour.co.uk), Scotland's smallest distillery, for a complementary "wee dram" with the 50-minute tour of this picturesque facility. The gift shop sells Edradour single malts, as well as various blends that use this whisky. The distillery is open January and February, Monday through Saturday 10am to 4pm; March, April, November, and December, Monday through Saturday 10am to 4pm, and Sunday noon to 4pm; and May to October, Monday through Saturday 10am to 5pm, and Sunday noon to 5pm. Tickets cost £5. Take the A924 1¾ miles east towards Braemar.

Exploring the Area

Pitlochry Dam was created because of the need for a power station, but in effect the engineers created a new loch. The famous **salmon ladder** was built to help the struggling salmon upstream. An underwater portion of the ladder has been enclosed in glass to give sightseers a fascinating look. An exhibition (✆ **01796/473-152**) is open from April to October, Monday through Friday from 10am to 5:30pm, and weekends as well in July and August. Admission to the salmon viewing chamber is free, but entrance to the visitor center with exhibition costs £4 for adults and £3 for seniors, though children go free.

There are terrific scenic hikes along the **Linn of Tummel,** with several signposted trails going along the river and into the forest directly to the north of the center. Just north of here you come to the stunning **Pass of Killiecrankie ★**. If you're driving, follow the A9 north. The National Trust has established the **Killiecrankie Visitor Centre** (✆ **01796/473-233**; www.nts.org.uk) here, open April to October daily from 10am to 5:30pm. Admission is free, though there's a charge for car parking. The exhibition inside the center tells of the story of the famous battle that occurred here during the 1689 Jacobite rebellion. John Graham of Cleverhouse (1649–89) rallied the mainly Highlander Jacobite army to meet government troops. Graham was killed, and the quest for Scottish independence soon fizzled out.

The B8019 leads to **Loch Rannoch,** almost 10 miles long and ¾ mile wide. Many consider this to be the most beautiful lake in the Highlands. The setting so impressed Robert Louis Stevenson that he wrote about it in *Kidnapped* (1886): "Much of it was red with heather, much of the rest broken up with bogs and hags and peaty pools." To see this desolate but awesomely beautiful spot, follow the B8019 to the Linn of Tummel north of Pitlochry, venturing onto the B846 at the Bridge of Tummel.

Anyone keen on golf shouldn't pass up the opportunity to play at the **Pitlochry Golf Course** (✆ **01796/472-792**; www.pitlochrygolf.co.uk). This 18-hole, par-69 course is one of the finest in Perthshire, benefiting from a spectacular undulating landscape that climbs up and up to some wonderful views and challenging holes. The club also has the advantage of a good restaurant in the stylish clubhouse. Open daily, year-round for lunch and dinner (except Sunday evenings in winter), the restaurant offers hearty main courses from £8 to £11, as well as a variety of reasonably priced snacks.

Blair Castle ★ CASTLE   Home to the Dukes of Atholl, this is one of the great historic castles of Scotland. Dating from 1269, it saw many alterations before it was finally turned into a Georgian mansion. Plan to spend about 2 hours viewing the palace's 18th-century interior filled with antique furniture and paintings, along with outstanding collections of arms, armor, and porcelain. After viewing the castle, you can stroll through the Victorian walled garden and take a long walk in the parklands. The restaurant serves a selection of hot and cold lunches as well as high tea in the afternoon.

Blair Atholl. © **01796/481-207.** www.blair-castle.co.uk. Admission £9.25 adults, £7.95 seniors and students, £5.65 children 5–16, £25 families. Apr–Oct daily 9:30am–5:30pm (last admission to Castle Tour 4:30pm); Nov–Mar Tues and Sat 9:30am–12:30pm. Closed Dec 22–Jan 4. From the town center, follow the A9 to Blair Atholl, where you'll see signs.

Where to Eat

East Haugh House ★★★ MODERN BRITISH   East Haugh House is as renowned for its restaurant as for its hotel and fishing beat. Meals can be taken in the cozy Fisherman's Bar beside the fire or in the more formal Two Sisters Restaurant. The menu relies exclusively on fresh Scottish ingredients, and, in season, may include local grouse, pheasant, and venison shot by the chef-patron himself. Of course, fine salmon and trout also feature prominently, as well as seafood from the Western Isles. The chef's specials might include zucchini stuffed with wild-mushroom duxelles, terrine of local pigeon with orange salad and mange tout, or wood pigeon and deer liver with Stornoway black pudding mash, creamed savoy cabbage, and rosemary jus.

Old Perth Rd., East Haugh, Pitlochry PH16 5JS. ©**01796/473-121.** Fax 01796/472-473. www.easthaugh. co.uk. Reservations recommended. Main courses £9–£19. MC, V. Restaurant daily 7–9pm. Bar daily noon–2:30pm and 6–9pm. Drive 1 mile south of Pitlochry on the A9 toward Inverness; East Haugh House is across the road from the Tummel River.

Victoria's ★★ ☺ SCOTTISH/INTERNATIONAL   Located toward the south end of the main street, Victoria's is something of an institution in Pitlochry. It's a place for all occasions, from breakfasts (Continental or full Scottish), to lunches (light or substantial), high teas (with delicious pastries and fine tea blends), pre-theatre dinners (from 5:30pm; the theatre is just a few minutes' walk away), and during the tourist season, hearty dinners. Its informal atmosphere, comfortable seats, and friendly service have ensured its long-standing success. The menu is unpretentious, but the quality of the ingredients and the cooking is excellent. Dishes include a superlative steak frites, fresh fish and chips, platters of fresh seafood, homemade burgers, and gooey chocolate desserts. Children are made to feel very welcome and have their own special menu.

45 Atholl Rd., Pitlochry PH16 5BX. © **01796/472-670.** www.victorias-pitlochry.co.uk. Reservations recommended. Dinner main courses £10–£18. MC, V. Dinner menu: mid-Mar–mid-Nov daily 5:30am–10:30pm; daytime menu: year-round, daily 10am–5:30pm.

Entertainment & Nightlife

The town is famous for the **Pitlochry Festival Theatre** (© **01796/484-626;** www. pitlochry.org.uk). Founded in 1951, it draws people from all over the world for its program of plays, concerts, and varying art exhibits, presented from April to October. The theatre complex opened in 1981 on the banks of the River Tummel, near the dam and fish ladder; it has a restaurant serving coffee, lunch, and dinner, along with other facilities for visitors.

Where to Stay

Acarsaid Hotel This graceful but solid-looking stone house dates from 1880, when it was the home of the Countess of Kilbride. Greatly expanded, the hotel contains cozy guest rooms with contemporary furnishings and immaculately kept bathrooms. The bar serves snacks at lunch (for guests only), while the more elaborate restaurant offers fixed-price dinners. The menu focuses on fresh locally sourced ingredients.

8 Atholl Rd., Pitlochry PH16 5BX. www.acarsaidhotel.com. © **0845/263-6855.** Fax 0845/268-6854. 29 units. £84–£110 double. MC, V. Free parking. **Amenities:** Restaurant; bar; access to nearby health club; Wi-Fi (free). *In room:* TV, hair dryer.

Craigmhor Lodge ★★ This is a family-run guest house of a very superior sort. The three bedrooms in the original Victorian house are complemented by 12 rooms in a stylish new courtyard building. While the Victorian rooms have high ceilings, fine traditional furniture, and views over the valley, the rooms in the new block are decorated in muted tones for a warm and contemporary look, and have balconies or terraces looking out over the wooded grounds. The new rooms also have chic designer bathrooms with underfloor heating. Docking stations for iPods connect to a surround sound system so you can listen to music while in the bath. Several of the rooms can accommodate extra beds for children for a modest surcharge; travel cots and high chairs are also available. Packed lunches and supper hampers can be supplied on request. Six of the courtyard rooms are suitable for guests with mobility difficulties.

27 West Moulin Rd., Pitlochry PH16 5EF. www.craigmhorlodge.co.uk. © **01796/472-123.** 15 units. £79–£140 double. MC, V. West Moulin Road is just off Pitlochry's main street, Atholl Road; the hotel is on your left. **Amenities:** Lounge; DVD library. *In room:* TV, DVD player, hair dryer, iPod docking station, Wi-Fi (free).

East Haugh House ★★★ 🏠 Warm and welcoming, and full of character, this family-run country hotel is highly recommended. It occupies a handsome turreted stone house, which was built in the 17th century by the Duke of Atholl for one of his tenant farmers. The 13 guest rooms are stylishly decorated with antique furniture; some have four-poster beds and their own open fires (lit for you by hotel staff while you're having your dinner downstairs). Attention to detail is evident everywhere, from the luxury toiletries to the quality of the smoked salmon at breakfast. The hotel's restaurant has a considerable reputation locally (see "Where to Eat," above). Children are welcome; dogs are too.

The public area of the hotel displays many vintage fishing trophies, paintings, and other memorabilia. Indeed, if you're interested in fishing, this place is something of a mecca. The hotel has its own fishing beat on the Tay (one of the finest on the river), complete with a full-time ghillie, a heated hut, two boats, and toilet facilities. Prices per rod per day range from £29 to £100. You can hire tackle and take lessons and courses. The hotel can also organize shooting and stalking activities.

Old Perth Rd., East Haugh, Pitlochry PH16 5JS. www.easthaugh.co.uk. © **01796/473-121.** Fax 01796/472-473. 13 units. £138–£238 double. MC, V. Drive 1 mile south of Pitlochry on the A9 toward Inverness; East Haugh House is across the road from the Tummel River. **Amenities:** Restaurant; bar; fishing beat. *In room:* TV, DVD/CD player, whirlpool spa bath (in some rooms), hair dryer, Wi-Fi (free.

Killiecrankie Hotel This typically Scottish country house, built in 1840 for the local church minister, is surrounded by lawns and woodlands, including a herbaceous border garden. The guest rooms are individually decorated in subtle tones. The restaurant serves formal dinners that feature fresh produce and seasonal meat, fish, and game. The Bar Conservatory offers a more informal setting for a quiet drink and lighter meals.

On the A924, Killiecrankie PH16 5LG. www.killiecrankiehotel.co.uk. © **01796/473-220.** Fax 01796/472-451. 10 units. £210–£270 double. Rates include half-board. MC, V. Free parking. Signposted from the A9 north of Pitlochry. **Amenities:** Restaurant; bar; room service. *In room:* TV, hair dryer, Wi-Fi (free).

Pine Trees Hotel This 19th-century country house is a 15-minute walk from the town center and 5 minutes from the golf course that hosts the Highland Open Championships. The family-run Pine Trees has spacious public rooms (decorated in a relaxed country-house style), an atmosphere of warmth, and a reputation for good food and wine. The guest rooms are in the main house as well as a 1970s annex designed to blend into the period of the central structure. Bar lunches and full lunch and dinner menus are offered, with fresh and smoked salmon always featured. Trout and salmon fishing nearby can usually be arranged.

Strathview Terrace, Pitlochry PH16 5QR. www.pinetreeshotel.co.uk. © **01796/472-121.** Fax 01796/472-460. 20 units. £104–£176 double. AE, MC, V. Turn right up Larchwood Rd., below the golf course on the north side of Pitlochry. **Amenities:** Restaurant; bar; Wi-Fi (free). *In room:* TV, hair dryer.

DUNDEE & GLAMIS CASTLE

63 miles N of Edinburgh; 67 miles SW of Aberdeen; 22 miles NE of Perth; 83 miles NE of Glasgow

The old seaport of Dundee, on the north shore of the Firth of Tay and Scotland's fourth-largest city, is now an industrial city. When steamers took over the whaling industry from sailing vessels, Dundee became the home port for ships from the 1860s until World War I. Long known for its jute and flax operations, Dundee is also associated with the production of rich Dundee fruitcakes and Dundee marmalades and jams.

Spanning the Firth of Tay is the **Tay Railway Bridge,** opened in 1888. Constructed over the tidal estuary, the bridge is 1¾ miles long, one of the longest in Europe. There's also a road bridge 1¼ miles long, with four traffic lanes and a walkway in the center.

Dundee itself has only minor attractions, but it's a good base from which to visit Glamis Castle (one of the most famous in Scotland) and the little town of Kirriemuir, which Sir James M. Barrie, author of *Peter Pan,* disguised in fiction as Thrums. Dundee also makes a good base for those who want to play at one of Scotland's most famous golf courses, Carnoustie (see chapter 4).

Essentials

GETTING THERE **ScotRail** (www.scotrail.co.uk) offers frequent train services from Perth and Aberdeen to Dundee. Phone © **08457/484-950** for schedules.

Citylink buses offer frequent services from Edinburgh and Glasgow. Contact © **08705/505-050,** or log on to www.citylink.co.uk.

The fastest way to drive to Dundee is to cut south back to Perth along the A9, and link up with the A972 going east.

VISITOR INFORMATION The **Tourist Information Centre** is at Discovery Point, Discovery Quay, Dundee (© **01382/527-527;** www.angusanddundee.co.uk). April to September, hours are Monday to Saturday 10am to 6pm, Sunday 10am to 4pm; October to March, Monday to Saturday 9am to 5pm.

Exploring the Area

For a panoramic view of Dundee, the Tay Bridge across to Fife, and the mountains to the north, go to **Dundee Law,** a 174m (571-ft.) hill, 1 mile north of the city. The hill is an ancient volcanic plug.

Broughty Castle CASTLE   This 15th-century estuary fort is 4 miles east of the city center at Broughty Ferry, a fishing village that was once the terminus for ferries crossing the Firth of Tay before the bridges were built. Besieged by the English in the 16th century and attacked by Cromwell's army under General Monk in the 17th century, the castle was restored in 1861 as part of Britain's coastal defenses. The museum has displays on local history, arms and armor, seashore life, and Dundee's past as a whaling port. The observation area at the top of the castle provides fine views of the Tay estuary and northeast Fife.

Castle Green, Broughty Ferry. ℰ **01382/436-916.** www.dundeecity.gov.uk/broughtycastle. Free admission. Apr–Sept Mon–Sat 10am–4pm, Sun 12:30–4pm; Oct–Mar Tues–Sat 10am–4pm, Sun 12:30–4pm. Bus: 75 or 76.

HMS *Unicorn* ★ HISTORIC SITE   This 46-gun ship of war, commissioned in 1824 by the Royal Navy, is now the oldest British-built ship afloat. It has been restored and visitors can explore all four decks: the quarterdeck, with its 32-lb. carronades; the gun deck, with its battery of 18-lb. cannons and captain's quarters; the berth deck, with its officers' cabins and crew's hammocks; and the orlop deck and hold. Various displays portraying life in the navy and the history of the *Unicorn* make this a rewarding visit.

Victoria Dock. ℰ **01382/200-900.** www.frigateunicorn.org. Admission £4 adults, £3 seniors and children 5–15 £9–£11 families. Apr–Oct daily 10am–5pm; Nov–Mar Wed–Fri noon–4pm, Sat–Sun 10am–4pm. Bus: 6, 23, or 78.

Verdant Works MUSEUM   This refurbished ex-mill, known as the Jute House, is dedicated to the history of an industry that sustained Dundee throughout most of the 19th and 20th centuries. The first level shows how raw jute from Bangladesh was processed, and includes a display on a weaver's loom. On the second level is a section about the socio-historical aspect of the city and how the different social classes lived in 19th-century Dundee. In the courtyard are 18th- and 19th-century street games, such as stilts, whips, and tops.

West Henderson's Wind. ℰ **01382/225-282.** Admission £5.95 adults, £4.70 seniors, £3.85 children 5–16. Apr–Oct Mon–Sat 10am–6pm, Sun 11am–6pm; Nov–Mar Wed–Sat 10am–5pm, Sun 11am–5pm. Lies a 15-min. walk north of train station (it's well signposted).

Where to Eat

Het Theatercafe INTERNATIONAL   Located within the Dundee Repertory Theatre building, the Het is both an upstairs cafe/bar and an excellent restaurant at street level. It's become one of the liveliest dining places in Dundee. Naturally, it's ideal for pre-theatre meals, and a special "Theatre Meal Deal" is offered, whereby you pay between £20 and £30 for a theatre ticket and dinner (ask at the box office for details). Freshly prepared, tasty food and reasonable prices make the restaurant a popular choice. The menu includes such favorites as steak frites and hot-and-spicy blackened chicken breast. There are also vegetarian options. The cafe upstairs offers light breakfasts, snack-lunches, and free Wi-Fi.

Tay Square. ℰ **01382/206-699.** Reservations recommended. Restaurant main courses £9–£15. MC, V. Mon–Sat noon–3pm and 5–9pm.

Jahangir Tandoori INDIAN Built around an indoor fish pond in a dining room draped with the soft folds of an embroidered tent, this is the best Indian restaurant in Dundee. Meals are prepared with fresh ingredients and run the gamut of recipes from both the north and south of India. Tandoori specials are also on offer, seasoned to the degree of spiciness you prefer. Both meat and vegetarian dishes are available.

1 Sessions St. (at the corner of Hawk Hill). ✆ **01382/202-022.** Reservations recommended. Main courses £9.50–£18. AE, MC, V. Daily 5pm–midnight.

Entertainment & Nightlife

The **Dundee Rep Theatre,** Tay Square (✆ **01382/223-530;** www.dundeerep theatre.co.uk), is likely to stage anything from *Peter Pan* to an opera, from plays to Scottish ballet or even flamenco. You can purchase tickets from the box office Monday through Saturday from 10am to 7:30pm (till 6pm on performance days). The theatre provides audio descriptions for people with visual impairments, and sign language is available for those with hearing impairments. On-site is the **Het Theatercafe** (see above).

Where to Stay

Craigtay Hotel This hotel is a useful option if you're traveling on a budget. Although this hotel was constructed around the core of an 18th-century farm building, few if any hints of its age are visible. In the 1960s, it was Dundee's first disco, before a local entrepreneur transformed it into a tearoom. Much enlarged and modernized, it's now a hotel. Its functional guest rooms have small but well-maintained bathrooms. The bar and restaurant serve moderately priced lunches and dinners daily.

101 Broughty Ferry Rd., Tayside, Dundee DD4 6JE. www.craigtay.co.uk. ✆ **01382/451-142.** Fax 01382/452-940. 18 units. £70–£98 double. AE, MC, V. Free parking. From Dundee, drive 1 mile east of town, following signs to Broughty Ferry. Courtesy pickup from train or airport. **Amenities:** Restaurant; bar; Wi-Fi (free). *In room:* TV, hair dryer.

Hilton Dundee This chain hotel helps to rejuvenate the once-seedy waterfront of Dundee. Although built in a severe modern style, the five-story block contains smart guest rooms, some of which overlook the Firth, the river, or the Tay Bridge. Both business and leisure travelers will find that the hotel's facilities—which include a restaurant, bar, cafe, fitness room, and swimming pool—make this a comfortable place to stay.

Earl Grey Place, Dundee DD1 4DE. www.hilton.com. ✆ **01382/229-271.** Fax 01382/200-072. 129 units. £70–£156 double; from £185 suite. AE, DC, MC, V. Parking £3. Bus: 1A, 1B, or 20. From the south, the hotel is on the left side as you come over the Tay Rd. Bridge into town. **Amenities:** 2 restaurants; bar; pool (indoor); health club w/sauna; room service. *In room:* TV, hair dryer, Wi-Fi (£6 1 hr., £15 24 hr.).

The Landmark ★ ☺ This restored Victorian mansion sits on 2.2 hectares (5½ acres) of well-landscaped gardens on the outskirts of Dundee. It's a good place to come if you have children; there's a nature trail and an adventure playground. It's also equipped with a leisure club, a gym, an indoor pool and Jacuzzi, and a beauty spa. Bedrooms are designed with a touch of boutique-hotel chic in tasteful colors.

Kingsway West, Invergowrie, DD2 5JT. www.thelandmarkdundee.co.uk. ✆ **01382/641-122.** Fax 01382/631-201. 95 units. £79–£114 double; £150 suite. AE, MC, V. Free parking. Signposted on the Dundee Kingsway, on the western outskirts of Dundee. **Amenities:** Restaurant; bar; pool (indoor); health club and spa; room service; babysitting; Wi-Fi (free). *In room:* TV, minibar, hair dryer.

IN search OF PETER PAN

You reach the little town of **Kirriemuir** by heading north of Glamis Castle for 4 miles or traveling 16 miles north of Dundee via the A929 and the A928. Thousands of visitors each year come here to pay their respects to Sir James M. Barrie (1860–1937), author of *Peter Pan.*

The little town of red-sandstone houses and narrow crooked streets, located in the heart of Scotland's raspberry country, was the birthplace of Barrie in 1860. His father was employed as a hand-loom weaver of linen. **Barrie's birthplace** still stands at 9 Brechin Rd. (© **0844/493-2142;** www.nts.org.uk) and is now owned by the National Trust for Scotland. The small house contains some of the writer's manuscripts and mementos. From April to June and September to October, the house is open Saturday to Wednesday noon to 5pm; in July and August, it's open daily 11am to 5pm. Admission is £6 for adults; £5 for seniors, students, and children 5 to 15; £15.50 for a family ticket.

Barrie first became known for his sometimes-cynical tales of Kirriemuir, disguised as Thrums, in such works as *Auld Licht Idylls* (1888) and *A Window in Thrums* (1889). He then turned to the theatre and in time became known for bringing supernatural and sentimental stories to the stage. It's said that talking to a group of children while walking his dog gave him the idea for the stories about Peter Pan, which were first presented to the public in 1904. It wasn't until 1957 that *When Wendy Grew Up: An Afterthought* was published.

He went on to write more dramas, including *Alice Sit-by-the-Fire* (1905), *What Every Woman Knows* (1908), *The Will* (1913), and *Mary Rose* (1920)—the latter a very popular play in its day. But, besides Barrie scholars, who remembers these works now? On the other hand, Peter Pan has become a legendary figure, known by almost every child in the Western world through films, plays, musicals, as well as the original book.

Although he spent most of his working life in London, Barrie is buried in Kirriemuir Cemetery. To reach **Barrie's grave,** turn left off Brechin Road and follow the cemetery road upward. The path is clearly marked, taking you to the grave pavilion. A camera obscura in the **Barrie Pavilion** on Kirriemuir Hill gives views over Strathmore to Dundee and north to the Highlands.

A Side Trip to Glamis Castle

The little village of Glamis (pronounced *Glams*) grew up around **Glamis Castle ★★** (© **01307/840-393;** www.glamis-castle.co.uk). Visitors to Scotland most want to see Glamis Castle for its link with the crown. For 6 centuries, the castle has been connected to members of the British royal family. The Queen Mother was brought up here; and Princess Margaret was born here, making her the first royal princess born in Scotland in 3 centuries. The current owner is the Queen's great-nephew. The castle contains Duncan's Hall, which the Victorians claimed was where Macbeth murdered King Duncan, but in Shakespeare's play the murder takes place at Macbeth's castle, Cawdor, near Inverness. (Incidentally, Shakespeare was wrong in naming Macbeth Thane of Glamis; Glamis wasn't made a thaneship—a sphere of influence in medieval Scotland—until years after the action in the play took place.)

The present Glamis Castle dates from the early 15th century, but there are records of a hunting lodge having been here in the 11th century. The Lyon family has owned Glamis Castle since 1372, and it contains some fine plaster ceilings, furniture, and paintings.

A self-service restaurant has been installed in the old kitchens, with a chalkboard featuring daily specials and excellent home-cooked dishes.

The castle is open to the public, with access to the Royal Apartments and many other rooms, as well as the fine gardens, from April to October, daily 10am to 6pm (last admission 4:30pm); and November and December, daily 10:30am to 4:30pm (last admission 3:30pm). Admission to the castle and gardens costs £9.50 for adults, £8.75 for seniors, £7 for children 5 to 15, and £28 for a family ticket. Tickets for entry to the grounds only are: £5.50 for adults, £5 for seniors, and £3.50 for children. Buses run between Dundee and Glamis; the journey time is approximately 35 minutes. **Note:** Buses don't stop in front of the castle, which is ⅔ mile from the bus stop.

EATING IN GLAMIS

Strathmore Arms CONTINENTAL/SCOTTISH   Try this place near the castle for one of the best lunches in the area. You might begin with the soup of the day or the fresh prawns. Then have steak pie or venison to follow—or, for something a little more diverse, go for the Indian chicken breast marinated in yogurt and spices. Vegetarians should try the filo parcels stuffed with asparagus and cauliflower.

The Square Glamis. ✆ **01307/840-248.** http://strathmorearmsglamis.com. Reservations recommended. Main courses £9–£21. AE, MC, V. Daily noon–2pm and 6:30–9pm.

WHERE TO STAY

Castleton House ★ 📷   This country-house hotel is run with great attention to detail. If the weather's cold, you're greeted by welcoming coal fires in the public lounge. Rooms of various sizes are furnished with reproduction antiques; the suite features a genuine Regency four-poster bed. Chef Andrew Wilkie presides over the award-winning restaurant, where most of the fruits and vegetables served are grown in the hotel's grounds. Dinner costs £30 for two courses and £35 for three courses. At lunch, you can enjoy a bargain-priced two-course menu for £10.

Eassie by Glamis, Forfar, Tayside DD8 1SJ. www.castletonglamis.co.uk. ✆ **01307/840-340.** Fax 01307/840-506. 6 units. £160–£200 double. AE, MC, V. Drive 3 miles west of Glamis on the A94. **Amenities:** Restaurant; bar; room service. *In room:* TV, hair dryer.

BALLATER & BALMORAL CASTLE ★

111 miles N of Edinburgh; 41 miles W of Aberdeen; 67 miles NE of Perth; 70 miles SE of Inverness

Located on the River Dee, with the Grampian Mountains in the background, Ballater is primarily a resort for visitors—although most people come here with only one goal in mind—to walk the grounds of Balmoral Castle, the Scottish home of the Windsors. The town still centers on its Station Square, where the royal family used to be photographed as they arrived to spend holidays. (The railway is now closed.) From Ballater, you can drive west to view the scenery of Glen Muick and Lochnagar, where you'll see herds of deer. Incidentally, the drive between Ballater and Braemar (see "Braemar," below) is very scenic.

Essentials

GETTING THERE   You can take the train to Aberdeen and continue the rest of the way by connecting bus. For rail schedules and information, call ✆ **08457/ 484-950.**

Buses run hourly from Aberdeen to Ballater. The bus and train stations in Aberdeen are next to each other on Guild Street (© **0871/200-2233;** or consult www. stagecoachbus.com for information). Bus nos. 201 and 202 from Braemar run to Ballater (trip time: 30 min.).

If you're driving from Braemar, go east along the A93.

VISITOR INFORMATION The **Tourist Information Centre** is at Station Square (© **01339/755-306**). July and August, hours are daily 10am to 1pm and 2 to 6pm; September, October, May, and June, Monday to Saturday 10am to 1pm and 2 to 5pm, Sunday 1 to 5pm. Closed November to April.

Balmoral Castle ★★★

"This dear paradise" is how Queen Victoria described Balmoral Castle, rebuilt in the Scottish baronial style by her beloved Albert. And Balmoral was the setting for the story of Victoria and her faithful servant, John Brown, as depicted in the film *Mrs. Brown.* Today, Balmoral is still a private residence of the British sovereign. Albert, Victoria's prince consort, leased the property in 1848 and bought it in 1852. As the original castle proved too small, the present edifice was built, completed in 1855. Its principal feature is a 30m (98-ft.) tower. Of the actual castle, only the ballroom is open to the public; pictures, porcelain, and other artworks are on display. There's also an exhibition in the Carriage Hall outside. In the grounds are many memorials to the royal family, along with gardens, country walks, souvenir shops, and a refreshment room.

Balmoral, Ballater. © **01339/742-534.** www.balmoralcastle.com. Admission £8.70 adults, £7.70 seniors, £4.60 children 5–16, free for children 4 and under, £23 families. Apr–July daily 10am–5pm. Closed Aug–Mar. Crathie bus from Aberdeen to the Crathie station; Balmoral Castle is signposted from there (a short walk).

Where to Eat

Green Inn ★★ SCOTTISH/FRENCH This family-run restaurant has won numerous awards and a significant reputation locally. Head chef Chris O'Halloran trained with Raymond Blanc at Le Manoir aux Quat' Saisons, the acclaimed Oxfordshire restaurant, and continues his principles of cooking locally sourced seasonal produce with a touch of French flair.

Appetizers might include terrine of filets of roe deer, teal, lamb, and pheasant wrapped in a mousse of their own livers, or a rabbit lasagna flavored with truffles. For your main course, you can have roasted organic pork tenderloin with braised cheek and wild rice, with fresh morels and a truffle cream sauce, or oven-roasted estate partridge with caramelized apples and pears. For dessert, there's warm chocolate tart with chestnut cream and orange sauce.

The Green Inn also offers two simply furnished double rooms on a bed-and-breakfast basis for £79 per night.

9 Victoria Rd., Ballater AB35 5QQ. ©/fax **01339/755-701.** www.green-inn.com. Reservations required. Fixed-price menu £35 for 2 courses, £39 for 3 courses. AE, DC, MC, V. Mar–Oct daily 7–9pm, Nov–Feb Tues–Sat 7–9pm.

La Mangiatoia ITALIAN This Italian restaurant is located within the unlikely setting of a converted early-18th-century stable beside the River Dee in the heart of Ballater. Amid a rustic decor that includes artfully placed bales of hay, lots of equine accessories, and a high wooden ceiling, you order from a menu that features chicken, veal, salmon, pastas, and baguette sandwiches, and favorite desserts such as sticky toffee pudding.

Bridge Square. © **01339/755-999.** Lunch main courses £8–£12; dinner main courses £11–£20. MC, V. Tues–Fri 5–10pm, Sat–Sun noon–10pm.

Oaks Restaurant BRITISH   The Oaks is located within a century-old mansion that was originally built by the marmalade kings of Britain, the Keiller family. Now owned by Hilton Hotels, the estate also has timeshare villas and access to a nearby golf course. The restaurant menu includes dishes such as venison and duck terrine flavored with orange and brandy, followed by roast rack of lamb, breast of Grampian chicken, or loin of venison. The dress code is "smart casual."

In the Hilton Craigendarroch Hotel, Braemar Rd. © **01339/755-858.** www.hilton.co.uk/craigendarroch. Fixed-price 4-course dinner £40. AE, DC, MC, V. Thurs–Sun 6:30–9pm.

Where to Stay

Darroch Learg Hotel ★ 📠   Built in 1888 as an elegant country home, this hotel stands in 2 hectares (5 acres) of lush woodlands opening onto views of the Dee Valley and the Grampian Mountains beyond. Constructed at the peak of the golden age of Victorian Royal Deeside, the hotel is imbued with halcyon charm. The individually decorated bedrooms (some with four-poster beds) are divided between the main house and Oakhall, a baronial mansion on the same grounds. Perhaps the hotel's main attraction, however, is the **Conservatory Restaurant,** which has views over the River Dee. Dishes include lamb, venison, halibut, and sea trout. The three-course a la carte dinner costs £43, and the seven-course tasting menu is £50.

Darroch Learg, Braemar Rd. (on the A93 at the west end of Ballater), Ballater AB35 5UX. www.darroch learg.co.uk. © **01339/755-443.** Fax 01339/755-252. 17 units. £140–£250 double. AE, DC, MC, V. Free parking. Closed Christmas and last 3 weeks in Jan. **Amenities:** Restaurant; room service. *In room:* TV, hair dryer.

Deeside Hotel   This well-managed guesthouse occupies an 1890 pink-granite house surrounded by late-Victorian gardens, and is a 3-minute walk west of the town center. The guest rooms are furnished in a low-key but comfortable way; one of them has a four-poster bed. The restaurant serves traditional fare, from roast beef to fillet of lamb.

45 Braemar Rd., Ballater AB35 5RQ. www.deesidehotel.co.uk. © **01339/755-420.** Fax 01339/755-357. 10 units. £90–£120 double. MC, V. Closed Jan. **Amenities:** Restaurant; bar. *In room:* TV, no phone.

BRAEMAR

85 miles N of Edinburgh; 58 miles W of Aberdeen; 51 miles N of Perth

In the heart of some of Grampian's most beautiful scenery is Braemar, known for its romantic castle. It's also a good center for exploring the area that includes Balmoral Castle (see above) and is home to the most famous of the Highland Gatherings. The village is set against a massive backdrop of hills, covered with heather in summer, where Clunie Water joins the River Dee. The massive **Cairn Toul** towers over Braemar, reaching a height of 1,287m (4,222 ft.).

Essentials

GETTING THERE   Take the train to Aberdeen, and then continue the rest of the way by bus. For information and schedules, call © **08457/484-950.**

Buses run six times a day from Aberdeen to Braemar (trip time: 2 hr.). The bus and train stations in Aberdeen are next to each other on Guild Street. (For information and schedules, call © 0871/200-2233, or go online to www.stagecoachbus.com.)

Driving to Braemar from Dundee, return west toward Perth, and then head north along the A93, following the signs into Braemar. The 70-mile drive takes between 70 and 90 minutes.

VISITOR INFORMATION   The year-round **Braemar Tourist Office** is in The Mews, Mar Road (© **01339/741-600**). In June, hours are daily 9:30am to 5pm; July and August, daily 9:30am to 6pm; and in September, daily 10am to 5pm. In the off season, hours are Monday to Saturday 10am to 1pm and 2 to 5pm, Sunday noon to 5pm.

SPECIAL EVENTS   The spectacular **Royal Highland Gathering** (© **01339/741-098;** www.braemargathering.org) takes place annually in late August or early September in the Princess Royal and Duke of Fife Memorial Park. The Queen herself often attends the gathering. It's thought that these ancient games were conceived by King Malcolm Canmore, a chieftain who ruled much of Scotland at the time of the Norman conquest of England. He selected his hardiest warriors from all the clans for a "keen and fair contest."

Braemar is overrun with visitors during the gathering—anyone thinking of attending would be wise to book tickets well in advance via the website and also to reserve accommodation anywhere in the vicinity of Braemar no later than early April.

Exploring the Area

You might spot members of the royal family, even the Queen herself, at **Crathie Church,** 8⅔ miles east of Braemar on the A93 (© **01339/742-208;** www.braemar andcrathieparish.org.uk), where they attend Sunday services when in residence. Services are at 11:30am; otherwise, the church is open April to October, Monday to Saturday 9:30am to 5:30pm and on Sunday 2pm to 5:30pm.

Nature lovers may want to drive 106 miles west of Braemar to the **Linn of Dee,** a narrow chasm on the River Dee and a local beauty spot. Other nature sites include Glen Muick, Loch Muick, and Lochnagar. A **Scottish Wildlife Trust Visitor Centre,** reached by a minor road, is located in this Highland glen, off the South Deeside Road. An access road joins the B976 at a point 16 miles east of Braemar. The tourist office (see above) provides maps.

Golfers will make for the **Braemar Golf Club** (© **01339/741-618;** www. braemargolfclub.co.uk). It's the highest golf course in the country. The 2nd-hole green is 380m (1,250 ft.) above sea level—this is the trickiest hole on the course. Pro golf commentator Peter Alliss has deemed it "the hardest par 4 in all of Scotland." Set on a plateau, the hole is bordered on the right by the River Clunie and on the left by rough. The only dress code is "be reasonable." The course is open only April to October daily (call in advance as hours can vary).

Braemar Castle CASTLE   This romantic 17th-century castle is a fully furnished private residence with architectural grace and scenic charm. The castle has barrel-vaulted ceilings and an underground prison and is known for its remarkable star-shaped defensive curtain wall.

On the Aberdeen-Ballater-Perth Rd. (the A93). © **01339/741-219.** www.braemarcastle.co.uk. Admission £6 adults, £5 seniors and students, £3 children 5–15, free for children 4 and under. Easter–Oct Sat-Sun only 11am–4pm; also Wed in July and Aug. Closed Nov–Easter. Take the A93 about ⅔ mile northeast of Braemar.

Where to Eat & Stay

Braemar Lodge Hotel   Whereas this hotel was in Victorian times used as a hunting lodge, today it's popular with skiers who frequent the nearby Glenshee slopes. Its setting is beautiful, amid extensive grounds at the head of Glen Clunie, near the cottage where Robert Louis Stevenson wrote *Treasure Island.* Bedrooms vary in shape and size, but each is comfortable and well equipped. On cool evenings, guests are greeted with log fires, and the wooden-paneled Malt Room with its hunting trophies is the ideal place for a quiet drink. The restaurant serves hearty comfort food. Three log cabins have been built in the grounds: Fully equipped with all modern conveniences, they sleep up to six persons. One of the cabins is also equipped for disabled guests.

6 Glenshee Rd., Braemar AB35 5YQ. www.braemarlodge.co.uk. ✆/fax **01339/741-627.** 7 units. £90–£100 double; £490–£665 weekly cabin rental (Sat–Sat). MC, V. Free parking. Closed Nov. Situated a 2-min. walk south from the bus station. **Amenities:** Restaurant; bar. *In room:* TV, hair dryer.

Callater Lodge Hotel 🛏   Full of rural charm, this house, built in the 1860s, is situated about ⅓ mile south of the center of Braemar, just off the A93. The book-lined sitting room downstairs offers a welcoming atmosphere, while the guest rooms are cozy. On request, the owners prepare packed lunches. Evening meals can also be arranged.

9 Glenshee Rd., Braemar AB35 5YQ. www.hotel-braemar.co.uk. ✆ **01339/741-275.** Fax 01339/741-345. 6 units. £75 double; £95 family room. MC, V. Free parking. From the center of Braemar, drive south on Glenshee Rd. *In room:* TV, hair dryer, no phone.

Invercauld Arms Hotel   The granite Victorian institution is Braemar's grandest hotel, even if its elegance is a little faded. It's a good base, however, for going hill walking and seeing deer, golden eagles, and other wildlife. Fishing and, in winter, skiing are also available close by. In the evening you can come back to a roaring fire in the lounge, and a drink at the Slainte Bar. Rooms are comfortably, if somewhat blandly, furnished. In the pub close by, you can meet the "ghillies" and "stalkers" (hunting and fishing guides), and then return to the hotel for the Scottish fare in its restaurant.

Invercauld Rd., Braemar AB35 5YR. www.shearings.com. ✆ **01339/741-605.** Fax 01339/741-428. 68 units. £79–£119 double. AE, DC, MC, V. Free parking. Bus: 201. **Amenities:** Restaurant; bar. *In room:* TV, hair dryer.

SPEYSIDE ★ & THE MALT WHISKY TRAIL ★

Much of the Speyside region covered in this section is in the Moray district, on the southern shore of the Moray Firth, a large inlet cutting into the northeastern coast of Scotland. The district stretches in a triangular shape south from the coast to the wild heart of the Cairngorm Mountains near Aviemore. It's a land steeped in history, as its many castles, battle sites, and ancient monuments testify. It's also a good place to fish and, of course, play golf. Golfers can purchase a 5-day ticket from Tourist Information Centres that gives them access to more than 11 courses in the area.

   One of the best of these courses is **Boat of Garten,** Speyside (✆ **01479/831-282;** www.boatgolf.com). Relatively difficult, the almost 6,000-yard course is dotted with many bunkers and wooded areas. In winter, call ahead to see whether the course is open. Dress smartly; blue jeans aren't acceptable.

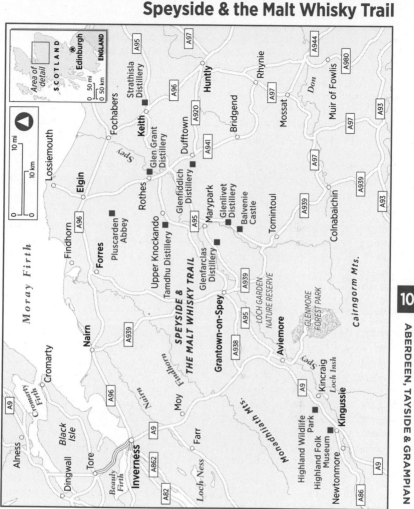

The valley of the second-largest river in Scotland, Strathspey, as it's also known, runs north and south of Aviemore, and is a land of great natural beauty. The Spey is born in the Highlands above Loch Laggan, which lies 40 miles south of Inverness. Little more than a creek at its inception, it gains in force, fed by the many "burns" that drain water from the surrounding hills. It's one of Scotland's great rivers for salmon fishing. Its major center is Grantown-on-Spey.

The primary tourist attraction in the area is the **Malt Whisky Trail,** 70 miles long, running through the glens of Speyside. Here, distilleries, many of which can be visited, are known for their production of *uisge beatha,* or "water of life." "Whisky" is its more familiar name.

Half the malt distilleries in the country lie along the River Spey and its tributaries. Peat smoke and Highland water are used to turn out single-malt (unblended) whisky.

There are five malt distilleries in the area: **Glenlivet, Glenfiddich, Glenfarclas, Strathisla,** and **Tamdhu.** Allow about an hour and a half to visit each of them.

The best way to reach Speyside from Aberdeen is to take the A96 northwest, sign-posted ELGIN. If you're traveling north on the A9 road from Perth and Pitlochry, your first stop might be at Dalwhinnie, which at 575m (1,886 ft.) has the highest whisky distillery in the world. It's not in the Spey Valley, but at the northeastern end of Loch Ericht, with fine views of forests and hills.

Keith

Keith, 11 miles northwest of Huntly, grew because of its strategic location, where the main road and rail routes between Inverness and Aberdeen cross the River Isla. It has an ancient history, but owes its present look to the town planning of the late 18th and early 19th centuries. Today it's a major stopover on the Malt Whisky Trail.

The oldest operating distillery in the Scottish Highlands, the **Strathisla Distillery,** on Seafield Avenue (© **01542/783-044**), was established in 1786. Hours are April to October, Monday to Saturday 9:30am to 4pm, and Sunday noon to 4pm. Admission is £5 for adults, free for children 8 to 18 (children 7 and under not admitted). The admission fee includes a £3 voucher redeemable in the distillery shop against a 70-cubic-liter bottle of whisky.

Dufftown

James Duff, the fourth Earl of Fife, founded Dufftown in 1817. The four main streets of town converge at the **clock tower,** which is also the **tourist office** (© **01340/820-501**). The office is open from April to October, Monday to Saturday 10am to 1pm and 2pm to 5pm.

A center of the whisky-distilling industry, Dufftown is surrounded by seven malt distilleries. The family-owned **Glenfiddich Distillery** is on the A941, ⅔ mile north (© **01340/820-373;** www.glenfiddich.com). It's open year-round Monday through Saturday from 9:30am to 4:30pm, and Sunday from noon to 4:30pm. Guides in kilts show you around the plant and explain the process of distilling. A film on the history of distilling is also shown. At the end of the tour, which is free, you're given a dram of malt whisky to sample. There's also a souvenir shop.

Other sights include **Balvenie Castle,** along the A941 (© **01340/820-121;** www.historic-scotland.gov.uk), the ruins of a moated 14th-century stronghold that lie on the south side of the Glenfiddich Distillery. During her northern campaign against the Earl of Huntly, Mary Queen of Scots spent 2 nights here. It's open from April to September, daily from 9:30am to 5:30pm. Admission is £4 for adults, £3.20 for seniors, and £2.40 for children 5 to 15.

WHERE TO EAT

Taste of Speyside ★ SCOTTISH   True to its name, this restaurant just off the main square avidly promotes Speyside cuisine as well as the products of Speyside's 46 distilleries. A platter including smoked salmon, venison, and trout, pâté flavored with malt whisky, locally made cheese, salads, and homemade oat cakes is offered at lunch and dinner. Wholesome soups are made daily and are served with homemade bread. There's also a choice of meat pies, including rabbit or venison with red wine and herbs. For dessert, try Scotch Mist, containing fresh cream, malt whisky, and crumbled meringue.

10 Balvenie St. ☎ **01340/820-860.** Reservations recommended for dinner. Main courses £18–£24; set menu £13 lunch, £24 dinner. AE, MC, V. May–Sept daily noon–9pm, Oct–Apr Tues–Sun noon–2pm and 6–9pm.

Grantown-on-Spey

This vacation resort, with its gray-granite buildings, is 34 miles southeast of Inverness in a wooded valley with views of the Cairngorm Mountains. It's a center for winter sports as well as for first-rate salmon fishing on the Spey. Founded on a heather-covered moor in 1765 by Sir James Grant, Grantown-on-Spey became the seat of Grant's ancient family. The town was famous in the 19th century as a Highland tourist center. From here, you can explore the valleys of the Don and Dee, the Cairngorms, and Culloden Moor, scene of the historic battle in 1746 when Bonnie Prince Charlie and his army were defeated. A **Tourist Information Centre** can be found on High Street (☎ **01479/872-773**). It's open from April to October only, Monday through Saturday 9am to 5pm and Sunday 10am to 4pm.

WHERE TO EAT

Craggan Mill BRITISH/ITALIAN   This licensed restaurant and lounge-bar, a 10-minute walk south of the town center, occupies a restored granite mill (the water wheel is still visible). The menu offers British and Italian cuisine at attractive prices. Your appetizer might be smoked trout or ravioli. Main courses include breast of chicken with cream or chicken cacciatore, and dessert may be rum-raisin ice cream or peach Melba.

On the A95, ¾ mile south of Grantown-on-Spey. ☎ **01479/872-288.** www.cragganmill.co.uk. Reservations recommended. Main courses £14–£23. MC, V. Wed–Mon noon–2pm and 6–11pm.

WHERE TO STAY

Garth Hotel   The elegant and comfortable Garth Hotel stands on 1.6 hectares (4 acres) of grounds beside the town square. Guests can enjoy afternoon tea in the spacious lounge, with its high ceilings, wood-burning stove, and vine-covered veranda. The handsomely furnished guest rooms have all the necessary amenities. The restaurant offers a menu that favors Scottish dishes—with a bit of French influence—made from fresh local produce. There are always several vegetarian options. Main courses cost from £12 to £16.

The Square, Castle Rd., Grantown-on-Spey, Morayshire PH26 3HN. www.garthhotel.com. ☎ **01479/872-836.** Fax 01479/872-116. 18 units. £90–£104 double. MC, V. Free parking. **Amenities:** Restaurant; bar; room service. *In room:* TV, hair dryer.

Tigh na Sgiath Country House Hotel ★ 🎒   This fine country home set amid private grounds and woods is a welcoming place for an extended stay. Built in 1902 as a Victorian hunting lodge for the Lipton tea family, the hotel overlooks the Cairngorm Mountains and retains many of its original Victorian features, including open fireplaces and wood paneling. Bedrooms are well decorated, with immaculate bathrooms.

3 miles south of Grantown-on-Spey by the A95 on the A938, Dulnain Bridge PH26 3PA. www.tigh-na-sgiath.co.uk. ☎ **01479/851-345.** Fax 01479/821-173. 9 units. £86–£150 double. MC, V. **Amenities:** Restaurant; 2 bars; lounge. *In room:* TV, hair dryer, no phone, Wi-Fi (free).

Tulchan Lodge ★★   This place offers a taste of grand living from the time of the British Empire. It was built in 1906 by the founder of the McCorquodale publishing empire as a sporting lodge, and many guests still come here for hunting, shooting, and fishing. The Edwardian atmosphere of the place lingers on, with the wood-paneled interior and the relatively formal dinners, where guests eat together at a communal dining table. Scattered across the undulating grounds are seven cottages, suitable for between four and nine occupants. Each of these has a fully equipped kitchen and decor that reflects the elegance of the main house. Favored mostly by people here for the fishing, the cottages don't include meal service, and are rented exclusively by the week.

Advie, near Grantown-on-Spey PH26 3PW. www.tulchan.com. ℂ **01807/510-200.** Fax 01807/510-234. 13 bedrooms in the main house, 7 outlying cottages. £400–£925 double. Rates include full board. Cottages £400–£3,750 per week for 4–12 occupants, without meals. MC, V. Closed Feb–Mar. Drive 8¾ miles northeast of Grantown on the B9102, following the signs to Elgin. **Amenities:** Tennis court; babysitting. *In room:* TV, hair dryer, Wi-Fi (free).

Glenlivet

As you leave Grantown-on-Spey and head east along the A95, drive to the junction with the B9008; go south and you won't miss the **Glenlivet Distillery.** The **Glenlivet Reception Centre** (ℂ **01340/821-720;** www.theglenlivet.com) is 10 miles north of the nearest town, Tomintoul. Near the River Livet, a Spey tributary, this distillery is one of the most famous in Scotland. It's open April to October, Monday to Saturday 9:30am to 4pm and Sunday noon to 4pm. Admission is free.

Back on the A95, you can visit the **Glenfarclas Distillery** at Ballindalloch (ℂ **01807/500-345;** www.glenfarclas.co.uk), one of the few malt whisky distilleries that's still independent of the giants. Founded in 1836, Glenfarclas is managed by the fifth generation of the Grant family. There's a small craft shop, and each visitor is offered a dram of Glenfarclas Malt Whisky. A 90-minute tour of the distillery costs £3.50 per person. There's also a special connoisseur's tour and tasting, which begins at 2pm on Fridays in July and August; tickets cost £15; advance booking is advisable. The distillery is open all year: October to March, Monday through Friday 10am to 4pm; April to June daily 10am to 5pm; and July to September Monday through Friday 10am to 5pm and Saturday 10am to 4pm.

Kincraig

Kincraig enjoys a scenic location at the northern end of Loch Insh, overlooking the Spey Valley to the west and the Cairngorm Mountains to the east. Near Kincraig, the most notable sight is the **Highland Wildlife Park ★** (ℂ **01540/651-270;** www.highlandwildlifepark.org), a natural area of parkland with a collection of animals, many of which roam the park at will. The collection includes herds of European bison, red deer, shaggy Highland cattle, wild horses, St. Kilda Soay sheep, and roe deer. In enclosures are wolves, polecats, wildcats, beavers, badgers, and pine martens. You can observe protected birds, such as golden eagles and several species of grouse—of special interest is the *capercaillie* ("horse of the woods"), a large Eurasian grouse that's native to Scotland's pine forests. There's a visitor center with a gift shop, a cafe, and exhibition areas. Ample parking and picnic sites are also available.

You need a car to go through the park; walkers are discouraged and are picked up by park rangers. The park is open every day at 10am. From April to October, the last entrance is at 4pm, except in July and August when it's at 5pm. From November to March, last entrance is at 3pm. All people and vehicles are expected to vacate the park within 2 hours of the day's last admission. The admission charge is £14 for adults, £11.50 for seniors and students, and £10 for children 5 to 15; children aged 3 and under go free. A family ticket costs from £44 to £50.

Kingussie

Your next stop along the Spey might be at the little summer vacation resort and winter ski center of Kingussie (pronounced "King-*you*-see"), located just off the A9. It's the capital of Badenoch, a district known as "the drowned land" because the Spey can flood the valley when the snows of a severe winter melt in the spring. Kingussie, 117 miles northwest of Edinburgh, 41 miles south of Inverness, and 11 miles southwest of Aviemore, practically adjoins Newtonmore directly northeast along the A86.

The **Highland Folk Museum ★**, Duke Street (© **01540/673-551;** www. highlandfolk.com), was the first folk museum established in Scotland (1934), and its collections are based on the life of the Highlanders. You'll see domestic, agricultural, and industrial exhibits. And the museum continues outside: There's a turf kailyard (kitchen garden), a Lewis "black house," and old vehicles and carts. Events, such as spinning demonstrations, music-making, and handicraft fairs, are held throughout the summer. Admission is free. The museum is open daily, April to August, from 10:30am to 5:30pm, and in September and October, from 11am to 4:30pm.

WHERE TO EAT

The Cross ★ SCOTTISH   This is probably the town's best restaurant, located in an idyllic setting in 1.6 hectares (4 acres) of grounds, with the Gynack Burn running through them. The main building is an old tweed mill. It has an open-beam ceiling and French doors leading to a terrace, over the water's edge, where alfresco dinners are served. Specialties include wild Scrabster seabass and breast of Gressingham duck.

Eight rooms are rented in a contemporary building. Two of the rooms have canopied beds, and another has a balcony overlooking the mill pond. Doubles, including half-board, cost from £210 to £280. Rooms don't have televisions.

Tweed Mill Brae, off the Ardbroilach road, Kingussie PH21 1TC.© **01540/661-166.** Fax 01540/661-080. www.thecross.co.uk. Reservations recommended. Fixed-price 3-course dinner £50. MC, V. Tues–Sat 7–9pm. Closed Dec–Feb.

WHERE TO STAY

Homewood Lodge ★ ☺   One of the best B&Bs in the area, this small house in a garden and woodland setting offers large, simply furnished rooms, with views of the countryside around. The sitting room has an open fireplace. Good traditional fare is served in the evening (reservations recommended). Summer barbecues are also offered, and children are welcome.

Newtonmore Rd., Kingussie PH21 1HD. www.homewood-lodge-kingussie.co.uk.© **01540/661-507.** 4 units. £50–£60 double. No credit cards. Free parking. **Amenities:** Restaurant. *In room:* TV, hair dryer.

Osprey Hotel   This 1895 Victorian structure, 275m (902 ft.) from the railway station, and next to the Duke of Gordon Gardens, is a convenient place to stay, with simple but comfortable bedrooms, decorated in a cottagey style. The hotel is primarily a bed-and-breakfast affair, though evening meals can be provided if arranged in advance.

Ruthven Rd. (at High St.), Kingussie PH21 1EN. www.ospreyhotel.co.uk.© /fax **01540/661-510.** 8 units. £60–£70 double. MC, V. Free parking. **Amenities:** Restaurant; bar; babysitting. *In room:* TV, hair dryer, no phone, Wi-Fi (free).

Rothes

A Speyside town with five distilleries, Rothes is just to the south of the Glen of Rothes, 49 miles east of Inverness and 62 miles northwest of Aberdeen. Founded in 1766, the town is situated between Ben Aigan and Conerock Hill. The town originally grew up around **Rothes Castle,** ancient stronghold of the Leslie family, who lived here until 1622. Only a single massive wall of the castle remains.

The region's best distillery tours are offered by the **Glen Grant Distillery** (© **01542/783-318;** www.glengrant.com). Opened in 1840 by a hardworking and hard-drinking pair of brothers, James and John Grant, and now administered by the Chivas & Glenlivet Group (a division of Seagram's), it can be found ⅔ mile north of Rothes, beside the Elgin-Perth highway (the A941). It's open from mid-March to October, Monday to Saturday 10am to 4pm, Sunday from 12:30 to 4pm. Admission is free (no children under 8). Visits include the opportunity to buy the brand's whisky at a discount.

Elgin ★

The center of local government in the Moray district and an ancient royal burgh, the cathedral city of Elgin is on the Lossie River, 38 miles east of Inverness and 68 miles northwest of Aberdeen. The city's medieval plan has been retained, with "wynds" and "pends" connecting the main artery with other streets. The castle, as was customary in medieval town layouts, stood at one end of the main thoroughfare, with the cathedral—now a magnificent ruin—at the other. Nothing remains of the castle, but the site is a great place for a scenic walk. Samuel Johnson and James Boswell came this way on their Highland tour and reported a "vile dinner" at the Red Lion Inn in 1773.

Lady Hill stands on High Street, opposite the post office. This is the hilltop location of what was once the royal castle of Elgin. **Birnie Kirk,** at Birnie, 3 miles south of Elgin and west of the A941 to Rothes, for a time was the seat of a bishopric. It dates from about 1140, when it was constructed on the site of a much earlier church founded by St. Brendan. One of the few Norman churches in Scotland still in regular use, it's open daily from 10am to 4pm.

On King Street are the ruins of the **Elgin Cathedral ★** (© **01343/547-171;** www.historic-scotland.gov.uk), off North College Street near the A96. It was founded in 1224 but destroyed in 1390 by the "wolf of Badenoch," the natural son of Robert II. After its destruction, the citizens of Elgin rebuilt their beloved cathedral and turned it into one of the most attractive and graceful buildings in Scotland. However, when the central tower collapsed in 1711, the cathedral was allowed to fall into decay. It's open April to September, daily 9:30am to 5:30pm; October, daily, 9:30am to 4:30pm; and November to March, Saturday to Wednesday 9:30am to 4:30pm. Admission is £5 for adults, £4 for seniors, and £3 for children 5 to 15.

After exploring Elgin, you can drive 6 miles southwest to **Pluscarden Abbey,** off the B9010. This is one of the most beautiful drives in the area, through the bucolic Black Burn Valley, where a priory was founded in 1230 by Alexander II. After centuries of decline, a new order of Benedictines arrived in 1974 and reestablished monastic life. You can visit restored transepts, monastic buildings, and the church choir. Admission is free to the home of this active religious community; it's open daily from 9am to 5pm.

If you're a fan of Scottish ruins, head for **Spynie Palace** (© **01343/546-358;** www.historic-scotland.gov.uk), reached via the A941. The former 15th-century headquarters of the bishops of Moray was used until 1573, when it was allowed to fall into ruins; for safety reasons, you can view them only from the outside. This is another great place for country walks, and from the top of a tower are magnificent vistas over the Laigh of Moray. It's open April to September daily from 9:30am to 5:30pm; and from October to March, Saturday and Sunday 9:30am to 4:30pm. Admission is £4 for adults, £3.20 for students and seniors, and £2.40 for children 5 to 15 (under-4s free).

WHERE TO STAY

Mansion House Hotel   This elegant hotel, built in the 19th-century baronial style, is located beside the River Lossie, about ⅓ mile from the center of Elgin. The guest rooms are furnished in old-fashioned country-house style, and some have four-poster beds. Lunch and dinner is served in the restaurant daily (main courses £15–£24), and the bistro is open in the evenings only.

The Haugh, Elgin IV30 1AW. www.mansionhousehotel.co.uk.© **01343/548-811.** Fax 01343/547-916. 23 units. £154–£202 double. AE, DC, MC, V. Free parking. Follow the A96 onto Alexandra Rd. to the turnoff onto Haugh Rd. **Amenities:** 2 restaurants; bar; health club w/Jacuzzi and sauna; room service. *In room:* TV, hair dryer.

Richmond Bed & Breakfast   For a homey stay on a budget, the Richmond is difficult to beat. This Victorian villa, located close to the town center, has three comfortable bedrooms, each with its own bathroom. The hearty Scottish breakfast will set you up for the day (vegetarians are catered for, too).

48 Moss St., Elgin IV30 1LT. www.elginbedandbreakfast.co.uk.© **01343/542-561.** Fax 01343/542-561. 3 units. £56–£88 double. Free parking. Located 2 blocks north of the railway station in Elgin. *In room:* TV, hair dryer, Wi-Fi (free).

INVERNESS & THE WEST HIGHLANDS

The romantic glens and rugged mountains of the West Highlands are timeless and pristine. Deer graze only yards from the highway, and at secluded lochs you can fish for trout and salmon or simply enjoy a picnic. The shadow of Macbeth still stalks the land—though locals may tell you that this 11th-century king was much maligned by Shakespeare. The area's most famous resident, however, is said to live in Loch Ness: first sighted by St. Columba in the 6th century, "Nessie" has eluded searchers ever since.

CITIES   The capital of the Highlands—and the only town of any great size—is **Inverness.** This royal burgh is situated at the north end of the Great Glen and straddles the Ness River just before it flows into the sea. It's a historic city; you can climb up to the castle and look out over the Victorian civic buildings below, or visit the nearby battlefield of Culloden, where Bonnie Prince Charlie suffered his final defeat.

COUNTRYSIDE   The landscape of the West Highlands is one of stark contrasts. It includes **Ben Nevis,** the highest mountain in Britain, but also **Loch Ness,** the deepest and most mysterious loch. The slopes around **Aviemore** provide Britain's best skiing, while the crags around **Knockan** interest geologists. And once you come down from the heights, there's the Flow Country of **Caithness** and **Sutherland**—the seemingly endless flatlands of Europe's largest peat bog.

EATING & DRINKING   The varied landscape of the region offers an equally varied cuisine. The fishing ports around the coast produce a breakfast of kippers with lemon and melted butter or haddock topped with a poached egg. The sheep flocks grazing on heather on the Sutherland moors provide a lunch of the sweetest lamb. At the end of the day, sporting estates in Caithness yield up freshly shot grouse, and people retire to bed after a glass or two of Speyside whisky.

COAST   For many visitors to the Highlands, their ultimate aim is to reach John o' Groats, popularly known as the northernmost tip of the British mainland. But before they get there, they can bask (or freeze) on the sandy beaches of Nairn, a pretty Victorian seaside resort, or watch dolphins and seals frolicking in the Moray Firth. Pleasure boats sail to the

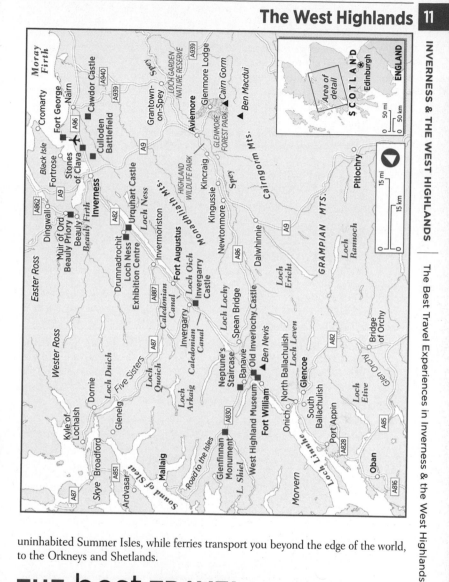

uninhabited Summer Isles, while ferries transport you beyond the edge of the world, to the Orkneys and Shetlands.

THE best TRAVEL EXPERIENCES IN INVERNESS & THE WEST HIGHLANDS

o **Drive through the breathtaking Glencoe Pass:** Running from Rannoch Moor to Loch Leven, this spectacular road sweeps between dramatic slopes on both sides, with occasional glimpses of hidden glens between snowy peaks. It was also the setting for one of the Highlands' most bloody historical events, the Massacre of Glencoe. See p. 317.

o **Dine in style at Inverlochy Castle:** This acclaimed hotel restaurant has been serving grand dinners since the days of Queen Victoria. Today, the freshest local produce is given the full fine-dining treatment. See p. 320.

o **Hike up Britain's highest mountain:** Ben Nevis looms over the nearby town of Fort William. In good weather, walkers ascend along the well-constructed path on the south side; climbers, however, take the more challenging routes up sheer cliff faces. See p. 318.

o **Enjoy the Cairngorms from the funicular railway:** While skiers are making their downhill dash in nearby Aviemore, you can sit back and relax as this mountain railway takes you up to a visitor center, restaurant, and magnificent views. See p. 324.

o **Play a round at the Royal Dornoch Golf Club:** The immaculate turf of the northernmost first-class course in the world is the perfect place for a civilized game of golf. See p. 344.

AROUND LOCH LINNHE & LOCH LEVEN

The area to the south of Fort William offers some of the most stunning scenery in Scotland. The landscape of lochs and moorland wilderness were memorably evoked by Robert Louis Stevenson in his novel *Kidnapped*. Of the villages that fringe Loch Linnhe and Loch Leven (not to be confused with the Loch Leven near Dunfermline), the best-known is **Glencoe,** the setting for the famous massacre in 1692, when the Campbells slaughtered the MacDonalds. The Glencoe Pass stretching inland provides a spectacular drive—as well as many wonderful walks that enable you to study flora and fauna unique to the West Highlands.

Around Ballachulish Bridge

Loch Linnhe meets Loch Leven at the narrows of Ballachulish. A steel cantilever bridge—known locally as "King Kong's coathanger"—connects Inverness-shire to the north with Argyll to the south.

On the northern side, on the shores of Loch Linnhe, is the charming village of Onich, 8⅔ miles southwest of Fort William. The waterfall of Inchree is only a short walk from the forest car park at Onich. To the south, the A828 follows the shoreline of the loch to Kentallen, with its fine views. Ballachulish and Kentallen are also connected by a cycle path that follows the old railway line and links up with a national cycle path network.

WHERE TO EAT & STAY

Allt-nan-Ros Hotel Allt-nan-Ros was built around 1885 as a hunting lodge for a wealthy industrialist. Today, the much-enlarged premises offer comfortable guest rooms and a restaurant that's also open to non-guests. The rooms have mahogany furniture and floral-patterned upholstery in an Edwardian country-house style, and most offer views of the loch or the stream running through the garden. In "The Stables," there are two spacious country-cottage-style bedrooms, with four-poster beds.

Onich, Fort William PH33 6RY. www.allt-nan-ros.co.uk. ⓒ**01855/821-210.** Fax 01855/821-462. 15 units. £120–£140 double. AE, DC, MC, V. From Fort William, drive 11 miles south along the A82. **Amenities:** Restaurant. *In room:* TV, hair dryer.

Holly Tree Hotel ★★ ☺   This hotel is an excellent choice as a base for a family holiday in Argyll, or as a stopping-off place on your way up north. Built out of an 1890s railway station on the former line between Oban and Ballachulish, the hotel retains the original station tearoom as a lounge, but otherwise has been significantly extended and equipped with the best modern comforts and facilities. There's a large heated indoor swimming pool and a Finnish sauna. Internet access is available throughout the hotel, and there's a large DVD library—with plenty of children's films, too. The spacious guest rooms (some with balconies) are bright and airy, and have wonderful sea views. All are furnished in a smart contemporary style, with sleek new bathrooms.

The award-winning Seafood Restaurant offers delicious cooking in generous portions. Unsurprisingly, given the name and location, its specialties are freshly caught scallops, lobster, and salmon. Next to the restaurant is a well-stocked lounge bar with a terrace outside for summer evenings. Reasonably priced bar meals are served at lunch and dinner daily.

Kentallen Pier, Argyll PA38 4BY. www.hollytreehotel.co.uk. © **01631/740-292.** Fax 01631/740-345. 20 units. £140–£200 double. Rooms can accommodate extra beds for children at £20 each. MC, V. From Fort William, take the A82 going south, and turn right on to the A828 after Ballachulish Bridge to follow the coast down to Kentallen. From Oban, head north on the A85, cross the bridge at Connel, and then continue up the coast on the A828. **Amenities:** Restaurant; bar; pool; sauna; bicycle rental; Wi-Fi (free). *In room:* TV, DVD player, hair dryer.

Glencoe: Spectacular Scenery ★★

The Glencoe Pass runs from Rannoch Moor to Loch Leven between majestic mountains, including 1,147m (3,763-ft.) **Bidean nam Bian.** In this spectacular setting of towering peaks and sweeping moorland, it's not difficult to imagine a fierce battle between kilted Highlanders.

Known as the "Glen of Weeping," Glencoe is where, on February 11, 1692, the Campbells massacred the MacDonalds—men, women, and children—who'd been their hosts for 12 days. Mass killings weren't uncommon in those times, but this one shocked even the Highlanders because it was a breach of hospitality. The **Monument to the Massacre of Glencoe,** at Carnoch, was erected by the chief of the MacDonald clan. After the incident, the crime of "murder under trust" was introduced into Scottish law as an aggravated form of murder that carried the same penalty as treason.

Glencoe Visitor Centre (© **0844/493-2222;** www.glencoe-nts.org.uk) is built on the site of the notorious massacre, 1 mile to the south of Glencoe village, just off the A82. The center tells the story of the massacre with the help of an audiovisual presentation. There's also an interesting exhibition on mountaineering and conservation in the Highlands, and advice and information for walkers. The center is open from April to October daily 9:30am to 5:30pm, and from November to March Thursday through Sunday 10am to 4pm. Admission charges are £6 for adults and £5 for seniors, students, and children aged 16 and under.

Glen Orchy, to the south, is well worth a visit for its wild river and photogenic mountain scenery. It was the birthplace of Gaelic bard Duncan Ban MacIntyre, whose masterpiece is the song "In Praise of Ben Doran."

WHERE TO EAT & STAY

Some visitors base themselves in Fort William (see "Fort William: Gateway to Ben Nevis," below) and explore the Glencoe area on day trips.

The **West Highland Way** (p. 61) is one of Scotland's most famous long-distance footpaths. It begins north of Glasgow in the town of Milngavie and winds a memorable 96 miles north along Loch Lomond before continuing through Glencoe and onto Fort William and concluding at the foot of Ben Nevis, Scotland's highest mountain. Walkers encounter a range of terrain along the way, from thick woodland to stark mountain, with the most dramatic stretch leading from the Bridge of Orchy to Glencoe.

Scotrail (✆ 0845/601-5929; www.scotrail.co.uk) operates a frequent and inexpensive train service from Glasgow's Queen Street station for the 25-minute journey to Milngavie. For more information on the walk, visit www.west-highland-way.co.uk.

The Clachaig Inn Although this hotel is built on the site where the famous massacre took place, it's like a tree-enclosed oasis amid the bleakness of Glencoe. The Daynes family offers Highland hospitality, good food, and an excellent selection of real ales. Weekly live folk music in the "Boots Bar" brings the place to life throughout the year. In addition to 23 simple but comfortable double, twin, and family rooms (all with bathrooms, all nonsmoking), the Clachaig also rents out 11 self-catering cottages around the glen.

Glencoe, Ballachulish PH49 4HX. www.clachaig.com. ✆ **01855/811-252.** Fax 01855/812-030. 23 units. £90 double. MC, V. Take the A82 south for 9½ miles from Fort William; the inn is signposted. **Amenities:** Restaurant; 3 bars; Wi-Fi (free). *In room:* TV, hair dryer.

King's House Hotel This remote hotel is open year-round and forms an excellent base for a walking or skiing holiday (it's only a 30-minute walk from a ski center with a chairlift). The inn's solid walls were built in the 1600s to withstand every sort of weather on this windswept plateau. It lies beside the A82, 12 miles southeast of Glencoe village, at the strategic point where Glencoe joins the Glen Etive, near the jagged mountain Buachaille Etive Mor. The rooms are very modestly decorated, but they do offer sweeping views of the surrounding landscape. Meals cooked with local ingredients are served in the bar.

Glencoe PA39 4HZ. www.kingy.com. ✆ **01855/851-259.** Fax 01855/851-216. 22 units, 10 with private bathroom. £64 double without bathroom; £70 double with bathroom. MC, V. You can arrange to be met at the Bridge of Orchy train station. **Amenities:** Restaurant-bar; laundry. *In room:* Hair dryer.

FORT WILLIAM ★: GATEWAY TO BEN NEVIS ★★

133 miles NW of Edinburgh; 68 miles S of Inverness; 104 miles N of Glasgow

Fort William, on the shores of Loch Linnhe, is a good place for an overnight stop if you're on your way to Inverness or going up to Skye. It's also a good base for exploring **Ben Nevis,** Scotland's highest mountain, and is well known for the nearby downhill mountain bike track.

Fort William stands on the site of a fort built by General Monk in 1655 in case of rebellion by the Highlanders. The town was later named after Prince William, Duke of Cumberland, who oversaw the crushing of the Jacobite Rebellion at the Battle of

Culloden in 1746. After several reconstructions, the fort itself was finally torn down in 1864 to make way for the railroad. Today, Fort William is a bustling town, living largely off the summer tourist trade, and is filled with hotels, shops, and cafes.

Essentials

GETTING THERE Fort William is a major stop on the scenic West Highland rail line that begins at the Queen Street Station in Glasgow and ends at Mallaig, on the west coast. Three trains a day run this route. For schedules, contact the tourist office (see below), or call **West Coast Railways** in Inverness at ℂ **01463/239-026.**

The leg of the West Highland line between Fort William and Mallaig is also served by The Jacobite, the only scheduled steam train service on the mainline in Great Britain. This scenic route is particularly popular with Harry Potter fans, because the Glenfinnan Viaduct section featured in the films. Services operate between mid-May and October from Monday to Friday, and during the weekends as well in July and August; visit www.westcoastrailways.co.uk.

Four buses per day run from Glasgow to Fort William, taking approximately 3 hours. Contact the **Citylink Bus Station** (ℂ **0870/550-5050;** www.citylink.co.uk) in Glasgow for schedules. If you're driving from Glasgow, head north along the A82.

VISITOR INFORMATION The **Tourist Information Centre** is at Cameron Centre, Cameron Square (ℂ **01397/701-801**). It's open year-round from Monday to Saturday 9am to 5pm and on Sunday 10am to 4pm, except in the summer months when it stays open until 7pm from Monday to Saturday, and till 6pm on Sundays.

Exploring the Area

You can reach **Old Inverlochy Castle,** scene of a famous battle, by driving 1¾ miles north of Fort William on the A82. Built in the 13th century, the ruined castle still has its round corner towers and a walled courtyard. The castle looms large in the pages of Scottish history as it was the scene of two famous battles. The first was in 1431, when clansmen of Alexander MacDonald, Lord of the Isles, defeated the larger army of King James I of Scotland. In the second battle, in 1645, the Royalist forces of the Marquess of Montrose won an important victory against the Covenanter army of the Marquess of Argyll. In all, 1,500 men were killed that day.

Neptune's Staircase, 3 miles northwest of Fort William, off the A830 at Banavie, is a series of nine locks that were constructed as part of Telford's Caledonian Canal, which connected the eastern seaboard at Inverness with the west coast at Fort William. This greatly shortened the distance that goods had to be transported from the North Sea to the Atlantic Ocean, avoiding the treacherous storms of Scotland's northern coast. This "staircase" of locks is one of the most prominent engineering triumphs in Scotland in the mid-19th century, raising boats up 19m (62 ft.) in total.

Fort William itself is relatively flat, and is therefore a good place for cycling. The best rentals are at **Alpine Bikes,** 117 High St. (ℂ **01397/704-008**). You need only your ID for the deposit. It's open Monday through Saturday from 9am to 5:30pm. If, however, you feel more adventurous, consider one of the many mountain bike trails in the countryside around the town (visit www.ridefortwilliam.com). There are routes for all abilities, culminating in the white-knuckle Off Beat Downhill Track (graded Orange Extreme). The latter is located at the Nevis Range resort, 7 miles north of Fort William on the mountain of Aonach Mor. The gondola takes you and your bike to the top, while gravity does the rest. The downhill track is open only in the summer, from May to September; bikes and protective gear are available for hire. In the winter season the resort offers skiing and snowboarding instead. See www.nevisrange.co.uk for details.

Glenfinnan Monument MONUMENT   Located at the head of Loch Shiel, at Glenfinnan, this monument marks the spot where Bonnie Prince Charlie unfurled his proud red-and-white silk banner on August 19, 1745, in his ill-fated attempt to restore the Stuarts to the British throne. The figure of a kilted Highlander tops the monument. At the visitor center, you can learn about the prince's campaign from Glenfinnan to Derby, which ended in his defeat at Culloden.

About 14 miles west of Fort William, on the A830, toward Mallaig. © 01397/722-250 for visitor center. www.nts.org.uk/Property/26. Free admission to site (open year-round). Visitor center admission £3.50 adults, £2.50 children. Apr–June and Sept–Oct daily 10am–5pm; July–Aug daily 9:30am–5:30pm.

West Highland Museum MUSEUM   This fascinating museum presents a variety of historical collections. There are exhibits on the 1745 Jacobite Rising, sections on tartans and folk life, items associated with Queen Victoria and the Victorian period (including gifts she gave to her beloved personal servant, John Brown), and artifacts that chart the history of mountaineering.

Cameron Square. © 01397/702-169. www.westhighlandmuseum.org.uk. Free admission. June–Sept Mon–Sat 10am–5pm (July–Aug also Sun 2–4pm); Oct–May Mon–Sat 10am–4pm.

Where to Eat

Crannog Seafood Restaurant ★ SEAFOOD   Occupying a converted ticket office and bait store in a quayside setting overlooking Loch Linnhe, this restaurant serves seafood so fresh that locals claim "it fairly leaps at you." Much of the fish comes from the owners' own fishing vessels or from their smokehouse. Bouillabaisse is a specialty, as are king prawns and langoustines. A vegetarian dish of the day is also on offer. The two-course lunch for £12 is a real bargain.

Town Pier. © 01397/705-589. www.crannog.net. Reservations recommended. Main courses £15–£20. MC, V. Daily noon–2:30pm and 6–9pm. Closed Jan 1–2 and Dec 25–26.

Inverlochy Castle ★★★ BRITISH   The cuisine at this grand hotel restaurant has been celebrated ever since Queen Victoria stopped in "for a good tuck-in." The kitchen uses local ingredients, including salmon from Spean, crabs from the Isle of Skye, crayfish from Loch Linnhe, and produce from the hotel's own gardens. Partridge and grouse are offered in season, and roast filet of Aberdeen Angus beef is a classic. The dining room is decorated with period furniture gifted to Inverlochy Castle from the king of Norway.

Torlundy, Fort William PH33 6SN. © 01397/702-177. www.inverlochycastlehotel.com. Reservations required. Fixed-price lunch £35; fixed-price dinner £67. AE, MC, V. Daily 12:30–1:30pm and 7–9pm. Closed Jan–Feb.

Shopping

Most of Fort William's shops can be found on the pedestrianized High Street that runs parallel to the shoreline. **The Whisky Shop** at 93 High St. (© 01397/706-164) is the place to peruse the considerable variety of single malts that Scotland produces. Nearby, the **Granite House** at 74–76 High St. (© 01397/703-651) is a family-run mini-department store. Here you can find a large selection of Scottish jewelry in traditional and contemporary designs, china, crystal, and other gifts. There's also a useful section on Scottish music with more than 1,000 Scottish music

CDs and an array of traditional instruments. For children, there's a well-stocked toy department.

Farther along is the **Highland Soap Company,** 48 High St. (℃ **01397/710-980**), which sells soaps and skincare products handmade in the Scottish Highlands using century's old traditional processes and fine natural ingredients. A very different sort of establishment is a few doors down: The **Rod and Gun Shop** at 18 High St. (℃ **01397/702-656**) is where those interested in country pursuits can get kitted out.

In the north end of town is the **Ben Nevis Woollen Mill,** Belford Road (℃ **01397/704-244**), where you can purchase a wide variety of clothing and accessories: wools, tweeds, tartans, and hand-knitted Arran sweaters.

Entertainment & Nightlife

Ben Nevis Bar, 103–109 High St. (℃ **01397/702-295**), offers free entertainment by rock, blues, jazz, and folk bands on Thursday and Friday evenings. The food and drinks are the usual pub fare, but the atmosphere is welcoming.

Grog & Gruel, 66 High St. (℃ **01397/705-078;** www.grogandgruel.co.uk), serves up regional cask-conditioned ales. There's occasionally a live band, with music ranging from rock and pop to folk and Scottish.

Where to Stay

There's no shortage of B&Bs in Fort William; the tourist office can supply you with a list if those recommended below happen to be full.

VERY EXPENSIVE

Inverlochy Castle ★★★   Inverlochy Castle, set against the scenic backdrop of Ben Nevis, once hosted Queen Victoria and remains the premier hotel in this part of Scotland. Now a Relais & Châteaux property, the Inverlochy offers a luxurious environment of art and antiques, plush furnishings, attentive service, and modern comforts—with prices to match. The **cuisine** here is some of the finest in Scotland (see "Where to Eat," above).

Torlundy, Fort William PH33 6SN. www.inverlochycastlehotel.com. ℃ **888/424-0106** in the U.S., or 01397/702-177. Fax 01397/702-953. 17 units. £440–£550 double; £590–£695 suite. AE, MC, V. Closed early Jan to late Feb. Take the A82 for 3 miles northeast of town. **Amenities:** Restaurant; tennis court; snooker room; room service; babysitting. *In room:* TV/DVD, CD player, PlayStation (on request), Internet (free).

MODERATE

Alexandra Hotel   The Alexandra, with its lofty gables atop formidable granite walls, is something of an institution in Fort William. Located across from the rail terminal, it's testimony to the Victorian fascination with touring the Highlands. Inside, the building has been completely modernized, offering unpretentious and comfortably furnished rooms. The restaurant is an enjoyable throwback to 1980s cuisine (fanned melon wrapped in Parma ham, for example). Guests can also use the facilities at the nearby Milton Hotel and Leisure Club.

The Parade, Fort William PH33 6AZ. www.strathmorehotels.com. ℃ **01397/702-241.** Fax 01397/772-441. 93 units. £109 double. AE, DC, MC, V. Free parking. From the north, take the A82 into Fort William, following signs for the town center. At the roundabout, turn right and drive straight over the next roundabout. The Alexandra is on the left side. **Amenities:** 2 restaurants; bar; access to nearby health club; room service. *In room:* TV, Internet (free).

The Lime Tree ★★   This beautiful 19th-century manse in the center of town now operates as a boutique hotel. The interior decoration offers not only style aplenty, but also comfort and calm. The popular restaurant (open daily 6–10pm) presents an acclaimed five-course dinner for £30. There's also an in-house art gallery exhibiting the work of Scottish painters.

The Old Manse, Achintore Rd., Fort William. www.limetreefortwilliam.co.uk. ✆**01397/701-806.** 9 units. £80–£110 double. DC, MC, V. Free parking. Follow the A82 into Fort William. **Amenities:** Restaurant. *In room:* TV, no phone.

INVERGARRY

25 miles NE of Fort William; 58 miles NW of Edinburgh

Invergarry, a center for exploring Glen Mor and Loch Ness, as well as for fishing, is located at the junction of the Fort William to Inverness road and the A87 or "Road to the Isles" that terminates at Kyle of Lochalsh and Skye.

Essentials

The nearest rail service runs to Fort William, where you can take a connecting bus to Invergarry, a half-hour ride away. Ask at the tourist office in Fort William for the **Highland Omnibuses** schedules. If you're driving from Fort William, proceed north on the Inverness road (A82) to Invergarry.

The nearest **Tourist Information Centre** is in Fort William (see "Fort William: Gateway to Ben Nevis," earlier in this chapter).

Exploring the Area

From Invergarry, it's a 3½-mile drive south on the A82 to the **Well of the Heads** (*Tobar nan Ceann* in Gaelic). The only sign indicating the well's position is a grocery store (Well of the Seven Heads Grocery & Convenience Mart). At the store, a staff member will direct you down a short forest path to the well itself. It was erected by MacDonnell of Glengarry in 1812 to commemorate the decapitation of seven brothers who had murdered the two sons of a 17th-century chief of Clan Keppoch at Glengarry. An obelisk supports the bronzed heads of the seven victims.

In the grounds of the Glengarry Castle Hotel (see below), you can see the grim ruins of **Invergarry Castle,** the stronghold of Clan MacDonnell of Glengarry. The site of the castle on Raven's Rock, overlooking Loch Oich in the Great Glen, was a strategic one in the days of clan feuds and Jacobite risings. To find the castle, drive 1½ miles south of Invergarry on the A82 toward Fort William, and then turn off to follow the signs pointing to the hotel. The ruins lie beside the hotel's very long main driveway, surrounded by trees.

Where to Eat & Stay

Glengarry Castle Hotel   This mid-19th-century mansion, with gables and chimneys, is an impressive sight. The hotel makes a pleasant base for fishing and walking. The spacious guest rooms are old-fashioned but comfortable, and some have four-poster beds. The dining room offers a fixed-price 30 menu of traditional home cooking.

Invergarry PH35 4HW. www.glengarry.net. ✆**01809/501-254.** Fax 01809/501-207. 26 units. £96–£176 double. MC, V. Closed mid-Nov to mid-Mar. From Invergarry, drive 1½ miles south, following the A82 toward Fort William; turn off to follow signs pointing to the hotel. **Amenities:** Restaurant; tennis court. *In room:* TV, hair dryer, Wi-Fi (free).

AVIEMORE ★

Aviemore, located on the Spey at the foot of the historic rock of **Craigellachie,** was established as a year-round resort in 1966. Although the center of Aviemore itself has little of the flavor of Scotland (with ugly concrete structures), visitors flock here for its access to the beautiful scenery of the Cairngorm Mountains, renowned for their skiing in winter and hiking in summer.

The Cairngorms form the largest national park in Britain, covering some (1,467 sq. miles). An area of outstanding natural beauty, the **Cairngorms National Park ★★** contains 52 mountain summits, including four of Scotland's highest peaks. Rivers, lochs, and forests are interspersed with farms and small hamlets. The park also embraces a number of old castles, a few rural museums, and some Scotch whisky distilleries.

With its cycling and walking trails, the park's most interesting stretch is the Victorian Heritage Trail that includes the royal family's Balmoral Castle. For more information, consult **www.castlesandwhisky.com**. For maps, advice on walks or hikes, and other information, contact **Cairngorms National Park Authority,** 14 The Square, Grantown-on-Spey PH26 3HG (*C* **01479/873-535;** fax 01479/873-527; www. cairngorms.co.uk).

Essentials

GETTING THERE   Aviemore is the major transportation hub for the area on the main Inverness–Edinburgh railway line. Some eight trains a day from Inverness pass through (trip time: 30–45 min.). Twelve trains per day also arrive from Glasgow or Edinburgh (trip time from each city: about 3 hours). For rail schedules in Aviemore, call *C* **01479/810-221.**

Aviemore is also on the main Inverness–Edinburgh bus line. The trip from Edinburgh takes about 3 hours. Frequent buses also arrive throughout the day from Inverness (trip time: 40 min.). For schedules, call *C* **08705/505-050,** or visit www. citylink.co.uk.

If you're driving from Edinburgh, after crossing the Forth Bridge Road, take the M90 to Perth, and then continue the rest of the way along the A9 to Aviemore.

VISITOR INFORMATION   The **Highlands of Scotland Tourist Office** (Aviemore branch) is on Grampian Road (*C* **01479/810-363;** www.visitaviemore.co.uk). It's open year-round from Monday to Friday 9am to 5pm, and on Sunday 10am to 4pm.

Exploring the Area

North of Aviemore, the **Strathspey Railway,** Dalfaber Road (*C* **01479/810-725;** www.strathspeyrailway.co.uk), offers the opportunity to experience the romance of steam trains in the Highlands. The line follows the valley of the River Spey between Boat of Garten and Aviemore, a distance of 5 miles. A round-trip takes about an hour. Consult the website for the full schedule, but trains generally run four times daily from April to October, though there are special trips around Christmas. You can also take afternoon tea or dine in the train's replica Pullman parlor car, the Amethyst. For reservations and hours of departure, call *C* **0800/085-7273.**

Skiers come to the Aviemore any time between December and April, when the prospects of good snow are high. They converge on the Day Lodge in Aviemore to arrange lessons and hire equipment. Check www.cairngormmountain.co.uk for information and the latest weather conditions.

There are several places to rent bikes in the area. **Speyside Sports,** Grant Road (© **01479/810-656**), and **Bothy Bikes,** 81 Grampian Rd. (© **01479/810-111;** www.bothybikes.co.uk), are both recommended.

The tourist office can give you hiking maps and offer advice, especially about weather conditions. One of the best trails is reached by following the B9760 to the signposted **Glenmore Forest Park,** in the vicinity of Loch Morlich.

For the grandest view of the Cairngorm peaks, you can take the **Cairngorm Funicular Railway** (© **01479/861-261**; www.cairngormmountain.co.uk). At the top is a visitor center and restaurant. Wear warm gear because it gets very cold at 900m (3,000 ft.) above sea level. The railway is signposted off the B9152. If weather permits, the train runs daily from 10am to 4:20pm.

Where to Eat

The Bar/The Restaurant SCOTTISH   Although the golf course, health club, and leisure facilities of this country club are open only to members, visitors are welcome in the cozy bar and restaurant. In the bar, there's a menu of venison cutlets, burgers, sandwiches, and steak pies. The restaurant serves seafood, steaks, and a limited number of vegetarian dishes.

In the Dalfaber Golf and Country Club, about 1 mile north of the center of Aviemore. © **01479/811-244.** www.macdonaldhotels.co.uk/resorts/dalfaber. Dinner main courses £10–£24. MC, V. Restaurant daily 6:30–9:30pm. Bar daily 11am–11pm.

Entertainment & Nightlife

The main nightspot in town is **Cafe Mambo,** 12–13 Grampian Rd. (© **01479/811-670**), which is both a restaurant and a bar, and on Friday and Saturday nights a nightclub (dancing to the latest music from 10pm to 1am). The restaurant and bar are open Sunday through Wednesday from 11am to 11pm, and Thursday through Saturday from noon to 1am. Food is served only until 8:30pm.

Where to Stay

Corrour House Hotel   This isolated Victorian granite house offers a haven from the modern commercialism of Aviemore itself. Built around 1880 in 1.6 hectares (4 acres) of gardens and woodland, it's a family-run affair with simple but comfortable rooms. A home-cooked dinner is available if arranged in advance.

Rothiemurchus, by Aviemore PH22 1QH. www.corrourhousehotel.co.uk. © **01479/810-220.** Fax 01479/811-500. 8 units. £80–£116 double. AE, MC, V. Closed mid-Nov to Christmas. From Aviemore, drive ⅔ mile east on the B970, following the signs to Glenmore. **Amenities:** Restaurant; bar. *In room:* TV, hair dryer.

Hilton Coylumbridge Aviemore ★ ☺   This is considered Aviemore resort's best hotel on account of its extensive sports and leisure facilities, spread across its 26 hectares (65 acres) of grounds. The guest rooms are smartly designed in a light and contemporary style. Children are especially welcome: There's a Fun House and adventure park to keep them busy, and the hotel even organizes special toddler breaks. If it's pampering you're after, the spa and Thai lodge offer a wide range of massage and beauty treatments. For sporting enthusiasts, there are two pools, a dry ski slope, a climbing wall, and a skate park. The hotel also offers a number of luxury self-catering lodges in the grounds; each accommodates up to eight people.

62, Grampian Road, Aviemore PH22 12N. www.hilton.co.uk:80/coylumbridge. ℭ **01479/810-661.** Fax 01479/811-309. 88 units. £116–£208 double. AE, DC, MC, V. In Aviemore, turn into the junction immediately opposite the railway station at the south end of the village. Follow the roundabout; the hotel is signposted. **Amenities:** 2 restaurants; 5 bars; babysitting; 2 pools (indoor); concierge; exercise room; spa; room service. *In room:* TV, hair dryer, Wi-Fi (free).

ALONG LOCH NESS ★★

Sir Peter Scott's *Nessitera rhombopteryx,* one of the world's great mysteries, continues to elude her pursuers. The Loch Ness Monster, or "Nessie" as she's more familiarly known, has captured the imagination of the world, drawing thousands of visitors every year to Loch Ness.

All types of high-tech underwater contraptions have gone in after the Loch Ness Monster, but no one can find her in spite of the photographs and film footage you might have seen in magazines or on TV. Dr Robert Rines and his associates at the Academy of Applied Science in Massachusetts maintain an all-year watch with sonar-triggered cameras and strobe lights suspended from a raft in Urquhart Bay. However, some people in Inverness aren't keen on collaring the monster: an old prophecy predicts a violent end for Inverness if it's ever captured.

The loch is 24 miles long, 1 mile wide, and some 229m (751 ft.) deep. In the summer, you can take boat cruises across Loch Ness from both Fort Augustus and Inverness.

If you're driving, take the A82 between Fort Augustus and Inverness running along Loch Ness. Buses from either Fort Augustus or Inverness also run to Drumnadrochit.

Drumnadrochit

The bucolic village of Drumnadrochit is about a mile from Loch Ness, at the entrance to Glen Urquhart. It's the nearest village to the part of the loch where there have been most sightings of the monster.

Although most visitors arrive at Drumnadrochit to see the Loch Ness Monster exhibition (see below), don't miss the opportunity to enjoy the beautiful countryside around the loch. One way of seeing it is on horseback at the **Highland Riding Centre,** Borlum Farm, Drumnadrochit (ℭ **01456/450-220;** www.borlum.co.uk). This 162-hectare (400-acre) sheep farm on the moorlands overlooking Loch Ness has a stable of 45 horses and organizes treks, lessons, and competitions for all ages and abilities. Depending on demand, tours depart almost every day in the summer, between 9:30am and 4:30pm; it's best to book in advance. An alternative way to get around is by bike. **Wilderness Cycles,** The Cottage, Drumnadrochit (ℭ **01456/450-223**), will rent you a bike so you can go exploring on your own. It's open daily 9am to 6pm.

Loch Ness Exhibition Centre MUSEUM This is Drumnadrochit's big attraction, featuring a scale replica of Nessie. Here you can follow the story of the monster from A.D. 565 to the present in photographs, audio, and video, and then climb aboard the sonar research vessel *John Murray.*

Drumnadrochit. ℭ **01456/450-573.** www.lochness.com. Admission £6.50 adults, £5.50 students and seniors, £4.50 children aged 6–18, £18 families, free for children ages 5 and under. Feb–May and Oct daily 9:30am–5pm; June and Sept daily 9am–6pm; July–Aug daily 9am–6:30pm; Nov–Jan daily 10am–3:30pm. Follow the A82 between Inverness and Fort William to the north shore of Loch Ness.

The latest evidence for the existence of the Loch Ness Monster came in June 2007, when a photograph taken by an amateur scientist was published. "I couldn't believe my eyes when I saw this jet black thing, about 45 feet long, moving fairly fast in the water," said Gordon Holmes, a lab technician from Yorkshire who shot footage of Nessie on May 26, 2007. The Loch Ness center at Drumnadrochit proclaimed this "as some of the best footage we've seen yet." Marine biologist Adrian Shine told news media that Holmes "panned back to get the background shore into the shot, so it's far less likely to be a fake and allows scientists to calculate the size of the creature and how fast it is going." Holmes estimated the monster's speed at about 6 mph.

Urquhart Castle RUINS   The romantic ruins of this castle are perched on a promontory overlooking Loch Ness. The chief of Clan Grant owned the castle in 1509, and most of the extensive ruins date from that period. In 1692, the castle was blown up by the Grants to prevent it from falling into the hands of the Jacobites. Rising from crumbling walls, the jagged keep still remains. The visitor center offers an audiovisual presentation, a cafe, and a shop.

Loch Ness. ✆ **01456/450-551.** www.historic-scotland.gov.uk. Admission £7 adults, £5.60 seniors, £4.20 children 5-15. Apr–Sept daily 9:30am–6pm; Oct daily 9:30am–5pm; Nov–Mar daily 9:30am–4:30pm. Drive 1½ miles southeast of Drumnadrochit on the A82.

WHERE TO EAT & STAY

Loch Ness Lodge ★★★   This award-winning family-run hotel is the finest luxury hotel in the area. It's ideal for a romantic getaway or a weekend of relaxation (children aged 16 and up are welcome). The white baronial-style building is set amid beautifully planted gardens looking out over Loch Ness. Guest rooms enjoy glorious views that change with the light and season. The interior has been designed with calm complementary colors, rich fabrics, and smart furniture to create a warm and relaxed modern take on country-house living. Guest rooms are equipped with designer bathrooms, and the hotel has its own spa and therapy suite, offering a hot tub, sauna, and a range of treatments. One of the guest rooms is suitable for disabled visitors.

In the evening, guests gather before the log fire in the drawing room for pre-dinner drinks (or on the terrace outside on summer nights). The hotel's cuisine is French-Scottish in style, with a "field-to-mouth" philosophy, whereby produce is harvested in season as locally as possible. Wild garlic is picked from the shores of the loch, vegetables and herbs come from the hotel's garden, and fish, seafood, meat, game, fruit, and cheese all come from local sources. The chefs also bake their own bread, make their own butter, and stew their own preserves. Dishes might include mixed grill of west coast seafood, with butternut squash, caviar, gnocchi, and caper butter, followed by prune and Armagnac soufflé with whisky cream. A five-course dinner is priced at 55 per person. Non-guests are welcome at dinner, subject to availability.

Brachla, on the A82, Loch Ness-side, near Inverness, IV3 8LA. www.loch-ness-lodge.com. ✆ **01456/459-469.** Fax 01456/459-439. 7 units. B&B £155–£320 double; DB&B £254–£419. During high summer, only DB&B is available. AE, MC, V. Free parking. Drive 9 miles southwest of Inverness on the A82 (about 15 min.). From Drumnadrochit, drive northwest on the A82 for 6 miles. **Amenities:** Restaurant; spa. *In room:* TV/DVD, DVD library, Wi-Fi (free).

Fort Augustus

Fort Augustus, 36 miles south of Inverness along the A82, stands at the head (the southernmost end) of Loch Ness. The town was fortified after the 1715 Jacobite rising. General George Wade, of road- and bridge-building fame, made his headquarters here in 1724, and in 1729 the government constructed a fort along the banks of the loch, naming it Augustus after William Augustus, the Duke of Cumberland and son of King George II. The Jacobites seized the fort in 1745 and controlled it until the Scottish defeat at Culloden. Long since destroyed, Wade's fort was turned into the Fort Augustus Abbey. A Benedictine order was installed in 1867, and the monks today run a Catholic secondary school on the site.

As well as being a convenient refueling stop for those visiting Loch Ness, Fort Augustus is noteworthy as the best place to see the locks of the Caledonian Canal in action. Bisecting the actual village of Fort Augustus, the locks of the **Caledonian Canal** are a popular attraction when boats are passing through. Constructed between 1803 and 1822, the canal runs right across the Highlands, almost in a straight line, from Inverness in the north, to Corpach, in the vicinity of Fort William. The canal is 60 miles long, consisting of 22 man-made miles and the rest natural lochs.

If you're interested in negotiating the canal, you can hire a boat from **Caley Cruisers,** Canal Road, Inverness (℃ **01463/236-328;** www.caleycruisers.co.uk). The company maintains a fleet of 50 cabin cruisers (with skippers), and groups of two to six people can rent them from March to October—even if their marine experience is relatively limited. Rentals last for 1 week, long enough to cover the 60 miles of the Caledonian Canal in both directions between Inverness and Fort William. (There are about 15 locks en route; tolls are included in the rental fee.) Depending on the craft's size and the season, a week's rental ranges from £512 to £2,142; the cost of fuel and taxes for a week will be an additional £100 to £200, plus another £45 to £85 for an insurance policy. Except for the waters of Loch Ness, which can be a little choppy, the canal is calm and doesn't pose any of the dangers of cruising on the open sea.

WHERE TO EAT & STAY

Inchnacardoch Lodge   Inchnacardoch Lodge is a family-run hotel with spectacular views over Loch Ness. It was built in 1878 as a hunting lodge by the Fraser clan's chief, Lord Lovat, and the bell used to call the hunters home at night is still in working order on the side of the building. The comfortable guest rooms are furnished in traditional style. The restaurant serves classic dishes using local Scottish ingredients; the hotel's manager is also its head chef.

Near Fort Augustus PH32 4BL. www.inchhotel.com. ℃ **01456/450-900.** Fax 01320/366-248. 15 units. £110–£130 double. AE, MC, V. Free parking. Drive ⅔ mile north of Fort Augustus on the A82. **Amenities:** Restaurant; bar. *In room:* TV/DVD, DVD library, Wi-Fi (free).

INVERNESS ★: CAPITAL OF THE HIGHLANDS

156 miles NW of Edinburgh; 134 miles NW of Dundee; 134 miles W of Aberdeen

The capital of the Highlands, Inverness is a royal burgh and seaport, situated where the river flows from **Loch Ness** into the North Sea. It's a historic town and a good base for touring around the surrounding countryside, with **Culloden Battlefield** and **Cawdor Castle** (of *Macbeth* fame) close by. Today, it's a fast-growing city, accommodating a quarter of the population of the Highlands, and boasts thriving shops, pubs, and music venues, as well as a famous annual gathering.

A day in Inverness might start with some sightseeing, taking in **St. Andrew's Cathedral,** walking up to the **Castle,** and learning about Highland life at the **Inverness Museum and Art Gallery.** After lunch, a round of golf at the **Dornoch Golf Club** may be just the thing, or if not, shopping in the emporia of the **Victorian Market** may suit you better. In the evening, there are restaurants, lively pubs, cinemas, and dance clubs to end a busy day.

Inverness has restaurants to suit all tastes and budgets, many of them situated on the banks of the Ness a stone's throw from the castle. For fine dining, try the hare filets with a passion-fruit compote at **Abstract,** or the lamb with polenta cake at **Rocpool Rendezvous,** while for comforting—and democratically priced—Italian fare, join the local clientele at **Riva.** Bear in mind too that lunchtime menus often offer particularly good value for money.

Inverness is by far the biggest center for shopping in the Highlands. The **Victorian Market** is a fascinating enclave of independent emporia, with jewelers and gift shops aplenty. The **Eastgate Shopping Centre,** on the other hand, has all the well-known chain stores. If you're tempted to get fitted with your own kilt, try **Duncan Chisholm & Sons** or **Boarstone Tartans,** where you can also buy deerstalker hats for days walking on the hills, and pewter flasks for your whisky.

Whereas most places in the Highlands offer only the pub or an early night, Inverness has plenty that's worth staying up for. **Hootananny** on Church Street offers live music, from local indie bands to Scottish and Celtic music, and on Saturdays there's often traditional dancing with a ceilidh. If that's not your style, try **Johnny Foxes** on Bank Street, for karaoke and DJ sets that continue long into the night.

Essentials

GETTING THERE   Domestic flights from various parts of Britain arrive at Inverness Airport. The flight time from London's Gatwick is 1¾ hours. Call ℂ **01667/464-000** in Inverness or visit www.invernessairport.com for flight information.

Some five to seven trains per day arrive at Inverness Station (Station Square, off Academy Street; ℂ **08457/484-950** for schedules) from Glasgow and Edinburgh (on Sun, two or three trains). The train journey takes 3½ hours from either city.

Scottish Citylink coaches (ℂ **08705/505-050;** www.citylink.co.uk) provides daily services from Edinburgh and Glasgow (a 4-hr. trip each way). The bus station is at Farraline Park, off Academy Street (ℂ **01463/233-371**).

Driving from Edinburgh, take the M9 north to Perth, and then follow along the Great North Road (the A9) until you reach Inverness.

VISITOR INFORMATION   The Inverness branch of the **Highlands of Scotland Tourist Board** is at Castle Wynd, off Bridge Street (ℂ **01463/234-353;** www.visithighlands.com). It's open mid-September to May from Monday to Saturday 9am to 5pm, and Sunday 10am to 4pm; April to May, Monday to Saturday 9am to 5pm, and Sunday 10am to 4pm; June hours are Monday to Saturday 9am to 6pm, and Sunday 9:30am to 4pm; from July to mid-September, it's open Monday to Saturday 9am to 6pm and Sunday 9:30am to 5pm (but only until 4pm in Sept).

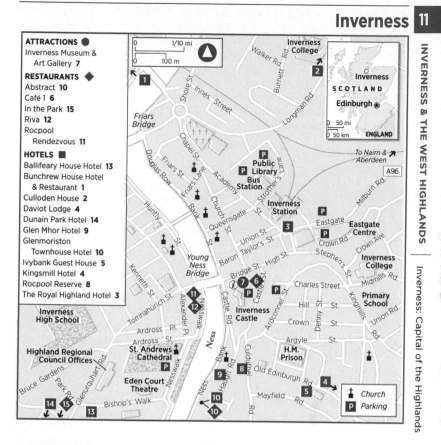

ATTRACTIONS ●
Inverness Museum &
Art Gallery **7**
RESTAURANTS ◆
Abstract **10**
Café 1 **6**
In the Park **15**
Riva **12**
Rocpool
Rendezvous **11**
HOTELS ■
Ballifeary House Hotel **13**
Bunchrew House Hotel
& Restaurant **1**
Culloden House **2**
Daviot Lodge **4**
Dunain Park Hotel **14**
Glen Mhor Hotel **9**
Glenmoriston
Townhouse Hotel **10**
Ivybank Guest House **5**
Kingsmill Hotel **4**
Rocpool Reserve **8**
The Royal Highland Hotel **3**

SPECIAL EVENTS   The summer season reaches its peak in Inverness with the **Highland Games** in July, when there are sporting competitions and festive balls. For more information and exact dates, consult the tourist office (see above).

Exploring Inverness

Inverness is one of the oldest inhabited sites in Scotland. On **Craig Phadrig** are the remains of a vitrified fort, believed to date from the 4th century B.C. One of the most important prehistoric monuments in the north, the **Stones of Clava,** can be found 6¼ miles east of Inverness on the road to Nairn. These cairns and standing stones date back to the Bronze Age.

The old castle of Inverness stood to the east of the street now known as Castlehill. King David I built the first stone castle in Inverness around 1141, and the **Clock Tower** is all that remains of the fort later erected on the site by Cromwell's army between 1652 and 1657. The rebellious Scots blew up the old castle in 1746 to keep it from falling to government troops, and the present **castle** was constructed by the Victorians in the 19th century. Today, this landmark houses the law courts of Inverness and local government offices.

West of the River Ness rises the wooded hill of **Tomnahurich,** known as the "hill of the fairies." Now a cemetery, it's the best place to go for a country walk in the vicinity of Inverness for panoramic views. The boat-shaped hillock is immediately to the southwest of the city center. From the hill's vantage point you can see wooded islands in the Ness that have been turned into parks and are now linked to Inverness by suspension bridges.

The 16th-century **Abertarff House,** Church Street, is now the headquarters of An Comunn Gaidhealach, the Highland association that preserves the Gaelic language and culture. Opposite the town hall is the **Old Mercat Cross,** with its Stone of the Tubs, said to be the stone on which women rested their washtubs as they ascended from the river. Known as "Clachnacudainn," the lozenge-shaped stone was the spot where early local kings were crowned.

St. Andrew's Cathedral (1866–69), Ardross Street, is the seat of the northernmost diocese of the Scottish Episcopal Church. The cathedral is a fine example of Victorian architecture, both imposing and richly decorated. Inside, you can see the icons given to Bishop Eden by the czar of Russia. The cathedral is open daily from 9:30am to 6pm. For information, contact the Provost's office at 15 Ardross St. (📞 **01463/233-535**).

If you're looking for a round, you can hit the links at the renowned **Royal Dornoch Golf Club** (📞 **01862/810-219;** www.royaldornoch.com), located 40 miles to the north of Inverness. Closer to town is the more modest 5,288-yard **Torvean Golf Course,** Glen Q Road (📞 **01463/225-651;** www.torveangolfclub.co.uk), an 18-hole, par-69 course.

Culloden Battlefield ★ HISTORIC SITE   At Culloden Battlefield, Bonnie Prince Charlie and the Jacobite army suffered their final defeat on April 16, 1746. A path leads from the visitor center through the Field of the English, where 52 men of the Duke of Cumberland's forces who died during the battle are supposedly buried. Features of interest include the **Graves of the Clans,** communal burial places with simple stones bearing individual clan names; the great **memorial cairn,** erected in 1881; the **Well of the Dead;** and the huge **Cumberland Stone,** from which the victorious "Butcher" Cumberland is said to have reviewed the scene. The battle lasted only 40 minutes; the prince's army lost some 1,200 men out of 5,000, and the Duke's army 300 of 9,000. In the visitor center is an audiovisual presentation on the background and history of the famous battle. There's also a restaurant and a bookshop.

Culloden Moor, 6¼ miles southeast of Inverness. 📞 **01463/790-607** for visitor center. www.nts.org.uk/culloden. Admission free to battlefield; admission to visitor center £10 adults, £7.50 seniors and children 5-15, £24 families. Battlefield open daily year-round; visitor center Apr–Oct daily 9am–6pm; Nov–Dec and Feb–Mar 30 daily 10am–4pm. Closed in Jan.

Fort George/Queen's Own Highlanders Regimental Museum MUSEUM   Fort George was called the "most considerable fortress and best situated in Great Britain" in 1748 by Lt. Col. James Wolfe, who went on to become famous as Wolfe of Quebec. Built after the Battle of Culloden, the fort was occupied by the Hanoverian army of George II and is still an active army barracks. The rampart, almost 1 mile around, encloses some 17 hectares (42 acres). Dr. Samuel Johnson and James

Boswell visited here in 1773 on their Highland trek. The fort contains the **Queen's Own Highlanders Regimental Museum,** with exhibits that date from 1778 to the present day and chart the history of a number of Highland regiments as well as its namesake. A new exhibition about the 1990s Gulf War has been recently added.

On Moray Firth by the village of Ardersier, 11 miles northeast of Inverness, 8 miles northwest of Cawdor along B9006. ⓒ**0131/310-8701.** www.armymuseums.org.uk. Free admission. Apr–Sept daily 9:30am–5:15pm; Oct–Mar Mon–Fri 10am–4:30pm.

Inverness Museum & Art Gallery MUSEUM   This centrally located museum documents the social and natural history, archaeology, art, and culture of the Scottish Highlands. Don't miss the important collection of Highland silver and reconstructed silversmith's workshop, a reconstruction of a local taxidermist's workshop, and a reconstructed 1920s Inverness kitchen.

Castle Wynd, off Bridge St. ⓒ**01463/237-114.** http://inverness.highland.museum. Free admission. Mon–Sat 10am–5pm.

Where to Eat
EXPENSIVE

Abstract ★ FRENCH/SCOTTISH   Relying on Scottish produce but using French cooking techniques, head chef Bruce Morrison has created one of the finest dining experiences in Inverness. Starters might include Scottish scallops with a hazelnut crust served with braised pork belly and white asparagus. For a main course you could have Ross-shire lamb with a rhubarb couscous or Scottish brown hare filets with a passion-fruit compote. As Inverness is near the coast, fish is also a specialty. The surroundings are luxurious and the service is formal.

20 Ness Bank St. ⓒ**01463/223-777.** www.abstractrestaurant.com. Reservations recommended. Main courses £26–£28; tasting menu £55 per person. AE, MC, V. Tues–Sat 6–10pm.

Rocpool Rendezvous ★★ BRITISH/MEDITERRANEAN   Located on the banks of the River Ness, just across from castle, this brasserie-style restaurant has injected new life into the once-sleepy culinary scene of the Highland capital. Sleek and modern in design, the restaurant is nevertheless comfortable and welcoming. And the food is no less stylish, comprised of Scottish fare with a continental (often Italian) accent. For example, rosemary-crusted lamb cutlets come with polenta cake, soft Italian cheese, broccoli, pancetta, and pine nuts. The bargain-priced lunch and early evening menus are simpler, but no less imaginative and delicious.

1 Ness Walk. ⓒ**01463/717-274.** www.rocpoolrestaurant.com. Reservations required. Main courses £16–£23; lunch menu £12 for 2 courses; early evening menu (5:45–6:45pm) £14 for 2 courses. AE, MC, V. Mon–Sat noon–2:30pm and 5:45–10pm.

MODERATE

Café 1 ★★ INTERNATIONAL/SCOTTISH FUSION   Behind the old stone facade of a building on Castle Street is one of the quirkiest and most enjoyable restaurants in town. The modern furniture and checkered ceiling hint at the unconventionality and informality of the place. The menus are eclectic, though relying first and foremost on good Scottish produce (including from the owner's own herds of sheep and cows). After starting with cocktails, you can then dine on tempura king prawns, Highland lamb with kale, halibut with santini tomatoes, and selected Scottish cheeses to follow. The lunch menu is very democratically priced, and there's plenty for vegetarians too.

75 Castle St. ☎ **01463/226-200.** www.cafe1.net. Reservations recommended. Luch main courses £8 for 1 course, £10 for 2 courses; dinner main courses £11–£23; 3-course dinner £27. MC, V. Daily 1–3pm and 7–11pm.

In the Park SCOTTISH   Head Chef Chris Crombie cooks high-quality Scottish ingredients with a few imaginative twists. Pan-fried pigeon breast comes with a haggis "scotch egg," and scallops are accompanied by black pudding bon-bons. For your main course you can have lamb cooked five ways, or baked cod with apple purée. There's always a vegetarian option as well. Prices are very reasonable given the smart surroundings.

In the Loch Ness Country House Hotel (see below), Dunain Park. ☎ **01463/230-512.** www.lochness countryhousehotel.co.uk. Reservations recommended. Dinner menu 30 for 3 courses. AE, DC, MC, V. Daily 7–9pm.

INEXPENSIVE

Riva ITALIAN/INTERNATIONAL   One of Inverness's best restaurants is also one of its most reasonably priced. Situated on the opposite bank from the castle, it's very popular with its local clientele. Upstairs there's a pizzeria (open Tues–Sat 5–9pm). Downstairs, the restaurant serves more refined dishes, such as pan-fried Highland beef with saffron fondant potato and buttered cepes, or risotto of smoked haddock and garden peas.

4–6 Ness Walk. ☎ **01463/237-377.** www.rivarestaurant.co.uk. Reservations required. Main courses £10–£20; 2-course set lunch £10; 3-course pre-theatre menu (until 6:30pm) £16. MC, V. Restaurant Mon–Sat noon–2:30pm and 5–9:30pm (last order).

Shopping

There are two major shopping areas in the center of Inverness: the **Eastgate Inverness Shopping Centre,** Millburn Road (www.eastgate-centre.co.uk), and the **Victorian Market** (constructed in 1870) on Academy Street, which offers a more traditional retail experience. The latter is open Monday to Saturday; some shops in the Eastgate are also open on Sundays.

Silvercraft, 5–7 Market Arcade (☎ **01463/232-686**), is a family-run jewelry store that opened in the Victorian Market in 1960. The friendly atmosphere and wide selection of diamond, gold, and silver jewelry make this a pleasant place to browse. Another useful jewelry store is **D&H Norval** at 88 Church St. (☎ **01463/232-739**). Its unusual selection of bangles and bracelets are inspired by the decorative traditions of Celtic Scotland.

If you're interested in getting your own kilt, try **Boarstone Tartans,** 14–16 New Market (☎ **01463/239-793;** www.boarstonetartans.co.uk). In fact, every traditional Scottish clothes item is available here—from kilt jackets to tartan trousers to Highland dress outfits. For outdoor enthusiasts, there's also shooting coats, tweed caps, deerstalker hats, tweed rugs, scarves, ties, and pewter flasks.

A worthwhile alternative is the family business of **Duncan Chisholm & Sons,** 47–51 Castle St. (☎ **01463/234-599;** www.kilts.co.uk). The tartans of at least 50 of Scotland's largest clans are available in the form of kilts and kilt jackets for men and women. If your heart is set on something more esoteric, the staff can acquire whatever fabric your ancestors would have worn to make up your garment. There's also a section devoted to Scottish gifts (ties, scarves, yard goods, kilt pins in thistle patterns), and you can visit the on-premises workshop.

Entertainment & Nightlife

One of the most popular places in town is **Hootananny,** Church Street (℗ 01463/ 233-651; www.hootananny.co.uk). Its three floors accommodate several bars, a Thai restaurant, and several venues for live music. The best time to show up is on a Friday at 10:30pm, when local singers and songwriters showcase their talents. Traditional Scottish music is featured on many nights, sometimes interspersed with video tracks. Every Saturday afternoon there is a ceilidh from 2:30 to 6pm. Most nights it closes at 1am, and, depending on the venue and entertainment, a £5 cover charge might be imposed.

Johnny Foxes, 26 Bank St. (℗ **01463/236-577;** www.johnnyfoxes.co.uk), is an Irish pub that draws the largest number of backpackers. Food is served and live music is presented Monday through Saturday, with Sunday nights devoted to karaoke. A range of popular and traditional music is offered, including Scottish and Irish tunes. It's open Monday through Tuesday 11am to 1am, Wednesday through Saturday 11am to 2am, and Sunday 12:30pm to 2am. Food is served daily from noon to 3pm. Downstairs there's also a cocktail bar and nightclub called The Den, with DJs most nights until 3am.

Love2Love, 9–11 Castle St. (℗ **0844/891-0856;** http://love2loveinverness. com), is the place to come for commercial dance music with no added sophistication. For the best atmosphere, show up on Friday and Saturday night to join a large crowd in their 20s. It's open Wednesday, Thursday, and Sunday 11pm to 3am, Friday and Saturday 10pm to 3am.

You can also spend an evening in the town's pubs sampling single-malt whiskies or beers on tap. Although the pubs here may not have the authentic charm of the isolated pubs in more rural areas, you'll still find a lot of Highlander flavor. Try **The Blackfriars,** 93–95 Academy St. (℗ **01463/233-881;** www.blackfriarshighland pub.co.uk); **Gellions Pub,** 8–14 Bridge St. (℗ **01463/233-648;** http://gellions. co.uk); or **Gunsmith's Pub,** 30 Union St. (℗ **01463/250-116**).

Where to Stay
EXPENSIVE

Bunchrew House Hotel & Restaurant This magnificent Scottish baronial-style mansion on the shores of Beauly Firth is the ancestral home of both the Fraser and the McKenzie clans. The house dates back originally to 1621 and is set in 8 hectares (20 acres) of landscaped gardens. You get a taste of a bygone era while relaxing in the paneled drawing room with roaring log fires. The guest rooms are individually decorated; the Lovat Suite, for example, has a canopied four-poster bed. Guests can dine in the candlelit restaurant on Scottish beef, fresh lobster and crayfish, and local game.

Bunchrew, Inverness IV3 8TA. www.bunchrew-inverness.co.uk. ℗**01463/234-917.** Fax 01463/710-620. 16 units. £170–£270 double. AE, MC, V. Drive 3 miles west of Inverness on the A862. **Amenities:** Restaurant; bar; room service. *In room:* TV, fridge, hair dryer, Wi-Fi (free).

Culloden House ★★ This is probably the most elegant country retreat in the area. Culloden House, a Georgian mansion with a much-photographed Adam facade, incorporates part of the Renaissance castle in which Bonnie Prince Charlie slept the night before Culloden, his last great battle. Set amid extensive gardens and parkland, it's perfect for a relaxed Highland holiday. At the iron gates to the broad front lawn, a piper in full Highland garb often plays at sundown, the skirl of the bagpipe accompanied by the barking of house dogs. Cozy yet sumptuously decorated rooms (think chandeliers and marble fireplaces) have fine views and modern comforts. The restaurant serves dishes based around fine local ingredients, and often cooked with a continental twist.

Culloden, Inverness IV2 7BZ. www.cullodenhouse.co.uk.© **01463/790-461.** Fax 01463/792-181. www.cullodenhouse.co.uk. 28 units. £250–£320 double; £395 suite. AE, DC, MC, V. Drive 3 miles east of Inverness on the A96. **Amenities:** Restaurant; bar; tennis court; croquet lawn; sauna and beauty spa; room service. *In room:* TV, hair dryer, Internet (free).

Glen Mhor Hotel ☺

This gabled Victorian hotel is set on the banks of the River Ness, and many of the guest rooms have views of the river, castle, and cathedral. Rooms are individually decorated, some in traditional style, others in contemporary fashion. Children are welcomed with games chests, Nintendo Wii, and excellent family room rates (children under 12 stay free in your room and also enjoy the free children's menu in the restaurant). The bistro-style restaurant and bar specializes in seafood and Scottish dishes. Main courses are priced from £11 to £19.

9-12 Ness Bank, Inverness IV2 4SG. www.glen-mhor.com.© **01463/234-308.** Fax 01463/218-018. 50 units. £70–£120 double; £135–£160 junior suite. AE, DC, MC, V. From Inverness, follow signs to Dores (on the B862); hotel is on the south bank. **Amenities:** Restaurant; bar; room service. *In room:* TV, CD player, hair dryer, Wi-Fi (free).

Glenmoriston Townhouse Hotel

Many of the guest rooms in this smart Victorian house have fine views over the river and town center, just a short walk away. The interior decoration creates a stylish and calm ambience. Your stay is further enhanced by the hotel's two restaurants: the upmarket Abstract (see above), and the more informal Contrast Brasserie (open for lunch and dinner daily), which offers hearty meals based around prime Scottish produce.

20 Ness Bank, Inverness IV2 4SF. www.glenmoristontownhouse.com. © **01463/223-777.** Fax 01463/712-378. 30 units. £105–£205 double. AE, MC, V. Free parking. Lies a 5-min. walk south of the train station. **Amenities:** 2 restaurants; bar; room service. *In room:* TV/DVD, hair dryer, Wi-Fi (free).

Kingsmill Hotel

The Kingsmill occupies a late-18th-century mansion situated about a mile from the center of Inverness. Over the years it has attracted royals, high-ranking government officials, film stars, and even Robert Burns himself. The guest rooms are comfortable, even if the styling is rather middle-of-the-road. Many of them do, however, benefit from views over the 1.6 hectares (4 acres) of parkland and the adjacent 18-hole golf course.

The hotel has 2 restaurants: a brasserie (main courses £11–£26) and the more formal Inglis Restaurant (£20 for 3 courses). Both make good use of the locally available meat, game and fish. A notice in the lobby tells you Robert Burns dined here in 1787, and the "Charles" who signed the guest register in 1982 was indeed the Prince of Wales.

Culcabock Rd., Inverness IV2 3LP. www.kingsmillshotel.com.© **01463/237-166.** Fax 0870/225-7208. 82 units. £80–£260 double. AE, DC, MC, V. Take Kingsmill Rd. 1 mile east of the center of Inverness. **Amenities:** Restaurant; bar; pool (indoor); health club w/sauna; room service. *In room:* TV, minibar, hair dryer, Wi-Fi (£4.95 1hr., £9.95 2½ hr., £14.95 24hr.).

Loch Ness Country House Hotel

The Dunain Park stands in 2.4 hectares (6 acres) of garden and woods between Loch Ness and Inverness. This 18th-century Georgian house is furnished with fine antiques, allowing it to retain an atmosphere of a private country house. Although Dunain Park has won particular renown mainly as a restaurant (see above), it also offers guest rooms with a host of thoughtful details and pretty furnishings.

Dunain Park, Inverness IV3 8JN. www.lochnesscountryhousehotel.co.uk. ℂ **01463/230-512.** Fax 01463/224-532. 15 units. £165 double; £195–£261 suite. AE, MC, V. Drive 1 mile southwest of Inverness on the A82. **Amenities:** Restaurant; bar; pool (indoor); room service. *In room:* TV, DVD, hair dryer, iPod docking station (in suites).

Rocpool Reserve ★★★   In the heart of Inverness, this boutique hotel, created from a restored 19th-century residence, is the epitome of modern hotel glamour. You might have expected this hotel to spring up in Glasgow or Edinburgh, but not in relatively dowdy Inverness. Bedrooms are not ultra-luxurious—with their contemporary, almost minimalist design—but they are comfortable and stylish (the bathrooms particularly so, with their "double-voyeur" showers). Rooms are categorized as Hip, Chic, Decadent, and Extra Decadent according to standard of luxury and price. The in-house restaurant (not to be confused with the Rocpool Rendezvous, p. 331) is among the very best in town. Main courses are priced at between £13 and £20; vegetarians have a dedicated menu.

Culduthel Rd., Inverness IV2 4AG. www.rocpool.com. ℂ **01463/240089.** Fax 01463/248431. 11 units. £185–£395. AE, MC, V. **Amenities:** Restaurant; bar; room service. *In room:* TV/DVD, CD player, minibar, hair dryer, MP3 docking station (in some), Internet (free). Moderate

The Royal Highland Hotel   The Royal Highland was built in 1859 across from the railway station to cater to the visitors pouring into the Highlands every summer on the new line. Today, this somber gray-stone pile has a slightly faded grandeur, though that can have its own sort of charm. The massive lobby contains the showiest staircase in Inverness. The ballroom is now used for weddings and corporate functions. The dining room retains its elaborate high ceiling and a sense of the Victorian age. The only concession to 21st-century taste is the new Ash Restaurant and Cocktail Bar, done out in cherry wood and with plush upholstery. Main courses are priced from £13 to £20, though the two-course set lunches for under £10 are hard to beat.

18 Academy St., Inverness IV1 1LG. www.royalhighlandhotel.co.uk. ℂ **01463/231-926.** Fax 01463/710-705. 86 units. £149–£189 double; £299 suite. DC, MC, V. **Amenities:** Restaurant; 2 bars. *In room:* TV, hair dryer, Wi-Fi (free).

INEXPENSIVE
Ballifeary House Hotel ★ 🏷   For a homey stay, you can't do much better than Mr. and Mrs. Luscombe's Victorian villa, just a short walk from the city center. Everything is immaculately turned out: the comfortable bedrooms, the neat bathrooms, even the pleasant gardens outside. The hotel discourages families with children under 15.

10 Ballifeary Rd., Inverness IV3 5PJ. www.ballifearyguesthouse.co.uk. ℂ **01463/235-572.** Fax 01463/717-583. 7 units. £70–£90 double. MC, V. From Fort William on the A82 as you're approaching Inverness, turn right on Ballifeary Rd. **Amenities:** Bar. *In room:* TV, hair dryer, no phone, Wi-Fi (free).

Daviot Lodge   For a really peaceful holiday, a stay at this farmhouse set in 32 hectares (80 acres) of farmland is ideal. From the windows of the traditionally styled guest rooms you'll see cows, sheep, and a pony named Seamus grazing. There's wheelchair access for disabled guests.

Daviot Mains Farm, Inverness IV2 53R. www.daviotlodge.co.uk. ℂ **01463/772-215.** Fax 01463/772-099. 7 units. £90–£100 double. MC, V. Lies 5 miles off Inverness on the A9. *In room:* TV, hair dryer, Internet (free).

Ivybank Guest House 🏷   Located off Castle Road about a 10-minute walk north of the town center, Ivybank was built in 1836 and retains many of its original features, including a grand oak-paneled hall with a rosewood staircase. The architecture is engagingly eccentric, with a tower and arched windows. The guest rooms are furnished in a reassuringly old-fashioned way, and the cozy atmosphere ensures a good night's sleep.

28 Old Edinburgh Rd., Inverness IV2 3HJ. www.ivybankguesthouse.com. ℂ/fax **01463/232-796.** 6 units, 3 with private bathroom. £56–£60 double. AE, MC, V. *In room:* TV, hair dryer.

Side Trips from Inverness
MUIR OF ORD

This small town, 10 miles west of Inverness, makes a good touring center for an area of the country north of Inverness that's particularly rich in historical sites. If you're holidaying in early August, it's also a good base for visiting the **Black Isle Show** (℃ **01463/870-870;** www.blackisleshow.info), one of the largest agricultural shows in Scotland; the showground is located just outside the town. Outdoors enthusiasts will also find the area around Muit of Ord attractive for its fishing, shooting, and golf.

Where to Eat & Stay
Dower House ★ 🏚☺   This charming 18th-century guesthouse is a perfect base for exploring the area. Rooms are decorated in a cottage style, with comfortable furnishings and flowers cut from the garden. A small three-bedroom cottage is perfect for families (£270 for 3 nights or from £350 to £520 per week). Be sure to make reservations well in advance; the home-away-from-home atmosphere is very much in demand. Even if you don't stay here, however, you can make a dinner reservation. A three-course meal (£42) cooked in the modern British style uses the best local seafood and game and as well as fresh herbs and vegetables from the hotel's own kitchen garden.

Highfield, Muir of Ord IV6 7XN. www.thedowerhouse.co.uk. ℂ/fax **01463/870-090.** 4 units. £135–£155 double; £155–£175 suite. MC, V. Drive 1 mile north of the A862. **Amenities:** Restaurant; bar; babysitting. *In room:* TV, hair dryer.

BEAULY ★
Beauly, 12 miles west of Inverness on the A862, is noted for the picturesque ruins of its monastery. French monks first settled here in the 13th century and gave the town its name: literally, "beautiful place".

Dating back as far as 1230, **Beauly Priory** (℃ **01463/782-309**) is the only one remaining of three priories built for the Valliscaulian order, an austere body that drew its rules from the Cistercians and Carthusians. Some of the intricate windows and window arcading remains intact among the ruins. Following the Reformation, the buildings passed into the possession of Lord Lovat, the local grandee. You can visit the priory at any time; if it's locked, ask for a key from the Priory Hotel across the way.

Visitors in the market for some tweeds might also be interested to visit **Campbell & Co.** at Highland Tweed House (℃ **01463/782-239;** www.campbellsofbeauly.co.uk) on the main street at the south end of the village square. The shop has been run by the same family since 1858, and offers a wide selection of fine tweeds and tartans, which you can then have tailored into the garment of your choice. Blankets, travel rugs, tweed hats, kilts, and cashmere sweaters are also on sale.

Where to Eat & Stay
Priory Hotel   The Priory Hotel is conveniently located on the historic main square of the town, a short walk from the ruins of the priory. The rooms are spacious but

modestly furnished. The hotel does benefit from its own in-house pub, "The Comm," where you can have a drink by the roaring fire. Afternoon tea can be taken in the lounge, and there's an a la carte menu for dinner in the restaurant.

The Square, Beauly IV4 7BX. www.priory-hotel.com. ✆**01463/782-309.** Fax 01463/782-531. 36 units. £105 double. AE, DC, MC, V. **Amenities:** Restaurant; bar; room service. *In room:* TV, hair dryer, Wi-Fi (free).

NAIRN & CAWDOR CASTLE ★

172 miles N of Edinburgh; 91 miles NW of Aberdeen; 16 miles E of Inverness

A favorite family seaside resort on the sheltered Moray Firth, Nairn (from the Gaelic for "Water of Alders") is a royal burgh at the mouth of the Nairn River. Its fishing harbor was constructed in 1820 by Thomas Telford, and golf has been played here since 1672—and still is today.

Essentials

GETTING THERE   Nairn can be reached by train from the south, with a change at either Aberdeen or Inverness. The service between Inverness and Nairn is frequent, and this is the most popular route. For train times and fares, consult **National Rail Enquiries** (✆ **08457/484-950;** www.nationalrail.co.uk). If you're driving from Inverness, take the A96 east to Nairn.

VISITOR INFORMATION   The **Tourist Information Centre** is at 62 King St. (✆ **01667/452-753;** www.visitnairn.com). Its opening times are April to mid-May and September to October, Monday through Saturday 10am to 5pm; mid-May to June, Monday through Saturday 10am to 5pm and Sunday 11am to 4pm; and July and August, Monday through Saturday 9am to 6pm and Sunday 10am to 5pm.

Exploring Nairn

Nairn's main appeal nowadays is as a seaside town, with a beautiful sandy beach and an attractive promenade. The pretty harbor area is also worth exploring, as is **"Fishertown"** just to the south, which with its narrow streets of fishermen's cottages remains much the same today as it was when first built.

Nairn is also well known as a golfing destination, with two 18-hole championship golf courses. The **Nairn Golf Club,** Seabank Road (✆ **01667/453-208;** www.nairngolfclub.co.uk), was established in 1887 and has come to be considered one of the finest traditional links courses in the world. In addition to the 18-hole championship course, there's also a 9-hole course. The **Nairn Dunbar Golf Club,** Loch Loy Road (✆ **01667/452-741;** www.nairndunbar.com) traces its history back to 1899; it too has a fine 18-hole course.

In the Footsteps of Macbeth

Nairn is great walking country, and the tourist office will give you a map and details about the various possibilities, including hikes along the banks of the River Nairn. The best walks are the five marked **Cawdor Castle Nature Trails.** They're signposted from Cawdor Castle, of Macbeth fame, and take you along some of the loveliest and most varied wooded areas in the Highlands.

Cawdor Castle ★ CASTLE Cawdor Castle has been home to the thanes of Cawdor since the early 14th century. Although the castle was constructed 2 centuries after his time, it has nevertheless been romantically linked to Shakespeare's *Macbeth*, once the thane of Cawdor. The castle has all the architectural ingredients you'd associate with the Middle Ages: a drawbridge, an ancient tower, and fortified walls. Its severity is softened by the handsome gardens and rolling lawns. Tours of the interior reveal grand rooms filled with fine paintings, furniture, and historical artifacts. The grounds accommodate five nature trails through beautiful woodland, a 9-hole golf course, a putting green, a picnic area, shops, and a restaurant.

Between Inverness and Nairn on the B9090, off the A96, Cawdor. ☏ **01667/404-401.** www.cawdor castle.com. Admission £9 adults, £8 seniors and students, £5.50 children, free for children 4 and under. May–Sept daily 10am–5:30pm.

Where to Eat

The Boath House Restaurant ★★ SCOTTISH/CONTINENTAL This acclaimed restaurant is located within a Georgian country-house hotel (see "Where to Stay," below). Its menus are based on the finest Scottish produce coupled with luxury ingredients. Scallops, sea bass, roe deer, and partridge are variously married with truffle, tapenade, or wild mushrooms. The dining room is decorated with antique furnishings, and in the evening is bathed in candlelight. The dress code is "casual smart," and so no jeans or tennis/training shoes.

In the Boath House, Auldearn. ☏ **01667/454-896.** www.boath-house.com. Reservations recommended. 3-course lunch £30; fixed-price 6-course dinner £70. AE, DC, MC, V. Daily 1–2:30pm and 7–8:30pm. On the A96, 2 miles east of Nairn.

Cawdor Tavern MODERN SCOTTISH This atmospheric restaurant occupies what was once the carpenter's shop for Cawdor Castle (which is only about 150m/ 490 ft. away). Many visitors opt for just a drink, choosing from the selection of real ales or single-malt whiskies served in the oak-paneled bar. Others come for the food, which includes generous portions of Scottish venison, pigeon, lamb, beef, and pork, as well as scallops, sea bream, and a number of vegetarian dishes.

The Lane, Cawdor. ☏ **01667/404-777.** www.cawdortavern.co.uk. Reservations recommended for dinner. Lunch main courses £9–£15; dinner main courses £11–£19. AE, DC, MC, V. Daily noon–2:30pm and 5:30–9pm.

Shopping

Nairn's High Street has a wide variety of shops and cafes, as well as several pharmacies (drugstores) and banks. Look out in particular for the independent **Nairn Bookshop** at 97 High St. (☏ **01667/455-528;** www.nairnbookshop.co.uk); **Wee Gooseberry**, 14 High St. (☏ **01667/452-500;** www.weegooseberry.com), for clothes and toys for children and babies; and **Bike Bug,** just off High Street on Falconers Lane (☏ **01667/455-416**), for bicycles and repairs.

Just north of High Street on St. Ninian Road, **Nairn Antiques** (☏ **01667/453-303**) carries a broad range of antiques, from Scottish pottery, silver, and fine porcelain to furniture and bric-a-brac from around the world. There's a stock of Lalique crystal. Just outside Nairn, off to the south of the Forres Road (the A96), is another worthwhile antiques emporium, **Auldearn Antiques** in Dalmore Manse, Auldearn (☏ **01667/453-087**).

Also east of Nairn on the A96 is **Brodie Countryfare** in Brodie (☏ **01309/641-555;** www.brodiecountryfare.com). This is a family-owned shopping complex with vendors selling everything from Scottish knitwear, gift items, and delicatessen foodstuffs.

Entertainment & Nightlife

A good place for an evening drink and some conversation is the bar of the **Braeval Hotel,** Crescent Road (© **01667/452-341;** www.braevalhotel.co.uk)—especially when it hosts its annual **Bandstand Beer Festival.** Although a good selection of beer and cider is on tap year-round, during the festival there are over 60 Scottish and English real ales on offer, and the jollity even spills over into a marquee in the beer garden.

Clifton House, 1–3 Viewfield St. (© **01667/453-119;** www.cliftonhousenairn. co.uk), presents classical concerts by solo artists and small ensembles about once every 3 weeks between September and March. This distinguished household also operates a small B&B.

Nairn also has its own theatre, **The Little Theatre,** King Street (© **01667/452-341;** www.nairndrama.org.uk), which stages productions throughout the year. Shows usually start at 7.30pm. During the month of August, the town plays host to the **Nairn Book & Arts Festival** (© **1667/451-804;** www.nairnfestival.co.uk), which organizes author events, films, exhibitions, plays, and workshops. The festival takes over numerous venues around town, including the Little Theatre.

Where to Stay

Boath House ★ Built in 1825, this Georgian mansion has all the advantages of genteel country living: It has a library, comfortable lounges with period furniture, and is set amid 8 hectares (20 acres) of lush greenery. There's also a salon open to both guests and non-guests—offering everything from aromatherapy to galvanic slimming treatments—and an **award-winning restaurant** (see "Where to Eat," above).

Auldearn, Nairn IV12 5TE. www.boath-house.com. ©**01667/454-896.** Fax 01667/455-469. 8 units. £230–£335 double. AE, DC, MC, V. On the A96, 2 miles east of Nairn. **Amenities:** Restaurant; exercise room; spa treatments. In room: TV, hair dryer, Wi-Fi (free).

Clifton House ★★ 🎒 This intimate guesthouse occupies a vine-covered, honey-sandstone Victorian house and reflects the dynamic personality of its long-standing owner, J. Gordon Macintyre. It stands on the seafront, 3 minutes from the beach and equidistant to both golf links. The interior is crammed with antique furniture, paintings, and engravings. Guest rooms are pleasantly idiosyncratic and comfortable, and all guests participate in the evening ritual of a family-style dinner. Mr. Macintyre also organizes a series of concerts and recitals open to all-comers (see above).

1–3 Viewfield St., Nairn, Nairnshire IV4 4HW. www.cliftonhousenairn.co.uk. ©**01667/453-119.** Fax 01667/452-836. 3 units. £220 double. Rates include breakfast and dinner. AE, DC, MC, V. Head east from the town's main roundabout on the A96. **Amenities:** Guest dining room. In room: Hair dryer, no phone.

Greenlawns 🐾 This Victorian house with its pretty garden is within easy reach of the beaches and golf courses. The guest rooms are spacious yet cozy, and are traditionally furnished. Children and dogs are welcome.

13 Seafield St., Nairn IV12 4HG. www.greenlawns.uk.com. ©**01667/452-738.** Fax 01667/452-738. 6 units. £55–£90 double. AE, MC, V. Turn down Albert St. from the A96. **Amenities:** Restaurant; bar. In room: TV, no phone, Wi-Fi (free).

THE BLACK ISLE PENINSULA ★

Cromarty: 23 miles NW of Inverness (via Kessock Bridge)

The Black Isle is one of Scotland's most enchanting and unspoilt peninsulas—a land rich in history, wildlife, and rugged coastline. Part of Ross and Cromarty County, it's situated northwest of Inverness, a 20-minute drive or bus ride away. If you're traveling by car, the distance from Inverness to Cromarty (on the western tip of the Black Isle) may be only about 23 miles, but be sure to allow plenty of time for stops and country walks along the way.

There's much confusion about the name of the peninsula, because it's neither black nor an island. Many hold that the name derives from the fact that, since snow often doesn't settle here in winter, the promontory looks black while the surrounding country is white. In summer, however, the land is green and fertile, with lush vegetation and deciduous woodlands. The district also has salt mudflats, fields of broom and whin, and scattered coastal villages. The peninsula has been inhabited for 7,000 years, as the 60-odd prehistoric sites testify, and Pictish kings, whose thrones passed down through the female line, once ruled the land. Subsequently, it was the Vikings who held sway, and the existence of many gallows hills testifies to their harsh justice.

Essentials

GETTING THERE The nearest railway station is at Muir of Ord; there are frequent trains between there and Inverness. **Stagecoach** runs a bus service from Inverness (nos. 26, 26A), making stops at North Kessock, Munlochy, Avoch, Fortrose, Rosemarkie, and Cromarty. Buses depart from Inverness bus station, Farraline Park (✆ **01463/233-371,** or visit www.stagecoachbus.com for schedules). Note that there are only two buses in either direction on Sundays.

If you're driving, head to Fortrose as your first stop (see below), taking the A9 north from Inverness. (Follow the signs toward Wick.) Stay on the A9 for 4 miles, until you see the Kessock Bridge. Go over the bridge and take the second road to the right, toward Munlochy. (Fortrose is 8 miles from this turnoff.) Follow the A832 through Munlochy, and at the junction take the road right, signposted FORTROSE. Continue straight on for Avoch and Fortrose.

VISITOR INFORMATION Ask at the **Inverness Tourist Information Centre** (see "Inverness: Capital of the Highlands," earlier in this chapter) for details on the Black Isle, because the peninsula is often included on a day tour from that city.

North Kessock

The village of North Kessock is the gateway to the Black Isle, and lies 4¾ miles from Inverness on the south coast at the narrows where the Beauly Firth becomes the Moray Firth. The village sits directly across the water from Inverness. North Kessock is bypassed by the A9, which crosses the Kessock Bridge, and consequently the village itself is spared heavy traffic and is rather peaceful. Most of the village lies along its Main Street, where there are several hotels and guesthouses.

The village offers a well-known vantage point for watching bottlenose dolphins, which live in the Moray Firth—and are, in fact, the most northerly group of bottlenose dolphins in the world. Alternatively, you can look out over the Firth from the **Dolphin and Seal Centre** (✆ **01463/731-866;** www.wdcs.org.uk), located just to the north of the village off the A9, and run by the Whale and Dolphin Conservation Society. There's the added bonus here of being able to listen to the whistles and clicks of dolphins via the Centre's link-up to an underwater microphone. The Centre is open daily from June to September between 9:30am and 4:30pm.

WHERE TO EAT & STAY

North Kessock Hotel ⚓ This is a family-run hotel, overlooking Beauly Firth, the Kessock Bridge, and Ben Wyvis mountain. The rooms are very simply furnished, but guests do have the advantage of either a sea or garden view. The hotel will lend you binoculars for dolphin spotting. The restaurant is open to guests and non-guests alike. The menu offers homestyle cooking, with main courses costing £9 to £15.

Main St., North Kessock IV1 3XN. www.northkessockhotel.com. (*)01463/731-208. 5 units. £65–£100 double. DC, MC, V. **Amenities:** Restaurant; bar. *In room:* TV/DVD, hair dryer, no phone.

Fortrose ★ & Rosemarkie

On your way to Fortrose, you'll pass a celebrated wishing well, or **clootie well,** festooned with rags. Dedicated to St. Boniface, the well dates back to pagan times. Rags, wool, and even human hair have used for generations here as charms against sorcery and as tokens of penance. It's said that anyone removing a rag will inherit the misfortunes of the person who placed it there.

In the sleepy village itself are the ruins of **Fortrose Cathedral.** Founded in the 13th century, the cathedral was dedicated to St. Peter and St. Boniface. You can still see fine detailing in the 14th-century remains. If the stones scattered about don't seem adequate to fill in the gaps, it's because Cromwell's men removed many of them to help build a fort in Inverness. There are no formal opening hours; you can wander through the ruins at any time.

Fortrose adjoins **Rosemarkie,** the next village along. The two villages share the **Fortrose & Rosemarkie Golf Club** ((*) 01381/620-529; www.fortrosegolfclub. co.uk). Set on the Chanonry Ness, the course juts out into the Moray Firth and offers fine views across to Fort George on the other side (see "Exploring Inverness," above). The golf course is also renowned for the **Chanonry Point Lighthouse** at the 4th hole. The lighthouse was designed by Alan Stevenson (the uncle of writer Robert Louis Stevenson) and came into operation in 1846. Fortrose and Rosemarkie also share the Chanonry Sailing Club, which hosts an annual regatta, bringing entries from all over Scotland.

The site of the village of Rosemarkie has been inhabited since the Bronze Age. A center of Pictish culture, the town saw the arrival of the first Christian missionaries, and it's reported that St. Moluag founded a monastery here in the 6th century. The **Groam House Museum** on High Street ((*) 01381/620-961; www.groamhouse. org.uk) tells the story of the region from prehistoric times. The museum's prize exhibits are 15 carved Pictish stones, some dating back to the 8th century A.D. when the area was a major center of early Christianity. The pride of the collection is the **Rosemarkie cross-slab ★**, decorated with enigmatic Pictish symbols. Visitors can also learn about the legendary prophet Brahan Seer, who was buried alive at Chanonry Point. The museum is open daily May to October Monday through Saturday from 10am to 5pm and Sunday from 2 to 4:30pm. In November, the museum opens only on the weekends from 2 to 4pm. From December to April, the museum is closed. Admission is free.

At the far end of the village you will find signposts for the mysterious **Fairy Glen.** This offers one of the most picturesque walks in the Black Isle.

Cromarty

Cromarty stands at the tip of the peninsula, where the North and South Sutors (the high rocky outcrops) guard the entrance to the Cromarty Firth, the second-deepest inland-waterway estuary in Europe. The village itself is well worth exploring, with its narrow lanes of terraced cottages that seem to hunch against the prevailing north winds. The town was once a flourishing port, and there are numerous larger merchants' houses, many of which are superb examples of domestic 18th-century architecture. In more recent times, the coast here has been home to a large facility for the manufacture and maintenance of North Sea oil platforms. The remnants of this industry can still be seen in the waters of Cromarty Firth, on the northern side of the town.

Cromarty is also noteworthy, though, for giving the world a famous son: Hugh Miller. Born here in 1802, in a little thatched cottage, Miller worked as a stonemason as a young man, but in time, though self-taught, he came to be recognized as an expert in the field of geology, as well as a powerful man of letters in Scotland. **Hugh Miller's Cottage,** Church Street (✆ **01381/600-245;** www.nts.org.uk/Property/34 and www.hughmiller.org), contains many of his personal belongings and collections of geological specimens. From April to September, it's open daily from noon to 5pm; in October on Tuesdays, Thursdays, and Fridays from noon to 5pm; and it's closed from November to March. Admission is £6 for adults, £5 for students and seniors, and £15.50 per family.

WHERE TO EAT & STAY

Royal Hotel Cromarty   The only hotel in town sits on an embankment overlooking one of the deepest estuaries in Europe. Around 1940, the British navy combined a series of waterfront buildings into living quarters for sailors. Today, the hotel is a cozy haven with wood-burning stoves and open fireplaces. The guest rooms are traditionally furnished. The dining room, which spills into a conservatory, offers lunch and dinner daily, with a menu of homely dishes such as steaks, stroganoff, burgers, and crepes.

Marine Terrace, Cromarty IV11 8YN. www.royalcromartyhotel.co.uk.✆ **01381/600-217.** Fax 01381/600-813. 10 units. £95–£125 double. AE, DC, MC, V. Bus: 26 or 26A from Inverness. **Amenities:** Restaurant; 2 bars. *In room:* TV, hair dryer, no phone.

SUTHERLAND

Sutherland has more sheep than people (a 20-to-1 ratio). It's genuinely off the beaten track, but if you have time to travel this far, you'll find it perhaps the most beautiful county in Scotland, with lochs and rivers, heather-covered moors and mountains—in all 2,000 sq. miles of unspoilt countryside. It may not offer many "attractions," but it's a wonderful setting for outdoor activities such as hiking, golf, and fishing.

Sutherland, situated to the northwest of Inverness, has three coastlines—on the north and west is the Atlantic, while to the east is the North Sea. Most villages have only 100 or so doughty inhabitants. Sutherland bore the brunt of the notorious 19th-century Highland Clearances, when many residents were driven out of their ancestral crofts. Some made their way to the New World. In certain remote glens, you can still see the ruins of the crofting villages they left behind.

Dornoch ★

The ancient cathedral city of Dornoch, 63 miles northwest of Inverness and 219 miles northwest of Edinburgh, is Sutherland's major town and the area's most interesting stop. Its most important landmark is **Dornoch Cathedral** (see below). Dornoch is also known for its sandy beaches, which are fine for long walks, but less good for swimming: The sea is icy cold for much of the year, even though a curious meander of the Gulf Stream as it bypasses northern Scotland keeps the local climate balmier than you'd expect.

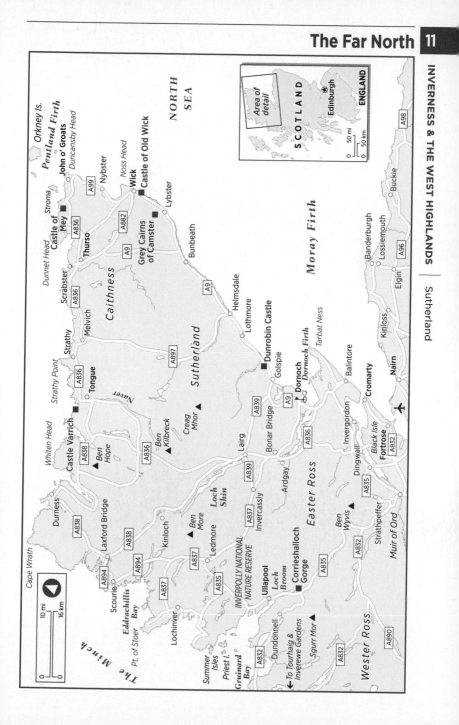

343

A **Tourist Information Centre** is at the Square (© 01862/810-400; www. visitdornoch.com). It's open November to March daily 10am to 1:30pm; April to May and September, Monday to Saturday 10am to 5pm and Sunday 10am to 4pm; June to July, Monday to Saturday 10am to 4:30pm and Sunday 10am to 4pm; August, Monday to Saturday 10am to 6pm and Sunday 10am to 4pm; and October, Monday to Saturday 10am to 5pm. From Inverness bus station at Farraline Park, off Academy Street (call © 01463/233-371 for schedules), three local companies run daily **buses** to Dornoch: Stagecoach, Scottish Citylink, and Highland Country Buses. The trip takes between 60 and 90 minutes.

EXPLORING DORNOCH

The village of Dornoch has long been known for its golf club on the sheltered shores of Dornoch Firth, the northernmost first-class course in the world. The turf of the **Royal Dornoch Golf Club,** Golf Road (© 01862/810-219), is considered sacred by aficionados; golf was first played here by monks in 1614. The club itself was founded in 1877, and a royal charter was granted by Edward VII in 1906. Prince Andrew and the Duchess of Sutherland are both members. Its SSS (Standard Scratch Score) is 73; its par is 70 for an 18-hole yardage of 6,185. Golf clubs and trolleys can be rented, and there's also a caddy service.

Dornoch Cathedral, Castle Street, was built in the 13th century and partially destroyed by fire in 1570. It has undergone many restorations, but its fine 13th-century stonework remains intact. The cathedral is famous for its modern stained-glass windows—three are in memory of Andrew Carnegie, the American steel magnate. The cathedral is open daily from 9am to dusk.

In the cathedral's cemetery, where the marketplace used to be, is the **Plaiden Ell,** a medieval measure for cloth. (An *ell* was a unit of measure equaling about 96cm/38 in.) The Ell is carved in stone in a flat shape similar to a tombstone's, but with two pieces of metal rising about 5cm (2 in.) above the level of the stone. The distance between those two pieces of metal is an ell. In one of the gardens is the 1722 **witch's stone** marking the spot where the last burning of a so-called witch took place in Scotland.

Shoppers should check out the **Dornoch Craft Centre,** Town Jail, Castle Street (© 01862/810-555), in the center of town opposite the cathedral. You can wander through the sections devoted to crafts, jewelry, and pottery, and then visit the Textile Hall and browse through the range of knitwear, tartans, mohair goods, and tweeds.

If the weather is fair, Dornoch is a good place for country strolls—the town is flanked by miles of clean sand sloping down into chilly waters. You often see migrant birds on these beaches.

At **Embo,** some 3 miles north of the beaches of Dornoch, are the remains of two funereal vaults believed to date from around 2000 B.C. Another 1¾ miles north of Embo are the shores of lovely **Loch Fleet,** where there's a meager ruin of **Skelbo Castle** on a lonely grassy mound. At one time, in the 14th century, Skelbo was a powerful fortification.

WHERE TO EAT & STAY

Dornoch Castle Hotel This unusual family-run hotel, close to the Royal Dornoch Golf Course, occupies what was once the residence of the bishops of Caithness. Located in the center of Dornoch, it dates back to the late 15th or early 16th century. Today, its winding stairs, labyrinthine corridors, and impenetrable cellars have been converted into a hotel and restaurant. The guest rooms are in both the original building and an extension overlooking the garden. The best rooms have four-poster beds, high ceilings, and views looking out over the cathedral. The restaurant serves mussels from Dornoch Firth, salmon from Loch Duart, and lamb and beef from local farms.

Castle St., Dornoch IV25 3SD. www.dornochcastlehotel.com. © **01862/810-216.** Fax 01862/810-981. 18 units. £94–£248 double. AE, MC, V. **Amenities:** Restaurant; bar. *In room:* TV.

Sutherland House SCOTTISH   This long-established restaurant is the best choice in the area for good traditional Scottish cooking, rather than the international fine-dining style of cuisine you find in so many places. The dishes on offer include the inevitable haggis, fine Scottish beefsteak, and the freshest seafood. The fresh mussels are particularly good, and the suprême of chicken Glenmorangie and the saddle of venison are recommended as well. There's also a wide selection of vegetarian options. The homemade desserts are worth saving space for.

Argyle St., Dornoch IV25 3LA. © **01862/811-023.** www.sutherland-house.co.uk. Main courses £8–£15. MC, V. Daily noon–2:30pm and 5:30–10pm.

2 Quail ★ 🏠   Occupying a Victorian townhouse in the middle of Dornoch, this is one of the best traditional bed-and-breakfast style hotels in the north of Scotland. It's no surprise to learn that one of the owners trained at London's Ritz Hotel. The attention to detail and service of a hotel are combined with a homey atmosphere and cozy rooms. You can relax in the library in front of the fire, or retire to your comfortable bedroom, which is decorated in muted colors and furnished in keeping with the period of the house.

Castle St., Dornich IV25 3SN. www.2quail.com. © **01862/811-811.** 3 units. £100–£130 double. AE, MC, V. **Amenities:** Lounge. *In room:* TV, hair dryer, Wi-Fi (free).

Golspie

This family resort town with a golf course is easily reached on the A9, and the journey is worth it for the pretty setting, looking out across the water to the Dornoch Firth, with a crescent of sandy beach. Situated some 228 miles northwest of Edinburgh and 72 miles northwest of Inverness, Golspie is most often visited, however, for the towering Dunrobin Castle.

EXPLORING GOLSPIE

Dunrobin Castle ★★ CASTLE   Home of the earls and dukes of Sutherland, Dunrobin is largest of the great houses in the northern Highlands, dating in part from the early 13th century. Some of the castle's 180 rooms are open to the public—the ornately furnished dining room, a billiard room, and the room with the gilded four-poster bed where Queen Victoria slept when she visited in 1872. The formal gardens were laid out in the manner of Versailles. There's also a museum in the grounds, which contains many relics from the Sutherland family. Falconry displays are put on at 11am and 2:30pm most days.

Golspie, Sutherland KW10 6SF. ⅔ mile northeast of Golspie on the A9. © **01408/633-177.** www.dunrobincastle.co.uk. Admission £9 adults, £7.50 students and seniors, and £5 children 5-16, £24 families. Apr-May and Sept-Oct Mon-Sat 10:30am-4:30pm, Sun noon-4:30pm; June-Aug daily 10:30am-5:30pm. Last entrance 30 min. before closing.

WHERE TO EAT & STAY

Golf Links Hotel   The best place to stay in Golspie dates from the early 1900s, when it was built as the rectory for the local minister. Many of the guests are golfers drawn to the nearby Golspie, Royal Dornoch, and Brora courses. The guest rooms are simply but comfortably furnished; each has a mid-size bathroom. The restaurant offers reasonably priced home cooking as well as fine views out of the windows towards Ben Bhraggie.

Church St., Golspie KW10 6TT. www.golflinkshotel.co.uk. (C) **01408/633-408.** Fax 01408/634-184. 9 units. £70–£80 double. MC, V. **Amenities:** Restaurant; 2 bars. In room: TV, DVD, hair dryer, no phone, Wi-Fi (free).

Tongue

Heading north along the A836, you cross high moors and brooding peaks to Tongue, 257 miles northwest of Edinburgh and 101 miles northwest of Inverness. For the nature lover and hiker, there's a lot to see, from the mighty cliffs of **Clo Mor,** near Cape Wrath (known for its large colonies of puffins), to waterfalls such as **Eas-Coul-Aulin** (the highest in Britain) and the **Falls of Shin,** where you can see salmon leap. Great mountains, including **Ben Loyal** (known as the queen of Scottish mountains), suddenly rise from a barren landscape. Any of the district's **Tourist Information Centres,** including the one in Dornoch, can provide a map of the local hills, valleys, and trails. The one closest to the places mentioned above is the office on Main Street in Bettyhill ((C) **01641/521-342**), a coastal village about 15 miles from Tongue.

West of Tongue, on a promontory, stands the ruin of **Castle Varrich,** said to have been built by the Vikings. Possibly dating from the 14th century, this castle was once the stronghold of the MacKays. It's now a good place for a walk.

A rather dramatic hike from Tongue leads you to the **Kyle of Tongue,** crossed by a narrow causeway. Protected from the wild and raging sea nearby, this is a long, shallow inlet. At low tide, wearing a pair of boots, you can wade out to Rabbit Island, lying at the mouth of Kyle of Tongue. You pass towering cliffs, sandy bays, odd rock formations, and deserted rocky islets.

WHERE TO EAT & STAY

Ben Loyal Hotel This small family-run hotel offers simple but comfortable guest rooms, some of which have fine views over the Kyle of Tongue to Ben Loyal itself. The hotel occupies buildings that were once a post office, a shop, a bakery, and some stables. The restaurant offers home-cooked meals based around local beef and produce grown on the grounds. The hotel also has its own fishing boats, and so the lobster on the menu doesn't come any fresher.

Main St., Tongue IV27 4XE. www.benloyal.co.uk. (C) **01847/611-216.** Fax 01847/611-212. 11 units. £70–£100 double. MC, V. **Amenities:** Restaurant; bar. In room: TV, hair dryer.

Tongue Hotel ★ Since Queen Victoria's day, the best place to stay in town has been the Tongue Hotel, 1 mile north of the village center beside the road leading to Durness. The hotel faces onto the Kyle of Tongue. Built of gray stone in 1850, it began life as a hunting lodge for the Duke of Sutherland, and retains much of its original character today. Both the public rooms and the guest rooms are decorated in Victorian style, with flowered curtains and plush upholstery.

The quality of the restaurant's food is well known locally. A moderately priced dinner usually includes a choice of game or fresh fish caught in the region. Affordable bar meals are served in the popular pub, with an open fireplace and an impressive collection of whiskies. There is also a more sedate cocktail lounge.

Tongue, Sutherland IV27 4XD. www.tonguehotel.co.uk. (C) **01847/611-206.** Fax 01847/611-345. 19 units. £80–£120 double. MC, V. **Amenities:** Restaurant; 2 bars. In room: TV, hair dryer.

CAITHNESS: UNSPOILED COUNTRY

It doesn't look like the Highlands at all, but Caithness is the northernmost county of mainland Scotland, where the ancient landscape is gentle and rolling. Within its 700 square miles, there are many relics of the Stone Age—most notably the enigmatic **Grey Cairns of Camster,** which date from 4000 B.C. The county is dotted with cairns, mysterious stone rows and circles, and standing stones. The Vikings once occupied this place too, with its natural harbors, craggy cliffs and stacks, and quiet coves; many of the place names derive from Old Norse. Caithness also has churches from the Middle Ages, as well as towering castles on cliff tops. The late Queen Mother's home, the **Castle of Mey,** which originally dates from 1570, is situated between John o' Groats and Thurso.

Rich in bird and animal life, Caithness is unspoiled country. Fishing draws many people to the area: wild brown trout are found in some 100 lochs, along with salmon in the Thurso and Wick rivers. Most people head for Caithness with **John o' Groats** as their final destination. John o' Groats is popularly referred to as the northernmost tip of the British mainland. In actual fact, Dunnet Head is farther north by a few miles.

Scrabster, a ferry harbor, is the main car-and-passenger service that operates all year to the Orkney Islands (see chapter 13 for more information). Boats offer day trips from here as well in the summer.

Wick

The famous old herring port of Wick, on the eastern coastline of Caithness, 287 miles northwest of Edinburgh and 126 miles northwest of Inverness, is a popular stop for those heading north to explore what's often called the John o' Groats Peninsula. The town itself, though, has some claim as a holiday resort. Robert Louis Stevenson spent part of his boyhood in Wick when his father worked here on an engineering project. Today, a sleepy nostalgia hangs over the town. There's a daily bus and rail service from Inverness; from there, train connections are possible via Edinburgh, Glasgow, or Stirling.

The **Wick Heritage Centre,** 20 Bank Row (© 01955/605-393; www.wick heritage.org), has many exhibits relating to Wick's herring-fishing industry in its heyday. From Easter to October, it's open Monday to Saturday 10am to 5pm; last entrance is at 3:45pm. Admission is £3 for adults and 50p for children 5 to 16.

Wick also produces its own whisky. The **Pulteney Distillery,** Huddart Street (© 01955/602-371; www.oldpulteney.com) has been in operation since 1826. A tour will take you on a journey back to discover the history and "art" of whisky making. A wide range of products, including the single malts produced on-site, are on sale in the distillery shop. Costing £4, tours are offered from Monday to Friday at 11am and 2pm; the tour time is 45 minutes. For real enthusiasts, there's also a "Master Class" tour costing £15 and involving three tastings, and a "Connoisseur" tour costing £30 and involving tasting the full range of Pulteney whiskies. These two tours must be booked in advance.

The most visited sites in the area are the two megalithic **Grey Cairns of Camster,** 6¼ miles north of Lybster on the Watten Road off the A9. The ruins of the **Castle of Old Wick** are also worth exploring, and they're always accessible. The castle is located just off the A9, 1½ miles south of Wick. Once known as Castle Olipant, the ruined structure dates back to the 14th century. You can still see three floors of the old castle rising up on a rocky promontory.

WHERE TO EAT & STAY

Breadalbane House Hotel This late-Victorian house on the southern outskirts of town, a 5-minute walk from the center, was once the home of a furniture maker (who's said to have done all the interior woodwork personally). It's now an unpretentious guesthouse with smartly decorated rooms. The friendly bar is a good place for a quiet drink on weekday nights, but comes alive on Saturday evenings when there are live music acts.

20 Breadalbane Crescent, Wick KW1 5AQ. www.breadalbanehousehotel.com. © **01955/603-911.** Fax 01955/603-911. 10 units. £70–£85 double. AE, MC, V. **Amenities:** Bar; babysitting. *In room:* TV, no phone, Wi-Fi (free).

Mackay's This refurbished hotel on the south shore of the River Wick is the home of the Lamont family, who have welcomed guests here for more than 40 years. All bedrooms are nicely decorated and have well-maintained bathrooms. Located in the heart of Wick, the hotel is a short walk to the Heritage Centre as well as to the swimming pool and leisure center. The restaurant, specializing in traditional Scottish fare (including locally caught seafood), offers both lunch and dinner, with main courses costing from £11 to £23.

Union St. (opposite Caithness General Hospital), Wick KW1 5ED. www.mackayshotel.co.uk. © **01955/602-323.** Fax 01955/605-930. 30 units. £105–£130 double. AE, MC, V. Closed Jan 1–2. **Amenities:** Restaurant; 2 bars. *In room:* TV, hair dryer, Wi-Fi (free).

John o' Groats

John o' Groats, 17 miles to the north of Wick, is the northern counterpart to Land's End, at the tip of the Cornish peninsula in England. The southern tip of England is 879 miles south of John o' Groats. From here, there are views north to the Orkney Islands and the Pentland Firth.

John o' Groats was named after a Dutch ferryman, Jan de Groot. His tombstone can still be seen at Cabisbay Church. The town abounds with souvenir shops, some selling small Arctic cowrie shells, once used as decoration by the first settlers in Caithness. You can take interesting walks along the coast to **Duncansby Head,** 1¼ miles east—one of the most dramatic coastlines in this part of Scotland. Many species of seabirds, including puffins, live among the jagged cliffs. A road leads out to a lighthouse perched on the cliffs; from there you can enjoy the panoramic view over Pentland Firth. These turbulent waters have claimed the lives of many mariners, with some 400 wrecks reported in the past century and a half.

The late Queen Mother's legacy to Scotland is the restored **Castle of Mey ★★**, lying 6 miles west of John o' Groats on the A836 (© **01847/851-473**; www.castleofmey.org.uk). Her Majesty first saw the castle in 1952 when she was mourning the death of her husband, King George VI. Hearing that it was to be abandoned, she set out to restore both the castle and its gardens. She returned every summer for the rest of her life, and one of her heirs, Prince Charles, now follows in her footsteps.

Looking out over the Pentland Firth towards the Orkney Islands, the castle was constructed on a Z-plan between 1566 and 1572, with jutting towers and corbeled turrets. It was built by the 4th Earl of Caithness and remained the seat of his family for a century. The castle is furnished just as it was when the Queen Mother departed

In an old converted country school, the Lyth Arts Centre (✆ 01955/641-270; www.lytharts.org.uk) stages performances of innovative and experimental works by small touring companies, from drama and dance to jazz, folk, and new music. There's also a permanent collection of art related to northern Scotland, and July and August bring touring exhibitions of contemporary art, photography, and some crafts. Special exhibitions are open daily from 10am to 6pm; admission is £2 for adults, £1 for seniors, and 50p for students and children 5 to 15. The center stages performances year-round; they usually start at 8pm. Advance booking is necessary for all shows, and so call ahead. Tickets typically cost £10 for adults, £8 for seniors, and £6 for students and children. Coffee, tea, and light snacks are available on performance evenings. The arts center is signposted, 4 miles off the A99, between Wick and John o' Groats.

from it. You can even see her gumboots beside the dog bowl and her blue coat hanging on the back of a chair. The walled kitchen garden in July is one of the most beautiful private gardens in Scotland.

The castle and gardens are open from May 1 to July 28 and August 8 to September 30 from 9:20am to last entry at 4pm daily. Admission is £9.75 for adults, £8.75 for seniors, and £5 for children 12 and under, with a family ticket costing £25. Tickets for the gardens and grounds only cost £5 each, for all ages. Allow at least 1½ hours for a visit.

John o' Groats has its own **ferry terminal** (✆ 01955/611-353; www.jogferry. co.uk), from where a passenger-only ferry service operates to Orkney everyday from May to September. The Orkney Islands are just a 45-minute sail away across the Pentland Firth (see chapter 13). The ferry company also offers tour packages that include bus trips around the Orkneys once you're there.

WHERE TO EAT & STAY

Seaview Hotel   The family-run Seaview is located only a few minutes' walk from where the ferries depart for the Orkneys. It's one of the very few places to stay in the vicinity of John o' Groats, and you can't miss it in the middle of a windswept landscape beside the town's only highway. Built in the 1950s, it's a simple but friendly place. The guest rooms are basic but clean, and reasonably priced lunches and dinners are available in the bar.

John o' Groats KW1 4YR. www.seaviewjohnogroats.co.uk. ✆/fax **01955/611-220.** 10 units. £40–£60 double. MC, V. **Amenities:** Restaurant; bar. *In room:* TV, hair dryer, no phone.

Thurso

Many visitors drive through the northern port of Thurso as they're heading for Scrabster, where ferries leave for the Orkney Islands (see chapter 13). The town, located on the River Thurso, is only mildly interesting; it's used mainly as a refueling stop for those who've made it this far north. It remains, however, a bustling holiday resort with a still-active fishing fleet. In the center, many restored sandstone town houses date from the 1700s.

Once an important Viking stronghold, Thurso—meaning "river of the god Thor"—had its greatest power and prestige in the 11th century, when it was ruled by Thorfinn, who defeated King Duncan's nephew in 1040. In medieval times, Thurso became the major trading town between Scotland and the Norse countries.

To the west are the cliffs of Holborn Head and Dunnet Head, where there's a lighthouse. Many visitors walk out to the northern point of mainland Britain for its panoramic views of the Orkneys. Thurso is 133 miles northwest of Inverness, 21 miles northwest of Wick, and 20 miles west of John o' Groats.

If you'd like to explore by bike, head for **Sandra's Back Packer Hostel,** 24 Princes St. (© **01847/894-575;** www.sandras-backpackers.co.uk). Open daily 9am to midnight. Accommodation rates are from £16 per bed, per night.

WHERE TO EAT & STAY

The Park Hotel With an almost Scandinavian style, this modern hotel is functional rather than stylish, but is a good place to base yourself for exploring the countryside around. Both the lounge and the restaurant offer reasonably priced meals. Children are welcome.

Thurso KW14 8RE. www.parkhotelthurso.co.uk. © **01847/893-251.** Fax 01847/804-044. www.park hotelthurso.co.uk. 21 units. £60–£65 double. AE, DC, MC, V. Closed Jan 1–3. Located on the right-hand side of the A9 on approach to the Thurso town center. **Amenities:** Restaurant; 2 bars. *In room:* TV, hair dryer.

The Weigh Inn & Lodges ★ This modern hotel overlooks the Pentland Firth, with views that extend (on a clear day) to the Orkney Islands. Many travelers planning to take the morning car ferry to the Orkney Islands stay overnight here. The rooms are simple but comfortable enough. There are three bars, including one for sports fans, where satellite coverage of major events is beamed in on the large screen.

Burnside, Thurso KW14 TUG. www.weighinn.co.uk. © **01847/893-722.** Fax 01847/892-112. 16 units. £50–£95 double. MC, V. Located on the outskirts of Thurso, at the junction of the A9 to Scrabster Harbour and the main artery leading to the western coast of the Highlands. **Amenities:** Restaurant; 3 bars. *In room:* TV, Wi-Fi (free).

Ullapool ★

Ullapool is the largest village in Wester Ross, and is situated 59 miles northwest of Inverness and 238 miles north of Glasgow. It was built by the British Fishery Society in 1788 as a port for herring fishers and is still a busy harbor. The original town plan, designed by Thomas Telford, hasn't been changed, and many of the buildings look much as they did at the time of their construction. Ullapool has long been an embarkation point for travelers crossing the Minch, a section of the North Atlantic separating Scotland from the Outer Hebrides. Weather permitting, at least two ferries depart every day for Stornoway on the Isle of Lewis (though only one on Sundays).

EXPLORING ULLAPOOL

Ullapool was founded on the shores of **Loch Broom,** with rugged mountains rising up in its hinterland. For those interested in conquering Munros (mountains over 3,000 feet), these include the peaks of An Teallach to the south and Beinn Dearg to the east.

One of the most dramatic and scenic drives in this part of Scotland is from Ullapool to the village of Lochiner (a 40-mile run north following the signposts). Take the A835 north from Ullapool, enjoying the views of Loch Broom as you go along.

You'll pass the hamlet of Armair on Loch Kanaird, and then come to the **Inverpolly National Nature Reserve,** comprising some 10,935 hectares (27,000 acres). As well as lochs and lochans (many with tiny islands), you can also see the peaks of Cul Mor (849m/2,785 ft.), Cul Beag (769m/2,523 ft.), and Stac Pollaidth (612m/2,008 ft.). It's good country for watching golden eagles and peregrine falcons during the breeding season.

At **Knockan** (www.knockan-crag.co.uk), 13 miles north of Ullapool, you can explore the landscape that first led geologists in the 19th century to theorize about plate tectonics. Here you can see "the Moine Thrust," which runs through the crag; geologists observed that the schists at the top of the crag were older than the limestone lower down. The colliding of the great plates of the earth's crust had caused the planes of rock to buckle, creating a fault where older rocks became exposed to the surface. A signposted nature trail along the cliff also offers most dramatic views of the countryside and is the best place to observe the area's flora and fauna.

Much of the countryside north of Knockan has now been designated North West Highlands Geopark (www.northwest-highlands-geopark.org.uk) by UNESCO on account of its special scientific interest. To explore farther, continue north on the A835 and at the Ledmore junction, take the A837 to the left, passing along **Loch Awe,** with the mountain peaks of Canisp (847m/2,779 ft.) and Ben More Assynt (984m/3,228 ft.) forming a backdrop. Eventually, you reach the spectacular 6¼-mile-long **Loch Assynt.**

You can take a number of day trips from Ullapool, including a jaunt to the nature reserve at **Corrieshalloch Gorge,** 12 miles to the southeast, along the A835 at Braemore. From this point, the Falls of Measach plunge 45m (148 ft.) into a 1-mile wooded gorge. A bridge over the chasm and a viewing platform offer panoramic views of the spectacular scenery.

Another interesting excursion is to the **Inverewe Gardens** (✆ **0844/493-2225;** www.nts.org.uk/Property/36). An exotic mix of plants from the South Pacific, the Himalayas, and South America gives the gardens year-round color. They can be reached along the A832, 6¼ miles northeast of Gairloch. Opening times are daily, April 10am to 5pm, May 10am to 5:30pm, June to August 10am to 6pm, September 10am to 5pm, and October 10am to 4pm. Admission is £9 for adults, £6.50 for seniors and children 5 to 15, £22 per family. From November to March, the visitor center is closed, but the gardens can still be visited from 10am to 3pm daily; during this period, admission is by donation.

From either Ullapool or Achiltibuie, you can take excursions in season to the **Summer Isles ★★,** a beautiful group of almost uninhabited islands off the coast. They get their name because sheep are transported here in summer for grazing; the islands are a mecca for bird-watchers. Boat schedules vary, depending on weather conditions. Information is available from the **Tourist Information Centre** at 6 Argyle Street (✆ **0845/225-5121**).

WHERE TO EAT & STAY

Dromnan Guest House ⚑   Mrs. MacDonald's 1970s guesthouse is a homey place on the southern outskirts of town, a 10-minute walk from the center. It's very well maintained, and Mrs. MacDonald describes the decor as a combination of Marks & Spencer department store goods and Shand-Kydd wallpapers and fabrics (designed by the mother of the late Princess Diana).

Garve Rd., Ullapool IV26 2SX. www.dromnan.com. ✆ **01854/612-333.** Fax 01854/613-364. 7 units. £65–£75 double. MC, V. **Amenities:** Access to nearby pool. *In room:* TV, hair dryer, no phone, Wi-Fi (free).

Royal Hotel The Royal sits on a knoll overlooking the harborfront. Designed with curved walls and large sheets of glass, it was reconstructed in 1961 from a 19th-century building. As a result, over half of the well-furnished guest rooms have balconies looking out onto Loch Broom. The restaurant offers an Italian menu, though local seafood does feature prominently. A three-course dinner costs £24.

Garve Rd., Ullapool IV26 2SY. www.royalhotel-ullapool.com. (*)**01854/612-181.** Fax 01854/612-951. 55 units. £84–£145 double. MC, V. Closed Nov to early Mar. **Amenities:** Restaurant; 2 bars; access to nearby pool; room service. *In room:* TV, hair dryer (on request), Wi-Fi (free).

THE HEBRIDEAN ISLANDS

12

Today, the Inner Hebrides are surprisingly accessible. A bridge takes you to Skye, and it's only a short ferry hop to Mull, so there's little to hinder visitors seeking luxury mini-breaks or challenging mountains to climb. On the very edge of Europe, the Outer Hebrides—Lewis, Harris, the Uists, and Barra—face the unforgiving winds of the Atlantic, yet are rich with archaeological treasures, clean beaches, and diverse wildlife.

SIGHTSEEING Your last stop before departing for the islands is the picture-postcard **Eilean Donan Castle** near the **Kyle of Lochalsh.** Across the bridge on **Skye,** head up to the **Old Man of Storr,** an extraordinary stone pinnacle on a mountainside. A ferry to Harris and Lewis takes you to the home of **tweed,** where you can visit the cottage of one of the 600 weavers. On **Mull,** visit **Torosay Castle & Gardens,** or take a boat across to the musical **Fingal's Cave** on **Staffa.**

EATING & DRINKING Gourmets flock to Skye to experience the Hebridean take on fine dining at the **Toravaig** and **Duisdale Hotels,** or the Michelin-starred **Kinloch Lodge.** Whisky enthusiasts make the pilgrimage to the **Tobermory Distillery** on Mull or Skye's **Talisker Distillery.** And the pub at the **Isle of Barra Hotel**—the most westerly in Scotland—is renowned as the "last dram before America."

HISTORY Preservation and tradition are vital to Hebridean life. The wonderfully intact Neolithic standing stones of **Callanish** on Lewis are the Hebrides' answer to Stonehenge. For quiet contemplation, you can stay at **Iona Abbey** (the religious community was founded here by St. Columba in A.D. 563). And on Skye, a visit to **Dunvegan Castle** is a must: Its massive walls have ensured the unbroken residence of the chiefs of Clan MacLeod for 800 years and counting.

NATURE Don't forget to pack your binoculars on your way to the islands. You'll need to keep your eyes peeled for **otters** on Skye, while guided walks on **Eigg** make it easier to spot **whales and porpoises** offshore. In early summer, observe **seals** with their pups at the breeding colonies on **Coll and Tyree.** Bird-watchers take a cruise from Dervaig on Mull, to the **Treshnish Isles,** a sanctuary for **puffins** and guillemots, and botanists make for **Barra**—reputed to have some 1,000 varieties of wild flowers.

THE best TRAVEL EXPERIENCES IN THE HEBRIDES

o **Explore Colonsay on two wheels:** Rent a bike from the Isle of Colonsay Hotel, and cycle at leisure around the 20 square miles of this tranquil island. See p. 379.

o **Stroll round the gorgeous Armadale Castle Gardens:** Take a guided walk or amble along at your own pace around these lush gardens in a sheltered corner of Skye. When you've finished, recuperate with afternoon tea in the stable-block cafe. See p. 363.

o **Wonder at the views from the Cuillin Hills:** These jagged peaks on the western side of Skye are a mecca for rock climbers, and a rewarding destination for walkers. See p. 356.

o **Enjoy the intimacy of the Mull Little Theatre:** Book in advance to avoid disappointment, because the smallest professional theatre in Britain seats only 43 people inside a former stables building. See p. 374.

o **Marvel at the winter spectacle at Balranald Nature Reserve:** This sanctuary on North Uist attracts bird-watchers in their droves to see the thousands of chattering Barnacle geese that winter there. See p. 387.

KYLE OF LOCHALSH

204 miles NW of Edinburgh; 82 miles SW of Inverness; 125 miles N of Oban

The popular Kyle of Lochalsh is the gateway to the Isle of Skye, which is now linked to the mainland by a road bridge. You can drive the length of Skye in a day, returning to the mainland by night if you want.

Essentials

GETTING THERE   Three trains per day (one on Sun) arrive from Inverness, taking about 2½ hours. For schedules, call © **08457/484-950,** or log on to www.scotrail.co.uk or www.nationalrail.co.uk.

Only **Scottish Citylink** (© **08705/808-080;** www.citylink.co.uk) coaches arrive daily from Glasgow at the Kyle of Lochalsh (trip time: 5 hours).

If you're driving from Fort William, head north along the A82 to Invergarry, where you cut west onto the A87 to the Kyle of Lochalsh.

VISITOR INFORMATION   The **Tourist Information Centre** is at the Kyle of Lochalsh Car Park (© **01599/534-276;** www.visitlochalsh.co.uk). It's open April to June, Monday to Saturday 9am to 5:30pm; July and August, Monday to Saturday 9am to 7pm and Sunday 10am to 4pm; September and October, Monday to Friday 9am to 5pm; and November to March, Monday to Friday 9am to 5pm and Saturday 10am to 4pm.

Exploring Kyle of Lochalsh

Eilean Donan Castle CASTLE   This romantic castle was built in 1214 as a defense against the Danes. In ruins for 200 years, it was restored by Colonel MacRae, of Clan MacRae, in 1932 and is now a clan war memorial and museum, containing

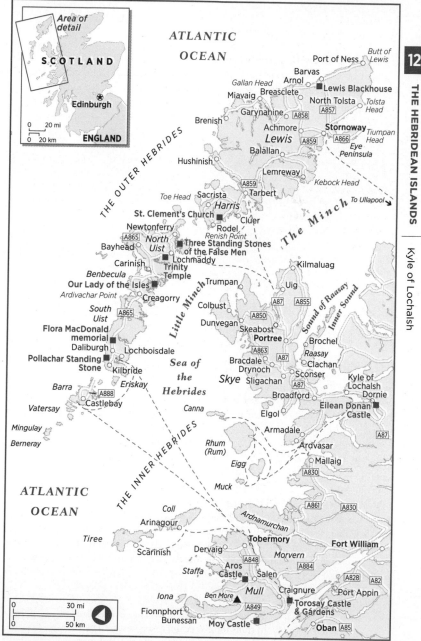

The Hebrides

ATLANTIC OCEAN

Butt of Lewis
Port of Ness
Barvas
Gallan Head Arnol
Miavaig Breasclete ■ Lewis Blackhouse
North Tolsta *Tolsta Head*
Garynahine A858 A857
Brenish
Achmore **Stornoway** *Tiumpan Head*
Lewis A859 A866
Balallan *Eye Peninsula*

Hushinish
Lemreway
Kebock Head

A859
Toe Head Sacrista Tarbert
St. Clement's Church *Harris* Cluer
Newtonferry Rodel *The Minch* To Ullapool
A865 *North* Renish Point
Bayhead *Uist* ■ Three Standing Stones
of the False Men
Carinish Lochmaddy Kilmaluag
Benbecula Trinity
Temple Uig
Our Lady of the Isles Trumpan A87 A855
Ardivachar Point Creagorry
Colbust *Sound of Raasay*
South A850 *Inner Sound*
Uist Dunvegan Skeabost
A865 **Portree** Brochel
Flora MacDonald Bracdale *Raasay*
memorial A863 A87 Clachan
Daliburgh Drynoch Sconser
Pollachar Standing Lochboisdale Sligachan Kyle of
Stone Kilbride *Skye* A87 Lochalsh
Barra Eriskay Broadford Dornie
Sea of A888 ■ Eilean Donan
Vatersay Castlebay *the* Castle
Mingulay *Hebrides* Canna A87
Berneray Elgol
Armadale
Rhum Ardvasar
THE INNER HEBRIDES *(Rum)*
Eigg Mallaig
A830
Muck

ATLANTIC OCEAN

Coll A861 A830
Arinagour *Ardnamurchan*
Tiree **Tobermory** **Fort William**
Scarinish Dervaig *Morvern*
Staffa Aros A848 A884
Castle Salen A828 A82
Iona *Ben More* *Mull* Craignure Port Appin
Fionnphort A849 Torosay Castle
Bunessan **Moy Castle** & Gardens
Oban A85

Area of detail

SCOTLAND

Edinburgh

0 20 mi
0 20 km **ENGLAND**

THE OUTER HEBRIDES

Little Minch

0 30 mi
0 50 km

Jacobite relics, mostly with clan connections. A shop here sells kilts, woolens, and souvenirs.

Dornie. ℂ **01599/555-202.** www.eileandonancastle.com. Admission £6 adults; £5 seniors, students, and children 5–16; £15 families. Mar–Oct daily 10am–6pm (open from 9am during July and Aug). Drive 8 miles east of the Kyle of Lochalsh on the A87.

Where to Eat & Stay

The lodgings here are limited, just barely adequate to meet the demand for rooms.

Kyle Hotel   This modernized stone hotel in the center of town, a 5-minute walk from the train station, is your best all-around bet in the moderate category. The mid-size guest rooms are furnished in a functional style, with neatly kept bathrooms. The hotel serves reasonably priced dinners in the "Old Chapel" restaurant and in the more informal Conservatory.

Main St., Kyle of Lochalsh IV40 8AB. www.kylehotel.co.uk. ℂ **01599/534-204.** Fax 01599/534-932. 30 units. £95–£170 double. MC, V. **Amenities:** 2 restaurants; 2 bars. *In room:* TV/DVD, hair dryer.

Lochalsh Hotel ★   This landmark hotel is the most refined nesting ground in the area. It was built as a luxury oasis when the British railway finally extended its tracks in this direction. The hotel's crafted small-paned windows with hardwood and brass fittings will remind you of those on an oceangoing yacht. The comfortable guest rooms have been stylishly overhauled and include state-of-the-art bathrooms. The restaurant offers a menu of traditional good Scottish cooking based on the best local ingredients; diners also have the advantage of panoramic views across the water to the mountains of Skye.

Ferry Rd., Kyle of Lochalsh IV40 8AF. www.lochalshhotel.com. ℂ **01599/534-202.** Fax 01599/534-881. 38 units. £80–£100 double. AE, MC, V. **Amenities:** Restaurant; bar; room service. *In room:* TV/VCR, hair dryer.

THE ISLE OF SKYE: STAR OF THE HEBRIDES ★★

83 miles W of Inverness; 176 miles NW of Edinburgh; 146 miles NW of Glasgow

Off the northwest coast of Scotland, the mystical Isle of Skye, largest of the Inner Hebrides, is 48 miles long and varies between 3–25 miles wide. It's separated from the mainland by the Sound of Sleat (pronounced "Slate"). At Kyleakin, on the eastern end, the channel is only ¼ mile wide.

Dominating the land of summer seas, streams, woodland glens, mountain passes, cliffs, and waterfalls are the **Cuillin Hills ★★★**, a range of jagged black mountains that are a mecca for rock climbers. The Sleat Peninsula, the island's southernmost arm, is known as the "Garden of Skye." There are many stories about the origin of the name *Skye*. Some believe it's from the Norse *ski,* meaning "cloud," and others say it's from the Gaelic word for "winged." There are in fact many Norse names on the island, as the Norsemen held sway here for 4 centuries ending in 1263. Overlooking the Kyle is the ruined **Castle Maol,** once the home of a Norwegian princess.

On the island you can explore castle ruins, *duns* (hill forts), and *brochs* (prehistoric round stone towers). For the Scots, the island will forever evoke images of Flora MacDonald, who conducted the disguised Bonnie Prince Charlie to Skye after the Culloden defeat.

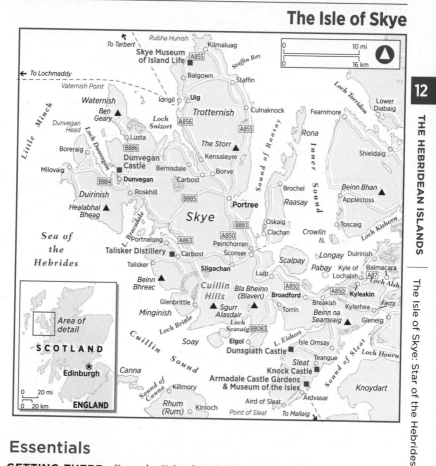

Essentials

GETTING THERE From the Kyle of Lochalsh, drive west along the bridge over the strait to Kyleakin.

VISITOR INFORMATION The **Tourist Information Centre** is at Bayfield House in Portree (© **01478/612-137;** www.skye.co.uk). It's open April to June and mid-August to October, Monday to Saturday 9am to 5:30pm; July to mid-August, Monday to Saturday 9am to 8pm and Sunday 10am to 4pm; and November to March, Monday to Friday 9am to 5pm and Saturday 10am to 4pm.

Outdoor Activities Around the Island

BIKING Gently undulating hills, coupled with good roads and a dearth of traffic, make the Isle of Skye appealing to cyclists. The island's premier rental outfits are **Island Cycles,** The Green, in the coastal town of Portree (© **01478/613-121;** the shop also sells fishing tackle), and **Fairwinds Bicycle Hire,** Elgol Road, Broadford (© **01471/822-270**). Both charge £10 to £18 a day. Island Cycles is open Monday through Saturday from 9am to 5pm; Fairwinds is open daily from 9am to 7pm.

BOATING   The coast of Skye is the most ruggedly beautiful this side of the Norwegian fjords, and several entrepreneurs offer boat trips letting you drink in the scenery. Foremost is **Bella Jane Boat Trips,** The Harbourfront, Elgol (© **0800/731-3089** toll-free in Britain, or 01471/866-244; www.bellajane.co.uk). From the piers in the village of Elgol, you board a sturdy vessel that sails daily (if there's enough business), between Easter and October, into the rock-ringed borders of Loch Coruisk, at the foot of the Cuillin Hills, which are rich in bird life. Most visitors opt for the standard return trip; you're carried to the base of the hills, deposited for 90 minutes of wandering, and then returned over water to Elgol. It lasts 3 hours and costs £22 per person, £12 for children 4 to 12 (children under 4 go free). If you're hardy and really interested in hiking, you can extend this experience to a full day.

GOLF   Golfing on Skye means an almost total absence of supervision, weather that can rain out or dry out a game with almost no notice, and, often, a lack of players. Whether you find this charming depends on your expectations, but overall, the island's best course is the 9-hole **Isle of Skye Golf Club** (© **01478/650-414;** www.isleofskyegolfclub.co.uk), adjacent to the hamlet of Sconser, on the southeast coast. Maintained by the local municipality, it has a simple snack bar and pub, and an on-again, off-again employee who cuts the grass whenever necessary. Less desirable, but appreciated by residents of the **Skeabost House Hotel** for its convenience (see "Skeabost Bridge," later in this chapter), is the hotel's 9-hole course. Non-guests can also play if they phone ahead.

HIKING   Any branch of Skye's **Tourist Information Centre** will offer advice on the many hikes available through the heather and glens of the island. If you enjoy walking, and you're stout-hearted and fit, consider extending a boat trip on the *Bella Jane* (see above) with an additional 14-mile overland hike from the Cuillin Hills back to more populated regions of the island. To do this, take the boat trip (one-way only) from Elgol to the Cuillin Hills. From here, brown-and-white signs direct you across an undulating, rock-strewn landscape to the Sligachan Hotel (see below), the premier hotel for trekkers. You can stay overnight at the hotel or take a bus or taxi the remaining 6¾ miles back to Portree.

Kyleakin

The seaport community of Kyleakin is the site of the old ferry terminal where the boats from the Scottish mainland used to arrive before Skye became linked by a bridge. Many visitors still prefer to stay here rather than on more remote, less convenient parts of the island.

Kyleakin opens onto a small bay and is dominated by a ruin, **Castle Maol,** on a jagged knoll. For a lovely walk, go from the town center up to this ruin, which dates from the 12th century, when it was a fortified stronghold of the Mackinnon clan.

WHERE TO EAT & STAY
The White Heather Hotel ☺   These two connected buildings provide good accommodation with up-to-date amenities. For more than half a century, this family-run guesthouse, with its panoramic views of the Torridon Mountains to the north, has provided accommodation to wayfarers. The small guest rooms are well maintained and comfortably furnished. The laundry service uses only environmentally friendly products, and in consideration of people with allergies, no feathers are used in pillows

or duvets. The lounge, licensed only to serve guests, has a pleasant view of the Castle Maol. The hotel is convenient for the bus terminals.

The Pier, Kyleakin, Isle of Skye IV41 8PL. www.whiteheatherhotel.co.uk. © **01599/534-577.** Fax 01599/534-427. 9 units. £68–£90 double. MC, V. Closed Oct–Feb. **Amenities:** Dining room; lounge/bar. *In room:* TV, hair dryer, no phone.

Sligachan

The village of Sligachan sits at the head of a sea loch in a setting of scenic beauty with views of the Cuillin Hills (pronounced "*Coo*-lin") to the west. It's one of the best bases for exploring Skye because of its central location. Visitors can enjoy sea-trout fishing, and an occasional salmon is caught on the Sligachan River. It's also possible to rent a boat from the Sligachan Hotel (see below) to explore the Storr Lochs, 15 miles from Sligachan, known for good brown-trout fishing from May to September.

A 10-minute drive directly west of Sligachan leads to the village of Carbost and the **Talisker Distillery,** along the B8009 (© **01478/614-308;** www.discovering-distilleries.com), opening onto the shore of Loch Harport. A distillery since 1843, the plant was mentioned by Robert Louis Stevenson in his 1880 poem *Scotsman's Return from Abroad*. Today, visitors can choose between two different tours of the distillery. The first is a 50-minute tour (£6 for adults and £3 for children) that includes a wee dram and a discount voucher to purchase a bottle of single malt. You will also no doubt meet members of the MacLeod clan, who make up more than half of the factory's 14 employees. The second "tasting" tour (£15; admission charge includes a nosing glass to take away) offers a more in-depth look at the distillery and includes a 5-sample nosing and tasting session of whiskies from the Talisker range of whiskies. This second tour starts at 1:45pm on selected weekdays. The center is open January to March and November to December, Monday through Friday, from 10am to 5pm (tours at 10:30am, noon, 2pm and 3:30pm); and from April to October, Monday through Saturday 9:30am to 5pm (tours throughout the day); during July and August, the distillery is also open on Sundays, from 11am to 5pm.

WHERE TO EAT & STAY

Sligachan Hotel ☺   This family-run hotel is nestled at the foot of the Cuillins, on the main road between Portree and Kyleakin, and has long been a base for mountaineering enthusiasts as well as those looking to explore Skye in a gentler way. It's one of the island's oldest coaching inns, built sometime in the 1830s, and even has its own museum of mountaineering memorabilia.

The guest rooms are modern and comfortable, but it's the facilities that make the difference, especially since there's nowhere else to go in Sligachan in the evening. The Cairidh Restaurant (also open to non-guests) offers traditional cooking, and vegetarians are also catered for. Mackenzie's Bar is the place for a quiet drink beside the log fire. The Seumas Bar, adjacent to the hotel, is a livelier affair, with about 200 malt whiskies and numerous real ales on offer (some brewed on site at the Cuillin Brewery). Food is served all day, and children are welcomed with toys and games in a play area and an outdoor play park.

The hotel runs a campsite nearby (www.sligachan.co.uk/sligachan-campsite) with 80 pitches and good facilities.

Sligachan, Isle of Skye IV47 8SW. www.sligachan.co.uk. © **01478/650-204.** Fax 01478/650-207. 21 units. £90–£150 double. MC, V. **Amenities:** Restaurant; 2 bars; room service. *In room:* TV, hair dryer, no phone.

CRAFTS ON skye

Edinbane Pottery, on the A850, 8 miles east of Dunvegan (☎ 01470/582-234; www.edinbane-pottery.co.uk), celebrated its 35th anniversary in 2007. The three artists working in this studio produce wood-fired stoneware and salt-glazed pottery, and they can fill custom orders in a wide range of finishes.

Artist Tom Mackenzie's etchings, prints, aquatints, and greeting cards are all inspired by the scenery and day-to-day life of the island. You can find his work at **Skye Original Prints at Portree,** 1 Wentworth St. (☎ 01478/612-544).

Since 1974, Stewart John Wilson has been designing and producing silver and gold jewelry, ceramic tiles, chessboards, platters, and clocks, all featuring intricate Celtic patterns. You can see his work at **Skye Silver,** in the Old School, on Glendale Road (B884), 6¾ miles west of Dunvegan (☎ 01470/511-263; www. skyesilver.com). The selection of tiles is especially vast.

Craft Encounters, in the old Post Office building in Broadford (☎ 01471/822-754), showcases many of Skye's talented artists. You'll find pewter jewelry, stained-glass light catchers, salt-dough bric-a-brac, folk and landscape paintings, tartan ties, and handmade jumpers (sweaters). Celtic patterns show up on glassware, tableware, linens, and pieces of marquetry. The island's musical talent is represented in a selection of traditional Scottish music CDs.

Skye Batik, The Green (☎ 01478/613-331; www.skyebatiks.com), is one of the best crafts shops in Scotland. It sells wall hangings and cotton, tweed, wool, and linen clothing hand-printed with Celtic designs from the 6th to the 8th century.

In **Harlequin Knitwear,** next to the Duisdale Hotel, on Sleat (☎ 01471/833-321), local knitter Chryssy Gibbs designs men's and women's machine-knit Shetland wool sweaters. Her work is bright and colorful.

For more knitwear, go to **Ragamuffin,** on the pier in Armadale (☎ 01471/844-217), featuring quality Scottish, Irish, and British hand-knits for the whole family, and such accessories as hats, gloves, and scarves.

Portree ★★

Skye's capital, Portree, is the port for steamers making trips around the island and linking Skye with the 15-mile-long island of Raasay. Sligachan, 8⅔ miles south, and Glenbrittle, 6¾ miles farther southwest, are centers for climbing the Cuillin Hills.

WHERE TO EAT

The Chandlery Restaurant SCOTTISH/SEAFOOD   This restaurant attracts visitors and locals alike. The highly skilled chef creates delicious, innovative dishes such as king scallops with green garlic butter and crispy bacon; rosemary roast loin of venison with fondant potatoes, puy lentils, and beans with light port sauce; and a dessert of ripe pear poached in port and flavored with cinnamon, served with a tartlet of whisky, honey, and oatmeal ice cream.

In the Bosville Hotel (see below), Bosville Terrace. ☎01478/612-846. www.bosvillehotel.co.uk. Reservations recommended. Main courses £17–£21. AE, MC, V. Daily 6–10pm.

WHERE TO STAY

Bosville Hotel   This well-established hotel stands in the center of Portree and commands panoramic views across the harbor to the Cuillin Hills. It's a bright, welcoming inn known equally for its cuisine. As well as the Chandlery Restaurant (see above), there's also a bistro-style restaurant and a bar serving more informal meals.

Bosville Terrace, Portree, Isle of Skye IV51 9DG. www.bosvillehotel.co.uk. © **01478/612-846.** Fax 01478/613-434. 15 units. £88–£340 double. AE, MC, V. **Amenities:** Restaurant; bar; room service. *In room:* TV, hair dryer, Wi-Fi (free).

The Cuillin Hills Hotel ★

This stone-sided manor was built in the 1820s as a hunting lodge for the MacDonald clan. Located almost ⅔ mile north of Portree's center, the comfortable hotel appeals to hikers and bird-watchers. Views from the guest rooms encompass the unspoiled Cuillin Hills, Portree's harbor, or the sea. Each unit is outfitted with reproductions of old-fashioned furniture against a backdrop of flowered wallpaper. Dinner is available in the upmarket "The View" Restaurant, which specializes in seafood. There's also a more relaxed brasserie serving steaks, seafood, and regional specialties.

Portree, Isle of Skye IV51 9LU. www.cuillinhills-hotel-skye.co.uk. © **01478/612-003.** Fax 01478/613-092. 27 units. £210–£310 double. AE, MC, V. **Amenities:** 2 restaurants; bar; room service. *In room:* TV, hair dryer, Wi-Fi (free).

Viewfield House ★ 🏠

For lovers of Victoriana, this is a good choice, offering old-world style and comfort. The house's original charm and interior have been preserved (complete with antique furnishings), and a stay here feels like a Scottish weekend party. Rooms are spacious, and offer pleasant views over the 8 hectares (20 acres) of woodland garden. Viewfield is only a 10-minute walk from the center of Portree.

Portree, Isle of Skye IV51 9EU. www.viewfieldhouse.com. ©**01478/612-217.** Fax 01478/613-517. 11 units. £110–£140 double. MC, V. **Amenities:** Breakfast room; communal TV; Wi-Fi (free). *In room:* Hair dryer.

Uig ★

The village of Uig is on Trotternish, the largest Skye peninsula. The ferry port for Harris and Uist in the Outer Hebrides, it's 15 miles north of Portree and 49 miles from the Kyle of Lochalsh. Many people like to anchor here because it's convenient for early departures. Uig is also one of the most beautiful places in Skye to spend the night, because it opens onto Uig Bay and is known for its **sunrises and sunsets.** Indeed, if you're an outdoors type of person, you can pitch your tent at the village campsite (© **01470/542-714;** www.uig-camping-skye.co.uk), which also, incidentally, rents bikes to visitors.

Once a virtual ruin and only of passing interest, the recently renovated **Monkstadt House,** 1½ miles north, is where Flora MacDonald brought Bonnie Prince Charlie after their escape from Benbecula. This famous Scottish heroine was buried in **Kilmuir churchyard,** 5 miles north.

While on the Trotternish peninsula, you can also visit the **Skye Museum of Island Life** (© **01470/552-206;** www.skyemuseum.co.uk), at Kilmuir. The old way of island life is preserved here, along with artifacts based on farming on the crofts. Some interiors from the 18th and 19th centuries have been reconstructed. Admission is £2.50 for adults, £2 for seniors and students, and 50p for children 5 to 16. The museum opens from Easter to October, Monday through Saturday from 9:30am to 5pm.

WHERE TO EAT & STAY

Ferry Inn This building was first a bank and later a post office, but today this hotel's main focus is its popular pub. You'll recognize this place in the town center by its Victorian gables. There are a handful of cozy guest rooms upstairs, each comfortably furnished. The restaurant serves dinner from 6pm daily.

Uig, Isle of Skye IV51 9XP. www.ferryinn.co.uk. © **01478/611-216.** Fax 01478/611-224. 6 units. £80–£88 double. MC, V. **Amenities:** Restaurant; 2 bars; lounge; Internet (free). *In room:* TV.

Dunvegan

The village of Dunvegan, northwest of Portree, grew up around Skye's principal sight: **Dunvegan Castle** ★ (© **01470/521-206;** www.dunvegancastle.com), the seat of the chiefs of Clan MacLeod, who have lived here for 800 years. Standing on a rocky promontory and said to be Britain's oldest inhabited castle, it was once accessible only by boat, but now the moat is bridged and the castle open to the public. It contains many relics, such as a "fairy flag" believed to have been given to the MacLeods by woodland spirits and reputed to have brought good luck in battle. The castle is open daily: mid-March to October, from 10am to 5pm, and November to mid-March, from 11am to 4pm. Admission to the castle and gardens is £9 for adults, £7 for seniors, and £4.50 for children aged between 5 and 15. A family ticket is £24. Admission to the gardens only is £7 for adults, £6.50 for seniors, and £3.50 for children.

WHERE TO EAT & STAY

Atholl House Hotel ☺ Opposite the post office and near Dunvegan Castle, this hotel was once the village's manse, and stands at the heart of the village, ⅔ mile from Dunvegan Castle. This well-run little hotel rents nicely furnished rooms. The best rooms have views of the mountain moorland and Loch Dunvegan. The chef prepares quality cuisine using an abundance of locally caught seafood.

Dunvegan, Isle of Skye IV55 8WA. www.athollhotel.co.uk. ©/fax **01470/521-219.** 9 units. £86 double; family room £120. AE, MC, V. **Amenities:** Restaurant; bar. *In room:* TV, hair dryer.

Three Chimneys Restaurant ★★ SCOTTISH The Three Chimneys, located in a stone crofter's house, has won multiple awards. In 2003, *Restaurant Magazine* proclaimed Chimneys as one of the world's top 50 restaurants. And the same high standards prevail today. Specialties are fresh seafood and Highland game, with dishes such as pan-fried Scottish salmon with asparagus and lemon sauce. The dessert menu includes scrumptious treats, including marmalade pudding and Drambuie custard.

Six luxurious suites are located a few steps away from the restaurant. The House Over-By boasts a panoramic view of the sea, and each suite is fully equipped with amenities such as a TV, VCR, CD player, phone, minibar, and hair dryer. They cost is not cheap, at £295 for a double and £590 for a family room, but the suites have been given a five-star rating by the Scottish Tourist Board.

Hwy. B884, Colbost, Isle of Skye IV55 8ZT. © **01470/511-258.** Fax 01470/511-358. www.threechimneys. co.uk. Reservations required for dinner. Fixed-price dinner £60 for 3 courses, £85 for 7 courses; lunch £28.50 for 2 courses, £37 for 3 courses. AE, MC, V. Dinner daily 6:15–9:45pm (last order); lunch mid-Mar–Oct Mon–Sat 12:15–1:45pm (last order). Drive 6.5km (4 miles) west of Dunvegan on B884.

Skeabost Bridge

Eastward from Dunvegan, Skeabost Bridge has an island cemetery of great antiquity. The graves of four Crusaders are here.

WHERE TO EAT & STAY

Skeabost Country House Hotel Built in 1851 as a private estate, Skeabost has been converted into a lochside hotel boasting dormers, chimneys, tower, and gables.

The Skeabost owns 8 miles of the bank of the River Snizort, and so it attracts many visitors who come to fish. In addition, guests can play the hotel's 9-hole golf course. The comfortable bedrooms come in a variety of shapes and sizes. The main dining room offers expensive table d'hôte menus concentrating on seafood.

Skeabost Bridge, Isle of Skye IV51 9NP. www.oxfordhotelsandinns.com. © **01470/532-202.** Fax 01470/532-761. 14 units. £90–£170 double. MC, V. **Amenities:** 2 restaurants; 2 bars; 9-hole golf course; room service; babysitting; Wi-Fi (free). *In room:* TV, hair dryer.

Sleat Peninsula

A lot of Skye can look melancholy and forlorn, especially in misty weather. For a change of landscape, head for the **Sleat Peninsula,** the southeastern section of the island. Because of the lushness of its vegetation (the shores are washed by the warmer waters of the Gulf Stream), it has long been known as the "Garden of Skye." As you drive along, you notice the intense green of the landscape and the well-kept grounds of locals' homes.

Off the A851, some 12 miles south of Broadford, is a ruined stronghold of the MacDonalds, **Knock Castle.** Another MacDonald stronghold, **Dunsgiath Castle,** has some well-preserved ruins open to view. They're found at Tokavaig on an unclassified road (watch for a sign) at a point 20 miles south and southwest of Broadford. You can visit both these evocative ruins for free, day or night. Inquire at the number given below for the Armadale Castle Gardens & Museum of the Isles.

Armadale Castle Gardens & Museum of the IslesMUSEUM   You don't have to have MacDonald as your last name to enjoy a stop at Skye's award-winning Clan Donald Visitor Centre. From Broadford, travel along a winding seaside road to the ruins of Armadale Castle and the rebuilt baronial stables. A multimedia exhibit tells of the lost culture of the ancient Gaelic world under the MacDonalds as lords of the Isles. The countryside ranger service offers a full summer program of guided walks and talks on the estate. A licensed restaurant in the stables offers good local food, from afternoon tea to a full meal. The drive from the ferry at Kyleakin is about 30 minutes, and the center is along the A851 (follow the signs) near the Armadale–Mallaig ferry.

Armadale. © **01471/844-305.** www.clandonald.com. Admission £7 adults, £5 seniors and children aged 5-15. Apr–Oct daily 9:30am–5:30pm (last entry at 5pm).

WHERE TO EAT & STAY

Ardvasar Hotel ☺   The oldest part of this 1800s coaching inn is a stone-trimmed pub in what was once a stable. The bar and restaurant are popular with locals as well as guests. The restaurant serves dinner every evening during the season; fish and seafood are the specialties. The lounge bar offers snacks and lighter meals throughout the day.

Ardvasar, Isle of Skye IV45 8RS. www.ardvasarhotel.com. ©**01471/844-223.** Fax 01471/844-495. 10 units. £126–£132 double. MC, V. **Amenities:** Restaurant; bar; room service. *In room:* TV, hair dryer.

Toravaig Hotel ★★★ 🎁   This intimate hotel is ideal for romantic breaks, peace and quiet, and gourmet dining. The rooms have stylish, contemporary fabrics and furnishings; they're not large but are well equipped, with smart bathrooms (and luxury toiletries). There are also spectacular views over the island's rugged coastline and the ruins of Knock Castle. In the lounge downstairs you can sink into a comfortable sofa and enjoy a glass of single malt by the crackling log fire.

The **Islay Restaurant** offers sumptuous cuisine—probably the best on the island—and a warm candlelit ambience. The menu changes daily, but dishes might include halibut with Stornoway black pudding, samphire, caper puree, cauliflower beignet, apple, and surf clams, or venison with hickory potato puree, girolles, baby carrots, spinach, and pineapple and plum chutney. The five-course dinner is £45 per person. The three-course lunch, at £23, offers remarkable value for money. The restaurant also welcomes non-guests.

Between April and September, the hotel owners offer guests sailing days on their 42-foot yacht (see also listing for the sister hotel, the Duisdale, below).

Sleat, Isle of Skye IV44 8RE. www.skyehotel.co.uk. © **01471/820-200.** Fax 01471/833-231. 9 units. £179–£230 double. MC, V. The hotel is located beside the A851 just to the north of the hamlet of Teangue. **Amenities:** Restaurant; lounge; sailing trips. *In room:* TV, hair dryer, Wi-Fi (free).

Isle Ornsay

Adjacent to Sleat Peninsula is the Isle Ornsay, also called Eilean Iarmain in Gaelic. It's a lovely, remote islet in a small, rocky bay with mountains of Knoydart in the background. Its heyday as Skye's main fishing port is long gone. Today you'll find little whitewashed cottages around the small harbor. The island's landlord is Sir Iain Noble, who also owns Hotel Eilean Iarmain (see below).

WHERE TO STAY

Duisdale Hotel ★★★   The Duisdale is the larger sister hotel to the Toravaig (see above). The same attention to detail and warm, comforting atmosphere are evident in both hotels; the staff is particularly welcoming. However, the grander guest rooms, and 14 hectares (35 acres) of gardens and woodland, make the Duisdale the number-one hotel choice on Skye. The 18 guest rooms all have different features: Some have four-poster beds, some have sea views, others garden views; some have their own dressing rooms, and one has a free-standing, double-ended bath with a view of the sea from an arched window.

The hotel is perfect for relaxing luxury breaks. There's a comfortable lounge with an open fire, where you can take afternoon tea and freshly baked scones with jam and cream (and maybe a glass of champagne too). In the garden is a hot tub. The Chart Room is a stylish bar for pre-dinner drinks and more informal lunches or evening meals. There's a cocktail menu, an impressive selection of unusual whiskies, and locally brewed beers. The glamorously designed **restaurant** serves the finest Scottish produce with a French twist. You might choose pheasant with fondant potato, Puy lentil and pancetta casserole, roast chestnuts, and smoked paprika jus, and follow it up with milk chocolate and Cointreau mousse with ice cream and citrus crisps. The five-course evening menu is £45 per person. Breakfast in the conservatory is also noteworthy: the full Scottish breakfast includes the option of porridge with cream and whisky.

Daily sailing trips are offered between April and September on the 42-foot luxury yacht, which is skippered by the hotel's owner, a former sea captain. Your trip might take you around Skye, or to Rhum, Eigg, or Loch Nevis.

Isle Ornsay, Sleat, Isle of Skye IV43 8QW. www.duisdale.com. © **01471/833-202.** Fax 01471/833-404. 18 units. £180–£300 double. MC, V. The hotel is located beside the A851 just to the north of the Isle Ornsay village. **Amenities:** Restaurant; bar; lounge; hot tub; sailing trips. *In room:* TV, DVD player, hair dryer, Wi-Fi (free).

Hotel Eilean Iarmain   Sir Iain and Lady Noble welcome guests to their century-old harborside retreat, Eilean Iarmain or, as it's more often referred to, "Isle Ornsay

Hotel." Inside, antiques, wood paneling, and chintz fabrics create a cottagey feel. In winter, the charming atmosphere is enhanced by log fires and the performances by guest musicians. The rooms are individually styled, though a little dowdy. The suites are housed in a former stable block dating back to the 1870s, while the Tower Room, with its pine-paneled walls and a great mahogany double bed, has views towards the sea.

Isle Ornsay, Sleat, Isle of Skye IV43 8QR. www.eilean-iarmain.co.uk. *©***01471/833-332.** Fax 01471/833-275. 16 units. £100–£200 double; £150–£250 suite. AE, MC, V. **Amenities:** Restaurant; bar; room service; babysitting. *In room:* TV, minibar (in suites), hair dryer, Wi-Fi (free).

Kinloch Lodge ★★ The white-stone walls of this manor are visible from across the scrub- and pine-covered hillsides bordering the property. Built in 1680 as a hunting lodge, it's now the elegant residence of Lord and Lady MacDonald. Portraits of the family's 18th-century forebears are a striking feature of the reception rooms, as are the open fireplaces and the scores of antiques. Guest rooms come in various shapes and sizes, and all are decorated with a traditional and cozy look. In 1998, a new house, also impressive architecturally, was completed 50m (164 ft.) from the main lodge; it contains five handsomely furnished bedrooms.

Every evening, you can enjoy drinks in the drawing room before sampling the fine cooking for which the hotel is famous. Head chef Marcello Tully has won a Michelin star for his efforts. Lady MacDonald herself is the author of 13 cookbooks, and runs cookery courses from the hotel.

Isle Ornsay, Sleat, Isle of Skye IV43 8QY. www.kinloch-lodge.co.uk. *©***01471/833-333.** Fax 01471/833-277. 15 units. £160–£200 double; £220–£250 suite. AE, MC, V. **Amenities:** Restaurant; bar. *In room:* TV/DVD, Wi-Fi (free).

RHUM (RUM)

8⅔ miles SW of the Isle of Skye

The enticingly named island of Rhum is only about 8 miles wide and 8 miles long. It's said to be the wettest island of the Inner Hebrides, with over 229cm (90 in.) of rainfall recorded annually. It's also one of the wildest and most beautiful islands, famed for its landscape and wildlife.

Since the mid-1950s, Rhum has been owned by the Edinburgh-based Nature Conservancy Council, an ecological conservation group. Attempts are being made to bring back the sea eagle, which inhabited the island in Queen Victoria's day. On this storm-tossed outpost in summer, mountain climbers meet challenging peaks and anglers come for good trout fishing. Bird lovers seek out the Manx shearwaters that live on the island in great numbers. Red deer and ponies, along with the wildflowers of summer, add color to an otherwise bleak landscape.

Before You Go

Before traveling to Rhum, you must contact **Denise Reed**, the reserve manager at the **Scottish Natural Heritage Nature Reserve** (*©* **01687/462-026;** www.snh.org.uk). The office will help you organize accommodation on the island.

Essentials

A passenger **ferry** from Mallaig, on the western coast of Scotland, leaves about five times a week. No cars are allowed on the island. For information, contact **Caledonian MacBrayne** (*©* **0800/066-5000;** www.calmac.co.uk). Sailings are from April to

October only, on Mondays and Wednesdays at 10:15am, on Fridays at 12:40pm, and on Saturdays at 7:20am. A round-trip is £16 to £20 for adults. **Arisaig Marine** (Ⓒ **01687/450-224;** www.arisaig.co.uk) sails from Arisaig to Rhum May through September on Tuesdays and Thursdays at 11am; there are also crossings on Saturdays during June, July, and August. A round-trip ticket is £24 for adults, £13 for children 11 to 16, and £10 for those aged 3 to 10. Schedules can vary, and so call to confirm. It takes about 2 hours to reach Rhum from one of these ports.

Where to Eat & Stay

Kinloch Castle ★ 🏨   You'll be astonished that in such a forbidding place, you can find a hotel that has been called "Britain's most intact example of an Edwardian country house." Of course, it's sadly run down and the bedrooms are a bit musty. But you get the feeling that you're living life as experienced back in 1901, maybe something from the pages of an Agatha Christie novel. Located on the seafront in the center of Rhum's biggest hamlet, Kinloch, this mansion was completed for Sir George Boullough, a wealthy Lancashire textile magnate. The castle still contains a ballroom, a massive Adam-style fireplace, and monumental paintings and stuffed animals. (This section is now part of an exhibit; to visit these areas, enter the front of the castle for a tour.) The former servants' quarters are now a simple and functional hostel, while the private rooms are furnished with four-poster beds (these share spacious bathrooms with tubs).

Because guests spend their days trekking around the island, lunches are packed picnics at £5.50 per person. The restaurant serves breakfast for £7 and a three-course dinner for £16.

Kinloch, Isle of Rhum PH43 4RR. www.isleofrum.com/placestostay-bb,.html. Ⓒ/fax **01687/462-037.** kinlochcastle@snh.gov.uk. 27 units, none with private bathroom; 52 hostel beds. Rooms £45–£80 double; hostel £16 per person in rooms with 2–5 beds. No credit cards. **Amenities:** Restaurant. *In room:* No phone.

EIGG & MUCK

Eigg: 4 miles SE of Rhum; Muck: 6¾ miles SW of Eigg

The tiny islands of Eigg and Muck lie in the Sea of the Hebrides, which separates the Inner from the Outer Hebrides. If you're doing the whirlwind tour of Europe, Eigg and Muck will hardly top your agenda. They appeal only to nature lovers seeking a variety of Hebridean scenery and a chance to look at life of long ago. If your time is limited and you can visit only one isle, make it Eigg, which has the most dramatic scenery.

Essentials

GETTING THERE   Before venturing to Eigg or Muck, confirm the schedule of the ferry's return. Because service isn't every day, you may find yourself staying at least 2 nights on either island. **Caledonian MacBrayne** (Ⓒ **01687/462-403** in Mallaig; www.calmac.co.uk) sails from Mallaig to Eigg on Monday and Thursday at 10:30am and Saturday at 1:40pm. The round-trip ticket is £15. From Arisaig, **Arisaig Marine** (Ⓒ **01687/450-224**) sails to Muck May through September on Mondays, Wednesdays, and Fridays at 11am; there are also crossings on Sundays during June, July, and August. A round-trip ticket is £19 for adults, £13 for children 11 to 16, and £10 for those aged 3 to 10. Sailings to Eigg are on Mondays, Tuesdays, Wednesdays, and

Fridays at 11am; during June, July, and August there are also crossings on Saturdays and Sundays. The round-trip fare is £18 for adults, and as above for children. Schedules can vary, especially if the weather is poor, and so call to confirm.

VISITOR INFORMATION For assistance in finding accommodation on Eigg or Muck, and for general information, contact the **Tourist Information Centre** in Mallaig (© **01687/462-064**).

Eigg

Eigg, about 4⅓ by 3 miles, is some 12 miles out in the Atlantic. The island is owned by the Isle of Eigg Heritage Trust (www.isleofeigg.net), which consists of about 70 island residents and the Highland Council and Scottish Wildlife Trust. The farmers, shepherds, fishermen, and innkeepers who live here raised the US$2.4 million to buy their island through a worldwide public appeal over the Internet.

The **Sgurr of Eigg,** a tall column of lava, is thought to be the biggest such pitchstone (volcanic rock) mass in the United Kingdom. Climbers on its north side try to reach the 394m (1,300-ft.) summit. It's said that the last of the pterodactyls roosted here.

After your arrival at **Galmisdale,** the principal hamlet and pier, you can take an antique bus to Cleadale. Once there, walk across moors to **Camas Sgiotaig,** with its well-known **beach of the Singing Sands.** Because the island is crisscrossed with paths and tracks, and access isn't restricted, you can walk in any direction that captures your fancy.

Visitors come to Eigg for the remoteness and the sense of living in the 19th century. The island is known for its plant, animal, and bird life, including golden eagles and seals. In summer, you can sometimes see minke whales and porpoises in the offshore waters. The island's resident warden leads guided walks of Eigg once a week in summer; call © **01687/482-477** for details.

Muck

Lying 6¾ miles southwest of Eigg, Muck has such an unappetizing name that visitors may turn away. However, the name of this 2½-square-mile island was originally a Gaelic word, *muic,* meaning "island of the sow." Naturalists come here to see everything from rare butterflies to otters. Large colonies of nesting seabirds can be viewed in May and June.

Muck is actually a farm (www.isleofmuck.com), and the entire island is owned by two brothers: the Laird of Muck, Lawrence MacEwan, and his younger brother, Ewen MacEwan. There are hardly more than 30 residents, and all are concerned with the running of the farm. There are no vehicles on the island except for bicycles and tractors. If you walk to the top of the highest hill, **Ben Airean,** at 137m (450 ft.), you have a panoramic view of Muck and the neighboring islands of Rhum and Eigg.

COLL & TYREE

90 miles NW of Glasgow; 48 miles W of Fort William

If you like your scenery stark and tranquil, try tiny Coll and Tyree. The outermost of the Inner Hebrides, they're exposed to the open Atlantic and are said to get the most sunshine in Britain. On Tyree (also spelled Tiree), the shell-sand *machair* (sand dunes) increase the arable area, differentiating it from the other inner isles.

Trees are scarce on both islands, but that doesn't mean the islands are barren. Both are rich in flora, with some 500 species. The islands' roughly 150 bird species, including Arctic skuas and razorbills, make them a bird lover's paradise. Both common and gray seals have breeding colonies on the islands. There are few cars for rent here, but visitors don't seem to mind biking around the islands or catching a ride on Tyree's least expensive method of transport; a mail bus serves most of the island. Boat rentals and sea angling can also be arranged.

Getting to the Islands

British Airways (© **0844/493-0787** in Glasgow) flies directly to Tyree from Glasgow, with about six 90-minute flights per week (none on Sun). A car ferry sails from Oban to Coll (a 3-hr. trip) and Tyree (an extra 45 min.), but in very rare instances gales may force cancellation of the trip. If the gale is very strong, you might be stranded on an island for a while, waiting for the next departure. Details and bookings, essential for cars, are available from **Caledonian MacBrayne** (© **0800/066-5000,** or 01631/566-688 for the port office in Oban; www.calmac.co.uk).

Coll

Lying in the seemingly timeless world of the Celtic west, the island of Coll has a population of some 130 hearty souls. The island averages about 3 miles in breadth; at its longest point, it stretches for some 13 miles.

Coll has a partially restored castle, **Breacachadh,** rising majestically from its southeastern side. A stronghold of the MacLeans in the 15th century, it's now a private residence. Immediately adjacent is the so-called **New Castle,** built for Hector MacLean in 1750. It provided shelter for Samuel Johnson and James Boswell when they were stranded on the island for 10 days because of storms at sea. The castle, still a private home, was altered considerably in the 19th century and embellished with pepper-pot turrets and parapets.

In the western part of the island at Totronald are two standing stones called **Na Sgeulachan ("Teller of Tales").** The stones predate the Druids and are thought to have been the site of a temple. The highest point on Coll is **Ben Hogh** (103m/338 ft.), which you can climb for a panoramic view.

On the road to Sorisdale, at **Killunaig,** stand the ruins of a church, from the late Middle Ages, and a burial ground. Going on to **Sorisdale,** you see the ruins of houses once occupied by crofters. Hundreds of families lived here. Some were chased away in the wake of the potato famine, and many were forced out in Land Clearance programs.

WHERE TO EAT & STAY

Isle of Coll Hotel This hotel enjoys the dubious honor of having been immediately rejected by Samuel Johnson and James Boswell as an inappropriate place to spend the night during their 18th-century tour of Scotland. (They eventually succeeded in securing lodgings with the laird of Coll.) Today, the small to mid-size guest rooms are far more comfortable, with electric blankets and simple but functional furniture. The dining room serves good but rather expensive dinners. The hotel contains the town's only pub, in which you're likely to meet locals over a pint of ale and a plate of reasonably priced bar food. There's also the Gannet Restaurant, where main courses range from £10 for quail egg curry to £18 for lobster. The hotel sits on a hilltop at the end of the Arinagour estuary, about a 10-minute walk north of town, next to the B8071.

Arinagour, Isle of Coll PA78 6SA. www.collhotel.com. ✆ **01879/230-334.** Fax 01879/230-317. 6 units. £95–£120 double. MC, V. **Amenities:** Restaurant; bar; children's play area; Wi-Fi (free). *In room:* TV, hair dryer, no phone.

Tyree (Tiree)

A fertile island, flat Tyree has a population of some 800 residents, mostly in farming communities, who enjoy its gentle landscape, **sandy beaches,** and rolling hills. As you travel about the island, you see many 1800s crofter's houses with thatched roofs. In 1886, the Duke of Argyll caused a scandal when he ordered marines and police to clear the crofters off the land. Many were sent, destitute, to Canada.

Most of the 800- to 900-strong population is based in **Scarinish,** with its little stone harbor where lobster boats put in. Fishing isn't what it used to be; the appearance of fast and dangerous squalls and storms are said to scatter the fleet as far as the shores of North America.

Bird-watchers are drawn to the shores of **Loch Bhasapoll,** a favorite gathering place of wild geese and ducks, and to a cave on the coast at **Kenavara,** where many seabirds can be observed.

Ancient duns and forts are scattered around Tyree. The best of these is a *broch* at **Vaul Bay,** with walls more than 3.5m (11 ft.) thick. At **Balephetrish,** on the northern rim of the island, stands a huge granite boulder. Locals call it the Ringing Stone—when struck it gives off a metallic sound. In the island's western part, at Kilkenneth, are the ruins of the **Chapel of St. Kenneth,** dedicated to a comrade of St. Columba.

WHERE TO EAT & STAY

Scarinish Hotel ★ ▥ Serving the best food in the area, this hotel also offers well-maintained and comfortable bedrooms in a superb location right on the sea. The Hebridean hospitality and service is another good reason for staying here; that and the succulent lobster served at the Old Harbour Restaurant, which also offers the best of local lamb and Scottish beefsteaks.

Bedrooms are done in a simple but comfortable style, and beds have crisp, white linen. Guests can use the Upper Deck Lounge with its views over the harbor, or the Lean To Bar, which is a friendly place where islanders gather at night in front of the fire. The full Scottish breakfast served here will fortify you for most of the day.

Scarinish, Isle of Tyree PA77 6UH. www.tireescarinishhotel.com. ✆ **01879/220-308.** Fax 01879/220-410. 5 units. £70–£80 double; £75 for 2 adults (children half-price) in family suite. DC, MC, V. **Amenities:** Restaurant; bar. *In room:* TV, no phone.

Tiree Lodge Hotel This is the nerve center of the island. Built as a simple hunting lodge around 1790, it was greatly enlarged in the 1970s with a modern addition. Located about 1 mile east of the island's only ferry landing, the hotel contains one of Tyree's two pubs and attracts a crowd of locals and visitors. The small guest rooms are well maintained and comfortable.

Kirkatol, Isle of Tyree PA77 6TW. www.tireelodgehotel.com. ✆ **01879/220-368.** Fax 01879/220-884. 14 units, 9 with private bathroom. From £50 for a double without bathroom, to £100 for a double with bathroom. MC, V. **Amenities:** Restaurant; bar; smoke-free rooms. *In room:* TV, no phone.

MULL ★

121 miles NW of Edinburgh; 90 miles NW of Glasgow

The third-largest island in the Hebrides, Mull is rich in legend and folklore, a land of ghosts, monsters, and the wee folk. The landscape is wild and mountainous, characterized by sea lochs and sandy bars. Mull was known to the ancient Greeks, and its prehistoric past is recalled in forts, duns, and stone circles. Be sure to bring a raincoat: the island is one of the wettest in the Hebrides, a fact that upset Dr. Johnson, who visited in 1773.

Many visitors consider Mull more beautiful than Skye. Mull has varied scenery with numerous waterfalls; the wild countryside provided the setting for many of David Balfour's adventures in *Kidnapped,* by Robert Louis Stevenson. The island's highest peak is **Ben More,** at 961m (3,153 ft.), but it also has many flat areas. The island's wildlife includes roe deer, golden eagles, polecats, seabirds, and feral goats. Mull is also a jumping-off point to visit Iona and Staffa (see "Iona & Staffa: An Abbey & a Musical Cave," later in this chapter).

Guarding the bay (you'll see it as you cross on the ferry) is **Duart Castle,** restored just before World War I. In the bay—somewhere—lies the *Florencia,* a Spanish galleon that went down laden with treasure. Many attempts have been made to find it and bring it up, but, so far, all have failed. To the southeast, near Salen, are the 14th-century ruins of **Aros Castle,** once a stronghold of the MacDonalds, lords of the Isles. On the far south coast at Lochbuie, **Moy Castle** has a water-filled dungeon.

At the end of the day, you might enjoy a dram from the **Tobermory Malt Whisky Distillery,** in Tobermory (© **01688/302-645;** www.tobermory.co.uk/distillery/tobermory_whisky.htm), which opened in 1823. Tours are given by appointment only. Be sure to call in advance, as the distillery seems to shut down from time to time.

Essentials

GETTING THERE It's a 45-minute trip by car ferry from Oban to Craignure, on Mull. For departure times, contact **Caledonian MacBrayne** (© **0800/066-5000;** www.calmac.co.uk). From Oban, there are about five or six sailings per day at a round-trip cost of about £10. The cost for a car is about £60 for a 5-day round-trip ticket.

GETTING AROUND Use **Bowmans Coaches Mull** (© **01680/812-313;** www.bowmanstours.co.uk) to go around the island. Coaches connect with the ferry at least three times per day and will take you to Fionnphort or Tobermory. Bowmans also offers tickets combining the cost of the ferry with a guided bus tour to Fionnphort and Iona. The tour begins when you board the 10am ferry and ends at about 5:40pm, back at Oban.

VISITOR INFORMATION The **Harbour Visitor Centre** in Tobermory provides information to visitors and will help with booking accommodation and boat trips (© **01688/302-182;** www.tobermory.co.uk). It's open from Easter to October, Monday through Friday from 9am to 6pm.

SPECIAL EVENTS In July, the **Mull Highland Games** feature traditional events such as bagpipes, caber tossing, and dancing. The **Tour of Mull Rally** is held in early October. Ask at the tourist office for exact dates.

Outdoor Activities Around the Island

BIKING   Its combinations of heather-clad, rock-strewn moors and sylvan forests make Mull especially appropriate for cycling. To rent a bike, try On Yer Bike, at Inverinate, Salen near Aros, not far from Tobermory (© **01680/300-501;** Easter–October only). In Tobermory itself, consider **Brown's,** High Street (© **01688/302-020;** www.brownstobermory.co.uk). Both are open daily from 8:45am to around 5:30pm.

GOLF   Just over 22 miles west of Tobermory is the isolated 9-hole **Craignure Golf Course,** with an honesty box into which you deposit the greens fees. For information about the course, contact the club's secretary, D. Howitt (© **01680/300-402;** www.craignuregolfclub.co.uk).

HIKING   Mull is wonderful for hiking. You'll probably drive off to a trail head, park your car beside the road (most residents boast that they haven't locked their car in decades), and then set off on foot in total isolation. The tourist office sells two books, *Walks in North Mull* and *Walks in South Mull.* They provide detailed options for specific routes with historic, ethnographical, scenic, or geological interest. Dress in layers, and wear something waterproof.

Craignure

The village of Craignure on the eastern side of Mull is the island's main ferry port, with five or six sailings per day to Oban during the summer months. Local buses connect the port to the villages of Fionnphort and Tobermory. There's also a railway station for the narrow-gauge Isle of Mull Railway (run by the owners of Torosay Castle), though services are currently suspended as the castle seeks a new owner.

EXPLORING CRAIGNURE

Duart Castle ★CASTLE   You can visit both Torosay Castle (see below) and Duart Castle on the same day. Located 3 miles west of Torosay, this castle dates from the 13th century and was the home of the fiery MacLean clan. A majestic structure, it was sacked in 1791 by the dukes of Argyll in retaliation for the MacLeans' support of the Stuarts in 1715 and 1745. It was allowed to fall into ruins until Sir Fitzroy MacLean, the 26th chief of the clan and grandfather of the present occupant, began restoring it in 1911, at the age of 76. It had been his ambition since he was a boy to see his ancestral home restored (he lived until he was 102).

 Close Encounters with Nature

Several operators will take you out to see whales, dolphins, and seals. Two of the best are **Sea Life Surveys,** Beadoun, Breidwood, Tobermory (© **01688/302-916;** www.sealifesurveys.com), and a **Mr. Laverty,** High Street (© **01688/302-048**), who maintains mid-size boats for 6 to 12 passengers each. Tours range from all-day whale-watching trips to 2-hour seal-watching cruises.

Visitors can also experience the wildlife-rich natural habitat on land with **Island Encounters** (© **01680/300-441;** www.mullwildlife.co.uk). Guided by a local expert, you can spend the day on a safari, exploring the most remote and scenic areas of the island in a comfortable eight-seat vehicle. Binoculars and lunch are included in the all-day package, and pickup can be arranged at all ferry terminals on Mull.

Off the A849, on the eastern point of Mull. ℂ **01680/812-309.** www.duartcastle.com. Admission £5.50 adults, £4.90 seniors and students, £2.75 children 3–15, £13.75 families. Apr Sun–Thurs 11am–4pm; May to mid-Oct daily 10:30am–5:30pm.

Torosay Castle & Gardens CASTLE/GARDEN   This is the only private castle and garden in the western Highlands that's open daily to visitors. The Victorian mansion was built in the mid-19th century by David Bryce, a famous Scottish architect. In his early years, Winston Churchill was a frequent visitor. One writer said a visit here was like returning to the Edwardian age of leisure, and so it is. To the surprise of visitors, the armchairs are labeled PLEASE SIT DOWN instead of PLEASE KEEP OFF. The portraits include examples by Sargent. Outside, you can wander through 4.9 hectares (12 acres) of Italian-style terraced gardens, and enjoy extensive views of the Appin coastline, from Ben Nevis to Ben Cruachan.

1½ miles south of Craignure on the A849. ℂ **01680/812-421.** www.torosay.com. Admission to castle and gardens £7.50 adults, £6.25 seniors and students, £4.25 children 6–16, £20 families. Admission only to gardens and tearoom £6 adults, £5 seniors and students, £3.50 children. Easter to Sept daily 10:30am–5:30pm.

WHERE TO EAT & STAY

Isle of Mull Hotel   This inn is situated near the ferry and the meeting point of the Sound of Mull and Loch Linnhe. From the picture windows of its public rooms, you have panoramic vistas of mountains and the island of Lismore. The guest rooms are small but smartly furnished. The chef serves British and Continental food in the attractive dining room. The spa and swimming pool provide welcome relaxation after a day touring round the island.

Craignure, Isle of Mull PA65 6BB. www.crerarhotels.com. ℂ **01680/812-544.** Fax 01680/812-462. 86 units. £50–£190 double. MC, V. **Amenities:** Restaurant; bar; indoor pool; spa; room service. *In room:* TV, hair dryer.

Salen

Near Salen are the ruins of **Aros Castle,** once a stronghold of the lords of the Isles, the MacDonalds. It dates from the 14th century and was last occupied in the 17th century. Most of the former castle has been quarried for building materials, but the ruins are still visible 11 miles southeast of Tobermory.

WHERE TO EAT & STAY

Glenforsa Hotel   This secluded seaside hotel was built in 1968 of Norwegian pine logs. It's near the Sound of Mull and the River Forsa, 11 miles southeast of

---

○ A Stunning View

Even locals sometimes drive out of their way to catch the sunset over the **Gribun Rock,** a large peninsula midway along the island's western coast, which has the windy uplands of Ben More as its centerpiece. The stretch of single-lane highway on the western flank of Ben More makes for a spectacular drive. To reach it from Tobermory or Craignure, follow the signs to the hamlet of Salen, and then drive west to Gribun. En route, you pass through the hamlets of Knock, Balnahard, and Balevuin. From dozens of points along the way, views stretch over the cliff tops, encompassing the setting sun (if your timing is right) as well as the isles of Staffa, Coll, and Tyree.

Tobermory, and visitors like to come here in late summer to fish for salmon. The guest rooms are well appointed, with pine paneling and white bed linens. The restaurant serves an array of tempting food, with venison, trout, and salmon offered in season for hotel guests and non-guests alike. Vegetarians enjoy dishes such as wild mushroom risotto. The hotel has its own grass airstrip, at which private and charter planes can land from dawn to dusk.

Salen, by Aros, Isle of Mull PA72 6JW. www.glenforsa.co.uk. ©**01680/300-377.** Fax 01680/300-535. 15 units. £84 double. MC, V. **Amenities:** Restaurant; bar; room service. *In room:* Hair dryer, no phone.

Tobermory

Founded as a fishing village in 1789, Tobermory, one of the most sheltered harbors in Scotland, is the unofficial capital of Mull. Its brightly painted houses facing onto a boat-filled harbor, and the backdrop of wooded hills, make the town wonderfully photogenic. Yachts and ferry boats to and from Kilchoan arrive here in the summer, and Tobermory becomes a bustling village with its shops, hotels, and pubs all catering to the island's visitors.

Mull Museum (© 01688/301-100; www.mullmuseum.org.uk) occupies an old bakery building on Main Street, and exhibits material relating to the island's history. From Easter to mid-October, it's open Monday to Friday from 10am to 4pm, and sometimes on Sundays too in the summer. Admission is free.

Established in the 1930s, the **Tobermory Golf Club** (© 01688/302-741; www. tobermorygolfclub.com) is a 9-hole course. Although the hilly terrain (and the wind) makes it challenging to play, it does have some of the best views of any course in the world.

WHERE TO EAT

Gannet's RestaurantSCOTTISH   Conveniently situated in a quayside setting in a 200-year-old stone building on Main Street, Gannet's is one of the best independent restaurants on the island. The specialty is fresh seafood, much of it caught locally, along with juicy steaks, several vegetarian options, and creamy desserts. During the day, you can stop in for sandwiches and fresh coffee.

25 Main St., Tobermory. ©**01688/302-203.** Main courses £10–£18. MC, V. Easter–Oct daily 10am–9pm; Nov–Easter daily 10am–3pm.

SHOPPING

Isle of Mull Silver, Main Street (© 01688/302-345; www.mullsilver.co.uk), stocks jewelry made by a number of Scottish designers. Among the unique items made on the premises are traditional Scottish silver *quaich* (drinking vessels) and christening spoons. **Mull Pottery,** Main Street (© 01688/302-057; www.mullpottery.com), sells tableware, ovenware, and lamps in seashore, seagull, and turquoise patterns. **Tackle & Books,** Main Street (© 01688/302-336; www.tackleandbooks.co.uk), carries fishing gear, bait, and an impressive array of reading materials—especially works by local authors and anything in print about Mull itself.

ENTERTAINMENT & NIGHTLIFE

Macgochan's Pub, Ledaig (© 01688/302-350), is a traditional pub that stages Scottish music most nights from 9pm to 1:30am. There's also a game room with a pool table. The **Mishnish Hotel,** Main Street (© 01688/302-009; www.mishnish. co.uk), is a faux-traditional pub also featuring Scottish music nightly. In pleasant weather, you can get a breath of fresh air in the beer garden.

WHERE TO STAY

Glengorm Castle ★★ 🧳 This is probably the best hotel on Mull. Built in 1860 and now restored, the castle is located at the northern tip of the island, near to Tobermory. It overlooks the Atlantic and is surrounded by green hills, forests, and lakes, with views from the guest rooms looking out to the Outer Hebrides up to 60 miles away on a clear day. At night, a roaring fire blazes while guests sample the various whiskies at the well-stocked bar. The bedrooms are luxuriously furnished, and each is individually decorated. The hotel has a stone bathing pool constructed in the early 1900s at the water's edge. In the grounds is the Glengorm Coffee Shop, selling freshly baked goods and excellent lunches often made with produce from the castle farm. It adjoins an art gallery displaying the work of local artists.

On the B8073, Tobermory, Isle of Mull PA75 6QE. www.glengormcastle.co.uk. ℭ **01688/302-321.** Fax 01688/302-738. 5 units. £120–£170 double. DC, MC, V. **Amenities:** Bar; pool (outdoor), library; coffee shop *In room:* TV, hair dryer, no phone.

Tobermory Hotel ☺ Occupying a converted row of 18th-century fishermen's cottages at the upper end of the town's main street, this hotel isn't short on character and atmosphere. Most of the guest rooms look out onto the harbor, which is usually dotted with fishing boats; the others have views of the tree-lined cliff, which rises abruptly behind the hotel. The dining room serves dinner nightly. Children are welcome here—a toy chest is ready for youngsters.

53 Main St., Tobermory, Isle of Mull PA75 6NT. www.thetobermoryhotel.com. ℭ **01688/302-091.** Fax 01688/302-254. 16 units. £76–£128 double. MC, V. Parking available on nearby streets. **Amenities:** Restaurant; room service. *In room:* TV, hair dryer, no phone.

Western Isles Hotel In a scenic location on a bluff above the harbor, the Western Isles is a large, gray-stone Victorian pile with gables and a baronial-style spire. It was built in 1882 as a hunting and fishing lodge. The current owners welcome guests with rooms that are comfortable, if a little old-fashioned. The price of the room relates to whether it has a seaview or looks inland. The hotel has a conservatory bar as well as an formal restaurant (3-course meal £30).

Tobermory, Isle of Mull PA75 6PR. www.mullhotel.com. ℭ **01688/302-012.** Fax 01688/302-297. 26 units. £90–£148 double. AE, MC, V. Closed Dec 18–28. **Amenities:** Restaurant; bar; room service; Wi-Fi (free). *In room:* TV, hair dryer.

Dervaig ★

The loveliest village on Mull, Dervaig (Little Grove) is a 8-mile drive west from Tobermory. The **Old Byre Heritage Centre** (ℭ **01688/400-229;** www.old-byre.co.uk) houses a charming museum of local life. The main exhibit features 25 scale models, painstakingly made by a local historian, showing the history of Mull from the first settlers to the Highland Clearances. A fully licensed tearoom serves light meals. Admission is £3 for adults, £2 for seniors and students, and £1.50 for children 5 to 12. From April to October, it's open from Wednesday to Sunday from 10:30am to 6:30pm. Take the twice-daily bus from Tobermory.

Just outside Dervaig is the 43-seat **Mull Little Theatre,** founded in 1966. According to the *Guinness Book of World Records,* this makes it the smallest professional theatre in Great Britain. See "Entertainment & Nightlife," below, for details.

From Dervaig, you can cruise to the lonely **Treshnish Isles,** a sanctuary for puffins, guillemots, and seals. From April to September, a local entrepreneur operates the *Turus Mara* (ℭ **0800/085-8786** or **01688/400-297;** www.turusmara.com), carrying up to 60 passengers on half-day visits, at £45 to £53 each. The boat departs from the Ulva Ferry Piers, on the west side of Mull. The Treshnish Isles are murky, muddy, and boggy, and so bring dry clothes, boots, and a sense of humor.

ENTERTAINMENT & NIGHTLIFE

Located in Druimfin, 8⅔ miles west of Tobermory, the **Mull Little Theatre,** Tobermory-Dervaig Road (ⓒ **01688/302-673;** www.multheatre.com), is indeed quite small, with an audience capacity of 43 people for the dramas staged inside a former *byre* (stable). The season runs from Easter to September, with visiting companies, as well as the small-but-capable Mull Theatre Company, filling the bill. Adult tickets cost £10; seniors and students pay £8, and children £6. Tickets should be reserved in advance. There's no seat allocation, so arrive early.

WHERE TO EAT & STAY

Druimnacroish Hotel   Visitors come here to leave modern life behind. Even though the owners have thoroughly refurbished and upgraded the place, they purposefully left TVs and phones out of the guest rooms (though they're available upon request). Families might be interested in the self-catering apartment, available for weekly stays. In summer, guests can enjoy a drink and views of the glen in the comfortable conservatory. The moderately priced menu features simple modern Scottish cuisine (set 3-course dinner £25).

Dervaig, Isle of Mull PA75 6QW. www.druimnacroish.co.uk. ⓒ/fax **01688/400-274.** 6 units. £56–£80 double. MC, V. Closed Nov–Mar. **Amenities:** Restaurant; bar; Wi-Fi (free). *In room:* Hair dryer, no phone.

Fionnphort

At the western tip of the Ross of Mull is Fionnphort, a tiny port that sees a lot of traffic. This is where the road ends, and regular ferry passages are available across the 1-mile Sound of Iona to the Isle of Iona, one of the most visited places in Scotland. Less than 1¼ miles to the south is the tidal island of Erraid, where David Balfour had adventures in Robert Louis Stevenson's *Kidnapped.*

WHERE TO EAT

Keel Row SCOTTISH   The undisputed leader in providing food and drink to passengers waiting for a ferry to Iona, this friendly place is in two connected buildings near the pier. Food is served in a cedar-clad building overlooking the waterfront, while drinks are offered in a 19th-century stone cottage with a blazing fireplace. Dishes include spicy fried crab with coriander, onions, tomatoes, and spices, or the national dish of haggis with *neeps and tatties* (turnips and mashed potatoes).

At the harborfront, at the end of the A849. ⓒ **01681/700-458.** Main courses £8–£12; sandwiches and burgers £4–£8. MC, V. Restaurant summer only, daily noon–3pm and 6–9pm; snacks and drinks year-round, daily noon–11pm. Meals served in the bar during winter, daily 6–8pm; drinks year-round, daily noon–11pm.

WHERE TO STAY

Achaban House ☺   Its almost indestructible walls (1m/3¼ ft. thick in places) were built in 1820 of pink granite for the supervisor of the local quarry. Shortly after, the building was converted into the manse for the local church. Today, it sits beside the town's only highway, a 10-minute walk east of the ferry landing. All rooms have private bathrooms, though some are across the hall. One family room is available. Fixed-price dinners are prepared on request and might include poached local salmon or locally reared lamb.

Fionnphort, Isle of Mull PA66 6BL. www.achabanhouse.co.uk. © **01681/700-205**. Fax 01681/700-649. 6 units. £32 double; £95 family room. MC, V. *In room:* Hair dryer, no phone.

Tiroran

Close to Ben More, Mull's highest mountain, Tiroran is isolated in the countryside. It's on the north shore of Loch Scridain, on the southern part of the island, and can be reached via the B8035.

WHERE TO STAY

Tiroran House ★ ☺ 🎁   Located on the north shore of Loch Scridain, standing in its own bucolic grounds, Tiroran House is ideal for a romantic getaway; it's surrounded by gardens and lawns that look out onto the wild sea. The bedrooms are decorated in an elegant cottage style, and each has its own distinctive character. To supplement the hotel business, the owners also rent out two beautiful cottages, ideal for a family vacation. The minimum rental period is usually at least 1 week.

Tiroran, Isle of Mull PA69 6ES. www.tiroran.com. © **01681/705-232.** Fax 01681/705-240. 6 units. £120–£195 double. MC, V. **Amenities:** Dining room. *In room:* no phone.

IONA ★ & STAFFA ★: AN ABBEY & A MUSICAL CAVE

Iona: ⅛ mile W of Mull; Staffa: 6¼ miles NE of Iona

A remote, low-lying, and treeless green island with high cliffs and rolling meadows, Iona is situated off the southwestern coast of Mull across the Sound of Iona. It measures only 1 by 3½ miles. Staffa, with its famous **musical cave,** is a 30-hectare (74-acre) island in the Inner Hebrides, lying to the west of Mull.

Iona

Iona has been known as a place of spiritual power and pilgrimage for centuries and was the site of the first Christian settlement in Scotland, preserving the learning that was nearly lost in the Dark Ages.

The island was owned by the dukes of Argyll from 1695, but in order to pay £1 million in real-estate taxes, the 12th duke was forced to sell it in the 1970s to Sir Hugh Fraser, former owner of Harrods department store. Fraser secured Iona's future and made it possible for money raised by the National Trust for Scotland to be turned over to the trustees of the restored abbey. The only village on Iona, **Baille Mor,** sits in the most sheltered spot, allowing some trees and garden plots to be cultivated. Walking is the best way to get around.

ESSENTIALS

Iona is accessible only by passenger ferry from the Island of Mull. (Cars must remain on Mull.) The service is informal but fairly frequent in summer. In the off season, transport depends on the weather. Contact **Caledonian MacBrayne** for times (© **0800/066-5000,** or **01688/302-017** for the port office in Tobermory; www.calmac.co.uk).

Today, the island attracts nearly 1,000 visitors a week in high season. Most come to see the Benedictine **Iona Abbey** ★, part of which dates from the 13th century. People also come to visit relics of the settlement founded here by St. Columba in

STAYING AT IONA abbey

Some people consider a visit to Iona the highlight of their trip to Scotland. Besides being impressed by the unique historical and archaeological heritage, many gain a renewed interest in the power of religion. If that's what you're seeking, you can contact the **Iona Community** (© **01681/700-404;** www.iona. org.uk), an ecumenical group that maintains a communal lifestyle in the ancient abbey and offers full board and accommodation to visitors who want to share in the community's daily life. The only ordained members of the group are its two wardens, one belonging to the Presbyterian Church of Scotland, the other to the Scottish Episcopal Church.

From March to October, the community leads a series of discussion seminars, each lasting from Saturday to Saturday. A recent seminar focused on the role of the Christian Church in the united Europe of the 21st century. The cost of a week's full board during one of these seminars is about £300 per person; there are significantly discounted rates for students and children. The abbey also opens to guests from late November to mid-December, although no seminars are offered then. The per-week price is the same as in summer. Guests are expected to contribute about 30 minutes per day to the execution of some kind of household chore. The daily schedule involves a wake-up call at 8am, communal breakfast at 8:20am, a morning religious service, and plenty of unscheduled time for conversation, study, and contemplation. Up to 44 guests can be accommodated at one time in bunk-bedded twin rooms without private bathrooms. In addition to the abbey, there's the Iona Community's center for reconciliation, the **MacLeod Centre,** built for youth, people with disabilities, and families. It accommodates up to 50 guests, during summer only.

A.D. 563, from which Celtic Christianity spread through Scotland and to Europe beyond. The abbey has been restored by the Iona Community and is run by Historic Scotland (www.historic-scotland.gov.uk), which leads tours and runs a coffee shop daily from 9:30am to 4:30pm in winter, and from 9:30am to 5:30 in summer. Admission is £5.50 adults, £4.40 students and seniors, £3.30 children 5 to 15. The community also offers room and board to interested visitors, conducts workshops on Christianity, sponsors a youth camp, and each Wednesday leads a 6¾-mile hike to the island's holy and historic spots.

Despite the many visitors, the atmosphere on the island remains peaceful and spiritual. You can walk off among the sheep and cows that wander freely everywhere to the top of **Dun-I,** a small mountain, and contemplate the ocean and the landscape as though you were the only person on earth.

WHERE TO EAT & STAY

Most of the islanders on Iona live by crofting and fishing, and supplement their income by taking in paying guests in season, usually charging very low or at least fair prices. Of course, you can check into the hotels below, but a stay in a private home may be an altogether more rewarding adventure.

Argyll Hotel ★ ⛳ Occupying a fine Victorian building constructed in 1868, the Argyll is located ⅓ mile from the ferry dock and overlooks the Sound of Iona and Mull. The small guest rooms are comfortably furnished, in a bright and simple style.

Lunches and dinners feature fresh fish and vegetables grown locally. The hotel also bakes its own bread, pastries, and cakes. Vegetarians are well catered for, too. The hotel is licensed to serve guests alcohol.

Isle of Iona PA76 6SJ. www.argyllhoteliona.co.uk. ℂ **01681/700-334.** Fax 01681/700-510. 16 units, 15 with private bathroom. £32–£185 double. MC, V. **Amenities:** Restaurant; lounge; Internet (free). *In room:* Hair dryer, no phone.

Martyr's Bay Restaurant ★ 🎁 SCOTTISH/SEAFOOD   Down by the docks, this is the best place on Iona for pub grub. One local said that it looks like a village hall from a 1970s British suburb, and so it does; but it warms considerably once you go inside, especially after you've had a pint or two of Guinness. The seafood (try the cold shellfish platter) is the best on the island. The owners not only secure the finest catch of the day, but also prepare dishes made from fresh local meat, with lamb being a particular specialty. Portions are huge, so come with a large appetite. There's seating outside for sunny days.

Isle of Iona. ℂ **01681/700-382.** www.martyrsbay.co.uk. Reservations recommended Fri–Sat. Main courses £15–£20. DC, MC, V. Restaurant daily 9:30am–5pm and 6–8:30pm. Bar daily 11:30am–11:30pm.

St. Columba Hotel   This hotel is located just uphill from the village and about ⅓ mile from the jetty. The oldest part of the hotel was originally built as a manse for Presbyterian clergy in 1846, but it has been greatly extended over the years. The guest rooms have been refurbished in a simple and contemporary style, with white walls and bare wood finishes. Try to get a room overlooking the sea, and reserve well in advance in summer. A set dinner is served nightly at 7pm, with wholesome food, including vegetables grown in the hotel gardens. Vegetarian meals are available on request.

Isle of Iona PA76 6SL. www.stcolumba-hotel.co.uk. ℂ **01681/700-304.** Fax 01681/700-688. 27 units. £98–£160 double. Rates include half-board. MC, V. Closed mid-Oct to Mar. **Amenities:** Restaurant; bar; Wi-Fi (free). *In room:* Hair dryer, no phone.

Staffa

The main attraction for visitors to the island of Staffa, 6¼ miles north of Iona, is **Fingal's Cave** ★★, which for more than 200 years has been the inspiration for music, poetry, paintings, and prose. Its Gaelic name, *An Uamh Ehinn,* means "musical cave." It's the only such formation known in the world that has basalt columns; over the centuries, the sea has carved a huge cavern in the basalt, leaving massive hexagonal columns. The sound of the crashing waves and swirling waters (the music) inspired Mendelssohn to write the *Fingal's Cave Overture.* Turner painted the cave on canvas, and Keats, Wordsworth, and Tennyson all praised it in their poetry.

Staffa has been uninhabited for more than 170 years, but you can still explore the cave, which is protected from development by the National Trust. Entrance is free, requiring only payment for boat passage from Mull or Iona at £25 for adults and £10 for children aged 13 and under. Between March and October the boat runs twice daily from Iona, at 9:45am and 1:45pm, and from Fionnphort on the Isle of Mull, at 10am and 2pm. The trip lasts about 3 hours, including about 1 hour ashore. Rubber-soled shoes and warm clothing are recommended. Reservations are important; telephone **Mrs. Carol Kirkpatrick,** whose husband, David, operates the boat, at *Tigh-na-Traigh* (House by the Shore), Isle of Iona (ℂ **01681/700-358;** www.staffatrips.co.uk).

COLONSAY

15 miles S of the Isle of Mull

The most remote of the islands of Argyll, Colonsay shares some of the same characteristics as Iona, Tyree, and Coll. To the west, it faces nothing but the open Atlantic—only a lighthouse stands between Colonsay and Canada. The island encompasses 20 sq.miles. It's more tranquil than Mull and Skye because it doesn't accommodate day-trippers.

Essentials

A ferry, operated by **Caledonian MacBrayne** (© **0800/066-5000** or **01951/200-308** for the port office on Colonsay; www.calmac.co.uk), sails between Oban and Colonsay daily except Tuesday. The 37-mile crossing takes 2½ hours, and costs £13 for passengers one-way and £68 for cars.

You can explore all parts of the island along its one-lane roads. Many visitors prefer to rent a bike than drive. You can also rent sailing dinghies and rowing boats and sail around the island, following in the grand tradition of the Vikings. Go to the **Isle of Colonsay Hotel** (see below), which rents bikes by the day or week. Hotel staff will also put you in touch with local fishermen and entrepreneurs who can either rent you a boat (prices start from around £20 per hour) or take you on a boat trips themselves.

Wildlife is one of the main attractions that draw visitors to the island. Golden eagles, falcons, gray seals, otters, and wild goats with elegant horns and long shaggy hair can all be seen on a good day. It's estimated that there are some 500 species of flora on the island. The gardens of the 1722 **Colonsay House** (the house isn't open to the public; www.colonsay.org.uk/gardens.html) are filled with rare rhododendrons, magnolias, eucalyptus, and even palm trees. From April to October, the gardens are open on Wednesday from noon until 5pm, and on Friday from 2 to 5pm (admission £3). The adjacent woodland gardens are open 7 days a week all year round.

The island also has plenty of archaeological remains. Prehistoric forts, stone circles, and single standing stones attest to the antiquity of Colonsay, which has been occupied since the Stone Age.

The little island of **Oransay** was named for Oran, a disciple of St. Columba. It's joined at low tide by the Strand, and you can wade across the sands during a 2-hour period. The ancient monastic ruins here date from the 6th century.

Where to Eat & Stay

Isle of Colonsay Hotel ★ 🍴 This is reputedly Great Britain's most isolated hotel and the social center for the Isle of Colonsay. Its mid-18th-century gables and chimneys rise above surrounding herb and vegetable gardens. The bedrooms aren't exactly spacious, but they are immaculately presented with bright yet simple furnishings. Some rooms have views out over the water to the neighboring island of Jura. Guests who want to get close-up views of the island's abundant flora and fauna can ask to be dropped off by courtesy car to go on rambles.

The smartly decorated restaurant serves lunch, dinner, and a pre-ferry set dinner. The chef's philosophy is to let the locally produced ingredients speak for themselves and to cook them simply, with a minimum of fuss. The results are delicious; you can feast on homemade soups, fresh oysters or mussels, sirloin steaks, vegetables from the garden, goat's cheese, and freshly baked bread. The tongue-and-groove-paneled bar is also stylishly designed. The warm ambience makes it popular with local people as well as hotel guests.

Isle of Colonsay PA61 7YP. www.colonsayestate.co.uk. ℗ **01951/200-316.** Fax 01951/200-353. 12 units, 9 with private bathroom. £70–£145 double. Half-board is £30 extra. MC, V. **Amenities:** Restaurant; bar; library; bike and scooter rental. *In room:* TV, hair dryer, no phone.

12 LEWIS ★: ISLAND OF HEATHER

209 miles NW of Edinburgh; 213 miles NW of Glasgow

The most northerly of the Outer Hebrides—and also the largest at 62 miles long and 18–28 miles across—Lewis is easily reached by ferry from Ullapool (see Chapter 11). The island was once known as Lews, or, more poetically, the "island of heather"—the sweet taste of the lamb raised here is said to come from their heather diet. Lewis and Harris (see "Harris," below) form parts of the same island, stretching for 95 miles north to south. Filled with marshy peat bogs, Lewis's landscape is relatively treeless, thanks in part to Norse raider Magnus Barelegs. He and his Viking warriors burned most of the trees, leaving Lewis as bare as his shanks.

Located on the eastern side of the island, **Stornoway** is the only real town in the Outer Hebrides; it's just inland from a natural harbor where you can see gray seals along with fishing boats. Even though the whole world has heard of Harris tweed, it might as well be called Lewis tweed, because Stornoway, with a population of 5,000, has taken over the industry. There are some 600 weavers on the island, and one of the attractions of this rather bleak port is visiting a mill shop or a weaver's cottage.

Essentials

GETTING THERE   An airport (www.hial.co.uk/stornoway-airport), which doubles as an RAF base, is (3½ miles from the center of Stornoway. The town receives flights from Glasgow and Inverness from Monday to Saturday, as well as a frequent service from Benbecula. Contact **British Airways** (℗ **0844/993-0787** in Glasgow) to make reservations.

Caledonian MacBrayne (℗ **0800/066-5000,** or 01851/702-361 for the port office at Stornoway; www.calmac.co.uk) operates one or two ferries from Ullapool to Stornoway each day; in July and August additional sailings are offered. One-way passage costs £7.50 for passengers, and £40 for cars. The journey time is 3½ hours.

VISITOR INFORMATION   The **Western Isles Tourist Board,** which has information about all the Outer Hebrides, is at 26 Cromwell St., Stornoway (℗ **01851/703-088;** www.visithebrides.com). It's open April to October Monday through Friday from 9am to 6pm and Saturday 9am to 5pm and 8 to 9pm; and October to April Monday through Friday from 9am to 5pm.

Exploring the Island

The island's major attraction is the Neolithic temple of **Callanish ★★**, 16 miles west of Stornoway, off the A858. Only Stonehenge, on Salisbury Plain in the south of England, equals these 13 standing stones in archaeological importance and visual splendor. The stones are laid out to depict a Celtic cross with a burial cairn at the center. They're approached from either north or south by a road lined with stone pillars. The site dates from about 1800 B.C. An old Gaelic legend claims that when the giants who were said to have once inhabited the island refused to convert to Christianity, St. Kieran turned them to stone. You can wander among the ruins for free, day

---

Boat Trips in the Outer Hebrides

You can take a day cruise with **Sea Trek**, 16 Uigen, Miavaig, Isle of Lewis (📞 01851/672-469; www.seatrek.co. uk); **Island Cruising**, 1 Erista, Uig, Isle of Lewis (📞 01851/672-381; www.island-cruising.com); or **Strond Wildlife Charters**, 1 Strond, Isle of Harris (📞 01859/520-204). All specialize in full- and half-day (or any amount of time you want) cruises that focus on the wildlife, bird life, and ecology of the Hebridean archipelago, usually with special emphasis on the seal colonies that thrive on some of the more remote islands.

---

or night. A **visitor center** (📞 01851/621-422; www.callanishvisitorcentre.co.uk), which provides historical information and an audiovisual presentation, charges £2. It's open from April to September, Monday through Saturday 10am to 9pm, and from October to March Wednesday through Saturday 10am to 4pm. The center has its own gift shop and cafe.

Just west of the harbor at Stornoway, you can visit the grounds of **Lews Castle** (which uses the old spelling), built in 1818. The castle itself is closed to the public, but you can wander through the garden, which is at its best in May.

At Arnol, 15 miles northwest of Stornoway, just off the A858, is the thatched **Lewis Blackhouse** (📞 01851/710-395), constructed without mortar and preserved to show what a typical Hebridean dwelling once looked like. It's called a "black house" because it was believed that the smoke from the open peat fires was good for the thatched roof—the Leodhasach (as the islanders are called) built their houses with no chimneys so the smoke could pass through the thatch. From April to September, it's open Monday to Saturday 9:30am to 6:30pm (to 4pm Oct–Mar). Admission is £2.50 for adults, £2 for seniors, and £1.25 for children 5 to 16.

At 6m (20 ft.) tall and 2m (6½ ft.) wide, the **Clach an Trushal** at Balanthrushal, Barvas, is the largest single monolith in northern Scotland. It's signposted beside the main highway leading north from Stornoway. Along the A858, 20 miles northwest of Stornoway, stands **Dun Carloway Broch,** a 9m (30-ft.) *broch* (round-sided stone tower) left over from the Iron Age. You can visit both sites at any time for free.

At Dun Borranish, near the village of Ardroil, the famous **Lewis Chessmen** were dug up in 1831 outside Uig Sands. Made of walrus tusks and reputed to have been carved around A.D. 500, they're now one of the prize exhibits of the British Museum in London. If you're a chess player, you can purchase a reproduction set on Lewis.

At Ness, toward that northerly outpost, the Butt of Lewis, is **St. Moluag's Church** (www.saintmoluag.com), a Scottish Episcopal church that still holds occasional services. The chapel, known in Gaelic as *Teampull Mhor* ("big temple"), is from about the 12th century, founded by Olav the Black during the Norse occupation.

Borgh Pottery (📞 01851/850-345; www.borgh-pottery.com), on the A857 at Borve, 17 miles from Stornoway on the road to Ness, has been in business for more than 20 years, producing hand-thrown stoneware in pink, blue, red, green, black, and cream. Its name is spelled with a *g,* the Gaelic spelling of Borve.

The Isle of Lewis's contribution to the world of golf is the 18-hole **Stornoway Golf Club,** Willow Glen Road, about a mile from Stornoway (📞 01851/702-240; www.stornowaygolfclub.co.uk). It's an isolated, windswept course carved out of the moors.

If you'd like to rent a bike, head for **Alex Dan's Cycle Centre,** 67 Kenneth St., Stornoway (℃ **01851/704-025;** www.hebrideancycles.co.uk).

Entertainment & Nightlife

Most of the pubs lining the waterfront have live music at weekends—usually featuring traditional Celtic or Scottish performers. There's generally no cover charge. An updated bar with live music is **Lewis Bar,** South Beach Street (℃ **01851/704-567**). On Saturday, the stage might present anything from a rock band to a traditional Scottish group.

An Lanntair Gallery, Town Hall, South Beach Street (℃ **01851/703-307;** www.lanntair.com), stages musical and theatrical events with a strong emphasis on Gaelic culture. The center also offers jazz, folk, and traditional music concerts, plus classic and contemporary drama, comedy, and children's shows. Tickets are generally priced at £10 to £15 for adults and £3 to £7 for children. Productions take place in either the gallery space, which seats 55, or the town hall, which holds 350.

Where to Eat & Stay

Cabarfeidh Hotel The Cabarfeidh stands about 1 mile north of Stornoway, midway between Laxdale and Newmarket, in a 3.2-hectare (8-acre) garden. Designed as a contemporary arrangement of cubes, it was built by a Mackenzie, who named it after the battle cry of his fighting clan, "stag antlers!"

The guest rooms are comfortable and well equipped, if a little corporate in style. One of the rooms is designed especially for disabled guests. The restaurant offers the best local produce: fresh fish and seafood, and local beef and lamb. The early dinner menu is particularly well priced at £17 for three courses. The convivial bar is shaped like a Viking longship.

Manor Park, Stornoway, Lewis, Outer Hebrides H51 2EU. www.cabarfeidh-hotel.co.uk. ℃ **01851/702-604.** Fax 01851/705-572. 46 units. £175 double. AE, DC, MC, V. Free parking. **Amenities:** Restaurant; bar; room service. *In room:* TV, hair dryer, Wi-Fi (free).

Caladh Inn ☺ A 5-minute walk from the town center, the Caladh is one of the most modern hotels—and the largest—in the Outer Hebrides. The public rooms have several full-size snooker tables; there's a bar as well as a basement nightclub open on Fridays and Saturdays. The guest rooms don't have a lot of charm but are well equipped. This hotel is a particularly good option if you have children. In addition to baby-changing facilities, high chairs, and a babysitting service, there are also plenty of toys to keep children amused.

The restaurant offers a reasonably priced lunches and dinners (main courses from £8). The menu features plenty of hearty fare, from scallops with black pudding to burgers or steaks.

9 James St., Stornoway, Lewis, Outer Hebrides HS1 2QN. www.caladhinn.co.uk. ℃ **01851/702-740.** Fax 01851/703-158. 69 units. £99–£119 double. AE, MC, V. Free parking. Closed Jan. **Amenities:** Restaurant; bar; babysitting. *In room:* TV, hair dryer, Wi-Fi (free).

Park Guest House ★ Occupying a century-old stone house about a 10-minute walk north of the ferry terminal, this hotel is one of the best places to stay on Lewis. Its restaurant, which is also open to non-guests, is renowned as the best in town. It has country-house decor and the furnishings throughout are carefully selected to correspond with the period of the building. The nine guest rooms, all with their own bathrooms, are immaculately outfitted.

The restaurant serves an "Early Bird" menu between 5pm and 6:30pm (two courses for £11), and an a la carte dinner menu from 6:30pm (main courses £14–£24). Dishes feature seasonal game, fresh seafood, and homemade desserts. A children's menu is available on request. The hotel offers cooking demonstrations (with lunch) on Saturdays during the season for £22.

30 James St., Stornoway, Lewis, Outer Hebrides H51 2QN. www.theparkguesthouse.co.uk. © **01851/702-485.** Fax 01851/703-482. 9 units. £110 double. MC, V. **Amenities:** Restaurant; bar. *In room:* TV, hair dryer.

HARRIS ★

218 miles NW of Glasgow; 56 miles NW of Mallaig; 246 miles NW of Edinburgh; 34 miles S of Stornoway

Harris is really part of the same island as its northern neighbor, Lewis, but it has a very different geography. North Harris is full of mountains, dominated by the **Clisham,** which at 789m (2,600 ft.) is the highest peak in the Outer Hebrides. Harris may not have as many ancient relics as Lewis, but most visitors agree that the mountains, beaches, and scenic vistas make up for it. The **beaches** in the west are good for strolling, swimming (if you're hardy), or camping; the bays in the east are ideal for fishing and sailing.

The locals, some 3,000 in all, are called Hearach, and they're different from the people of Lewis, even speaking with a different accent. If you arrive in Lewis, you can drive to Harris on a single-lane road that connects the two. As you drive through the rugged terrain, you might meet another car, in which case you'll need to use one of the "passing places." No matter what, however, drive slowly, because sheep might suddenly scamper in front of your wheels. The distance from Stornoway, the capital of Lewis, to Tarbert, the capital of Harris, is 34 miles. Many visitors prefer to take the ferry from the little port of Uig on the Isle of Skye. From Harris you can also make connections to Lochmaddy on North Uist (see "North & South Uist," below). Even in the busiest season, Harris isn't overrun.

Harris has long been known for its hand-weaving and tweed. Although that industry has now passed to Stornoway (see "Lewis: Island of Heather," above), you can still buy Harris tweed jackets in Harris. In summer, you see them displayed on the walls of roadside sheds, selling for very good prices.

The island is bisected by two long sea lochs that meet at Tarbert, the single-street main village. Whatever you need in the way of supplies, you should pick up in the town here—otherwise you'll be out of luck. If you're touring by car, also make sure you fill up with petrol (gas) here. Ask at the tourist center (see below) about the island bus tours conducted in summer. For an adventure, take the car ferry, which runs regularly across the sound to the little fishing community of **Scalpay,** an offshore island.

Essentials

GETTING THERE   You can take a car/passenger ferry to Tarbert, capital of Harris, from Uig on the Isle of Skye, Monday to Saturday. There are one or two ferries per day; a one-way ticket for the 1¾-hour trip costs £5.35 (£24 with car). Contact **Caledonian MacBrayne** (© **0800/066-5000** or **01859/502-444** for the port office in Tarbert; www.calmac.co.uk).

Buses run from Stornoway to Tarbert daily (a 70-min. trip). Call **Harris Coaches** (© **01859/502-441**) for schedules. At least five buses per day make the run, Monday to Saturday, but fewer on Sundays.

If you're driving from Stornoway on Lewis in the north, head south along the A859 to reach Tarbert.

VISITOR INFORMATION A **Tourist Information Centre** operates from the port at Tarbert (✆ **01859/502-011;** www.visithebrides.com). April to October, it's open Monday through Saturday 9am to 5pm; November to March, it's open Monday and Friday 11am to 1pm, and Tuesday, Thursday, and Saturday 11am to 2pm.

Exploring the Island

The lack of roads makes it impossible to take a circular tour of Harris. However, using Tarbert as your base, you can set out northwest along the coast of **West Loch Tarbert,** with the Forest of Harris to your north. Or you can go south from Tarbert, hugging the western coast road along the Sound of Taransay, with Rodel as your final destination.

Taking the northwesterly route first, you come to an **Old Whaling Station** at Bunavoneadar. In the early 20th century, Norwegians set up the station, but because of dwindling profits it was abandoned in 1930. If you continue north along the B887, you arrive at the **Amhuinnsuidhe Estate,** a Scottish baronial castle built in 1868. The river to the left has one of the most beautiful salmon leaps in Scotland. The road beyond the castle continues to **Hushinish Point,** from where you can see the little island of Scarp, which is no longer inhabited.

Returning to Tarbert, now take the A859 south. Some of the South Harris coastline might remind you of Norway, with its sea lochs and fjord fingers. The main road to Rodel is mostly two lanes and well surfaced; the east-coast road, however, is a winding single lane. Along the way, you pass the **Clach Mhicleoid** ("MacLeod's Stone") standing stone.

From here you can look out across the Sound of Taransay, to the **Island of Taransay,** named after St. Tarran. It has several ancient sites, including the remains of St. Tarran's Chapel. Like Scarp, it was once populated, but now its fields have been turned over to sheep for grazing. Continuing on the coastal road along the wild Atlantic—actually the Sound of Taransay—you'll find another ancient stone, the **Scarista Standing Stone.** Before reaching it, you pass **Borve Lodge,** the former home of Lord Leverhulme, the soap tycoon.

The road south passes the little promontory of Toe Head, which juts into the Atlantic. An ancient chapel, **Rudhan Teampull,** stands about ¾ mile west of Northton and is reached by a sand track. Many prehistoric sites were uncovered and excavated on the tiny *machair*-studded peninsula of Toe Head.

The next village is **Leverburgh,** named after Lord Leverhulme. He's credited with trying to bring the people of the area into the 20th century, but his efforts to rejuvenate the economy largely failed. From here you can take a small passenger ferry to North Uist and Berneray.

Finally, drive east to Rodel, where **St. Clement's Church** ★ stands high in the village. Overlooking Loch Rodel, this church is one of the most important monuments in the Western Isles. Cruciform in plan, it has a western tower, a nave, and two cross aisles. Some of the masonry work in freestone is similar to that used at Iona Abbey. It's believed that the church was built in the late 15th or very early 16th century.

In the Sound of Harris, separating Harris from North Uist, lie the islands of **Ensay, Killegray,** and **Pabbay.** Again, they were once populated, but now are the domain of grazing sheep.

The island has a 9-hole **Golf Club,** Scarista (☏ **01859/550-226;** www.harris golf.com), an isolated, windswept course carved into the Hebridean moors. The course isn't staffed; you're asked to put £20 into the honesty box for playing 9 holes.

Where to Eat & Stay

Harris Hotel ★　This hotel, a landmark since it was built in 1865, remains one of the most popular places to stay in the Outer Hebrides. In the 1920s, the novelist J.M. Barrie visited and found inspiration for his story *Mary Rose*. He even etched his initials on the dining room window. Each guest room has lots of old-fashioned comfort. Some family rooms are available, many overlooking the garden.

The pub is a social center for local people, and you can order pub grub here throughout the day. The more formal restaurant offers lunch and dinner, with a good-value set dinner menu (£27 for 3 courses) as well as an a la carte one.

Tarbert, Harris, Outer Hebrides HS3 3DL. www.harrishotel.com. ☏ **01859/502-154.** Fax 01859/502-281. 23 units. £80–£150 double. MC, V. **Amenities:** Restaurant; bar; Wi-Fi (free). *In room:* TV, hair dryer, no phone.

Rodel Hotel ★ 🎒　Built at land's end in the shadows of the 500-year-old St. Clement's Church, this hotel is at the southernmost tip of Harris. Because it fronts a harbor with an anchorage, the Rodel is a favorite retreat for anglers seeking trout and salmon. The exterior dates to the 18th century, but its interior has been comfortably and somewhat luxuriously modernized. Bedrooms are all nonsmoking and elegantly furnished, each decorated with a charming character and ambience. Harris tweed bedcovers and matching curtains are used throughout.

In the restaurant, the best local produce is used, including island lamb, beef, and venison as well as, when available, rabbit and goose. Fish and seafood is caught locally: scallops from the Sound of Harris, salmon from Lewis, lobster and crab from out in the Atlantic. A wide selection of Highland malts, along with good local ales, is available in the bar, where you can join the locals.

Rodel, Harris, Outer Hebrides HS5 3TW. www.rodelhotel.co.uk. ☏ **01859/520-210**. Fax 01859/520-219. 4 units. £120–£135 double. MC, V. From Tarbert head south for 2 miles. **Amenities:** Restaurant; bar. *In room:* Hair dryer.

Scarista House ★★　Built long ago as a Georgian manse, this is now a lovely hotel with handsome guest rooms and two self-catering cottages. Some summer guests enjoy a bracing dip in the icy water of Scarista Beach, while others prefer to read in the well-stocked library. Guests get the best breakfast around: organic oatmeal porridge with cream, Lewis kippers, fresh herring rolled in oatmeal, full English breakfast, and a variety of baked goods. A packed lunch is provided for those who want to go hiking. Most guests return for a drink by the fireplace, and then, at 8pm, enjoy a four-course dinner of local shellfish and heather-fed lamb.

Scarista, Harris, Outer Hebrides HS3 3HX. www.scaristahouse.com. ☏ **01859/550-238.** Fax 01859/550-277. 5 units. £190–£210 double; £580–£820 per week cottage. MC, V. 24km (15 miles) SW of Tarbert on the A859. **Amenities:** Restaurant; library; CD library; babysitting. *In room:* Hair dryer.

NORTH & SOUTH UIST

90–100 miles NW of Glasgow

Standing stones, chambered cairns, ruins, and fortresses bear testimony to the rich histories of North Uist and South Uist, and the smaller island of Benbecula, which sits in between and connects the two.

Essentials

GETTING THERE British Airways flies daily from Monday to Saturday to **Benbecula Airport** (the nearest connection for North Uist) from Glasgow, a 1-hour trip. Call ℂ **0141/887-1111** at Glasgow Airport for flight information.

Lochboisdale is the site of the ferry terminal (ℂ **0800/066-5000;** www.calmac. co.uk) that provides a link between South Uist and the mainland at Oban, which takes 5½ hours. Ferries depart from Oban for Lochboisdale on Tuesdays, Thursdays, Saturdays, and Sundays in summer, costing about £12 one-way. Some of these ferries stop at Castlebay, on Barra. Other ferries run from Uig, on the Isle of Skye, to Lochmaddy, North Uist, once or twice daily. The most popular connection, this car/passenger ferry trip takes anywhere from 2 to 4 hours and costs £6.50 one-way. For information, consult **Caledonian MacBrayne** (ℂ **01876/500-337** in Lochmaddy; www.calmac.co.uk).

North Uist is linked to Benbecula and South Uist by causeways and bridges, so you can drive to or from either of these islands along the A867, which becomes the A865.

VISITOR INFORMATION Consult the **Western Isles Tourist Board** in Stornoway (see "Lewis: Island of Heather," earlier in this chapter). There's also a **Tourist Information Centre** at the pier in Lochmaddy, on North Uist (ℂ **01876/500-321;** www.visithebrides.com), open Monday through Friday 9am to 5pm; Saturday 9:30am to 1pm and 2 to 5:30pm; and Monday, Wednesday, and Friday 7:30 to 8:30pm. The staff can arrange a place to stay if you've arrived without a reservation. On South Uist, the **Tourist Information Centre** at the pier at Lochboisdale (ℂ **01878/700-288**) is open Easter to October only, Monday to Saturday 9am to 5pm. It's also open for late ferry arrivals, usually Monday to Thursday and Saturday 9 to 10pm and Friday 7:30 to 8:30pm. Accommodation can be arranged through this office as well.

North Uist

A real bogland where hardy crofters try to wrestle a living from a turbulent sea and stubborn ground, North Uist is one of the lesser-known islands in the Outer Hebrides, but it's beautiful nonetheless. Its antiquity is reflected in the *brochs,* duns, wheelhouses, and stark monoliths, all left by the island's prehistoric dwellers.

The population of North Uist is about 1,300. Before the Highland Clearances, it had been as high as 5,000. The island is about 12 miles wide by 35 miles at its longest point, and is served by a circular road, usually a single lane with passing places, and several minor roads that branch east and west.

The main village is **Lochmaddy,** on the eastern shore. Whatever you need, you're likely to find it here (if it's available on North Uist at all), from a post office to a petrol station. Lochmaddy is also the site of a ferry terminal. Ferries operate between here and Uig on the Isle of Skye daily during the summer. In addition, a small private ferry runs from Newton Ferry, north of Lochmaddy, to Leverburgh, on Harris. This isn't a car ferry, but it does allow small motorcycles and bikes. A small vehicular ferry takes you to the island of Berneray. In keeping with the strict religious tradition of these islands, this ferry doesn't operate on Sunday—and neither, seemingly, does anything else.

EXPLORING THE ISLAND

North Uist may be small, but its scenery is extremely varied. The eastern shores possess an untamed beauty. The coastline is dotted with trout-filled lochs, and everything is set against a backdrop of rolling heather-clad hills. Nights come on fast in winter; sunsets linger in summer. The western side of North Uist is a land of rich meadows filled with wildflowers. Here you find **long white beaches,** where Atlantic rollers attract hardy surfers.

Heading northwest from Lochmaddy for 2½ miles, you come to the hamlet of **Blashaval,** where you find the **Three Standing Stones of the False Men.** Local tradition has it that this trio of stones, known in Gaelic as *Na Fir Bhreige,* were actual men, wife deserters from Skye turned into stone by a witch.

Continuing along the road for 4 miles, you approach uninhabited **Dun Torcuill Island,** rising above the west side of **Loch an Duin.** Access to the island is possible on foot only during low tide; exercise caution. On the island is a *broch;* it's a ruined, though still fine, example of the circular towers that provided living accommodation and perhaps also defensive fortification during the Middle Ages. Most visitors prefer to admire it from across the water.

Turning north on the B893, you come to **Newton Ferry.** A 15-minute crossing takes you to the little offshore island of **Berneray,** which has some ancient sites, including the mysterious-looking **Borve Standing Stones.** There's a privately run hostel here (www.gatliff.org.uk) offering 20 beds. The 140 or so people who live on the island are mainly engaged in crofting and fishing and may regard *you* as a sightseeing attraction.

After you return to Newton Ferry, head south on the same road. As the road forks, bear left to **Trumisgarry** to see the ruins of an old chapel where an early Christian settlement was founded. Look out also here for **St. Columba's Well** (*Tobar Chaluim Chille* in Gaelic).

Return to the main road and head west toward Sollas. On both sides of the road are cairns and standing stones, many from 2000 B.C. Pass through **Hosta,** a site of the Highland Games, heading for the **Balranald Nature Reserve** (www.rspb.org.uk) 3 miles northwest of Bayhead. At a reception cottage at **Goulat,** near Hougharty, you can learn more about the birds inhabiting the Outer Hebrides. The reserve itself is particularly noted for the large numbers of Barnacle geese that winter there; in summer you may be lucky enough to see the elusive corncrake, one of Britain's rarest birds. You can walk through the reserve at any time at no charge, but guided tours (£5) are given at 2pm on most Mondays during the summer.

Back on the main road, heading southeast, you pass through **Bayhead.** Again, the area is filled with an astonishing number of ancient monuments. At the junction, take the A867 back toward Lochmaddy. You'll see a sign pointing to **Ben Langass.** On the mountain slopes is a chambered cairn, thought to be at least 3,000 years old and one of the best preserved on the island. Some historians believe a warrior chieftain was buried here, but others suggest it was a communal burial ground. Bones and pottery fragments removed from excavations were sent to the National Museum in Edinburgh.

Returning to the main road again, retrace your trail and head south for Carinish, a hamlet known for the **Carinish Stone Circle** and the **Barpa Carinish,** the site of the major attraction on the island, **Trinity Temple** (*Teampull na Trionad* in Gaelic), off the A865 some 8 miles southwest of Lochmaddy. Admission is free and it's open at all times. The monastery is said to have been founded in the 13th century by Beathag, the first prioress of Iona, daughter of Somerland, an Irish mercenary and the founding father of the MacDonalds.

WHERE TO EAT & STAY

Langass Lodge ★ 📖 This hotel's spaciousness and comfort come as a welcome surprise after the miles of windswept, barren countryside you traverse before reaching it. The nearby sycamores are apparently among the few trees on all North Uist. Built as a hunting lodge in 1876, the hotel today attracts hunters, anglers, and nature lovers. The guest rooms have been completely refurbished with smart furniture and warm fabrics. Each has views of the nearby loch. The restaurant specializes in fish dishes: a three-course meal costs £34. There's also a bar, where more informal meals can be taken; main courses here range in price from £10 to £17.

Locheport, North Uist, Outer Hebrides HS6 5HA. www.langasslodge.co.uk. 📞 **01876/580-285.** Fax 01876/580-385. 12 units. £90–£135 double. MC, V. Closed Feb. **Amenities:** Restaurant; bar. *In room:* TV, DVD (in some), CD player, fridge (in some), hair dryer.

Lochmaddy Hotel You can't miss the peaked gables of this white-walled hotel, a few steps from the ferry terminal. Those who come to fish for the area's brown trout, sea trout, and salmon often stay here, and guests are welcome to use the hotel's scales to weigh the catch of the day. This is one of the few places on the island where you can buy fishing permits; prices are £6 to £52 a day, depending on the season, what kind of fish you're seeking and whether a boat is required.

The guest rooms are comfortable, if not exactly luxurious. The bar offers a fine collection of single-malt whiskies, and the dining room serves fresh locally caught lobster, king prawns, mussels, cockles, mackerel, trout, and salmon.

Lochmaddy, North Uist, Outer Hebrides HS6 5AA. www.lochmaddyhotel.co.uk. 📞 **01876/500-331.** Fax 01876/500-210. 15 units. £98–£135 double. AE, MC, V. **Amenities:** Restaurant; 2 bars; watersports. *In room:* TV, hair dryer, Wi-Fi (free).

South Uist

South Uist holds a rich treasure-trove of antiquities. A number of ecclesiastical remains are scattered along its shores, and Clan Ranald left many ruins and fortresses known as *duns.* Ornithologists and anglers alike are attracted to this island. It's the breeding habitat for a large variety of wading birds, and is also a good place to see otters. Part bogland, the island is 20 miles long and 6¼ miles wide at its broadest, and has a resident population of around 2,000 people. A main road, the A865, bisects the island, with minor roads branching off east and west.

EXPLORING THE ISLAND

The biggest village in South Uist is **Lochboisdale,** at the head of a deep-sea loch on the southeastern part of the island. It was settled in the 19th century by crofters who had been forced off their land in the notorious Land Clearances. The ruins of a small medieval castle can be seen at the head of the loch, on the island of Calvay, one of the many places Bonnie Prince Charlie used as a hideout.

Leaving Lochboisdale, the A865 goes west for 3 miles to Daliburgh, where you can pick up the B888 south to Pollachar, on the southern shore—a distance of 6¼ miles. The village is named after the **Pollachar Standing Stone,** a jagged dolmen rising a few paces from the hamlet's center. Continue east along a minor road for 2½ miles to find the Ludag jetty, where a private ferry goes to the islands of Eriskay and Barra.

The next stop is the **Klipheder Wheelhouse,** 1¾ miles west of the A865. These evocative ruins of a circular building date back to A.D. 200. On the main road again, you come to Askernish, site of an 18-hole **golf course** (📞 **07900/387-167;** www. askernishgolfclub.com).

About 3 miles north from Daliburgh, at Airidh Mhuilinn, is the **Flora MacDonald memorial.** She's revered for helping Bonnie Prince Charlie escape from George II and his supporters. Located to the west of the A865, 182m (600 ft.) up a little farm track about ⅔ mile north of Milton, the memorial consists of a cairn atop a little hill; it was here that Flora MacDonald was born in 1722. Not far away, on the other side of the main road, is the **Kildonan Museum** (ⓒ **01878/710-343;** www.kildonan museum.co.uk). It contains archaeological finds, including the famous Clan Ranald Stone, which dates from the late 1500s. The museum also has its own cafe and a shop selling crafts produced by islanders. It's open from April to October Monday through Saturday 10am to 5pm, and on Sundays from 2pm to 5pm.

If you stay on the minor roads, you'll see the dramatic *machair*-fringed shoreline and pass through the hamlets of Bornish, Ormiclete, and Stoneybridge. At Ormiclete are the ruins of **Ormiclete Castle,** constructed by the Clan Ranald chieftains in the early 18th century.

Rejoin the main road at Howbeg. The part of the island directly north of Howbeg is rich in archaeological remains. Ruins of several **medieval chapels** are all that's left of a major South Uist ecclesiastical center.

Farther north, the A865 passes the **Loch Druidibeg National Nature Reserve,** the most significant breeding ground in the country for the native grayleg goose. Attracting dedicated bird-watchers, it's a setting of *machair* and brackish lochs. At Drimsdale lie the ruins of a big dun, a fortification in a loch where the villagers retreated when under attack. It continued as a stronghold for the Clan Ranald until the early 1500s.

The road continues past the Royal Artillery Rocket Range. On the flank of Reuval Hill stands **Our Lady of the Isles,** a 9m (30-ft.) statue of the Virgin and Child. Erected in 1957, it's the largest religious statue in Britain. **Loch Bee,** inhabited by mute swans, nearly bisects the northern part of South Uist.

At the north end of the Iochdar Road you'll find signposts for **Hebridean Jewelry,** Garrieganichy, Iochdar (ⓒ **01870/610-288**). This shop produces silver and gold pendants, and brooches featuring Celtic patterns. The artists here create custom pieces on request.

If you'd like to explore the island by bike, head for **Rothan Cycles,** 9 Howmore (ⓒ **01870/620-283;** www.rothan.com).

WHERE TO EAT & STAY

Borrodale Hotel Located near the center of the island, 2½ miles west of Loch Boisdale along the A865, this gabled hotel stands in a landscape of freshwater lakes, heather, and gorse. The hotel has undergone extensive renovations, and the guest rooms, common areas, and the upmarket restaurant have all been updated. The owners can assist in arranging fishing and golf expeditions.

Daliburgh, South Uist, Outer Hebrides HS8 5SS. www.isleshotelgroup.co.uk. ⓒ**01878/700-444.** Fax 01878/700-446. 14 units. £90–£106 double. MC, V. **Amenities:** Restaurant; 2 bars; babysitting; smoke-free rooms. *In room:* TV, hair dryer.

BARRA ★: GARDEN OF THE HEBRIDES

118 miles NW of Edinburgh; 88 miles NW of Glasgow

Barra lies at the southern end of the Outer Hebrides. Since the days of the conquering Vikings, it has been associated with the Clan MacNeil. The island is one of the most beautiful in the Hebridean chain, with heather-clad meadows, beaches, sandy grasslands, peaks, rocky bays, and lofty headlands. Locals claim it has some 1,000 varieties of wildflowers.

Most of the 200 inhabitants of Barra are centered at **Castlebay,** its capital, a 19th-century herring port and the best place to stock up on supplies. In the background of the port is **Ben Heaval,** Barra's highest mountain (379m/1,243 ft.). A circular road of 10 miles takes you around the island, which measures about 4 by 8 miles.

Essentials

GETTING THERE   At the northern end of Barra is **Cockle Strand,** the airport. A long and wide beach of white sand, it's the only runway in Britain that's washed twice daily by sea tides. The Scottish airline **Loganair** (© **0871/700-2000;** www.loganair.co.uk) flies here from Glasgow and from Benbecula, on the Isle of Lewis.

From the mainland at Oban, Barra can be reached by the **Caledonian Mac-Brayne** car ferry (© **08705/650-000;** www.calmac.co.uk), which docks at Castlebay. Subject to weather conditions, ferries depart daily from Oban in the summer. Note that on most days the ferries leave in the afternoon from Oban; the return trips from Castlebray depart in the mornings or evenings. The sailing time is about 5 hours.

VISITOR INFORMATION   The **Castlebay Tourist Information Centre** (© **01871/810-336**) is near the pier where the ferry docks. From Easter to mid-October, it's open Monday to Saturday 9am to 5pm, and Sunday 1 to 4pm. The staff will help you locate a room should you arrive on Barra without a reservation.

Exploring the Island

The most important attraction sits on a rocky islet in the bay: **Kisimul Castle** (© **01871/810-313;** www.historic-scotland.gov.uk), built for strategic purposes, was the longtime stronghold of the notorious MacNeils of Barra, a clan known for piracy and lawlessness. The oldest part of the castle is a tower dating from 1120. In 1938, the 45th chieftain, the late Robert Lister MacNeil of Barra, began restoration work on his ancestral home. Weather permitting, a boatman can take you over to the castle, and back again, between April and September, daily from 9:30am to 5:30pm, Entrance is £5 for adults, £4 for seniors, and £3 for children 5 to 15, including the boat ride.

To drive around the island, head west from Castlebay until you reach Kinloch. On the left is **Loch St. Clair,** reached by a tiny track road. In the loch, on an islet, stand the ruins of St. Clair Castle, called **MacLeod's Fort.** Continuing north toward Borve, you see the **Borve Standing Stones** on your left. At Borve, the north fork leads to a chambered cairn and the hamlet of **Craigston,** which has a church dedicated to St. Brendan, the Irish navigator whom many cite as the discoverer of America. There are two interesting ruins in the area: **Dun Bharpa,** a collection of stones encircled by standing stones, and **Tigh Talamhanta,** a ruined wheelhouse.

Continue north to Allasdale. **Dun Cuier** is one of the few excavated Hebridean Iron Age forts, better preserved than most. Opposite Allasdale is **Seal Bay,** a beautiful spot where the seals do as much inspecting of you as you of them.

At **Northbay,** at Loch an Duin, the remains of an old dun protrude from the water. Continuing north to Eoligarry, you come to a small ferry terminal taking passengers to Ludag on South Uist. Eoligarry's main landmark is **St. Barr's Church,** named after St. Findbarr of Cork (A.D. 550–623), who, it's said, converted the islanders to

Christianity after finding many of them practicing cannibalism when he arrived. The original 12th-century chapel was restored by Fr. Callum MacNeil.

For bike rentals and advice on scenic routes, head for **Barra Cycle Hire,** 29 St. Brendans Rd. (© **01871/810-284**).

Where to Eat & Stay

Castlebay Hotel   Built around 1890, this gabled hotel overlooks the bay and the ferry terminal where most of the island's visitors disembark. The small guest rooms are simply but comfortably furnished, each with a neat bathroom. There's a cocktail bar and a 60-seat restaurant, where lunch and dinner are served daily. Main courses cost from £9 to £15; the menu includes numerous options for vegetarians. Adjacent to the hotel and under the same management is the Castlebay Bar, the island's most popular gathering place. There's often live music in the evenings.

Castlebay, Barra, Outer Hebrides HS9 5XD. www.castlebay-hotel.co.uk. © **01871/810-223.** Fax 01871/810-455. 14 units. £79–£180 double. MC, V. Closed Dec 22–Jan 5. **Amenities:** Restaurant; 2 bars. *In room:* TV, hair dryer.

Isle of Barra Hotel ★ ▟▊   This architecturally striking seashore hotel is—for the Outer Hebrides at least—a luxury choice. The hotel is a favorite with the yachting crowd and commands views of the tranquil, less-populated western shore of the island. It serves the best food on Barra, and its pub, the most westerly in Scotland, is widely touted as the "last dram before America." From the dining room and many of the well-furnished guest rooms, you can see everything that's coming and going at sea.

Tangusdale, Castlebay, Barra, Outer Hebrides HS9 5XW. www.isleofbarrahotel.co.uk. © **01871/810-383.** Fax 01871/810-385. 39 units. £74–£137 double. MC, V. Closed Oct 18–Mar 20. **Amenities:** Restaurant; bar; cinema room; Wi-Fi (Free). *In room:* TV, no phone.

ORKNEY & SHETLAND

Collectively known as the Northern Isles, the far-flung Orkney and Shetland archipelagos consist of about 170 wild and windswept islands, 34 of which are inhabited. Don't expect kilts and the Saltire here: The people refer to themselves as Orcadians and Shetlanders rather than Scots. Their heritage lies to the east, in Scandinavia, with Celtic culture playing a role only in the last few centuries.

SIGHTSEEING   While Orkney's antiquities put it in a league of its own, Shetland is better known for its coastal scenery and bird colonies. Prepare to crawl through tunnels and climb ladders to explore some of Europe's best-preserved prehistoric sites as well as castles, Pictish forts, and long-abandoned settlements. Binoculars will come in handy on dramatic cliffs where puffins, gannets, and great skuas nest.

EATING & DRINKING   Chefs use a wealth of local meat, seafood, and vegetables to create fresh, tasty, and wholesome dishes. Shetland is known in particular for its excellent salmon, which makes an important contribution to the local economy; eat it fresh or smoked. Watch out for Orkney's North Ronaldsay lamb: The sheep feed exclusively on seaweed, giving the meat a distinctive flavor.

HISTORY   Until they were ceded to Scotland by the Danes and Norwegians as part of the 1469 dowry of Princess Margaret of Denmark when she married James III, both sets of islands had been a gathering place for Viking fleets. Before the Norsemen, Stone Age people and Picts occupied Orkney and Shetland, all leaving their marks on the landscape.

NATURE   Isolated by the sea and lashed by wind and waves, nature has a profound influence on these bleak but beautiful islands. The seabird colonies are the largest in the U.K. and the cliffs among the highest. Otters, dolphins, and the occasional pod of orca whales can be seen in the crystal clear waters. Orkney is also known for its flora, including the rare Scottish primrose.

THE best TRAVEL EXPERIENCES IN ORKNEY & SHETLAND

o **Exploring the Heart of Neolithic Orkney:** This World Heritage Site includes atmospheric standing stones, a 5,000-year-old village, and one

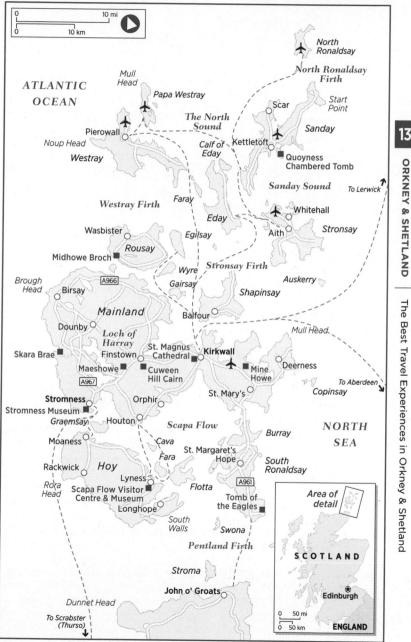

The Orkney Islands

0   10 mi
0   10 km

North Ronaldsay

North Ronaldsay Firth

ATLANTIC OCEAN

Mull Head

Papa Westray

Scar

Start Point

The North Sound

Sanday

Pierowall

Calf of Eday

Kettletoft

Noup Head

Quoyness Chambered Tomb

Westray

Sanday Sound

To Lerwick

Faray

Westray Firth

Eday

Whitehall

Wasbister

Egilsay

Aith

Stronsay

Rousay

Midhowe Broch

Wyre

Stronsay Firth

Brough Head

Gairsay

Auskerry

Birsay

A966

Shapinsay

Mainland

Balfour

Dounby

Loch of Harray

Mull Head

Skara Brae

St. Magnus Cathedral

Kirkwall

Finstown

Maeshowe

Cuween Hill Cairn

Mine Howe

Deerness

A967

To Aberdeen

Stromness

Orphir

St. Mary's

Copinsay

Stromness Museum

Graemsay

Houton

Scapa Flow

NORTH SEA

Moaness

Cava

Burray

Fara

St. Margaret's Hope

Rackwick

Hoy

Lyness

South Ronaldsay

Rora Head

Scapa Flow Visitor Centre & Museum

Flotta

A961

Longhope

Tomb of the Eagles

South Walls

Swona

Pentland Firth

Area of detail

Dunnet Head

Stroma

SCOTLAND

To Scrabster (Thurso)

John o' Groats

Edinburgh

0   50 mi
0   50 km

ENGLAND

393

of the largest and best-preserved chambered cairns in Europe. It would take months to visit all the prehistoric sights in Orkney, but these are some of the best. See p. 394.

o **Experiencing the simmer dim:** The Northern Isles, particularly Shetland, are known for their long twilights with the sun barely setting at midsummer. The "simmer dim" is a magical time of the day. Golfers can even enjoy a round of their favorite game at midnight on Orkney. See p. 410.

o **Being part of Up Helly Aa:** In winter, Shetlanders take part in Europe's largest fire festival. Dressed as Vikings, they march through Lerwick and set fire to a replica longboat, lighting up the long January night in dramatic fashion. See p. 412.

o **Watching wildlife:** Shetland is one of the best places in Europe to see the elusive otter. Bird-watchers also flock to the islands, particularly Fair Isle with its famous bird observatory where it's possible to see huge seabird colonies and watch for rare migrants. See p. 409.

o **Walking the magnificent coast:** The islands have some of the best and most unusual coastal scenery in the British Isles. The U.K.'s highest vertical cliff is on Hoy (see p. 394). Take a day trip to Papa Stour to see gloups, stacks, arches, and mysterious subterranean passages. See p. 418.

ORKNEY ★

6¼ miles N of Duncansby Head (mainland Scotland), across Pentland Firth; 280 miles N of Edinburgh

The islands of Orkney are an archaeologist's dream. The entire archipelago is covered in Stone Age burial cairns, Neolithic villages, mysterious standing stones and stone circles, Pictish brochs, Norse settlements, and ancient churches. Every few miles, you come across a brown sign indicating the way to yet another historical site; and, when you reach it, there's a good chance it's unlocked and a torch provided so that you can explore it easily.

At least 50 of Scotland's 500 known *brochs*—often called the "castles of the Picts"—are found here. Thought to have served a defensive purpose, these round constructions are characterized by double walls, the outer one of which was several meters thick.

Stretching about 50 miles from the tip of South Ronaldsay to the far north of North Ronaldsay, the islands lie 6¼ miles north of the Scottish mainland. The mostly low-lying terrain has lots of rich farmland, but there's also some dramatic scenery: Britain's highest vertical cliffs rise to 335m (1,099 ft.) on Hoy. The population of the entire chain is about 20,000, spread sparsely across 19 inhabited islands. The people are warm and laid-back, happy to help strangers, and rarely lock their doors at night.

The climate is milder than the northerly location would suggest because of the warming influence of the Gulf Stream, but the almost constant wind does temper things slightly. From May to July the sunsets are astonishing, with the midsummer sun remaining above the horizon long into the night. There's even enough light for golfers to play at midnight. There are two 18-hole golf courses on Mainland: **Orkney Golf Club** at Kirkwall (② 01856/872-457; www.orkneygolfclub.co.uk) and **Stromness Golf Club** (② **01856/850-772;** www.stromnessgc.co.uk). The nine-hole **South Ronaldsay Golf Club** (② **01856/831-395;** www.southronaldsaygolf.com) is in the village of St. Margaret's Hope. In addition, there are courses on Westray, Sanday, and North Ronaldsay. All operate a turn-up-and-play policy.

Essentials

GETTING THERE **Loganair** operates several flights a day from Aberdeen, Glasgow, Inverness, and Lerwick on Shetland to Kirkwall Airport on Mainland (the largest Orkney island). Reservations are made through **Flybe** (✆ **0871/700-2000,** or ✆ +44/1392-268-5290 from outside the U.K.; www.flybe.com).

For motorists, the shortest ferry crossing is **Pentland Ferries'** regular route from Gill's Bay in Caithness to St. Margaret's Hope. It takes about an hour and costs £30 for a car (one-way) and £13 per adult (✆ 01856/831-226; www.pentlandferries. co.uk). **NorthLink** runs frequent sailings from Scrabster on Scotland's north coast to Stromness (✆ **0845/600-0449;** www.northlinkferries.co.uk); the trip takes just over 2 hours, and single fares are £46 to £51 per car and £15 to £17 per adult. Three times a week (four in summer), the company's overnight Aberdeen–Shetland service also stops in at Kirkwall; single fares are £71 to £97 per car and £18 to £27 per adult, and the journey takes 6 hours.

If you don't have a car, you can take one of the **John o' Groats Ferries** (✆ **01955/611-353;** www.jogferry.co.uk), which operate May through December twice daily (trip time: 40 minutes). Round-trip fares are £28 per passenger.

GETTING AROUND **Loganair** (✆ **01856/872-494;** www.loganair.co.uk) operates flights from Kirkwall Airport to Sanday, Stronsay, Westray, Eday, North Ronaldsay, and Papa Westray.

Orkney Ferries Ltd. (✆ **01856/872-044;** www.orkneyferries.co.uk) operates scheduled services from Kirkwall to Eday, Papa Westray, Sanday, Stronsay, Westray, North Ronaldsay, and Shapinsay. From Houton, there's a service to Flotta and Lyness (Hoy), and from Tingwall to Rousay, Egilsay, and Wyre. There's also a passenger-only ferry from Stromness to Graemsay and Moaness (Hoy).

The **Churchill Barriers,** erected to impede enemy shipping in World War II, have been turned into a road link between the islands of Mainland, Burray, and South Ronaldsay. To rent a car, try **Colin Gregg Cars** on Hatston Industrial Estate, Kirkwall (✆ **01856/870-900;** www.a1carhireorkney.com); **J.D. Peace Cars,** Junction Road, Kirkwall (✆ **01856/872-866;** www.orkneycarhire.co.uk); or **W.R. Tullock,** Castle Street, Kirkwall (✆ **01856/875-500;** www.orkneycarrental.co.uk), which also has an office at the airport.

If you'd like to explore the region on two wheels, stop by **Bobby's Cycle Centre,** Tankerness Lane, Kirkwall (✆ **01856/875-777**). Rates are £15 daily or £70 weekly. It's open Monday through Saturday from 9am to 5:30pm. If you're based in Stromness, head to **Orkney Cycle Hire,** 52 Dundas St. (✆ **01856/850-255;** www. orkneycyclehire.co.uk), which charges £7.50 to £10 daily.

VISITOR INFORMATION To find out what's going on during your visit, consult *The Orcadian,* a weekly newspaper published since 1854 and viewable online at www.orcadian.co.uk. There are **Tourist Information Centres** in Kirkwall and in Stromness (see below). You can also get information at www.visitorkney.com.

SPECIAL EVENTS These sparsely populated islands generate quite a bit of cultural activity, especially in celebrating the region's music. Information is available through the Kirkwall Tourist Information Centre (see below), which publishes an annual list of events. One of the biggest is the 4-day **Orkney Folk Festival** (www. orkneyfolkfestival.com), which normally takes place at the end of May. This features lively ceilidhs and relaxed concerts of traditional music performed by artists from all around the globe. Based in Stromness but with some events in Kirkwall, tickets range from £6 to £15. June brings a change of pace in the form of the **St. Magnus Festival** (www.stmagnusfestival.com), which celebrates classical music and the dramatic arts. Tickets average £6 to £20.

At Christmas and New Year, the streets of Kirkwall host a chaotic game of mass football, known as the **Ba'** and said to date back at least to the 17th century. With no rules to speak of and most of the town's men joining in, it can look a little unruly to visitors.

Kirkwall

Kirkwall, established by Norse invaders on the island called Mainland, is the capital of Orkney and Britain's most northerly cathedral city. Its name comes from the old Norse "Kirkjuvagr," which means "church bay" and refers to an 11th-century church dedicated to King Olaf Haraldsson, who became the patron saint of Norway. The church no longer stands.

Away from the harbor, the old town is built around two ancient palaces and a striking red sandstone cathedral. Narrow, winding streets add to the feeling of stepping back in time as you explore this tiny city.

The **Tourist Information Centre** is at West Castle Street (℗ 01856/872-856; www.visitorkney.com). September through May it's open Monday through Friday 9am to 5pm and Saturday 10am to 4pm; during June, July, and August, it's open daily from 9am to 6pm.

EXPLORING KIRKWALL

Probably the most beautiful building on Orkney is **St. Magnus Cathedral ★**, on Broad Street (℗ 01856/874-894; www.stmagnus.org). Earl Rognvald, nephew of the martyred St. Magnus, the islands' patron saint, founded the cathedral to honor him in 1137. The remains of the saint and Rognvald were interred within pillars of the choir. Built by the same masons as Durham Cathedral in the north of England, its sense of grandeur inside is totally out-of-keeping with the simple sandstone exterior. The walls are lined with a large, interesting collection of grave slabs dating from the 17th century and earlier. Tours of the upstairs galleries take place on Tuesdays and Thursdays at 11am and 2pm; cost £5. Admission to the cathedral is free, although donations are welcomed. There's more information, including a video presentation, on its history at the nearby **St. Magnus Centre** on Palace Road, open Monday through Saturday from 8:30am to 6:30pm, and Sunday from 1:30 to 6:30pm.

Across the street on Palace Road are the ruins of two fortified medieval residences: the 12th-century **Bishop's Palace** and the 1606-built **Earl Patrick's Palace** (℗ 01856/871-918; www.historic-scotland.gov.uk). King Haakon of Norway died in the Bishop's Palace in 1263, following the Battle of Largs and his attempt to invade Scotland. The facade of the Earl's Palace, with its oriel windows and elaborate entrance, inevitably draws the eye. Inside, the Great Hall is dominated by a 5m-wide (16-ft.) fireplace. Both palaces are open April through October daily from 9:30am to 5:30pm. Admission for both is £3.70 for adults, £3 for seniors and students, and £2.20 for children.

Nearby on Broad Street is the 1574-built **Tankerness House,** home to the **Orkney Museum** (℗ 01856/873-191). This sprawling townhouse illustrates Orkney's history from Neolithic times to the 20th century. It consists of a maze of rooms, each dedicated to a different period of history, and includes children's activities. Exhibits range from the bones of the earliest inhabitants to Pictish domestic utensils. One gallery is devoted to temporary exhibitions by local artists. The museum is open Monday through Saturday from 10:30am to 5pm. Admission is free, but donations are welcome.

Highland Park Distillery, Holm Road (© 01856/874-619; www.highlandpark. co.uk), runs informative guided tours of the buildings it has been using to create one of the world's best-known whiskies since 1798. As well as the still room, visitors get to see the peat kiln and the malting floor. The Orkney distillery is one of only a handful in Scotland that still uses traditional malting floors to allow the grain to germinate. Visitors can also sample a wee dram of the 12-year-old malt at the end of the tour. There are hourly tours (costing £6) from April to September, including weekends from May to August. October through March, tours are given at 2pm and 3pm on weekdays only.

Orkney Wireless Museum, Kiln Corner, Junction Road (© 01856/871-400; www.orkneywirelessmuseum.org.uk), is dedicated to both wartime and domestic radio memorabilia. It's open from April to September, Monday through Saturday from 10am to 4:30pm and Sunday from 2:30 to 4:30pm. Admission is £3 for adults and £2 for children 5 to 15.

SHOPPING

As well as selling fine wines and gifts, the **Longship,** 7–15 Broad St. (© 01856/888-790; www.thelongship.co.uk), is the retail outlet of Ola Gorie jewelry. This family business has a wide range of high-quality pieces, including some inspired by items uncovered at archaeological digs.

Sheila Fleet, 30 Bridge St. (© 01856/876-900; www.sheila-fleet.co.uk), is the leading competitor to Ola Gorie, and is also regarded as one of the best jewelry designers in Scotland. Her collections reflect the colors of Orkney's landscape, as well as the islands' folklore and history.

Judith Glue, 25 Broad St. (© 01856/874-225; www.judithglue.com), is one of Orkney's best-known craft and knitwear designers. The shop, opposite the cathedral, also stocks an interesting selection of handmade pottery, jewelry, greeting cards, soaps, and food and drink.

WHERE TO EAT & STAY

Albert Hotel Unassuming from the outside, the Albert Hotel has a range of smart, modern rooms of varying shapes and sizes, all equipped to a high standard and with contemporary decor. The adjoining Bothy Bar is a pleasant, homely place to enjoy a drink. On Sunday nights, it hosts informal gatherings of local musicians.

Mounthollie Lane, Kirkwall, Orkney, KW15 1JZ. www.alberthotel.co.uk. © 01856/876-000. Fax 01856/875-397. 18 units. £131–£152 double; £163 suite. AE, MC, V. **Amenities:** Restaurant; bar. *In room:* TV, hair dryer, Internet (free).

Kirkwall Hotel The standard rooms in this harborfront hotel are small. Go for one of the bright and airy superior or superior-plus rooms and watch the fishing boats come and go below. The restaurant and bar are very popular with locals and visitors alike; main courses range from £8 to £19.

Harbour St., Kirkwall, Orkney, KW15 1LF. www.kirkwallhotel.com. © 01856/872-232. Fax 01856/872-812. 36 units. £80–£130 double. MC, V. **Amenities:** Restaurant; bar. *In room:* TV, hair dryer, Wi-Fi (in some; free).

Orkney Hotel Although the Orkney Hotel has been fully refurbished and the guest rooms have been modernized, the overall style is traditional. Superior rooms have a spa bath, while the suite also has a four-poster bed. The restaurant specializes in local produce such as roast Orkney lamb (£11) and Westray haddock and chips (£9.95).

40 Victoria St., Kirkwall, Orkney, KW15 1DN. www.orkneyhotel.co.uk. © **01856/873-477.** Fax 01856/872-767. 30 units. £79–£110 double; £129 suite. AE, MC, V. **Amenities:** Restaurant; 2 bars; room service; Wi-Fi (free). *In room:* TV/DVD, hair dryer.

Shore Inn ★   The Shore has a friendly, casual feel about it. Its stylish, contemporary rooms are simple but comfortable and include bathrobes. The loft suite sleeps five, making it perfect for a family group. The hotel has two relaxed bars and a popular restaurant. Main courses are priced from £7.95 to £17, and reservations are essential during the summer. Ask about winter deals in the hotel.

Shore St., Kirkwall, Orkney, KW15 1LG. www.theshore.co.uk. © **01856/872-200.** 12 units. £75–£90 double; £135 suite. MC, V. **Amenities:** Restaurant; 2 bars. *In room:* TV, hair dryer, Wi-Fi (free).

West End Hotel   There's an air of cozy exclusivity about the West End Hotel, tucked away in a quiet area of Kirkwall. All the spacious rooms feature antique or reproduction furniture. The tiny, but comfortable, bar has a roaring fire in the winter. As well as meat, the restaurant serves a good range of fish and vegetarian dishes (main courses £7.50–£18). During the summer, diners can eat in the pleasant garden.

14 Main St., Kirkwall, Orkney, KW15 1BU. www.westendkirkwall.co.uk. © **01856/872-368.** Fax 01856/876-181. 10 units. £96 double. MC, V. **Amenities:** Restaurant; bar. *In room:* TV, hair dryer, Wi-Fi (free).

ENTERTAINMENT & NIGHTLIFE

Fusion, Ayres Road (© **01856/873-359;** www.fusionclub.biz), is Kirkwall's main nightclub and music venue. Located in a former fish-processing warehouse on the waterfront, it caters for a variety of musical tastes. As well as local and visiting DJs, it hosts live performances by Orkney bands. Doors open Thursday through Saturday at 10pm (last entry at 11:45pm). Admission on club nights is £3 to £7.

Exploring Mainland from Kirkwall to Stromness

Most of the attractions on Mainland are to the west of Kirkwall, although **Mine Howe** ★ (© **01856/861-209**), just off the A960 on the way to Deerness, makes a detour to the east well worthwhile. This mysterious subterranean chamber has archaeologists puzzled. They think it dates from the Iron Age, but they're not sure. They think it might be a shrine, but they're not sure. Armed with hard hats, visitors descend 29 almost vertical steps into the dark, damp unknown. About halfway down, there's a "landing" with chambers off to the side. Like many of the ancient, underground sites on Orkney, Mine Howe isn't recommended for people with claustrophobia. Open daily in June, July, and August from 10am to 4pm; May and September, it's open Tuesday and Friday from 11am to 3pm. There's a small admission charge.

Heading west from Kirkwall along the A965, **Wideford Hill,** about 3 miles outside the town, is home to a prehistoric cairn. Unlike many similar sites on Orkney, some of the exterior stonework is still visible, giving the site a stepped appearance made up of three concentric rings.

Lift up the heavy trapdoor in a nearby farmyard and go down the short metal ladder to reach the **Rennibister Earth House.** About 3,000 years old, this underground chamber, supported by four pillars, may have been used for storage or for ritualistic purposes.

An air of mystery hangs over the lochs of Stenness and Burray, about 4¼ miles northeast of Stromness. Scattered throughout this landscape are the monuments left by prehistoric peoples: enigmatic stone circles, huge burial chambers, and even villages. This is the **Heart of Neolithic Orkney**, designated as a World Heritage Site.

The showpiece attraction, without a doubt, is **Maeshowe ★★★** (✆ **01856/ 761-606; www.historic-scotland.gov. uk)**. More than 5,000 years old, this is one of the biggest and best chambered cairns in the whole of western Europe. Knowledgeable guides lead small parties down the low, narrow entrance passageway to the magnificent main chamber. Lighthearted runic inscriptions grace the stone walls—graffiti left by Norse raiders who broke in 1,000 years ago and now one of the largest collections of runes in the world. Come the winter solstice, the setting sun shines straight down the passageway, illuminating the back wall, a hackle-raising phenomenon that can be viewed via a webcam at **www.maeshowe.co.uk**. Reservations for the hourly tours are a must; spaces on the winter solstice tours are sometimes snapped up months in advance. From October to March, tours start daily at 10am and finish at 3pm; April through September, they're given daily from 10am to 4pm; and special twilight tours are offered in June, July, and August at 6pm, 7pm, and 8pm. Admission is £5.20 for adults, £4.20 for seniors and students, and £3.10 for children.

The **Ring of Brodgar ★★**, stands on a raised mound, dominating the narrow isthmus of land between the two lochs and visible for miles around. One of the largest stone circles in Britain, it consists of 36 stones and is thought to date from about 2500 B.C. Its purpose remains a mystery, though some believe that it was a lunar observatory. Predating Brodgar by almost 1,000 years are the **Stenness Standing Stones ★**, possibly Britain's earliest henge monument. A 200m (650 ft.) walk from the four remaining stones is **Barnhouse**, the site of a Neolithic village discovered in 1984. The walls have been partially reconstructed on top of the original structures.

Last occupied about 5,000 years ago, **Skara Brae ★★** (✆ **01856/841-815; www.historic-scotland.gov.uk)**, 6 miles northwest of Stenness, is a collection of Neolithic houses joined by covered passages. You can see the remains of several houses, magnificently preserved beneath the sand until a storm revealed the ruins in 1850. The hearths are still evident in the center of the homes; beds are placed against the side walls. The visitor center houses a cafe and an excellent series of displays that put the site into historical context and explain what life might have been like here in Neolithic times. Just outside is an excellent, full-size replica of one of the houses. It's then a 200m (650 ft.) walk to the village itself. Open from April to September daily from 9:30am to 5:30pm, and October through March daily from 9:30am to 4:30pm. Admission, including entry to nearby Skaill House, is £6.70 for adults, £5.40 for seniors and students, and £4 for children.

About ¾ miles southeast of Finstown is the **Cuween Hill Cairn ★**. After a short climb from the road, visitors take a torch from the box near the entrance and crawl along a tunnel to reach the 5,000-year-old burial chambers. The skulls of at least eight adults were discovered here when the cairn was excavated in 1901.

Ignoring the road to Stromness and Maes Howe for now, continue on an anti-clockwise circular tour of the island. The **Gurness Broch** site (ℂ **01856/751-414;** www.historic-scotland.gov.uk), 9¼ miles north of Finstown, consists of substantial remains of an Iron Age broch and farmstead at the end of a windswept peninsula. A series of defensive ditches is still clear to see. There's free access to the site in the winter, but the visitor center is open only April through October daily from 9:30am to 5:30pm. Admission is £4.70 for adults, £3.80 for seniors and students, and £2.80 for children.

Close to the northern tip of Mainland, and about 23½ miles from Kirkwall, is the **Brough of Birsay** (ℂ **01856/841-815;** www.historic-scotland.gov.uk). This tiny island—which is accessible only for 2 hours on each side of low tide via a concrete causeway—has ruins of Pictish and Norse homes as well as the remains of a 12th-century chapel. As at Gurness, there's free access in the winter, but the visitor center, which houses sculptures and Viking artifacts, is open only June through September daily from 9:30am to 5:30pm. Admission is £3.20 for adults, £2.70 for seniors and students, and £1.90 for children.

Nearby are the attractive ruins of the **Earls' Palace** at Birsay, a substantial mansion constructed in the 16th century for the Earls of Orkney.

About 2¾ miles inland from Birsay is **Kirbuster Farm Museum** (ℂ **01856/771-2680**), said to be the last unrestored "firehoose" in northern Europe. Built around a central hearth and containing a rare stone bed, the site dates to the 16th century and admission is free. It's open from March to October Monday through Saturday from 10:30am to 1pm and 2 to 5pm, and Sunday from noon to 5pm.

Click Mill, 2½ miles northeast of Dounby, is the only still-functioning example of an old horizontal water mill on the island (ℂ **01856/841-815;** www.historic-scotland.gov.uk).

About 3 miles southeast of Dounby is **Corrigal Farm Museum** (ℂ **01856/771-2680**), providing an insight into life on Orkney in Victorian times. The museum is open March to October Monday through Saturday from 10:30am to 1pm and 2 to 5pm, and Sunday from noon to 5pm. Admission is free.

Heading south from Kirkwall along the southern coastal road toward Stromness, you come to **Orphir Church,** about ½ mile off the A964. Here are the ruins of the country's only circular medieval church, built in 1123 and dedicated to St. Nicholas. Next to the parking area is the **Orkneyinga Saga Centre,** which tells the story of the Norse Earls of Orkney. It's open daily from dawn till dusk, and admission is free.

WHERE TO EAT & STAY

Foveran Hotel ★ SCOTTISH   The Foveran Hotel is one of the best places to eat in Orkney. Chef Paul Doull and his partners have created a smart restaurant with a relaxed, friendly atmosphere—a place that's popular with locals year-round. The excellent monkfish in soy, ginger, and chili sauce is served on a bed of tender pak choi with a good selection of vegetables (£18). Passion fruit, mango, and papaya create the perfect combination of flavors for a pavlova. Ask for a table in the window for excellent views over Scapa Flow. Reservations are essential, particularly in summer. The hotel also rents eight pleasant guest rooms; doubles go for £104 to £110.

St. Ola, Orkney, KW15 1SF. www.foveranhotel.co.uk. ℂ **01856/872-389.** Fax 01856/876-430. MC, V. **Amenities:** Restaurant. *In room:* TV, Internet.

Woodwick House   This rambling old house is surrounded by beautiful grounds, including almost 5 hectares (12 acres) of bluebell woods and its own beach. Woodwick

House has a reputation for being draughty and old-fashioned, but the new managers are working hard to make it brighter and more colorful. Note that not all rooms are en-suite. There are plans to open the restaurant and delightful conservatory for light, bistro-style lunches. Evening meals are available.

Evie, Orkney, KW17 2PQ. www.woodwickhouse.co.uk. © **01856/751-330.** Fax 01856/751-383. 8 units. £75–£110 double. MC, V. **Amenities:** Restaurant. *In room:* Wi-Fi (in some units).

Stromness

With its interesting mix of old buildings, waterfront homes, jetties, and steep, narrow lanes, **Stromness** is an enchanting town to explore. It's situated on the western side of Mainland, opposite the island of Hoy. With its sheltered anchorage, Stromness is the main port of Orkney, and was once known as Hamnavoe ("haven bay") in Old Norse. In the 18th century, vessels belonging to the Hudson's Bay Company could often be seen here, and many young Orcadians went to Canada to man the company's fur stations. **Login's Well,** at the southern end of the town's winding main street, is where many of these ships, and Captain's Cook's *Discovery,* took on fresh water for their long voyages to the New World.

Stromness has a **Tourist Information Centre** in the ferry terminal building (© **01856/850-716**), open April, May, and September Monday through Friday 9:30am to 3:30pm and Saturday 8:30am to 2:30pm; in June, July, and August, it's open daily from 9am to 5pm.

The **Pier Arts Centre,** Victoria Street (© **01856/850-209;** www.pierartscentre. com), puts on a dynamic range of exhibitions throughout the year. It's open Monday through Saturday from 10:30am to 5pm; admission is free.

At the **Stromness Museum,** 52 Alfred St. (© **01856/850-025**), you can see artifacts relating to the history of Orkney. Maritime subjects, such as the Hudson's Bay Company and the sinking of the German fleet in nearby Scapa Flow, form an important part of the collection. There's also an excellent section on natural history. It's open April through September daily from 10am to 5pm; and October through March Monday to Saturday from 11am to 3:30pm. Admission is £3.50 for adults, £2.50 seniors and students, £1 for children, and £7 for a family ticket.

Unstan Cairn, 3 miles northeast of Stromness along the A965, is a large burial mound dating from about 2500 B.C. Slabs of rock divide the main chamber into "cells." Two skeletons in a crouching position were discovered in a smaller side chamber.

Stromness is one of the major dive centers for exploring the wrecks of **Scapa Flow.** After being captured at the end of World War I, the German fleet was held at Scapa Flow, one of the world's largest natural harbors. Not wanting the vessels to fall into British hands, the German officer in charge gave the order for them to be scuttled, creating what

is today one of the best dive sites in the northern hemisphere. Divers must be PADI-qualified to explore the wrecks, which vary in depth from 26 to 46m (85–151 ft.). Many other ships were sunk during the building of the nearby Churchill Barriers in World War II. Lying in shallower waters, some of these are accessible to less experienced divers. If you'd like a diving adventure, call **Scapa Scuba,** Stromness (© **01856/851-218;** www.scapascuba.co.uk). Guided dives cost £140.

WHERE TO EAT & STAY

Mill of Eyrland ★ 🏠 This 19th-century watermill has been beautifully restored and converted into an upmarket B&B. Surrounded by well-tended gardens, it's 4¼ miles from Stromness, close to the A964. Warm and kitted out with comfortable furniture, the rooms are very welcoming at the end of the day. Packed lunches are made for those setting out for a day's exploration of Orkney.

Stenness, Orkney, KW16 3HA. www.millofeyrland.com. ℂ **01856/850-136.** Fax 01856/851-633. 5 units. £60–£90 double. MC, V. *In room:* TV, hair dryer, Wi-Fi (free).

Royal Hotel Ask for one of the recently refurbished and more spacious rooms upstairs in this busy hotel in the town center; they have chic new bathrooms and sumptuous wool carpets. If you're staying for dinner, try the delicious Thai-poached salmon (£9.75) or the North Ronaldsay lamb (£13). A bar menu is also available (main courses £7.80–£9.50).

53–57 Victoria St., Stromness, Orkney, KW16 3DS. www.royalhotel.biz. ℂ **01856/850-342.** Fax 01856/ 850-999. 10 units. £90 double. MC, V. **Amenities:** Restaurant; 2 bars; beer garden. *In room:* TV, hair dryer, iron, Wi-Fi (free).

Burray & South Ronaldsay

Burray and **South Ronaldsay** are connected to Mainland by the Churchill Barriers causeways, which are occasionally closed in strong wind. The first of the four barriers leads on to the tiny island of **Lamb Holm.** There's really only one reason to stop here, but it's a compelling one: the **Italian Chapel** ★ doesn't look like much from the exterior, but step inside and you're greeted by a riot of color. Built by Italian prisoners of war during World War II, the eastern end of the plasterboard-lined interior of this Nissen hut has been painted with dazzling Biblical scenes. The artist responsible, Domenico Chiocchetti, returned to Orkney in 1960 to restore the paintwork.

Two more causeways lead on to **Glimps Holm** and then **Burray.** The latter is home to the **Fossil and Heritage Centre** (ℂ **01856/731-255;** www.orkneyfossil centre.co.uk). Reflecting one family's passion for collecting, the items on display include fossils from around the world and objects used by Orcadians in daily life throughout the 20th century. The Community Café on site is run by volunteers. The Centre is open April through September daily from 10am to 5pm; admission is £3.50 for adults and £2 for children.

Continuing south across the final causeway, you reach South Ronaldsay and the picturesque village of **St. Margaret's Hope,** possibly named after a young Norwegian princess and heir to the Scottish throne. She died here in 1290, on her way to England to become Edward II's child bride; her death prevented the early union of the Scottish and English crowns.

About 2½ miles west of the village is the **Hoxa Tapestry Gallery** (ℂ **01856/831-395;** www.hoxatapestrygallery.co.uk), housing Leila Thomson's large, hand-woven tapestries.

The **Orkney Marine Life Aquarium** ☺ (ℂ **01856/831-700;** www.orkney marinelife.co.uk) is located in Grimness, about 3 miles east of St. Margaret's Hope. Particularly entertaining for younger visitors, it's open April through October daily from 10am to 6pm; admission is £6 for adults and £4.25 for children.

Tomb of the Eagles ★ (ℂ **01856/831-339;** www.tomboftheeagles.co.uk), near the southern tip of the island, is a fine chambered burial cairn dating from 3000 B.C. Local farmer Ronnie Simison rediscovered it in 1958 by accident; he and his family still run the site. The tomb is located about a mile from the simple visitor center. Allow up to 2 hours for your visit. Entry through the narrow passageway has been made easier by the installation of a wheeled trolley. It's open to visitors in March daily from 10am to noon; April through October, it's open daily from 9:30am to 5:30pm.

Winter visits are possible by advance arrangement. Admission is £6.80 for adults, £5.80 for seniors and students, and £3 for children.

WHERE TO EAT & STAY

Creel Restaurant with Rooms   This cozy restaurant overlooking the bay has won several awards over the years, including one for Scottish Restaurant Chef of the Year. The kitchen uses a large variety of local products. Specialties include smoked haddock and roasted monkfish tails with ratatouille and a chervil sauce. The strawberry shortcake, made with homemade shortbread, cream, and fresh Orkney strawberries in season, is a treat. The restaurant also rents three guest rooms at £110 for a double.

Front Rd., St. Margaret's Hope, South Ronaldsay, KW17 2SL. © **01856/831-311.** www.thecreel.co.uk. Reservations recommended. All main courses £21. MC, V. Apr–Oct Wed–Sun 7–9pm.

Murray Arms   Here you'll find simple rooms in a friendly pub in the middle of St. Margaret's Hope. Good, hearty pub food, including haddock and chips (£8.50) and Orkney crab salad (£12), is served in the evenings. During the summer, the Murray Arms is also open to non-guests for morning coffee, lunch, and afternoon tea.

Back Rd., St. Margaret's Hope, South Ronaldsay, KW17 2SP. www.murrayarmshotel.com. © **01856/831-205.** 6 units. £70–£80 double. MC, V. **Amenities:** Restaurant; bar. *In room:* TV, hair-dryer, Wi-Fi (free).

Roeberry House ★ ☺ 🎁   You'll feel at home as soon as you walk into this grand old house. The owners have opened up the whole of the downstairs area—including several reception rooms, a conservatory, and well-equipped kitchen—of this sprawling and beautifully renovated 150-year-old building to their guests. There are dozens of books and games as well as a trampoline to keep children entertained. Four-course evening meals (£35) are available if booked in advance, as are simpler dinners. There's a helipad if you decide to arrive by helicopter.

St. Margaret's Hope, South Ronaldsay, KW17 2TW. www.roeberryhouse.com. © **01856/831-228.** 3 units. £70–£90 double. No credit cards. *In room:* TV, hair dryer, Wi-Fi (free).

Sands Hotel Bar & Restaurant ★   Immaculate rooms, all with sea views, are offered in a building that was originally a fish-processing plant. Each of the two light and airy suites, ideal for small families, has a downstairs lounge area and handy kitchenette with two bedrooms upstairs. The restaurant has a good reputation with local diners. Bar meals (main courses £6.25–£9.50) and an a la carte menu (mains £9.50–£18) are available.

Burray Village, Burray, KW17 2SS. www.thesandshotel.co.uk. © **01856/731-298.** 6 units. £100 double; £150–£160 family room. MC, V. **Amenities:** Restaurant; bar. *In room:* TV, hair dryer, Wi-Fi (in some; free).

Hoy ★

Hoy is undoubtedly an island of two halves: The southern end is not unlike Mainland, but more sparsely inhabited, while the northern end consists of bleak heather moorland and rugged cliffs. The highest point in the Northern Isles, the 479m (1,571 ft.) **Ward Hill,** is located here, as are Britain's highest vertical cliffs at **St. John's Head** (335m/1,099 ft.). Visitors without cars can take the passenger-only ferry (© **01856/850-624;** www.orkneyferries.co.uk) from Stromness to **Moaness** at the northern end of the island. There are four crossings per day during the week (two at weekends) and the journey takes 30 minutes. The adult fare is £7.20 round-trip. The more frequent vehicle ferry (© **01856/811-397;** www.orkneyferries.co.uk) leaves from

Houton and arrives in **Lyness** at the southern end of the island about 35 minutes later. The adult fare is £7.20 round-trip; cars are £23.

With the British fleet based in Scapa Flow, Lyness was the location of a huge naval base during both world wars. The **Scapa Flow Visitor Centre and Museum** (✆ **01856/791-300;** www.scapaflow.co.uk) tells the story of the base and houses a collection of military equipment, including guns salvaged from German ships. The museum is open March and April, Monday through Friday from 9am to 4:30pm; May through September daily from 9am to 4:30pm; and October, Monday through Saturday from 9am to 4:30pm. Admission is free. Nearby is a large **naval cemetery.**

At South Walls is the **Hackness Martello Tower and Battery** (✆ **01856/701-727;** www.historic-scotland.gov.uk), a relic of earlier wars. This was built in 1813 to protect British merchant ships against French and American privateers. Visitors can see the barracks and climb to the top of the tower. It's open April through October daily from 9:30am to 5:30pm; admission is £4.20 for adults, £3.40 for seniors and students, and £2.50 for children.

Heading north, the island's main road hugs the east coast; the interior consists of nothing but bleak and boggy hills. There's only one tiny settlement on the west coast: the beautiful **Rackwick Bay ★**, about 4½ miles from Moaness and reached via a narrow road that cuts through the dark, atmospheric hills here. Penned in by high, almost vertical cliffs, and with the waves pounding the long beach, only a few hardy souls live in the few old crofthouses that dot the landscape in this remote spot. Walkers and climbers come here to explore the cliffs and the hills. A well signposted path leads from Rackwick to the **Old Man of Hoy ★**, a 137m (449 ft.) sea stack that has become a mecca for climbers since it was first climbed in 1967. The dramatic walk takes about 90 minutes. The **Cra'as Nest Museum,** an 18th-century crofthouse that's open during the summer, can be visited en route to the Old Man. It's also possible to continue along the cliffs for 2 miles to St. John's Head. Watch for mountain hares on the hills here. Assuming there's no snow on the ground, they're easy to spot in the winter because their coats turn white.

The **Dwarfie Stane,** a Neolithic burial chamber neatly hewn from the rock at the foot of the hills, is located beside a minor road 3 miles east of Rackwick Bay. It takes about 10 minutes to reach the site using a boardwalk that leads across boggy ground from the parking area.

WHERE TO EAT & STAY

Stromabank Hotel This friendly hotel has good views over the southern end of Hoy. The rooms are simple but cheerful; the one downstairs is suitable for travelers with disabilities. Decent bar meals (£7.25–£12) are served in the conservatory restaurant, but in the winter, are available to non-guests only during weekends.

Longhope, South Walls, Hoy, KW16 3PA. www.stromabank.co.uk. ✆ **01856/701-611.** 4 units. £70 double. MC, V. **Amenities:** Restaurant; bar. In room: TV, hair dryer.

Wild Heather ★ 🎒 This is a delightful bed-and-breakfast located right at the edge of Mill Bay. Rise in the morning to the smell of home-baked bread and take breakfast on the terrace below your room—with nothing between you and the seals and otters in the water below. The homey rooms are bright and comfortable, with under-floor heating, power showers, and huge windows. Three-course evening meals are available (£16). Most produce is sourced locally, including delicious Westray kippers.

Millhouse, Lyness, Hoy, KW16 3NU. www.wildheatherbandb.co.uk. ✆ **01856/791-098.** 2 units. £55–£59 double. No credit cards. In room: TV, hair dryer.

Rousay

Known as the "Egypt of the North" because of its huge number of archaeological sites, the island of Rousay lies off the northwest coast of Mainland. A 13-mile road runs right around the island, making for an interesting bike ride. The regular ferry (✆ 01856/751-360; www.orkneyferries.co.uk) leaves from Tingwall and takes about 20 minutes to reach Rousay. Adult fares are £7.20 round-trip; cars are £23.

The island's most significant site, the 5,000-year-old **Midhowe Chambered Cairn ★**, is located almost 5 miles northwest of where the ferry comes in. Excavated in the 1930s, the cairn is more than 23m (75 ft.) long and is divided into 12 stalls or compartments. The bones of 25 people, along with their livestock, were found inside. Nearby is **Midhowe Broch,** occupied from 200 B.C. to A.D. 200. One of the best-preserved brochs on Orkney, its walls are up to 4m (13 ft.) high.

The **Blackhammer Cairn** lies within easy walking distance of the ferry terminal. Dating from the same period, it's similar to the cairn at Midhowe but smaller. Entry is via a sliding roof door and a short ladder. Nearby is the unusual, two-story **Taversoe Tuick** burial cairn.

Golden plovers, snipe, curlews, great skuas, red grouse, red-throated divers, merlins, and hen harriers can be found on the RSPB's reserve at **Trumland.** Rising to a height of 227m (745 ft.) at Knitchen Hill, these wild moors provide good views of the surrounding islands.

Eday

Made up of heather-clad moorland, peat bogs, sheer cliffs, coastal dunes, and long sandy beaches, Eday is a rewarding and tranquil destination for the few visitors who make it to this remote northern island. During the summer, there are two ferries a day from Kirkwall (✆ 01856/872-044; www.orkneyferries.co.uk). The journey takes 75 minutes direct (or more than 2 hours if the ferry is going via Stronsay and Sanday); adult fares are £14 round-trip; cars are £34. **Loganair** flies from Kirkwall every Wednesday; fares are £70 round-trip.

To see the main archaeological sites, walk the 5-mile **Eday Heritage Trail** at the northern end of the island. Pick up a leaflet from the **Eday Heritage and Visitor Centre** (✆ 01857/622-288), about 3½ miles north of the ferry terminal. The route takes in the distinctive **Setter Stone,** Orkney's largest standing stone, and several burial cairns, the most impressive of which is the **Vinquoy Chambered Cairn** built from red sandstone. The walk continues right out to **Red Head,** the northernmost tip of the island where fulmars nest on the cliffs. The tiny island of the **Calf of Eday** sits just off the coast, home to large, noisy colonies of puffins, kittiwakes, razorbills, and guillemots.

On its eastern coastline, Eday opens onto Eday Sound, where notorious pirate John Gow was captured in 1725. (After a trial in London, he was executed later that year.) He was thought to be attempting a raid on **Carrick House,** which you also pass on the Heritage Trail. Built in 1633, it's a fine example of a laird's house. The current owners sometimes open it to visitors, by appointment only, on Sundays from late June until mid-September (✆ 01857/622-260).

WHERE TO STAY

Sui Generis   Sui Generis is Latin for "unique" and this island bed-and-breakfast is definitely that. With furniture and designs created by the Kerr family, the rooms are full of color and imagination. The en-suite shower in the twin room, for example, features reclaimed Victorian tiles and a fantasy landscape. Sui Generis is located just a few minutes' walk from the ferry terminal. Three-course evening meals are available if booked in advance (£15 per head).

Redbanks, Eday, KW17 2AA. www.suigenerisfurniture.co.uk. ℂ/fax **01857/622-219.** 2 units. £90 double. No credit cards. *In room:* TV, hair dryer.

Sanday

Sanday means "sand island," which is fitting: The island's long white beaches have grown as tides have changed over the past century. With few residents or visitors, the stretches of seashore are often deserted—perfect for long, solitary walks. Some 13 miles long, Sanday is the largest of Orkney's north isles.

During the summer, there are two ferries a day from Kirkwall (ℂ **01856/872-044;** www.orkneyferries.co.uk). The journey takes 1 hour and 15 minutes direct (or nearly 2 hours if the ferry goes via Eday); adult fares are £14 round-trip; cars are £34. **Loganair** flies a daily service (except Sundays) from Kirkwall (£70 round-trip).

On Elsness, a peninsula jutting south from the bulk of Sanday, is one of the most spectacular chambered cairns in the entire archipelago: the **Quoyness Chambered Tomb ★.** This well-preserved tomb and its principal chamber, which reaches a height of some 4m (13 ft.), date from around 3000 B.C. The narrow entrance tunnel would originally have been a massive 9m (30 ft.) long, but during reconstruction the first section was left unroofed, so that visitors only have to crawl the last 3.5m (11 ft.). There are many other burial cairns on the island, but most of them remain unexcavated.

In 1991, a rare Viking boat burial was found at **Scar,** on the north side of the island. During one of Orkney's most important 20th-century digs, archaeologists discovered buried in the sand 300 rusted iron rivets marking out the shape of a 6.5m-long (21 ft.) wooden boat. The remains of three people were found alongside a treasure trove of grave goods, including combs, swords, brooches, and a decorated whalebone plaque, which is now on display in Orkney Museum (p. 396).

Start Point is the far eastern tip of Sanday. Migratory birds such as waxwings and crossbills, blown off course during their spring and autumn migrations, can sometimes be seen here. Walk out to the end of the peninsula to see Scotland's first revolving lighthouse, built in 1806 by Robert Stevenson, one of the famous family of lighthouse engineers. It now sports black and white vertical stripes. On a clear day, it is possible to see the lighthouses on North Ronaldsay and even Fair Isle.

One of the most interesting beaches is **Doun Helzie,** a 2-mile walk from the ferry terminal. The beach's natural arch and caves can be explored at low tide.

WHERE TO EAT & STAY

Belsair Hotel   This family-run inn is located in the village of Kettletoft, about 7½ miles northeast of Sanday's ferry pier. Kettletoft consists of about 15 buildings and is the most central of the island's four communities. The Belsair's functionally furnished guest rooms all have sea views. Gardens across the road produce many of the vegetables served in the dining room, where dishes include straightforward but flavorsome preparations of fish, beef, and lamb (main courses £8.95–£13).

Kettletoft, Sanday, KW17 2BJ. www.belsairsanday.co.uk. ℂ **01857/600-206.** 3 units. £60 double. No credit cards. **Amenities:** Restaurant; bar. *In room:* TV, Wi-Fi (free).

Kettletoft Hotel   This lively hotel offers simple but comfortable accommodation. Like the neighboring Belsair Hotel, the Kettletoft also has a bar and restaurant. Main courses are priced at about £8.50.

Kettletoft, Sanday, KW17 2BJ. www.kettletofthotel.co.uk. (©) **01857/600-217.** 6 units. £70 double. No credit cards. **Amenities:** Restaurant; bar. *In room:* TV.

Westray

The main tourist attractions on Westray can be seen in a day, but it's worth staying at least a night or two to soak up the island's relaxed atmosphere and explore its delights on foot. From north to south, it's about 11¾ miles long, the main settlement being Pierowall, which makes a good base for visitors.

In the summer, there are two to three ferries a day from Kirkwall to Rapness at the southern end of the island (© **01856/872-044;** www.orkneyferries.co.uk). The journey takes 90 minutes; adult fares are £14 round-trip; cars are £34. **Loganair** operates up to three flights a day from Kirkwall (£70 round-trip).

The **Westray Heritage Centre** in Pierowall (© **01857/677-414;** www.westray heritage.co.uk) has exhibitions and interactive displays about the island. It's open May through September on Sunday from 1:30 to 5:30pm, Monday from 11:30am to 5:30pm, and Tuesday through Saturday from 10am to noon and 2 to 5pm. Admission is £2.50 for adults and £0.50 for children.

The island's best-known attraction is **Noltland Castle,** the grey sandstone ruins overlooking Pierowall. It was built in the 16th century by Gilbert Balfour, a man with many powerful enemies. He built it with defense in mind: with 2m (7 ft.) thick walls, no accessible windows at ground level, and a grand total of 71 gunloops. A kitchen, a stately hall, and a grand, winding staircase are still standing. To explore inside, get the key from the farmhouse nearby.

At Pierowall itself are the ruins of the 17th-century **St. Mary's Church** or **Lady Kirk.** The churchyard contains some finely lettered grave slabs.

The island's other medieval church is about 4 miles south of Pierowall. A grassy path leads from the car park overlooking the Bay of Tuquoy to the picturesque ruins of **Cross Kirk** about ½ mile away. The church dates from about 1140, although it was enlarged in the 17th century.

The cliffs of Westray are well worth exploring. The western coastline is the steepest, rising to 76m (249 ft.), from which you can enjoy panoramic vistas. Below the cliffs is the **Gentleman's Cave,** where the lairds of Westray, supporters of the 1745 Jacobite rebellion, took refuge after the defeat at Culloden in 1746.

The island is great for bird-watchers: As well as large, smelly seabird colonies around **Noup Head,** you might be lucky enough to hear or even see a corncrake, one of Britain's rarest birds. Listen for their harsh, rasping call on summer evenings. One of the best places to get a close-up view of puffins, known on the Northern Isles as *tammy nories,* is on the **Castle O'Burrian** in the south of the island. Between April and August, up to 300 birds nest on this sea-stack.

For botanists, the rare Scottish primrose can be seen on the cliffs near **Fitty Hill.** Look out to sea and you may catch sight of dolphins or whales, particularly towards the end of the summer.

WHERE TO EAT & STAY

Cleaton House Hotel   A little old-fashioned in terms of decor and furnishings maybe, but Cleaton House in the best hotel on Westray. This Victorian manse has spacious, comfortable rooms. It also serves excellent evening meals in the rather grand Stewart Room, which has the family coat of arms above the fireplace. A four-course meal is £35.

Cleaton House Hotel, Westray, KW17 2DB. www.cleatonhouse.co.uk. © **01857/677-508.** Fax 01857-677/442. 6 units. £95–£120 double. MC, V. **Amenities:** Restaurant; lounge bar. *In room:* TV, Wi-Fi (free).

No. 1 Broughton Now an artist's home, this Victorian house has recently been extensively renovated. It offers modest bed-and-breakfast accommodation overlooking the Bay of Pierowall. A sauna is available for a small extra charge.

Pierowall, Westray, KW17 2DA. www.no1broughton.co.uk. © **01857/677-726.** 3 units. £60 double. MC, V. *In room:* TV.

Pierowall Hotel This cozy hotel, about 7 miles north of the roll-on/roll-off ferry terminal, offers simple rooms in the heart of Westray's main settlement. The pub also serves up affordable bar meals such as fish and chips (£8.45) and homemade curries (£8.50).

Pierowall Village, Westray, KW17 2BZ. www.pierowallhotel.co.uk. © **01857/677-472.** Fax 01857/677-707. 6 units, 2 with private bathroom. £64 double without bathroom, £80 double with bathroom. MC, V. **Amenities:** Restaurant; 2 bars. *In room:* TV, hair dryer.

Papa Westray

Papa Westray, known locally as Papay, is one of the remotest and smallest of Orkney's inhabited islands, measuring just 4¼ miles from north to south. Like much of the archipelago, it's rich in archaeological sites as well as being popular with bird-watchers. It also gets a mention in the Guinness Book of World Records for having the world's shortest scheduled flight: It's just a 2-minute hop from Papay to neighboring Westray. The daily flight, operated like other inter-island services by **Loganair,** costs £20 round-trip (or £14 if you're staying overnight). Loganair also operates daily flights from Kirkwall (£34 round-trip). A vehicle ferry (© **01856/872-044;** www.orkney ferries.co.uk) runs from Kirkwall on Tuesday and Friday. Journey times differ according to the route taken, but adult fares are £14 round-trip and cars are £34. There's also a passenger ferry from Pierowall on Westray that runs between three and six times a day; the journey takes about 30 minutes and costs £7.40 round-trip.

You can see most of the main sites in a day, but if you have time for nothing else, the must-see attraction is the **Knap of Howar,** the oldest standing house in Europe. Radiocarbon dating suggests it was occupied as long ago as 3500 B.C. The site, which is open at all times, is on the west coast, near the airfield.

About ⅔ mile north of the Knap of Howar is **St. Boniface Church,** one of the earliest Christian sites in the whole of Scotland. It's possible that a chapel stood here as early as the 8th century. A Norse hogback gravestone has been found, as well as two early Christian cross-slabs. The church itself has been restored, and its spartan stone interior now hosts services and occasional concerts.

The ruins of **St. Tredwell's Chapel** are located on a peninsula jutting out into the **Loch of St. Tredwell.** The chapel, now in ruins, was dedicated to Triduana, an 8th-century saint who traveled from Northumberland to convert the Picts to Christianity. When a Pictish king, Nechtan, admired her lovely eyes, she is said to have been so angry that she plucked them out and sent them, impaled on a branch, to the king. For many decades, the chapel was a place of pilgrimage for those with eye problems and the waters of the loch were regarded as medicinal.

The northern end of the island has been turned into an **RSPB bird reserve.** Along with significant numbers of guillemots, puffins, kittiwakes, and Arctic skuas, **North Hill** is the site of Europe's largest breeding colony of Arctic terns. The resident warden leads walks across this wild, windswept maritime heath during the summer.

SHETLAND ★★

60 miles NE of the Orkneys

Shetlanders proudly tell visitors: "Wir closser ta Norwa as we ir ta Scotland, du kens." Roughly translated, it means: "We're closer to Norway than we are to Scotland, you know." The Shetland archipelago is the northernmost part of the British Isles, about 600 miles from London but only 220 miles from Bergen in Norway. Historically and culturally, these islands are closely linked with their Scandinavian neighbors and ancestors. Many place names are Norse in origin, and Viking heritage is still celebrated in events such as the dramatic Up Helly Aa, Europe's largest fire festival.

The islands have been inhabited for some 6,000 years, but the Vikings have had the most enduring influence. They first started arriving in the 8th century, marauders looking for a base from which to launch further raids on the British Isles. Having subdued the local Pictish peoples, though, they began to settle here. Shetland was ruled by the Norwegians and the Danes until 1469 when it was "pawned" to enable the Scandinavians to pay a wedding dowry to the Scots.

Shetland's 100-plus islands cover 50 sq. miles of land, but only 15 of them are inhabited. The main island is called Mainland, as in Orkney. About 55 miles long and 20 miles wide, it's home to the capital, Lerwick.

Also like Orkney, Shetland has a number of important historical sites, but that's where the comparison ends: Shetland's main pulling power in terms of visitor attractions is its landscape and wildlife. At first glance, this treeless place seems bleak and barren, but the stark beauty soon becomes apparent. Wild and rugged, its complex coastline is battered by both the Atlantic Ocean and the North Sea. The waves have sculpted the rock into weird and wonderful shapes, creating stacks, natural arches, blow-holes, caves, and tunnels. At no point in Shetland are you more than 3 miles from the sea.

Although the human population of the entire archipelago totals just 22,000, the islands' towering cliffs are home to 54,000 gannets and more than 200,000 puffins. Local specialties include the tiny storm petrel, great skuas (or *bonxies*), and the red-necked phalarope, one of Britain's rarest breeding birds. This is paradise for bird-watchers and walkers alike. Shetland is also famous for being one of the best places in the British Isles for spotting otters. Seals, both the gray and the common variety, can be seen bobbing up and down in the sea or lounging about on the rocks and beaches. If you're lucky, you may spot porpoises, white-sided dolphins, and even orcas.

Tiny **Shetland ponies** have roamed freely among the hills and common grazing lands for at least 4,000 years. Some are shipped south to mainland Britain, where they were once used in coal mines but are now popular as children's mounts.

Anglers will find some 300 freshwater lochs in Shetland, home to brown trout. Permits, costing £25, are required and can be bought from **Lerwick's Tourist Information Centre** or online at www.shetlandtrout.co.uk. Chartering a boat locally for a deep-sea angling trip makes for a memorable day out. Mackerel and haddock can be caught, or for a more challenging experience, halibut.

There are three main golf courses on the islands, each with simple facilities and modest fees to match. The two 18-hole courses are **Shetland Golf Club** (✆ 01595/840-369; www.shetlandgolfclub.co.uk), about 3¾ miles west of Lerwick on the A970, and **Whalsay Golf Club** (✆ 01806/566-705; www.whalsaygolfclub.com), the U.K.'s most northerly. The nine-hole **Asta Golf Club** is 1¼ miles north of Scalloway.

Exposed to the full blast of Atlantic systems, the weather on Shetland is never boring. The rain may come in quickly, but it usually disappears just as rapidly, making this a land of countless rainbows. It's worth remembering that the archipelago has considerably less rain than the Scottish Highlands; it also benefits from the warming influence of the Gulf Stream, and so isn't as cold as you might expect. In summer, there's almost continuous daylight, a phenomenon Shetlanders call "simmer dim." In midwinter, there are fewer than 6 hours of daylight but, thanks to the northerly latitude, it's a beautiful, crystal-clear light, much loved by photographers.

The islands' craftspeople are noted for their creativity, reflected in their handicrafts, jewelry, and knitwear. In some places, you can watch these items being made in artists' workshops. **Hand-knitted sweaters** are still produced in great numbers, and can be bought throughout the islands.

Essentials

GETTING THERE   By air or sea, Aberdeen is the major departure point from the U.K. mainland. The flight to the islands' main airport at **Sumburgh,** on the southern tip of Mainland, takes just less than an hour. **Loganair** operates several services a day from Aberdeen, Edinburgh, Glasgow, Inverness, and Kirkwall on Orkney. Reservations are made through **Flybe** (© **0871/700-2000,** or © +44/1392-268-5290 from outside the U.K.; www.flybe.com).

Large roll-on/roll-off car ferries leave Aberdeen every evening throughout the year to arrive in Shetland at 7:30am the next day. Single fares are £95 to £128 per car and £23 to £36 per adult. Comfortable cabins cost from £61 to £121. Good on-board facilities include a restaurant, cafeteria, bars, lounges, a movie theatre, and gift shops. For information, contact **NorthLink** (© **0845/600-0449;** www.northlinkferries. co.uk). Three times a week (four in summer), these ferries also stop at Kirkwall in Orkney, departing at 11:45pm.

GETTING AROUND   **Direct Flight** (© **01595/840-246;** www.directflight. co.uk) operates services to the islands of Papa Stour and Foula (see below) as well as Out Skerries and Fair Isle. These depart from Tingwall, 6 miles northwest of Lerwick. Although flying is a bit more expensive than taking a ferry, the bonus is that you can go and return on the same day, which isn't always possible on some ferry routes.

The heavily subsidized inter-island ferries are operated by **Shetland Islands Council** (www.shetland.gov.uk/ferries). Regular vehicle services operate to the islands of Unst, Yell, Whalsay, Fetlar, Skerries, and Bressay. Passenger services operate to Papa Stour, Foula, and Fair Isle. For more information on scheduled services, see the relevant sections below. Boat trips to the islands of Mousa, Noss, and Foula can also be arranged (see below).

In summer, **buses** travel around Mainland to all the major places of interest as well as several of the larger islands. To download a full timetable, visit www.zettrans. org.uk.

Driving around Shetland is a pleasant, relaxing experience—no traffic jams, few traffic lights, and some 500 miles of excellent roads. Many of the smaller islands are connected by road bridges, and for those that aren't, there are car ferries. Renting a car might be the best solution if you want to cover a lot of ground in the shortest time. You can bring a car from mainland Scotland or pick one up in Lerwick. As yet, no major international car-rental firm maintains an office in Shetland. However, Avis has as an on-island agent, **Bolts Car Hire** at 26 North Rd. in Lerwick (© **01595/693-636;** www.boltscarhire.co.uk). Its main competitors are **Grantfield Garage,** North

The Shetland Islands

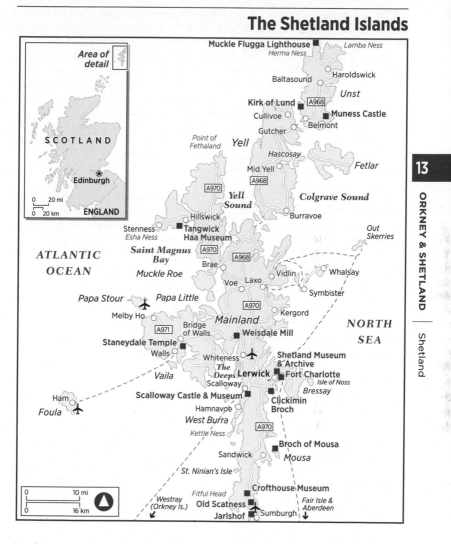

Road, Lerwick (© **01595/692-709;** www.grantfieldgarage.co.uk), and **Star Rent A Car,** 22 Commercial Rd., Lerwick (© **01595/692-075;** www.starrentacar.co.uk), which is the agent for Alamo, Sixt, and Europcar.

If you're intent on using pedal power to get around, **Grantfield Garage** also rents bikes for £5 per day or £30 per week.

VISITOR INFORMATION The **Shetland Visitor Information Centre** is at Market Cross in Lerwick (© **01595/693-434;** www.visit.shetland.org). The helpful staff can arrange rooms and provide information on ferries, boat trips, car rentals, local events, and visitor attractions. It's open from April to October, Monday through Saturday from 9am to 5pm and Sunday 9am to 4pm; and November to March, Monday through Saturday from 10am to 4pm.

Up Helly Aa Fire Festival ★★

On the last Tuesday in January each year, a thousand-strong horde of loud, bearded men dressed as Vikings and carrying flaming torches march through the streets of Lerwick. Cheered on by onlookers, they reach the harbor where they storm a 10m (30 ft.) replica of a Viking longboat and set it alight. This is the islands' **Up Helly Aa**, descended from the Norse festival of Yule and now Europe's largest **fire festival**.

When Christianity came to the islands, Yule became Christmas and the Norsemen weren't allowed to hold their celebrations until 24 days later, after the Christian holy period ended. This time of feasting, drinking, and bonfires became known as "Uphalliday"—the end of the holidays.

Today, the islanders still feel the almost pagan need to light up the seemingly endless winter night with fire. The harbor blaze is followed by a long night of eating, drinking, playing music, and dancing. The celebrations spread out from here, and more remote communities hold local versions over the coming weeks.

During the summer, the **Galley Shed,** St. Sunniva Street, Lerwick is home to an exhibition about the festival, including displays of the costumes used. Opening times differ from year to year; admission is £3 for adults, £1 for children (www.uphellyaa.org).

SPECIAL EVENTS Music-loving Shetlanders don't need much excuse for a festival or general party. Pubs and community centers regularly schedule music and dancing, and on most weekend nights, all you have to do to find live traditional music is go in search of a pint of beer.

The **Shetland Folk Festival** (© **01595/ 694-757;** www.shetlandfolkfestival. com) usually takes place on the last weekend in April. Young fiddlers and accordion players on the islands take part, and international artists fly in for 4 days of concerts, workshops, and informal jam sessions. Foot-stomping reels, contemporary Celtic, bluegrass, excellent musicianship, and strong vocals are all part of the package. Past performers have included Sharon Shannon, Mary Black, and Elvis Costello. Lerwick forms the focus of the festival, but concerts, often incorporating dinner and dancing, take place in local halls throughout the islands.

Other music-based annual events include the **Fiddle Frenzy** (www.shetlandfiddle frenzy.com) program of concerts and workshops in August; the **Shetland Blues Festival** (www.shetlandblues.info) in September; and October's **Shetland Accordion and Fiddle Festival** (www.shetlandaccordionandfiddle.com).

In June, the **Bergen–Shetland Races** take place, an annual North Sea yachting challenge. Summer weekends are also the time for local **regattas,** in which different communities compete in sailing and rowing competitions.

Lerwick

The capital of Shetland since 1708, Lerwick, on the east coast of Mainland, is home to more than 7,000 people, a third of the population of these islands. It owes its existence—and its wealth—to its natural harbor. Sheltered by the small island of Bressay, it developed in the 17th century as a trading port for Dutch herring fishermen and became a haven for smugglers. Today, it serves as a base for North Sea oil rig workers, whose presence ensures most of the town's hotels remain open all year.

The attractive center of Lerwick is based on Commercial Street, the principal artery and main shopping street. From here, a network of steep and narrow lanes runs up into the residential areas. The oldest buildings, the *lodberries* sitting right on the seafront, are at the southern end of the town.

EXPLORING LERWICK

Your first stop should be the Shetland Visitor Information Centre (see above) where you'll find the staff is helpful and knowledgeable.

The new **Shetland Museum & Archive** ★, in the restored Hay's Dock, is a 10-minute walk north of Lerwick's center (℡ **01595/695-057;** www.shetland-museum.org.uk). It covers the islands' history from prehistoric times to the modern day, including fascinating sections on folklore, traditions, and language as well as good interactive displays for children. Admission is free. It's open Monday through Friday from 10am to 4pm, Saturday from 10am to 5pm, and Sunday from noon to 5pm.

Entered via Charlotte Street, pentagonal **Fort Charlotte** (℡ **01667/460-233;** www.historic-scotland.gov.uk), built in 1665 and restored in 1781, is constructed of high, robust walls pierced with gun slits pointing out to sea. There's not a great deal to see as you wander the fort precincts, but it does provide excellent views across the sound. Open daily from 9am to sunset; admission is free.

Clickimin Broch, about a mile southwest of the town center, is located on the Loch of Clickimin (℡ **01667/460-233;** www.historic-scotland.gov.uk). A good path leads to this Iron Age tower, excavated in the 1950s. Before being fortified, the site was home to a Bronze Age farm.

A 12m (39 ft.) replica of a Viking longboat, *Dim Riv* (**"Morning Light"**), is available for a tour of the harbor on Monday evenings in the summer. Ask at the Visitor Centre (see above).

Of the many shops in Lerwick, you may want to drop in at **The Spider's Web** (℡ **01595/695-246**) opposite the Queen's Hotel. It sells Shetland knitwear, including sweaters, hats, scarves, and intricate, hand-knitted shawls that cost anything up to £250. The **North Rock Gallery** on Commercial Street (℡ **01595/694-644;** www.northrockgallery.co.uk) displays photographs, mostly moody local seascapes, by local artist Mark Sinclair. The shop also sells other crafts and gifts.

The **Böd of Gremista Museum** is about ½ mile north of the ferry terminal (℡ **01595/695-057;** www.shetland-museum.org.uk). This restored 18th-century fishermen's home was the birthplace in 1792 of Arthur Anderson, co-founder of the P&O shipping company. It's open May through September Wednesday to Sunday from 10am to 5pm; admission is free, but donations are welcome.

WHERE TO EAT

Hay's Dock Cafe Restaurant ★ ☺ SCOTTISH   The best to place to eat in Lerwick, this bright, modern restaurant is located in the Shetland Museum. Tuck into delicious tagliatelle with scallop, squid, monkfish, and langoustine in a vanilla cream and cherry tomato sauce, while gazing out at the town's harbor. Also open for lunch. A toy box is available to keep children entertained.

Hay's Dock. ℡ **01595/741-569.** www.haysdock.co.uk. Reservations recommended. Main courses £14–£19. MC, V. Mon–Thurs 10:30am–3:30pm, Fri 10:30am–3:30pm and 6:30–11pm, Sat 10:30am–4:30pm and 6:30–11pm, Sun noon–4:30pm.

Monty's BISTRO   At both lunch and dinnertime, the young serving staff in this colorful, lively restaurant always seem to be rushed off their feet—a good sign. The food's a little pricey, but this is another excellent place to eat. If you're here in the evening, try the pan-fried Shetland king scallops. The desserts are gorgeous.

5 Mounthooly St. © **01595/696-555.** www.montys-shetland.co.uk. Reservations recommended. Evening main courses £12–£20. MC, V. Tues–Sat noon–2pm and 5–9pm.

Peerie Shop Cafe SCOTTISH   This is a bustling little cafe tucked away at the back of an interesting gift shop close to the harborfront. Serving excellent coffee and a variety of sandwiches, paninis, and other snacks, it's tremendously popular with local people throughout the day.

Esplanade. © **01595/692-816.** www.peerieshopcafe.com. MC, V. Mon–Sat 9am–6pm.

ENTERTAINMENT & NIGHTLIFE

If you want to know the best places to go to hear traditional music, pay a visit to **High Level Music** (© **01595/692-618**), up the steps close to Market Cross. The shop is run by Brian Nicholson, who is a mine of information on the subject.

At the time of writing, Lerwick has only one theatre—the **Garrison** on Market Street, which hosts live drama, stand-up comedy, concerts, and movies (© **01595/743-843;** www.shetlandarts.org). There are plans to open a new, larger arts complex next to the Shetland Museum in Hay's Dock. With two movie screens, an auditorium for live performances and a cafe, the **Mareel** is already getting local people talking (http://www.shetlandarts.org/venues/mareel/).

WHERE TO STAY

Glen Orchy House   Built as a convent in 1904 and extended in 1997, this hotel has clean, tidy, and pleasantly decorated rooms about 5 minutes' walk from the town center. There are several spacious public areas, where guests can unwind after a hard day's sightseeing. Computers are available with Internet connection.

20 Knab Rd., Lerwick, Shetland, ZE1 0AX. www.guesthouselerwick.com. ©/fax **01595/692-031.** 25 units. £90 double. MC, V. **Amenities:** Thai restaurant, bar. *In room:* A/C (some rooms), TV, hair dryer.

Grand Hotel   This grand old Victorian building, with its pointed turrets and solid walls, lies a block from the waterfront on the town's main thoroughfare. The guest rooms are perfectly pleasant, although the dark stairways and frayed hall carpets could do with updating. The four-poster room is particularly spacious with good views out over the harbor, a spa bath, and a large, widescreen TV. Home to Lerwick's only nightclub, Posers, the Grand can be a noisy spot at weekends.

149 Commercial St., Lerwick, Shetland, ZE1 0AB. www.kgqhotels.co.uk. © **01595/692-826.** 24 units. £113 double; £148 family room. AE, DC, MC, V. **Amenities:** Restaurant; 2 bars; room service. *In room:* TV, hair dryer.

Lerwick Hotel   The unprepossessing exterior and rather dull reception area (due to be refurbished at press time) don't prepare visitors for probably the best views of any hotel in Lerwick. As you sit and enjoy your hearty, full Scottish breakfast, you gaze out over the sound to the island of Bressay. The rooms are well appointed and the swish bathrooms, with attractive, slate-style paneling, have been recently updated. The main brasserie is open to non-residents (mains £8.95–£19); and the traditional Sunday lunchtime carvery (mains £7.25–£8.95) is very popular with locals; you need to reserve in advance.

15 South Rd., Lerwick, Shetland, ZE1 0RB. www.shetlandhotels.com. © **01595/692-166.** Fax 01595/694-419. 35 units. £120 double; £135 suite. AE, DC, MC, V. **Amenities:** 2 restaurants; bar; room service. *In room:* TV, hair dryer, Wi-Fi.

Queens Hotel   Located in the oldest part of town, the Queens is about as close to the sea as you get and receives many a salty soaking. Needless to say, most of the rooms have harbor views. They're small and simple but functional, and the location is relatively quiet considering it's just a short walk from Market Cross.

24 Commercial St., Lerwick, Shetland, ZE1 OAB. www.kgqhotels.co.uk. © **01595/692-826.** Fax 01595/694-048. 26 units. £113 double; £148 family room. AE, DC, MC, V. Amenities: Restaurant; bar; room service. *In room:* TV, hair dryer.

Westhall 🎁   A 20-minute walk from Market Cross, Westhall is worth the extra effort it takes to reach it. This spacious, family-run guesthouse is located down a quiet lane with the sea on one side and fields on the other. Its bright, airy rooms feature traditional wooden floors and dreamy views. The comfy downstairs guest lounge comes complete with sumptuous sofas, piano, and open fire.

Lower Sound, Lerwick, Shetland, ZE1 ORN. www.bedandbreakfastlerwick.co.uk.© **01595/694-247.** 3 units. £90 double. MC, V. *In room:* TV, Wi-Fi (free).

South Mainland

This narrow isthmus south of Lerwick is home to some of Shetland's most popular tourist attractions. The main A970 heads down the eastern side of the 25-mile peninsula, surprisingly crossing Sumburgh Airport's runway and ending near Jarlshof. The western side consists mostly of barren peatlands, but there are interesting sights here too.

EXPLORING SOUTH MAINLAND

Leaving Lerwick, the first attraction you come to is on the tiny offshore island of Mousa: the **Broch of Mousa** ★★. This Iron Age tower, the best preserved of its kind in Britain, has guarded Mousa Sound for more than 2,000 years. Constructed of local stones, with two circular walls, one within the other, it stands more than 13m (43 ft.) tall. Visitors can climb the narrow internal staircase and look out from an open parapet at the top. The unusual, cat-like noise of tiny storm petrels nesting in the walls of the broch is an added bonus. The daily, 15-minute ferry crossing to Mousa starts from **Sandwick,** 6¾ miles south of Lerwick. There's a daily bus service between Lerwick and Sandwick. The ferry operates April through September only. The cost is £13 for adults and £6.50 for children (© **01950/431-367;** www.mousa boattrips.co.uk).

Continuing south, and crossing to the west of the peninsula, you reach **St. Ninian's Isle** ★, near Bigton, just off the B9122. Visitors can walk to the island on the *tombolo,* a narrow, crescent-shaped sandbar that connects it to Mainland. The island became famous in 1958 when a local schoolboy helping on an archaeological dig uncovered a rich cache of Celtic artifacts, including silver bowls and brooches, in the ruins of its 12th-century chapel. The treasure is in the Museum of Scotland in Edinburgh, but there are replicas in the museum in Lerwick.

At Boddam, part of the parish of Dunrossness, is the **Crofthouse Museum** (© **01595/695-057;** www.shetlandmuseumandarchives.org.uk). It's east of the A970 on an unmarked road 25 miles south of Lerwick. This quaint thatched crofthouse, complete with box beds and farm implements, gives a taste of what life was like on Shetland in the 1870s. The museum also has a functioning water mill. It's open May through September daily from 10am to 5pm; admission is free.

The recently restored mill at **Quendale** (© **01950/460-969;** www.quendalemill. shetland.co.uk) can be found at the end of a minor road 2 miles west of the A970 near Boddam. Guided tours are available and there are refreshments at the site. Open mid-April to mid-October, daily 10am to 5pm. Admission is £2 for adults, £1 for seniors, and £0.50 for children.

To watch an ongoing archaeological dig, continue south to **Old Scatness** ☺ (www.shetland-heritage.co.uk), where an Iron Age broch, Pictish homes, Norse dwellings, and crofthouses are being unearthed. A Pictish wheelhouse has been rec-reated and guides, dressed in period costume, give demonstrations of ancient crafts and skills. Children can dress up as Vikings and join in a variety of activities. It's open May through September daily 10am to 5:30pm. Admission is £4 for adults and £2 for children.

Shetland's most impressive—and most popular—attraction is **Jarlshof** ★★ (© **01950/460-112;** www.historic-scotland.gov.uk), near Sumburgh Airport. In 1897, a violent storm performed the first archaeological "dig" here, washing away sections of the low cliffs and revealing huge stone walls. Excavations soon followed, uncovering human habitations spanning 4,000 years. On this unique, relatively small site, Neolithic houses, a Bronze Age village, and an Iron Age broch brush shoulders with a Norse longhouse, medieval farm, and 16th-century laird's house. Jarlshof is open April through September daily from 9:30am to 5:30pm. Admission is £4.70 for adults, £3.80 for seniors, and £2.80 for children.

WHERE TO EAT & STAY

Hayhoull   Mary and Les Andreas opened this small bed-and-breakfast establish-ment in 2010, having built an extension on to their own home. The smart, spacious guest lounge, complete with under-floor heating, is just the sort of place you want to sit and relax in after sightseeing. The modern, tastefully decorated bedrooms all have lovely views. Two-course evening meals (£15 per head) are available for guests.

Hayhoull, Bigton, Shetland, ZE2 9JA. www.hayhoull.co.uk. © **01950/422-206.** 4 units. £60 double. No credit cards. **Amenities:** Guest lounge. *In room:* Wi-Fi (free).

Spiggie Hotel   Small but well-equipped rooms are the order of the day at this peaceful spot overlooking the Loch of Spiggie. The best room is the airy family room with windows on three sides. When the candles are burning and the fire is lit on a cold autumn evening, what could be nicer than relaxing on one of the comfortable sofas in the little bar downstairs? The restaurant serves up hearty meals (mains £6.50–£14) and is open to non-guests Thursday to Saturday nights and Sunday lunch. Ask for the table in the bay window overlooking the loch.

Spiggie Hotel, Scousburgh, Dunrossness, Shetland, ZE2 9JE. www.thespiggiehotel.co.uk. © **01950/ 460-409.** Fax 01950/460-674. 6 units. £65–£100 double. AE, MC, V. **Amenities:** Restaurant; bar. *In room:* TV, hair dryer, Wi-Fi (free).

Sumburgh Hotel   The standard rooms in the Sumburgh Hotel are just that—stan-dard. Only if you upgrade to a superior room do you get the sort of luxury you expect of a 19th-century laird's house complete with turrets and towers. With high, ornate ceilings, comfortable sofas, and big bay windows, these rooms ooze comfort. The hotel's West Voe restaurant offers a good table d'hôte menu (£22), and simpler meals are available in the bar.

Sumburgh Head, Sumburgh, Shetland, ZE3 9JN. www.sumburghhotel.com. © **01950/460-201.** Fax 01950/460-394. 32 units. £90–£100 double. AE, MC, V. **Amenities:** Restaurant; bar; room service. *In room:* TV, hair dryer, Wi-Fi (free).

Scalloway & Central Mainland

Shetland's second largest town and former capital, Scalloway, lies on the west coast, about 6¼ miles west of Lerwick. The buildings, a mixture of fish merchants' homes, 18th-century lairds' houses, and colorful 19th-century cottages, huddle around its sheltered natural harbor where fishing boats come and go.

Dominating the town are the ruins of the forbidding tower of **Scalloway Castle** (© **01667/460-233;** www.historic-scotland.gov.uk), commissioned by Earl Patrick Stewart in the last years of the 16th century and built with local slave labor. The Earl was hated for his tyranny and the exorbitant taxes and fines he imposed on the islanders. In 1615, he was executed in Edinburgh for treason. The key to the castle is available from the Scalloway Hotel (see below); admission is free.

The nearby **Scalloway Museum** (© **01595/880-608**) contains an informative exhibition on the town's role in Norway's Resistance movement during World War II. The port was used by the "Shetland Bus," a fleet of fishing boats and, later, U.S. submarine chasers, that brought refugees out of Nazi-occupied Norway and shipped arms and agents to the Resistance. It's open May to September Monday through Saturday from 10am to noon and 2pm to 4:30pm; admission is free.

Heading north from Scalloway, along the B9074, you come to the pretty **Loch of Tingwall** where "parliament" used to sit during Norse rule.

You can watch high-quality jewelry being made at **Shetland Jewellery,** Soundside (© **01595/830-275;** www.shetlandjewellery.co.uk), where the artisans base many of their designs on ancient Celtic and Viking patterns. It's open Monday through Friday from 9am to 1pm and 2 to 5pm.

The nearby valley of Weisdale is home to the restored **Weisdale Mill,** which houses the **Bonhoga Gallery** (© **01595/745-750;** www.shetlandarts.org). This purpose-built venue runs a dynamic program of local, national, and international art and craft exhibitions. It also has a popular cafe and shop. It's open Tuesday through Saturday from 10:30am to 4:30pm and Sunday from noon to 4:30pm; admission is free.

WHERE TO EAT & STAY

Scalloway Hotel ★ The bright, airy rooms in this harborside hotel are pleasant enough at the moment, but if what owners Peter and Caroline McKenzie have done with the superb restaurant are anything to go by, the planned refurbishment (which should be partially complete by the time you read this) will make the Scalloway Hotel *the* place to stay on Shetland. The hotel has already acquired a reputation for being the best place to eat on the islands—and deservedly so. Local chef Colin Maclean's cooking can't fail to impress. His perfectly pink venison melts in the mouth and his vegetarian dishes are tasty and imaginative. Diners can also eat in the comfortable bar where they can choose from the main restaurant menu (mains £12–£22) or a selection of good, gastro-style pub food (mains £8.75–£12).

Main St., Scalloway, Shetland, ZE2 OTR. www.scallowayhotel.com. © **01595/880-444.** Fax 01595/880-445. 24 units. £100 double. AE, DC, MC, V. **Amenities:** Restaurant, bar. *In room:* TV, hair dryer.

West Mainland

West Mainland's landscape consists of rolling moorland and rocky knolls divided by sparkling freshwater lochans; long sea lochs, or voes, make big dents into the coastline; and the few settlements are small and scattered. Like much of Shetland, it's a great area for walking, one of the best spots being **Deep Dale** and **Sandness Hill** in the far west. The pretty hamlet of **Walls** hosts an agricultural show in the summer.

An 800m (½ mile) walk across damp, moody moors brings you to **Staneydale,** the site of an ancient settlement occupied as far back as the late Neolithic. This lonely but intriguing place is dotted with the remains of houses and cairns, but the most interesting feature is the **Staneydale "Temple,"** thought to have been a meeting hall. The site is about 4 miles east of Walls.

WHERE TO STAY

Burrastow House ★ A superb waterside setting many miles from the nearest village provides a peaceful, idyllic location for Burrastow House. This is the place to come if you want to escape the stresses of the modern world and relax in serene surroundings. Some of the rooms in this 18th-century house look out over the sound to low-lying grassy islands. Excellent dinners are available for an extra £35 per person.

Walls, West Mainland, Shetland, ZE2 9PD. www.burrastowhouse.co.uk. © **01595/809-307.** 6 units. £90–£100 double. AE, DC, MC, V. Closed Nov to Mar. **Amenities:** Restaurant. *In room:* TV, hair dryer.

A Side Trip to Papa Stour ★

Papa Stour, the "great island of priests," is a 40-minute ferry journey off the coast of West Mainland. It's thought to have been home in the 6th century to Celtic missionaries. Since the middle of the 20th century, the island has battled depopulation. People from other parts of the U.K. were encouraged to settle here in the 1970s, and things were looking positive for a while, but the island now has only nine permanent residents.

As far as visitors go, its attraction lies in its birdlife and amazing geology. Facing the full force of the Atlantic, its volcanic rocks have been sculpted by the raging sea into some of the most remarkable coastal scenery in the British Isles. On a walk around the island, you will see stacks, natural arches, and long subterranean passages. **Kirstan's Hole** is one of the most striking features. Here, the roof of a cave that extends some 73m (240 ft.) inland has collapsed, forming a "gloup" and providing a glimpse of the tumultuous waves far below. In June and July, watch for common seal pups on the beaches.

You can fly to Papa Stour (© **01595/840-246;** www.directflight.co.uk), but most people arrive by boat from West Burrafirth. For a full day on the island, travel on Friday or Saturday. The cost is £3.40 each way (© **01957/722-259**).

A Side Trip to Foula

The towering cliffs of the tiny, remote island of Foula have to be seen to be believed. Take a cruise to the base of Da Kame and you have to crane your neck to see the top of this 370m (1,214 ft.) wall of rock. Noisy colonies of sea birds live on these windlashed ledges—it's easy here to see how Foula (which means "bird island" in local dialect) got its name.

The island lies 27 miles west of Scalloway, and its isolation has a profound effect on the local population. Only 31 people live here now, but Norse tradition remains important to them. Curiously, they still follow the old Julian calendar, which means Christmas Day falls on January 6.

If you want to explore Foula's steep-sided hills or wander the exposed clifftops to do some bird-watching, it's possible to arrange a bed-and-breakfast stay on the island (try **Marion Taylor** at © **01595/753-226**).

Atlantic Ferries runs a weather-dependant, twice-weekly service from Walls (© **01595/743-9760;** www.atlanticferries.co.uk). **Direct Flight** (© **01595/840-246;** www.directflight.co.uk) operates six flights a week during summer. Alternatively, on Wednesdays, **Cycharters** runs a day trip that includes a circumnavigation of Foula and a tour of the island's main settlement. The cost is £60 for adults, £30 for under-16s (© **01595/696-598;** www.cycharters.co.uk).

North Mainland

Heading north from Lerwick, you enter some of Shetland's most rugged scenery. The road divides at **Voe,** a tiny village with colorful, wooden buildings that have a hint of Norway about them.

To the east, the B9071 leads to **Laxo** and **Vidlin,** for ferries to Whalsay and Out Skerries respectively. Nearby **Lunna Kirk** is the oldest church on the islands still used for worship. Parts of it date back to the 12th century. The church has a "leper squint," from which victims could watch the sermon without coming into contact with the rest of the congregation.

North of Voe, visitors reach **Brae,** an unattractive village but a good base for touring. The presence of contractors servicing nearby Sullom Voe, Europe's largest oil terminal, means there are several places to stay and eat here and in **Busta** on the other side of the voe. For interesting **coastal hiking,** take the minor road south from Busta and over Roe Sound to the island of **Muckle Roe.**

Continuing north, visitors cross **Mavis Grind,** a narrow isthmus where it's said you can throw a stone from the North Sea into the Atlantic Ocean.

Some of the islands' most unusual cliff scenery, including stacks, natural arches, and steep-sided clefts or "geos," can be found on the **Ness of Hillswick** and the spectacular **Esha Ness** ★ at the end of the B9078. These are great areas for **hiking.** The nearby **Tangwick Haa Museum,** housed in a 17th-century laird's home, tells the story of life in these remote parts; it's open May to September daily from 11am to 5pm, and admission is free but donations are welcome.

WHERE TO EAT & STAY

Brae Hotel   Here you'll find clean, simple, and well-equipped rooms in a modern hotel that mainly serves the oil industry. Ask for a room with a view of the voe.

Brae, Shetland ZE2 9QJ. www.braehotel.co.uk. © **01806/522-456.** Fax 01806/522-026. 36 units. £100 double, £120 suite. AE, MC, V. **Amenities:** Restaurant; bar. *In room:* TV.

Busta House   Shetland's oldest continuously inhabited house, Busta House has been a hotel since 1972. Overlooking Busta Voe and with its own private harbor, the hotel's lounge retains a period feel with oil paintings and antique furniture, while the bar and restaurant have a traditional ambience. The comfortable dining areas are open to non-guests all day, and there are two menus from which to choose, including a £35 per head evening menu in the restaurant. The chef prides himself on using only the best local produce as well as herbs and salad from the hotel's gardens.

Busta, near Brae, Shetland, ZE2 9QN. www.bustahouse.com. © **01806/522-506.** Fax 01806/522-588. 22 units. £110–£120 double. AE, DC, MC, V. **Amenities:** Restaurant; bar; room service. *In room:* TV/DVD, hair dryer, Wi-Fi (free).

Frankie's Fish & Chip Café   Britain's most northerly fish and chip shop is located beside the voe in Brae. Bright, clean, and popular, it's open all year and serves fish from sustainable sources, mussels, burgers, and other light meals.

Brae, Shetland, ZE2 9QJ. © **01806/522-700.** www.frankiesfishandchips.com. Meals £4–£6.90. Mon-Sat 9:30am–8pm, Sun 1–8pm.

Pierhead   Wooden floors and a chilly public bar give this Voe pub a basic feel, but the meals are anything but basic. Delicious mussels and a great pork stroganoff are just two of the dishes on a good, but very reasonably priced, evening menu. Weekend diners can enjoy their meal in the upstairs restaurant, with views over the harbor.

Voe, Shetland, ZE2 9PX. © 01806/588-332. Main courses £7.50–£11.

St Magnus Bay Hotel   This 110-year-old timber-clad building was brought over from Norway for an exhibition in Glasgow in the late 19th century. It's now being enthusiastically returned to its former glory by new owners Paul Bird and Andrea Manson. With wood paneling on the walls, the rooms in the quirky main building are warm and full of character. The rooms in the more modern annex aren't as interesting, but are equally comfortable. Many rooms have magnificent views, as does the rather grand drawing room, where guests can sit and watch otters and even the occasional pod of orcas in the bay below. The poet W.H. Auden created a stir locally when he stayed here with his lover in the 1930s.

Hillswick, Shetland, ZE2 9RW. www.stmagnusbayhotel.co.uk. © **01806/503-372.** Fax 01806/503-707. 27 units. £95–£145 double. DC, MC, V. **Amenities:** Restaurant; bar. *In room:* TV, hair dryer.

Unst

Unst is the U.K.'s most northerly inhabited island. Beautiful and remote, it takes two ferry journeys to reach it. The first is from **Toft,** 10 miles north of Voe on Mainland, to **Ulsta** on **Yell,** Shetland's second largest island. The crossing takes about 20 minutes, with ferries leaving at half-hour intervals (© 01957/722-259). The fare is £8.40 round-trip for a car and driver. This crossing is followed by a 17-mile drive north to **Gutcher** for another "roll-on/roll-off" ferry to **Belmont** on Unst. With boats leaving about every half-hour, the journey takes about 10 minutes and is free.

About 5 miles east of Belmont is **Muness Castle,** constructed in 1598 by Laurence Bruce, a relative of the notorious Earl Patrick Stewart. Admission to the ruins, known for their fine architectural detail, is free (© 01667/460-233; www.historic-scotland.gov.uk). Visitors can pick up the key from a nearby cottage; details provided at the site.

A 1-mile walk from here leads to **Sandwick,** one of Unst's beautiful and tranquil white beaches and home to the ruins of an old **Norse longhouse.** Other good beaches can be found at **Burrafirth** in the north of the island and **Lunda Wick,** 4¼ miles from Belmont. Here, a narrow, gated road leads to the **Kirk of Lund,** a ruined church and graveyard next to the lonely beach—a wild but romantic setting.

Visitors go to **Haroldswick** to mail their cards and letters in the most northerly post office in the British Isles. At the time of writing, a **replica Norse longhouse** was being built on the edge of the village. There are plans to open this to the public with people in Viking costume showing visitors what life would have been like for the early settlers (www.vikingshetland.com). Next to it is a full-size replica of a Viking longboat.

The highlight of any visit to Unst is the **Hermaness Reserve ★**, one of the most important ornithological sites in the U.K. Ideal for scenic **hikes,** its 182m (600 ft.) cliffs are filled with kittiwakes, gannets, razorbills, guillemots, and the inevitable puffins. Great skuas have a tendency to dive-bomb walkers in the nesting season; hold your arm up to prevent them from attacking your head. Walk to the end of the peninsula to see the lighthouse on the islet of **Muckle Flugga** and, farther north, **Out Stack,** the northernmost tip of Britain.

WHERE TO EAT & STAY

Baltasound Hotel   This place consists mainly of a group of log cabins arranged around a lawn in front of the hotel. Pine-style paneling on walls and ceilings gives a bright atmosphere to the simple rooms. Inside the main building are an additional six rooms.

Baltasound, Unst, ZE2 9DS. www.baltasound-hotel.shetland.co.uk. © **01957/711-334.** Fax 01957/711-358. 23 units. £84–£95 double. MC, V. **Amenities:** Restaurant; bar. *In room:* TV, hair dryer (on request).

Buness House 🎁   This ancient laird's house has remained in the same family since Norse times. Today, it's the home of the friendly, knowledgeable Jennifer and David Edmondson, who will make you feel at home as soon as you enter their charming house. Guests are free to make use of the family's drawing room and library. Four-course evening meals are served in the conservatory, from where you can watch otters playing in the water below.

Baltasound, Unst, ZE2 9DS. www.users.zetnet.co.uk/buness-house. © **01957/711-315.** Fax 01957/711-815. 3 units. £122 double. Discount for stays of 4 nights or more. No credit cards. *In room:* TV (on request).

Fair Isle ★

45 miles S of Lerwick, Shetland

Britain's most isolated inhabited island, Fair Isle, lies about halfway between Orkney and Shetland, but is administered by the latter. It's about 3 miles long and never more than 2 miles wide. Relentless seas pound its rocky coast in winter, and powerful westerly winds fling Atlantic spray from one side of the island to the other. Fair Isle is home to about 70 rugged, self-reliant souls, most of whom live at the southern end of the island.

An important staging point for migrating birds, Fair Isle is a dream destination for most British ornithologists. It's also an important breeding ground for everything from the puffin and the Arctic skua to the razorbill and the storm petrel. More than 340 different species have been recorded at the **bird observatory,** which was built in 1948 (and then completely rebuilt in 2010). Fair Isle is also full of botanical rarities, and thanks to traditional crafting methods, comes alive with color in the late spring and early summer. In 1954, the entire island was acquired by the National Trust for Scotland.

Fair Isle is also well known for its **pullovers,** made from fine yarns stranded into a double layer. In stores around the world, you see these intricately patterned garments retailing at high prices. The homegrown product, produced by the co-operative Fair Isle Crafts, is sold at half the price. First worn by fishermen in the 19th century, the pullovers' fame was spread in the 1920s by the then Prince of Wales after he was seen sporting one while playing golf at St. Andrew's.

GETTING THERE

Direct Flight (© **01595/840-246;** www.directflight.co.uk) flies to Fair Isle from Shetland twice daily on Monday, Wednesday, and Friday, and once on Saturday. Flight time is 25 minutes and the economy fare for visitors is £60 round-trip. Flights depart from Tingwall, 6 miles northwest of Lerwick.

The *Good Shepherd* sails at 11:30am on Tuesday, Thursday, and Saturday from Grutness Pier, Sumburgh Head, on Mainland. It's advisable to check sailing times by phoning before 9:30am on the day of the scheduled departure, in case of weather delay. Bookings for the trip can be made through the skipper, **Neil Thomson** (℡ **01595/760-363**). A one-way fare is £3.40; the journey takes 2½ hours.

WHERE TO EAT & STAY

Fair Isle Bird Observatory Lodge   A stay at this smart newer lodge is an interesting experience even if you're not a bird-watcher. Located near the sea at the northern end of the island, the original bird observatory was the dream of a well-respected ornithologist, George Waterston. It's a sociable place to stay, with keen bird-watchers swapping notes in the bar and the dining room. All guests are invited to join the staff for the "Bird Log," which takes place at 9:30 every evening.

The lodge is most busy during the spring and autumn bird migrations. It's wise to reserve well in advance, especially during those seasons.

Fair Isle, Shetland, ZE2 9JU. www.fairislebirdobs.co.uk. ℡/fax **01595/760-258.** 12 units. £100 double, full board. MC, V. Closed Nov to late Apr. **Amenities:** Dining room, bar, laundry room.

PLANNING YOUR TRIP TO SCOTLAND

A wealth of practical information is available to help ensure that your trip to Scotland goes smoothly. Whether it's understanding how local taxes work or how much you can take home through customs, it always mation on the practicalities of everyday life, which seem so simple at home and yet in another country can sometimes be perplexing.

GETTING THERE

By Plane

FROM THE U.K. A choice of airlines operates regular and often inexpensive flights from cities around the U.K. including all London airports, Manchester, Birmingham, and Bristol. These services link with both Edinburgh Airport (EDI; www.edinburghairport.com) and Glasgow Airport (GLA; www.glasgowairport.com), and to a lesser extent Aberdeen (ABZ; www.aberdeenairport.com), Inverness (INV; www.hial.co.uk/inverness-airport), and Dundee (DND; www.hial.co.uk/dundee-airport). The most frequent services are run by **easyJet, British Airways, BMI, Flybe,** and **CityJet.** These airlines also run regular services from Ireland and many other European destinations.

FROM NORTH AMERICA Limited flights from the U.S. and Canada connect directly with Scotland. **Continental Airlines** operates direct flights between Newark and Glasgow and Edinburgh airports; **Virgin Atlantic Airways** connects Orlando with Glasgow in the summer; and **Canadian Affair** flies directly to Glasgow from Calgary, Toronto, and Vancouver.

Most other services between the U.K. and U.S. operate out of London Heathrow (LHR; www.heathrowairport.com) or Gatwick (LGW; www.gatwickairport.com). **Virgin Atlantic Airways** is known for consistently offering excellent fares and flies directly to Heathrow from Boston, Los Angeles, Miami, New York, San Diego, San Francisco, and Seattle and to Gatwick from Orlando, Las Vegas, San Diego, and Seattle. **American Airlines** offers flights to Heathrow from many U.S. gateways including New York, Newark, Chicago, Boston, Miami, and Los Angeles and to Gatwick from Orlando and Tampa.

Depending on the season, **Delta Air Lines** runs nonstop flights from Atlanta, Boston, Detroit, and New York to Heathrow and between Atlanta and Gatwick. **Continental Airlines** operates direct flights from Houston, Newark, Chicago, and San Francisco to Heathrow. **United Airlines** fly nonstop from Chicago, San Francisco, Los Angeles, and Dulles Airport near Washington, D.C. to Heathrow.

For travelers departing from Canada, **Air Canada** flies nonstop to Heathrow from a number of major cities including Vancouver, Montreal, and Toronto. **Canadian Affair** flies directly to Gatwick from Calgary, Toronto, and Vancouver. **American Airlines** offers flights to Heathrow from Toronto, Calgary, and Vancouver. **British Airways** has direct flights from Toronto, Montreal, and Vancouver.

Some passengers opt for flights into Manchester, England because it's closer than London and has good air, rail, and coach connections with Scotland.

FROM AUSTRALIA & NEW ZEALAND   For travelers departing from Australia, **British Airways** operates flights to Heathrow from Sydney, Melbourne, Perth, and Brisbane. **Qantas** offers flights from Sydney and Melbourne to Heathrow. Many flights between Australia and the U.K. have the bonus of a stopover in Singapore.

Departing from Auckland, **Air New Zealand** flies to Heathrow via Shanghai or Hong Kong.

By Car

If you're driving to Scotland from London or anywhere in eastern England to Edinburgh, the **A1** is the fastest route. This road heads directly north from the **M25,** London's ring road, and crosses into the Scottish Borders before leading into Edinburgh from the east. For Glasgow from London take the **M1,** which leads northwest from the M25. At junction 19 of the M1 head west to join the M6 which journeys west through Birmingham before heading directly north up the west side of England into Scotland. If you're traveling from the southwest of England the **M5,** which begins at Exeter (Devon), leads into the M6 at Birmingham. As the M6 crosses the border into Dumfries and Galloway in Scotland, it becomes the M74 and heads directly north into Glasgow. All major routes into northern Scotland lead from either Edinburgh or Glasgow.

By Train

Two main rail lines link London to Scotland. The **East Coast Mainline** connects London's **King's Cross Station** with Edinburgh via York, Newcastle-upon-Tyne, and Durham. Trains depart at regular intervals throughout the day and cross from England into Scotland at Berwick-upon-Tweed. The journey from London to Edinburgh takes around 4¼ hours with some services traveling an additional hour on to Glasgow, and others continuing north to Dundee (an additional 1½ hr.) and Aberdeen (an additional 2½ hr.).

Rail Information
National Rail Enquires (☎ 08457/484-950; www.nationalrail.co.uk) is a central service offering information on all routes, timetables, and fares in England, Scotland, and Wales.

The **West Coast Mainline** leads from London's **Euston Station** for Glasgow by way of Preston, Oxenholme in England's Lake District, and Carlisle. Trains depart roughly every hour throughout the day and take around 4½ hours to reach Glasgow.

In addition, a **Cross Country** route leads from Penzance in Cornwall,

Getting There

PLANNING YOUR TRIP TO SCOTLAND

| Scenic Scotland by Motor Home |

When it comes to exploring Scotland, many visitors prefer to rent a motor-home. **Car Rental Scotland** (✆ **0141/ 427-5475; www.carrentalscotland.com)** rents four-, five-, and six-berth motor homes and can arrange transfers from Edinburgh, Glasgow, and Prestwick airports. Fill out an online enquiry form for details on rates and all the optional extras.

England through Plymouth, Exeter, Bristol, Birmingham, Leeds, and other cities to Scotland. For more information on this service, contact ✆ **08477/369-123** (www. crosscountrytrains.co.uk).

Train routes from Edinburgh and Glasgow lead across the rest of Scotland and are mostly operated by **ScotRail** (✆ **08457/550-033**; www.scotrail.co.uk). ScotRail also operates **Caledonian Sleepers,** overnight trains between London and Scotland that offer both seated and sleeping berth accommodation. Services can be booked up to 12 weeks in advance either by telephone or online.

To truly travel to Scotland in style, consider a trip on the **Orient Express'** *Northern Belle.* Each carriage is as sumptuous as a stately home, and the trains—which carry a maximum of 252 passengers—feature six luxury dining carriages. For more information and to make a reservation, call ✆ **0845/217-0799** in the U.K. or 800/524-2420 in the U.S., or go to **www.orient-express.com**.

BY TRAIN FROM CONTINENTAL EUROPE London's fully restored, iconic **St. Pancras Station** is the hub for high-speed Eurostar train services from Paris and Brussels traveling to the U.K. from Belgium and France via the multibillion-dollar **Channel Tunnel.** Recent upgrades to the line mean you can now reach London from Brussels in 1 hour and 51 minutes and from Paris in 2 hours and 15 minutes. In London, make reservations for **Eurostar** by calling ✆ **0843/2186-186;** in North America, book online at **www.eurostar.com** or contact **Rail Europe** (✆ **800/622-8600,** or 800/361-7245 in Canada; www.raileurope.com). U.S. visitors arriving from Continental Europe should remember that the validity of the Eurorail pass ends at the English Channel. You need to purchase a separate BritRail pass if you plan to tour the U.K. by train; visit **www.britrail.com**.

By Bus (Coach)

Long-distance buses, or "coaches" as they're more generally known in Britain, are the least expensive means of reaching Scotland from other parts of the U.K. but also take the most travel time. The majority of routes and services are operated by **National Express** (✆ **0871/781-8181;** www.nationalexpress.com), which links with most decent-sized communities in the U.K. The budget operator **MegaBus** (✆ **0871/266-3333;** www.megabus.com) also runs long-distance coach services to Scotland from a limited number of U.K. destinations. In London most coaches depart from **Victoria Coach Station** at 164 Buckingham Palace Rd. (✆ **020/7730-3466**), and take 8 to 8½ hours to reach Edinburgh or Glasgow. Regardless of the company you travel with, it's always wise to make reservations in advance, especially during peak times such as the summer months and over the festive season. National Express also offers three different **Brit Xplorer** passes that allow unlimited travel on their services for a set period of time and for a set fare; the Hobo ticket costs £79 and is valid for 7 days, the

Footloose ticket costs £139 for 14 days, and the Rolling Stone ticket costs £219 and lasts for 28 days.

GETTING AROUND
By Car

Driving in Scotland is straightforward and often enjoyable as, once you get away from the central belt around Edinburgh and Glasgow, you encounter far less traffic than in many other parts of the U.K. A small network of motorways link the main urban areas in the middle of the country and, where the landscape allows, "A" roads that are often "dual carriageways" (divided highways) spread out over the rest of Scotland. In more remote areas—especially the islands of western Scotland—single-lane roads are often the only link to small communities or off-the-beaten-track attractions. Passing places are provided but caution is important because many of these roads are unfenced and livestock such as sheep often wander into the road.

> ### Look Both Ways!
>
> **North American visitors should remember that in Great Britain, cars drive on the left. Always look both ways before stepping off a curb.**

CAR RENTALS If you're considering hiring a car in Scotland shop around, compare prices, and have a clear idea of your needs. Rates are often discounted if you reserve in advance and return the vehicle to its point of origin, although many companies will pick you up and drive you to their location. Some companies require drivers to be at least 23 years old, although 21 is more standard. To rent a car in Scotland, you must present your passport and driver's license along with a deposit; special British or international licenses aren't needed. Be aware that a further 20% VAT (Valued Added Tax) will be added to your bill. For a list of car rental companies, see "Car-Rental Agencies" at the end of this chapter.

Car-rental rates vary even more than airline fares. The price you pay depends on the size of the car, where and when you pick it up and drop it off, length of the rental period, whether you purchase insurance against excess in the event of a claim, and a host of other factors. For a useful car rental comparison website, see **www.carrentals. co.uk** and consider asking a few key questions that could save you hundreds of dollars:

- Are weekend rates lower than weekday rates? Ask if the rate is the same for pickup Friday morning, for instance, as it is for Thursday night.
- Is a weekly rate cheaper than the daily rate? If you need to keep the car for 4 days, it may be cheaper to keep it for 5, even if you don't need it for that long.
- Does the agency assess a drop-off charge if you don't return the car to the same location where you picked it up? Is it cheaper to pick up the car at the airport compared to a downtown location?
- Are special promotional rates available? If you see an advertised price, be sure to ask for that specific rate; otherwise, you may be charged the standard cost. The terms change constantly, and representatives may not volunteer information.
- Are discounts available for members of AARP, AAA, frequent-flier programs, alumni organizations, or trade unions? If you belong to any of these organizations, you could be entitled to a discount.
- What is the cost of adding an additional driver's name to the contract?

Car-Rental Excess

It's illegal to drive without insurance in the U.K., and the cost is included as standard in rental rates. However, the excess (deductible) against this insurance is often as high as £600 unless you pay for a reduced excess which can, if you take the car rental company's policy, often be as much again as the cost of the car. A number of companies offer insurance against car-rental excess. Under these policies you still have to pay the excess to the car rental company, but you then claim it back from the insurance company. You can often choose between annual and single trip coverage. Companies that provide this insurance include **Insurance 4 Car Hire** (℄ **01883/724-001; www.insurance4carhire.com**) and **Car Hire Excess** (℄ **0818/444-447; www.carhireexcess.com**).

- How many free miles are included in the price? Free mileage is often negotiable, depending on the length of your rental.
- How much does the rental company charge to refill your gas (petrol) tank if you return with the tank less than full? Though most rental companies claim these prices are "competitive," fuel is almost always cheaper in town. Try to allow enough time to refuel the car yourself before returning it.

GASOLINE   There are plenty of gas ("petrol") stations in and around main urban areas, but in more remote locations they're few and far between and so always make sure you have a good supply before venturing away from larger towns and cities. At press time, prices charged for gasoline in the U.K. stand at around £1.35 per liter (1 U.S. gallon = 3.785 liters) and are ever increasing.

DRIVING RULES & REQUIREMENTS   In Scotland and the whole of the U.K., *you drive on the left* and pass on the right and always give way to traffic coming from the right at a roundabout. If you're driving on a single lane road, you must use the passing places on the left side of the road, give priority to traffic traveling uphill, and never park in a passing place. Pedestrian crossings not controlled by traffic lights are marked by white striped lines (zebra striping) on the road and sometimes flashing lights near the curb. Drivers must stop and yield the right of way to any pedestrian waiting to cross or has already stepped out into the zebra crossing. Before driving in the U.K., it's a good idea for overseas visitors to read the British *Highway Code,* which can be bought at most gas stations and bookshops or viewed online at www.direct.gov.uk.

MAPS   Up-to-date maps can be bought at most gas stations, bookstores and newsagents, or online from the **Automobile Association** (℄ **0870/600-0371; www.theaa.co.uk**). The best maps, especially if you're trying to locate some obscure village, are produced by **Ordnance Survey** (www.ordnancesurvey.co.uk) and can be bought via the website or at most bookstores. Other excellent maps include the *Collins Touring Map of Scotland.*

BREAKDOWNS   Breakdown coverage is normally included as standard with any car rental. Otherwise a number of organizations offer this service, including the **Automobile Association (AA)** (℄ **0161/333-0004;** www.theaa.com), the **Royal Automobile Club (RAC)** (℄ **08000/722-822;** www.rac.co.uk), and **Green Flag** (℄ **0845/246-1558;** www.greenflag.com). All these organizations also provide online route planners via their websites, and the **Highways Agency** features online traffic news via its website at www.highways.gov.uk. Roadside emergency telephone boxes are located roughly every mile along motorways. If you don't see one, walk in either direction until you spot a blue-and-white marker with an arrow that points to the nearest box. The 24-hour number to call for the AA is © **0800/887-766;** for the RAC, it's © **0800/82-82-82;** and for Green Flag, call © **0800/051-0636.**

By Plane

Scotland's relatively small scale makes internal flights between cities impractical. However, to reach some of the farthest flung regions of the Highlands and Islands, an internal flight is often the quickest option. **Flybe** operate routes from Glasgow and Edinburgh to destinations including the Shetland Islands, Stornoway, Wick, and Tiree. For information on traveling to Scotland by plane, see "Getting There" on p. 423.

By Train

Traveling by train is one of the best ways to see Scotland and travel between different regions. The cost of rail travel is generally quite low and services are normally frequent, punctual, and reliable, while some routes such as the line from Glasgow to the West Highlands are among the most scenic in the world.

The main train operator in Scotland is **ScotRail** (© **0845/601-5929;** www.scotrail.co.uk), with a network of rail routes around the country. Information on routes, timetables, and fares is available through its website or at any staffed station; some of the smaller stations are unstaffed and tickets must be purchased on the train from the conductor. In addition to standard single and return fares, ScotRail offers a number of ticket deals. With the Kids Go Free deal (www.scotrail.co.uk/kidsgofree), two children between ages 5 and 15 can travel free with an adult as long as you

> ### Eurorail Pass Warning
>
> Note that your Eurorail pass is *not* valid on trains in Britain.

travel during off-peak hours and make the return journey on the same day. A number of attractions in Scotland are linked with this deal and allow free entry for children traveling on these tickets. Tickets can be bought in advance on the day of travel. Discount fares are also available for groups of three or four adults traveling together, and vary depending on whether you book in advance or travel during off-peak hours; to find out more about possible savings, ask about **Friends Fare** and **GroupSave** when purchasing your tickets.

Young adults between ages 16 and 25 can purchase an annual **16-25 Railcard,** which saves a third of the price on all rail tickets for a year. A yearlong pass costs £26 and can be bought in advance online at www.16-25railcard.co.uk or at any staffed station. You need to have two passport-sized photographs and to show your actual passport as proof of age and identity.

Hop aboard the **Royal Scotsman** (© **800/524-2420** or 401/884-0090; www.royalscotsman.com) and you can truly experience the romance of rail travel and Scotland's scenic rail routes in style on one of the most luxurious trains in the world. Known as "a country house hotel on wheels," the Royal Scotsman offers a choice of routes that depart from Edinburgh's Waverley station and sweep past ancient mountains and misty lochs and through glens and villages. The train carries a maximum of

36 guests, allowing each passenger plenty of sumptuous space to spread out, and travelers can expect plush beds and opulent en-suite bathrooms. Tours range from the 2-night Highland Journey at £2,140 per twin cabin to the 7-night Grand North Western Journey at £6,360 per twin cabin. Prices include all meals, drinks, and sightseeing excursions.

BRITRAIL TRAVEL PASSES   BritRail Passes allow unlimited travel in England, Scotland, and Wales on any scheduled train over the whole of the network during the validity of the pass without restrictions. **BritRail Consecutive Pass** allows you to travel for a consecutive number of days for a flat rate; a more versatile pass is the **BritRail FlexiPass** allowing you to travel when you want during a 2-month period of time. Prices can vary significantly between first and second class (with second class anywhere from £100 to £250 less expensive), and discounts are available for seniors age 60 and over. Passengers age 25 and under qualify for a 2nd Class Youth Pass; one child between ages 5 and 15 can travel free with each adult and any additional children pay only half the regular adult fare. All children aged under five travel for free.

> ### Traveline Scotland
>
> Traveline Scotland is a centralized service that assists travelers in planning their journeys across the whole country and all forms of public transport. Routes can be planed either online at www.travelinescotland.com or via the helpline at ℂ 0871/200-2233.

BritRail Passes and trip packages are available through www.britrail.com. To call BritRail in the United States, dial ℂ **877/677-1066.**

OTHER TRAIN PASSES FOR SCOTLAND   ScotRail (ℂ **0845/601-5929;** www.scotrail.co.uk) offers a selection of passes across Scottish rail networks. The **Freedom of Scotland Travelpass** allows unlimited travel across all routes in Scotland from Carlisle, England (near the western Scotland–England border) and from Berwick-upon-Tweed, England (near the eastern Scotland–England border). This pass also includes rides on ferries operated by Caledonian MacBrayne (www.calmac.co.uk) and travel on a limited selection of bus (coach) routes operated by Scottish Citylink (www.citylink.co.uk), Stagecoach in Fife and Inverness (www.stagecoach-bus.com), and First Edinburgh (www.firstgroup.com). Passes for 4 days of unlimited travel over 8 consecutive days cost £122, and 8 days of unlimited travel over 15 consecutive days cost £164. Children aged 5 to 15 travel for half the cost of an adult ticket and under-5s travel for free.

Five other similar ScotRail touring passes are available, each covering a different section of the country and working with different ferry and bus operators. With a couple of exceptions, travel isn't permitted on any train before 9:15am Monday through Friday. Anyone planning to travel on ScotRail's Caledonian Sleeper trains with these passes is strongly advised to make reservations. More information is available on ScotRail's website or pick up their *Touring ticket guide* leaflet. Tickets can be bought online via ScotRail's website or from any staffed station.

By Bus (Coach)

Bus or coach travel is one of the cheapest ways to travel around Scotland, but it's also one of the slowest. All major towns and cities operate their own **bus services,** and these are often the best way to travel around urban areas. Also in rural areas buses

If you're planning to visit a number of Scotland's many historic properties, you could save money by purchasing one of Historic Scotland's **Explorer Passes** (www.historic-scotland.gov.uk/index/places/explorer.htm). Passes allow entry into their most visited historic attractions, including Edinburgh, Stirling, and Urquhart castles, Iona Abbey, and Skara Brae. There are two types of passes: The first is good for 3 days within a 5-day period and costs £25 for adults, £20 for seniors, £15 for children aged 5 to 15, and £50 for families. The second pass is available for 7 days within a 14-day period and costs £34 for adults, £27 for seniors, £21 for children and £68 for families. Explorer Passes can be bought at any staffed Historic Scotland property, at **Tourist Information Centres (TICs)** across the country, or online at Historic Scotland's website at www.historic-scotland.gov.

uk. For more information, call ✆ **0131/668-8600.**

Another good choice for visitors on a budget is the **Great British Heritage Pass,** which allows entry to around 400 heritage attractions across Britain including the Palace of Holyroodhouse, Edinburgh, Balmoral and Blair castles, and many National Trust for Scotland properties. In addition to free entry, pass holders also receive a 40-page guidebook and a map of Great Britain. Passes start at 4 days for £39 for adults and £23 for children; for 7 days it's £69 for adults and £40 for children; and for 15 days it's £89 for adults and £52 for children. The month-long pass costs £119 for adults and £70 for children. You must use the pass on consecutive days, and it can be purchased online at www.british-heritagepass.com. For more information, call ✆ **0870/242-9988.**

are often the only means of reaching smaller communities unless you rent a car. In very remote regions, Royal Mail post buses provide a lifeline of public transport for locals and visitors and are one of the most fascinating ways to travel around Scotland. For more information on this service, visit www2.royalmail.com/you-home/your-community/postbus or ✆ **08457/740-740.** Local post offices can also provide details of routes.

Scottish Citylink (✆ **08705/505-050**; www.citylink.co.uk) operates a frequent and inexpensive coach service for all Scotland's cities and large towns. **Explorer Passes** allow unlimited travel on a set number of days within a consecutive time period; for example, 3 travel days within 5 days costs £35, 5 travel days within 10 days costs £59, and 8 travel days within 16 days costs £79. Tickets can be bought on the day of travel, or you can save by purchasing in advance via Citylink's website or customer service telephone line (see above).

Stagecoach also runs many services across Scotland; for full details of its routes and timetables, visit www.stagecoachbus.com. **Megabus** (✆ **0871/266-3333;** www.megabus.com) also operates a number of routes between many of Scotland's towns and cities.

TIPS ON PLACES TO STAY

There's a vast amount of styles and types of accommodation to choose from in Scotland: modern city center boutique hotels to remote farmhouses and lighthouse cottages. It's advisable to book as far in advance as possible even in what might be considered the slow months from November to April, because these times of the year are now often popular with retired travelers. Also the farther in advance you can book, the greater the discounts you can bag. If you're particular about the type of room you require, always ask at the time of booking; for example if you're sensitive to noise, request a quieter room, perhaps at the rear or garden side of the hotel so you won't hear street noise. Remember that in the older hotels and inns, guest rooms tend to be small and some en-suite bathrooms come with only a shower, and so confirm that your room has a bathtub if it's important to you.

Visit Scotland provides an accommodation booking service, **Advance Reservations Service** (*©* 0845/225-5121). It's free to use, but 10% of the accommodation fee is required to secure your accommodation, which can be booked last minute or secured as soon you like.

Accommodation prices quoted throughout this guide include breakfast unless otherwise stated and represent the hotels' rack rates, the maximum price charged. However, when it comes to the larger hotels and chains, it's unlikely you'll end up paying that rate. Booking online through the hotel's website often brings significant discounts, especially at quieter times when you can get up to 75% off the rack rates particularly at the luxury end of the market. Booking through websites such as www.laterooms.com or www.expedia.com can also save a significant amount of money. For tips on surfing for hotel deals online, visit www.frommers.com/planning.

Classifications

In Britain regional tourist boards classify the standard of accommodation through a star rating system, with five stars being the highest rating and one star the lowest. Each property is judged on its standards, facilities, and quality, and its rating is usually posted on its website and via a plaque at the entrance. All establishments from two stars upward are required to provide en-suite bathrooms, and in one-star accommodation hot and cold running water must be provided in all rooms. Rating is voluntary and some hotels choose not to participate. However, the vast majority do and although some accommodation still lags behind when it comes to modern standards, on the whole most have upped their game and provide a good standard of amenities, customer service, and comforts. If you have any doubts on the facilities provided, always check and request confirmation at the time of booking.

Bed & Breakfasts

A mainstay of accommodation in all areas of Scotland and the U.K. are bed-and-breakfasts, which can be found all over the country from big cities to the most remote

Dear Visa: I'm Off to Aberdeen!

Some credit card companies recommend that you notify them of any impending trip abroad so that they don't become suspicious when the card is used numerous times in a foreign destination and block your charges. Even if you don't call your credit card company in advance, you can always call the card's toll-free emergency number if a charge is refused—a good reason to carry the phone number with you. But perhaps the most important lesson here is to carry more than one card with you on your trip; a card might not work for any number of reasons, and so having a backup is the smart way to go.

biking IN SCOTLAND

For details on biking around the country, see "Biking, Walking & Other Outdoor Activities," in chapter 4.

o **The Galloway Region:** South-western Scotland doesn't draw the most visitors, but its beauty is unrivaled. A land of fields, verdant forests, and mist-shrouded hills, Galloway offers endless biking possibilities. All tourist offices in the area carry *Cycling in Dumfries and Galloway,* which describes the best routes. A free leaflet published by the Scottish Forest Enterprise gives trail routes through the various forests. See chapter 6.

o **The Isle of Arran:** The largest of the Clyde Islands, Arran has been called "Scotland in minia-ture." And indeed, if you don't have time to see the whole country, you can get a preview of its various regions by biking this island. The northern part is mountainous, like the Highlands, while the south, with scenery akin to the Borders, resembles the Lowlands. The full circuit around the island takes about 9 hours. The tourist office distrib-utes the free *Cycling on Arran,* which indicates the best routes. See "Exploring the Island," on p. 209.

o **The Trossachs:** Scotland's most scenic stretch for biking (not to mention for driving and bucolic walks) is the Trossachs, famed as Rob Roy MacGregor country. The ideal biking spot is along Loch Katrine, 10 miles long and 1¾ miles at its widest. See chapter 9.

o **Glencoe:** Site of a famous 1692 massacre, Glencoe features stark and grandiose mountain scenery. Rent a bike in the village and embark on an adventure, though you're likely to get rained on, as some 100 inches of rain a year are recorded. But as one local said, "Biking through Glencoe in the rain is when it's at its most mystical—we Scots have done that for years." See "Glencoe: Spectacular Scenery," in chapter 11.

o **The Isle of Skye:** Part of the Hebrides, Skye is the land of the Cuillins, a brooding mountain range you see at every turn as you pedal along. The most unusual place to bike is the 20-mile Trotternish Peninsula. It's known for its odd rock forma-tions, and its coastal road passes an area of beautiful but often rocky seascapes, opening onto Loch Snizort and the Sound of Raasay. See chapter 12.

communities. Sometimes this type of accommodation can be an extension of a family home; at other times the property can be a modern stylish guesthouse. What they all have in common is that they're small, typically offering between two and 15 rooms, and they rarely offer evening meals or any restaurant or bar facilities. Rates for this type of accommodation are often on a per person per night basis rather than per room, and usually with a single person supplement. As such, although they're often touted as one of the cheapest types of accommodation going, it's worth doing the math to check that the price per head is actually cheaper than an alternative that charges per room. However, economy isn't the only reason to stay in bed and break-fasts, because they can also be far friendlier than many big chains or large hotels.

Bed and Breakfast Nationwide (☏ 01255/672-377; www.bedandbreakfast nationwide.com) is an agency specializing in privately owned bed-and-breakfasts all over Britain. Properties range from small cottages to large manor houses and prices vary accordingly. Remember that these are often private homes and that hotel-level services aren't available. You will, however, be assured of a warm welcome, a comfortable bed, a hearty breakfast, and, for foreign visitors in particular, a glimpse of British life. Properties can be searched online or you can request a copy of their brochure, which features all 160 homes and can be mailed for US$5 to addresses outside the U.K.

A unique take on bed-and-breakfast accommodation is **Bed and Fed** (www. bedandfed.co.uk), a network of affordable guest rooms throughout the U.K.—often in private homes—through which guests are provided with dinner, a bed for the night, and breakfast at rates from £30 per person per night.

Farmhouses

Many farmhouses across Scotland and the U.K. set aside rooms for paying guests on a bed-and-breakfast basis. These traditional farmhouses might not boast all the modern conveniences and luxuries of hotels but they're packed with rural charm, provide a unique insight into Scottish life off the beaten track, and are famous for some of the best home-cooked breakfasts in Scotland. Staying in farmhouses, which are often also private homes, can be cheaper than many other types of accommodation, and many farms also offer self-catering accommodation in converted barns or cottages as well as camping and caravan sites on their land.

Farm Stay UK (☏ 024/7669-6909; www.farmstayuk.co.uk) is the main national organization that deals with accommodation of this type and you can search all the farm stay accommodation options registered with them via the website, which also provides details on what do in the area around the properties. Alternatively you can order a free copy of the annual directory (published in early December) through the Farm Stay UK website; listings include quality ratings, number of bedrooms, nearby attractions and activities, and prices, as well as images of each property. Also listed are special details, such as rooms with four-poster beds or activities on the grounds (fishing, for example). Many farms are child-friendly and young guests are often invited to tag along when gathering eggs or at feeding times.

The approximate prices range from £30 to £60 per person per night and include a full home-cooked breakfast and usually private facilities. Farm stay self-catering accommodation costs from £200 per week and usually include amenities such as dishwashers and central heating. Each property is inspected annually by both Farm Stay UK and regional tourist boards, and most are open year-round.

Holiday Cottages & Villages

Throughout Britain, fully furnished studios, houses, cottages, "flats" (apartments), and even trailers suitable for couples, families, or groups can be rented by the day, week, or for longer periods. This type of holiday accommodation can often be an economical option, not least because you can cook all your own meals and rental rates are generally far cheaper outside of school holidays.

Companies that offer this type of accommodation include **Cottages 4 You** (☏ 0845/268-0760; www.cottages4you.co.uk), representing thousands of rental properties in the U.K. from thatch-roofed cottages to castles. Companies specializing in Scotland accommodation include **Embrace Scotland** (☏ 01866/822-122;

www.embracescotland.co.uk), **Unique Cottages** (℃ **01835/822-277**; www. unique-cottages.co.uk), and **Wilderness Cottages** (℃ **01456/486-358**; www. wildernesscottages.co.uk).

The **National Trust for Scotland** (℃ **0844/493-2108;** www.ntsholidays.com) also rents many incredible historic properties around the country from flats in old tenements on Edinburgh's Royal Mile to lighthouse cottages and castles. In addition, the **Landmark Trust** (℃ **01628/825-925;** www.landmarktrust.org.uk), a national building preservation charity, also has a large collection of historic buildings available for holiday lets.

Also search the "self catering" options listed in the "Accommodation" section of Visit Scotland's website at www.visitscotland.com for details of local companies.

Chain Hotels

Major chains such as Best Western, Hilton, Sheraton, and Travelodge, are found throughout Britain. In addition, Britain has a number of leading chains with which North American travelers are generally not familiar. These include **Thistle Hotels** (www.thistle.com; ℃ **020/7138-0000**), a well-regarded chain of moderate-to-upscale full-service hotels that caters to business and leisure travelers alike, and **Premier Inn** (www.premierinn.com; ℃ **0871/527-8000**), a chain of modern, moderately priced accommodation located across the U.K., each one featuring a licensed restaurant. See "Major Hotel & Motel Chains" at the end of this chapter for a full list of options.

House Swapping

A number of companies organize home exchanges. Florida-based **HomeLink International** (℃ **800/638-3841** or 954/566-2687; www.homelink.org) is the oldest and largest home-exchange holiday organization in the world. Membership costs $119 for 1 year or $190 for 2 years. Competitors include **Intervac U.S. & International** (℃ **800/756-HOME** [4663]; www.intervacus.com), with membership rates of $100 for 1 year or $180 for 2 years, and **Home Exchange** (℃ **800/877-8723;** www. homeexchange.com), with fees of $10 a month for an annual membership or $16 a month for a 3-month membership.

[FastFACTS] SCOTLAND

American Express   There's an office at 69 George St. in Edinburgh (℃ **0131/718-2505**); hours are Monday through Friday from 9am to 5:30pm and Saturday from 9am to 4pm. Another office is at 115 Hope St. in Glasgow (℃ **0141/225-2905**); it's open Monday through Friday from 9am to 5:30pm, Saturday from 9am to 5pm.

Area Codes   The telephone country code for Britain is **44**. The area code for Edinburgh is **0131;** for Glasgow, **0141;** for Aberdeen, **01224;** and for Inverness, **01463.**

Business Hours   With many exceptions, business hours are Monday through Friday from 9am to 5pm. In general, stores are open Monday through Saturday from 9:30am to 5:30pm, and on Sunday from 11am to 5pm. In country towns, there's usually an early closing day (often on Wed or Thurs), when the shops close at 1pm, and most shops don't open at all on Sundays.

Car Rental   See "Getting There by Car," earlier in this chapter.

Cellphones   See "Mobile Phones," later in this section.

American Express | PLANNING YOUR TRIP TO SCOTLAND

Customs **Non-E.U. nationals** can bring into Scotland duty-free 200 cigarettes, 100 cigarillos, 50 cigars, or 250 grams of smoking tobacco. You can also bring in 4 liters of wine and either 1 liter of alcohol over 22% proof or 2 liters of fortified wine under 22% proof. In addition, you can bring in up to £390 of other goods (including perfume) without having to pay tax or duty. Check www.hmrc.gov.uk/customs/arriving/arrivingnoneu. htm for further details. (Customs officials tend to be lenient about general merchandise, realizing that the limits are unrealistically low.)

For information on what you're allowed to take home from Scotland, contact one of the following agencies:

U.S. Citizens: U.S. Customs & Border Protection (CBP), 1300 Pennsylvania Ave., NW, Washington, D.C. 20229 (✆ **877/CBP-5511;** www.cbp.gov).

Canadian Citizens: Canada Border Services Agency (✆ **800/461-9999** in Canada, or 204/983-3500; www.cbsa-asfc.gc.ca).

U.K. Citizens: HM Customs & Excise at ✆ **0845/010-9000** (from outside the U.K., 020/8929-0152), or consult the website at www.hmce.gov.uk.

Australian Citizens: Australian Customs Service at ✆ **1300/363-263,** or log on to www.customs.gov.au.

New Zealand Citizens: New Zealand Customs, The Customhouse, 17–21 Whitmore St., Box 2218, Wellington (✆ **04/473-6099** or 0800/428-786; www.customs.govt.nz).

There are no restrictions on the amount of goods (including alcohol and tobacco) that **E.U. nationals** can bring into Scotland. However, you must transport the goods yourself, the goods must be for your own use or intended as a gift (any form of payment received invalidates this claim), and the goods must be duty and tax paid in the E.U. country where they were acquired. Failure to meet any of these conditions may result in the goods being seized.

Disabled Travelers Facilities for disabled people in Britain are improving all the time. Legislation requires that new public buildings are fully accessible to wheelchair-users. It is not, however, permitted for listed buildings to widen entrances or build permanent ramps. New public buses and black taxis are generally wheelchair-friendly. Many theatres and cinemas have induction loops available for the hard of hearing. People with disabilities are often granted special discounts ("concessions") at attractions and, in some cases, nightclubs. It always pays to ask. Free information and advice are available from **Tourism for all,** c/o Vitalise, Shap Road Industrial Estate, Shap Road, Kendal, Cumbria LA9 6NZ (✆ **0845/124-9971;** www.tourismforall.org.uk).

Flying Wheels Travel (✆ **877/451-5006;** www.flyingwheelstravel.com) offers escorted tours and cruises that emphasize sports, and private tours in minivans with lifts. **Access-Able Travel Source** (✆ **303/232-2979;** www.access-able.com) offers extensive access information and advice for traveling around the world with disabilities. **Accessible Journeys** (✆ **800/846-4537** or 610/521-0339; www.disabilitytravel.com) caters specifically to slow walkers and wheelchair travelers and their families and friends.

Organizations that offer assistance to travelers with disabilities include the **Moss Rehab Hospital** (✆ **800/CALL-MOSS** [225-5667]; www.mossresourcenet.org), which provides a library of accessible-travel resources online; and **SATH** (Society for Accessible Travel and Hospitality; ✆ **212/447-7284;** www.sath.org), which is now partnered with **AirAmbulanceCard.com** (allowing you to preselect top-notch hospitals in case of an emergency). **Flying with Disability** (www.flying-with-disability.org) is a comprehensive information source on airplane travel, and the **American Foundation for the Blind** (AFB; ✆ **800/232-5463;** www.afb.org) provides information on traveling with Seeing Eye dogs.

Also check out the quarterly magazine *Emerging Horizons* (www.emerginghorizons. com) and *Open World Magazine,* published by the Society for Accessible Travel and Hospitality (see above for contact details).

Drinking Laws   The legal drinking age is 18. Children 15 and under aren't allowed in pubs, except in certain rooms, and then only when accompanied by a parent or guardian. Don't drink and drive; the penalties are stiff. Pub opening hours are generally from 11am to 11pm, but within these limits there's wide variation, according to the discretion of the pub owner. Licensed premises in certain areas are allowed extended opening hours—up to 4am, on a "local need" basis. On Sundays, some pubs, particularly in city centers, are closed; those that do remain open usually do so from noon to 10:30 or 11pm. Restaurants are allowed to serve liquor during these hours, but only to people who are dining on the premises. The law allows an additional 30 minutes for "drinking-up time." In hotels, liquor may be served from 11am to 11pm to both guests and non-guests; after 11pm, only guests may be served.

Driving Rules   See "Getting There" and "Getting Around," earlier in this chapter.

Drug Laws   Both hard and soft drugs are illegal in Britain. People arrested for possession of even very small quantities of marijuana can be refused entry to the country. Possession of larger quantities or of harder drugs such as heroin and cocaine carry much stiffer penalties including fines and imprisonment.

Drugstores   There are very few 24-hour pharmacies in Scotland (none in Edinburgh, for example). Some large supermarkets remain open until very late (or even 24 hours) and may have in-store pharmacy counters. Every police station in the country has a list of emergency chemists. Dial "0" (zero) and ask the operator for the local police, who will give you the name of one nearest you.

Electricity   British electricity is 240 volts AC (50 cycles), roughly twice the voltage in North America, which is 115 to 120 volts AC (60 cycles). American plugs don't fit British wall outlets. Bring suitable transformers and/or adapters—if you plug an American appliance directly into a European electrical outlet without a transformer, you'll destroy your appliance and possibly start a fire.

Embassies & Consulates   All embassies are in London. However, there's a **U.S. Consulate** in Edinburgh at 3 Regent Terrace (© **0131/556-8315;** http://edinburgh.usconsulate. gov), open Monday through Friday from 1 to 5:30pm; appointment required. The **Canadian High Commission** is at 50 Lothian Rd. (© **0131/473-6320;** http://canada.embassy homepage.com), open Monday through Friday from 8am to 4pm. The **Australian Consulate** is at 5 Mitchell St. (© **0131/538-0582;** www.uk.embassy.gov.au), open Tuesday through Friday from 9am to 11:30am and noon to 4:30pm. The **Irish Consulate** is at 6 Randolph Crescent (© **0131/226-7711;** http://ireland.embassyhomepage.com). New Zealand doesn't have a consulate in Scotland.

Emergencies   For police, fire, or ambulance, dial © **999.** Give your name, address, phone number, and the nature of the emergency. Misuse of the 999 service will result in a heavy fine.

Family Travel   Note that all children must have their own passport for entry into the U.K. See "Passports," below, for further information about acquiring or renewing passports.

It's worth asking hotels whether they have family suites available. Otherwise, there are plenty of self-catering options (cottages, cabins, and apartments) in Scotland, particularly in rural areas. To locate hotels, restaurants, and attractions that are particularly child-friendly, refer to the "Kids" icon throughout this guide. Note that some castles and some luxury hotels don't receive young children as guests. Such instances are noted in reviews.

Recommended family travel websites include **Take The Family** (www.takethefamily. com), **Family Travel Forum** (www.familytravelforum.com), **Family Travel Network** (www. familytravelnetwork.com), **Family Travel Files** (www.thefamilytravelfiles.com) and **Kids Can Travel** (www.kidscantravel.com). Also, check out Frommer's *Scotland With Your Family*, packed full of advice.

Health Travel in Scotland does not pose any extraordinary health risks for a Western European country.If you need a doctor, your hotel can recommend one, or you can contact your embassy or consulate. Most health treatment is free for E.U. nationals (including maternity care). However, it may still be worth acquiring additional medical insurance so that you're covered for unforeseen needs such as dental care, mountain rescue, and repatriation.

U.S. visitors who become ill while in Scotland are eligible for free emergency care only. For other treatment, including follow-up care, you'll be asked to pay. Contact the **International Association for Medical Assistance to Travelers (IAMAT;** © **716/754-4883** in the U.S. or 416/652-0137 in Canada; www.iamat.org) for tips on travel and health concerns, and for lists of local doctors. The United States **Centers for Disease Control and Prevention** (© **800/232-4636;** www.cdc.gov) provides up-to-date information on health hazards by region or country and offers tips on food safety. **Travel Health Online** (www.tripprep.com), sponsored by a consortium of travel medicine practitioners, can also offer helpful advice on traveling abroad. You can find listings of reliable medical clinics overseas at the **International Society of Travel Medicine** (www.istm.org).

See also "Emergencies," earlier in this section for further information.

Holidays The following public holidays are celebrated in Scotland: New Year (Jan 1–2), Good Friday and Easter Monday, May Day (May 1), spring bank holiday (last Mon in May), summer bank holiday (first Mon in Aug), St Andrew's Day (Nov 30), Christmas Day (Dec 25), and Boxing Day (Dec 26). Almost everything is closed on Christmas Day, and most business (except pubs) are closed on New Year's Day. Many shops remain open on other public holidays.

Insurance Before leaving home, find out what medical services your health insurance covers. You may have to pay all medical costs up front and be reimbursed later. As a safety net, you may want to buy travel medical insurance, particularly if you're traveling to a remote or high-risk area where emergency evacuation might be necessary. If you require additional medical insurance, try **MEDEX Assistance** (© **410/453-6300;** www.medexassist.com) or **Travel Assistance International** (© **800/821-2828** or 410/987-6233; www.travelassistance.com).

Canadians should check with their provincial health plan offices or contact **Health Canada** (www.hc-sc.gc.ca) to find out the extent of their coverage and what documentation and receipts they must take home if they're treated overseas.

Travelers from the **U.K.** should carry their European Health Insurance Card (EHIC), which replaced the E111 form as proof of entitlement to free/reduced-cost medical treatment abroad (www.ehic.org.uk). Note, however, that the EHIC covers only "necessary medical treatment," and for repatriation costs, lost money, baggage, or cancellation, travel insurance from a reputable company should always be sought (www.travelinsuranceweb.com).

For information on traveler's insurance, trip cancellation insurance, and medical insurance while traveling, please visit **www.frommers.com/planning**.

Internet & Wi-Fi There are abundant opportunities to connect to the Internet in cities and major towns, with plenty of Wi-Fi access as well Internet-connected terminals in cafes and many hotels. In most airports and at some chain cafes (such as Starbucks), wireless access is available for a subscription charge. You can log on for free, however, at numerous hotspots in towns and cities; visit **www.myhotspots.co.uk** or use an iPhone/iPod Touch Wi-Fi finder app such as **www.jiwire.com/iphone**.

Although even most of the Scottish islands have Internet connectivity, you may find that some hotels in remote areas don't offer access to their guests. Likewise, in small towns and villages, there may not be any connections that are readily accessible to visitors.

Legal Aid   Contact your consulate, embassy, or high commission (see above) if you run into trouble. They can advise you of your rights and even provide a list of attorneys (whom you'll have to pay if services are used), but they can't interfere on your behalf in the legal processes of Great Britain. For questions about American citizens arrested abroad, including ways of getting money to them, call the **Citizens Emergency Center of the Office of Special Consulate Services,** in Washington, D.C. (📞 **202/647-5225**). Other nationals can go to their nearest consulate or embassy.

LGBT Travelers   Edinburgh and Glasgow have thriving gay communities, with bars, clubs, shops, and gyms. Gay and lesbian visitors may sometimes experience bigoted attitudes in rural areas. There are also occasionally incidents of gay bashing, mostly in the grimier industrial areas of towns and cities. Governments have introduced tougher legislation to try to combat such occurrences. Generally, though, visitors will find the Scots open and welcoming to all comers.

Useful resources for visitors include ScotsGay (www.scotsgay.co.uk) and QSLifestyle (www.qsmag.com) magazines. There's also the **LGBT Youth Scotland** organization (www.lgbtyouth.org.uk) and the **Strathclyde Gay and Lesbian Switchboard** (📞 **0141/847-0447;** www.sgls.co.uk) for advice, information, and social events.

The **International Gay & Lesbian Travel Association** (**IGLTA;** U.S. head office: 📞 **954/630-1637;** contact in Scotland: **0131/220-5353;** www.iglta.org) is the trade association for the gay and lesbian travel industry, and offers an online directory of gay- and lesbian-friendly travel businesses; go to the website and click on "Members." Many agencies offer tours and travel itineraries specifically for gay and lesbian travelers. **Now, Voyager** (📞 **800/255-6951;** www.nowvoyager.com) is a well-known San Francisco–based gay-owned and operated travel service. Within the U.K., try **Amro Holidays** (📞 **01462/434-663;** www.amroholidays.com).

Mail   Most post offices and sub post offices are open Monday through Friday from 9am to 5:30pm and Saturday from 9:30am to noon. British mailboxes are painted red and carry a royal coat of arms. All post offices accept parcels for mailing, provided they're wrapped properly and securely.

Mobile Phones   The three letters that define much of the world's wireless capabilities are **GSM** (Global System for Mobile Communications), a big, seamless network that makes for easy cross-border cellphone use throughout Europe and dozens of other countries worldwide. In the U.S., T-Mobile and AT&T use this quasi-universal system; in Canada, Microcell and some Rogers customers are GSM, and all Europeans and most Australians use GSM. GSM phones function with a removable plastic SIM card, encoded with your phone number and account information. If your cellphone is on a GSM system, and you have a world-capable multiband phone such as many Sony Ericsson, Motorola, or Samsung models, you can make and receive calls across the habitable areas of most of the globe. Just call your wireless operator and ask for "international roaming" to be activated on your account. Unfortunately, per-minute charges can be high—usually $1 to $1.50 in western Europe.

In Scotland, it's often cheaper, however, to purchase a cellphone. In general, tariffs run from as low as £25 a month, or even less, for unlimited calls with a pay-as-you-go card. Alternatively, if you have an unlocked phone, you can also purchase just a SIM card with a local Scotland phone number. For more information, contact **Mobal** (📞 **888/888-9162;** www.mobal.com) or **Cellular Abroad** (📞 **800/287-5072;** www.cellularabroad.com), or visit a mobile phone shop (of which there are many in major towns and cities).

Money & Costs   Britain's monetary system is the pound Sterling (£). There are 100 pence (written as "p") to a pound. Colloquially, pounds are also referred to as "quid". Scotland issues its own pound notes, but English and Scottish money is interchangeable.

Coins come in denominations of £2, £1, 50p, 20p, 10p, 5p, 2p, and 1p. Banknotes are issued in denominations of £5, £10, £20, and £50.

It's always advisable to bring money in a variety of forms on your trip: a mix of cash, credit cards, and perhaps, if you're particularly worried about security, traveler's checks. You should also exchange enough petty cash to cover airport incidentals, tipping, and transportation to your hotel before you leave home, or withdraw money upon arrival at an airport ATM.

In Scotland, ATMs usually offer the best exchange rates. Avoid exchanging money at commercial exchange bureaus and hotels, which often have the highest transaction fees. You can find ATMs at almost all bank branches, as well as at most large supermarkets, some petrol stations, in shopping malls, and some post offices. Small towns and villages may not have banking or ATMs, and so take care to have enough cash with you if traveling in rural areas. ATMs require you to input a four-digit personal identification number (five- or six-digit numbers aren't valid), so be sure to request the valid PIN (personal identification number) from your card issuer before traveling.

Frommer's lists exact prices in the local currency. The currency conversions quoted below were correct at press time. However, rates fluctuate, so before departing, consult a currency exchange website such as **www.oanda.com/convert/classic** to check up-to-the-minute rates. Alternatively, for help with currency conversions, tip calculations, and more, download Frommer's convenient Travel Tools app for your mobile device. Go to www.frommers.com/go/mobile and click on the Travel Tools icon.

THE VALUE OF THE BRITISH POUND VS. OTHER POPULAR CURRENCIES

UK£	US$	Can$	Euro (€)	Aus$	NZ$
£1.00	US$1.60	C$1.60	1.16€	A$1.60	NZ$2.10

Chip & PIN is the system adopted in Britain for the use of credit and debit cards. Vendors ask customers for a four-digit PIN, which will be entered into a keypad near the cash register. In some cases, a waiter will bring a hand-held model to your table to verify your credit card.

In order to use a credit card in Britain, the following tips may be useful:

o Typically, only a card with an embedded computer chip can be used.
o Get a four-digit PIN from your credit card's issuing bank before leaving home, or call the number on the back of your card and ask for a four-digit PIN.
o Keep an eye out for the right logo displayed in a retailer's window.
o Know that your Amex card will work where an Amex logo is displayed, but the card isn't as widely accepted as Visa and MasterCard.
o As a last resort, make sure you have enough cash to cover your purchase.

Beware of hidden credit-card fees while traveling. Check with your credit or debit card issuer to see what fees, if any, will be charged for overseas transactions. Recent reform legislation in the U.S., for example, has curbed some exploitative lending practices. But many banks have responded by increasing fees in other areas, including fees for customers who use credit and debit cards while out of the country—even if those charges were made in U.S. dollars. Fees can amount to 3% or more of the purchase price. Check with your bank before departing to avoid any surprise charges on your statement.

Newspapers & Magazines   Each major Scottish city publishes its own newspaper. All newsagents (newsstands) carry the major national papers as well. In summer, you can generally pick up a copy of the *International Herald Tribune,* published in Paris, along with the European editions of *USA Today, Time,* and *Newsweek.*

WHAT THINGS COST IN EDINBURGH	U.K.£
Airlink bus into the center of Edinburgh	3.50
Average bus fare within Edinburgh	2.00
Double room (very expensive)	360.00
Double room (expensive)	200.00
Double room (moderate)	130.00
Double room (inexpensive)	60.00
Dinner (expensive)	45.00
Dinner (moderate)	20.00
Dinner (inexpensive)	12.00
Average price of a drink in a nightclub	4.00
Average cover charge at a nightclub	5.00–12.00
Average theatre seat	15.00
Average movie ticket	9.00
Admission to Edinburgh Castle	14.00

Packing   If you're venturing beyond the major cities, bring robust footwear and some waterproof clothing. Many smarter restaurants in Scotland request that customers don't wear jeans or trainers (sneakers), and so do bring nice clothing.

Passports   All U.S. citizens, Canadians, Australians, New Zealanders, and South Africans must have a passport with at least 2 months' validity remaining. South African visitors must also have a visa. For all non-E.U. visitors, the immigration officer will also want proof of your intention to return to your point of origin (usually a round-trip ticket) and visible means of support while you're in Scotland. If you're planning to fly from the United States or Canada to the United Kingdom and then on to a country that requires a visa (India, for example), you should secure that visa before you arrive in Britain.

For information on how to get a passport, consult the relevant national passport office. The websites listed provide downloadable passport applications, as well as the current fees for processing applications.

Australia   **Australian Passport Information Service** (☏ **131-232,** or visit www.passports.gov.au).

Canada   **Passport Office,** Department of Foreign Affairs and International Trade, Ottawa, ON K1A 0G3 (☏ **800/567-6868;** www.ppt.gc.ca).

Ireland   **Passport Office,** Setanta Centre, Molesworth Street, Dublin 2 (☏ **01/671-1633;** www.foreignaffairs.gov.ie).

New Zealand   **Passports Office,** Department of Internal Affairs, 47 Boulcott St., Wellington, 6011 (☏ **0800/225-050** in New Zealand or 04/474-8100; www.passports.govt.nz).

United Kingdom   Visit your nearest passport office, major post office, or travel agency, or contact the **Identity and Passport Service (IPS),** 89 Eccleston Square, London, SW1V 1PN (☏ **0300/222-0000;** www.ips.gov.uk).

United States   To find your regional passport office, check the U.S. State Department website (http://travel.state.gov/passport) or call the **National Passport Information Center** (☏ **877/487-2778**) for automated information.

Petrol (Gasoline)   Pumps dispense in liters, not gallons. Expect to pay over £1.30 per liter (subject to change, of course). The British Imperial gallon is about 20% more in volume than the gallon as measured in the United States. One British gallon is about 4.5 liters. Most petrol stations in Scotland are self-service; almost all accept major credit cards.

Police   The best source of help and advice in emergencies is the police. For non-life-threatening situations, dial "0" (zero) and ask for the police; dial 999 for emergencies. If the local police can't assist, they'll usually have the contact details of a person who can. Losses, thefts, and other crimes should be reported immediately.

Safety   Although rural Scotland is quite safe, the big cities are no more immune from crime than any other European city. If visitors do find themselves victims of a crime, it's likely to be one of pickpocketing; mugging; "snatch and grab" theft of mobile phones, watches, and jewelry; or theft of their unattended bags, especially at airports and from cars parked at restaurants, hotels, and resorts.

Pickpockets target tourists at historic sites and restaurants, as well as on buses and trains. Unattended cars are targeted, too. Visitors in Scotland aren't expected to produce identity documents for police authorities, and so feel free to secure your passport in the hotel or room safe.

Senior Travel   Many discounts are available to seniors. Be advised that in Scotland you often have to be a member of an association to get discounts. Public-transport reductions, for example, are available only to holders of British Pension books. However, many attractions do offer discounts for seniors (women 60 or over and men 65 or over). Even if discounts aren't posted, ask if they're available.

If you're over 60, you're eligible for special 10% discounts on **British Airways (BA)** through its Privileged Traveler program. You also qualify for reduced restrictions on APEX cancellations. Discounts are also granted for BA tours and for intra-Britain air tickets booked in North America. British rail companies offer seniors discounted rates on first-class rail passes around Britain.

Don't be shy about asking for discounts, but carry some kind of identification that shows your date of birth. Also, mention you're a senior when you make your reservations. Some hotels offer seniors discounts. In most cities, people over the age of 60 qualify for reduced admission to theatres, museums, and other attractions, and discounted fares on public transport.

Smoking   Since 2006, smoking has been banned in public places, including pubs, restaurants, workplaces, and public transportation. Ignoring the ban may incur a fine of £50.

Student Travel   Check out the **International Student Travel Confederation (ISTC)** website (www.istc.org) for comprehensive travel services information and details on how to get an **International Student Identity Card (ISIC),** which qualifies students for substantial savings on rail passes, plane tickets, entrance fees, and more. It also provides students with basic health and life insurance and a 24-hour helpline. The card is valid for a maximum of 18 months. You can apply for the card online or in person at **STA Travel** (© **800/781-4040** in North America; 132-782 in Australia; 087/1230-0040 in the U.K.; www.statravel.com), the biggest student travel agency in the world; check out the website to locate STA Travel offices worldwide. **Travel CUTS** (© **866/246-9762;** www.travel cuts.com) offers similar services for both Canadians and U.S. residents. Irish students may prefer to turn to **USIT** (© **01/602-1906;** www.usit.ie), an Ireland-based specialist in student, youth, and independent travel.

Taxes   Although there's no local sales tax in Britain, a standard value-added tax (VAT) of 20% is imposed on most goods and services. Hotel rates and meals in restaurants are taxed at 20%; the extra charge will show up on your bill unless otherwise stated. For non-EU residents, this amount can be refunded if you shop at stores that participate in the Retail Export Scheme (signs are posted in the window). When you make a purchase, show your passport and request a Retail Export Scheme form (VAT 407) and a stamped, pre-addressed envelope. Show the VAT form and your sales receipt to British Customs when you leave the country—they may also ask to see the merchandise. After Customs has stamped the form, mail it back to the shop in the envelope provided *before you leave the country.* Your VAT refund will be mailed to you.

Remember: Keep your VAT forms with your passport; pack your purchases in a carry-on bag so that you have them handy; and allow yourself enough time at your departure point to find a mailbox.

Several readers have reported a VAT refund scam. Some merchants allegedly tell customers they can get a refund form at the airport on their way out of the country. *This is not true.* The form must be completed by the retailer on the spot, or you won't get a refund later. For information, contact **Global Blue,** (*©* **866/706-6090** in the U.S. or 800/3211-1111 in E.U. countries; www.global-blue.com).

Britain imposes a flight departure tax (Air Passenger Duty). The rate depends on destination and the airline class in which you're traveling. At the time of writing, economy-class passengers pay £12 for short-haul flights, whereas passengers traveling standard-class (or above) pay up to £170 for the longest international flights. This tax is accounted for in your ticket.

Gasoline (petrol) is subject to combined fuel duty and VAT.

Telephones   To call Scotland: If you're calling Scotland from outside of the U.K.:

1. Dial the international access code: 011 from North America; 00 from Ireland, Europe, or New Zealand; or 0011 from Australia.

2. Dial the country code 44.

3. Dial the local 3- or 4-digit area code (drop the initial "0").

4. Dial the 7-digit number. The whole number you'd dial for a number in Edinburgh would be 011-44-131-000-0000.

To make calls within Scotland: Cities and localities have area codes. If you're calling within the same area code inside Scotland, simply dial the local 7-digit number. However, if you're calling from one area code to another, you must dial 0 and then the area code.

To make international calls: To make international calls from Britain, first dial 00 and then the country code (U.S. or Canada 1, Ireland 353, Australia 61, New Zealand 64, South Africa 27). Next, dial the area code and number. For example, if you wanted to call the British Embassy in Washington, D.C., you would dial 00-1-202-588-7800. Or call through one of the following long-distance access codes: **AT&T USA Direct** (*©* **1800/CALL-ATT** [225-5288]), **Canada Direct** (*©* **0800/890-016**), **Australia** (*©* **0800/890-061**), and **New Zealand** (*©* **0800/890-064**).

For directory assistance: For U.K. **directory enquiries**, dial *©* **118-500;** for international directory enquiries, dial *©* **118-505**. Note that these are premium-rate numbers. Consult www.192.com for a free online service.

For operator assistance: If you need an international operator or to call collect, dial *©* **155.**

Pay phones & phone cards: There are three types of common public pay phones: those taking only coins, those accepting only phone cards (called Cardphones), and those taking phone cards and credit cards alike. At coin-operated phones, insert your coins before dialing. The minimum charge is 20p. Phone cards are available in varying denominations, from £2 to £20, and are reusable until the total value has expired. Cards can be purchased from newsstands and post offices. Finally, the credit-call pay phone operates on credit cards—Access (MasterCard), Visa, American Express, and Diners Club—and is most common at airports and large railway stations.

Caller beware: Some hotels routinely add outrageous surcharges onto phone calls made from your room. Inquire before you call! It'll be a lot cheaper to use your own calling card number or cellphone, or to find a pay phone.

Time   The United Kingdom follows Greenwich Mean Time (GMT), which is 5 hours ahead of Eastern Standard Time, with British summertime lasting (roughly) from the end of March to the end of October. For most of the year, including summer, Britain is 5 hours ahead of the time observed in the eastern United States. Because of different daylight-saving-time practices in the two nations, there's a brief period (about a week) in autumn when Britain is only 4 hours ahead of New York, and a brief period in spring when it's 6 hours ahead.

Tipping   For **cab drivers,** add about 10% to 15% to the fare shown on the meter. If the driver personally unloads or loads your luggage, add 50p per bag.

You should tip hotel **porters** at least a couple of pounds even if you have only one small suitcase; give £5 to £10 if you have substantial amounts of luggage. Hall porters are tipped only for special services. **Maids** receive £1 per day. In top-ranked hotels, the **concierge** often submits a separate bill, showing charges for newspapers and the like; if he or she has been particularly helpful, tip extra.

Hotels often add a **service charge** of 10% to 15% to bills. In smaller B&Bs, the tip isn't likely to be included. Therefore, tip for special services, such as the waiter who serves you breakfast. If several people have served you in a B&B, a 10% to 15% charge will be added to the bill and divided among the staff.

In upmarket **restaurants** and **nightclubs,** a 15% service charge is often added to the bill. To that, add another 3% to 5%, depending on the quality of the service. **Sommeliers** (wine stewards) get about 10% of the cost of the wine served. Tipping in **pubs** isn't common, although in cocktail bars the waiter or barmaid usually gets about £1 per round of drinks.

Barbers and **hairdressers** expect 10% to 15%. **Tour guides** expect £2, but it's not mandatory. **Theatre ushers** don't expect tips.

Toilets   Public toilets are usually clean and often have an attendant. Hotels can be used, but they discourage non-guests. Garages (filling stations) generally don't offer toilet facilities. There's no need to tip, except to a hotel attendant.

VAT   See "Taxes," earlier in this section.

Visas   See "Passports," earlier in this section.

Visitor Information   Before you go, you can get information and maps from **Visit Britain** (www.visitbritain.com). Offices in other countries can be contacted as follows: USA and Canada, ✆ **212/850-0321;** Australia, ✆ **02/9021-4401;** and New Zealand, ✆ **09/357-6620.**

Within the U.K., the main Britain and London Visitor Centre is at 1 Regent Street, London SW1Y 4XT (✆ 0870/1566-366). It's open Monday through Friday 9:30am to 6pm and at weekends from 10am to 4pm. If you're in London and are contemplating a trip north, you can visit the **Scottish Tourist Board,** 19 Cockspur St., London SW1 Y5BL (✆ **020/7930-2812;** www.visitscotland.com); it's open Monday through Friday 9:30am to 5:30pm and Saturday noon to 4pm. Once you're in Scotland, you can stop by the **Edinburgh & Scotland Information Centre,** Princes Mall, 3 Princes St., Edinburgh EH2 2QP (✆ **0131/473-3800;** www.edinburgh.org). In July and August, it's open Monday through Saturday 9am to 8pm and Sunday 10am to 8pm. May, June and September, hours are Monday through Saturday 9am to 7pm and Sunday 10am to 7pm. In April and October, hours are Monday through Saturday 9am to 6pm and Sunday 10am to 6pm. From November to March, opening times are Monday through Saturday 9am to 5pm and Sunday 10am to 5pm.

There are more than 170 **tourist centers** in Scotland, all well signposted in their cities or towns; some are closed in winter, however.

Water   Tap water is considered safe to drink throughout Scotland.

Websites   A wealth of information is available at **www.travelbritain.com**, which lets you order brochures online, along with travel cards and rail passes. There's even an e-mail service that provides prompt answers to any queries. All of Great Britain is covered. If you're surfing the Web for hotels, a good site to browse is **www.visitscotland.com** (site of the Scotland Tourist Board).

Several regional tourist board websites are also helpful. The best include **www.scot-borders.co.uk**; **www.visithighlands.com**; **www.ayrshire-arran.com**; **www.visitscottish heartlands.com** (for Argyll and the Isles, Loch Lomond, Stirling, and the Trossachs); **www.perthshire.co.uk**; **www.angusanddundee.co.uk**; **www.seeglasgow.com**; **www.edinburgh.org**; and **www.aberdeen-grampian.com**.

Travel information for the whole of Scotland is offered on Visit Scotland's national telephone hot line, available for inquiries from the U.K. and overseas. Travel advisors are available to help you book accommodation throughout Scotland—hotels, guesthouses, or bed-and-breakfasts—or find out about special offers, events, and attractions to visit. Advisors are available Monday through Friday 8am to 8pm and Saturday 9am to 5:30pm (U.K. time). In the U.K., call ✆ **0845/225-5121;** from overseas, call ✆ **+44-845/225-5121** or go online to www.visitscotland.com.

Other useful websites include **www.bbc.co.uk** for news and weather; **www.streetmap.co.uk** for locating addresses; and **www.theaa.com**, especially for its route planner for drivers.

Wi-Fi   See "Internet & Wi-Fi," earlier in this section.

AIRLINE, HOTEL & CAR-RENTAL WEBSITES

MAJOR AIRLINES

Air Canada
www.aircanada.com

Air Europa
www.aireuropa.com

Air France
www.airfrance.com

Air New Zealand
www.airnewzealand.com

Alitalia
www.alitalia.com

American Airlines
www.aa.com

British Airways
www.britishairways.com

China Southern Airlines
www.cs-air.com

Continental Airlines
www.continental.com

Delta Air Lines
www.delta.com

Etihad Airways
www.etihadairways.com

Finnair
www.finnair.com

Gulf Air
www.gulfair.com

Iberia Airlines
www.iberia.com

Japan Airlines
www.jal.co.jp

Lufthansa
www.lufthansa.com

Malaysia Airlines
www.malaysiaairlines.com

North American Airlines
www.flynaa.com

Northwest Airlines
www.nwa.com

Qantas Airways
www.qantas.com

Qatar Airlines
www.qatarairways.com

Royal Dutch Airlines
www.klm.com

SAS Scandinavian Airlines
www.flysas.com

South African Airways
www.flysaa.com

TAP
www.flytap.com

Thai Airways International
www.thaiair.com

United Airlines
www.united.com

Virgin Atlantic Airways
www.virgin-atlantic.com

BUDGET AIRLINES

Aegean Airlines
www.aegeanair.com

Aer Arann
www.aerarann.com

Aer Lingus
www.aerlingus.com

Air Malta
www.airmalta.com

Austrian Airlines
www.aua.com

BMI
www.flybmi.com

Brussels Airlines
www.brusselsairlines.com

Canadian Affair
www.canadianaffair.com

Cimber Air
www.cimber.com

CityJet
www.cityjet.com

easyJet
www.easyjet.com

Flybe Flights
www.flybe.com

Germanwings Airlines
www.germanwings.com

Loganair
www.loganair.co.uk

LOT
www.lot.com

Malèv Airlines
www.malev.com

Norwegian
www.norwegian.com

Ryanair
www.ryanair.com

Thomson
http://flights.thomson.co.uk/

Wizz
wizzair.com

MAJOR HOTEL & MOTEL CHAINS

Apex Hotels
www.apexhotels.co.uk

Best Western International
www.bestwestern.com

Clarion Hotels
www.clarionhotel.com

Comfort Inns
www.comfortinn.com

Courtyard by Marriott
www.marriott.com/courtyard

Crerar Hotels
www.crerarhotels.com

Crowne Plaza Hotels
www.crowneplaza.com

Days Inn
www.daysinn.com

De Vere Hotels
www.devere.co.uk

Doubletree Hotels
www.doubletree.com

Embassy Suites
www.embassysuites.com

Hilton Hotels
www.hilton.com

Holiday Inn
www.holidayinn.com

Hyatt
www.hyatt.com

Marriott
www.marriott.com

Novotel Hotels
www.novotel.com

Quality
www.qualityinn.com

Radisson Hotels & Resorts
www.radisson.com

Ramada Worldwide
www.ramada.com

Residence Inn by Marriott
www.marriott.com/residenceinn

Scotland's Hotels of Distinction
www.hotels-of-distinction.com

Sheraton Hotels & Resorts
www.sheraton.com
Swallow Hotels
www.swallow-hotels.com
The Townhouse Collection
www.townhousecompany.com
Thistle Hotels
www.thistle.com
Travelodge
www.travelodge.com

CAR-RENTAL AGENCIES
Alamo
www.alamo.com
Arnold Clark
www.arnoldclarkrental.com
Avis
www.avis.com

Budget
www.budget.com
Dollar
www.dollar.com
Enterprise
www.enterprise.com
Europcar
www.europcar.com
Hertz
www.hertz.com
Kemwel (KHA)
www.kemwel.com
National
www.nationalcar.com
Thrifty
www.thrifty.com

14

Index

See also Accommodations and Restaurant indexes, below.

General Index

A

Abbey House (Melrose), 134
Abbey Mill (Melrose), 136
Abbot House (Dunfermline), 239
Abbotsford House (Melrose), 135
Abercrombie & Kent, 33
Aberdeen, 41–42, 274–284
  accommodations, 280–282
  entertainment and nightlife, 279–280
  exploring, 276–277
  getting there, 276
  restaurants, 277–278
  shopping, 278
  side trips from, 282–284
  visitor information, 276
Aberdeen Angus Cattle Show (Perth), 30
Aberdeen Art Gallery, 277
Aberdeen Arts Centre, 279
Aberdeen Family History Shop, 278
Aberdeen International Youth Festival, 279–280
Aberdeen Maritime Museum, 277
Aberfoyle, 265–267
Abertarff House (Inverness), 330
Access-Able Travel Source, 435
Accessible Journeys, 435
Accommodations. See also Accommodations Index
  types of, 430–434
  websites, 445–446
Achamore House Gardens (Gigha), 218
Active in Scotland (brochure), 60
Active vacations, 53–64
Adam, James, 23, 132
Adam, Robert, 23, 84, 109, 121, 131, 132, 205
Adam, William, 23, 130–132
Advance Reservations Service, 431
Adventures in Golf, 57
Afternoon Tea Tour (Edinburgh), 35, 118
AirAmbulanceCard.com, 435
Air Canada, 424
Air New Zealand, 424
Air travel, 423–424, 428
  websites, 444–445
Albert Halls (Stirling), 260
Alexandra Park (Glasgow), 191
Alex Scott & Co. (Aberdeen), 278
Alhambra Theatre (Dunfermline), 240

Alistir Tait (Edinburgh), 97
Alloway, 198
Alloway Auld Kirk (Ayr), 200
American Airlines, 423, 424
American Express, 434
  Edinburgh, 71
American Foundation for the Blind (AFB), 435
Amhuinnsuidhe Estate, 384
Amro Holidays, 438
Ancestral roots, tracing your, 87
Andrew Carnegie Birthplace Museum (Dunfermline), 239
Angus beef, 28
An Lanntair Gallery (Lewis), 382
Annan Water Valley Road, 146
Anstruther, 245–246
Anta (Edinburgh), 100
Antiques
  Aberdeen, 278
  Corrie, 212
  Glasgow, 185
  Nairn, 338
Antonine Wall, 121
The Arches (Glasgow), 189
Architecture, 24, 25–26
Arctic Penguin Heritage Centre (Inveraray), 226
Ardfern Riding Centre (Argyll), 213
Ardkinglas Woodland Garden (Inveraray), 226
Area codes, 434
Argyll, 207–235
Argyll Arcade (Glasgow), 184
Argyll Forest Park, 227
Argyll Peninsula, 41
Argyll's Lodging (Stirling), 257–258
Armadale Castle Gardens & Museum of the Isles (Skye), 363
Armstrong's (Edinburgh), 99
Aros Castle (near Salen), 370, 372
Arran, Isle of, 208–213
Arran Fine Foods, 212
Arthur's Seat (Edinburgh), 73
Arts Festival (Pittenweem), 245
Association of National Park Authorities, 33
Asta Golf Club (Shetland), 409
ATMs (automated-teller machines), 439
Auld Brig o' Ayr, 200
Auldearn Antiques, 338
Auld Kirk of Ayr, 200
Australia
  consulate, 436
  customs regulations, 435
  passports, 440
Automobile Association, 427
Aviemore, 323–325
Aye Write! (Glasgow), 187
Ayr, 198–201
Ayr Racecourse, 200

B

Ba' (Orkney), 396
Back Walk (Stirling), 256
Bagpipes, 20–21
Bagpipes Galore (Edinburgh), 100
Balcomie Golf Course (Crail), 247
Balephetrish, 369
Balgove (St. Andrews), 248
Balgownie, the Royal Aberdeen Golf Club (Aberdeen), 279
Balhousie Castle (Perth), 285
Ballachulish Bridge, 316
Ballater, 302–304
Balloch, 268–270
Balloch Castle, 269
Balloch Castle Country Park, 269
Balmaha, 269
Balmoral Castle (Ballater), 303
Balmoral Spa (Edinburgh), 109
Balquhidder Church (near Callander), 263
Balranald Nature Reserve, 387
Balvenie Castle (Dufftown), 308
Bandstand Beer Festival (Nairn), 339
Bannockburn, 257
Bannockburn Heritage Centre, 257
Barnhouse (Orkney), 399
Barpa Carinish (North Uist), 387
Barra, 389–391
The Barras (Glasgow), 185
Barrie, James M., 24
  sights associated with (Kirriemuir), 301
Barrowland (Glasgow), 189
Bass Rock (North Berwick), 119
Battle of Culloden, 21
Bayhead, 387
BBC Scottish Symphony Orchestra (Glasgow), 189
Beaches
  Harris, 383
  North Uist, 387
  Sanday, 406
  Shetland, 420
  Troon, 202
  Tyree (Tiree), 369
Beauly, 336–337
Beauly Priory, 336
Bed and Breakfast Nationwide, 433
Bed & breakfasts, 431–433
Bed and Fed, 433
Bella Jane Boat Trips (Skye), 358
Belleisle Golf Course (Ayr), 201
Beltane Fire Festival (Edinburgh), 31
Ben Airean, 367
Ben Arthur, 227
Benbecula, 385
Ben Cruachan, 229
Ben Heaval, 390
Ben Hogh, 368

Restaurants

RESTAURANT INDEX